MANAGEMENT OF HUMAN RESOURCES

Edwin L. Miller
University of Michigan

Elmer H. Burack
University of Illinois
Chicago Circle

Maryann H. Albrecht
University of Illinois
Chicago Circle

PRENTICE-HALL, INC.   Englewood Cliffs, New Jersey 07632

Library of Congress Cataloging in Publication Data

Main entry under title:
Management of human resources.

    Includes bibliographical references.
    1. Personnel management—Addresses, essays, lectures. I. Miller, Edwin, (date)
II. Burack, Elmer H. III. Albrecht, Maryann H.
HF5549.M3133   658.3   79-23992
ISBN 0-13-549410-9

Editorial/production supervision
and interior design by Natalie Krivanek
Cover design by Saiki/Sprung Design
Manufacturing buyer: Tony Caruso

© 1980 by Prentice-Hall, Inc., Englewood Cliffs, N.J. 07632

All rights reserved. No part of this book
may be reproduced in any form or
by any means without permission in writing
from the publisher.

Printed in the United States of America

10 9 8 7 6 5 4 3 2 1

Prentice-Hall International, Inc., *London*
Prentice-Hall of Australia Pty. Limited, *Sydney*
Prentice-Hall of Canada, Ltd., *Toronto*
Prentice-Hall of India Private Limited, *New Delhi*
Prentice-Hall of Japan, Inc., *Tokyo*
Prentice-Hall of Southeast Asia Pte. Ltd., *Singapore*
Whitehall Books Limited, *Wellington, New Zealand*

CONTENTS

Contributors vii
Introduction 1

1 THE CHANGING ORGANIZATIONAL ENVIRONMENT 9

Environmental Changes and Organizational Adaptation

1. Human Resource Planning: Technology, Policy, Change, 12
   Elmer H. Burack and Thomas J. McNichols

2. The 1980s and Beyond: A Perspective, 22
   William Lazer

3. The New Labor Force: Implications for Better Personnel Practices, 41
   Maryann H. Albrecht

Labor Relations and The Future

1. What's Coming in Labor Relations, 53
   George S. McIsaac

2 HRM AS A PROFESSION 65

Assessments and Predictions

1. The Personnel Function: Marching to the Beat of a Different Drummer, 69
   George A. Rieder

2. Personnel Management in the 1990s, 74
   Thomas H. Patten, Jr.

3. The Personnel Function in Transition, 91
   Elmer H. Burack and Edwin L. Miller

Professionalism and Personnel

1. Professionalism and Accreditation in the Field of Personnel and Industrial Relations, 102
   Drew M. Young

2. Organizational Research and Organizational Change: GM's Approach, 106
   Howard C. Carlson

3 PLANNING DIMENSIONS OF HUMAN RESOURCE MANAGEMENT 119

Approaches to the Planning Functions

1. Human Resource Planning—Responding to Changing Needs, 122
   James W. Walker

2. The Nature of Managerial Manpower Planning, 136
   Eric Vetter

3. An Integrated Research and Development Program for Enhancing Managerial Effectiveness, 145
   Walter W. Tornow and Timothy C. Gartland

4. The Careers of Individuals and Organizations, 165
   John J. Leach

4 MAINTAINING THE HUMAN RESOURCE MANAGEMENT SYSTEM 187

Basic Personnel Management Activities

1. On the Road to Equal Opportunity, 190
   George T. Milkovich and Frank Kryztofiak

2. Training and Development Programs: What Learning Theory and Research Have to Offer, 212
   Craig E. Schneier

3. Employee Growth Through Performance Management, 219
   Michael Beer and Robert A. Ruh

4. Influencing Employee Behavior Through Compensation, 231
   Richard I. Henderson

5. Individual and Organizational Correlates of Pay System Preferences, 247
   Michael Beer and Gloria J. Gery

Supporting Human Resource Processes

1. Job Analysis: Objectives, Approaches, and Applications, 269
   Melany E. Baehr

2. Organizational Best Fit: Survival, Change, and Adaptation, 292
   Kenyon B. DeGreene

3. Human Resources Development Through Work Design, 308
   Richard O. Peterson

4. The Design and Implementation of Human Resource Information Systems, 315
   Robert D. Smith

5 ASSESSING INDIVIDUAL QUALIFICATIONS 333

The Selection of Human Resources

1. Legal and Effectiveness Issues in the Personnel Selection Process, 336
   Helen LeVan and Peter F. Sorensen, Jr.

2. Assessment Centers: Background and Human Resource Planning Applications, 350
   Cabot Jaffee and Stephen Cohen

Training and Learning

1. Executive Development in the Department of Agriculture, 380
   Thomas W. Gill

6 EMPLOYEE BEHAVIOR 391

Motivation of the Worker

1. Concerning the Application of Human Motivation Theories in Organizational Settings, 395
   Craig C. Pinder

Alcoholism and Drug Addiction

1. Long-Term Experience with Rehabilitation of Alcoholic Employees, 412
   Fern E. Asma, Raymond L. Eggert and Robert R.J. Hilker

2. Rehabilitation of the Problem Drinker, 420
   Illinois Bell Telephone Company

Retirement: Problems and Programs

1. Dealing with the Aging Work Force, 429
   Jeffrey Sonnenfeld

2. The Problems Retirement Can Bring, 442
   J. Roga O'Meara

Dedication

To Anne who has been my window to what can be in terms of understanding human behavior and encouraging others to develop their potential.

Edwin L. Miller

This is a note of appreciation and thanks to Ruth. Her sensitivity and insights into people and an understanding of their needs and concerns have helped to bring to me a greater awareness and appreciation of behavioral processes and relationships. And what more fitting place for the expression of some of those concerns than a book about human resource management.

Elmer H. Burack

To Gary Louis Albrecht whose patience and support have encouraged my career and directed the excellence of many young scholars.

Maryann H. Albrecht

Contributors

Albrecht, Maryann H.
  University of Illinois, Chicago Circle

Asma, Fern E.
  Illinois Bell Telephone Company

Baehr. Melany E.
  University of Chicago

Beer, Michael
  Harvard Business School

Burack, Elmer H.
  University of Illinois, Chicago Circle

Carlson, Howard C.
  General Motors Corporation

Cohen, Stephen L.
  Assessment Designs, Inc.

De Greene, Kenyon
  University of Southern California

Eggert, Raymond L.
  Illinois Bell Telephone Company

Gartland, Timothy C.
  Control Data Corporation and USAF, Human Factors Branch

Gery, Gloria J.

Gill, Thomas W.
  Department of Agriculture

Henderson, Richard I.
  Georgia State University

Hilker, Robert R.J.
  Illinois Bell Telephone Company

Jaffee, Cabot L.
  Assessment Designs, Inc.

Kryztofiak, Frank
  State University of New York, Buffalo

Contributors

Leach, John J.
University of Chicago

LaVan, Helan
DePaul University

Lazer, William
Michigan State University

McIsaac, George S.
McKinsey & Company

McNichols, Thomas J.
Northwestern University

Milkovich, George T.
University of California, Los Angeles

Miller, Edwin L.
University of Michigan

O'Meara, J. Roga
National Industrial Conference Board

Patten, Thomas H.
Michigan State University

Peterson, Richard O.
AT&T

Pinder, Craig C.
University of British Columbia

Rieder, George A.
Indiana National Bank

Ruh, Robert A.
American Hospital Supply Corporation

Schneier, Craig E.
University of Maryland

Smith, Robert D.
Kent State University

Sonnenfeld, Jeffrey
Northeastern University

Sørensen, Peter F., Jr.
George Williams University

Tornow, Walter W.
Control Data Corporation

Vetter, Eric
Gould Inc.

Walker, James W.
Towers, Perrin, Forster & Crosby

Wanous, John P.
Michigan State University

Young, Drew M.
Atlantic Richfield Company

INTRODUCTION

Performance! The managerial "bottom line" once grew by adjusting workers to the demands of technology. This response is being challenged today because theories and findings from empirical behavioral science research have produced a different image and understanding of workers. The concept of performance has been broadened to include an awareness of employee needs and expectations as well as new and interactive changes in law, social values, and technology. These forces, among others, establish the impact of both environmental and organizational systems on performance.

The challenge has become the creation of new relationships and practices that help to increase performance by managing the impact of change on the interrelated activities within the organization. Out of this ferment has emerged a better understanding of the human resource activity and the management of these new relationships and practices. This newer, more comprehensive approach is termed **Human Resource Management** (HRM), and this area of study promises to bring major changes for personnel practitioners and for the educational preparation of the large number of people moving into this field.

The field of human resource management has a major anchor in the discipline of personnel management. Yet, importantly it goes beyond this area because it seeks to achieve coordination and integration with overall enterprise planning and supportive structures such as information systems and performance appraisal. Not surprisingly, the coordination and integration of people-related activities require modern human resource management to draw upon a variety of ideas, methods, and information.

2 Introduction

The objective of HRM is to help make an organization more effective. It seeks to achieve this objective by means of (1) integrating comprehensive human resource planning with overall organization plans and strategies, and (2) by implementing responsive human resource programs with a growing sensitivity to the economic and policy needs of the organization. The central activities associated with HRM are defined by those functions needed to meet both the requirements of the organization and the needs of people who staff these organizations. Organizational requirements of "bottom-line" performance or improved delivery of services to customers or clientele are seen as related to the economic requirements of organization members and to improving the human experiences. These central functions of HRM include the following:

1. *Professionalism and human resource development* which guide other functions, relate professional activities to other fields, and contribute to professional training and knowledge.
2. *Human resource planning* which involves identifying the numbers, types, and timing for future personnel requirements.
3. *Organizational design* which serves to analyze work tasks, develop the people-related requirements of work activity, and then to design the job and work systems needed to meet organizational and individual objectives.
4. *Personnel maintenance and development* which has been a mainstream of personnel activity in the past and now provides the wide range of activities needed to secure and maintain the work force while meeting numerous (and growing) legal requirements. These activities include recruiting, selection, training and development, compensation, industrial relations, and health and safety matters.
5. *Evaluation, research, and control* which represent the ever-present need to monitor and guide work activity, assess results, and redirect activity where needed.

Unfortunately, these activities and areas of information often develop in haphazard fashion. Thus, an important objective of this book is to provide a framework for understanding these interrelated activities and to provide a representative body of information, procedures, and concepts which describe the current and future events in the management of human resources.

The organization of the HRM function within the institution is a point which needs to be addressed, and it is substantially developed in Part II, which deals with professionalism. Within organizations special terminology exists for describing the functions that concern people and their interrelationships. Personnel, personnel and industrial relations, human relations, and human resources are common descriptive terms. Thus, the term human resource management is often likely to be what managers and professionals in those functions actually (should) do. Additionally, HRM refers to that line management responsibility of thinking about and planning for human resources.

A number of well known academics and practitioners have contributed papers focused on many key topics identified with this field, and these developments are likely to have a major impact on organizational policies and programs now and, even more decisively, in the future. This book focuses on human resource areas of major concern to business and service enterprises today—areas which are likely to be of even greater concern tomorrow. Organizations are concerned with improving "bottom-line," economic performance. People are concerned with their economic welfare and the quality of life within the enterprise. Thus, the organization provides a common ground to meet its own as well as member purposes. The contents of this book, though highly selective because of space limitations, convey important ideas, information, and emphasis to three groups of readers: (a) students considering the human resource field for employment or simply general interest; (b) practitioners already in the field; and (c) members of organizations who may be considering the human resource management field for job purposes.

The coverage of the book has been narrowed to topics which communicate the new(er) sense of human resource management thinking and concerns. A complete treatment of this field would be unworkable in "reader form." However, the number of papers, the areas covered, and the depth of treatment provide ample material for students and a significant number of ideas for practitioners. Classes and seminars concerned with "modern" personnel management, human resource development, organization development, and human resource management would be likely to find these materials applicable and interesting.

HUMAN RESOURCE MANAGEMENT CONCEPT

The notion of human resource management as described in this book includes those sets of people-related activities designed to deal with the (1) *environment*, (2) *orgnization*, (3) *group*, and (4) *individual*. The professional function of HRM is to plan, coordinate, and administer the personnel resource and matters at four different organization levels. Exhibit 1 shows how these HRM activities relate to each other as work, activities, and developments in one area affect the focus and activities ·of other units. For example, initiation of government regulations affecting compensation practice, insurance, and retirement funds in organizations was a result of changed social and economic values and the importance assigned to them. In turn, these regulations have affected organizational policies, compensation and benefits administration, work design, group bonus plans, and individual rewards. Other external developments and organizational functions express these same interdependent relationships. Human resource management, then, is as simple and as difficult as using key HRM functions to orchestrate (manage) the key relationships affecting human resources, for example, forces generated within the environment, organization, work group, and/or individual.

ABOUT THE CONTRIBUTORS

The practitioners, academicians, and researchers who have contributed to this book have all had considerable experience in the human resource and personnel fields, and they effectively bridge research, experience, and application. The very newness of many human resource developments has left little time for the full development of this field. At the same time it should be stated that the authors demonstrate quite different approaches in their papers. Some represent state-of-the-art papers, integrations of research findings, or examinations of a particular research question. Other papers report on noteworthy activities of a particular organization, emphasizing ideas and applications. As an integrated description with a well-defined body of knowledge, our book represents an important step in forging the substantive base of this field.

The thrust of the contributors' practical experiences, insights, and conceptualizations shape an exciting future for HRM, but one which will impose major demands on current practitioners and those entering the field. The authors have presented their ideas with a minimum of specialized language and exhibits so that their contributions can be understood by practitioners and students with a variety of educational backgrounds and experience levels. Also, some other published materials have been included to round out certain topics, and part introductions have been developed to assist in identifying the contributions of each part and integrating these into the HRM theme. The final product is a reasonable representation of modern HRM policies, strategies, and techniques.

Many people have helped us develop and complete our book, and we are very appreciative. About one half of the articles are original contributions especially written for inclusion here. A special thanks goes to our colleagues who have contributed these articles as well as to those authors who gave us permission to reprint articles they have published elsewhere.

Our book can be used as a single course text or as a reference resource. The readings supplement and combine with many of the topics covered in the leading personnel textbooks. In Exhibit 2, we have cross-referenced the articles in our reader to the topics covered in selected personnel books. We hope this will prove useful in supplementing and updating the materials presented in basic textbooks, and that students will find the perspectives presented in our book helpful in rounding their understanding of the HRM field.

ORGANIZATION OF THE BOOK

In Exhibit 3 the central activities of HRM are related to the contents of our book of readings. It is organized into six major parts. Part I considers the changing organizational environment—the broad economic trends, the changing composition of the labor force, the emerging legislation and its influence on institutional factors, and the consequences of social changes. In Part II, HRM is considered as a profession, and the articles focus on the current status and likely future directions of the field. Part III deals with the human resource planning process. This part includes articles on human resource planning, career planning, and planning for improved managerial effectiveness. Jointly considered, these elements form the foundation of emerging personnel planning activities. Part IV focuses on maintaining the HRM system and, of course, members of the organization. The articles in this part identify the newer areas of concern and contribution which support human resources. Included are articles on job analysis and design, personnel information systems, and personnel research. The papers in Part V reflect the high priority assigned to identifying and developing managerial resources to assure organizational continuity and renewal. These activities involve assessment of individual potential, formulating individual career approaches, the design of management development programs, and basic selection decisions. Finally, Part VI presents a view of modern human resource practices concerned with employee motivation, well-being, and performance.

EXHIBIT 1   Human Resource Management: Integrating Organizational Activities

Personnel Professionalism
Development—Education
Planning—Organization Design
Management—Administration
Evaluation—Research Control

Inputs	Impact	Outcomes

Environment
  Economic Change
  Social Change
  Legislative Change
  Technological Change
	Work Force, Values Needs
	Legal Requirements, Restraints
	Technology: Information, Work
	Community Relations
		Resource Allocation
		Work Force Composition
		Policy, Organizational Goals

Administrative
  Goals
  Finances
  Technology
  Human Resources,
    Know-How
	Change Strategies, Coping
	Planning
	Decision Making
	Structure: Organization &
	  Communications
	Personnel Management
		Budgetary Allocations
		Personnel Maintenance System
		Planning Activities
		Development Systems
		Compensation Systems
		Appraising Performance
		Assessing Potential

Group
  Staffing
  Budget
  Work Arrangements
  Organization Structure
	Work/Job Structure
	Group Activities: Technical,
	  Social
		Design: Work, Jobs
		Assignment, Groups
		Relationships: Work,
		  Communications

Individual
  Job Structure
  Work Environment
  Opportunity
  Information
	Skills, Development
	Values, Motivating
	Career Focus, Goals
	Productivity
	Value of Organization
	  Membership
		Work Performance
		Career Development
		Personal Returns:
		  Economic, Psychological

EXHIBIT 2

	Part I The changing organizational environment	Part II Human resource management as a profession	Part III Planning dimensions of human resource management	Part IV Maintaining the HRM system	Part V Performance potential and career development	Part VI Employee behavior
Burack, Elmer H. and Robert D. Smith, *Personnel Management A Human Resource Systems Approach.* St. Paul, Minn.: West Publishing Co., 1977.	Chpt. 3 Chpt. 4 Chpt. 7 Chpt. 13	Chpt. 1 Chpt. 2	Chpt. 5 Chpt. 16	Chpt. 6 Chpt. 9 Chpt. 15	Chpt. 7 Chpt. 9 Chpt. 12 Chpt. 16	Chpt. 11 Chpt. 14
Chruden, Herbert and Arthur W. Sherman, Jr. *Personnel Management* (5th ed.). Cincinnati, Ohio: South-Western Publishing Co., 1976.	Chpt. 5 Chpt. 15 Chpt. 16	Chpt. 4 Chpt. 24	Chpt. 4 Chpt. 9 Chpt. 10	Chpt. 2 Chpt. 4 Chpt. 24	Chpt. 6 Chpt. 7 Chpt. 10 Chpt. 9	Chpt. 11 Chpt. 14 Chpt. 19 Chpt. 20
Glueck, William F. *Personnel: A Diagnostic Approach.* Dallas, Texas: Business Publication, Inc. 1974.	Chpt. 3 Chpt. 4 Chpt. 6 Chpt. 17 Chpt. 18	Chpt. 1 Chpt. 3 Chpt. 20	Chpt. 4 Chpt. 8 Chpt. 9	Chpt. 4 Chpt. 20	Chpt. 6 Chpt. 9 Chpt. 11 Chpt. 12	Chpt. 2 Chpt. 13 Chpt. 15 Chpt. 16
Miner, John B. and Mary Green Miner, *Personnel and Industrial Relations A Managerial Approach* (3rd ed.). New York: Macmillan, 1977	Chpt. 4 Chpt. 5 Chpt. 19	Chpt. 1 Chpt. 3 Chpt. 22	Chpt. 6 Chpt. 8 Chpt. 15	Chpt. 7 Chpt. 22	Chpt. 10 Chpt. 11 Chpt. 12 Chpt. 13 Chpt. 14	Chpt. 16 Chpt. 17 Chpt. 20
Pigors, Paul and Charles A. Myers, *Personnel Administration A Point of View and A Method* (8th ed.). New York: McGraw-Hill, 1977.	Chpt. 1 Chpt. 4 Chpt. 8 Chpt. 17	Chpt. 1 Chpt. 2 Chpt. 23	Chpt. 3 Chpt. 16 Chpt. 17	Chpt. 6 Chpt. 11 Chpt. 14	Chpt. 3 Chpt. 4 Chpt. 15	Chpt. 6 Chpt. 20 Chpt. 22
Robbins, Stephen P. *Personnel The Management of Human Resources.* Englewood Cliffs, N.J.: Prentice-Hall, 1978.	Chpt. 1 Chpt. 5 Chpt. 14	Chpt. 1 Chpt. 2 Chpt. 15	Chpt. 3 Chpt. 6 Chpt. 7	Chpt. 3 Chpt. 10	Chpt. 5 Chpt. 6 Chpt. 7	Chpt. 8 Chpt. 10 Chpt. 11 Chpt. 13
Sayles, Leonard and George Strauss, *Managing Human Resources.* Englewood Cliffs, N.J.: Prentice-Hall, 1977.	Chpt. 4 Chpt. 10 Chpt. 11 Chpt. 14	Chpt. 2 Chpt. 3	Chpt. 7 Chpt. 12	Chpt. 2 Chpt. 3	Chpt. 5 Chpt. 8 Chpt. 9 Chpt. 12	Chpt. 15 Chpt. 16 Chpt. 17 Chpt. 19

EXHIBIT 3 HRM Model and Book Sections

	Human Resource Management	
The Concept	The Systems Activities	Book Sections
Planning	Environment	1. The Changing Organizational Environment
Organization Design	Administration (Organization)	2. HRM as a Profession
Personnel Maintenance and Development		3. Planning Dimensions of HRM
Evaluation, Research, Control	Group	4. Maintaining the HRM System A. Basic Functions B. Support Activities
Professionalism	Individual	5. Performance, Potential, and Career Development
		6. Employee Behavior

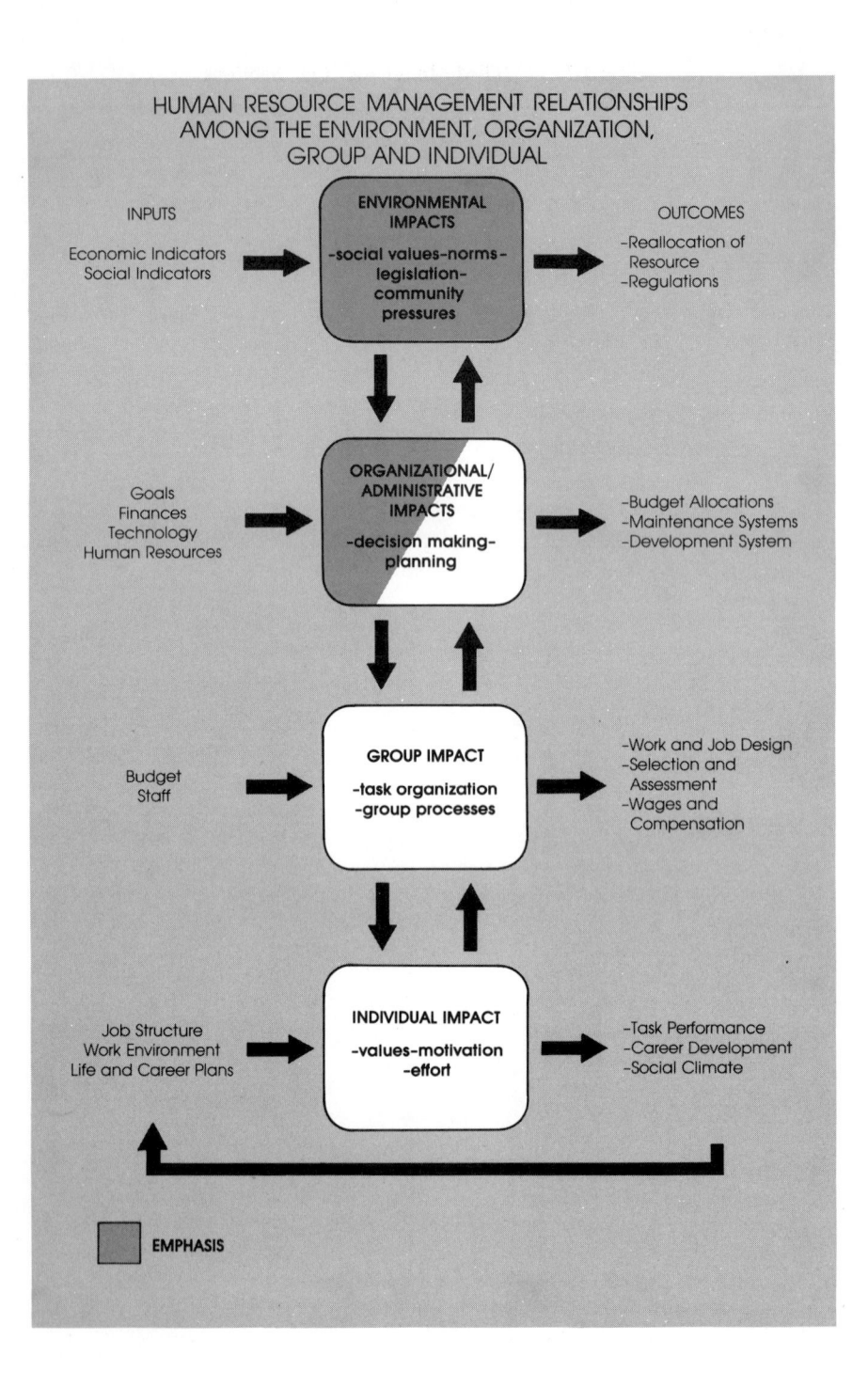

HUMAN RESOURCE MANAGEMENT RELATIONSHIPS AMONG THE ENVIRONMENT, ORGANIZATION, GROUP AND INDIVIDUAL

INPUTS

Economic Indicators
Social Indicators

→ **ENVIRONMENTAL IMPACTS**
-social values-norms-
legislation-
community
pressures →

OUTCOMES
-Reallocation of Resource
-Regulations

Goals
Finances
Technology
Human Resources

→ **ORGANIZATIONAL/ ADMINISTRATIVE IMPACTS**
-decision making-
planning →

-Budget Allocations
-Maintenance Systems
-Development System

Budget
Staff

→ **GROUP IMPACT**
-task organization
-group processes →

-Work and Job Design
-Selection and Assessment
-Wages and Compensation

Job Structure
Work Environment
Life and Career Plans

→ **INDIVIDUAL IMPACT**
-values-motivation
-effort →

-Task Performance
-Career Development
-Social Climate

■ **EMPHASIS**

1

THE CHANGING ORGANIZATIONAL ENVIRONMENT

Human resource managers are becoming increasingly alarmed at the scope and depth of system adaptations organizations must make to remain technologically and socially competitive. Currently, pressures for change are generated by advances in technology, by a variety of specialized interest groups, and by legislation which reflects basic shifts in societal values. As a result, managers must determine the priority of requests made by vocal and concerned representatives from government agencies, consumer groups, community and employee groups, and unions. In addition, managers are called upon to redesign and shape core personnel systems to respond to sweeping legislation involving fair employment opportunities, health and safety regulations, and modifications in mandatory retirement programs.

Implementing massive system changes at each level of the organization has made many managers aware that change is the only predictable condition of their current work environment. It is also understood that when the dust settles, the transformation of human resource systems will also have shaped a new managerial role, work force, work system, and organizational environment. Managers realize that if they can control these change processes, rather than be controlled by them, they have an opportunity to design a vital, stimulating, and rewarding work environment. The challenge of this opportunity has led professionals to develop procedures and approaches that should help human resource managers and specialist practitioners understand, stabilize, and direct the transformation of their organization.

Personnel people are faced with two types of demands: one has to do with guiding current organizational changes and the other with developing a blueprint for future change designs. The articles we have chosen for Part I provide a clear view of organizational possibilities for the future. They speak particularly to the **information needs** of human resource managers by identifying those perspectives, strategies, and facts which relate the organization to its community, work force, and unions.

Our first selection, "Human Resource Planning: Technology, Policy, Change," helps us to analyze the truly dramatic impact that environmental change has had on organizational policy, processes, and human resources. One of the more volatile aspects of this change, technology, is described in terms of both production processes and computers. The authors, Elmer H. Burack and Thomas J. McNichols, have used the analyses and research findings from some six years of research and work with organizations to show how institutional planning emerges in response to technological change and how needs give rise to appropriate modifications and accommodations in activities related to human resource planning. Yet it is clear that the needed plans and programs often don't take place and thereby result in uneconomic use of resources and frustrating experiences for organization members.

Demographic factors and social trends have a tremendous impact on organizations, and human resource management officials should be apprised of impending demographic and social changes, the implications of these trends for the organization, and available means to cope with these changes. William Lazer explains what basic shifts in demographic factors and social trends portend for business. This article presents a perspective of some fundamental factors and forces that will shape business opportunities during the 1980s. The prospect of a second baby boom, the changing mix of the population, the increasing affluence of households, and growing participation of women in the work force will impact organizational goals as well as individual needs. Thus, HRM will be faced with an increasingly complex set of challenges.

One of the major contributing factors to change in organizational environments is the dramatic shift that is taking place in the composition of the work force. Encouraged by equal opportunity legislation, larger numbers of women and minority groups are entering the work force, all of which necessitates a rethinking of managerial assumptions, activities, and policies regarding personnel practices and policies. Maryann H. Albrecht describes the changing composition of the new labor force and some of its implications for personnel programs. Her work suggests programs of planning, analysis, education, and research which can improve hiring, training, and employment stability. These approaches are especially timely in the light of continuing difficulties encountered by minority groups and women as they seek even-handed treatment in **both** employment and promotion opportunities.

Unions have come to play an important yet complex role in organizational policies and programs. Union membership and union-management relationships are important in the HRM framework, just from the viewpoint of members alone. But aside from this factor is the realization that the character of union membership and labor-related legislation have assumed an important new thrust.

In the concluding article of Part I, McIsaac specifies the changes already occurring in management-union relationships as a result of changes in the organizational environment. Although organizational profits, ability to pay, and worker productivity have usually been key issues in management-union confrontations, the author suggests that the war over compensation is ending. Greater managerial concern for a stable work force and increased worker demands for a secure job have resulted in a common goal: the stabilization of the work force. This shared goal has helped to foster cooperation and focus attention on the worker as a productive individual whose total work career will contribute to the long-term growth of the organization. McIsaac's documentation of the effectiveness of such a program highlights the points made in previous papers which suggest that the forces of external change can be controlled and directed—that systems can be created which (re)vitalize and benefit the organization as well as its members.

On balance, the articles in Part I provide an overview of some of the major forces and considerations leading to the pressures for organizational accommodation and change. In this context, the term **dynamic environment** is distinguished by a number of characteristics: technological change, shifts in the composition of the work force, changing demographic characteristics of the population, and new directions in union-management relationships and activities. In terms of the HRM model presented in the introduction, all of these change forces lead to organizational adjustments in decision activities, policies, and functional programs, and these in turn affect individuals, communities, and so on. HRM planners attempt to anticipate the thrust of these developments within work systems and administrative systems through which organizational affairs are conducted. Work groups, departments, and other collective arrangements of people may be enlarged. curtailed, or created. Work technologies and attendant work skills may also shift and thus alter the demands imposed on individuals as well as their career possibilities for the future.

ENVIRONMENTAL CHANGES AND ORGANIZATIONAL ADAPTATION

Human Resource Planning:
Technology, Policy, Change

Elmer H. Burack
Thomas J. McNichols

BACKGROUND

Twentieth-century technology, accelerated by the electronic explosion and the computer, is one of the most significant advances in the history of mankind. Modern literature and philosophy have praised and criticized the good and evil inherent in our automated industrial society. Forebodings that the scientific revolution would outpace man's ability to adapt to his new technology are a reality which has affected all functions and levels of society.

While the impact of technical change on the social and economic structure of modern civilization has been widely studied, the effects of new technologies on the changing role of management and professional (technical) groups have not been clearly stated or understood. The effects of change on manpower requirements and manpower planning at the managerial level have not been delineated or thoroughly researched. The subtle, cumulative effects of rapidly advancing process-technology, together with computer analysis and direction, have created significant need for new levels of education, training, and technical skills. In companies which utilize advanced technologies, the day of the foreman, supervisor, and maintenance chief nurtured on experience and longevity has already passed. That day is rapidly approaching for all types of process manufacturing, and for many service institutions maintained on the basis of information systems.

The advance of technology has dictated new responsibilities and roles for technical, operational, administrative, and support groups. Engineers with college degrees now serve as high-level foremen and maintenance supervisors in many manufacturing firms. Computer-trained systems personnel direct various operational and functional units. The number and stature of technical support groups (systems, control, planning) have increased—they now occupy a signifi-

Adapted with permission from Comparative Administration Research Institute Series No. 6, College of Business Administration, Kent State University.

cant and crucial place within the managerial structure of various institutional and industrial complexes. This trend toward greater demands for technical managers has changed the industrial organization, shifted the locus of decision making, redefined job characteristics and skill requirements, and altered the relationships of supervisory and staff roles. To date, industry has not fully recognized the organizational implications of these technological changes, nor has it kept pace with the manpower planning and career development necessary for managing a highly complex, automated, industrial society.

Research projects probing the interaction of technological change with occupations, job structure, and work skills—together with special U.S. Department of Labor analyses—have provided the know-how for formulating Departmental policies and programs. It was out of this ferment that the research project emerged. The present study is based on six years of field research in manufacturing and service units, including a major three-year field research study ("Management and Automation") undertaken by the authors (1966–68) for the U.S. Department of Labor under the authority of the Manpower Development and Training Act. This study focused on managerial manpower and its response to technological change. In addition, a support base was provided from a large group of industrial research studies conducted over a three-year period under the direction of Elmer Burack at the Illinois Institute of Technology. The results from this study are used to illustrate important, emergent trends affecting contemporary organizations and key manpower groups.

Information for the Management and Automation study was based on data from 44 companies and 72 plant sites, which represented nine major industrial classifications. Six hundred interviews were made and 400 responded to questionnaires. Approximately one-fourth of the research sites included advanced areas of technical achievement in petroleum refining, chemical plants, and power generation. Approximately three-fourths of the companies studied constituted industrial sectors where widespread technological change was taking place. These areas included steel making and rolling, manufacturing of building products, meat processing, processing of fruits and vegetables, packaged food specialities, and mechanical and computer-based communication systems. Information on computer-based changes emerged from the research studies at Illinois Institute of Technology and the authors' consulting experiences.

ORGANIZATIONAL CHALLENGE IN AN ERA OF CHANGE

Computer Advances

The era of the seventies has been a period of unparalleled excitement and opportunity for the organization, operation, and management of business activities. This development was paced by newer technologies and a growing need for and recourse to information and understanding of the business and operational environment.

Newer manufacturing technologies achieve unprecedented rates of output at high levels of product quality and uniformity. Included are newer concepts in control instrumentation and engineering approaches in equipment design, cross-fertilization of new technologies (control, production, and information), and advances in material technology which help to standardize system inputs.

A second major dimension of the technological promise of the future is the information explosion and computer usage. Optimism about new management opportunities comes from the ability to obtain information at great speed, in substantial volume, and in a form suitable for direct use. For example, customer demands for order status and billing information are met by "customer information systems," and computer usage in accounting transactions and routine managerial calculations is well established. Advances associated with digital computers span a range of application from use in direct production and business support to aerospace applications and national information networks. Insurance companies, banks, retail stores, city governments, manufacturing concerns, and federal agencies have already put the computer to use. It is estimated that more than 70,000 computers were in operation in 1970. The computer is leading to the development of new operational techniques and business strategies. The rapid advances in newer technologies sometimes exceed the pace of managerial advances. New problem areas are created by unique situations which were infrequently encountered in the past or by developments previously considered unimportant. Newer information opportunities for supervisors and managers to gain an immediate picture of ongoing operations as they occur means more meaningful decision making and tighter control of business variables and benefits. These improvements should be considered an interim step leading to increased understanding and potential manipulation of the entire business environment.

Training devices simulating operating conditions and systems provide opportunities to plan procedures for handling nonstandard or emergency conditions as well as providing for more routine development by accelerated training assignments. An added awareness of man's reaction to particular operation situations is also gained.

Computers and Organization Planning

Computers have fostered substantial modifications in work procedures, allocation of responsibilities, attendant work qualifications, and the distribution of managers and supervisors. The incorporation of computer systems in plant design and the installation of computers in plant and headquarter facilities indicate even more widespread changes for the future. These trends will have a great impact on organizational structure and managerial manpower demands.

Computers have a substantial impact on the amount, quality, and timeliness of information received. New corporate strategies emerge with regard to decision making, management function, and the structuring of the management organization. There are new possibilities for determining the locus of managerial functions as well as the distribution of responsibilities between operating and staff support personnel. In some manufacturing areas, the incorporation of computer-based systems of management information may proceed irrespective of advancements in the technology of the production process. In other areas, production variables may be difficult to quantify and this would be the limiting factor.

Computers in Production

A second important point of entry for the computer is the production system. Explicit incorporation of the computer in higher level production systems poses problems for supervisory and managerial personnel in experimental uses (such as data logging applications) and in more conventional production applications (analysis, interpretation, and/or rapid response). Computer technology presents higher level management with a wide variety of managerial manpower problems. Changing manpower demands give rise to problems in job training and in broader managerial development. The approach to these problems is conditioned by the experience and educational base of incumbent personnel, the availability of computer specialists, and the background of new employees.

Problems and Issues

Introduction of newer technologies into a firm creates a complex series of problems. These are aggravated if the managerial group is only partially aware, or wholly unaware, of the emerging issues. The cumulative effects of slow change over time are subtle and may lead to an attitude of "business as usual." The problems arising from lack of recognition are just as bad as solutions which lack expertise or reflect premature response. The problems arising from the newer technologies include man-to-man and man-to-technology relationships, functions, or activities; processes of decision making; and communications and planning. New challenges arise when emergent technologies are affixed to older existing systems. Functional managers are frequently under severe administrative or economic pressure to capitalize on the promise or potential of newer technologies—especially in communications.

Growing organizational complexity of production, distribution, and sales functions complicates the generation, dissemination, and use of information. The growing interdependencies of process and distribution facilities demand levels of coordination and control less frequently encountered in the past. In the communication of complex ideas among plant operations and support personnel, or between plant personnel and those stationed at physically removed headquarters, new problems arise in timing, distance, selection of a communication vehicle, and authority power. An increased dependence on staff support personnel arises from the newer technological systems and the growing interdependencies among personnel. This higher rate of interaction represents another area of communication difficulty and organization conflict.

The acceleration and incorporation of newer technologies does not provide sufficient time to eliminate potential difficulties between younger professional and older experience-based personnel. Threats to power, position, prestige, or authority are frequently a part of the veiled issues underlying tension, conflict, and poor employee relationships which accompany the introduction of change. These same general types of problems arise when newer approaches are applied to decision making or problem solving, or when newer communication technologies are adapted to existing systems.

Computer procedures promise more effective operations. However, industries which use computers and analytical models as guides to more effective performance will still have to communicate results to potential users and incorporate the results into work-related activities.

Communication problems also arise within the framework of newer organizational designs. "Project management" and "task force management" describe some of the newer concepts representing various functional areas which cut across traditional company lines. Key factors in instituting these new designs are problem solving in the newer technologies and developmental work within operational areas. Reaching these goals is totally dependent on communication among organizational members who have different interests, functional orientation, age, skills, and education.

More comprehensive approaches to manpower planning are needed as operations become faster-paced and manpower is intertwined with procedure and process. Such planning may be viewed by some as manipulative or as a depersonalization of jobs or as a loss of authority or responsibility. Management's traditional preoccupation with the economic and technological details often excludes the human factor or places it in a secondary position. The supervisor or manager is often bewildered by the many interacting factors affecting his job and job security, factors over which he may exercise little control.

Manpower Planning and Administration

"Planning" is often viewed as a panacea for avoiding the pitfalls of change or for producing a design for more effective operation. The secondary position often assumed by managerial and supervisory personnel counteracts the expected therapeutic effects of the planning process. The threat to individual competency is often overlooked or underestimated. Erosion of individual competence, diminishing relevance of early schooling and job experience, and needed mental abilities relative to emerging job demands pose direct threats to today's managers. The individual, his job, his superior, and the organization as a whole relate to this problem of incipient obsolescence in a complex fashion. Personnel displacement or early retirement emerge as additional consequences of technological change. The issues posed in manpower retraining or anticipation of problems are easily obscured by the higher priority of business projects and the traditionally lower prestige of personnel manpower functions, or by a lack of understanding about the dynamics of these issues.

The manpower problems which emerge from an organizational viewpoint are paralleled by those of the individual. Indifference to his job, lack of motivation, tension, and frustration are among the many problems faced by the man who is confronted with obsolescence of his job skills. Sometimes the person is not completely aware of the sources of his tension or uneasiness. In other cases, the forces of change have already been set in motion and there is insufficient time for the individual to mentally and emotionally adjust to the new skill requirements. Since managerial personnel are a critical part of the organizational-operational system, their problems affect that whole system.

POLICY MAKING AND MANPOWER PLANNING

The significance of investment decisions which drastically change the nature of the production process and the importance of manpower planning are recognized by industry. However, examination of companies included in the Management and Automation (M&A) Study, for example, showed that important manpower considerations were omitted in the policy-making process. In the following discussion, traditional policy procedures on capital expenditures are described and logical points of manpower interest and involvement are detailed. The effect of Research and Development and the tie-in of policy-launched technological change on manpower programming are explored.

Perspective in Policy Formulation and Manpower

M & A research indicates the interrelationship of policy procedures and manpower issues. Figure 1 shows existing arrangements for policy formulation. Top management is charged with overall responsibility for long-range planning. Closely related to technological planning is the Research and Development

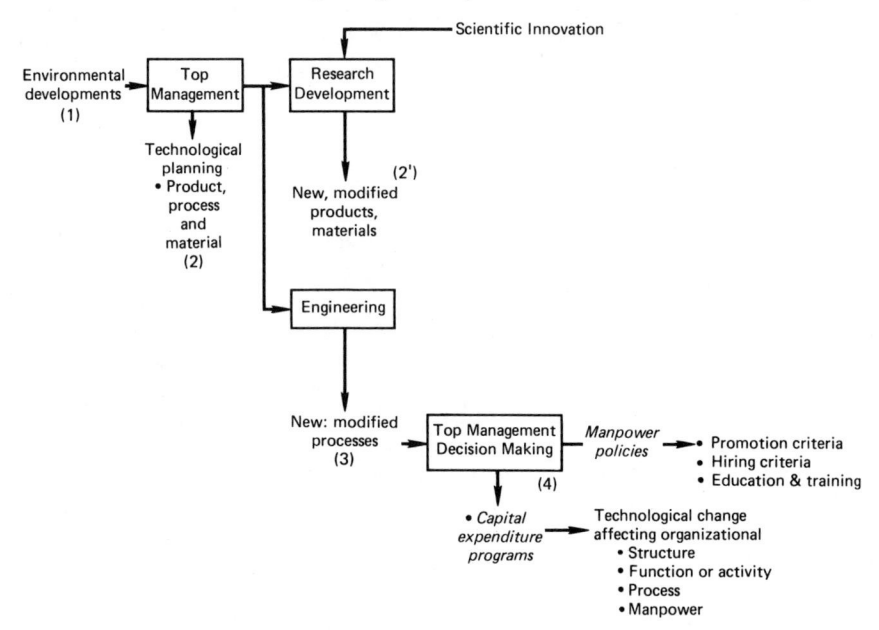

FIGURE 1 *Policy Formulation: Establishing the Base for Change*

(R&D) unit. A plan for the future embodying product, process, and material is the result of the interplay of top-level managers, financial and cost personnel, R&D talent, and the applied technologists and engineers. The initiation of a capital expenditure program brings with it a concomitant need for consideration of manpower resources, which includes far more than simply the number needed. Forces are set in motion which directly affect the need for specific education, skills, and experiences. This in turn dictates a time sequencing of manpower programs. Some of the individual company considerations leading to capital programs are described in the following sections.

Influence of Capital Expenditure Policies on Technological Change

Because of the large investment involved in any significant technological advance, top management usually reserves the right of final decision. For large companies, the financing of the installation may be a minor problem. For medium-size and small firms, committing a large amount of funds is more critical, particularly if the older equipment is performing satisfactorily. Even relatively large companies are slow to introduce technological change if their earnings and return on invested capital are unattractive. In those industries with a low return, capital expenditures are directed mainly to maintaining the status quo and any change in the production process is on a more gradual basis. Such firms also pay more for their capital on a present value basis. Industries and firms which are most in need of technological change to improve their earnings position are least likely to initiate significant new production processes. "Glamor" industries and those industries which have good cash flow positions (such as petroleum) are more likely to introduce technological change.

Response to the Environment

Besides capital budgeting policies, the interpretation of and the response to the environment are significant factors in initiating technological change. Firms in a rapidly growing industry must respond quickly to the competitive environment to keep pace. Although firms in less attractive industries may delay technological improvements, when drastic changes are necessary for survival management finds a way to acquire the necessary funds. As an alternative, a merger takes place. There have been a number of take-overs and acquisitions in the coal industry. This is a declining industry, beset with labor problems. It has had to introduce technological change to remain competitive with other forms of energy.

In more mature industries, firms are likely to wait until a crisis situation develops before introducing significantly new production processes. The steel industry continued to operate submarginal plants until the cost-price squeeze and foreign competition forced significant technological changes. In the printing industry, the introduction of high-speed automatic presses was in direct response to cost pressures from a strong and demanding union. It is expected that the use of the computer to operate the complete printing process will continue to make gains in this industry.

Many technical discoveries are made outside the industries most affected by them. The adaptation of nuclear power for commercial use has affected the electrical utility industry. This industry spent a lot of time formulating its decisions to adopt nuclear power, but it had to rely on the expertise of those who produce nuclear generating equipment for the installation and training of operating crews, technical analysis, economic operating conditions, and trouble shooting. In the initial stages of planning, more attention was given to capital budgeting and cost analyses than to manpower. Educational programs were finally planned which helped to provide the staff specialists and operational managers required by these advanced installations.

Changes as Affected by Research and Development Policies

Many companies cause technological change through Research and Development policies. Expenditure on R&D is a function of the profitability and cash flow of the firm. The more successful firms are likely to be more progressive in making technological improvements in their production process. R&D effort, size, cash flow, and profitability all affect the firm's ability to launch change and the time-related pattern of the changes.

If R&D effort is directed toward the development of new products and materials, new technologies will probably have to be found to produce the new products. As noted in Figure 2, the character of the R&D effort determines the scope and depth of manpower and organization changes.

In many cases, new skills are needed for the operation of new production processes. While the new technology may be developed internally, the production equipment is probably manufactured by a specialist in the production of automated equipment or machine tools. This is a logical point for manpower efforts related to the programmed changes.

Companies which adopt a policy of product improvement (the "me too" or follower philosophy noted in Figure 2) with a minimum of R&D effort on the discovery of new products, are in a position to benefit from the experiences of "trail blazers." Introduction of the basic oxygen furnace in Europe and subsequently in Canada and the United States provided several sites where manufacturers were willing to share operating experiences. Technical assistance, training, and discussion of experiences were sufficiently detailed to alter company managements to the following:

1. gross manpower needs
2. qualitative requirements in terms of work experience and education
3. need for new job classifications
4. problem-solving approaches for confronting a wide variety of operating problems
5. labor displacement possibilities with subsequent implications for both the union and managerial personnel

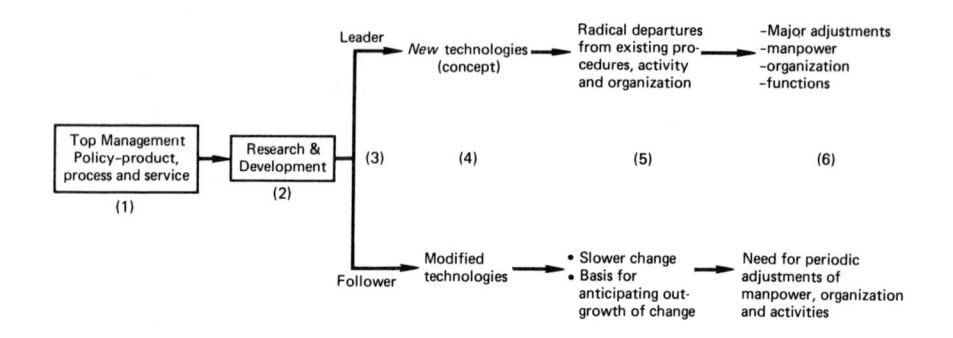

FIGURE 2 *Research Roles and Degree of Change*

Some firms are only concerned with modification of the production process while other firms introduce major departures from existing processes. The policy on new products and processes has a direct bearing on manpower needs.

Policy Making and Manpower Planning

In many companies included in the M&A and related studies, overall corporate planning activities (for example, product, service, and facility) took precedence over manpower planning. Manpower planning generally took place shortly before or after a new operation was underway. In the more sophisticated technologies associated with computer-based operations, the full impact of manpower requirements was not felt until the new equipment was introduced into the production lines.

The more drastic the change in technology, the greater the impact on the organization adopting the new process. Technical support groups created to provide the expertise needed for new manufacturing processes were often without a basis in the organization. Some of these staff support groups assumed line authority and caused organizational conflict. In many instances, educational requirements for personnel servicing and operating new advanced equipment proved to be a serious problem. Long-time supervisors and employees lacked the basic education to direct and operate the sophisticated equipment, and training programs did not always provide the necessary upgrading of skills. There was often a change in educational background and skills of an entire organizational level.

Policy and Manpower Problems— A Case Illustration

Many firms in the food industry have not made major technical improvements because of financial considerations and the low state of technical knowledge (food chemistry). The events that took place when a large, diversified processor of food products underwent extensive changes are discussed below.

This company was of substantial economic size, but the profitability and cash resources of former days had given way to low profits, poor reserves, and plant technologies covering a wide range of technical sophistication. An occasional up-to-date production unit was intermixed with outmoded processes. A "follower, me too" philosophy had permitted certain facilities to lose technical or competitive positions. Manpower activities were at a low state of accomplishment and the *personnel* role at corporate headquarters was traditional, providing limited training and servicing of job evaluation and wage needs. Plant management directed their own personnel operations. Manpower administration in the firm was *reaction* rather than *planned* management. Personnel were allowed to fend for themselves when technological changes were introduced and remedial measures took place after the fact.

Economic considerations were important in the fortunes of this company, but problems were compounded by inept handling of manpower matters and a lack of rationalization of capital budgeting procedures.

Policy and Organization Design

Careful attention to design options can have important manpower benefits for the organization. The following list of items suggests some of the possibilities in this area:

1. Organization for introducing new technologies—For example, the staffing of a group for specialized technical study affords a seat of technical expertise. Options exist to ensure wide dissemination of acquired experiences to resident groups. A decision to build on the capabilities of line or support elements has important implications for maintaining the relevancy of these personnel.
2. Training options—Critical examination of traditional on-the-job approaches and informal guidance by line supervisors. New learning technologies for accelerating individual experiences are possible.
3. Balancing older, experienced-based and younger degree trainees to meet change demands.

Summary

Policy considerations affect the manpower picture and a wide range of matters touch on emergent personnel problems. The traditional view of policy-making processes requires reinterpretation and extension to more fully identify the effect of these activities on the character and frequency of managerial problems. Economic size, profitability, and cash flow influence capital expenditure patterns and the resulting manpower problems. A fundamental point of departure in manpower programming is the interplay of capital expenditure policy and the options available to the architects of organization structure, relationships, and activities.

The 1980s and Beyond: A Perspective

William Lazer

The decade of the 1960s witnessed a most remarkable and extended period of continuous business growth.[1] The "soaring sixties" reached unprecedented heights in the expansion of population, income, employment, housing markets, business investments, and profits. It led to consumer expectations of a bigger and better future.

In striking contrast, the 1970s have been marked by rising unemployment, inflation, scarcity, declining productivity, contracting markets, a sharp recession, and a climate of considerable self-doubt and retrenchment. The following paraphrases of statements made in business publications about our economy in the last two years are examples:

> The United States is steadily sliding down the path to decline.
>
> Our long-term growth trend has slowed and we are confronted with permanent stagflation.
>
> We are entering a period of scarcity in energy and raw materials.
>
> The United States will have difficulty generating sufficient economic growth to satisfy consumer demand.
>
> Our economic and political system is designed to cope with short-term problems, and it cannot cope with the long-term demands placed upon it.
>
> We are entering a new period of our history—a no-growth economy.
>
> The good life and high living brought about by the affluence of the 1960s have now come to an abrupt halt.
>
> Consumers in the future will be forced to lower their life-style expectations.
>
> By conquering nature, Americans have squandered their natural resources. Soon they will have to live austerely.

There seem to be three tendencies on the part of business prognosticators. First, forecasts of future markets and business opportunities seem unduly influenced by the most immediate events, especially when those events show a sharp break with the recent past. This was the case with double-digit inflation, high unemployment levels, the quadrupling of petroleum prices, and our falling productivity levels. Second, greater weight seems to be given to negative market forces and economic difficulties than to positive or supporting factors. One need only review the lack of emphasis on declining interest rates, moderate levels of inflation, and increasing productivity of 1976, as compared to the notice given to their opposites during

William Lazar, "The 1980s and Beyond: A Perspective," pp. 21–35, *MSU Business Topics*, Spring 1977. Reprinted by permission of the publisher, Division of Research, Graduate School of Business Administration, Michigan State University.

1974. Third, American events do not seem to be placed in a balanced perspective. Our economic problems, difficult social issues, and disturbances are not viewed as happenings. They are treated as crises and are presented as precursors of a rapidly deteriorating future. For example, in the past few years in the United States, attention has been given to our energy crisis, environmental crisis, unemployment crisis, population crisis, international monetary crisis, hospital crisis, pollution crisis, medical crisis, food crisis, urban crisis, farm crisis, housing crisis, gun crisis, water crisis, credibility crisis, and, of course, Watergate crisis.

What do the basic shifts in demographic factors and social trends portend? What are the myths, and what are the realities? This article presents a perspective of some fundamental factors and forces that will shape business opportunities during the 1980s.

DECLINING BIRTHS OR ANOTHER BABY BOOM?

There seems to be as much misunderstanding about actual births, zero population growth, the desire to have children, and fertility rates as there is about any aspect of demographics. Such mistaken statements as the following are illustrative:

> We have now reached zero population growth (ZPG), and our population is declining.
> The young people no longer wish to have children.
> Ours is an era of the childless marriage.
> Young marrieds desire freedom, not entrapment with family responsibilities.
> Given the pill and abortion, the number of babies born will continue to decline rapidly.

Our population growth depends on the rate of births, deaths, and migration. Death rates are quite predictable, and net migration to the United States averages about 400,000 persons per year. The controlling factor is the birthrate. Misconceptions about actual births and birthrates stem from a misunderstanding of technical terms used in reporting birth statistics, such as total fertility and zero population growth (ZPG).

In the United States, ZPG is estimated to occur when a rate of birth of 2.1 children per woman of childbearing age—women aged 15 to 44—is maintained over a considerable period. At that rate, our population growth will eventually level off or just replace itself. Moreover, our current birthrate is below ZPG, being approximately 1.8 to 1.9. As a result, an erroneous conclusion is often drawn that the number of babies born is decreasing and our population is declining.

For our population to level off, it is estimated that a rate of 2.1 children per woman of childbearing age must be maintained for several decades. Will this occur? It could, but that may be unlikely. Even if it did occur, this would not mean that the number of babies born over the next 15 years will decline. In fact, the potential is present for a *second baby boom*. But it should also be recognized that if the current tendency to defer marriage and births is maintained, eventually the United States will have an excess of deaths over births.

During the late 1950s and early 1960s, the postwar baby boom generated an average of about 4 million births per year, reaching a high point of 4.3 million births in 1957. That factor helped stimulate the growth years of the 1960s, leading to rapidly expanding markets and levels of great economic accomplishments. A second baby boom is likely to occur even if the birthrate remains at a low rate of 1.9 children per woman of childbearing age. The actual number of live births in the United States from 1940 on, with projections for 1980 and 1985, using a 2.1 birthrate, is given in Table 1. Obviously, the 1980–1990 total occurs on a larger population base.

The next baby boom, however, will have some marked differences from that of the 1960s. The previous boom resulted from relatively fewer women having large families, almost four children each. The new baby boom will comprise about twice the number of women having one-half the number of children. A larger proportion of babies of the second baby boom will be firstborn. That, of course, has significant market ramifications.

Considerable attention has been paid by the news media to the childless couple. This is sometimes highlighted in terms of the two-career family. But such families are very small in number, and while they are expected to grow in the 1980s, their overall impact on births will remain insignificant. The main reasons for our relatively low birthrate are (1) smaller families, (2) later starts for families, (3) postponement of marriage by the young, and (4) a decline in the proportion of women of childbearing age in the population.

But even if the number and proportion of women of childbearing age are increasing, the question is whether women have changed in their desire to bear children. Survey results continue to indicate that married women want to have children. The expected number of children for wives 18 to 24 in June 1974 was reported to be: 0 or one child, 17 percent; two children, 55.7 percent; three children, 19.4 percent; four or more children, 7.8 percent.[2]

The average number of children desired, however, has decreased significantly, and families are smaller. The norm now seems to be a matched set—a girl and a boy. Given the uncertainty associated with predetermining the sex of children, the birth of several children will be required by many couples to achieve the desired mix. Hence, it seems likely that a birthrate of more than two children per woman of childbearing age may be realized in the near future, contributing to the second baby boom. Also, it should be noted that more babies are being born to unwed mothers.

Some of the characteristics of the second baby boom of interest to business are:

1. An average of about 4 million babies per year will be born between 1975 and 1990. This parallels the baby boom of the 1960s.
2. Previously, 25 percent of all babies were firstborn. By 1980 this may reach 40 percent. Thus, expenditure on children's furniture, clothing, housing needs, baby foods, and accoutrements will be affected.
3. Family size will be smaller.
4. Declining birthrate will result from fewer higher order births and not from childless couples.
5. The proportion of families expecting no children will continue to be small, and this will not be the norm.

men aged 15 to 24 will have three-fourths of the firstborns, while women aged 20 to 29 will account for two-thirds of higher order births. These groups are increasing absolutely and proportionately.

7. Families will realize higher per capita income.[3]

TABLE 1 Live Births in the United States

Year	Births (100's)
1940	2,570
1945	2,873
1950	3,645
1955	4,128
1960	4,307
1965	3,801
1970	3,725
1974	3,160
1980	4,000 (estimated)
1985	4,250 (estimated)

Source: Based on data from Bureau of the Census, *Current Population Reports*, Series P-25, using Series E for projection purposes.

POPULATION INCREASE OR DECLINE

Related to the major misunderstandings about births are some of the general statements made about changes in our total population. For example:

Since our birthrate is below ZPG, our population has leveled off.
Our population has peaked and is now declining.
Ours is becoming more of a child-centered and teen-aged population.
Senior citizens are becoming less significant as a proportion of the total population.

Table 2 presents an estimate of expected growth in population from 1970 to 2000 using the assumption of a ZPG birthrate. While our population is increasing at a lower rate than it did during the 1960s, it is still showing substantial gains. Conservative census projections indicate that the United States will add over 19 million people, more than four-fifths of the Canadian population, for example, during the 1970–1980 decade. It will add a little more, about 23 million, roughly the total Canadian population, between 1980 and 1990. By the year 2000 our population is expected to reach 264 million.

To gain perspectives on future market opportunities, a most important factor to note is the varying growth rate of different age groups. During the 1970s the relative rate of growth of the 25–34 age group stands out. This group is expected to account for 46 percent of the growth over the decade.

TABLE 2 Population Shifts in the United States, 1960–2000

	Population in Millions				
Age	1960	1970	1980	1990	2000
Under 20	69	77	73	77	81
20–24	11	17	21	18	19
25–34	23	26	37	42	36
35–44	24	23	26	37	41
45–54	21	23	22	25	36
55–64	16	19	21	20	22
65 and over	17	20	24	28	29
	181	205	224	247	264

Percentage Change			
1960–1970	1970–1980	1980–1990	1990–2000
+11.1%	− 5.2%	+ 5.7%	+ 4.3%
+54.3	+22.6	−15.4	+ 7.8
+10.4	+46.1	+13.1	−14.6
− 4.5	+ 9.6	+45.5	+13.0
+13.3	− 3.9	+ 9.9	+45.1
+19.4	+13.0	− 3.4	+10.6
+20.4	+19.8	+15.4	+ 3.9
+13.4%	+ 9.4%	+10.0%	+ 7.2%

Source: Based on data from Bureau of the Census, *Current Population Reports*, Series P-25, using Series E for projection purposes.

The decade of the seventies is an era of the young marrieds. Their proportionate growth does not portend a revolution in values or upheaval in our society, as is often projected. Rather, the young marrieds are interested in establishing themselves in their communities, homes, families, and jobs. They support extended market growth for such items as houses, home furnishings, cars, appliances, and furniture. They are net borrowers, not net savers.

In gross terms, each of the decades from 1950 to 2000 may be characterized according to a "core market thrust"—that market which reflects the largest proportional growth. This trend is shown in Table 3. Obviously, there is some overlap between decades, but the table illustrates the ripple effect as people move through the age cycle.

A few highlights of expected trends in the growth of various age categories during the 1980s are pointed up in Table 4.

Population statistics reveal that even with a relatively low birthrate, our population will realize substantial growth. The young marrieds and middle agers will become more important in the next 15 years. Both males and females are living longer, and the population is aging. The life expectancy at birth for women in 1974 was almost 76 years, compared to 68 years for men. This will result in an increasing number of women living alone. The proportion of senior citizens, which is increasing and will continue to do so through the year 2000, will make itself felt.

TABLE 3 Characterization of Decades

Decade	Core Market Focus
1950–1960	Babies and young children
1960–1970	Teen-agers and young adults
1970–1980	Young marrieds
1980–1990	Early middle agers
1990–2000	Middle agers

TABLE 4 Trends in Age Groups in the 1980s

Age Category	Projected Trends
0–4	Although they have been contracting since 1960, between 1980 and 1985 *they will grow almost four times as fast* as the average for the whole population.
5–15	They realized great growth during and since the 1950s and were one-fourth of the population in 1970. *They will decline relatively* and account for less than 20 percent of the population in 1985.
18–24	They are currently expanding and represent the age category of first marriage and first child for many Americans. *They will decline relatively* during the 1980s.
25–34	The young marrieds *will continue to realize the greatest growth rate of all groups* through 1980. They are expected to grow by 46 percent over the decade of the 1970s.
35–44	The early middle-agers have high income, high home ownership, and teenagers at home. *They will expand at a rate of four times that of the general population from* 1980 to 1985.
45–54	The middle-age group is the one which enjoys the highest income and rate of savings. *It has been contracting* since 1970 and will continue to do so during the 1980s but will expand greatly in the 1990s.
55–64	The late middle-agers and younger senior citizens have high savings and buying power. They are empty nesters and *will grow at about the same rate as the general population* during the 1980s.
65 and over	The senior citizens present a growth market. Their incomes are lower than those of other adult population segments. The growth rate through 1985 is expected to *be twice that of the population rate*, and the proportion of women in this category is increasing.

Let us highlight some of the characteristics of two age groups of interest to business people; those aged 25–34 (young adults) and those 65 and over (senior citizens).

25–34—Young Adults

1. Single most important market to 1980.
2. A generation raised in affluence.

3. Expect bigger and better.
4. Will number about 31 million or 21 percent of the adult population in 1975.
5. Are in major growth phase of family.
6. Are married (over 75 percent).
7. Are in best educated population segment.
8. Included 12.7 million family heads in 1975.
9. 24 percent of family heads have college degree.
10. 45 percent of heads have white-collar job.
11. 80 percent of homes have children.
12. 23 percent of homes have three or more children.
13. Have one-third of the nation's children.
14. 38 percent of families earn $15,000 and over.
15. Over 50 percent of families own their premises.

65 and over—Senior Citizens

1. Are "younger older," not decrepit.
2. Amount to 10–12 percent of population in 1990.
3. Have considerable resources—pensions.
4. Have more active and full retirement.
5. Political power will increase.
6. Are interested in maintenance of self.
7. Have more surviving children.
8. Family ties remain.
9. Live apart from children.
10. Higher proportion of women will be evident by 1990.
11. Are relatively free of work and want.
12. Are not disadvantaged, unskilled, uneducated, blue-collar.
13. Will become more visible.
14. Will live longer.

AN AFFLUENT OR A NO-GROWTH ECONOMY?

A signal characteristic of our economy for the past 30 years has been the continuous and substantial increase in real family income. It has been estimated that the standard of living enjoyed by the average U.S. family during that time has almost doubled. In addition, there has been some redistribution of income from the wealthiest to the poorest population segments. Relatively, however, the poor have not gained ground.

Since the economic downturn of 1973, many statements have been made questioning the viability of our economy and its capability of delivering an increased standard of living. The following are typical of the comments that have been made:

> Americans in the future will be forced to cut back on their standard of living.
> The high growth rates of the 1960s are over, and we are faced with permanent stagflation.
> Real income in the future will continue to decrease.
> Productivity rates are now declining and will continue to decline.
> Americans will no longer be able to enjoy the good life of the previous two decades.

The reasons for such dire statements are understandable and include our severe recession, the high rates of inflation with the erosion of real personal income, the oil and energy situations, and rising prices and high unemployment. But what of the future? Two important determinants will be the rate of productivity realized and the rate of inflation.

Estimates of productivity increases tend to be colored by the negative figures of 1974, which was an atypical year. It was affected by such factors as the quadrupling of oil prices, scarcity of some raw materials, and the extended and deep recession. In 1974, two-thirds of the selected industries studied by the Bureau of Labor Statistics recorded declines in output, and more than 85 percent of them also had decreases in productivity.[4] That year was a cyclical peak, a stage at which productivity gains usually have been hard to sustain. But all of these industries realized productivity gains between 1950 and 1974, with increases ranging from a high of 6.9 percent to a low of 1 percent. From 1950 to 1969 productivity grew at an average rate of over 3 percent. During the five years 1969 to 1974, however, covering a rather difficult and atypical period, productivity grew at only an average rate of 2.1 percent. In 1975, productivity was just 2.1 percent, while in 1976 it was 3.6 percent, and in 1977, 1.5 percent.

Increasing attention is now being given to productivity by government, labor, and business. Productivity is highly correlated with both educational levels and past expenditures on research and development. Both of these factors should add a positive thrust in the future. For projection purposes an average productivity increase of 3 percent per year has been assumed and used as a basis for income projections. While this seems realistic, some readers may be more comfortable assuming rates of 2 or 2.5 percent. This would affect the amount but not the direction of the increase in income and would not invalidate references to family affluence.

But what about inflation levels which erode income? In 1974, as measured by increases in the Consumer Price Index, inflation for the first time in modern history reached double-digit levels—12.2 percent. In 1976, however, it had dropped drastically to 4.8 percent. Yet, by 1977, the inflation rate was on the rise again, measuring 6.8 percent. For 1978 the rate is estimated to reach 9.0 percent. Table 5 presents data on inflation since 1960. The given rates indicate that inflation has averaged about 6.8 percent a year since 1970.

The actual income growth rates of the 1960s, which were quite high, are expected to slow a little. But even with a lower than average 3 percent productivity increase per annum, and a rate of inflation of about 6 percent, real family income

TABLE 5 Inflation Levels as Measured by Percentage Point Changes in the Consumer Price Index

Year	Percentage Point Changes
1960	1.5
1965	1.9
1970	5.5
1971	3.4
1972	3.4
1973	8.8
1974	12.2
1975	7.0
1976	4.8
1977	6.8
1978	9.0 (est.)

over the decade 1975–1985 will increase markedly. The following statements are indicative of the income perspective:

1. In the past decade, while households grew by 25 percent, families with incomes of $15,000 and over almost doubled.
2. A larger number and proportion of American families will move into the upper income brackets between 1975 and 1985.
3. Even if productivity increases do not reach their long-run average of more than 3 percent per year and decline to an average figure such as 2.5 or 2.75 percent, real economic growth will still be substantial.
4. Families in the income bracket $20,000 and over in 1974 included one out of every four families as compared with one out of 20 in 1945.
5. Families with incomes over $20,000 in 1974 averaged more than $29,000 per year.
6. A median income family today enjoys a standard of living realized by only the top 10 percent of families in 1950.
7. Factory foremen and operatives head more than one-fourth of the families in the $20,000 and over category.

Three major points should be noted. First, even with higher inflation rates, there has been a substantial increase in the real incomes of American families, and on the average they are much more affluent than in the 1960s. This trend is reflected in Table 6. Second, over the next decade this trend will continue. We are, in fact, fast becoming a nation of upper-middle-income families. Third, the market segments that will enjoy inordinate growth are those households with incomes over $25,000 headed by persons aged 25–44.

A *Conference Board* study using census data as a basis for income projections and assuming an average real growth in income of 3.5 percent per year noted the striking fact that by 1985 the income pyramid will be reversed.[5] This is shown in Table 7, which indicates that the largest proportion of family income will be controlled by upper income families—those in the $25,000 and over and $35,000 and

TABLE 6 Changes in Family Income
1970 Dollars

	In Percentages		
Income	1960	1970	1980
$15,000 and over	8.5	21	35–38
10,000–15,000	21.5	27	26–29
7,000–10,000	23.5	21.5	14.5
5,000– 7,000	17	11.5	8.5
3,000– 5,000	14	10	7
Under 3,000	15.5	9	6

Note: These estimates were made using Department of Commerce data and assuming an annual real growth in income of 3 percent.

over income categories. Note that the percentage of family income controlled by families with income less than $10,000 is reduced from 12 percent in 1975 to 6 percent in 1985. Similarly, families with less than $15,000 per year controlled 30 percent of income in 1975 but will control only 18 percent in 1985. Moreover, similar changes will occur if one assumes a real growth rate in incomes of 2, 2.5, or 3 percent.

These projections suggest that markets for luxury goods and services will enjoy above-average growth. At the same time, notice should be taken of the poor and disadvantaged families in our population. It seems likely that the bottom 20

TABLE 7 Changing Distribution of Family Income, 1975 Dollars

Family Income Category	Percentage of Family Income	
	1975	1985
$35,000 and over	16	28
$25,000 to $35,000	16	26
$20,000 to $25,000	17	16
$15,000 to $20,000	21	14
$10,000 to $15,000	18	10
Under $10,000	12	6

Source: Fabian Linden, "Age and Income—1985," *Conference Board Record*, 13 (June 1976).

TABLE 8 Women at Work

Year	Female Population 16 and Over in Millions	Women in Labor Force in Millions	In Percentages
1947	52.5	16.7	.318
1951	54.9	19.0	.346
1955	57.6	20.6	.358
1959	60.5	22.5	.372
1963	64.5	24.7	.383
1967	69.0	28.4	.412
1971	74.0	32.1	.434
1973	80.0	37.1	.464

Source: John E. Smallwood and Ronald L. Ernst, *Distribution Demographics Research Report* (Manhattan, Kan.: Management Horizons, Inc., 1975); pp. 37–38.

TABLE 9 Working Wives

Year	Husband Employed	Husband Unemployed
1955	28.4%	37.9%
1961	33.9	40.6
1965	36.7	44.4
1969	42.3	44.5
1971	43.6	51.7
1973	45.8	48.4

Source: John E. Smallwood and Ronald L. Ernst, *Distribution Demographics Research Report* (Manhattan, Kan.: Management Horizons, Inc., 1975), pp. 37–38.

widows—for whom a job may be very important. Also, 47 percent of all wives with husbands earning $3,000 to $5,999 per year in 1970 were in the labor force.[7] On the average, in 1974 working wives contributed between 26 and 30 percent of total family income. In more than one-fourth of the husband and wife families, wives contributed 40 percent or more of the family income.[8] The earnings of working wives have tended to become a permanent part of total family income and a basis for life style expectations. Even where it is not a necessity, the economic contribution of the wife is often important to the whole family.

On the other hand, there is a large proportion of wives who work as a matter of choice rather than economic necessity. Some enter the labor force to get away from the home and family for a regular period. Sometimes wives take jobs outside the home which yield very little by way of net monetary gains. Sometimes work outside the home is seen as glamorous, challenging, exciting, and personally rewarding in contrast to the ill-defined, unpaid work in the home. In any event, whether induced by economic pressures or by choice, work outside the home is becoming a vital part of many women's lives.

Observers have often assumed that wives work when they are young and reenter the labor force later in life; that they work when there are no preschool or school-age children at home, and that they work to supplement the husband's income. None of these assumptions seems to be supported, as shown by the data in Table 10. Note that the age of the wife, the number of schoolchildren, and the amount of the husband's earnings have little if any impact on whether wives are in the labor force. A higher proportion of wives with school-age children work than do wives without children of school age. Husbands with higher earnings have a greater proportion of wives who are working. The factor most directly correlated with labor force participation of wives is their education level. Increasing educational accomplishments, particularly of minority wives, portend a larger proportion of them entering the job market.

TABLE 10 Labor Force Participation Rates for Women With Selected Characteristics, 1975

Age°	Percentage of Women in the Labor Force
16–19	49.3
20–24	63.2
25–34	52.4
35–44	54.7
45–54	54.6
55–64	40.7
65 and over	8.2

Total Family Income	Percentage of Wives in the Labor Force
under $2,000	21.03
$ 2000–2999	17.21
3000–3999	16.23
4000–4999	20.33
5000–5999	20.17
6000–6999	25.91
7000–7999	31.61
8000–8999	32.07
9000–9999	37.89
10000–10999	34.47
11000–11999	41.31
12000–12999	41.89
13000–13999	45.19
14000–14999	48.08
15000–15999	46.58
16000–16999	52.91
17000–17999	51.21
18000–19999	54.37
20000–24999	57.83
25000–49999	58.70
50000 and over	29.80

TABLE 10 (Continued)

Educational Attainment	Percentage of Women in the Labor Force
Not a high school graduate	31.6
High school graduate	52.5
1–3 years of college	53.5
College graduate	64.1

Ages of Children	Percentage of Wives Employed
Less than 3 years	32.7
3–5 years	41.9
6–17 years	52.3
None under 18	43.9

Husband's Income	Percentage of Wives in the Labor Force
$ 999 or less	46.11
1000–1499	50.58
1500–1999	51.85
2000–2499	46.94
2500–2999	54.35
3000–3499	56.72
3500–3999	62.47
4000–4999	62.29
5000–5999	57.69
6000–6999	62.10
7000–7999	61.79
8000–8999	62.72
9000–9999	62.87
10000–11999	59.29
12000–14999	57.93
15000–19999	53.43
20000–24999	47.43
25000 and over	36.55

° 1974 survey
Source: Bureau of the Census, *Current Population Survey,* Series P-23, no. 58 (1976); Series P-60, no. 105 (1977).

The life styles and purchase behavior of working wives are only beginning to be felt by business. The full-time working wife may work an average of 60 to 70 hours each week both on the job and at home. This affects the products and services she wants and needs. Studies indicate that the working wife tends to be

1. more conscious of her appearance and concerned with dress and fashions
2. very interested in maintaining a youthful posture (the young get ahead in business)
3. more confident, sure of herself, secure, and individualistic

4. more adept at dealing with the external world and making decisions
5. more concerned with convenience and ease in performing household duties
6. more cosmopolitan in tastes, more knowledgeable, and a more demanding customer
7. interested in leisure, travel, and exposure to the world outside the home
8. concerned with improving herself and her educational background
9. concerned with equal rights
10. less concerned with small price differences in purchases than with convenience, time, and service

Business should consider the impact, current and future, of the working wife on the demand for one-stop shopping, repair service on weekends and at night, Sunday store openings, evening sales, prepared foods, convenience items, products that require little service, and products that stress youthfulness, individualism, maintenance of self, and self-improvement.

MARRIAGES AND FAMILIES IN A DIVORCE-ORIENTED SOCIETY?

There is much discussion today about whether young people have given up on marriage. Recently, marriage trends have declined slightly. Also, divorce has become more prevalent, reaching a high point in the United States in 1976. Typical of the comments made are

> The outmoded institution of marriage is being replaced by the commune.
> Alternative life styles to marriage have arrived.
> Women are giving up marriage and families to further their own careers.
> The young no longer choose to marry.
> We now have more divorces than marriages.

The following quotation, which like the above statements is untrue, is humorously misleading: "All our traditions are crumbling. Look at the Catholic Church. The only people who want to get married today are Catholic priests."[9]

The Census Bureau has found that the number of unmarried persons living with a member of the opposite sex in a two-person household in March 1976 was 1,320,000, double the number reported in 1970. It appears that there have been important changes in marriage and living arrangements, that later marriages have gained general acceptance, and that a higher proportion of adults may never marry. However, despite the attention directed to singles, communes, and alternative living arrangements, marriage today is still very popular. Approximately 93 percent of all American adults marry at some time in their lives. It is true that the total number of marriages in the United States has declined slightly in the last few years, from 2,277,000 in 1973, to 2,223,000 in 1974, to 2,126,000 in 1975.

Accompanying this decline is the fact that the proportion of marriages among women ages 20–24, which have generally constituted about 43 percent of first marriages, has also declined. In 1970, almost 40 percent in this age group were single. Does this indicate a rejection of marriage?

The more likely conclusion seems to be that a postponement rather than an abandonment of marriage is occurring. Factors such as the current recession, inflation, and unemployment tend to encourage the young to postpone getting married. Postponement of marriage, rather than rejection, is supported by the fact that the percentage of single females 25 and over actually declined between 1970 and 1974, from 7.2 percent to 6.4 percent.[10]

The relevant statistics suggest that in the future there likely will be a continuing rise in first marriages resulting from the number of women now in the 18-24 age category, the pressure built up by the postponement of marriage in the past few years, and the central position that marriage, the family, and home still maintain in our society. It seems reasonable to expect an increase to 2,500,000 marriages per year by 1985, an increase of about 20 percent from the 1975 level of 2,100,000.

The structure and way of life of the family are being affected markedly by such factors as birthrates, age at marriage, size of family, developments in contraception, and the working wife. As was mentioned, family size has fallen dramatically. The average number of children per woman (total fertility rate) has dropped from a high of 3.7 in 1957 to about 1.8 in 1975. The five-year average for 1966-1971 was 2.4 children per woman. The impact is now being felt of the decreasing number of children per family, increasing number of women living alone, higher life expectancy of women as compared to men, growing number of young people living away from their families, and rapid increase in the number of divorces.

Young adults have a later marriage age, declining birthrates with fewer children, and a later age for the birth of the first child. Yet, they are having their children in a shorter span of years and planning the number and spacing of children. This is coupled with a decline in the age at which children leave home. The result is that adults in the future, who are living longer, will spend less time as "full nesters" and more time as "empty nesters." Also, future grandmothers and grandfathers may be relatively young, in their late 40s and early 50s, knowledgeable, well educated, more financially secure, and well traveled.

Traditionally, the usual dwelling unit, or household, has been perceived as a husband-wife family. Of the total number of households in 1960, 75 percent were husband-wife. By 1974, however, this proportion had declined to less than two-thirds. During this 15-year period, primary individual households—those headed by people living with their families—grew almost four times as fast as husband-wife households. They now comprise 22 percent of the total. Some of the important shifts in the distribution of household classes in the 1980s are identified in Table 11.

A disproportionate growth is occurring in households headed by unmarried people. The average size of the household continues to decrease and is expected to reach 2.8 people per household in 1980. As divorces increase, the number of individual households expands; as divorced people remarry, individual households contract. It is interesting to note that to just maintain the quality of our housing, not to improve it, it has been estimated that we will need a minimum of 2 to 2.5 million net new households each year for the next ten years. Delivering them will be a major economic challenge.

A discussion of marriage and household trends must consider statistics on divorce. Both the rate and the number of divorces have accelerated greatly in the last 10 years. From 1967 to 1975, divorces almost doubled. Divorces totaled 913,000 in 1973, 970,000 in 1974, and 1,026,000 in 1975. It is estimated now that one in three marriages will end in divorce.

Increasing divorce rates should not be misconstrued as indicating a decline in the desire for marriage. Divorce represents not a rejection of marriage, but dissatisfaction with a specific partner.

Some of the tendencies gleaned from a study of divorce statistics are

1. Divorces are likely to increase substantially.
2. The rate of increase in divorce is likely to remain higher than the rate of increase in marriage through 1985.
3. The average duration of marriage that ends in divorce is six to seven years.
4. Divorced people tend to remarry.
5. Divorced people tend to remarry other divorced people.
6. Divorced women wait longer for remarriage than divorced men.
7. A higher proportion of second marriages, as compared with first marriages, end in divorce.
8. Lower socioeconomic groups tend to account for a large proportion of second divorces.

TABLE 11   Distribution of Households in the 1980s

Household Category	Projected Trends
Husband-wife households	They will continue to decline relative to singles' households. Most of their growth to 1980 will be in the under 35 age group. From 1980 to 1990, it will be in the 35–44 age group.
Female family heads	These households, headed by women where no husband is present, have realized a high rate of growth. They will continue to do so through 1985. Most of the growth is in the under 35 age group, which is expanding at a rapid 7 percent growth rate.
Male family heads	Families headed by men with no wife present comprise only about 2 percent of all households. They will continue to be a relatively small proportion.
Primary female individuals	These households headed by single women, divorcees, and widows were made up largely of women over 35 in 1970. While the over 35 group comprised over 80 percent of such households, the under 35 group has doubled in numbers over the last 5 years and will continue to grow at a rapid rate through 1985. However, women over 35 living alone will still represent 12 percent of all households in 1980, more than four times as many as those under 35.
Primary male individuals	Households with single and divorced men living alone have doubled since 1970. Much of the growth has occurred in the under 35 group. Whereas, in 1970, these households were mostly headed by men over 35, by 1980 the balance will start to move in the direction of men under 35.

CONCLUDING OBSERVATIONS

Projections of some of the fundamental population and income statistics suggest that the longer run business climate is a cautiously optimistic one. Despite declining birthrates, we are likely to realize a second baby boom. The population will increase by about 42 million over the 1970s and 1980s. Real family income will continue to increase significantly, and we will become an even more affluent society.

While the proportion of single women and wives in the labor force will grow and add to our productivity, the family will remain a central focus. By 1985, marriage will be more popular than ever, as will divorce. There will be a significant growth in households accompanied by shifts within household categories.

American society is often characterized as being in a state of flux, with major pressures influencing and shaping totally new and different life styles, wants and needs, and markets. The changes are described as crises and rebellions. But the most striking fact resulting from an investigation of trends and projections is that life styles of Americans have, in reality, demonstrated great stability and are likely to continue to do so. The developments of the 1980s will continue to highlight the dominant characteristics of the existence of the core American values of permanence and stability.

This does not mean that demographic and social changes will not occur, or that unexpected trends will not evolve, for they will. Rather, the data, past and future, seem to suggest that our basic values and patterns of relationships will be adapted readily to new social, environmental, economic, and political situations that will present expanding markets and business opportunities. The result will be stability within change—a factor often disguised by the emphasis given when highlighting the disruptions and deviations that are caused by immediate events.

Notes

[1] All of the statistical data for this article, except where specifically noted, have been selected from U.S. government sources. The basic references are the monthly *Current Population Reports* of the Bureau of the Census, the 1970 Census, and the new publication *Status;* the U.S. Department of Labor, Bureau of Labor Statistics publications; and reports of government surveys and vital statistics. Interested readers are directed specifically to the *1970 Census of Population*, vol. 1, Part IB; *Current Population Reports*, Series P–25, nos. 614 and 493; U.S. Department of Labor, *Manpower Report to the President 1975;* Bureau of Labor Statistics, *Marital and Family Characteristics of Workers*, March 1973, and *Employment and Earnings*, April 1973; and Bureau of the Census, *A Statistical Portrait of Women in the United States, Current Population Reports*, Special Studies P–23, no. 58.

[2] Bureau of the Census, Series P–20, no. 277.

[3] This was reported by a Gallup poll of 1,562 adults age 18 or over, in 1974, as mentioned in "A Study of the American Family and Money," in *The General Mills American Family Report 1974-75*, conducted by Yankelovich, Skelly & White, Inc.

[4] Bureau of Labor Statistics, *Productivity Indexes for Selected Industries* (Washington, D.C.: 1975), Bulletin 1890, 1976, p. 3.

[5] "Age and Income—1985," by Fabian Linden, *Conference Board Record*, 13 (June 1976).

[6] As quoted in the *Wall Street Journal*, March 8, 1976, p. 1.

[7]Bureau of the Census, *U.S. Census of Population: 1970, Employment Status and Work Experience* (Washington, D.C.: 1972), pp. 182-84.
[8]See Thomas F. Bradshaw and John F. Stinson, "Trends in Weekly Earnings: An Analysis," *Monthly Labor Review* 98 (August 1975), 25-26.
[9]As quoted in *Business Week*, March 10, 1975, p. 60.
[10]For data on marital status, readers are referred to Bureau of the Census, *Current Population Reports*, Series P-20 (Washington, D.C.), nos. 212, 225, 287, 144, and 87; and U.S. Department of Health Education and Welfare, National Center for Health Statistics, *Vital Statistics Reports* (Washington, D.C.: various years).

The New Labor Force: Implications For Better Personnel Practices*

Maryann H. Albrecht

Human resource managers are increasingly aware of the impact of federal regulations on the composition of their work force. By translating such affirmative action phrases as "utilization of the relevant labor force" and "shall not discriminate . . . in any term, condition or privilege of employment" into job opportunities for underutilized groups of men, women, and ethnic minorities, they have helped to shape this social transformation. Although the most substantial change in the labor force in recent years is the relatively large numbers of women seeking employment, many of these workers have not advanced into positions of authority. Consequently, the responsibility of human resource managers has expanded to include not only a concern for the entry level jobs of the underutilized worker, but also a concern for their career development. This concern is shared by federal regulatory agencies. Recognizing the limited success of affirmative action programs, federal agencies are now monitoring the recruitment, training, and advancement of all employees, particularly those in legally protected categories.

But affirmative action alone will not remedy situations in which behavioral, cultural, and work design issues are (also) a part of improved personnel practice. This new phase of affirmative action complements the manager's recognition that traditional personnel programs are not motivating large segments of the labor force. Today, many men and women share work values which demand recognition of their individuality. Thus, managers are challenged to design work experiences and personnel systems which respond to current human needs for greater self-development, job responsibility, and growth (Hrebiniak and Alutto, 1973; Renwick and Lawler, 1975). In order to design more flexible work experiences and

°The author wishes to thank Elmer H. Burack for his advice and clarifying comments on an earlier version of this manuscript.

Prepared especially for this book and printed with permission of the author.

recruitment, selection, training, and compensation programs, managers must be aware of the social composition of the emerging labor force and be able to relate this social structure to both employee and organizational needs. This paper has the purpose of providing human resource managers with (1) a view of the social characteristics of the labor force as it affects their analyses; (2) an overview of employment opportunities for underutilized males, women, and minority group members; and (3) bases for developing strategies which jointly consider new work force entrants and their developmental needs.

THE NEW LABOR FORCE: A SOCIAL PERSPECTIVE

Historically, most personnel programs have been designed to serve workers in specific occupational categories. At one time, generalized approaches were taken for individuals in differing occupational groupings including executives, professionals, clerical and sales workers, or even laborers. Recent changes in the social composition of the labor force and a series of findings from the behavioral sciences have necessitated a more individualized approach. Differences in education, marital and family statuses, work values, ages, and health are some of the variables that require more individualized personnel programs which at the same time cut across occupational categories. One of the most recent and significant changes in the labor force is the rapid entry of large numbers of women.

Women in the Labor Force: Implications for General HRM Programs

During the past 25 years, the number of women in the labor force has more than doubled, and over the last 15 years alone the ranks of working women have grown by more than 40 percent. Today women constitute over 40 percent[1] of the civilian labor force. The scope and rapidity of this change have in many cases caught management thinking and programming unprepared. Information in Table 1 provides an overview of this new segment of the labor force and shatters a melange of myths which have already grown regarding the working woman. The reality is that large numbers of women are entering and remaining in the labor force, that they are an important source of family income, and that most mothers with children aged six to 17 are employed. It is expected that these trends will continue through the mid-1980s. Even though the rate of increase of women employees will slow down during this period, it is noteworthy that new women workers and managerial candidates will have approximated male characteristics of education and age for holders of their jobs. Most working women will be aged 20 to 34 and 80 percent will have completed high school. Later in the 1980s, the aging of the "baby boom" generation and the lowered fertility rate of women will mean that three-fourths of all newly employed workers will be aged 35 to 54. Through the 1980s, then, new employees will require entry and employment programs which speak to their needs for individual career development, varied wage and compensation programs, and those flexible work arrangements which allow them to meet both family and employee responsibilities.

TABLE 1 The Age, Marital Status, and Family Status of Women in the Labor Force

Age
More than half of all women aged 18 to 64 are in the labor force.
More than 75 percent of all women employees work full time.
63 percent of all women aged 20 to 24 are employed.
Trends suggest a substantial proportion of young women will remain employed throughout their life-career cycle.

Marital Status
The husband is the sole provider in only 36 percent of all intact families.
43 percent of all married women are employed and bring in 25 percent of their family's income. Those married women who are employed full time account for 40 percent of their total family's income.
Employed women include: 73 percent of all divorced women   58 percent of all single women   25 percent of all widowed women

Family Status
More than 50 percent of all mothers with children aged 6 to 17 are in the labor force.
38 percent of all mothers with children under age 6 are employed.
35 percent of black families and 10 percent of white families are headed by women.
25 percent of all black families and 7 percent of all white families live below the poverty level. The majority of youth living below the poverty level live in families headed by women.

Sources: Department of Labor, *1975 Handbook on Women Workers, Manpower Reports to the President;* Kreps, *Women and the American Economy,* 1976; EEOC, *Equal Opportunity Report,* 1975, U.S. Department of Labor Reports, 1978.

The Occupations of Women and Minorities

The racial and ethnic characteristics of the general population and work force are not proportionally represented in different occupational groups or in levels of authority or responsibility. The racial and ethnic combination of the civilian labor force is as follows:

  84.0 percent white

  11.0 percent black

  4.1 percent Spanish-surnamed Americans

  0.8 percent Asian Americans

  0.4 percent American Indian

However, substantial differences exist in occupational distributions which in turn affect the income and unemployment rate of workers in these social categories. Clearly a matter of continuing national concern and gross inequity, these comparisons are brought out more clearly by considering the distribution of employees by race and sex and examining how many positions within given occupations are held by workers who differ in gender and race. Figure 1 presents this information. Some of the following ideas indicate important points to be inferred from this exhibit.

White males hold 83 percent of both the highest ranked white- and blue-collar occupations, and comprise the majority of American professionals, technicians, sales workers, and operatives. By contrast, minorities and women are generally in both industries and positions with low pay scales, little opportunity for advancement, and high unemployment rates. Only 28 percent of minority workers, for example, are in white-collar jobs and only 16 percent are service workers. With the exception of blacks and Asian professional workers, minority males are concentrated in blue-collar occupations while minority females occupy lower paying office, clerical, and operative positions.

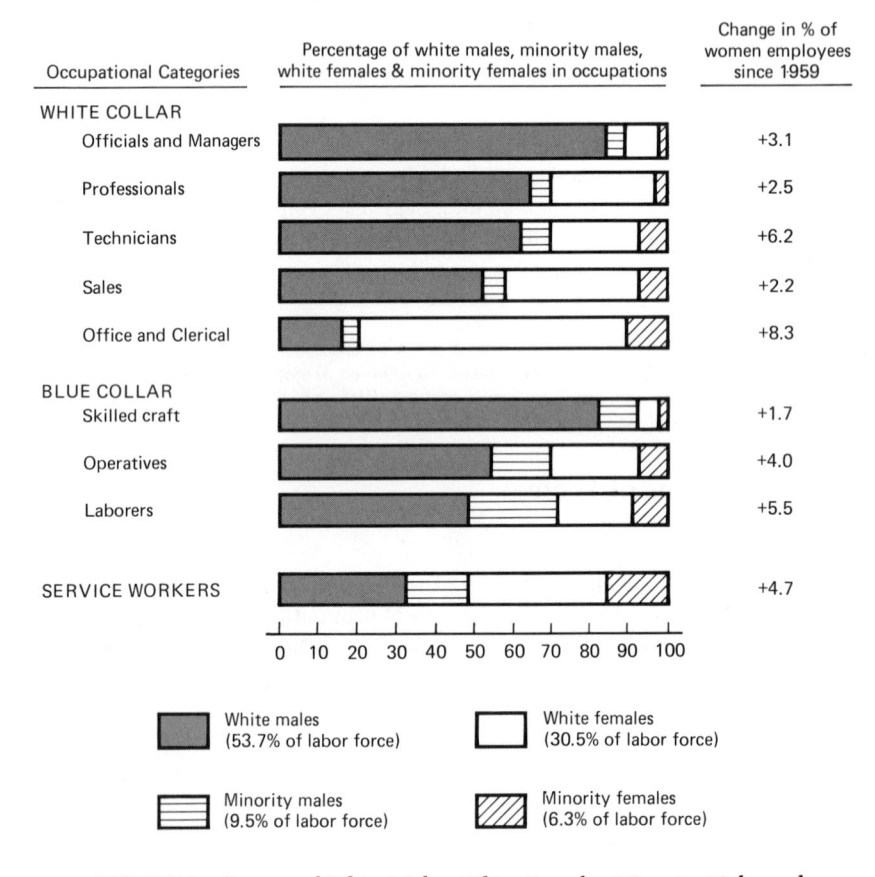

Occupational Categories	Percentage of white males, minority males, white females & minority females in occupations	Change in % of women employees since 1959
WHITE COLLAR		
Officials and Managers		+3.1
Professionals		+2.5
Technicians		+6.2
Sales		+2.2
Office and Clerical		+8.3
BLUE COLLAR		
Skilled craft		+1.7
Operatives		+4.0
Laborers		+5.5
SERVICE WORKERS		+4.7

Legend:
- White males (53.7% of labor force)
- White females (30.5% of labor force)
- Minority males (9.5% of labor force)
- Minority females (6.3% of labor force)

FIGURE 1 *Percent of White Males, White Females, Minority Males and Minority Females in Broad Occupational Groups*

Occupational distributions are further revealing of disparities in employment opportunities for women. Changes in the occupational distribution of women are listed in the right-hand column of Figure 1. Over the past 20 years, more women have entered occupations traditionally held by women rather than occupations historically considered "male." Only among laborers, traditionally a male position, has there been a marked increase in women employees (+ 15.3 percent). Currently, a greater percentage of office and clerical workers are female than in 1959 (+ 8.3 percent), while only 3.1 percent more managers are female. Women also remain concentrated in a few occupations; more than 40 percent of women employees are clustered into 10 traditional occupations (secretary, retail sales, bookkeeper, private household workers, elementary school teacher, waitress, typist, cashier, weaver and stitcher, and registered nurse). Males reach out to six times as many occupations. Differences in the salary level and unemployment rates of males and females are due, in large part, to these differences in occupational distribution and to the lower job positions of females and minority group members within each occupation.

The current salary and employment status of women and minorities is summarized in Table 2. At present women with the same education, occupation, and employment status as males earn only 44 to 65 percent of the income of males. However, important adjustments are taking place and current salary trends are expected to continue until the occupational position and seniority level of women and minorities approximates that of white males.

TABLE 2   The Salary and Unemployment Status of Women and Minorities

Salary

Women who are employed full time, and have the same education and occupation as males, earn only 44 to 65 percent of the income of males.

Minority females earn:

  50 percent of the salary of white males
  70 percent of the salary of minority males
  89 percent of the salary of white females

Black males earn 72 percent of the income of white males.

Gaps between the incomes of males and females are narrowing, but there is a continuing and slightly increasing gap between the income of black females and white males.

Unemployment

Minority males and females have twice the unemployment rate of white males and females.

Within each racial group, the unemployment rate for females is twice that for males.

Within each racial group, the unemployment rate for youth aged 16 to 19 is four times that for adults. The majority of unemployed minority teen-agers lost their jobs.

Sources: Department of Labor, *1975 Handbook on Women Workers, Manpower Reports to the President;* Kreps, *Women and the American Economy,* 1976. U.S. Department of Labor Reports, 1978.

Whatever inroads have been made by women and racial minorities can be drastically altered by the shifting economic scene. For example, a general decline in economic activity can (as proven historically) alter the unemployment rate of these groups—first hired and part-time workers (predominantly women, minorities, and teen-agers) suffer most from a constricting economy. Confounding these correlations is the fact that until the mid-1980s there will also be increased pressure for women to shift from teaching at the primary and secondary levels to other occupations, as the number of school-age children declines. Thus, projected high unemployment rates and large numbers of youth currently being raised below the poverty level by divorced and separated women indicate that national attention be directed to the educational preparation, employment, and advancement of women.

Currently, nationally funded programs are helping the youth identify various career choices and are also assisting underutilized and disadvantaged workers to prepare for entry into the labor market. The majority of these public training and counseling programs are sponsored under CETA and the Department of Labor; others emanate from the Department of Health, Education and Welfare. The major portion of funds under the Comprehensive Employment and Training Act of 1973 (CETA) is used to provide the disadvantaged, unemployed, and underemployed with job training and employment opportunities. CETA programs developed on a local level include outreach, intake and assessment, job referral, counseling, education, on-the-job training, employer and employee subsidies, and support services. Other programs such as WIN (Work Incentive) for families with dependent children continue to operate independently. Most of these programs include referral, counseling, and support services for organizations which employ extremely disadvantaged workers. These programs are complemented by industrial affirmative action programs that encourage the employment and advancement of workers in "protected categories." This system of public and private programs forms a feeder network for the development of future human resources. The quality of the labor force of the future depends to a great extent on the jobs, incomes, and values transmitted by the current generation of parents. Nevertheless, the relatively slow occupational advancement of underutilized employees suggests that organizations may need to overcome another source of resistance to employee development—the employees themselves.

THE NEW LABOR FORCE: PERSPECTIVES OF THE "UNDEREMPLOYED"

New employees are a product of many environments. Their behavior is shaped by values and beliefs taught in neighborhoods, schools, churches, families, and friendship groups. When brought to a work environment, these beliefs perpetuate the stereotypes attacked by civil rights and fair employment legislation. Personnel managers have also discovered that such beliefs prevent many women, minorities, and underutilized males from accepting some work opportunities. Even when the firm provides a supportive environment, personnel directors report that many workers hesitate to accept positions traditionally held by those of another sex or race (O' Leary, 1974; Hall and Albrecht, 1977). Separate studies of 450 women and 250 males in all occupational categories confirm this employment problem. [2] Fully a third of "promotable" women stated they would refuse a promotion. Listing their reasons in order of importance, these women first mentioned their reluctance to accept additional responsibility. Those who visualized the role of women as primarily one of a housewife felt that they lacked necessary skills needed for advanced positions, or that supervisory and managerial roles are inappropriate for women. Those who listed a second reason cited their own problems in coping simultaneously with work and family obligations. However, none of these women mentioned solving such role problems by obtaining additional help from training programs, informal advice networks, or other members of the family. This self-isolation from potentially useful sources of advice has been noted in other observational studies of women employees (Hennig and Jardim, 1977; Kanter, 1978), and is apparently related to a broader work-identity problem. In the study of 450 women already cited, women at work were asked to identify all of the important people in their lives; less than 1 percent mentioned a co-worker or superior. By contrast, a matched sample of males in similar occupations listed someone in their organization, usually a "boss," as a significant figure in their lives. Interestingly, males in occupational fields traditionally dominated by females also experienced both feelings of isolation from potential sources of help and difficulties in establishing a work identity.

This research suggests that many underutilized employees probably share one or more of the following identity problems: (1) lack of awareness of personal skills, (2) an inability to visualize oneself in a job that uses these skills, and (3) a psychological, mental, and/or physical unpreparedness to use one's skills in an appropriate job.

SPECIALIZED ENTRY AND EMPLOYMENT PROGRAMS: BETTER PERSONNEL PRACTICES

Programs designed to (af)firm or strengthen an organization's commitment to workers are often diluted by traditional approaches. When traditional programs fail to accomplish their goals, problem-location strategies can redirect efforts to reach "hard to find," "hard to promote," or "difficult" employees.

Barriers of skill, attitudes, and behavior often cripple the effectiveness of hiring and development programs. Needs analyses and flow charting often help pinpoint these problems by quantifying in number and percent those employees of different social characteristics who enter and leave the different stages of a recruitment process or are promoted, advanced, or transfer into different positions at the completion of training or work cycles. Practices that have traditionally barred classes of individuals from entry level opportunities include (1) rejecting their applications, (2) providing lower starting salaries, (3) preventing them from entering higher skill level jobs, or (4) not recruiting among members of that subgroup. Employee discrimination is often inferred when classes of individuals have slower rates of promotion, assignment to less attractive or less challenging tasks, lower or less frequent raises, or fewer training opportunities (Terborg and Ilgen,

1975). Once the location of the problem is identified, managers can flow chart each stage in that process in order to identify the individuals and/or practices which restrict employee growth. The analyses may point to the need for specialized programs that update employee attitudes, behaviors, or skills.

Recent Innovations in Personnel Programs

The most effective responses to personnel programs spring from a realistic juxtapositioning of the specific needs and resources available to organizations. Such reviews usually begin with information that outlines (1) the organization's long-range, intermediate, and short-term staffing needs; (2) the skill levels and social composition of the available labor force; (3) the location and types of work problems that limit (potential) employees. In many cases, different levels of programs must be devised to reach out in general fashion to the community and organization at large and then provide specialized information for targeted groups of employees.

Figure 2 presents some innovative programs used in over 80 organizations to overcome current human resource problems.[3] To combat discriminatory tendencies of co-workers and managers, these programs were originally aimed at attracting and advancing women, minority groups, and underutilized males. Currently, these programs are also used to meet the needs of those veterans, aged, disabled, or handicapped individuals whose skill levels, motivation, or attitudes toward work are limited by stereotyped beliefs. In general, the programs encourage positive attitudes to entry and employment opportunities by demonstrating modern work practices and by providing opportunities to enrich skill levels.

Entry Opportunities. Corporations whose resources and positions allow them to make use of national and regional recruitment devices find traditional programs effective. Organizations located in smaller, more isolated geographical areas need specialized programs to meet their long-term, intermediate, and immediate hiring goals. Strong public relations campaigns allow these organizations to project their (new) image to the community at large and to specific media that reach targeted groups in the labor force. Well-placed ads proceed beyond the typical AA/EEOC statement to stress commitment to the individual and thus capture the attention of younger or less experienced workers. Organizations that can help market these communications to "hard to find" applicants include unions, employment agencies, schools, public welfare agencies, churches, professional associations, employees, and community groups. Within the same geographical area and industry, smaller firms often share the costs of general programs for recruiting, research on selection criteria, and employee development. Such shared cost programs might include joint community-organization efforts to establish a day care center. In such cooperative situations, no one organization would recruit before publicity appeared showing how women workers make use of the jointly sponsored center.

As a part of their efforts to meet long-term hiring goals, organizations are helping communities build and maintain a talented labor pool. Contests, part-time jobs, internships, grants, instructional programs, and scholarships are used to

ROUTINE PROGRAMS	SPECIALIZED PROGRAMS	EMPLOYEE PROBLEMS
Entry • Recruitment • Selection • Training • Placement • Monitoring **Employee** • Assessment • Compensation • Advancement/ 　Promotion/ • Training/ 　Counseling • Discipline/ 　Grievances • Support Systems • HRIS/Planning	**Entry Opportunities** • Forecasting/Utilization 　Planning • Targeted Long Range, 　Intermediate and 　Immediate Hiring Goals • Education/Development • Public Image • Cooperative Joint Effort 　Research and Education **Employee Opportunities** • System Networks • Information Systems • Counseling Programs • Targeted Information • Targeted Advancement • Job Analysis • Job Design/Bridges	**Entry** "Who am I?" • Expectations/Goals • Realistic Self-Image "What Can I Do?" • Knowledge of Job/Training • Visualization of Self 　in Job "Can I Do It?" • Role Conflicts • Fears/Anxieties • Counseling/Support Needs **Employee** "Who am I?" • Identity with Organization 　(Past, Present, Future) • Unit Structure/Jobs • Work/Life Values "What Can I Do?" • Organization Structure/ 　Jobs/Future • Task Values/Skills • Ability to Perceive 　Opportunities "Can I Do It?" • Ability to Use 　Opportunities • Ability to Try New Roles • Ability to Handle 　Multiple Role/Conflicts

SOCIAL COMPOSITION OF THE NEW LABOR FORCE

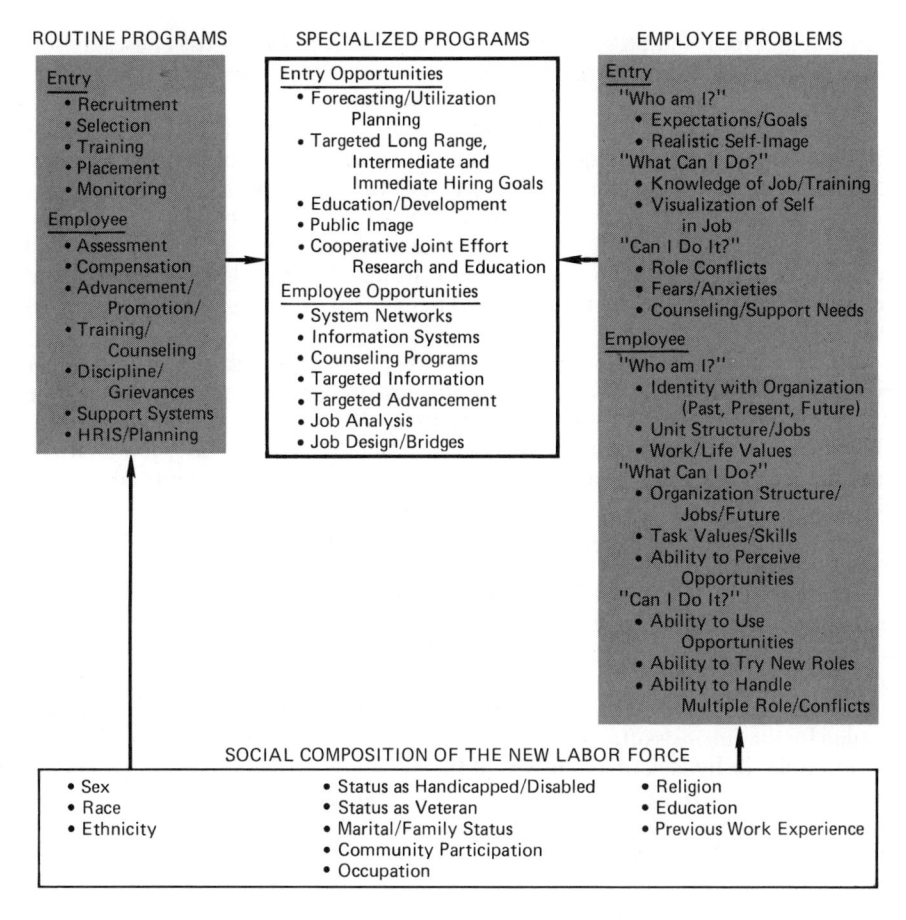

• Sex • Race • Ethnicity	• Status as Handicapped/Disabled • Status as Veteran • Marital/Family Status • Community Participation • Occupation	• Religion • Education • Previous Work Experience

FIGURE 2　*Specialized Personnel Programs*

develop organizational visibility while building the skills of potential employees. Where employees are limited by personal problems, organizations help to develop a "building block" approach to community development. After identifying the problems, they encourage the growth of housing, public transportation, child care, schools, health, banking and/or legal agencies which meet employee needs and result in broader applicant pools.

Opportunities for Employee Growth. To encourage employees' professional growth, managers have designed programs to broaden their knowledge and skill levels and to foster a positive attitude toward career development. In addition to broad efforts to instill some sense of organizational identity, special programs attempt to expand employees' knowledge of the organization and of potential paths to upward mobility within it. In some programs, for example, workers are encouraged to visit special job information centers where staff provide an understanding of posted job openings, discuss the training needed for such jobs, and solicit employee applications. A more personalized information network relies on unit representatives to identify workers with unique skills. These advisors discuss career plans with targeted employees and, when appropriate, help them identify useful training and enrichment opportunities.

Information networks and training programs designed for subordinates simultaneously help managers channel their personnel efforts in the right direction. For example, if an organization discovers that attitudes of co-workers or subordinates block the mobility of disabled workers, it may develop information networks and training programs to combat this problem. Such programs will necessarily include a general information format for high-level managers and more detailed information, training, and behavioral experiences for managers of disabled workers.

Other employee development programs use job analysis, job design, and career counseling to help "dead-ended" employees prepare for new positions. The opportunities of clerical workers, for example, are often restricted by technical skills that do not easily transfer to other positions. In such a case, job analysis, training, and new work designs slowly enrich the worker's decision-making and supervisory skills while bringing her into contact with those in higher level jobs. These enrichment and transformation structures bridge the gap between "no-growth" jobs and work with greater potential for career mobility.

Programs that help individuals direct their own career growth often begin with career planning. Initially, guided inventories help workers assess their potential and prepare realistic career goals. All too often, however, this guided examination of employee problems (see column 3 of Figure 2) leaves out any reference to the larger social context in which individuals shape their careers. Employees' ability to plan for the future is often impaired by a limited knowledge of their capabilities, for example, or by lack of awareness of the job market, the processes that lead to advancement, or those strategies which help them match personal and career plans. Often, "reality checks" can help these individuals test the validity of their planning. In reality checking, those who know the individual help examine both the appropriateness of a career goal and plans made to develop the expertise necessary to achieve that goal (Burack, 1977; Burack, Albrecht and Seitler, 1979). In many organizations, self-directed materials (Burack, 1978) or guided discussions are then used to link these plans to the reality of an organization's present and future staffing needs.

Programs presented in Figure 2 have general themes of communication, training, or career development. By design, some reach into the community while others operate at different levels of the organization. For this reason, different types of programs, some more general than others, can be combined to build more efficient and effective solutions to human resource problems. For example, programs designed to recruit maintenance workers would be formulated *after* analyzing the flow of applicants through different stages of the recruitment and selection processes. When increasing the size of the applicant pool becomes a key objective, organizations should stress those aspects of the job to which workers can relate known skills and abilities. As a result of more detailed information, specific recruitment strategies might portray common on-the-job experiences, cite employee benefits, or project the firm's commitment to providing employees with career development opportunities. These programs can be combined with targeted hiring programs aimed at both the community and lower level employees. Visits to junior colleges that offer courses in maintenance and networks of communication within the firm, as well as targeted counseling, encourage semi-skilled workers to train for maintenance positions. Personnel managers who have used combinations of programs find them particularly effective when changes in technology, consumption patterns, or social values prevent them from reaching established hiring and advancement goals.

Future Directions

During the past 25 years, relatively large numbers of women and minority group members have reshaped the social composition of the work force. To attract and develop employees, human resource managers have enriched the design of communication, compensation, work flow, and support systems. Because these newer programs speak to basic needs shared by groups of employees, they cut across occupational and social categories to strengthen linkages between employee skills and organizational opportunities. The clearer identification of these work relationships motivates employees whose previous social and work experiences prevented them from fully identifying their own skills, relating them to specific jobs, or moving into different occupations. Managers have discovered that work-related problems of attitude, skill, and behavior are shared by many employees during different phases of their personal and professional careers.

At present, values that stress the quality of work experiences encourage young people to seek out jobs with opportunities for greater self-determination and individual development. This need for a more responsive work environment is also a topic of growing concern among experienced workers. Rapid growth in work technologies, greater demand for service skills, and a lengthening work career provide older workers with increased opportunities for job mobility. Newer methodologies, springing from an awareness that social and work histories shape employee behavior, provide methodologies which more effectively identify needs among newer and more experienced classes of employees. For this reason, these programs can (af)firm more than the opportunities of the socially and physically disabled. Since they establish a realistic dialogue between the organization and the employee, they provide methodologies which bridge gaps between the knowledge, skills, and attitudes of employees and the staffing needs of the organization.

Notes

[1] Unless otherwise specified, the majority of data on the labor force used in this paper comes from the following sources: United States Department of Labor, *Handbook on Women Workers, 1975.* United States and *Employment and Training Report to the President, 1976.* Kreps, *Women and the American Economy* (1976); EEOC, *Equal Opportunity Report* (1974).

[2] These studies include research on the motivation of 200 men and 290 women and a separate study of the advancement problems of 50 men and 160 women. Both samples included all nine occupational categories used by the Department of Labor. In each case, samples were chosen with the use of stratified random cluster techniques using a grid method to sample from the population of organizations located in a large midwestern metropolitan area.

[3]Information on these programs comes from studies on the effectiveness of AA related programs (Hall and Albrecht, 1977, 1979) as well as conferences and consulting experiences concerned with the design of modern personnel systems.

References

Albrecht, Maryann. "Women, Resistance to Promotion and Self-Directed Change," *Human Resource Management*, 17, No. 1 (Spring 1978), 12–17.

Bardwick, Judith. *The Psychology of Women*. New York: Harper and Row, 1975.

Burack, Elmer H. "Career Paths—Why All the Confusion?" *Human Resource Management*, 16, 2 (Summer 1977, 21–24.

Burack, Elmer H. "Self-Directed Inquiry: A Newer Developmental Tool," *Training and Development Journal*, 1978.

Burack, Elmer H., Maryann H. Albrecht, and Helene Seitler. *Growing: A Guide to Career Development*. Belmont, California: Lifetime Learning Publications (Wadsworth), 1979.

Epstein, Cynthia F. "Bringing Women In; Rewards, Punishments, and the Structure of Achievement." In *Women—Volume 1: A PDI Research Reference Work*, ed. Florence L. Denmark et al. New York: Psychological Dimensions, Inc., 1976.

Equal Employment Opportunity Commission. *Affirmative Action and Equal Employment*. Washington, D.C.: U.S. Government Printing Office, 1974.

Hall, Francine, and Maryann H. Albrecht. "Training for EEO: What Kinds and for Whom?" *The Personnel Administrator*, 22, No. 8 (October 1977), 25–28.

Hall, Francine, and Maryann H. Albrecht. *The Management of Affirmative Action*. Santa Monica, Cal.: The Goodyear Publishing Co., 1979.

Hennig, Margaret, and Anne Jardim. *The Managerial Woman*. Garden City, N.Y.: Doubleday, 1977.

Horner, Matina S. "Toward an Understanding of Achievement Related Conflicts in Women," *Journal of Social Issues*, 28 (1972), 157–175.

Hrebiniak, L. C., and J. A. Alutto. "Personal and Role-Related Factors in the Development of Organizational Commitment," *Administrative Science Quarterly*, 18 (1973), 555–572.

Kanter, Rosabeth. *Men and Women of the Corporation*. Englewood Cliffs, N.J.: Prentice-Hall, Inc., 1978.

Kreps, Juanita. *Women and the American Economy*. Englewood Cliffs, N.J.: Prentice-Hall, Inc., 1976.

O'Leary, Virginia E. "Some Attitudinal Barriers to Occupational Aspirations in Women," *Psychology Bulletin*, 81 (1974), 809–826.

Renwick, Patricia A., and Edward E. Lawler. "What Do You Really Want from Your Job?" *Psychology Today*, 11 (1978), 53–65, 118.

Terborg, James R., and Daniel R. Ilgen. "A Theorectical Approach to Sex Discrimination in Traditionally Masculine Occupations," *Organizational Behavior and Human Performance*, 13 (1975), 352–376.

Tresmer, David. "Fear of Success: Popular but Unproven," *Psychology Today*, March 1974, pp. 82–85.

United States Department of Labor. *Handbook on Women Workers, 1975; Manpower Reports to the President*. Washington, D.C.: U.S. Government Printing Office, 1975.

United States Department of Labor. *Employment and Training Report to the President, 1976*. Washington, D.C.: U.S. Government Printing Office, 1975.

LABOR RELATIONS AND THE FUTURE

What's Coming in Labor Relations?

George S. McIsaac

For the lifetime of most U.S. executives, American production and managerial skills have set the pace for the industrial nations of the West. Indeed, the preeminence of the United States as an exporter of management know-how has long been virtually taken for granted on both sides of the Atlantic.

In at least one vital area, however—that of labor relations—this situation may soon be reversed. Growing evidence suggests that recent developments on the labor relations scene hold important lessons for U.S. industry—lessons that many European companies have already mastered. Powerful pressures for job security and income stability are sweeping the industrialized economies of Western Europe and resulting in far-reaching changes in the climate as well as the institutional structure of labor relations. Some observers call what is happening a second Industrial Revolution. By any name, its implications are immense.

Before we are well into the 1980s, the new European labor relations model promises to challenge some of U.S. business's most deeply rooted assumptions and practices. The changes that are on the way will inevitably be painful for many American managers. But the pangs of the transition will be less severe for companies that have begun to anticipate it by studying the historical background of the European labor relations developments and by considering their relevance for U.S. industry in terms of not only human resources but national stability as well.

The basic European model for labor-management cooperation was erected in Germany after World War II by novel legislation that installed labor representatives on supervisory boards of steel and mining companies. The partnership thus established permitted rational planning to meet emerging economic threats and allowed companies to deal with problems of industrial rationalization and dislocation (as in the soft coal industry) and at the same time to maintain a relatively stable employment base. Although it takes somewhat different forms in Germany, Italy, Britain, and the Low Countries, the new industrial revolution is

George S. McIsaac, "What's Coming in Labor Relations?" Harvard Business Review, September-October 1977, Copyright © 1977 by the President and Fellows of Harvard College; all rights reserved.

Reprinted with permission from *Harvard Business Review* (September–October 1977), pp. 22–36.

fundamentally a single phenomenon: the fact that job rights and, in particular, an individual's right to have both secure employment and stable income are being elevated to political and legal parity with property rights, notably including the rights of investors.

This change usually finds institutional expression in a restructuring of the organs of corporate governance and control. (For examples of different forms of this restructuring in Europe, see Exhibit 1.)

"It may be the shareholders' money, but it's our lives." This remark of a young French supervisor, quoted to me by his boss, sums up the attitude of the labor-oriented battalions of voters who constitute the political force behind this new industrial revolution. The responses of European companies reflect a sober recognition that their profits depend on political stability and that political stability in turn is now tied closely to employment security. Preferring accommodation to costly confrontation, they are adjusting their strategic plans and investment programs as best they can to take due account of the new realities.

When weighing investment and divestment alternatives, sophisticated European corporate strategists no longer simply extrapolate current labor cost trends to determine ranges of future manpower expense, as most of their U.S. counterparts still do. Instead, European managers now routinely project in detail the manpower requirements of each strategic option and often revise product-market development programs and capital investment decisions in order to maintain employment stability, even at the cost of dampening profits. (Volkswagen's long delay in investing in a U.S. assembly plant is a notable case in point.)

The demonstrated willingness of these companies to assume the social responsibility of providing secure jobs is more than a defensive response to political realities. In many cases, it also reflects a sense that management may, after all, have something positive to gain: namely, genuine employee commitment to the economic well-being of the enterprise and, ultimately, higher productivity.

In this article I shall try to show why the European experience holds important lessons for U.S. management, indicate some significant parallels that may emerge in the near future in the United States, and identify some possible elements of a timely management response.

EMERGING U.S. TRENDS

Until quite recently, the relevance of the European labor relations revolution for American industry has been debatable. During more than three decades of almost uninterrupted economic growth in the United States, employment has been readily available for nearly all Americans except the indigent, the unwilling, or the unskilled—groups with little or no political clout. And up to the present, few American unions have shown much interest in codetermination. As one key labor spokesman put it not long ago, "We've watched codetermination and its offshoot experiments with interest . . . but it is our judgment that it offers little to American unions."[1]

Moreover, until recently the growth in demand for labor has absorbed new entrants to the labor force as well as those displaced by new technology. Partly as a result of this absorption, the U.S. labor movement has put a higher priority on purchasing-power and fringe-benefit gains than on job and income security

Exhibit 1 Forms of Employee-Management Cooperation in Europe

In West Germany, the economy most competitive with our own, new forms of employee involvement in top management decision making were legislated in 1975. Following long experience with workers' councils and persistent pressure from the German labor movement for *Mitbestimmung* (codetermination), union and employee group representatives will now by law participate in nearly all fundamental top management decisions—including, of course, all those affecting employment levels and job security—in every company employing more than 500 workers.

In the Netherlands, new works council legislation designed to give labor a strong voice in determining future corporate courses of action is currently before Parliament, and a proposed excess profits tax aimed at enabling Dutch employees to acquire a substantial ownership position in their companies is moving toward adoption. Meanwhile, the government has not hesitated to intervene directly to maintain employment security by stopping planned plant closings such as the proposed shutdown of an outmoded fiber plant by the giant chemical and fibers company Akzo. Not surprisingly, in response to union pressures for job security, large Dutch companies such as KLM are devoting much management attention to the design of new manpower redevelopment schemes for employees displaced by automation or plant and product obsolescence.

In France, following an eight-year period of mounting government intervention, implicit job security guarantees were strengthened by the government in 1974, and it is now virtually impossible for any large company to cut back its work force. French managers have thus been compelled to work out detailed long-range (five- to ten-year) manpower plans, some of which work surprisingly well.

In Sweden, since January 1971, it has been mandatory for management in every Swedish factory to consult employees on important operational decisions. Experiments with employee participation in decision making at Volvo evolved into a complete reorganization of assembly operations.°

Even in Great Britain, beset by crippling labor relations problems—fragmented bargaining structures, a turbulent labor relations climate, and uncertain employee motivation—some managements have been finding ways to ease the impact of redundancies through extensive job retraining and redeployment measures, and others have preserved a measure of strategic flexibility through mechanisms for informal consultation with responsible labor leaders. Moreover, although no one expects labor representation on corporate boards to become law overnight (least of all in the form recommended by the government-appointed Bullock Committee on Industrial Democracy), some form of employee participation in board-level decisions is almost certainly on the way.

° See Nancy Foy and Herman Gadon, "Worker Participation: Contrasts in Three Countries," Harvard Business Review, May–June 1976, p. 71; and Pehr G Gyllenhammar, "How Volvo Adapts Work to People," Harvard Business Review, July–August 1977, p. 102.

guarantees or on overall employment levels. In the "pressure bargaining" preceding contract settlements, labor spokesmen usually soften job security demands for the sake of wage gains.

More important perhaps, top management's attention has simply been absorbed by other matters. For most of the past three decades, the chief executive officers of large U.S. companies have been deeply involved in issues of growth, diversification strategy, and related financial and legal concerns. In consequence, labor-management relations and employment matters have been relegated to down-the-line managers and staff to a degree rare in Europe, where organized labor has much more political influence than here and employees tend to vote as a bloc. In general, American managers have been less respectful of labor's power and far less mindful than their European counterparts of the possible impact of any contemplated strategic move on sensitive labor interests.

Subtly but surely, all this is now changing. Indeed, some evidence suggests that U.S. business may have already begun tracing the European path. Because the pressures are less well defined and compelling than in Europe, the movement is less rapid. But it is probably no less inexorable.

The U.S. employment problem now looms large in public discussion. American labor leaders—aging veterans for the most part—are under growing pressure from a younger generation to champion the interests of labor's rank and file, with special emphasis on job availability and security. Meanwhile, inflation (fueled by demands for higher wages and benefits) and lagging productivity growth are giving labor relations matters a much higher priority in the minds of senior U.S. managers. Demands for job creation and employment maintenance have begun to be heard in the executive suite. And U.S.-based multinational companies, noting the labor productivity growth levels enjoyed by their competitors in Germany, France, Holland, and Japan, are beginning to take a keen interest in the employee relations aspects of that phenomenon.

The Ballooning Work Force

Among the domestic forces that are drawing the attention of U.S. industry and government to developments in Europe, the most persuasive is quite simply the demand for more jobs. Unemployment levels in the United States, as a percentage of the labor force, have for some years been about one-third higher than in Europe. The baby boom of the postwar years surfaced in the 1970s as an explosion in work force entries. Enlarging the demand for jobs, women of all ages continue to seek employment in unprecedented numbers. In consequence, by the early 1970s the U.S. labor force was growing by over 2 percent per year—just about twice as fast as during the two previous decades.

Fortunately, a little-noticed boom in jobs coincided with this expansion in the available work force. Though interrupted by the 1974–1975 recession, a rise in employment absorbed the great majority of labor force entrants. From 1969 to 1975, employment increased from 77.9 million to 84.8 million—a compound annual growth rate of 1.4 percent versus one of approximately 1.0 percent in the 1950s and 1960s. Of the 6.9 million new jobs created in those years, 5.7 million, or more than 80 percent, came from increases in three sectors: state and local government (2.5 million), health services (1.7 million), and education (1.5 million).[2]

Recent projections by the Bureau of Labor Statistics suggest that from 1976 to 1980 the labor force will continue to grow by roughly 1.9 percent annually—somewhat more slowly than in the recent past, but still rapidly enough to add more than 9 million Americans to the work force over the five-year period.[3]

How will this continuing pressure for jobs be accommodated? In the future, public and health services will not be able to absorb the growing work force. Throughout the nation, school enrollments and, consequently, opportunities in education are dropping; municipal fiscal problems have halted the growth of state and local government employment; and with the cost of health care under intense public scrutiny, a sharp slowdown of mushrooming health services employment is in sight. Armed forces employment is shrinking. The civilian federal establishment is going to be put through a budget wringer, so employment growth in that quarter also looks most improbable. Even if the federal government should undertake some form of youth corps program, no significant or enduring effects on job creation can be expected.

Even to hold unemployment levels at the current 7.0 percent, then, it appears that private industry must provide nearly 6 million jobs in the next three years. To bring unemployment down to the Carter administration's stated target level of 4.5 percent, the private sector would have to create close to 8 million jobs by 1980, a feat that would mean expanding employment by nearly 2.8 percent per year. Since the rate of increase between 1969 and 1975 was about half that, or 1.4 percent, achieving this rate is as likely as shooting the moon in a game of Hearts. (In the short term, we may be doing just that. The Bureau of Labor Statistics has reported that the private sector added over 1 million employees from November 1976 through March 1977. This recent upsurge, however, is probably traceable to the belated recovery of the construction industry.)

To add to the challenge, both management and government will be pressing for higher productivity. Concerned with the lag in U.S. productivity growth in comparison with that of Western Europe and Japan, the federal government is seeking ways to get rid of excess manpower as well as to provide incentives to encourage productivity-boosting (and labor-saving) investments.

Few students of twentieth-century history would quarrel with the proposition that high and continuing unemployment poses the gravest possible threat to a nation's political stability. Hence, if President Carter's program of mild economic stimulus, including the recently signed Public Works Employment Act, proves ineffectual or at least insufficient, renewed attention to job creation is a certainty. Ideas already proposed include a revival of activities like the Civilian Conservation Corps of the 1930s, a two-year period of required public or community service for young adults, and government subsidies for private-sector job creation programs.

Even the enactment of some form of private-sector job subsidy program—anathema to most professional managers but presumably the least costly of these choices—would compel companies to face up to some daunting questions in the manpower planning area. Where would management draw the line between "essential" jobs and "marginal" jobs—that is, those in excess of corporate economic requirements? Under what conditions could an essential job be redesignated as marginal? How would managers determine and account for the profit impact of marginal jobs? How would subsidies be arranged? At the moment, there are no answers to these questions in sight.

New Labor Priorities

Current trends in union rank-and-file priorities are another major factor underlying the growing appeal of job security. Most recently, the Steelworkers, spurred on by outgoing president I.W. Abel's call for "uninterrupted steady work and steady, uninterrupted wages," decided that a demand for some form of guaranteed career employment security should be the cornerstone of their future annual negotiations. This year, the union settled for increased protection against layoffs and plant closedowns for employees with more than 20 years of service, who comprise about 40 percent of the industry's labor force. Further discussion of the income security issue is due to be resumed by a joint industry and union task force.

Significantly, this settlement came on the heels of the Steelworkers' innovative "experimental negotiating agreement" (ENA). With its no-strike clause, which is tied to a program to establish shop-floor communication committees, the ENA signaled a dramatic turn from confrontation to cooperation across a broad sector of the American labor movement. The defeat last February of the insurgent district leader, Edward Sadlowski, and his anti-ENA, anitcooperation platform by the pro-ENA forces of Abel's hand-picked successor, Lloyd McBride, amounted to rank-and-file ratification of a strategy that could eventually reshape the U.S. labor movement's approach to collective bargaining. This strategy, offering labor peace in return for employment and income security, clearly parallels the European model.

Nor is the growing preoccupation with job security confined to the Steelworkers. The United Auto Workers' (UAW) drive to reduce yearly work hours and career lengths as a means of maintaining both employment and job security reflects another emerging trend in U.S. labor's thinking. Moreover, in its 1976 pact with General Motors, which requires GM to keep a "hands off" attitude toward organizing attempts in the South, the UAW had also signaled renewed labor interest in expanding membership.

Precedents for job and income security guarantees are already well established, of course, in government employment. In a contract that commits management to rely on normal attrition to achieve work force reduction, the U.S. Postal Service, with nearly 700,000 employees, has in effect guaranteed employment security to current full-time postal employees. Employment security guarantees to blue-collar employees were preconditions of the political deals that resulted in Amtrak and Conrail. But beyond these massive, government-sponsored precedents, company after company in the private sector has accepted—either explicitly in contracts or implicitly in de facto "understandings" relating to work force adjustments—the concept that specified groups of employees will be entitled to employment security until retirement.

Behind the government precedents, we should remember, runs a strong current of public sympathy for bedrock union interests. In a recent national opinion poll by Louis Harris, 85 percent of those interviewed agreed that "unions are needed ... so that legitimate ... complaints can be heard and action taken," and 76 percent thought that "most unions in the United States have been good forces working for ... desirable social needs."[4] Probably the majority of Americans regard employment as one of those individual rights that government has an obligation to secure.

Not surprisingly, many Democratic political leaders have maintained this position over the years. But it is not a view confined to politicians. Even among company presidents, if the findings of one survey are to be credited, almost three out of five think that the government ought in some circumstances to act as an employer of last resort.[5] Thus no one should have been surprised when President Carter announced his intention, as one of three or four top goals, of bringing unemployment down to 4.5 percent by 1980, a level close to full employment by most U.S. economists' standards.

A well-defined sentiment in favor of employee ownership, another concept that has been gaining ground in Europe, emerged from a 1975 poll carried out for the People's Bicentennial Commission by Peter D. Hart Research Associates.[6] Of those questioned, 67 percent said they believed it would do "more good than harm" for employees to own a majority of their companies' stock and that they would prefer to work for a company in which they could hold shares. A slightly larger majority—75 percent—thought business had done badly at preventing joblessness. Also in 1975, employee stock ownership plans received the government's blessing in the form of a tax credit.

NEW MANAGEMENT CONCERNS

Partly, but not wholly, as a result of pressures from blue-collar workers, the government, and the public at large, business leaders themselves are beginning to take a keen new interest in employment matters. Executives are becoming aware of the concept of employee "life-cycle costing" and concerned about the full impact of the employment commitment on competitive unit labor costs. (Note General Motors' recent statement that employee health-care cost commitments now account for more of the price of a Chevrolet than the steel the car contains.)

But beyond purely economic concerns, there are also the stirrings of a new compassion. Some observers note that managerial values are changing and that management "humanism" is growing.[7] More and more American executives, indeed, seem sympathetic to the idea that employees are or should be entitled to some form of employment security and that management therefore bears the responsibility of maintaining stable employment. For example, the chief executive of a large Western utility told me categorically, "I think that, once he's proved himself, an employee should be guaranteed a job."

For that matter, many industrial chief executives have still not fully recovered from the shock of finding themselves compelled three years ago to order massive layoffs affecting not just anonymous numbers at some remote plant but familiar faces from the same floor. They are more preoccupied than before with long-term employment maintenance matters, and some are already taking steps to upgrade their companies' manpower forecasting and planning at both the executive and the blue-collar levels. Executives are beginning to suspect that employment security has a good deal to do with the success of companies like Eastman Kodak and IBM in attracting the cream of the manufacturing labor force in their plant areas.

Effective manpower planning programs have enabled these companies to provide their employees with security benefits. The respect the companies have thus earned among wage-earning families in their plant areas is reflected in genuine employee loyalty and labor force commitment to the success of the enterprise. Convinced of management's genuine concern for employment stability and individual job rights, these companies' employees rarely have a confrontation with management and give no evidence of feeling any need of unions.

Meanwhile, the climate of relations between management and organized labor has also been changing in many industries. Collective bargaining in the United States, both across the table and in less formal exchanges, has gradually evolved into a forum for discussion of issues ranging far beyond wages and work rules.

Already more than a dozen large U.S. companies, including Procter & Gamble and Weyerhaeuser, have experimented with new ways of organizing work and getting employees involved in the management process. These experiments have included mechanisms for encouraging employees' participation in decision making at the plant level and for planning and controlling work activity by organized work groups instead of by first-level supervisors. And following experiments with new forms of employee-management dialogue at Chrysler's U.K. subsidiary, the UAW and management have discussed employees' representation on the company's U.S. board of directors.

Usually, management has undertaken such initiatives in order to reduce labor-management tensions as well as to increase productivity. Many of those experimenting with new organization and communication forms are not motivated solely by "heart"; they are also concerned about missing a good competitive bet. In any case, the growing willingness of U.S. executives to experiment with greater employee involvement in matters once regarded as strictly management's province unmistakably reflects a worldwide trend.

A Time for Action

Not long hence, U.S. management may, for the first time in decades, find itself facing an unemployment crisis of really ominous proportions. Over the next five to seven years, the growth in our labor force could easily outstrip employment opportunities by a politically unacceptable margin. If this should happen, businessmen who have been upset by past government interventions in the economy will need to brace themselves for far worse. Only by learning some lessons now from the European labor relations revolution and by taking accommodative action in advance can management and labor prepare themselves, I believe, to meet that challenge.

Neither management nor labor can afford to walk away from the near-term problem of expanding private-sector employment. Along with greater retirement and medical benefits, labor unions want employment security and hope to enlarge the work force by cutting hours worked per employee without reducing earnings. Moreover, unions intend to place a renewed emphasis on organizing to expand membership. Management, faced with competitive cost pressures, is unwilling to absorb the added costs that would result from labor's desires. Government wants to reduce unemployment sharply yet balance the budget. Both management and government are fearful about adding to inflation.

Something has to give. My view is that before government, with its demonstrated capacity for ham-handedness, moves to solve the problem, management and labor ought to begin hammering out some experimental approaches that are based on cooperation rather than on confrontation.

Fortunately, as job security agreements are negotiated, management's own interests require that its corporate labor force requirements be closely attuned to carefully worked-out, long-term labor demand projections. Within corporations, decisions on investment and product-market strategy will have to be weighed with an eye to the long-term economic well-being of the labor force, not merely to financial return and profitability. Just as in Europe today, labor force planning in the United States will share top billing with financial planning on management's strategic priority list.

Quite apart from defensive considerations, there are positive benefits to be gained. Speaking privately, the chief executive officer of a large well-known German manufacturing company remarked to me: "Despite what we say for public consumption, codetermination isn't all that bad; we know how to make it work for us. We give a little here and there, but we don't have strikes. Our manufacturing costs are in control, productivity is going up, and our labor force understands that everybody's bread is buttered on the same side."

Issues and Imperatives

If an American chief executive officer decides that action is indeed called for, what possibilities should he or she explore? First, in my opinion, he might well begin by examining the incentive value of guaranteed employment security. Precedents exist. For instance, Delta Airlines has long had a policy of no furloughs when traffic falls off. Management at Delta feels that the resulting employee morale has a positive effect on productivity.[8] Also, a chief executive officer might investigate the degree to which employees and their unions are willing to trade on other interests (including rising wages and benefits) to achieve employment security. Is there a way this principle might be constructively applied, in view of a company's perceived current and future problems?

Experience suggests that employees are fully aware of the declining orders as well as the earnings problems inherent in business downturns. The reader may recall that in 1975, to counter the cash drain brought about by a recession-induced drop in revenues, Eastern Airlines employees agreed to postpone expected salary increases.

In some European countries, management and labor have agreed on contingency plans (such as short workweeks at reduced wages) designed to have employees share available work and avoid layoffs in case of a downturn. So far, these plans have a generally encouraging history. The concept might be applied in the United States.

Second, I think a concerned chief executive officer ought to consider how his or her company's work force might be better educated about the actual economics of the organization on which their jobs depend. European managers have long since learned that fully informed employees make the best business partners. In many German companies, for example, unions hold classes on company time to instruct and inform their members on a variety of management topics. Top executives should also consider how the work force—including the company's management group—can be made aware of the economic problems linked to guaranteed job security.

A third possibility for an executive is to examine the effectiveness of his or her current corporate manpower planning approaches. Are the employment aspects of every key investment and divestment decision carefully weighed? Are they accommodated within the company's overall employment and job security policies? Starting with a detailed profile of the current labor force (for example, job skill categories broken down by product line and location), management ought to be able to project the long-term impact on employment of the expected growth of the company, changes in production levels, and capital investment alternatives.

These projections will make it possible for management to anticipate potential manpower shortages and surpluses far enough ahead to avoid the usual stop-and-go employment patterns. Such foresight is particularly vital whenever employment-level goals are to be given greater weight in strategy.

Fourth, the action-minded chief executive officer should give some thought to ways of including labor in the resolution of problems that are demonstrably related to broad national employment issues. In Europe, labor involvement has helped to solve many seemingly intractable problems such as the massive shutdown of the inefficient Ruhr coal mines. But a few hasty or ill-conceived attempts to engage labor cooperation have misfired and left ill will and distrust in their wake. Success in any such venture clearly requires that both parties to the attempted dialogue base their positions on incontrovertible information and sincerely recognize each other's legitimate interests and concerns. In Europe, this form of dialogue has on occasion been actively sought by governments as an alternative to formal government intervention.

Finally, it is vitally important for business and labor leaders to understand national priorities, interests, and problems as seen from the political leader's perspective. Our government, with its responsiveness to popular will, cannot and will not recede into the background on matters of national interest. That is why the adversary mode typical of today's labor-management dialogues with its shortsighted disregard for the national interest, is a luxury that neither side can much longer afford.

Recently, a French steel company initiated a long-range strategic effort to build economically meaningful jobs for 4,500 currently superfluous employees. "We may not agree with the government," one of its senior executives told me, "but we've got to come to terms with the way things are. Everyone here is in the same boat. The quicker we develop jobs, the more respect we get from our employees and the sooner we can set more competitive prices. Meanwhile, all this planning information serves a triple purpose. It tells us precisely where we're going, it provides the basis for an informed dialogue with our employee representatives, and it gives us the documentation to get the government help we need to accommodate to the situation."

When I was a youngster, my father worked in an upstate New York manufacturing plant of the American Locomotive Company, once the leading

U.S. builder of steam locomotives and one of the giants of the Dow Jones industrial list. Visiting my father at the plant, I got to know a few of the Alco executives and many of the union leaders. Short-term interests—profits on one side, increasing wages on the other—seemed to be the sole preoccupation of both groups. So absorbed was each side with gaining even the smallest advantage at the expense of the other that the technological changes threatening Alco's very existence went virtually unnoticed. It was the obstinate refusal of both parties to put aside even for a moment, the quest for tactical gains that prevented them from recognizing and reacting to the trends that were engulfing them.

The demise of that once-great company disrupted the lives of hundreds of its workers and scores of its managers. In my view, what is now happening in Europe and the trends I see in the United States could prove as relevant for America's industrial future as the rise of General Motors diesels was for Alco.

Notes

[1] Thomas R. Donahue, executive assistant to the president, A.F.L.-C.I.O., in a speech before the International Conference on Trends in Industrial and Labor Relations, Montreal, May 26, 1976

[2] See Leonard A. Lecht, "Employment Growth in the 1970s—An Uneven Pattern," *The Conference Board Record*, July 1976, p. 2.

[3] See Howard W. Fullerton, Jr. and Paul O. Flair, "New Labor Force Projections to 1990," *Monthly Labor Review*, December 1976, p. 3.

[4] As reported in "Mixed Views About Unions," *Chicago Tribune*, January 6, 1977.

[5] See Frank G. Goble, "Toward 100% Employment," *AMA Survey Report* (New York AMACOM, 1973), p. 42.

[6] See Jeremy Rifkin, *Own Your Own Job* (Des Plaines, Illinois: Bantam Books, 1977), pp. 114-124.

[7] See Kurt R. Student, "Coping with Psychological Responsibility," *The Conference Board Record*, July 1975, p. 61.

[8] See "Delta's Flying Money Machine," *Business Week*, May 9, 1977, p. 84.

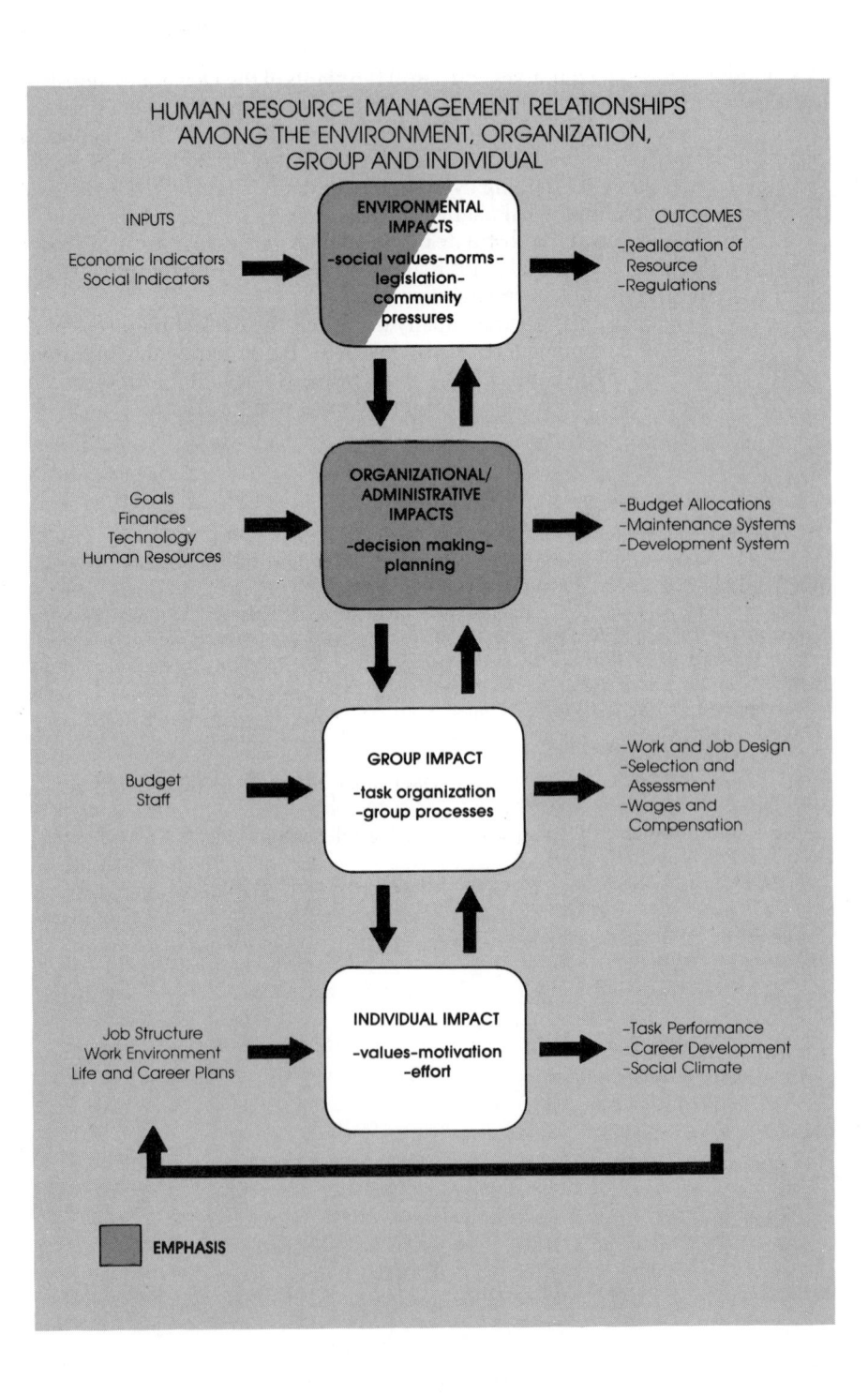

HUMAN RESOURCE MANAGEMENT RELATIONSHIPS AMONG THE ENVIRONMENT, ORGANIZATION, GROUP AND INDIVIDUAL

INPUTS

Economic Indicators
Social Indicators

→ **ENVIRONMENTAL IMPACTS**
-social values-norms-
legislation-
community
pressures

OUTCOMES

-Reallocation of Resource
-Regulations

Goals
Finances
Technology
Human Resources

→ **ORGANIZATIONAL/ ADMINISTRATIVE IMPACTS**
-decision making-
planning

-Budget Allocations
-Maintenance Systems
-Development System

Budget
Staff

→ **GROUP IMPACT**
-task organization
-group processes

-Work and Job Design
-Selection and Assessment
-Wages and Compensation

Job Structure
Work Environment
Life and Career Plans

→ **INDIVIDUAL IMPACT**
-values-motivation
-effort

-Task Performance
-Career Development
-Social Climate

■ **EMPHASIS**

2

HRM AS A PROFESSION

Human resource management is emerging as the dominant model in the field of personnel management. For those organizations which have incorporated the HRM perspective, it has signaled the growth of the personnel function into one of the organization's major corporate staff units. The human resource management staff is becoming responsible for services needed by management for organizational planning and control, and it is exercising significantly more influence over the direction and utilization of the organization's human resources. Human resource management workers not only strive to integrate the personnel function into overall organization planning, they are also participating in a vital way in organization-wide planning. Clearly, there is an important interdependency between HRM and traditional management functions: Not only does an improved understanding of the business by the HRM person encourage the sharing of organizational policy and planning responsibilities with policy makers; more importantly perhaps, the more HRM people become involved with major institutional decisions, the greater their influence in **the incorporation of human resource thinking in virtually all business affairs.**

Human resource management demands that the HRM professional become and remain familiar with the findings and application of behavioral science research to human problems in organizations, the use of quantitative methods, computer applications and forecasting techniques, employee assessment techniques, social trends, and judicial decisions as they apply to organizations' human resource systems. Furthermore, the HRM staff unit must be committed to organizational effectiveness. Winning the confidence of top management as well as access to overall organizational planning requires that HRM professionals demonstrate in convincing terms the merit of the programs they propose and the value of their contributions to the organizational decision-making process. In short, professional competence must be the goal toward which the human resource management specialist must continuously strive.

The first article of Section One, "The Personnel Function Marching to the Beat of a Different Drummer" by George Rieder, has as its theme the need of the HRM function to respond actively to the requirements of the organization. Organizational effectiveness is the criterion for judging HRM activities, and Rieder identifies three ways in which HRM contributes to this effectiveness:

1. Personnel services provided to line and staff groups should be designed to maintain an organization's human resource system.
2. Profit improvement is a positive indicator of the personnel function's success in identifying and resolving human resource problems within the constraints of the organization.
3. The attitude of human resource management is that an organization's employees are its principal resource rather than problems or costs.

For Rieder, the personnel function must become responsive to organizational objectives and it must do so in a creative fashion.

According to Thomas H. Patten, the activities of the personnel department of the future will be recognizable and will be strikingly congruent with those of HRM. Patten writes in "Personnel Management in the 1990s" that greater professionalism will be a distinguishing characteristic, and this will be evident by the significantly greater emphasis on planning. There will be an integration of human resource planning with the dual concerns of compensation and individual employee career planning, and all three aspects will be incorporated into the overall organizational blueprint. Although there will be ebbs and flows in the demands placed on the HRM function, the practitioner will have a broad range of skills. An area of controversy cited by Patten concerns the accreditation of personnel professionals. (Additional information on this subject is provided in the article by Burack and Miller and the subsequent one by Drew Young.) Accreditation is, of course, an important part of the professionalization of any field, but Patten feels that the key to HRM professionalization is the expansion of research into the personnel function.

In their article, "The Personnel Function in Transition," Burack and Miller examine the need for personnel generalists and specialists to update both know-how and methodology in response to new and growing demands in both public and private sector organizations. From a systems perspective, they identify both external and internal pressures acting upon organizations and the coping responses of HRM. Another point they make reinforces a theme in Rieder's article, namely, that HRM must center its attention on contributing to organizational effectiveness. As HRM moves into activities more closely aligned with contributions to the destiny of the organization, personnel managers and technicians alike will be expected to demonstrate a high degree of professionalism. The authors conclude that instead of merely administering traditional personnel activities, HRM personnel will be expected to plan for the continued growth of the individual employee, the total utilization of the organization's human resources and the overall effectiveness of the organization.

The next section of Part II begins with an article by Drew M. Young, "Professionalism and Accreditation in the Field of Personnel and Industrial Relations." He focuses on the American Society for Personnel Administration's (ASPA) accreditation program. Young notes that ASPA is the nation's largest association of personnel and industrial relations executives, with over 22,000 members. The ASPA Accreditation Program was launched in 1973 and administered its first accreditation tests in 1976. In this article, Young reviews the mechanics and consequences of the accreditation program. It is his contention that ASPA's accreditation activities represent a breakthrough in the HRM field. He lists several reasons: First, the accreditation program has produced a set of professional standards in a field which is going to command increasing attention. Second, the accreditation program provides a process whereby individuals working in the field can broaden their perspective and technical competence. Third, participants in the program will undoubtedly bring a higher level of professional competence to their jobs because of their efforts to keep abreast of current organizational developments.

Obviously this approach for furthering professional competence is not without its opponents among both practitioners and academicians. Since 1950, credentialing programs have sprung up among various professional and technical societies, and most are no longer regarded as innovative devices. Whether the ASPA model is an appropriate and durable vehicle for the HRM field remains to be seen. Nonetheless, the program has formalized important aspects of the personnel function and crystallized issues which are bound to have an important impact on the future of the field.

The commitment of human resource management to the evolving needs of the organization includes a pledge to develop more effective research strategies. Forces for organizational change require the ongoing development of new research technologies that allow the professional to be one step ahead of rapid organization-environment interactions. The concluding article of Part II presents a new research model which places research in the mainstream of the organizational development process. In "Organizational Research and Organizational Change: G.M.'s Approach," Howard C. Carlson shows how organizational research can direct ongoing processes of adaptation. At General Motors, traditional research strategies often created artificial results and negative attitudes toward new programs. In response to this problem, researchers developed a framework that integrated concepts of change and related them to action-oriented research strategies. The result is a model of dynamic strategies which can be used to guide the choice, monitoring, and evaluation of research conducted in a change context. The core model presented by the author relates the problem, technique, and program dimensions of research to "real world" time frames and the constructs of the organization. Examples and short cases illustrate the use of each strategy presented in the general model and stress the importance of involving line managers in each phase of the research process. The author concludes by relating these interactive research designs to current professional needs for technologies which bridge the worlds of theory and reality while helping organizations respond more effectively to change processes.

ASSESSMENTS AND PREDICTIONS

The Personnel Function—Marching to the Beat of a Different Drummer

George A. Rieder

What do demographics, individual rights, monkey jars, internal marketing, political savvy, quantitative techniques, and profitability analyses have in common? They are all part of the emerging bag of imperatives for personnel practitioners. Signs of the times include unprecedented problems of inflation, widespread youth unemployment, energy supply, environmental improvement, consumerism, minority rights, gray power, and political activism. The tide of working women continues unabated, with altered family and workplace values in its wake. Government no longer concentrates merely on legislating new benefits or protecting traditional ones, but instead increasingly regulates to assure compliance with administrative law and to cater to the sentiments of special interest groups. Users of human resources in our nation are learning to manage enterprises successfully in a slow-growth economy where productivity gains are harder to find and where relatively expensive capital and credit continue to be funneled to clean up the environment and develop domestic supplies of energy. The times have changed and many segments of our society are marching to the beat of a different drummer.

A 1972 LOOK AT 1977

Decisions made today regarding the organization of the personnel function are futuristic in effect. They impact tomorrow's results by channeling the enterprise's resources either toward constructive ends or merely toward marking time. Long-range planning may be thought of as the process of making assumptions about possible, probable, and preferable futures. It is at the same time theoretical and practical. For some substantiation of this, let's go back to 1972 and examine the work of ASPA's Long-Range Planning Committee. The members concluded that the 1977 priorities would be

1. *Personnel planning and development*, with special emphasis on discovering those workers with a number of skills or abilities; implementing effective affirmative action

Prepared especially for this book and printed with permission of the author.

programs; designing and using practical employee data systems; and developing successful training and career pathing techniques that hit the bottom line

2. The "*conscience function*," which by scrupulous adherence to fairness in recruiting, promoting, disciplining, compensating, and negotiating with employees via their union, would assure management of credibility within the organization; and by extending organizational concern to business-related social problems of the community would serve notice of management's wider perspective

3. *Interpersonal communications* within the individual organization in a role of internal facilitator and harmonizer of a kaleidoscope of functions, groups, and employees

4. *Competence in public affairs*, especially with regulatory and governmental bodies but also with media, educators, and consumer groups

5. *Compensation management*, as this relates to direct cash compensation and pay for performance, with a secondary emphasis on benefit plans

THE THREE FACES OF THE PERSONNEL FUNCTION

Given the projection of HRM priorities for 1977, what can we conclude about the emerging personnel function? Essentially, that it is in a state of change. Whether the personnel executive prefers it or not, the cross-currents of change have cast him or her in the role of hybrid psychologist–sociologist–economist–anthropologist–political scientist–lawyer–moralist. Recently, more than a tinge of the accountant–financial analyst has been added with data-processing systems and procedures not far behind. Increasingly, quantitative techniques are necessary to validate practices and programs—from selection, placement, and compensation to performance appraisal, promotion, training, and development. Applied research becomes vital in a competitive and regulated business environment, not to mention its role in unlocking doors to higher productivity and creativity. Above all, the weight of practicality has moved the personnel profession from concern with theory to the practice of business management; fortunately for HRM personnel, this has meant acceptance as a full-fledged partner in serving the multiple resources of an enterprise. This dimension has been addressed recently by two executives. Cummins Engine's Chief Executive Officer provided the following insights:

> The job ahead for both top management and the personnel department can be summed up very simply as: fewer people, better people, and leadership. That is, fewer people to do a given amount of work, thereby increasing productivity and ultimately cash flow; better people, in order to cope successfully with a less favorable environment and find new ways to do the job; and leadership, in order to make major changes in the way we do business. Management can be static; leadership is making change.[1]

Walter E. Burdick, IBM's vice-president of personnel plans and programs, reinforced this bottom-line sentiment when he observed: "Our [personnel's] achievements must be measured against how well we contribute toward meeting our organization's goals."

The line manager's organization concepts and jargon, therefore, have become an integral part of the personnel professional's daily operation. Terms such as benefit-cost studies, information systems, marginal costs, regression analyses, make-or-buy decisions, and productivity indexes are common lingo in today's personnel office.

Generally speaking, the three faces of the personnel function cluster around the performances required by an enterprise today and over time. They are geared to both efficiency and effectiveness and are tempered by the organization's dual needs for stability and qualitative (if not also quantitative) growth.

1. *Personnel services* is the first and perhaps most familiar face of personnel. These services, provided to line and other staff groups, constitute the meat and potatoes of the personnel function. Users of personnel services expect timeliness, cost effectiveness, and consistent quality when it comes to assistance in hiring, orientation, training, evaluating, rewarding, counseling, promoting, and terminating employees at all levels. The users expect a quick response to their requests—and at an affordable overhead cost. In many respects the organizational principles that apply to this aspect of personnel are similar to unique-product production, where the tools and materials used are standardized and the staff person renders services by stages; for example, a clerk may be able to process most salary recommendations within guidelines set by management and need only refer exceptional items to a higher authority. The wonderful worlds of methods and procedures, information technology, and sound policy guidelines combine to add productivity dimensions to the personnel services' tasks. This is not to suggest that everything is done in a cookbook fashion but only points to the value of production-line approaches to the service industry.[2]

Since most personnel services directly affect the majority of workers as well as prospective employees, they can be termed "conscience functions" and require audit and control. Placement, pay, promotion, training, discipline, and layoff decisions test whether a firm does what it says it is going to do. Well-publicized Equal Employment Opportunity Commission audits including those relevant to equal pay or wage-hour matters are only the tip of the iceberg. Below the water line is the real mass of transactions—work assignments, performance appraisals, testing, salary reviews, opportunities for development, and good faith efforts on behalf of affected groups. These transactions must be monitored against commitments, using a panoply of personnel talents ranging from the legal paraprofessional to the behavioral scientist to the auditor.

Without a qualified work force whenever needed, without constant attention to a mountain of required governmental reports, without prompt and efficient processing of benefit claims, without instruction to update employees on new skills, without remedying health and safety deficiencies, and without realistically resolving grievances or complaints there will be a bevy of practical emergencies that can suffocate an organization. Just as with a McDonald's restaurant, service must be delivered NOW. Things are accomplished because a viable personnel system is in place and operating. Importantly, the system must be efficient and economical enough to support a firm's profit requirements. It must be down-to-earth, function reliably, and deliver results whenever needed, which usually is today.

for the monkey, he wants the food so desperately that he won't let go. Eventually, he's captured. That is one lesson for practitioners, too. People change. Corporate goals and objectives change. Externalities are moving targets. The personnel function's accountabilities are a part of the enterprise, not its reason for existence. One starts with desired organizational results and then designs structure, priorities, and methods. Food is only food when it is consumed. Potentials or competencies are just that until converted to accomplishments.

Notes

[1]J.A. Henderson, "What the Chief Executive Expects of the Personnel Function," *The Personnel Administrator*, May 1977, p. 42.
[2]See Theodore Levitt, "Production-Line Approach to Service," *Harvard Business Review*, September-October 1972, pp. 41–52.
[3]Dr. Neil H. Jacoby, "Six Big Challenges Business Will Face In The Next Decade," *Nation's Business*, August 1976, p. 37.
[4]For more about the hazards or dangers of being a "change agent," see Fred K. Foulkes and Henry M. Morgan, "Organizing and Staffing the Personnel Function," *Harvard Business Review*, May-June 1977, pp. 150–151.
[5]Peter F. Drucker, "Management: Tasks, Responsibilities, Practices," New York: Harper & Row, 1973, pp. 308–309.
[6]George S. Odiorne, "Personnel Management for the '80s," *The Personnel Administrator*, August 1977, p. 22.

Personnel Management in the 1990's

Thomas H. Patten, Jr., Ph.D.

Personnel management has, not surprisingly, always been concerned about its future; and there is a literature expressing this concern.[1] In this paper we attempt to envisage panoramically what lies ahead in the next two decades. Only time can confirm the accuracy of our predictions, but our goal is to *extrapolate presently discernible trends* to the year 2000 rather than to make wild guesses about the possible detailed contents of personnel work.

Topics reviewed are the overall structure of the personnel department, human resource planning, recruitment, selection, compensation, training and individual development, organizational development and planned change, occupational safety and health and environmental engineering, labor relations, plant-community relations, and personnel research and audits. This overview highlights rather than exhaustively delineates the future of personnel processes/systems in the private sector (with minimal attention given to the public

Prepared especially for this book and printed with permission of the author.

sector). In the interest of brevity, we will not discuss the relationship of underlying social, economic, political, and technological factors to changes in the personnel function. However, the reader should keep in mind that the world of the year 2000 will probably be one in which only 15 to 20 percent of the American population will be employed in the manufacturing sector of the economy, 30 percent will be employed by various levels of government, and the remainder will be employed in services, except for a handful in farming and some other traditional industries of the past.[2]

OVERALL STRUCTURE OF THE PERSONNEL DEPARTMENT

If we were magically transported to the future, we would still easily recognize the personnel department of the twenty-first century by its title—"personnel," "industrial relations," "employee relations," or perhaps "human resource." In small firms (those employing less than 150 people), the personnel manager will be a generalist. In large firms (those employing 150 to 5,000 employees), the personnel staff will include a number of specialists; and in the largest firms, including the multinational corporations (those employing 5,000 to 600,000 or more), there will not only be specialization, but *ultra-specialization* within the personnel staffs. In the largest firms which are decentralized by geography and/or product lines, we will continue to see functional supervision exercised by the corporate personnel staff over the divisional personnel staff and by the divisional personnel staff, in turn, over the plant personnel staff.

There will also be a dramatic increase in the number of persons employed as specialists and ultra-specialists graduating from the better undergraduate and graduate business schools who will find personnel attractive as a career field for a major portion of their work lives even if they aspire to careers subsequently in general (multi-functional) management.

The issue as to whether personnel management should be centralized or decentralized will never be settled definitively, now or in the 1990s. Some firms that operate in a highly centralized, bureaucratic manner will generally continue in that way. Yet organizations built by "conglomerateurs" will be more numerous and characteristically quite decentralized with very lean corporate staffs, including the personnel staff.

Discussions of organizational design and structure are almost always conjectural because in the real world of day-to-day business and agency life, organizational planning is carried out under the governance of a multitude of subjective notions. Yet the personnel department of the future will seek to integrate human resource planning with compensation, career development, and organizational planning. There are many ways in which this integration can be accomplished and many organizational arrangements for interrelating the personnel specialties and ultra-specialties so that the overall goals of the business or agency can be accomplished.[3] The important point is that they will be planned, controlled, and integrated through rational, calculated policies and procedures rather than treated in isolation or opportunistically left to chance. Perhaps the dominant theme of all personnel work of the future will be planning, whether that concept is applied to the systems already mentioned or to the implementation of equal employment opportunity and affirmative action, training programs, safety, or any other facet of the personnel field.

Overall, we expect to see a continuing role redefinition of the personnel department away from the "trashcan hypothesis" to the "treasury hypothesis." This observation signifies that in the 1990s the top personnel staff official in a private sector organization will be entitled Vice-President–Personnel and his counterpart in the public sector will be the agency Director of Personnel. The former will report to the president and the latter to the agency head. Both will have administrative responsibility not over a trashcan of disparate functions but rather over the management of human resources in the organization, unquestionably the most precious of all resources. Both will be treasurers of human resources much as today the top financial and control officer subsumes the financial treasury in his area of responsibility. The private sector Vice–President–Personnel will in many cases also sit on the corporate board of directors.[4]

HUMAN RESOURCE PLANNING

The reason we see the treasury concept taking hold today is that we have been experiencing a "manpower revolution"[5] for a decade or two and have seen manpower planning and the development of human resources come to center stage several times.

Human resource planning is a bona fide concern of contemporary work organizations, large and small, because of the changing modes of production and job structure in our economy and society. One evidence of this new approach to the human factor of production is the establishment in 1977–78 of the Human Resource Planning Society. In the future even more than now, companies and agencies must look ahead to have the right people in the right place at the right time to perform work for organizational goal attainment. We require highly educated people in great numbers who must be provided with work experiences and careers so that they properly add to and augment the corporate or agency treasury of human resources.

The computer has proven to be of great value in many facets of human resource planning: providing a personnel data bank and skills inventory; periodic reports of the impact of such personnel transactions as promotions, retirements, layoffs, and changes of employee status; and printouts of individual employee records that can be used in succession planning, consideration for overseas assignments, and the like. We can expect still other, more sophisticated uses of the computer in the future, as in modeling for various types of planning purposes and in further reducing some of the manual drudgery of paperwork that still exists in very large firms. In making managerial decisions regarding employees, for example, computers can be programmed to coordinate executive succession planning with the career pathing of younger managers and professional employees on the high-potential list.

There may be a gradual demise of such relatively promising techniques as human resource accounting, either because the technology for such accounting leads to a blind alley (it has no legal standing as does financial accounting) or because some of the concepts are still quite murky in the human translation (return on investment in people or depreciation of people).[6] On the other hand, there is likely to remain an interest in the economic evaluation of human resource programs of all kinds in the 1990s.[7] The key perhaps to the success of any of these people-organization-jobs programs is the planning phase, because the attainment of beneficial or harmful results is often traceable to the adequacy of initial planning.

To make this prediction is not to deny, however, that any number of fads may dominate planning concepts for short periods. In the past we have seen an emphasis upon cost-benefit analyses of human resource programs, particularly in the public sector when Robert S. McNamara was in the U.S. Department of Defense.[8] Program planning and budgeting systems (PPBS) were made popular in the last decade, and it appears that zero-based budgeting (ZBB) will be ascendant for the next few years.[9] But these may well prove to be merely flashes in the managerial pan that had some potential for rational human resource planning and in time were either institutionalized or forgotten (or both!).

RECRUITMENT POLICY AND PRACTICES

It is fair to say that until the early 1960s, recruitment, selection, and placement (roughly what collectively used to be called "the employment function") were a stodgy part of personnel work. With the onset of the manpower revolution and the passage of the Civil Rights Act of 1964, recruitment policies and practices received much governmental scrutiny and the step-daughter of personnel became its princess. There is much controversy today over the upward mobility and socioeconomic progress of minority group members in America.[10] Yet we will be closer to a society of true socioeconomic mobility for all in another generation (roughly the year 2000); and by the time still another generation has matured, we may look back on the middle decades of the twentieth century as the breaking point for eliminating all types of irrational discrimination.

By 2000 what we today identify as equal employment opportunity and affirmative action programs will have changed their character so drastically as to be unrecognizable. Having passed through the era of quotas, goals, and timetables in EEO-AA, we shall look back upon the cries of reverse discrimination hurled by white males at college recruiters, corporate personnel administrators, and the management establishment generally as the turning point in human resources management. Recruitment policies and practices will be significantly more egalitarian, and American society will have continued to become more fluid, throwing status achievement open to competition rather than ascription from birth. The federally mandated EEO-AA requirements that appear onerous today will have become institutionalized and a new way of life in recruiting will have emerged.

The days of laissez faire in personnel management expired during the early 1970s, and many types of personnel decisions which were strictly at the discretion or prerogative of management have long since become channelized because of legislation, federal executive orders, and collective bargaining agreements.[11] The continuing reduction of managerial discretion will probably remain characteristic of personnel decision making, coincident with the trend of American society to move from one of exclusion to inclusion. Hence, a strictly legalistic approach will no longer be needed.

Demographics themselves will, of course, play a major part in this inevitable transition. In addition, younger personnel executives will have been brought up under the new values of the open society and neither resent nor consider EEO-AA as burdensome or out of the ordinary.

Labor supply sources will remain about the same as at present, but executive search firms will play a steadily increasing role in the recruitment of executive, managerial, and high-level professional personnel. The federal government will continue its attempts to rationalize the labor market through improvements in the federal-state employment service, and there may indeed be some advances made in managing disadvantaged and unskilled workers. But no significant inroads will be made in rationalizing the executive labor market or in improving the recruitment, selection, and placement of managerial, professional, and technical personnel.

The availability of people for work in the 1990s will be markedly affected by changes already underway in mandatory retirement policies. Two crosscurrents are presently competing: a strong interest by some industrial unions in early retirement (symbolized in the slogan "30 and out"—thirty years' service and optional retirement regardless of age) versus a strong interest by individuals for removal of compulsory retirement at 65 (or any age in the case of some zealots). These currents will remain, giving employees wide options for second careers (if their health stands up), early retirement, or no retirement. Widespread clogging of positions by older people who have reached the higher levels of the job pyramid or top management could have a stultifying effect on the mobility of younger people who aspire to move up. There would also be important implications for the funding of federal social security (Old-Age, Survivors, Disability, and Health Insurance—OASDHI) and private pension and benefit plans. We shall resume our discussion of these aspects of the personnel function in a later section.

SELECTION POLICY AND PRACTICES

Closely related to the new recruitment philosophy of including rather than excluding people is a similar notion in selection policy. Until the emergence of the EEO-AA era, it is accurate to note that initial selection for employment was governed more by possible reasons to reject applicants than by creative thinking on the part of the interviewer as to how the applicant could be hired, made qualifiable, and trained to be job-proficient.[12] Certainly, in times of extreme labor shortage there has often been a willingness on the part of employers to be inclusive rather than exclusive. The shift to more general acceptance of inclusion has meant the virtual abandonment of the use of paper-and-pencil tests in initial selection.[13] In large part this shift was caused by the requirement that to be lawfully used in selection, written tests must be validated in one or more acceptable ways.[14] The decline in use of commercially available and home-made tests will continue in the years ahead.

Selection procedures for initial employment will continue to place high emphasis on the interview even though it too is a "test." For employees who are being considered for transfer or promotion, the interview is of course a commonly used device. It is used in assessment centers, together with paper-and-pencil tests, simulations, in-baskets, and a variety of other techniques and tools for making promotional decisions and for the assessment of potential of various kinds—for example, for supervisory work, advancement as a nonsupervisory individual contributor, and for long-range career potential.[15] The interview will continue to serve these purposes in the future. However, the spread of assessment centers themselves over the next two decades will be relatively slow because of the cost involved in establishing and maintaining them. Yet there is little doubt that the assessment center is the best tool personnel researchers have so far been able to devise for estimation of that elusive quality called "potential," which is at the center of the notion of human resources: the quality of the individual human being in relation to job and career performance.

The last aspect of selection policy and practices which we discuss is the reference check. Until recent years it was common practice for employers to check an applicant's list of references before the final employment decision. Often checks made of friends, neighbors, and clergymen listed by applicants were worse than useless in divulging job-performance or even character data about an applicant, because the sources applicants listed were positively biased. Checks with former employers were generally more fruitful, but again, if carried out by telephone, they might fluctuate from being superficial and downright erroneous to extremely candid and even strongly derogatory. By the year 2000 meaningful data in reference checks will have all but disappeared for the aforementioned reasons and for others that loom even larger: privacy legislation.

Privacy legislation is designed to protect individuals against improper divulgence of information to outsiders.[16] At present, the Privacy Act of 1974 covers only employees of the federal government. Of the 50 states, only one (California) has a privacy of information act (which applies to all records except letters of reference). However, legislation on this topic is being drafted in many states and will obviously be more of a central concern to the personnel manager of the 1990s. (Paradoxically, it could coexist with freedom of information legislation—as it does in federal employment—where recognition is given to the public's right to know myriad details about people, programs, budgets, policies, and the like in an effort to let "the sun shine in" on such matters, rather than keep them privy to the bureaucracy.)

In practice, privacy legislation means that employers are likely to maintain more concise, to-the-point personnel records on individuals, to make these available to employees and their supervisors, and to include only those data that are correct and defensible. These records will constitute a hard core of factual and performance data verifiable by an employee before inclusion in the file.

Privacy legislation will also have an important effect on the computerization of employee records and, in turn, on the employee's career development. All personnel transactions after initial hiring (promotion, transfer, demotion, reinstatement after leave, layoff, and retirement) will come under employee scrutiny and may well be challenged on the grounds of unfairness or incorrect timing. However, the ethical soundness and quality of personnel decision making will

tion is ideological. Freedom could be traded off for the security of a place on the payroll. This will also be a costly security for the employer to bear in both dollars and the transformation of human resources. Are we likely to engender cautious and overly job-conscious attitudes rather than energetic and risk-taking behavior in human resources? The threat presented by such a situation will thoroughly challenge the personnel manager to take forfending action to assure that any personnel policies, programs, and procedures he or she implements are not dysfunctional for either employee or organization.

Legislative change will also have a powerful effect on indirect compensation; and projecting such changes is conjectural, except that undoubtedly the trend will be toward liberalization and higher employer cost. We can expect slow growth in ESOPs (Employer Stock Ownership Plans).[26] Formal cost-of-living allowances will be needed on pensions in the next two decades and will be formularized somehow, although the design requirements involved will give actuaries nightmares.

Future changes in the Employee Retirement Income Security Act of 1974 (ERISA) will result in the cancellation of pension and profit-sharing plans by smaller employers, but we can expect the liberalization of vesting and the formalization of portability. By 2000 most of the ERISA concepts will also be mandated for public sector employees, such as those for funding, vesting, rollovers, and guaranty insurance.[27] We can expect OASDHI to be a very expensive proposition. Under 1977 legislation, social security taxes are scheduled to rise horrendously to a maximum of 7.10 percent for both employers and employees on wage bases up to $42,600.00 annually. If over the next two decades future congresses follow the paths of past congresses in election years, OASDHI benefits and eligibilities will be liberalized, placing the social security system in a continuing series of financial crises. Sharply higher payroll taxes to fund OASDHI plus, eventually, federal contributions from the general revenue are very likely.

There will be some form of national health insurance within a decade; but at this point no one can envisage the form this will take.[28] The only certainty is that owing to OASDHI increases, ERISA liberalization, and the launching of national health insurance, the percent of payroll attributable to fringes will skyrocket along the lines previously discussed. Quite possibly the skyrocketing will trigger levying individual ordinary income taxes on the cost value of fringes paid by employers.

If inflation continues as predicted, "indexation" (or the application of formal cost-of-living formulas to compensation) will become common not only for pensions and OASDHI but also for adjustments in the minimum wage under the Fair Labor Standards Act and wages and salaries throughout the economy. Such formal indexation on wages already exists in a few industries such as automobiles, steel, and rubber.

TRAINING AND INDIVIDUAL DEVELOPMENT

The training and development function will remain fundamentally the same between now and the year 2000. Training directors will become increasingly professionalized, and the American Society for Training and Development will continue to grow. Any changes in training will be more apparent than real, although the creative genius of people in this personnel specialty is remarkable. One has only to witness the plethora of new human resource development techniques (assertiveness training, transactional analysis, and est-Erhard Seminar Training among others), innovative phrases ("buying in," becoming "sensitized," or getting top management "ownership" of the training effort, for example), and diverse programs (two weeks back-to-back of nonverbal centering, value clarification sessions, and career life planning seminars).[29]

The bread-and-butter of training will remain: apprenticeship programs; trainee foreman and new first-level staff supervisory programs; college graduate orientation and induction efforts; on-site and off-site middle management seminars; specialized training for sales and marketing personnel; and refresher training for engineers, technicians, and skilled trades employees. Such programs will continue for the next two decades, although formal programs for highly educated employees in management positions (defined as those who supervise the work of others) may actually be less numerous than today. There will instead be greater use made of on-the-job training and senior executive coaching, well-arranged job rotation, fast track programs especially for minority group members, and sophisticated career planning.

ORGANIZATIONAL DEVELOPMENT AND PLANNED CHANGE

As American industry absorbs more and more highly educated people in employee roles, notions of proper recruitment, selection, placement, compensation, and career development change correspondingly. At one time managerial ideology held that only the best-qualified people should be hired and then required to socialize themselves to the work organization through a one-way accommodative process. In the past decade we have seen poorly qualified individuals hired and brought into the mainstream while work organizations accommodated to them. Changes in an organization's accommodative behavior which lead to improved management of human resources via increased diffusion of problem-solving capabilities among managers and employees is what organizational development (OD) is all about.

We flatly predict much more extensive use of OD in the years ahead and the building of a strong network between academia and work organizations through the export and import of applied behavioral science knowledge. Such a network will be regarded as indispensable in the future planning and control of compensation, in performance reviews, collective bargaining and labor relations, in safety, and in other personnel systems so far only lightly touched by OD.

In the years ahead, the term organizational development may be replaced by alternate terms, such as organizational studies, organizational research and development, human resource management, or personnel operations. However, the phenomenon itself will remain vital, alive, and dynamic, underscoring a common denominator among all organizations—a commitment to the improvement of organizational management through the planned utilization of behavioral science knowledge.

Today's well-rounded personnel generalist is in command of the full range of technical nonbehavioral skills, including the ability to conduct job analyses, prepare training conferences, design incentive plans, and so forth. The generalist of the future will need all these skills, plus the ability to apply the practical findings of behavioral science, so that, for example, interdepartmental conflicts can be identified and resolved, jobs enriched, employees motivated to perform better, and the work culture made more receptive to change. Personnel managers will themselves become competent agents of planned social change, using human resource development and improved management techniques to accommodate the demands of employees, the environment, legislative innovations, expanding technology, and the various contiguous publics to which the company or agency must relate. This is obviously a tall order in job performance requirements but underscores once again what is meant when we suggest that personnel management is rapidly moving away from preoccupation with trashcan concerns toward treasury priorities. In the future OD (whatever it may then be called) will be on a permanent par with compensation and collective bargaining–labor relations as central systems in personnel work.

OCCUPATIONAL SAFETY AND HEALTH AND ENVIRONMENTAL ENGINEERING

Anyone familiar with the Pittsburgh Survey of 1908 conducted by the Russell Sage Foundation is likely never to forget that microeconomic study of Eastern urban-industrial America for its revelation of the horrors of industrial accidents, diseases, child labor exploitation, long hours, low wages, callous personnel practices, job insecurity, and utter lack of protection of employees and families from the contingencies of life.[30] We have come a long way in 70 years, and the next two decades offer the possibility of still greater progress in the improvement of occupational safety and health. But, significantly, such advances are not automatic!

Today employees should be advised that work, like cigarette smoking, is definitely dangerous to their health and safety, even though conditions comparable to those in Pittsburgh at the turn of the century are rare. We seldom hear about anthrax and phossy jaw anymore; but silicosis, asbestosis, byssoniosis, radiation diseases, and physical deterioration caused by carcinogenic substances in the workplace (such as in the manufacture of polyvinyl chloride) have taken their places. Coal mine explosions caused by methane gas may be fewer, but black lung disease is more common than years ago. Workers' compensation, a type of social insurance cushion funded solely by employer contributions, is in effect in all 50 states to pay for employees' anatomical losses and impairment of earning capacity for accidents arising in and out of the course of employment. Yet we still have too many disabling accidents and industrial diseases in America because we have not used the resources within our power to reduce the number and extent of calamities and personal disasters.

Federal legislation intended to deal with health and safety problems was enacted in 1970 in the Occupational Safety and Health Act. For personnel managers who aspired to be change agents in firms where health and safety problems were severe and correctable, OSHA meant quite literally "*our savior has arrived.*" Some thought OSHA compliance could be used as leverage to get top management to act. Personnel managers were doomed to disappointment, however, because the unit of the federal Department of Labor that administers OSHA was and has remained under-funded and under-staffed for the magnitude of the task before it.

In the absence of first-rate government assistance, personnel managers have typically been assigned company and agency responsibility for safety. In the years ahead, employee well-being will be somewhat better controlled through safety and environmental engineering. The process will be slow and steady. As the 50 states enact "baby OSHAs," we can expect more frequent and thorough factory and workplace inspections. Yet there are literally hundreds of thousands of work locations to be inspected in the United States, and small business turnover is high. Thus, by the year 2000, unless there are unforeseen changes, OSHA and the baby OSHAs may have made only a slight overall impact. Business concerns over the impact of OSHA from a cost standpoint (the expenditure of billions on new safety equipment, changes in plant facilities and layout, and environmental change), at a peak in the early 1970s, is now low and will remain there for at least the short term unless OSHA receives an unexpected injection of new funds.

LABOR RELATIONS POLICY AND PRACTICES

Collective bargaining has been a central concern of unionized firms ever since the AFL organized skilled tradesmen, and particularly since the CIO organized mass-production industry in the 1930s and 1940s. Although unions are here to stay in the private sector, only 25 percent of the U.S. labor force of 96 million is unionized. Perhaps it is the "crucial" 25 percent in some sense, but it is nevertheless a minority of the labor force.

By the year 2000, we can expect unions to be burgeoning in the public sector but little more than holding their own in the private sector. There is little or no drive today toward unionization on the part of private-sector managerial, professional, technical, and clerical employees, the so-called white-collar worker. The number of blue-collar employees in manufacturing will be dropping both absolutely and relatively in the years ahead. Blue-collar unions in all industry will be important in the year 2000 because personnel management in unionized industries has become institutionalized through a history of consecutive collective bargaining contract negotiations. The issues of the past have been wages, hours, and conditions of employment; and the governing concepts have been "more" for wages (direct and indirect compensation), "less" in the sense of fewer hours per week, and "improvement" (from the employees' standpoint) of working conditions. None of these directions is expected to change from now to 2000, except that some outer limits may have been reached beyond which any addenda to "more," "less," or "improvement" look less like pioneering than iterations and minor embellishments of the past.

Proposals of the past 15 years for creative collective bargaining, long-range committees, and union-management study groups functioning between periods of contract negotiation have yielded some innovative change but altered very little the institutions which grew out of the Wagner, Taft-Hartley, and Landrum-Griffin acts in the private sector.[31] Current proposals for modifying the National Labor Relations Act are not likely to interfere in the future with established institutions of collective bargaining, only the lesser important administrative details.

Acknowledging the institutional rigidity of collective bargaining in America, we must also note its adaptability and malleability within limits. Some critical students of personnel view collective bargaining as based upon outmoded assumptions and have proposed changing these while injecting some of the recent ideas borrowed from the behavioral sciences into existing collective bargaining relationships.[32]

Various experiments with collective bargaining have suggested that relationships between the parties can mature to the extent that third-party intervention may become unnecessary. More recently quality of work-life committees (which incidentally are often misnomers for committees for union-management cooperation) have been established which encourage the parties to be more open and authentic with one another and to build durable trust into their relationship.[33] These committees abjure tough adversary-style relations and substitute maturity for childlike trust in split-the-difference philosophies of rights and interest arbitration. Even the federal Mediation and Conciliation Service seems to be swinging this way, since it has for several years been working with conflict-ridden companies to improve union-management relations in a program dubbed "relations-by-objectives," which partakes of both MBO and OD.[34] In the future we are likely to see further extensions of applied behavioral science in labor relations and more sophisticated use of RBO.

We predict greater acceptance of such approaches as Scanlon plans, community labor-management committees, and long-range, between-negotiations study committees for the improvement and maturation of union-management relations. Behavioral science will have great impact upon labor relations when the present older guard generation of labor relations practitioners retires, forever breaking direct links with World War II industrial relations ideas.

PLANT-COMMUNITY RELATIONS POLICY AND PRACTICES

Public relations is not labor relations. However, the plant manager or personnel manager of the local branch of a multi-plant corporation is *the* company in the eyes of the local community.[35] In the future personnel managers will increasingly be responsible for representing "the company" or "the agency" before publics of all kinds, particularly in localities remote from headquarters in these far-flung, faceless, complex organizations. Such publics could be identified as racial/ethnic, special interest, educational, professional, or general community. A public can be defined simply as a group having one or more characteristics in common; hence, under the treasury of human resources concept, the personnel manager as a people specialist will be expected to represent the employing organization before any number of publics. This responsibility is bound to loom large in the 1990s because there will be greater involvement of firms and agencies in the solution of social problems caused by possible new welfare/workfare laws, programs for the control of alcoholism and substance abuse, continued efforts for the upward mobility of minorities, and for contributing to the physical and socioeconomic well-being of communities.[36]

In a word, personnel managers of the 1990s must keep abreast of developments in a wide variety of newly evolving, complex areas. Those who are lucky may obtain professional assistance from headquarters public relations staffs or purchase help from outside public relations consulting firms. But if this assistance is limited to the provision of canned position statements, speakers' bureaus, press releases, and the traditional paraphenalia of public relations, it is not going to be of much use in solving the day-to-day problems the personnel manager will encounter in the rapidly changing environment of the 1990s.

PERSONNEL RESEARCH AND AUDITS

We have already discussed the importance of evaluating training programs, however, *all* personnel systems should be periodically evaluated in terms of their efficiency and effectiveness. The systems should be economically sound and fulfill their purpose within the context of broader organizational goals. In order to measure or appraise the systems in these two ways, personnel managers in the 1990s will have to make successful quantum leaps over today's state of the profession. Inasmuch as personnel research and auditing are closely related we discuss both together.

There are at least three types of personnel research: theory-based and oriented toward contributing to the fund of scientific knowledge in a basic social science discipline (basic research); theory-based but oriented toward problem solving in a particular work organization (service research); and statistical and essentially descriptive with no theory base. Personnel research is done by academicians in universities, professionals in work organizations of all kinds, and private consultants. Personnel research varies greatly in quality, quantity, topics investigated, funding, publication or lack of publication of findings, and so on.

We predict that by the year 2000 service research rather than basic research in human behavior will be a predominant aspect of the personnel manager's job. For the most part, research will be conducted only by the largest companies or agencies, and it will be oriented toward the personnel program itself or toward further defining the personnel function. It will frequently take the form of audits and be designed to gather facts on how well an organization's personnel programs are being administered in its various far-flung divisions. For this reason the research of the future will most accurately be described as of a service nature, designed primarily to aid in planning and controlling the quality of personnel operations, much as is the case today.

Personnel research studies that investigate basic concepts in human behavior are typically conducted by academically based researchers, not by those employed in work organizations. Basic personnel research will predominantly be conducted by professionals with a background in industrial and organizational psychology or by individuals with a multidisciplinary organizational behavior/management background. This, too, is a prediction that follows directly from current trends and practices. Similarly, attitude surveys and feedback will continue to loom large in the 1990s but will be more sophisticated than those of the past and typically fed back to employees in a participative action-research mode.

More prosaic research will still abound in the year 2000. The computerization of personnel records will take much of the drudgery out of manual procedures and statistical report preparation, as well as provide a wealth of data in a timely manner for planning and controlling the administrative side of personnel work.[37] This will, of course, be service or institutional research of a relatively low order of complexity.

Top management, by and large, hungers for knowledge of results; and this is as true for the personnel function as it is for production, marketing, finance, or engineering. There is a great challenge for personnel managers of the future to satisfy this hunger of the cost-conscious management who sees human resources as crucial to enterprise success. In reality, management is waiting to bestow the mantle of treasurer of human resources on the personnel manager who can make research relevant to improved management and communicate this relevance to his/her organizational superiors in understandable management language.

Research in any field is in many ways the key to professionalization. While future personnel managers will have a much greater familiarity with the uses and methods of research, it is not likely they will become research or computer experts. The power of the chief personnel executive in any work organization, and the respect he or she commands, rests upon personal credibility and competence. Subjectively and objectively this individual must know the parameters of the personnel function and communicate this know-how to both superiors and subordinates. Adequate research properly utilized can be symbolically and organizationally important in this context—and will be even more so in the 1990s.

CONCLUSION

At a time when the ability of the labor market to absorb college graduates and offer them a challenging career is being debated and many graduates are disappointed in obtaining a job that connects with their educational and occupational choice, there can be no doubt that college graduates with in-depth education in personnel managment are eminently placeable. The proliferation of legislation has itself been a stimulus to job creation in the personnel field—witness the rising number of EEO coordinators, safety inspectors, pension consultants, group insurance administrators, workers' compensation claim analysts, job analysts, wage administrators, and the like. The personnel field in all its many facets appears to offer rich opportunities for employment from now through the 1990s.

To work in the personnel field—as a vice-president, salaried personnel supervisor, training coordinator, or in any personnel subspecialty—is to have an important impact on people. For the future, these impacts are likely to intensify as our society continues to place greater value on human beings, the human condition, and shaping the direction of human destiny through planned change. A professional career in personnel offers a unique opportunity to contribute to these changes and presents both an intellectual and managerial challenge for the individual who enters this important field of human endeavor.

Notes

[1] See, for example, Thomas H. Patten, Jr., "Personnel Management in the 1970s: The End of Laissez-Faire," *Human Resource Management, 12,* 3 (Fall 1973), 7-19; Fred K. Foulkes, "The Expanding Role of the Personnel Function," *Harvard Business Review, 53,* 2 (March-April 1975), 71-84; Elmer H. Burack and Edwin L. Miller, "The Personnel Function in Transition," *California Management Review, 18,* 3 (Spring 1976), 32-38; and Edwin L. Miller and Elmer H. Burack, "The Emerging Personnel Function," *MSU Business Topics, 25,* 4 (Autumn 1977), 27-32.

[2] Daniel Bell, *Toward the Year 2000: Work in Progress* (Boston: Beacon Press, 1967).

[3] For expansion of these thoughts, see Thomas H. Patten, Jr., *Pay: Employee Compensation and Incentive Plans* (New York: Free Press, 1977), pp. 20-51.

[4] See Foulkes, "The Expanding Role of the Personnel Function," pp. 78-79.

[5] Garth L. Mangum, *The Manpower Revolution* (Garden City, N.Y.: Doubleday, 1968).

[6] One of the best detailed discussions of this subject can be found in Eric Flamholtz, *Human Resource Accounting* (Belmont, Calif.: Dickenson, 1974). See also, Jacob B. Paperman and Desmond D. Martin, "Human Resource Accounting: A Managerial Tool?" *Personnel, 54,* 2 (March-April 1977), 41-50; James A. Craft and Jacob G. Birnberg, "Human Resource Accounting: Perspective and Prospects," *Industrial Relations, 15,* 1 (February 1976), 2-12; and John Grant Rhode et al., "Human Resource Accounting: A Critical Assessment," *Industrial Relations, 15,* 1 (February 1976), 13-25.

[7] A sign of the continuing interest is Ray A. Killian, *Human Resource Management: An ROI Approach* (New York: AMACOM, 1976), esp. pp. 42-48.

[8] Michael E. Borus and William R. Tash, *Measuring the Impact of Manpower Programs: A Primer* (Ann Arbor: Institute of Labor and Industrial Relations, University of Michigan-Wayne State University, 1970). See also, Rodney H. Brady, "MBO Goes to Work in the Public Sector," *Harvard Business Review, 51,* 2 (March-April 1973), 65-74.

[9] Logan M. Cheek, *Zero-Based Budgeting Comes of Age* (New York: AMACOM, 1977). See also his "Cost Effectiveness Comes to the Personnel Function," *Harvard Business Review, 51,* 3 (May-June 1973), 96-105.

[10] Stuart H. Garfinkle, "Occupations of Women and Black Workers, 1962-74," *Monthly Labor Review, 98,* 11 (November 1975), 25-35; and Curtis L. Gilroy, "Black and White Unemployment: The Dynamics of the Differential," *Monthly Labor Review, 97,* 2 (February 1974), 38-42.

[11] See Patten, "Personnel Management in the 1970s," pp. 9-12.

[12] *Ibid.,* pp. 7-10.

[13] See Donald J. Peterson, "The Impact of Duke Power on Testing," *Personnel, 51,* 2 (March-April 1974), 30-37.

[14] For a discussion of test validity, see Frank Erwin, "The New OFCCP Guidelines: What Happened?" *Personnel Administrator, 22,* 2 (February 1977), 30-34. In 1978 new guidelines were published in the Federal Register.

[15] For studies of assessment centers, see Robert B. Finkle and William S. Jones, *Assessing Corporate Talent* (New York: Wiley 1970); and Douglas W. Bray et al., *Formative Years in Business: A Long-Term AT&T Study of Managerial Lives* (New York: Wiley, 1974).

[16] Virginia E. Schein, "Privacy and Personnel: A Time for Action," *Personnel Journal, 55,* 12 (December 1976), 604-607; and Mordechai Mironi, "The Confidentiality of Personnel Records," *Labor Law Journal, 25,* 5 (May 1975), 270-292.

[17] Alvar O. Elbing et al., "Flexible Working Hours: The Missing Link," *California*

Management Review, 17, 3 (Spring 1975), 50–57. See also, Riva Poor, ed., *4 Days, 40 Hours* (Cambridge: Bursk and Poor, 1970).

[18] Frederick Herzberg, "One More Time: How Do You Motivate Employees?" *Harvard Business Review*, 46, 1 (January–February 1968), 53–62; and his "The Wise Old Turk," *Harvard Business Review*, 52, 5 (September–October 1974), 70–80.

[19] For information on cafeteria pay plans, see J. Taylor, "A New Approach to Compensation Management," *Compensation Review*, 1, 1 (First Quarter 1969), 25–28; L. M. Baytos, "The Employee Benefit Smorgasbord: Its Potential and Limitations," *Compensation Review*, 2, 1 (First Quarter 1970) 16–18; Robert V. Goode, "Complications at the Cafeteria Checkout Line," *Personnel*, 51, 6 (November–December 1974), 45–49; and William B. Werther, Jr., "Flexible Compensation Evaluated," *California Management Review*, 19, 1 (Fall 1976), 40–46.

[20] Edward E. Lawler, III, "New Approaches to Pay: Innovations That Work," *Personnel*, 53, 5 (September–October 1976), 11–23; and his and Raymond N. Olsen's, "Designing Reward Systems for New Organizations," *Personnel*, 54, 5 (September–October 1977), 48–60.

[21] See Wendell L. French and Robert W. Hollmann, "Management By Objectives: The Team Approach," *California Management Review*, 17, 3 (Spring 1975), 13–22; Rensis Likert and M. Scott Fisher, "MBGO: Putting Some Team Spirit into MBO," *Personnel*, 54, 1 (January–February 1977), 40–47; and Richard E. Byrd and John Cowan, "MBO: A Behaviorial Science Approach," *Personnel*, 51, 2 (March–April 1974), 42–50.

[22] Thomas H. Patten, Jr., "Linking Financial Rewards to Employee Performance: The Roles of OD and MBO," *Human Resource Management*, 15, 4 (Winter 1976), 2–17. For parallel ideas, see Milton L. Rock, ed., *Handbook of Wage and Salary Administration* (New York: McGraw-Hill, 1972).

[23] Many personnel experts bemoan the sad state of job evaluation. See, for example, Robert E. Sibson, "New Practices and Ideas in Compensation Administration," *Compensation Review*, 6, 3 (Third Quarter 1974), 40–41.

[24] Thomas H. Patten, Jr., "Job Enrichment and Job Evaluation: A Collision Course?" *Human Resource Management*, 16, 4 (Winter 1977), 2–8. See also, Sar A. Levitan and William B Johnston, "Job Redesign, Reform, Enrichment—Exploring the Limitations," *Monthly Labor Review*, 96, 7 (July 1973), 35–41.

[25] *Employee Benefits 1977* (Washington: Chamber of Commerce of the United States, 1978).

[26] For more information on ESOPs, see W. Robert Reum and Sherry Milliken Reum, "Employee Stock Ownership Plans: Pluses and Minuses," *Harvard Business Review*, 54, 4 (July–August 1976), 125–132; and Donald E. Sullivan, "ESOPs: Panacea or Placebo?" *California Management Review*, 20, 1 (Fall 1977), 55–61.

[27] For a summary of ERISA and a nontechnical explanation of these terms, see Patten, *Pay: Employee Compensation and Incentive Plans*, pp. 532–540.

[28] See such references as Committee for Economic Development, *Building a National Health-Care System* (New York: CED, 1971); Edward M. Kennedy, *In Critical Condition* (New York: Simon and Schuster, 1972); and Abraham Ribicoff, *The American Medical Machine* (New York: Saturday Review Press, 1972).

[29] For an up-to-date review of trends in training and development, see Craig, ed., *Training and Development Handbook: A Guide to Human Resource Development*, 2nd ed. (New York: McGraw-Hill, 1976).

[30] For a summary, see Thomas H. Patten, Jr., "Materials for the History of Community Development: Social Stratification in Pittsburgh in 1908," *International Review of Community Development*, No. 2 (December 1963), pp. 153–167.

[31] James J. Healey et al., *Creative Collective Bargaining* (Englewood Cliffs, N.J.: Prentice-Hall, Inc. 1965). For a still fresher point of view which applies MBO thinking to labor relations, see Reed C. Richardson, *Collective Bargaining by Objectives* (Englewood Cliffs, N.J.: Prentice-Hall, Inc. 1977).

[32]Thomas H. Patten, Jr., "Collective Bargaining and Consensus: The Potential of a Laboratory Training Input," *Management of Personnel Quarterly, 16,* 1 (Spring 1970), 29–37; Irving Stern and Robert Pearse, "Collective Bargaining: A Union's Program for Reducing Conflict," *Personnel, 45,* 3 (July–August 1968), 61–72.

[33]Some of this experience is reviewed in Edgar Weinberg, "Labor-Management Cooperation: A Report on Recent Initiatives," *Monthly Labor Review, 99,* 4 (April 1976), 13–22; and William L. Batt, Jr., and Edgar Weinberg, "Labor-Management Cooperation Today," *Harvard Business Review, 56,* 1 (January-February 1978), 96–104.

[34]John J. Popular, "U.S. Mediators Try to Build Common Objectives," *World of Work Report, 1,* 7 (September 1976), 1–3. See also, "U.S. Mediators Try a New Role," *Business Week,* No. 2377 (April 25, 1975), p. 108.

[35]Dave Hyatt, *Public Relations: A Handbook for Business, Labor and Community Leaders,* Bulletin 48 (Ithaca: New York State School of Industrial and Labor Relations, Cornell University, 1963).

[36]An excellent discussion of the social audit showing the role of the personnel department in such audits can be found in Clark C. Abt, *The Social Audit for Management* (New York: AMACOM, 1977), esp. pp. 60–110.

[37]See Glenn A. Bassett and Harvard Y. Weatherbee, *Personnel Systems and Data Management* (New York: American Management Association, 1971).

The Personnel Function in Transition

Elmer H. Burack
Edwin L. Miller

This article examines some of the steps that should be taken for updating knowledge and approaches of the personnel function in organizations in response to new and growing demands in the public and private sectors of our economy. A parallel theme and need is one of substantial modification of personnel curricula; changes are needed to prepare students to cope successfully with changing job requirements and new functions within the personnel field or human resource management. This study emerges from the authors' intensive involvement in personnel research, curricula study as a part of a national study group, writings, and professional contacts with clients in business and government.[1]

Various changes in technology, environment, and social attitudes have emerged that dictate substantial modifications in job knowledge and functions for managerial personnel working in functional areas with such descriptions as personnel, industrial relations, and manpower. In turn, shifting organizational needs forecast redevelopment of various educational programs. An important factor here is that the relevance of these understandings applies equally to general management and various specialties. The growing pace of innovation and technological change, combined with increasing institutional size and forms (such

Reprinted by permission from *California Management Review.* Copyright 1976 by The Regents of the University of California.

as multinationals and conglomerates) and competitive and legislative thrusts, has made business and public-sector activity far more complex than in past years. These have affected career paths, deployment of people, and need for management and technical specialties, to name a few. Also, emerging social trends signal considerable changes in work-related expectations, such as work commitment and life style and including multiple careers and employers, manner of dress, and behavior of work entrants.[2]

Compounding the problems of those who deal with personnel is a vast new body of legislation such as equal employment, manpower, and occupational health and safety acts. Furthermore, difficult planning problems have emerged because of heightened turbulence in the environment from the uncertainties of national and international incidents, scientific innovation, and change itself. Underlying these trends and changes are even more fundamental structural shifts in the character and disposition of the labor force.[3]

By the year 2000, 15 to 20 percent of the American population will be employed in the manufacturing sector of the economy, 30 percent will be employed by the government, and the remaining 50 percent will be employed in services of one type or another.[4] Thus, work-force composition indicates further declines in the manufacturing sectors and continuing growth and attraction of people to the governmental and service sectors. Occupational shifts are also likely for current work-force members.

Importantly, the basis for securing performance will also be changing. Even in the manufacturing sector, where automated facilities have grown in importance, their delicate balance, complexity, and need for continuity place a high premium on human capabilities (training, selection, and motivation). The relative growth in the service and governmental sectors suggests growing dependence on interpersonal processes if productivity gains are to be realized, computer uses notwithstanding.

As the transition in the labor force occurs, different skills and expertise will be required of those persons in (or entering) the contemporary firm who are engaged in the management of human resources as compared to job roles in traditional personnel departments. Personnel maintenance functions increasingly must acknowledge the need for new capabilities in planning and personnel programming technology. Consequently, the educational needs of managers and human resource/personnel specialists are already beginning to differ from the product of many university or college personnel management courses or curricula.

BASES FOR STRATEGIC CHANGES IN PERSONNEL PLANNING— MANAGEMENT

Four key characterizations concerning personnel activities warrant the attention of policy makers and officers of both private- and public-sector firms.

1. The definition and thrust of personnel administration as a concept and function is undergoing vast modifications in response to a variety of forces and pressures.
2. Personnel as a function is evolving toward a comprehensive resource system both dependent upon and contributing substantially to the various organizational work

systems and significantly affecting economic performance, institutional welfare, and employee realizations.
3. Personnel is increasingly exhibiting the potential to make contributions to vital organizational decisions, performances, and accomplishments.
4. Of necessity, personnel is moving into higher levels of professional activity; matters confronting it are of a higher order of complexity; its affairs are more sensitive; and personnel's tools, appropriately, have grown more sophisticated.

PERSONNEL'S MISSION: CONCEPT AND THRUST

Personnel has moved beyond the traditional functional boundaries where its activities were largely concerned with maintaining people in organizations. It is not that the functions of maintaining people in organizations such as hiring, processing, and keeping records have become less important (Figure 1). Their successful accomplishment is still critical to the ongoing activities of the institution. Yet, as noted previously, the cumulative impact of vast societal changes, legislation, governmental surveillance, and growing need for acceptable social and economic performance have mandated change. Also, the reality of newer life styles, people expectancies, and advanced economic achievement suggests bilateral decisions on the part of individuals and units—such as to join organizations or maintain affiliations—where either party to the decision may opt to withdraw or simply not initiate the relationship.[5]

Figure 1 suggests that various pressures are pushing organizational interests beyond securing and maintaining people to growing concerns with the post-work welfare and the lot of former employees. Disinterest or superficial programming of various benefits and activities will no longer suffice to meet regulative necessity or socially responsible activity.

The newer profile of personnel administration displays a growing capability and need to plan and mesh with the long-standing planning systems that encompass marketing, financial, and operational concerns. Competitive thrusts and technical innovations portend far more than new packaging, engineering, or merchandising programs. The people component provides an indispensable partner in this game of survival. Personnel specialists must display a high order of analytical ability in providing useful counsel for a wide range of marketing situations or complex sociotechnical problems.[6]

For example, a large steel firm was confronted with a number of competitive thrusts and technical innovations that led to the need to introduce and formulate a new marketing organization, develop a formal research capability, and introduce several new production systems. Profit objectives and achievement of business plans became dependent on the abilities of key personnel officials to develop a blueprint for manpower development and organizational changes to effectuate planning goals.

In addition, part of the shifting focus of personnel relates to its utilization as an instrument of research in probing difficult organizational problems. Problems of productivity, creativity, and administrative ineptness call forth a posture of inquiry and ability in problem definition and resolution.[7] A case in point is a recent matter concerning a private university.

THE TRADITIONAL ROLE   THE EMERGING ROLE

Personnel Administration and Control

- Hire, Fire
- Training and development
- Records
- Government reporting
- Wages, benefits
- Industrial-Labor relations safety

A. People in Society

B. Environmental Monitoring Forecasting

C. Inter-Firm "Exchanges"

D. Post Work

Change Innovation Law

I Personnel Administration and Control

II Institutional Policy and Planning

Personnel Planning System Organization

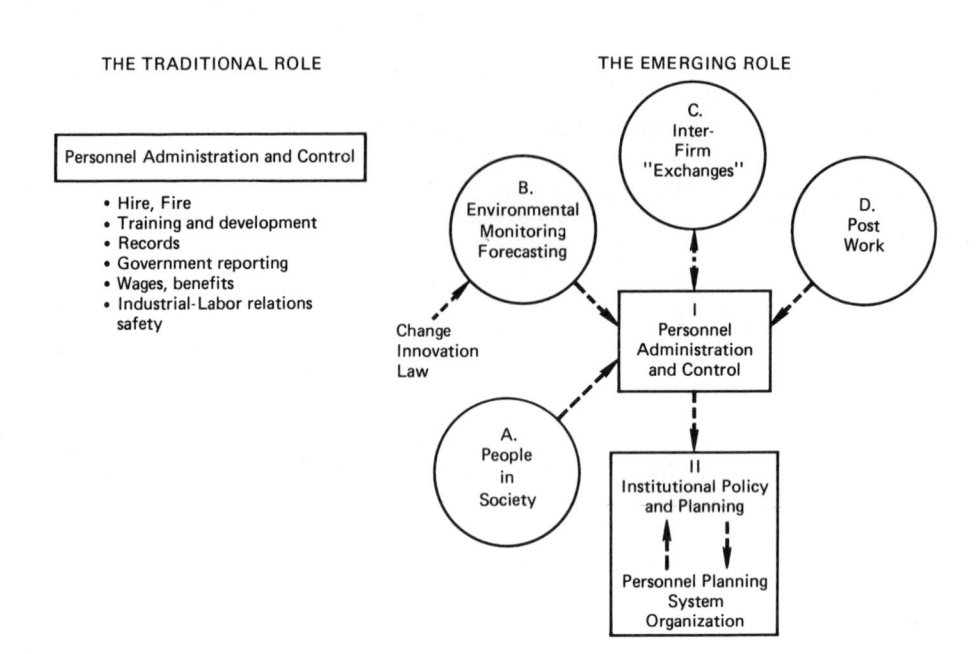

FIGURE 1   *The Personnel Function in Transition*

The personnel department had largely concerned itself with routine matters for many years. The growing fabric of legal compliance regarding minority (race and sex) employment and opportunity was acknowledged by officials. But they had little feel for the current state of affairs regarding personnel deployment, let alone how people fared within the system. Several legal suits and adverse publicity in several newspapers demonstrated the vulnerability of institutional practices. Comparatively nominal researching of salary and career development of academic and nonacademic personnel could have easily headed off this situation.

PERSONNEL AS A COMPREHENSIVE RESOURCE SYSTEM

The age of specialization has witnessed the formulation and undertaking of a vast array of activities for securing organizational goals and maintaining people in the organization, but the vital interdependency of these undertakings is often overlooked. Thus, compensation, benefits, and programs of employee appraisal may evolve and be highly developed. So, too, many programs of management by objectives and job enrichment have been launched without regard for the critical interdependencies between these.

A large manufacturer of electronic systems and components maintained a big human relations department with specialists in numerous personnel-related areas. Compensation programming was highly advanced in procedures and specifications, but salaries and promotions were made independently of an employee performance-assessment program, which never got off the ground.

Senior managers had resisted assessment efforts and the program was never fully activated.

Effective personnel work requires a comprehensive programming effort but also necessitates a commensurate display of maturity and understanding to identify needs and integrate these into an organization's planning and administrative systems and successfully launch undertakings.[8]

Comprehensive programming also necessitates an initial awareness of needs. A monitoring and interpretative capability provides the initially vital input of information for exerting a personnel systems effort.

A medium-sized manufacturer and distributor of consumer products possessed a decentralized, multistate operation for the manufacture of its products. Failure to anticipate the impact of new minimum wage legislation on its cost structure, job rates, and employee motivation led to considerable disruption of its internal operations and poor economic performance before balance could be restored.

Another instance of the critical nature of information inputs and their interpretation concerns a large engineering firm. Here, the need was to "read" important changes in life style; this had an adverse effect on younger engineers' decisions to join and resulted in poorer performance in recruiting efforts. It was incumbent upon personnel in this situation to develop the relevant information and evidence the professional capability to propose modifications in institutional policy and propose programs and strategies to attract younger people to the organization for continuing renewal of its design concept.

Another dimension of personnel's comprehensive effort pertains to the understanding of organizational administration and the behavioral implications of its procedures and actions. Internal programs must be formulated that are responsive to these needs and realities.

A large hospital with many medical and supporting departments continued to place primary responsibility for training on its functional heads. Although these professionals were well qualified in technical skills, many were poor teachers and still fewer had an understanding of the management or administrative side of their operation and how these tied to other functions and systems of the hospital. Not surprisingly, continuing growth brought disproportionate increases in costs, and internal tensions mounted as duplication or lack of execution continued to plague operations.

PERSONNEL, PERFORMANCE, AND ORGANIZATIONAL DECISION MAKING

Human resource–related needs continue to grow more varied and complex as performance must be improved, competing objectives must be resolved, deficiencies clarified, and talent identified and developed to meet these needs. It takes a little effort to establish the point that compelling payoffs exist where the batting average can be improved in the selection of managerial and supervisory candidates. In one situation with which we are familiar, systematic approaches in employee assessment led to a gain from one of three successful candidates to one of two. Absenteeism, tardiness, drug problems, and turnover require innovative job designs and work-performance–related research that truly reflects system and behavioral insights.

Consistency in performance and equitable treatment indicate the formulation of reward systems where individual and group efforts are tied more closely to performance, compensation, and nonmonetary returns. Individual needs vary greatly such that the development of a more flexible structure of reward and benefits can bolster the recruiting and retention of people. Better approaches in these areas can serve to examine the returns of various undertakings and the possible economics or higher returns through the rebalancing of expenditure programs.

The performance of an organization's decision system, technology aside, is vitally dependent on its human resource members. Facilitating identification of job need and information of a manpower data base can prove responsive to the demands of the decision system. Also, these approaches can serve to meet business needs that impose special talent requirements as in venture analysis, multinational operations, and managerial talent for diversification.

PERSONNEL'S GROWING PROFESSIONALIZATION

The growing complexity of personnel functions increasingly signals higher levels of professionalization and sophistication. Growing professionalization indicates expanded needs in terms of perspective, attitude, and tool knowledge. The inclination to utilize and capitalize on various mathematical and statistical approaches, plus the computer, requires a working knowledge of the assumptions, usefulness, and limitations of these approaches. Their use grows more indispensable in career planning, job design, forecasting, planning designs, and productivity approaches. Also, further signs of professionalization are found in the growing criticality of knowledge related to such things as system concepts, newer tools and models for assessment, bases for job evaluation, and incorporation of behavioral models in performance programs.[9]

The leading edge of personnel's newer activities indicates an important extension and perhaps a redefinition of activity. Experience continues to play a central role in professionalization, but it must be acknowledged that formal education and special training in supportive disciplines are becoming more than a desirable additive. The addition of new responsibilities congenial with the model presented previously and a more appropriate organizational positioning suggesting greater authority and scope of responsibility are concomitant, and indispensable to the realization of personnel's potential.

The Manpower Division of the National Academy of Management formulated a curriculum study group in 1974 to study personnel-related curricula for undergraduate and graduate programs. New text materials, courses, and greatly modified programs are some of the key ingredients in the report presented to the academicians making up this division.

To meet the changing needs and circumstances of organization, substantive changes in the orientation of personnel specialists, let alone curriculum, faculty preparation, and pedagogical techniques, will be demanded. For example, the descriptive and recipe approaches to personnel or human resource management should be replaced by a more comprehensive approach, which incorporates policy, environment, and people and particularizes these to specific organizational or situational conditions.

The new curriculum should be designed to emphasize the significance of an organization's human resources and the need to develop and utilize these valuable resources more effectively. The perspective of the curriculum should be upon organizational and manpower planning rather than upon a limited emphasis stressing technique. Although there will continue to be a need to familiarize students with the descriptive and recipe approach to personnel or human resource management, the main thrust of the educational program should be more comprehensive in nature. Programs in personnel/human resource management as well as overview courses should increasingly deal with the breadth of processes, structure, and capabilities.

Updating of current department members, acquisition of new personnel specialties, and academic preparation for students interested in the personnel/human resources area will reflect personal development or course work that focuses on four major areas. Figure 2 shows these areas and their interrelationships; they are *the environment, the individual and society, the organization,* and *the public sector.*

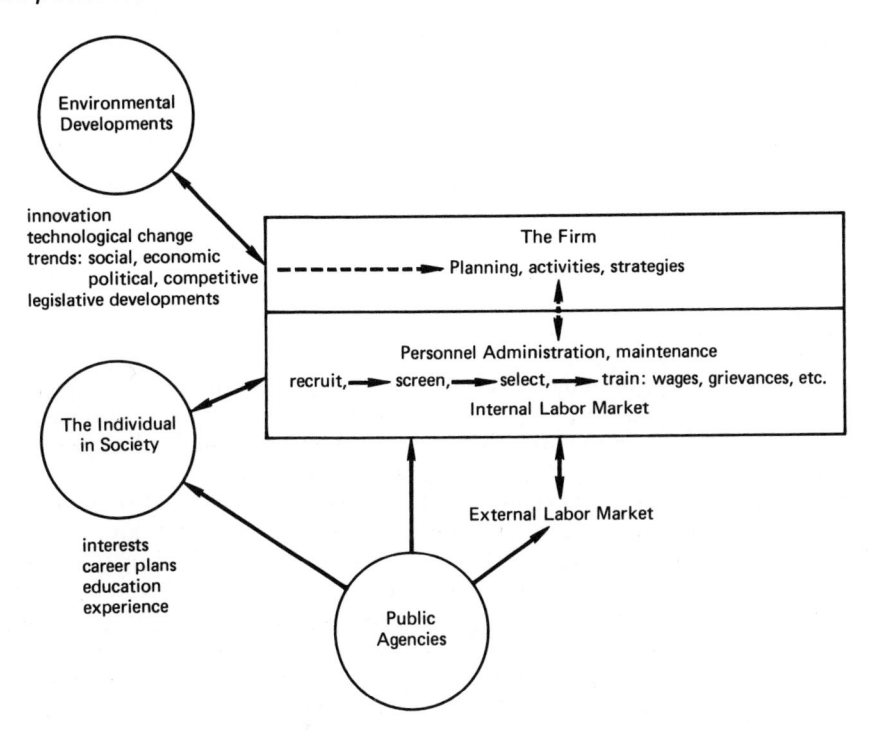

FIGURE 2 *A Personnel/Human Resource Perspective*

Based on Elmer H. Burack, "Perspective on Personnel Manpower Planning," Illinois Institute of Technology, working paper (1974).

Environment

Environmental monitoring, technological forecasting, and interpretation of these events will be critical inputs to the human resource/personnel system. The translation of environmental developments in technical, economic, and social areas will provide key information and data for manpower forecasts and maintenance of an organization's human resources. The monitoring capability need not reside within personnel's functional responsibilities but the information is crucial to human resource designs for the future.

Individual and Society

The personnel–manpower processes within the organization will of necessity integrate more closely with business planning and strategy processes. Shortages of managerial talent in the prime age level of thirty-five to forty-four, and an increased willingness on the part of many managers and professionals to change employers, if necessary, to facilitate their career development is a factor organizations are being forced to contend with. Furthermore, the attitudes of new employees as well as established employees are pressuring management to examine and in many cases to accept obligations to implement meaningful career planning programs, create physically and psychologically healthy work climates, and consider their individual needs, goals, and desires when personnel decisions are made.

Organization

Personnel/human resource specialists will increasingly have to take into account the individual himself as a decision unit, as the decisions *to join, to stay,* and *to produce* continue to grow in significance for productivity and desired economic and social performance.

Public Sector

Educational programming will need to deal explicitly with the public agencies and actions affecting the external labor market (labor supply, wages, and distribution of various professions and job specialists), as well as those impinging on the organization and its internal maintenance activities involving recruiting and training, for example. Legislative action, the role of agencies in training and employment preparation, external-internal labor market relationships, and the public sector's role and responsibility in manpower forecasts and analysis are of growing significance for personnel officials and are needed in curriculum design.

In more formal educational programs, the focus will be that of producing graduates who are prepared first with a general management orientation and second with competencies in personnel or human resource specialties. That is, the graduate will be a broad-based individual who understands the dynamics of management and the calculus of organization. The skills and competencies of the personnel or human resource management specialist will complement the graduate's general management perspective.

IMPLICATIONS FOR PERSONNEL/HUMAN RESOURCE SPECIALISTS

We can expect to see several distinct modifications in the personnel/human resource area, and these changes will have significant influence upon the work and the environment in which the personnel/human resource specialist will operate. It is our expectation that the personnel official will move into those types of activities much more closely aligned with contributing to the destiny of the organization. Specifically, we propose the following implications for the personnel/human resource area:

1. Within organizations there will be structural modifications and potential creation of new jobs built around manpower planning, manpower forecasting, career planning, and manpower information systems. Although specific approaches to manpower planning are varied, there is an awareness of the need for planning to enable an "organization to attain its goals and objectives more surely, faster, better, and perhaps cheaper."[10] As a result the personnel/human resource people will have an opportunity to assume a more important role in the management and administration of the organization. No longer will a personnel activity be able to justify itself only on the basis of the number of interviews conducted during the year or the acquisition of watermelons and name tags required for the company's annual picnic. Rather, the personnel/human resource area will be oriented toward planning and policy making in the areas of overall manpower planning, utilization of personnel, development, employment, and compensation. The overriding emphasis of the personnel/human resource area will be less on programs and gadgetry and more on what will actually be required to help the organization meet its goals.

2. As a corollary to the impending structural modifications for the personnel/human resource functional area, there will be an emphasis upon in-house programs focusing on updating personnel's technology for forecasting an organization's human resource needs as well as assessing and evaluating the qualifications of the organization's present work force. Specifically, the personnel/human resource specialist will be expected to become more sensitive to what operating managers find to work best rather than what is easiest or most comfortable for the personnel function. Thus, there will be increased emphasis placed upon developing employees in ways that are meaningful and challenging to the individual and provide for the future of the organization. The theme must be one in which personnel/human resource officials are concerned with making an organization more effective rather than maintaining an organizational climate or environment that can be objectively justified only on the basis of being familiar and comfortable.

3. Personnel's program for maintenance functions must be reexamined, and a more comprehensive scheme must be designed to translate the corporate or institutional plans and objectives into future quantitative and qualitative manpower requirements together with plans to fulfill those requirements over both the short and long terms. Those personnel activities concerned with recruiting, employment, compensation, and training must be integrated into the organiza-

tion's overall planning process. Instead of a melange of diverse activities or specialties, the personnel department's responsibilities will be regarded as an integral, integrated general management activity responsible for the effective utilization of the organization's human resources, sensitive to the requirements of the organization and committed to making the organization more effective. Specifically, the personnel/human resource function will be directly responsible for coordinating the planning, employment, utilization, and compensation functions so as to maintain an equilibrium between the organization and the external environment.

4. The personnel/human resource specialist will be called upon to assist top management in initiating different organizational approaches to the effective utilization of human resources and the capabilities of the personnel/human resource function. Chief executives of a growing number of organizations are becoming increasingly aware of the significance of their organization's human resources; they are reviewing the efficient use of the organization's existing manpower at its present level of development, assessing the level of performance of their employees, and concerning themselves with the enhancement of the individual's skills and talents, and thus contributing to the productivity and overall contribution of the work force.

As a result of this interest expressed by chief executives, it becomes increasingly apparent that personnel/human resource specialists have an excellent opportunity to contribute to the growth and success of their organization in still other ways. The personnel specialist must be able to help to identify and ease potential pressure points and adverse trends related to an organization's human resources. For example, the personnel specialist should be able to provide management with the type of counsel and assistance that can help to meet the intense pressure generated by equal employment legislation and affirmative action programs. No longer can equal employment be indiscriminately lumped in with the sundry group of activities included under the rubric of corporate social responsibility. With expanded responsibility in this area it is imperative that personnel people be qualified to provide the advice desperately needed by organizations.

The personnel/human resource function must also be able to spot adverse trends in turnover and absenteeism. Yet responsibility will not end with problem identification. The goal must be to determine the causes of these problems and what's actually needed to help the organization solve its manpower problems. As we see it, the personnel department will become much more creative or proactive in those areas of its responsibilities and the personnel specialist must become involved in providing managers with advice that is workable and useful.

It is our conviction that the role of personnel is changing rapidly and that the responsibilities of the personnel activity are being redefined. The personnel specialist must become increasingly oriented toward growth and efficiency of the organization instead of merely administering traditional personnel activities. This will mean greater emphasis upon planning the structure of the future organization and its personnel requirements, identifying and selecting personnel to meet these expected needs, developing and utilizing the organization's human resources, and assessing and rewarding performance. These activities will be undertaken with the purpose of ensuring growth of both the individual employee and the organization.

To handle these responsibilities, many personnel specialists will be required to engage in professional development, self-renewal types of activities. If personnel departments and specialists fail to meet these challenges, there is the distinct possibility that the personnel function will be relegated to an employee services activity limited to serving the needs of lower-level employees and maintaining those traditional personnel activities. It is our hope that personnel will begin turning its energies toward making the organization more effective now and into the future.

Notes

[1] Professor Miller has chaired a national study committee on behalf of the Manpower Division, Academy of Management, of which Professor Burack was a member. In addition, both authors have established continuing contacts with personnel/manpower officials and specialists. Burack has directed several research projects on the personnel function and is president of the Industrial Relations Association of Chicago.

[2] Adam Smith, "The Last Days of Cowboy Capitalism," *The Atlantic Monthly*, September 1972, pp. 43-55.

[3] D. Zand, "Managing the Knowledge Orientation," in *Preparing Tomorrow's Business Leaders Today*, P. Drucker, ed. (Englewood Cliffs, N.J.: Prentice-Hall, Inc., 1969).

[4] D. Bell, *Toward the Year 2000: Work in Progress* (Boston: Beacon Press, 1967).

[5] An excellent example is in the "Last Days of Cowboy Capitalism," cited in footnote 2.

[6] F. H. Cassell, "Manpower Planning: State of the Art at the Micro Level," *MSU Business Topics, 21*, 4 (Autumn 1973), 13-21.

[7] M. D. Dunnette and B. Bass, "Behavioral Scientists and Personnel Management," *Industrial Relations, 2*, 3 (May 1963), 115-130.

[8] F. E. Fischer, "The Personnel Function in Tomorrow's Company," *Personnel, 45* (1968), 64-71.

[9] *Ibid.*

[10] E. Burack, *Strategies for Manpower Planning and Programming* (Morristown, N.J.: General Learning Corporation, 1972).

PROFESSIONALISM AND PERSONNEL

Professionalism and Accreditation in the Field of Personnel and Industrial Relations

Drew M. Young, AEP

Currently, we are witnessing a rapidly growing interest in professionalism and accreditation in the total field that is known by such names as personnel and industrial relations (PAIR), employee relations, or human resources management. This is not an unexpected development when one realizes that with the growing recognition of the importance of the human element in the world of work, there is also the increasing necessity for improving and assuring the professionalism and competency of its practitioners.

The interest in and concerns about professionalism and accreditation in the PAIR field are far from new. For many years, personnel practitioners have asked themselves, Is our occupation a profession? In 1967 the American Society for Personnel Administration (ASPA) joined with Cornell University to examine the degree of professionalism in the PAIR field. Specifically, the investigation was intended to obtain answers to such questions as

1. How professional are individual personnel managers?
2. What are the various dimensions of the "professional model" in PAIR?
3. Where are we?
4. Where do we go from here?

The findings of the study appeared in ASPA publications and set forth in greater detail in Ritzer and Trice's book, *An Occupation in Conflict: A Study of the Personnel Manager*.[1]

CHARACTERISTICS OF A PROFESSIONAL OCCUPATION

Basically, there are five characteristics which differentiate a professional occupation from a nonprofessional one. First, does the occupation demand the

Prepared especially for this book and printed with permission of the author.

full-time attention of its practitioners? Second, has it been able to set up a series of training schools aimed at educating people in the basic ideas of the occupation—the common body of knowledge? Third, can it point to the existence of a national professional association? Fourth, has the occupation provided for standards of certification or accreditation of practitioners in the field? And finally, has it been able to establish a regulative code of ethics?

RESULTS OF THE STUDY

The results of the ASPA-Cornell study indicate that PAIR had met the first criterion of a professional occupation—it was a full-time employment. This goal was achieved by PAIR in the early 1900s. The second criterion of a profession was partially met. There were a number of colleges and universities with majors in PAIR. However, despite the existence of training in the specialty, there was still a question as to exactly what body of knowledge or theory was the domain of PAIR. There seemed to be no distinct or well-defined body of theory at that time which belonged exclusively to personnel and industrial relations.

The third criterion, evidence of a national professional association, was also fulfilled to some degree. PAIR did have a national personnel association as well as regional personnel groups. One of the characteristics of a professional occupation is the existence of *a single* authoritative professional body. Although the American Society for Personnel Administration (ASPA) was the largest national association of personnel and industrial relations executives, it did not completely fulfill the bill at that time.

PAIR also failed to meet the fourth criterion, standards of certification or accreditation. Although it did have codes of ethics developed by professional associations, these codes of ethics seemed to have little impact on the behavior of personnel administrators, nor were they in any sense regulative.

Thus PAIR had some of the characteristics of professionalism, yet was either wholly or partially lacking a number of the other dimensions. ASPA responded to these deficiencies by establishing an accreditation institute, and the institute set out to eliminate the voids of the PAIR professional model at the occupational level. Specifically, the first order of business for ASPA's Accreditation Institute (AAI) was to

1. Define and delineate a common body of knowledge
2. Provide for the accreditation of practitioners in the field

After considerable discussion among practitioners, consultants, and educators, the following functional areas were agreed upon as being within the field of personnel and industrial relations:

employment, placement, and personnel planning	personnel research
training and development	management practices
compensation and benefits	
health, safety, and security	
employee and labor relations	

Once the functional areas had been agreed upon, a series of tests were developed to measure qualifications of candidates for certification. These tests were designed to measure the candidates' level of technical competence in each of the seven functional areas.

THE ACCREDITATION REQUIREMENTS

The AAI accreditation program was launched when the definition and delineation of the common body of knowledge had been accomplished. Also a process was developed whereby practitioners in the field could obtain accreditation.

The requirements for becoming accredited are determined by the applicant's educational background and experience. For *specialists* (practitioners, educators, and consultants), accreditation requires experience and demonstration of knowledge through successful completion of an examination in one of the six PAIR functional areas plus current practice in the area. For *generalists,* accreditation requires experience and demonstration of knowledge through successful completion of an examination in multiple PAIR functional areas and in management practices plus current practice in personnel and industrial relations.

The accreditation program provides for four categories of accreditation, two for specialists and two for generalists:

Specialist	*Generalist*
Accredited Personnel Specialist (APS)	Accredited Personnel Manager (APM)
Accredited Personnel Diplomate (APD)	Accredited Executive in Personnel (AEP)

WHY ACCREDITATION?

In attempting to justify the need for accreditation, we should first note that an accreditation program is basically a vehicle for raising and maintaining professional standards in the field of personnel and industrial relations. Through the involvement of highly experienced professionals, it seeks to identify people who have superior knowledge and meaningful experience in the various functions and levels of personnel and industrial relations. By qualifying for accreditation, the candidate can measure and maintain his or her knowledge and expertise in the field.

In a general sense, the accreditation program is designed to help improve performance in and foster increased acceptance of the personnel and industrial relations field as a profession. More specifically, the total program of accreditation offers various benefits to several different groups. For *colleges and universities,* the development of the body of knowledge required for successful practice in the various areas of PAIR will provide invaluable assistance in curriculum design. The breakdown of the field into its specialties will provide guidance for *students* so that they may better understand the various career alternatives available and be able to select applicable courses.

Young practitioners will have sound guidelines and information to assist them in their career development, in improving their level of competency, and in establishing their long-range career goals. For *senior practitioners*, it provides the opportunity to continue their education and development. By participating they will be able to maintain and improve competence in their chosen area, obtain recognition, and present documentation of their accomplishments. Employers may look upon accreditation as an important factor in identifying qualified practitioners within and outside of their organizations.

During 1977, the ASPA Accreditation Institute (AAI) commissioned Professor Edwin L. Miller of the University of Michigan to do a research study of "Professionalism and Its Impact on Accreditation Type Programs." He studied the credentialing programs of ten different professional institutes and associations, and his findings were most informative. In one section of his report to the AAI Board of Directors, Miller described the value of the credentialing process to the candidate seeking accreditation.

From the professional association's perspective, credentialing is one means that a field can use to differentiate itself from competing fields. This becomes a useful strategy in this day of overlapping fields and the ensuing competition for members. The process of determining the boundaries of a field and reaching agreement on the functional areas to be included within the domain provide growth experiences for the profession. Once the field has staked out its content areas, the development of comprehensive definitions of competence and the construction of valid measures for predicting proficiency within the areas of specialization are excellent exercises in and of themselves. Credentialing benefits the associations and societies that sponsor such activities because it highlights an educational and research focus within such organizations. Finally, certification programs should provide the means for upgrading the overall quality of practice within the field.

Regardless of the market value of certification to the individual, the candidates preparation for certification is perhaps the greatest benefit to be derived. Professionally, the individual should grow because he or she will be required to master and demonstrate proficiency in certain selected areas. This knowledge should have an impact on the person's job performance as well. To many individuals, certification has also had a payoff in terms of salary increases and promotions. Finally, the public and personal recognition for reaching a stated level of professional accomplishment can prove psychologically rewarding. A less tangible but perhaps more meaningful result of the credentialing process is the enhancement of the individual's feeling of self-worth.

As an overall assessment of the credentialing process, Ralph St. John has said it best:

> It is in the preparation for certification that its greatest benefit is realized. This emphasis on self-improvement and education is satisfying to the individual, valuable to his employer, and ultimately to the quality of product and services to everyone.[2]

While many practitioners in the PAIR field have degrees, relatively few have specialized in personnel or industrial relations studies. Therefore, earning an accreditation certificate will be a significant accomplishment. It will indicate that the accredited professional has mastered a validated, recognized, and agreed-upon common body of knowledge.

As the PAIR accreditation program continues to evolve, it is essential that it be aware of new developments both within the organization and its social environment and that it maintain the relevance and integrity of its accreditation process. This is an important responsibility, one that will require drawing on the combined resources available through practitioners, educators, and consultants. There must be increased liaison and cooperative efforts with representatives from colleges and universities, other associations in the PAIR field that specialize in discrete functional areas, the Academy of Management, and other related organizations—plus corporations and government.

The ASPA Accreditation Program represents a bold and significant breakthrough for the personnel and industrial relations field. It represents the work of many professionals who have dedicated their talents, knowledge, and efforts to establish professional standards in this important field. It has provided practitioners, educators, and consultants with the opportunity to raise their sights and achieve at a higher level of competency.

Notes

[1] G. Ritzer and H.M. Trice, *An Occupation in Conflict: A Study of the Personnel Manager* (Ithaca, N.Y.: New York State School of Industrial and Labor Relations at Cornell University, 1969).

[2] Ralph St. John, *A Study of Voluntary Certification Programs in Emerging Professions* (unpublished Master's thesis, Arizona State University, 1976) pp. 50–51.

Organizational Research and Organizational Change: GM's Approach

Howard C. Carlson

Practical problem-solving and action strategies probably have never been more welcome in industry than they are today. Increasingly serious problems pose complex requirements, a seemingly endless array of new demands, and the need to deal rapidly and effectively with change in almost every industrial organization. In this action-oriented context, traditional modes of personnel research inevitably seem to fall short of producing the fundamental changes necessary for enhancing

Reprinted, by permission of the publisher, from PERSONNEL, July–August 1977, © 1977 by AMACOM, a division of American Management Association. All rights reserved.

the profitability, growth, or survival of an organization or for enhancing the quality of work life of its members.

Thus many behavioral scientists in industry have attempted to reorient their research to important issues in the context of change. Dr. Michael Beer, for example, found it useful to distinguish research action (traditional) from action research (change-oriented) in his work at Corning Glass. The model to be described here—which evolved out of an experimental change program initiated in 1969 at four General Motors plant sites—attempts to provide an organizing framework for doing research in the context of change.

BACKGROUND AND PURPOSES OF THE MODEL

From the outset, research was closely tied into the experimental change program at General Motors. For example, a careful research design guided the selection of the four plant sites that participated in the first effort. This design called for plants that had similar geographical location, labor-market and workforce composition, products, and production technology but markedly different operating performance.

Two assembly plants in Atlanta and two foundry plants in Saginaw, Michigan, met these requirements. Each city provided what later became casually identified as a "good" plant and a "poor" plant in terms of operating performance, making possible the program's research objective of learning what elements of leader behavior, organizational climate, and structure accounted for the difference.

Unfortunately, however, the research design also had an unanticipated impact on the program: It actually got in the way of using the research findings effectively in bringing about change. Upon being informed of the design, one of the "good" plants found it difficult to see why it should change at all. A "poor" plant, on the other hand, found it easy to reject the very basis for its inclusion and participation in the change program. These difficulties were never completely overcome.

Other growing pains also became apparent in early attempts to couple research and the change process at General Motors. But perhaps the program's most serious mistake was neglecting to consider research as an *intervention* in itself. Since then, however, recognition of this mistake has helped to recast the traditional employee research perspective at General Motors. For example, the company no longer uses any systematic procedure for gathering research information without giving considerable thought to its impact on either the present functioning or potential modifiability of the organizational unit involved. Beyond this, research at General Motors has been given a more direct action orientation to the business of change.

Nevertheless, persisting stereotypes about research can easily operate to cloud such an orientation. They can make it difficult to find full acceptance among managers, OD consultants, trainers, and even researchers of the potential value of research as an intervention. Most of these stereotypes are already familiar: Research is academic, impractical, never-ending, not tied to profits, a quest for knowledge, an elegant design, an anal-compulsive interest in precise measurement, or the technical ability perhaps to record change but certainly not to help bring it about. It might even be expected, so the stereotype goes, that some researchers have never really accepted World War II because there was no control group!

The research model that grew out of the GM experimental change program was designed to help eliminate some of these stereotypes. It attempted:

> To begin to pull together the concepts and strategies of research as an intervention, providing an organizing framework for a total research program likely to reduce internal barriers to change
>
> To assist in "reaching" managers and OD specialists with a way of looking at and thinking about research as a dynamic, action-oriented process
>
> More generally, to provide a guide for people who want to use research, watch research, or evaluate research in the context of change

In each of these ways, the GM research model has proved useful. Its main drawback as a framework for research is that it is abstract; the model is concerned only with broad kinds of research strategies and their assumed relationship to change. It is free of specific "how-to" content. A research manager or specialist must specify the projects and project mechanisms required in any real application of the model to change in an organization.

MODEL DESIGN

In general appearance, the GM research model has led some people to call it a "Paper Airplane (Delta Wing, no less) Model of research strategies that will hopefully fly." However, some of its lines have been neatly drawn for effect and should not be interpreted too literally (see Figure 1). The real importance of the design is its attempt to portray research as a multifaceted process or framework of different strategies—and not as just one stereotypic approach.

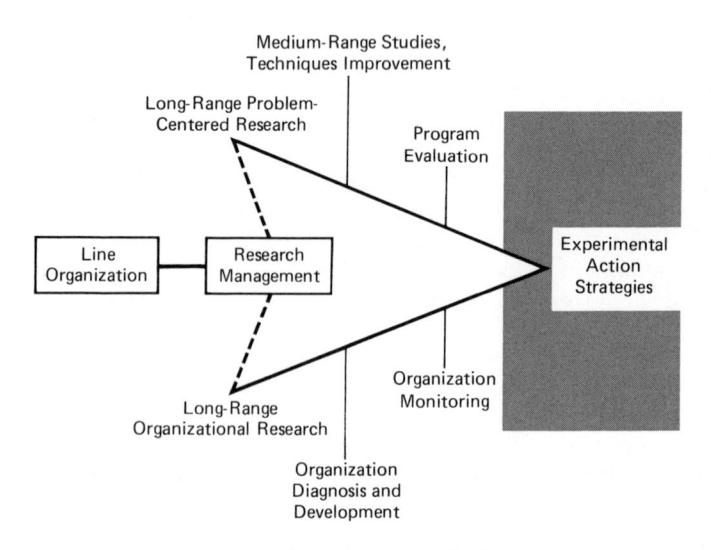

FIGURE 1 *Breaking the Internal Change Barrier*

At the top of the model is a problem-techniques-program dimension to the framework of research strategies. At the base is an organizational dimension. Along either dimension, strategies to the right are regarded as short range and operating closer to the cutting edge of change. Strategies to the left are regarded as long range in nature (typically six months or longer in the auto industry).

Although each strategy and its relationship to change will be described separately, the total framework must be considered in thinking about research as an intervention. Consequently, a continuous single example or case experience will be presented to illustrate each strategy that is embodied in the model. Briefly, the case involves one of GM's car divisions that had experienced a consistently increasing rate of employee absenteeism and turnover over a period of five years. In late 1969, this division decided to take some research action even though its current absolute levels of absenteeism and turnover were neither the worst nor the best being demonstrated at that time in General Motors.

Involvement of the Line Organization

An important feature of this research model is the involvement of key representatives of the line organization from the beginning and throughout all stages of the research process. This involvement should not be merely token in nature but rather should provide line representatives the chance to *influence* project design and implementation, analysis or interpretation of results, and development of recommended action steps. It also should enable line people to *get up front* in the process when it comes to related internal presentations and communication steps, implementation planning and action, and follow-up assurance of effective action.

Put simply, the basic assumption underlying this model is that only people, and not research per se, can bring about any needed changes in an organization. This is evident whenever reports of research findings and recommendations simply gather dust in someone's desk drawer. Researchers in the context of change can thus ill afford to sit in their offices or next to their computers designing and carrying out projects without real involvement of the line organization.

At the GM car division that will serve as an example, an absenteeism and turnover task force was formed at the start. It comprised representatives of line management, production, industrial engineering, and personnel from within the division along with representatives of GM's supporting staffs from employee research, education and training, and manufacturing development. An industrial engineer from the manufacturing development staff chaired meetings of this task force while also performing a liaison and integrative role between meetings. The task force designed a multifaceted research program, deciding to focus the total effort solely upon the engine and assembly plants to permit later comparisons of any progress with the experience of other plant operations in the car division.

Long-Range Problem-Centered Research

When a specific and narrowly defined problem or felt need is apparent to the line organization and when it also seems likely that any real solution will be complex or long range in nature, long-range problem-centered research may be applied. Some specific problems to which this kind of research can be addressed include excessive grievances, low or declining productivity, poor quality, rising absenteeism, and declining employee morale.

In adopting this research strategy, whether the problem appears symptomatic or seems more fundamental in nature is of little immediate consequence. The idea is to begin research where the organization is or where it is "hurting" and to be aware of this in some way. As an intervention, research should clearly *not* begin with a problem defined primarily by the researcher, with a new concept in the theoretical literature, or with an armamentarium of techniques seeking to fit and thus define their own problem.

At GM, preliminary analysis by the car division's task force suggested that the great bulk of turnover occurred during the first four weeks of employment. It also suggested that early job experiences might predispose employees who were retained longer to exhibit either high or low rates of absenteeism. The problem for research, then, was to identify critical factors in the early job experiences of new hires that contributed to turnover and led to different levels of absenteeism among employees who were retained.

An in-depth tracking study of 200 randomly selected new hires was conducted over a six-month period. Results showed, for example, that persons oriented in their new jobs as individuals (rather than as members of a group) and assigned to an above-average operator for training (rather than to one rated by the foreman as average in performance) were less likely to be absent. In addition, the results showed that foremen could predict very accurately—on the first day of a new hire's employment—whether a person would or would not be frequently absent in the future. Perhaps as a kind of self-fulfilling prophecy, foremen behaved differently (in their orientation and training assignments, for example) toward persons identified as a future problem. These and other results of the long-range research endeavor led to a number of specific changes in how new hires were treated early in their work experience with the car division.

Medium-Range Studies:
Techniques Improvement

Research interventions can also begin where the line organization is impeding techniques already operating, believed to be operating, or existing largely on paper and in the minds of their authors for solving people problems. Techniques of human resource planning, recruitment, selection, orientation, training, career planning and counseling, management development, communication, and motivation are but a few of these. In other words, research can be aimed not only at changes in personnel management techniques but also at identifying factors that constrain a given technique from achieving its intended result, confronting the organization with data on such constraints to bring about needed change, and integrating the technique into other organizational processes more effectively.

For example, research in the GM car division had sought improvement in the orientation and training foremen were expected to give new employees. The results pointed to many constraints upon the foreman, including one introduced by his own reward system. Any time spent by a new employee in orientation would weigh against the efficiency of a foreman's area. Upon recognizing the constraint, management was easily moved to apply no charge against an area for the first day a new hire was on the job. Foremen were thus given greater latitude to orient an employee without jeopardizing their efficiency. Additionally, special training aids were provided the foremen to ensure more consistent attention to the adjustment of all new employees to their jobs.

Program Evaluation

Any new program or technique introduced into the line organization should be systematically evaluated. Unfortunately, this step is often regarded as "something we really should do as professionals" and also as a kind of academic concern or check on "something we already know intuitively or from our experience." Since neither of these points of view is very compelling, evaluation is usually neglected as an intervention in itself.

The basic intent of this strategy, however, is to provide the initiators or authors of a new program with some kind of objective feedback mechanism that will lead to real change and needed revision in the program. Furthermore, whether or not a program is evaluated is likely to have an important impact on the climate for change in an organization. The model shown in Figure 2, for example, points out some expected consequences of evaluating versus not evaluating training programs.

As this model shows, two things can obviously happen to training: Management can either increase funds or reduce funds during the life of a given program. These two possibilities, in turn, are related to a "liberal" loop and a "conservative" loop of management attitudes toward the use of expenditures of time or money for training. Under the same general conditions and economic climate, one or the other loop will be dominant in the thinking of managers making decisions about training.

The model shows that whenever evaluation is *not* carried out, the conservative loop is strengthened 100 percent of the time. And when evaluation is carried out but unreliable data (data not permitting us to know whether or not the training worked as intended) are used, the effect is still one of feeding into the conservative loop. On the other hand, using reasonably dependable data in carrying out an evaluation will always contribute to increasingly progressive management attitudes. When success is indicated, of course, this will happen almost by definition. But even when a failure becomes evident, alternative proposals for a revision in the training program can be expected to feed into the progressive loop. The major point of the model, then, is that evaluation affords at least some possibility of a progressive change in management climate, while the lack of evaluation will always contribute to increasingly conservative attitudes among managers.

In the car division's absenteeism and turnover research program, for example, an evaluation plan developed by the task force produced at the start some knowledge of results and later an expanding interest in going beyond the program as it was originally designed. An industrial engineer within the division was assigned full time to logging and tracking absenteeism, turnover, and many other indicators that might potentially affect the indices of concern. By 1971, the results showed a demonstrable decline in absenteeism in the engine and assembly plants (8 to 9 percent drop in absenteeism without prior notice), while absenteeism

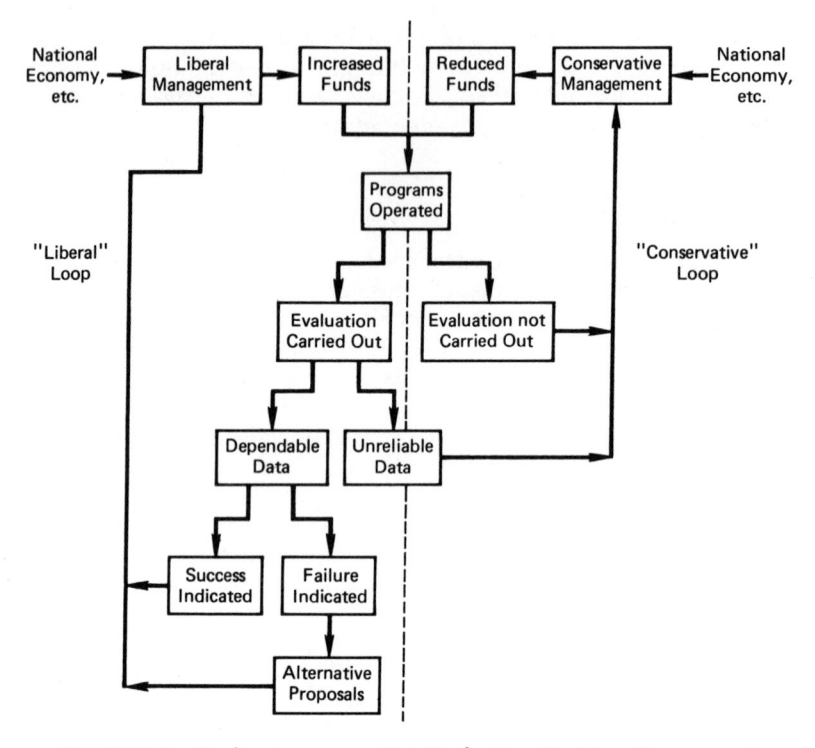

FIGURE 2   *Evaluating versus Not Evaluating Training Programs: A Model of Some Expected Effects*

continued to rise throughout the rest of the division (25 percent increase in absenteeism without prior notice) and also in another plant in the same city.

Experimental Action Strategies

This strategy emphasizes initiatives or response to the line organization—helping the organization *now* rather than proposing a lengthy study or very elaborate research design. In effect, it involves "shooting from the hip" with whatever immediate action appears to have some potential on the basis of past research, experience, sheer intuition, or an accidental opportunity available in the present situation. Ideally, a member of the line organization itself will suggest trying something and perhaps put into operation a practical application of some principle of the behavioral sciences—one that might have entered the picture along with the researcher.

Any such experimental actions should probably be introduced in a limited and reasonably controlled way and not applied across the board in an organization. Efforts should then be directed toward measuring how well the strategy works and, if it does, toward diffusing it into other parts of the organization. Thus the emphasis in taking the action initially should not be entirely on getting results but also on getting experience and educating members of the line organization who can assist effectively in diffusion later.

For example, while not part of the original GM car division program design, four experimental employee task forces were established in the engine plant to put some group involvement and dynamics immediately to work on the problem of absenteeism. Each task force included a foreman and six to eight hourly employees, including a union committeeman. After two days of preparatory training for the foreman, a series of five meetings—each lasting two hours or longer and held about a week apart—was structured for each task force.

At the first meeting, the approach was introduced and task forces formed. Although an effort was made to control the mix of groups in terms of seniority, sex, race, and individual absenteeism rates, final participation was voluntary—which, of course, limited conclusions that would later be drawn from this research. At the second meeting, the task forces discussed how absenteeism was not only a problem to management but also a problem to the employees who did come to work. Subsequent meetings were structured around identifying causes, brainstorming possible solutions or corrective actions, and evaluating these possible solutions to arrive at specific recommendations for management.

Absenteeism at meetings of the four groups of employees was virtually nonexistent. While comparison groups of employees displayed typical rates of absenteeism, some (but not all) of the experimental groups showed reduced rates of absenteeism during a scheduled work period of five months after their taskforce participation. None of the recommendations made by the task forces were rejected by management, and meetings with all employees in the departments involved were used to provide feedback on the work of the task forces and on what short- and long-range actions would be taken. Subsequently, with both management and employees enthusiastic about this approach, employee task forces were set up to deal with a wide range of other operating and employee relations problems in the car division.

Organizational Monitoring

The next strategy, organizational monitoring, really parallels and ties in with the evaluation of programs. The difference, obviously, is its focus on monitoring or tracking the status of organizational units instead of programs. Doing this effectively requires adequate measures not only at the level of results or relevant end-state variables (such as profits, cost savings, product quality, or employee morale) but also at the level of organizational processes essential to these results (such as leader behavior, decision-making and information systems, or the operational readiness of a work team).

Virtually all the measures now widely used in industrial organizations are historic in nature. That is, they evaluate yesterday's, last month's, or last year's performance, making it difficult to see a problem until it already exists. But once the results begin to dip substantially, organizations monitoring them begin to experience internal pressures or forces for change. By developing measures of the processes behind such a dip, it should be possible to predict or project future levels of results and thus mobilize internal forces for change earlier—hopefully to get ahead of the problem.

Beginning steps have been taken to develop lead-time indicators in the case of the GM car division under discussion as well as in other GM units. It is already clear that absenteeism, turnover, and grievances can be predicted reasonably accurately on a monthly, quarterly, or even yearly basis. In addition, a well-controlled study showed that absenteeism is functionally related to in-process quality. Once defect detection and repair systems have operated, however, the relationship of absenteeism to final quality measures prior to shipment drops to zero (debunking, incidentally, the popular speculation in some quarters that cars built on a Monday or Friday are of lower quality because of higher absenteeism on those days).

Organizational Diagnosis and Development

A broad organizational diagnosis and development strategy is probably the most essential element in a viable and ongoing research program. Its users in the line organization seem to become more receptive to behavioral science research in general and to the utilization of specific research findings when such an overall strategy exists.

This strategy enters the model parallel to techniques improvement. Yet while it may seem that OD is technique-oriented in its present state, any techniques being applied are usually hooked together in some sort of process that makes sense to the OD consultant and, it is hoped, to people in the line organization. To summarize the literature on the subject: We know a great deal about many different intervention techniques, something about their effects, and very little yet about the change process that we seek to tap into or accelerate through organization development.

By 1972, and even earlier than that, the GM car division was institutionalizing many of the principles and techniques developed in the course of its research. Additionally, different programs seeking to reemphasize the individual's sense of doing an important job, to provide for a regular interchange of ideas, information, and problems between hourly employees and their supervisor, and to adopt interdepartmental problem-analysis task forces utilizing hourly employees and technical resources were all beginning to take form outside the research program. At this point, the industrial engineer who chaired the absenteeism and turnover task force accepted and received intensive training for a broader role in the division as coordinator of organizational development. By now, he has a very small staff, and the car division has an expanding program of organizational development that extends to plants beyond the original engine and assembly plants.

Long-Range Organizational Research

Long-range organizational research is a far more encompassing strategy than its parallel on the problem-techniques-program dimension. Generally, this strategy attempts to focus research on problem combinations or complexes, underlying causal variables, and broad issues of sociotechnical and structural relevance to the organization. Some of the targets for this strategy might include the design of new plants, new organizational structures or forms, and organic problem-solving systems.

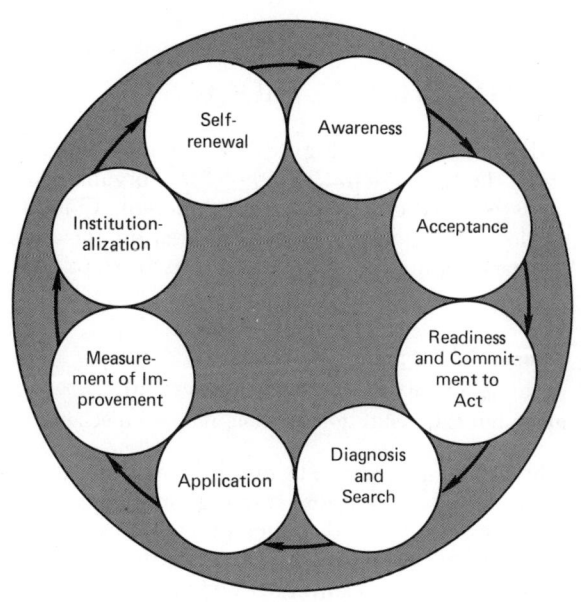

FIGURE 3 *Process of Organizational Development*

Awareness of a disturbance, of organizational problems of growth, identity, destiny and revitalization, of human satisfaction and utilization of human resources; and of problems of organizational effectiveness.

Acceptance of the nature of organizations, of the existence of alternative modes of organizational management and of the range and depth of human and organizational potentialities.

Readiness and commitment to act, to undertake change process and provide required resources and actions beyond mere verbal support.

Diagnose problems, search solutions, to gain understanding of where the organization is, what produces disturbances, where the organization should be, and which improvement strategies are most appropriate to its needs and goals.

Application of new behavior, to experimentally test new methods of operating, to modify organizational processes, and to seek congruency between organizational goals and individual needs.

Measurement of the degree of improvement, of the means by which effective change occurs and of the standards and methods by which organizations should be evaluated.

Institutionalize as an integral part of the enterprise, to incorporate into the management system the principles of human resources management and the mechanism and strategies of organizational development.

Renewal mechanism, to introduce a means of activating steps to renew awareness of problems, of recycling the entire organizational development process as the principal means by which organizations carry out day-to-day operations, and of incorporating relevant values and practices into the management system to ensure the continuity of the enterprise.

A MODEL OF THE CHANGE PROCESS

The model and outline shown in Figure 3 describe the change process as it was hypothesized by Dr. D. L. Landen, GM's director of organizational research and development. It is conceived as a naturally inherent, though in some ways, perhaps, often a slowed or blocked, process in every organization. A short-hand description of the overlapping stages (as opposed to the steps) of the model might include:

Unfreezing (awareness, acceptance, readiness)
Planned intervention (diagnosis and search, application)
Refreezing (measurement, institutionalization, renewal mechanism)

Research might seek to *describe* in terms of the model techniques such as job enrichment, human resource planning, training, or team building to determine which elements of the hypothesized change process are well covered and which elements are not. Given knowledge of a technique's descriptive status in terms of the model, relating this status to results obtained with the technique might—over many such comparisons—establish the utility of the model. Improvement in the techniques themselves could also result from this process.

IMPLICATIONS OF THE MODEL

While other models are imbedded within the overall model that has been proposed here as a framework of research strategies, it is the overall model that carries implications for a total research program. This model should lead us to organize research and select projects in terms of all the elements described. In these times, long-range research will simply not survive without action strategies operating in the short range and up front on current issues relevant to the organization. On the other hand, "shooting from the hip" is not likely to survive very long either without some more fundamental and long-range research coming along behind it.

From the model, it is also clear that research may fall into disuse and perhaps atrophy without real involvement of the line organization. And finally, it seems clear that coupling organizational development into the program will help research acquire a more dynamic and integrated posture with respect to both the theoretical and real world.

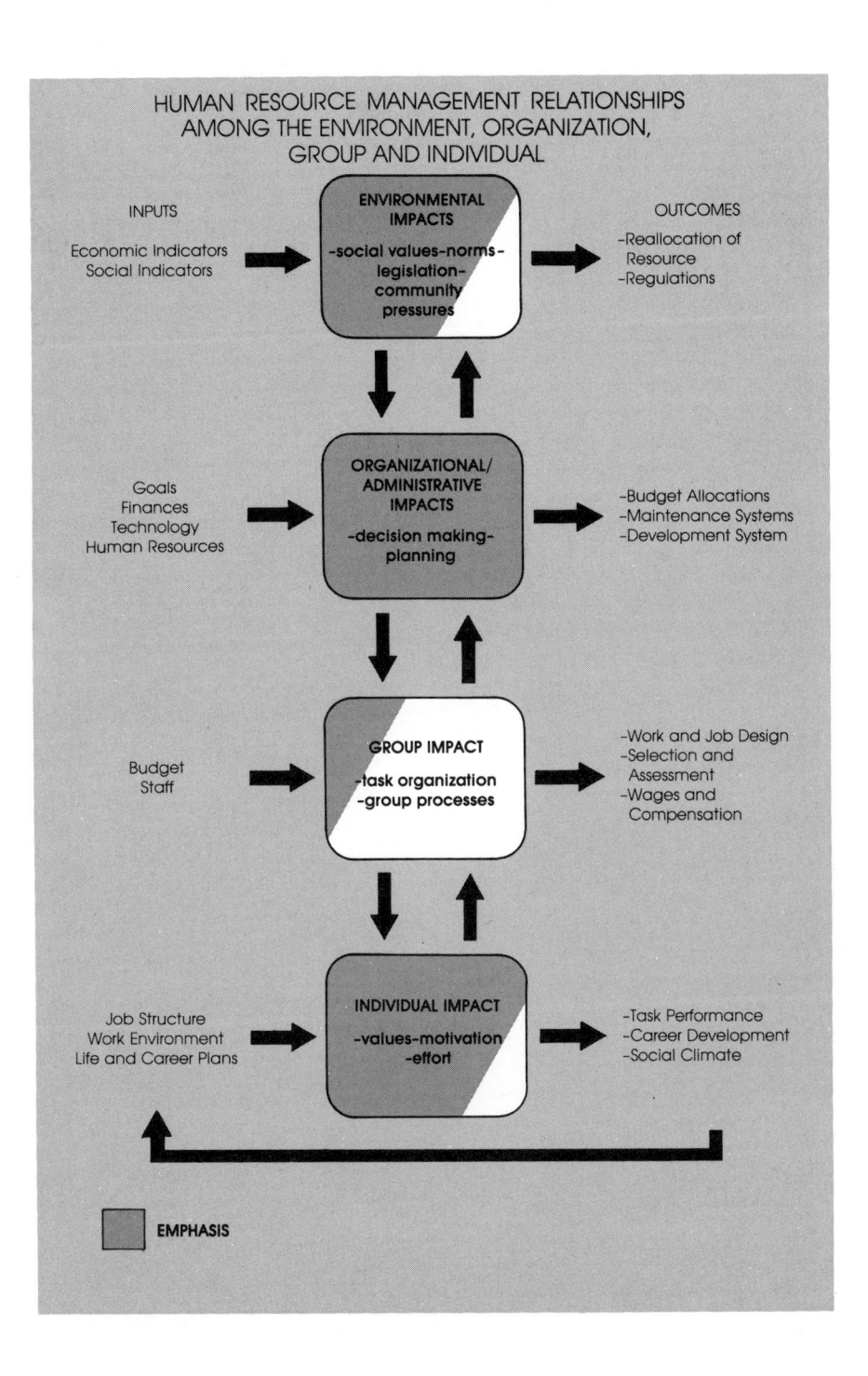

HUMAN RESOURCE MANAGEMENT RELATIONSHIPS AMONG THE ENVIRONMENT, ORGANIZATION, GROUP AND INDIVIDUAL

INPUTS

Economic Indicators
Social Indicators

→ **ENVIRONMENTAL IMPACTS**
-social values-norms-legislation-community pressures

OUTCOMES
-Reallocation of Resource
-Regulations

Goals
Finances
Technology
Human Resources

→ **ORGANIZATIONAL/ ADMINISTRATIVE IMPACTS**
-decision making-planning

-Budget Allocations
-Maintenance Systems
-Development System

Budget
Staff

→ **GROUP IMPACT**
-task organization
-group processes

-Work and Job Design
-Selection and Assessment
-Wages and Compensation

Job Structure
Work Environment
Life and Career Plans

→ **INDIVIDUAL IMPACT**
-values-motivation
-effort

-Task Performance
-Career Development
-Social Climate

EMPHASIS

3

PLANNING DIMENSIONS OF HUMAN RESOURCE MANAGEMENT

A distinguishing characteristic of human resource management is its involvement in the organizational planning process. HRM is charged with integrating comprehensive human resource planning with overall organizational plans and strategies, and consequently implementing responsive human resource programs sensitive to organizational needs.

Planning requires that the HRM activity broaden its perspective to encompass the total organization, and that its strategies and programs contribute to productivity, profit/cost improvement, and the quality of human resource experiences. Human resource planning must always be oriented toward the accomplishment of the organization's goals; however, if proper planning and execution are occurring, individual needs and expectations will concurrently be fulfilled.

Although approaches to the planning responsibility of HRM will vary, there is inherent in the human resource management model a central emphasis on planning as a facilitator of organizational goals. Of course, HRM's planning responsibility will be oriented toward planning and policy making in the areas of forecasting human resource needs, utilization of personnel, career management and development, employment, and compensation. Specifically, HRM will be responsible for coordinating the various planning and maintenance activities so as to maintain an equilibrium between the organization and its internal and external environments. In order to do so, human resource management must involve itself with people-related activities vis-a-vis the **environment,** the **organization,** the **group,** and the **individual.**

Part III contains four articles, all of which deal with various HRM activities related to the forecasting and programming of future activities and some of the research and information required to carry out planning responsibilities.

In the first article, "Human Resource Planning: Responding to Changing Needs," James W. Walker discusses the evolving nature of human resource planning in response to changing conditions. Thus, this paper extends the themes introduced in Part I, but it refocuses the reader's thoughts on the specifics of human resource planning and programming undertakings. Basic concerns in this area include forecasting future requirements, performance management, career management, and management development. Human resource planning establishes a link between the more sweeping forces that act both outside of and within the organization and specific personnel programs. HRM approaches, therefore, make use of systems analysis as well as various models and activities that contribute to organizational performance. The author concludes that effective human resource planning is based on an analysis of the factors representing change—change that potentially affects the survival, growth, profitability, or efficiency of the business.

The relationships between planning, career management, and future organizational needs presented in the article by Walker are developed more fully in our second selection, "The Nature of Managerial Manpower Planning," by Eric Vetter. Vetter presents a classic analysis of planning as a process which integrates all these traditional approaches to training future executives: management development, forecasting, and planning. The phases of the planning process may be outlined as (1) analyzing data through inventories and forecasting, (2) establishing manpower objectives and policies, (3) designing and implementing plans and action programs, and (4) controlling and evaluating organizational plans and policies. This perspective enables manpower planners to consider the historical context of an organization and to relate the specific developmental needs of organizations to those of talented employees. The remaining two articles in Part III consider those analytical techniques which further specify the linkages between career development and manpower planning.

Our third selection is an extremely important piece because it demonstrates how an effective personnel research program can contribute to the conduct of human resource activities and assist in integrating HRM functions. Since job analysis is the basic underpinning for all personnel activities, it follows that it is critical in planning functions. In an article entitled "An Integrated Research and Development Program for Enhancing Managerial Effectiveness," Walter W. Tornow and Timothy C. Gartland present some of the results from a major job analysis program at Control Data Corporation. Their results suggest that **most** managerial jobs can be described and compared on the basis of scores along 13 behavior-based position factors. These results are striking because they point toward common denominators among seemingly diverse jobs and open the way to integrate comprehensive job descriptions with the human resource system activities unrestrained by job titles and functional designations. For example, comprehensive job description can provide basic data for such applications as staffing (analyses), management development, and performance measurement. The authors conclude that a program that integrates research, development, and programming activities for increasing managerial resource utilization can bring human resource management a step closer to using common standards for hiring, appraising, developing, promoting, and compensating managers.

In our last selection, "The Careers of Individuals and Organizations," John Leach examines career notions in a broad life and work framework. A central question addressed is, What is it about a person's movement through an organization that produces satisfaction, challenge, growth, and commitment for the individual and superior performance and contribution for the organization? This question is basic to HRM and provides a common theme that helps establish bonds between the organization and various groups and individuals along the lines of the HRM model that we presented in the introductory notes. Utilizing his framework to study individual career behavior, Leach argues that "career planning **is** human resource planning and career development **is** organization development."

Another theme presented in Leach's paper is that an **organization's career** changes over time and that such shifts have an impact on individual careers. This, along with the other concepts Leach proposes, is quite compatible with Walker's thinking as well as Tornow and Gartland's rationale. Whatever one's particular interest in human resource management, it is important to recognize that the issue of careers is fundamental to an understanding of individuals as they relate to work climates, leadership styles, and inspiration. Career thinking serves to integrate the individual into various organizational work and group processes and thus functions in harmony with both forecasting and various human resource planning activities. Of course, human resource planning in turn connects to enterprise planning and so constitutes one in a series of interrelated events and undertakings.

APPROACHES TO THE PLANNING FUNCTIONS

Human Resource Planning: Responding to Changing Needs

James W. Walker

A decade ago, manpower planning was cited as an emerging managerial function concerned with responding to organizational demands for talent and an improved development and utilization of available talent (Geisler, 1967). What has happened in the interim? Has this function come into its own? In what ways has it changed? What has become of this promising new dimension of human resource management? This article briefly describes how human resource planning has evolved and how it is taking shape to meet the changing needs emerging in the decade of the eighties. Topical areas include origins and evolution, state of the art, needs forecasting, performance management, career development, and management development and HRM planning.

Techniques have become more sophisticated through years of applications and research, but the raison d'etre of human resource planning has been its capacity to help managers satisfy their needs for talent which will achieve organizational objectives. The effectiveness of human resource planning practices depends largely on how *relevant* they are to *pratical* managerial concerns and the prevailing demands upon an organization. Planning for human resource needs is more than a set of techniques and a "system" that is part of the personnel function. Today it is widely viewed as *the* way management comes to grips with ill-defined and tough-to-solve human resource problems.

ORIGINS AND EVOLUTION

However informal its recognition, human resource planning has been a function of management since the origins of the modern industrial organization. Economist Alfred Marshall observed in 1890 that "the head of a business must

---

Adapted from Chapter One *Human Resource Planning* by James W. Walker (New York: McGraw Hill Book Co., 1979). All rights reserved.

assure himself that his managers, clerks, and foremen are the right men for their work and are doing their work well." Division of labor, specialization, organization of management into levels, work simplification, and application of standards for selecting employees and measuring their performance were all principles applied early in industrial management. They were also applied in large nonindustrial organizations, including religious, governmental, and military organizations.

Planning for the staffing of work is not a recent notion. The relatively sophisticated techniques available to management today are the outcome of a long period of evolution in practices, beginning decades ago with simple, pragmatic, short-term planning. As shown in Table 1, the techniques used by management tended to fit contemporary conditions and events. During the first part of this century, for example, the focus in manpower planning was upon the hourly production worker. The aim of improving efficiency through work engineering and early industrial psychology applications was consistent with the need to improve productivity and introduce greater objectivity to personnel practices (Merrill, 1959; Ling, 1965; Yoder, 1952).

During World War II and the postwar years the HRM focus intensified on employee productivity and on the availability of competent managerial personnel. These needs resulted from a civilian talent shortage in combination with an increasing demand for goods and services. New technologies and a new awareness of and interest in behavioral aspects of work also complicated the manpower planning task.

The expanded demand for high-potential personnel in the 1960s resulted from high-technology programs (the space race) and rapid corporate expansion and diversification. In response, manpower planning practices attempted to balance supply with demand, particularly for managerial, professional, and technical personnel. The shortages of men aged 30 to 40 and of specific engineering and scientific skills were noteworthy during this period. The textbooks written during the latter part of the decade document well these conditions and concerns, as manpower planning come to be viewed as a system linking the organization with its environment (Vetter, 1967; Patten, 1971; Walker, 1969).

Emerging Concept of Manpower Planning

The prevailing view of manpower planning at that time and one that has dominated the literature ever since, was that "companies forecast their needs for manpower into the future, forecast their internal labor supply for meeting these needs for manpower into the future, and identify the gaps between what will be needed and what will be available." Manpower planners develop plans for recruiting, selecting, and placing new employees, plan for training and development, and anticipate necessary promotions and transfers (Heneman and Seltzer, 1968; Wilkstrom, 1971; Geisler, 1967; Burack and Walker, 1972).

TABLE 1 The Evolution of Human Resource Planning

Periods and Emphasis	Conditions and Events	Techniques Introduced or Emphasized
1900–1940 **Work Engineering** (hourly personnel)	Search for efficiency in production Labor intensive, unskilled Modern work organization, division of labor, professional management Union movement Depression years	Task measurement/simplification Output-related incentive pay Testing for employee selection Skills training Payroll budgeting and control Manning tables for workloads Labor relations Welfare programs
1940–1960 **Productivity and Continuity** (hourly/managerial)	Talent shortage due to war Emphasis on productivity for wartime and postwar demand Increased mechanization, automation Job satisfaction/productivity studies	Organization charting Management backup charting for replacements University executive development programs Work group effectiveness and leadership style changes Workload forecasting using ratios and regression analysis Attitude surveys, human relations programs
1960s **Balancing Supply and Demand** (managerial, professional, and technical employees)	Sputnik-stimulated demand for highly talented personnel Age 30–40 gap; shortage of scientists and engineers Rapid organizational expansion and diversification Multinational expansion Rapid technological change, risking obsolescence Civil Rights Act Student/youth activism Vietnam war	Intense college recruitment Fast-track programs; career ladders Skills inventories Matrix organizations Assessment centers Disadvantaged/hard core programs Formalized forecasting activity Experiments with mathematical models Job enrichment projects Performance goal-setting
1970s **Affirmative Action** (salaried employees, particularly the protected classes)	Court and government imposed goals and timetables New Legislation (OSHA, Age Discrimination, ERISA, Privacy, etc.) Slowing of business expansion Concern for retention, utilization of present staff; cost control Women's Liberation movement "Discovery" of mid-life crisis Energy crisis	Models used in setting AA goals Computer-based information systems Human resource planning functions established Human resource analysis related to business planning and budgeting Assessment of human resource costs and benefits Early retirement and outplacement Quality of work life and productivity programs "Zero-base" budgeting Broadening of managerial development (**multifunctional**) Job posting/bidding systems

TABLE 1 (Continued)

Periods and Emphasis	Conditions and Events	Techniques Introduced or Emphasized
1980s **Work and Career Management** (all employees)	Consolidation of federal law governing personnel practices and administration Aging of the work force Competition among young managers for responsibility Accelerated unionization of professionals and managers Expansion of adult education Stronger pressures for egalitarian practices in pay and employment Participation in management more commonplace Increased pressures on human resources for cost control and profit contribution	Job-related criteria for personnel decisions (hires, promotions, pay, terminations, etc.) Individual career planning Activity analysis as a tool for designing jobs, forecasting needs, organization, etc. Flexible work schedules Direct access to computer systems Clarification of management commitments in human resource management; policy changes
1990s and beyond **Individual Autonomy Within Large-scale Work Organizations** (all employees)	Energy, food, other resource shortages Limited work available; increased leisure time Stress on family, privacy, personal independence Extended life expectancy, improved health Legislation governing pensions, health insurance, and lifetime income security Political/social challenge to large institutions; drive for individual freedom, autonomy, and recognition	Reshaping of work environments and customs Work sharing; shortened workweek Job matching/career guidance aided by government and employers New careers in emerging fields of communications, health, energy sciences, etc. Measurement and auditing of human resource changes as part of management accounting Extended vacations, sabbaticals

New Demands on Manpower Planning

With new legislation, court decisions, and governmental regulations, management attention turned in the 1970s to affirmative action planning and other aspects of compliance. Although many firms adopted the techniques that had been introduced by leading companies during the previous decades, others experimented with such new devices as career planning, activity analysis, and reshaping of work. Most organizations, however, have been concerned primarily with compliance with the significant new regulations governing discrimination, safety, and pensions. Attention was also directed toward the updating and refinement of salary administration practices to assure competitive and motivational compensation in an era of rapid inflation. Generally, it has been an unsettled decade, during which managers have attempted to cope with the energy crisis, uncertain costs and profits, slowed business expansion, and heightened employee anxieties about women's liberation, reverse discrimination, and the mid-life crisis.

Emergence of "Human Resource Planning"

However, during these years, manpower planning—now broadly termed "human resource planning"—became widely established as a staff function in major business and governmental organizations. The term *human resource planning* implied a concern with broader issues than merely trying to balance supply and demand or project quantitative estimates. The new term shifted attention from these more narrowly conceived parts of the process to a more comprehensive view of personnel as both needs forecasting and program planning. The term *human resource* also had the advantage of minimizing the sexist implication of *man*power and of emphasizing the positive aspects of personnel as a basic corporate *resource*.

STATE OF THE ART

In the decade ahead there may be less new legislation, but administration and enforcement of laws will likely be strengthened, and diverse regulations affecting company human resource practices will be consolidated. At the same time, employee desires for participation in decisions that affect their work and careers will become stronger, as will management desires for improved control over costs and profitability. As a result, companies will adopt work and career management practices of the type reflected in innovations under affirmative action programs. Needs forecasting, work/job analysis, and career planning will become commonplace.

The 1990s and Beyond

Beyond 1990 and the turn of the century, practices considered radical today will likely become conventional. For example, job sharing, reduced working hours, significant reshaping of work and work customs—possibly not going to an office—are all projected. It is possible that the government will have more direct involvement in matching individuals with jobs, both across organizations and within organizations under "equal opportunity" objectives. The conditions anticipated by futurists indicate continued work-force expansion, limited availability of work, and strong desires for individual autonomy within large and complex work organizations (Dunnette, 1973).

Relating Techniques and Practice

Techniques and practices have, therefore, been developed and applied to satisfy needs resulting from managerial concerns and, indirectly, from economic, social, and technological changes in the environment. The state-of-the-art practices applied in a few leading organizations indicate emerging needs and priorities that may ultimately affect many organizations (Churchill and Shank, 1976;

Grinold and Marshall, 1976). For example, Sears, Bank of America, AT&T, and General Motors have led the way in developing advanced career management techniques, in part because of their EEO/Affirmative Action commitments. Many other retailers, banks, utilities, and large manufacturers have not felt the same degree of pressure to move so boldly into broad new programs. It takes time for the majority of organizations to catch up to the leading edge of practice, as they come to feel the pressures detected earlier by their forerunners (Walker, 1974).

THE CONTEMPORARY APPROACH

Effective human resource planning is a process of analyzing an organization's human resource needs under changing conditions and developing the activities necessary to satisfy these needs. It is essentially a two-step process, as shown in Table 2. The emphasis is upon a responsiveness to needs emerging within and outside the organization rather than upon the techniques or systems which can be applied. The forecasting of needs allows the determining of priorities and allocating of resources where they can do the most good.

Analysis of needs leads to the planning of programs to be conducted. While the activities and programs may run the gamut of human resource management, new programs tend to emphasize those areas that relate directly to current issues. During the seventies and eighties, four basic areas appear to be of primary concern to management (Walker, 1976). These concerns reflect issues identified in the above discussion of changing conditions and events:

Needs forecasting: Improved planning and control over staffing and organizational requirements, based on analysis of conditions

Performance management: Improving the performance of individuals and of the organization as a whole

Career management: Activities to select, assign, develop, and otherwise manage individual careers in an organization

Management development: Activities to assess and develop the managerial talent needed to satisfy future succession needs

In focusing on these four areas, the contemporary approach to human resource planning establishes a link between the broad range of environmental and organizational factors, on the one hand, and specific personnel programs on the other. The planning approach defines human resource needs in the context of the organization's overall needs and defines a strategy by which they will be satisfied. In this way, individual development, recruitment, compensation, and other activities become integral parts of a dynamic process. Training programs, for example, are no longer warranted if they are not shown to be pertinent to prevailing skill or knowledge needs. College recruitment is tailored to satisfy specific forecasted needs.

Coordinating Decisions

Today's personnel manager tries to coordinate decisions in different parts of an organization or in different functional areas within the same planning framework.

TABLE 2 Human Resource Planning: Contemporary Approach

1. Needs Forecasting	2. Program Planning		
	Performance management	Career management	Management development
Analysis of external conditions economic, social, political governmental, legislative population, work force markets, competitive technological	Performance planning goal setting appraisal	Selection and placement criteria systems and practices	Assessment and individual development Succession planning
Analysis of internal conditions plans and budgets management policies technology and systems organization structure inventory of talent results of past forecasting and human resource programs	Shaping the work activities time utilization work environment	Career planning and development self-analysis career information career development	
EEO/Affirmative Action goals and plans	Rewards incentives compensation	Training and development on-the-job training internal/external programs	
Forecast of staffing requirements forecasted demand forecasted talent supply net needs		Retirement/termination programs policies preparation/alternatives	
Future organizational changes structure, positions job requirements, career paths			

Thus, termination of employees for poor performance cannot logically follow sizable bonus awards or salary increases for these individuals. Laying off employees in one quarter while recruiting comparable employees in another would also be a logical contradiction. All programs are measured against affirmative action plans and against the other tests of necessity.

Linking Individual and Organizational Plans

The contemporary approach also features a strong link between individual goals and plans and those of the organization. Historically, programs have been designed to meet organizational needs. But in the years ahead, it will be increasingly important to balance organizational needs against those of employees and society in general. Employee career interests, relocation preferences, and development plans will be weighed in needs forecasting. Societal pressures for disclosure of company policies and practices for hiring of minorities, job sharing, more flexible work schedules, and other new programs will also be evaluated. In the future, what is considered good for individuals may increasingly be regarded as beneficial to the organization.

NEEDS FORECASTING

Few executives today are unconcerned about controlling personnel costs. In an era of continuing inflation, rapidly rising costs, and increased competitive pressures on profits, personnel costs loom large. In banks, personnel costs rank second only to cost of capital, and in many manufacturing firms, labor costs have risen more rapidly than any cost except energy. There is, therefore, considerable interest in improved forecasting and control of staffing at all levels, but particularly with respect to professionals and managers.

Commonly, the problem of staffing has been solved by planning and budgeting at each successive level of management. Properly conducted planning and budgeting yields estimates of future demand, supply, and net human resource needs accepted as valid by managers. In the past, forecasting has been enhanced by

- including human resource forecasting in the budgeting cycle and requiring submission of plans along with financial budgets
- requiring estimates of needs from each organizational unit (bottom up), so that unit managers are committed to them
- analyzing supply through computerized models (forecasting flows of employees in, up, over, and out of the organization)
- careful reviews of facts and forecast assumptions by senior executives before approving future staffing proposals

To improve the objectivity of staffing plans, companies are also including human resource planning at an earlier stage in the planning cycle. It is not enough, many executives argue, for staffing plans to be budgeted. Human resource needs must be considered in the context of longer range, strategic planning. A number of firms have found themselves short of talent when they were all set to implement broad capital expansion programs. Others have found themselves heavily overstaffed with employees whose talents no longer fit the company's changing needs, and thus in the uncomfortable position of having to terminate many individuals or force them to retire early. In the years ahead, increased lead time will be provided, to allow advance planning for staffing and related career development and organizational changes (Walker 1976; Bell, 1974).

Work and Staffing

Concurrent with these developments is the greater emphasis being placed on the qualitative aspects of human resource needs. In many cases improved control of staffing is being achieved through closer attention to the actual nature of the work. Analysis and planning of work activities, organizational changes, and specific job requirements is an increasingly important part of needs forecasting. In an effort to manage the actual tasks as well as the people who perform them, companies are giving studies of work activities high priority in planning. Numbers alone simply don't tell the whole story; for example, an agency in Washington reviews its staffing levels and utilization each year using information on activities and output indicators provided by job incumbents. The analysis yields guidelines for staffing via the budget process and also points out specific areas deserving in-depth study and reorganization of the work.

Computer-Supported Systems

Computers are also being used more extensively as reliable personnel data are maintained. Introduced early in the seventies in many companies, personnel data systems are just now starting to be used for analysis and planning purposes. Companies are now providing computer-generated analyses of personnel complement, attrition, movement, and projected requirements. The use of mathematical models, largely experimental in the seventies, will become more common in the years ahead. An impelling force for the use of models has been the need for projecting career opportunities in affirmative action planning. To date, most models have focused on the forecasting of talent supply. In the future, models will be used extensively for forecasting staffing needs in relation to both changing demand and changing supply. To achieve this, data on changing work activities, workload demands, and organizational patterns will be necessary elements in the data systems. In large, complex organizations (such as the military services), large-scale modeling is relied upon to assure optimal staffing and organization to meet planned objectives.

Overall, improved forecasting of needs precedes other substantial changes in organizations. The analysis of current and projected personnel supply provides a chart management can follow in adapting job designs and organization structures to changing requirements, adjusting business plans where talent clearly is unavailable, and planning the kinds of activity programs needed to develop and maintain a work force capable of achieving the organization's objectives.

PERFORMANCE MANAGEMENT

Many executives are convinced that company productivity can be increased through better management of employee performance. Individual employee motivation is seen as a key factor, but other factors such as the structure of jobs, individual competencies, and appropriateness of performance goals and standards of measurement are also considered important. The results of programs specifically designed to motivate employees to improve performance have, by and large, been disappointing. For this reason, companies are trying alternative approaches for obtaining closer control over performance.

For many years, managers have relied on job descriptions and performance appraisals as basic tools in managing performance. But, no matter how frequently revised, job descriptions are often out-of-date and are not really descriptive of the actual tasks involved. Appraisals, too, often fail to address the employee's actual performance—quality of work, initiative, cooperation, and so forth. To strengthen managerial skills in this area, companies are modifying their performance planning and performance appraisal systems. New guidelines are simpler to understand and easier to use and designed to avoid pitfalls experienced in the past. Training and coaching for appraisers have been stepped up in many companies to help managers carry out their part of the process. In some large companies, for example, workshops help appraisers conduct the most difficult part of appraisal: actually discussing performance and future plans with the individual employee. On the other side of the coin, employees are being brought more actively into the process by being asked to prepare their own plans and past performance reviews in advance of discussions with their managers. Management policies and statements of philosophy are being liberalized to encourage open and constructive discussions of performance plans and results. Too often, goal-setting systems were forced into organizational settings that simply weren't prepared to make them work.

An understanding of the work to be performed is viewed as a critical element in good performance. Many companies are supplementing their job descriptions with additional tools for analysis of the actual work requirements. Time sheets, activity reporting, special studies, and supplemental job analysis questionnaires are being used to build a broader picture of the activities *actually performed* and those *desired* on a job. Such activity/work analysis is becoming more common in part as a response to requirements for improved job-relatedness of employee selection, promotion, pay, termination, and other personnel decisions under EEO regulations.

Finally, companies are making noteworthy changes in working conditions. Experiments to improve the "quality of working life" have pointed the way toward flexible job design, flexible working hours, flexible benefits and compensation, more open communications, open posting/bidding for job assignments, and other innovations. Many companies are working to build rewards into the design of jobs, and to make compensation incentives more meaningful to employees.

Overall, practices in managing performance are changing significantly as organizations come to realize they can improve their productivity through improved management of people. Such traditional practices as performance appraisal and job description are being reexamined and given new vitality through new approaches. As an important management concern, human resource planning focuses on improving performance.

CAREER MANAGEMENT

Another trend that is gaining momentum is management's increased concern with employee careers. With high turnover, a limited supply of competent talent, and changing requirements, career development has become an important aspect of human resource planning. Retention and improved utilization of talent are taking precedence over external recruitment. And this means greater attention to selection, appraisal, individual counseling, career planning, and innovative training and development programs.

Another factor prompting heightened interest in career management has been the more prominent role of government through EEO and Affirmative Action programs. To achieve EEO/AA objectives, companies have developed new job-matching/career progression systems, explicit career paths and job requirements, more objective ways to identify and evaluate prospective candidates for promotions and transfers, and expanded employee development programs. To achieve specific targets for utilization of protected classes, procedures are being adopted in recruitment, selection, placement, and development.

Recruiting and selection practices are focused on job criteria. What are the skills, knowledge, and experience really needed on a job? Can these requirements be demonstrated to be job related? Executives are increasingly concerned with the quality, not only the quantity, of talent employed. And this concern persists beyond the initial candidate selection to each new assignment.

Facilitating Individual Career Planning

For many employees, the focus of human resource planning is upon career development. Everyone has a contribution to make to an organization. The challenge is to develop these talents fully and to match them with opportunities that best fit the organization's needs. The organization can help by providing developmental resources and job-matching vehicles, but responsibility for career development rests largely upon the employee (Hall, 1976).

Some companies are providing their employees with tools for individual career planning—workbooks, workshops, counseling, and career information. In all these devices the focus is upon self-analysis and development planning. It normally includes examination of personal goals, interests, and values; capabilities and limitations (assets); career options and how they relate to personal goals, values, and assets; current job performance—so that development can proceed realistically and not be dependent on future openings; and specific development action plans.

Companies are expanding the resources available in support of individual career planning and development. Training programs are being redesigned and expanded to meet identified needs. Tuition aid programs are being used more extensively to meet both company and individual needs. More job rotation and special assignments are allowing mutual assessment of individuals as candidates for different kinds of jobs. Data systems are being used to provide practical inventories of available job candidates, often as a complement to open job posting or bidding systems. Appraisal programs are being expanded (or sometimes split into dual programs) to give improved consideration of individual development progress and plans.

Career development programs have been expanded. For example, special programs have focused on the needs of women and minority groups to acquire career planning skills that will set them on an equal footing with white males. Nonetheless, the trend is toward broadly based programs open to all employees. Even "fast-track" management development programs, popular in the 1960s to move young managers into executive ranks, have waned as the supply of managerial talent has become greater and the lead time for development planning has extended.

But companies are turning attention to the needs of one new "minority group"—older workers. Careers of employees approaching retirement were never considered an issue until the Age Discrimination in Employment Act began to be enforced. Performance appraisals are now essential in terminating employees over 40 if there is any possibility of age discrimination having been a factor. Also, companies are providing special counseling and more flexible work/retirement options to employees facing retirement or career changes. Career planning is a natural way of life in many companies, and is likely to become commonplace in the future.

Overall, companies are working toward applying more objective systems for appraising individual capabilities and potential, identifying candidates for position vacancies, and guiding individual career development. While many ways remain uncharted, the trend is toward providing employees with more resources to aid in their career planning.

MANAGEMENT DEVELOPMENT

Developing future managers has long been a concern of executives, but contemporary leadership has evidenced more interest in developing managerial capabilities from among different segments of the work force and also in finding new ways of developing them. Competition, rapid change, financial pressures, and the many other strains on an organization, all lead toward a need for more broadly experienced and seasoned managers.

In the past, the key question was, Do we have back-ups for our key positions? The right answer was assured through one of several alternate techniques. In many companies, the "cream" was assumed to rise naturally; if high-potential individuals were recruited, they would develop themselves. In others, back-up charting techniques have been used to spot the "comers" and help management plan promotions and transfers to aid them in getting necessary experience. In still others, committees or staff officers have maintained files of data on key management candidates and advised on developmental moves.

The primary concern today, however, is to develop broadly experienced and seasoned managers in a way that is simple, practical, meaningful, and fair. Companies are focusing on a talent pool, rather than on individual back-ups for key positions. This allows greater flexibility in planning developmental assignments across organizational and functional lines.

Planning for management development begins today with clarification of job requirements—exactly what do specific management positions require? Yet requirements are constantly changing; rarely do executives feel their successors will closely "fit their own image." Rather, new skills, knowledge, and types of experience will be called for.

A number of companies have developed position profiles, a sort of behavioral job description for each key position based on inputs from job incumbents and senior management.

Assessment information on candidates is also changing. The trend is toward more specific job-related appraisals rather than global assessment of managerial qualities. Of course, the search continues for those "absolute" qualities possessed by "every effective manager," and assessment programs and appraisals necessarily focus on those qualities currently demanded by an organization or job. But the emphasis today is upon the skills, knowledge, and experience that candidates may obtain through career development. Less weight is given to ratings of "potential" or "personal promotability" than to specific development needs and plans.

Also, there is greater consideration of individual goals, interests, and preferences in management development. Many companies have acknowledged that they have little "hold" on highly talented individuals. To keep them in the organization and keep them motivated, executives are listening to individual desires regarding career paths, location, and other factors. Young managers are particularly vocal about their personal career goals and plans, and they are being heard.

HRM PLANNING

Setting Goals and Priorities

So where does a company begin? The varied needs for human resource planning come from both internal organizational sources and from external pressures. As a first step, therefore, it is necessary to weigh the various needs and determine their relative priority for management attention. It would be an extraordinary organization that could do all of the things described in this article. Few organizations ever *try* to respond to *all* of the concerns felt important to human resource planning.

Of course, many external forces are compelling, such as affirmative action agreements and lawsuits. But labor shortages, economic pressures to reduce staff, technological changes, and even changing social attitudes are not evenly felt across companies. One organization may be particularly impressed by its difficulty in recruiting high-potential employees; another may have difficulty recruiting but not consider it a noteworthy problem. Those companies that are "in the crunch" respond with action; others direct attention to other concerns.

Pressures and Priorities in Human Resource Planning

Even the pressure of competitive employment practices is unevenly felt. Some companies, and some industries in particular, are more sensitive to competition than others. For example, the shortage of petroleum engineers, particularly females, is a concern of only a few companies that are aggressively competing to attract them. Retention and motivation of clerical employees tends to be a problem in urban areas and locations with a concentration of businesses.

Some companies have levels of profitability that allow them to implement human resource programs whether they are demonstrated to be essential or not. Utilities, oil companies, and other capital-intensive businesses allocate staff and money to human resource programs simply because personnel expenses are low relative to other costs. Smaller, rapidly growing companies also tend to support innovative human resource programs under the philosophy that continued growth requires extraordinary attention to the development of required talent. In the first instance, human resource needs and costs are not felt to be particularly significant to the realm of business operations; in the second instance, human resources are felt to be a potential key factor affecting future growth and profitability.

In many companies, the concerns, attitudes, values, and personal managerial styles of key senior executives tend to set the priorities among human resource needs. In these cases, changing internal organizational conditions affect planning far more than any change in external conditions. Preserving the status quo is often a number one priority in the mind of conservation executives. Only when external factors or changing internal conditions result in mounting pressures do human resource policies and programs begin to change.

Naturally, executives have primary responsibility for identifying, sorting, and initiating action upon human resource needs. But it is important that their judgment be based on objective analysis of conditions and not upon their personal biases or assumptions. In many cases, priorities for human resource planning are selected on the basis of

minimum costs and lowest risk of upsetting existing practices

previous personal experiences (for example, practices of a previous employer)

practices and concerns of other companies, especially industry leaders

consultant advice, which itself is dependent on results achieved in other companies

package approaches readily available on the market

Although all these factors commonly play some role in human resource planning, they should never obscure current needs. Goals and priorities should be determined by business plans, obstacles, and changing external demands on the organization.

The key to effective human resource planning is an analysis of the factors representing change—change that potentially affects the survival, growth, profitability, or efficiency of the business.

References

Bell, D. J. *Planning Corporate Manpower*. London: Longmans & Harlow, 1974.

Burack, Elmer H., and James W. Walker. *Manpower Planning and Programming*. Boston: Allyn and Bacon, 1972.

Burdick, Walton. "A Look at Corporate and Personal Philosophy," *Personnel Administrator*, July 1976, 21–26.

Churchill, Neil C., and John K. Shank. "Affirmative Action and Guilt-Edged Goals," *Harvard Business Review*, (March–April 1976), 111–116.

Dunnette, Marvin D., ed. *Work and Nonwork in the Year 2001.* Monterey, Calif.: Brooks/Cole Publishing Company, 1973.

Foulkes, Fred K., and Henry M. Morgan. "Organizing and Staffing the Personnel Function," *Harvard Business Review,* 55, 3 (May–June 1977), 142–154.

Geisler, Edwin B. *Manpower Planning: An Emerging Staff Function.* New York: American Management Association, 1967.

Grinold, Richard C., and Kneale T. Marshall. *Manpower Planning Models: Modelling of Long Range Manpower in Large Operations.* New York: Elsevier North-Holland, 1976.

Hall, Douglas T., *Careers in Organization.* Pacific Palisades, Calif.: Goodyear Publishing, 1976.

Heneman, Herbert G., and George Seltzer. *Manpower Planning and Forecasting in the Firm: An Explanatory Probe.* Minneapolis: Industrial Relations Center, University of Minnesota, 1968.

Ling, Cyril C. *The Management of Personnel Relations: History and Origins.* Homewood, Ill.: Irwin, 1965.

Merrill, Harwood E., ed. *Classics in Management.* New York: American Management Associates, 1959.

Patten, Thomas A. *Manpower Planning and Development of Human Resources.* New York: John Wiley & Sons, 1971.

Vetter, E. W. *Manpower Planning for High Talent Personnel.* Ann Arbor: Bureau of Industrial Relations, University of Michigan, 1967.

Walker, James W. "Evaluating the Practical Effectiveness of Human Resource Planning Applications," *Human Resource Managment,* 13, 1 (Spring 1974), 19–27.

Walker, James W. "Human Resource Planning: Basic Managerial Concerns and Practices," *Business Horizons* (June 1976), pp. 55–59.

Walker, James W. "Forecasting Manpower Needs," *Harvard Business Review,* 47, (March–April 1969), 152–175.

Wilkstrom, Walter S. *Manpower Planning: Evolving Systems.* New York: The Conference Board, 1971.

Yoder, Dale. *Personnel Principles and Policies.* Englewood Cliffs, N.J.: Prentice-Hall, Inc., 1952.

The Nature of Managerial Manpower Planning

Eric Vetter

WHAT IS MANPOWER PLANNING?

Manpower planning means different things to different organizations. To some companies, manpower planning means management development. It involves helping executives to make better decisions, communicate more effectively, and know more about the firm. The purpose is qualitative—to make men and women better managers. The emphasis is on having current managers (whatever their number) who are skilled in their functions and reasonably qualified for promotions. Too frequently the acquisition and development of the skills and knowledge needed for the future are lacking. The goal is often only to make the manager a better manager today.

The expenditure of large sums of money on management development in such cases does not insure a sound future manpower structure. Provision for the quantitative aspects of future management is not an essential part of such management development programs, yet without quantitative information on future manpower needs, the development programs cannot be geared to developing the numbers of managers who will be required in the future. Too, when management development programs are tied to short-range needs, they frequently fail to produce the qualitative product needed for the future.

In other firms, the approach to manpower planning is reversed. Here the problem is defined as estimating future manpower needs. The goal is to hire persons today to meet future requirements. The qualitative aspect of development is somehow to be met by a "natural" development process, even though future knowledge and skill requirements are ignored in the planning efforts. The guiding principle is to insure that enough "bodies" are available when needed. This quantitative-only approach is supported by a belief that the organization has never suffered because people were not capable—that manpower hardships can only result from a numerical manpower shortage.

Unfortunately, this type of thinking may exist because the organization does not evaluate the quality of its manpower carefully. A low managerial turnover rate may be considered to mean that managers are performing well. Another interpretation of the same statistic might be that these managers are not wanted by other firms and so are unable to relocate. The emphasis on numerical projections results in a lack of attention to necessary future managerial and professional qualities, to the level at which these qualities will be needed, or to the education and experience quotients that lead to the possession of these qualities. In addition, the lack of attention to qualitative problems may lead to the neglect of the career development of current managerial and professional personnel.

Eric Vetter, "The Nature of Managerial Manpower Planning," *High Talent Manpower*, University of Michigan, Graduate School of Business Administration, 1967.

Research in the aerospace industry, for example, indicates that many professional employees change jobs because of a neglect in manpower planning of these individual qualitative career factors.

The problems posed by overemphasis on either quantitative or qualitative approaches are partially overcome by a third group of planners who define manpower planning as organization planning. Their approach is to code the current organization chart with color chips after each manager's name to indicate his/her current performance quality and his/her promotion potential. The planner then designs an "idealized" organization structure for some future time period. If a long-range organization plan—for example, five years—is desired, the focus tends to be on higher management ranks because the planner lacks quantitative data on the probable structure and size of middle and lower management. If a detailed organization plan is desired, a short-run approach is adopted because of a lack of information on long-range needs.

Once the future organization is conceived, the planner allocates existing manpower to the future positions in view of their promotability, capability, and availability. This approach focuses attention on potential manpower problems arising from probable changes in the nature and structure of the organization. The planner tries to cope with external and internal forces at work on the organization which tend to make it behave in certain ways. Forces such as new markets, new production methods, and new competitive influences, for example, are considered.

Like the other two approaches to manpower planning, organization planning fails to provide the assurance that future manpower requirements are considered satisfactorily. The organization planner is restricted in his/her design work because of a lack of quantitative data, and because he/she does not have responsibility for programs that would develop managers to fill future organization positions.

Each of these approaches—management development, manpower forecasting, and organization planning—is inadequate by itself, yet each approach contains information needed for the other approaches. When combined with other aspects of manpower planning they become key links in an integrated manpower planning effort.

Our definition of manpower planning incorporates elements of all these approaches. It is defined as: *The process by which management determines how the organization should move from its current manpower position to its desired manpower position. Through planning, management strives to have the right number and the right kinds of people, at the right places, at the right time, doing things which result in both the organization and the individual receiving maximum long-run benefit.*

It is a four phased process. The first phase involves the gathering and analysis of data through *manpower inventories and forecasts*. The second phase consists of establishing *manpower objectives and policies* and gaining top management approval of these. The third phase involves designing and implementing *plans and action programs* in areas such as recruitment, training, and promotion to enable the organization to achieve its manpower objectives. The fourth phase is concerned with *control and evaluation* of manpower plans and programs to facilitate progress toward manpower objectives.

The emphasis in manpower planning is to benefit both the organization and the individual. The long-run view means that gains may be sacrificed in the short run for future benefits. The justification for the planning rests on economic grounds. The planning process enables the organization to identify what its manpower needs are and what potential manpower problems require current action. This leads to more effective and efficient performance.

Because of the economic rationale in manpower planning, the entire process should be carefully grounded in profit planning. Manpower planning is more than an interesting exercise in forecasting numbers, in managing the flow of managerial resources through the organization, or in introducing new personnel management methods. Manpower planning should result in benefits that justify its cost, or it should not be undertaken.

If manpower planning can yield a positive economic return, why isn't it more widely practiced? The answer probably rests in the amount of "felt pressure" for the activity in the past. Although some firms have planned for manpower needs for many years, most companies have been able to achieve a reasonably satisfactory manpower structure without such planning. Increasingly, however, firms are feeling pressure on their ability to perform effectively. New strains are being placed on their manpower resources. The causes of this pressure? It is difficult to identify all of them. It appears, however, that perhaps the most fundamental reason is the current rate of increase in the production of knowledge—a rate that will increase in the future.

THE CURRENT NEED FOR MANPOWER PLANNING

Although many of the effects of new knowledge upon organizations are easily seen, the most important impact is the increased rate at which change takes place in the organization and its environment. Unless the firm is able to change successfully as its environment changes, it faces economic loss and possible extinction. In a competitive environment, economic strength is quickly lost by the company unable to keep pace with its rival. An ability to cope with changing conditions is usually a mark of the company which performs well economically. The awareness by higher management that economic success requires a work force capable of adapting to new conditions leads to planning for that work force.

The knowledge revolution is most clearly seen in the new products that result from advancing science and technology, but the effects are everywhere. They appear in the management area where decision-making models and advanced analytical approaches (for example, simulation techniques) can result in a competitive advantage for their users. The insights gained by social scientists into the behavior of people and organizations under various conditions form another result of the knowledge revolution contributing to change in organizations. The quest for knowledge and some of the early findings are altering the attitudes of government bodies toward the social problems of communities, and are leading to legislation and government pressures on organizations to engage in a wide range of different practices. The business organization, too, must effectively adapt to these new pressures or suffer from its lack of flexibility.

The drive for new knowledge is spurred by researchers in industry, universities, and government. Each new finding opens avenues for further research and new applications. As this occurs, the business firm is forced to even more intense efforts in order to survive. Schumpeter's concept of "creative destruction"[1] serves as a driving force in research laboratories, offices, and computer centers across the nation. As competitors demonstrate ability to adapt to change and to initiate further change with new ideas, products, and methods, rivals face potential "destruction" unless they also develop new ways of creating demand, reducing costs, and serving society.

Today, changes to which much of the work force has had little time to adapt are occurring. Compared with the past, competitive forces are now felt more keenly, economic opportunities appear more rapidly, and society is requiring better performance in economic and social areas. These pressures are causing managers to plan more carefully in the areas of finance, marketing, and production. The realization of the planning objectives in these areas is dependent upon the company's having the manpower resources that are implicit in the plans.

The pressures of change also result in a demand for new manpower skills and abilities. The utilization of new and different equipment to produce new products and the need to operate in new markets, is shortening the life span of jobs. The change in demand for manpower skills is occurring more rapidly than many realize, and the prospect is for even greater changes in the future. As the authors of one study said, "It seems clear, however, that the American industrial system has not as yet experienced the full effect of automation since relatively little automation has occurred in the total American industrial scene. The full story of automation and job displacement has yet to unfold."[2]

The "Change Agents"

The knowledge revolution stimulates demand for the person who is capable of providing new knowledge and is able to convert knowledge into economic or social uses. This person can be considered the "agent of change" in the organization. He/she is found in the laboratory engaged in an analysis of chemical phenomena for new products, in the office studying the economic significance of the balance of payments on company investment decisions, and in the factory evaluating the feasibility of introducing new electronic control equipment. He/she is a "very high talent" person—whether scientist, engineer, or manager—who possesses specialized knowledge as well as the ability to utilize it within an organizational context.

A shortage of "very high talent" manpower cannot be met through intense company training because the knowledge required by these individuals is not quickly acquired. Offering premium salaries to attract them from other organizations may fail because they are relatively scarce and because money is only part of their personal complex motivation and reward system. In short, the organization must be increasingly concerned with insuring it has the necessary "very high talent" manpower it needs both to cope with change and to initiate change.

Professional Obsolescence

The formation rate of new knowledge has still another influence on manpower. The rapid advances in knowledge make it increasingly difficult for the professional man to maintain his proficiency. Returning experienced engineers and managers to the college classroom is the method by which some companies try to meet this problem. Other firms are doing nothing about it, sometimes because they are unaware of the growing obsolescence of their highly trained manpower. The unsolved problem of professional obsolescence posed by the production of knowledge is a threat to the growth potential of organizations and to the nation as a whole.

While the advance in knowledge generates forces that mean change in company manpower requirements, a sizable portion of the academic community lags behind in its teaching efforts. Educational institutions encourage the exploration of knowledge frontiers by the individual scholar and researcher, yet at the same time, many curricula are strongly tied to the past. Most keenly felt at the secondary school level, this situation exists at all levels in our educational system. The problem arises in part from a lack of knowledge of how to communicate the "new knowledge" to students.

A more discouraging reason is the inability of many educators to recognize the need for curriculum change. Employers in all types of organizations should inform educators of their changing manpower needs; they should demand better prepared graduates—persons who are capable of coping with the future effectively. Manpower planning requires that the company look to the future to identify its future needs. Hopefully this looking will result in an improved exchange between the "real" world of work and the "academic" world of education with respect to the educational needs of society.[3]

THE STATISTICAL CASE FOR MANPOWER PLANNING

The pressure felt by all types of organizations to employ high talent manpower is also seen in a quantitative way. Historic trends show an increase in professional employment, and projections for the future show still greater increases. In addition, the next decade will be unusual because of the relative shortage of persons in the 35- to 44-year-old age group.

The Supply and Demand for Professional Manpower

Estimates of future national manpower needs point to the professional, technical, and kindred workers groups as the fastest growing occupational groups during the next ten years. Also projected is a large increase in managerial employees for the large and medium-size organization.[4] Table 1 shows the post–World War II growth in these two employment groups and estimates of future growth.

TABLE 1   Professional and Managerial Employment
(in thousands)

| | Professional, Kindred, and Technical Occupational Group || Managerial Occupational Group ||
	Number employed	Percent of total employment	Number employed	Percent of total employment
1947	3,795	6.6	5,795	10.0
1950	4,490	7.5	6,429	10.8
1955	5,782	9.2	6,442	10.2
1960	7,475	11.2	7,067	10.6
1965	8,883	12.3	7,340	10.2
1970	11,000	13.5	8,400	10.3
1975	12,900	14.5	9,200	10.4

Statistics such as these, however, do not indicate what the relationship will be between the supply and demand for qualified persons. Making such estimates is admittedly difficult. Factors such as participation rates of older persons in the labor force, mobility into and out of occupational groups, the future role of the space program in our economy, the increasing use of women in managerial jobs, and utilization of those who enter the labor force without college degrees must be considered.

The 1965 *Manpower Report of the President* projected a probable balance of supply and demand for professional and related occupations through 1975. It added, however, that "In some fields, persistent personnel shortages are likely unless special efforts are made to increase the number of new entrants."[5] Science and engineering are given special attention in the yearly manpower reports because of possible shortages. In addition, any balance of supply and demand in professional occupations apparently will be achieved through the use of perhaps as many as 3,000,000 persons without college degrees.

During the early and mid-1960s, the labor market for professionals was greatly affected by the demands of the aerospace industry for highly trained manpower. For one large corporation, the competitive bidding for well-qualified persons pushed recruiting costs up to as high as $13,000 per engineering graduate hired. The rapid rise in starting salaries for engineers, scientists, and MBA's upset some salary administration systems. The differential between salaries paid new college hires and experienced manpower shrank because starting salaries rose faster than average salary increases for experienced personnel.

Government and Educational Demands for Manpower

Additional support for the statement of recent shortages of professional manpower is the large number of unfilled government positions for professional and managerial manpower. In New York City, for example, a study revealed that 20 percent of the budgeted professional, managerial, and technical positions were unfilled and many others were filled by persons not fully qualified.[6]

Examination of available statistics indicates that under economic growth conditions, the future supply of those qualified for professional, technical, and managerial positions will, at best, barely satisfy the demand. Each new projection of employment in these occupational groups is usually greater than the previous projection.[7] Despite their own increased efforts and skill in college recruiting, business firms are finding government agencies and educational institutions more important as competitors in the labor market.

The demand by government agencies at all levels for planners, systems analysts, computer specialists, management scientists, health specialists, traffic engineers, social welfare experts, economists, and other professionals will grow rapidly in the next decade. The starting salaries for those positions, particularly those paid by federal agencies, are increasing; recruiting literature and techniques employed by many federal government groups now compare favorably with industry's efforts.

Fewer Middle-aged Persons

The low birth rate during the 1930s means that the 35- to 44-year-old age group will be a relatively small one during the next ten years. In 1950, this group constituted over 14 percent of the population; in 1970 it will represent 11 percent; and by 1975 it will be less than 10 percent. In actual numbers, it is estimated, for example, that there will be 800,000 fewer males in the work force aged 35 to 44 in 1975 than there were in 1965. In addition nearly two million fewer persons of both sexes in this age group will be in the population in 1975 than in 1965.[8]

What is the significance of this information to manpower planning? The 35- to 44-year-old age group is perhaps the most important one in management staffing. Men in this group have ten to twenty years of experience in specialized and varied assignments, which result in abilities that cannot be learned in the classroom: a sharpening of decision making skills, an ability to live with mistakes, and a growth in self-confidence as a result of past successes. This kind of management talent, which is especially important to an organization as it tries to cope successfully with the demands of change, is also the kind of experience that must be gained by persons selected for top management. And it is from the 35- to 44-year-old age group that most of the new top managers appointed in the 1970s will be selected.

Some organizations have discovered that this age distribution factor already poses a problem. During the depression years of the 1930s, these firms were trying to protect current managers' jobs and did little, if any, hiring. Manpower shortages in World War II meant another five years of reduced hiring of young management talent. These factors have combined with a short supply of middle-aged persons to create staffing problems. As retirements in the late 1960s and early 1970s drain off personnel hired during the 1920s, these firms will lack persons with adequate experience to move into higher level vacancies.

Because many organizations are short of experienced manpower it is increasingly difficult to recruit capable persons in this age group. Their short supply inside an organization increases their opportunities for promotion there and lowers their desire to relocate. At the same time, the organization that does not utilize persons in this age group intelligently may find them leaving because of opportunities elsewhere.

INVESTMENT IN HUMAN RESOURCES

Another, and very compelling, reason for manpower planning is the investment an organization makes in its manpower resources. Unlike most other assets of the company, manpower can increase in value through utilization. In fact, the more intensively it is utilized with respect to its capability and capacities, the more valuable it tends to become. A manager who is forced to use his/her abilities to the fullest develops into an even better manager. The manager operating below his/her capacity in a nonchallenging assignment, however, may depreciate in value through a lack of use.

This fact that manpower is an asset that can appreciate through careful utilization is another argument for manpower planning. A manpower plan that increases the value of manpower has demonstrable economic returns. Such a plan might involve planned job assignments of those managers with promotion potential. Placing men and women in positions to provide necessary experience for future positions is an investment in them, even though it may entail reduced short-run efficiency. But highly qualified and experienced top executives are needed to make future major resource and policy decisions.

Because an organization makes investments in its personnel either through direct training or job assignments, it is important that employees are utilized effectively throughout their careers. Computer information retrieval systems may effectively identify manpower with the proper qualifications for particular assignments. This facilitates their placement on the basis of skill and ability—something which is often not possible when the organization is ineffective in screening its personnel records manually.

Decisions on the assignment of manpower can be regarded from an opportunity-cost point of view. By placing a manager in a particular job the planner sacrifices the opportunity of that manager's being in another position where he/she might perform better or where he/she might better learn and develop for future utilization. In the same vein, the planner sacrifices the opportunity of having another person in the position in order to realize the learning and development opportunities that exist in the position.

The dollar value of a trained, flexible, motivated, and productive work force is difficult to determine. The quality of the work force, however, can be responsible for significant differences in the short- and long-run performances among firms. Money may enable a company to duplicate a competitor's physical facilities, but money cannot enable a company to duplicate the quality of a competitor's manpower. Needed for that, in addition to money, is a management that recognizes the asset role of manpower and is willing to make provision for future manpower.[9]

CONCLUSION

As Ralph Besse of the Cleveland Electric Illuminating Company once said, "There is nothing we can do about the performance of past management or the qualifications of today's management. But tomorrow's management can be as good as today's managers care to make it."[10] This helps to sum up the need for manpower planning.

A final benefit results from the activity. In providing good management for the future, the organization also better services society. Its improved overall economic performance and its better utilization of scarce manpower resources are direct results. Its development of information of value to educators developing entrants to the labor force is another result. As important a benefit as any is the increased opportunity for individuals to utilize their special talents and to find self-expression in their work.

A great deal of manpower planning attention is directed toward individual managers. Enriching the opportunities for individual growth and development is a major objective of manpower planning. To have managers correctly placed in the organization on the basis of both present and future organization considerations, careful attention must be given to the individual and his/her needs. In this area of manpower planning, the behavioral scientist contributes significantly. His understanding of motivation, personality, attitudes, and organization behavior is helpful in successfully integrating the needs of the individual with the needs of the organization.

Success in manpower planning is not seen in the accuracy of a manpower forecast or in the uniqueness of an action program. The use of forecasts, objectives, and programs helps in the identification and avoidance of serious manpower problems. Success, instead, is measured by whether the organization has the management personnel it requires when needed. This is both a quantitative consideration and a qualitative one.

Notes

[1] Joseph A. Schumpeter, *Capitalism, Socialism and Democracy* (New York: Harper & Brothers, 1950), chap. 7, "The Process of Creative Destruction."

[2] William Haber, Louis Ferman, and James R. Hudson, *The Impact of Technological Change* (Kalamazoo, Mich.: W. E. Upjohn Institute, 1963), p. 8.

[3] An interesting and valuable source of information on this topic is in Fritz Machlup, *The Production and Distribution of Knowledge in the United States* (Princeton, N.J.: Princeton University Press, 1962). See particularly chap. 4, "Education," and chap. 5, "Research and Development." See also, Gary S. Becker, *Human Capital*, National Bureau of Economic Research, General Series No. 80 (New York: Columbia University Press, 1964).

[4] Government statistics include proprietors of small business in the general classification of managerial employment. The number of proprietors is not expected to increase during the next decade. This means that the percentage growth of managers and officials of organizations will increase rather rapidly. See *Manpower Report of the President—1965* (Washington, D.C.: Government Printing Office, 1965), p. 54.

[5] *Ibid.*, p. 114.

[6] *Ibid.*, p. 81.

7For example, see *Manpower Reports of the President.*

8*Manpower Report of the President—1967* (Washington, D.C.: Government Printing Office, 1967), p. 268.

9The idea of investment in human resources was given impetus by Theodore W. Schultz of the University of Chicago. Dr. Schultz' interest has been in the investment the nation as a whole makes in its manpower resources through education and other programs including company-sponsored or supported training and education. See T. W. Schultz, "Capital Formation by Education," *Journal of Political Economy*, December 1960, pp. 571–583; and "Investment in Human Capital," *American Economic Review*, March 1961, pp. 1–17. Rensis Likert develops the asset role of manpower in small organization units in his *New Patterns of Management* (New York: McGraw-Hill Book Company, 1961).

10Ralph M. Besse, "Tomorrow's Managers." Address before the Edison Electric Institute, New York, June 7, 1961.

An Integrated Research and Development Program for Enhancing Managerial Effectiveness

Walter W. Tornow
Timothy C. Gartland

OVERVIEW

The purpose of this paper is to present a conceptual model for empirically investigating the practical question, How can one specific organization (for example, Control Data Corporation) become a more effective organization? It is asserted that managers are the key link for maximizing the positive relationship between individual performance and organizational effectiveness. The model focuses on what steps can be taken to improve managerial performance. Each of five major research and development areas is discussed as well as their interrelationships and practical applications. The areas are *job description, performance measurement, management development, staffing,* and *compensation*. The status of current research and development efforts in each of these areas is briefly reviewed. This review also shows how research, development, and program applications must work together in a coordinated way to assure synergy among the tools and procedures used across the entire personnel function. Finally, the paper highlights the major directions of future research and development efforts toward achieving the desired goal: an integrated program for enhancing managerial effectiveness in a given target organization.

Prepared especially for this book and printed with permission of the authors.

INTRODUCTION

Managers play a key role in determining an organization's effectiveness by virtue of their function, influence, and expense. They set the goals and procedures such that the combined efforts of individual employees result in the products and services of direct importance to the organization's well-being. In so doing, managerial actions can have far-reaching consequences on the employee climate they produce as well as the economic well-being of the organization. In short, managers represent one of an organization's most important resources.

It is for this reason that Control Data Corporation (CDC) has encouraged an integrated approach of systematic and empirical research toward the development of human resource programs designed to effectively enhance the utilization of CDC's managerial resources. The conceptual framework of this R&D approach has its basis in a model of determinants for managerial effectiveness developed by Campbell, Dunnette, Lawler, and Weick (1970). A slightly modified version of this model is presented in Figure 1.

The basic points of this model are

Individual job performance (2) is the result of a complex interaction between the job (1) and the individual (3). This interaction is influenced by the organization's environment (6) and by human resource programs such as staffing (1 and 3), compensation (5), and management development (4).

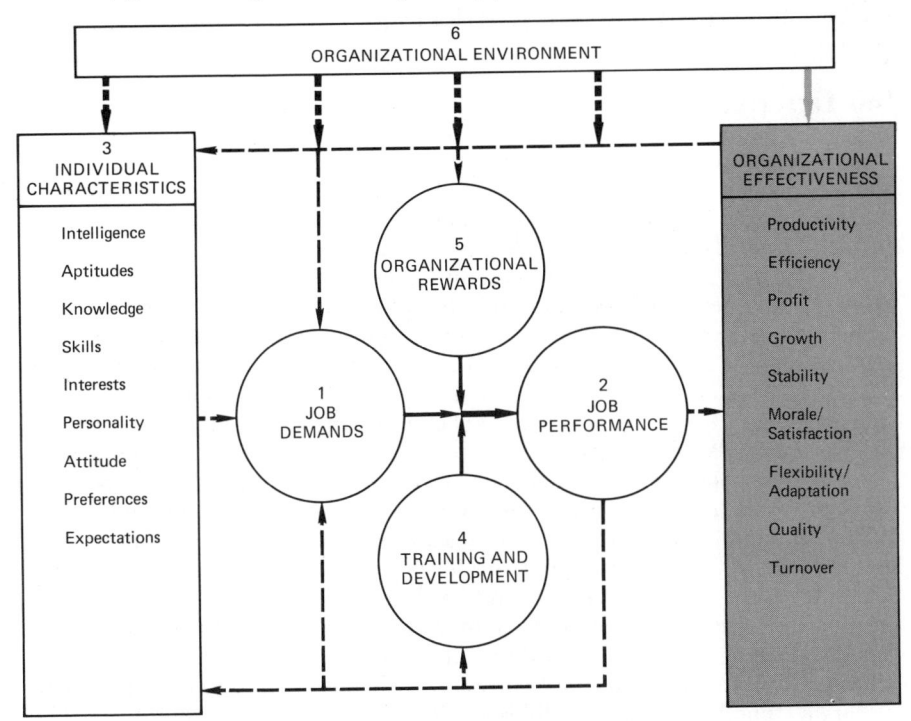

FIGURE 1 *Determinants of Managerial Effectiveness*

There is a difference between individual job performance and organizational effectiveness. Certainly the performance of individuals contributes to organizational effectiveness; however, factors beyond the control of individuals also impact organizational effectiveness.

Individual job performance and organizational effectiveness will be enhanced when all human resource systems act in a coordinated fashion to select, train, evaluate, promote, and compensate on the basis of similar standards.

Systems for objectively describing jobs and people are the key tools for integrating human resource programs.

In short, for human resource programs to be effective, data bases must be designed to give reliable and valid results. This in turn calls for sound data-gathering tools that help describe, at a minimum, the characteristics of the manager's job and his or her performance, since these two factors provide the key foundation for management development, staffing, and compensation.

This paper describes an ongoing management R&D program started at CDC several years ago. The first section focuses on the systems being developed for objectively describing managerial job content and managerial performance. The second section shows how these descriptive systems are applied and can enhance, integrate, and ensure the organizational relevance of human resource programs in management development, staffing, and compensation.

DEVELOPMENT OF DESCRIPTIVE TOOLS

Job Description

Job description is of central importance to the development of organizationally relevant human resource programs. Describing managerial jobs is difficult because (1) there are many management jobs differing in title, function, and level and (2) any given job or position changes from time to time, from person to person, and from situation to situation. Since job descriptions are used by a variety of personnel programs, it is desirable that such descriptions be comprehensive so that each application can draw from a common data base. What is needed, then, is a set of fundamental factors that can be used to describe and classify management jobs in terms of their similarities and differences.

Over the past few years, a major R&D effort by the Corporate Compensation and Corporate Personnel Research departments has developed a system for objectively describing executive and management jobs in terms of their responsibilities, concerns, restrictions, demands, and activities (Tornow and Pinto, 1976). The initial efforts of this project were devoted to the development of a standardized, diagnostic questionnaire for objectively describing management jobs differing in content, function, and level. Responses of 41 carefully selected position incumbents were used to reduce an original 505-item pool to a 208-item Position Description Questionnaire (PDQ). The PDQ was then administered to 433 managers and consultants from different organizations with disparate functions, and at different levels within the corporation. The responses were then analyzed to identify the basic job content factors. Results revealed that 13 behavior-based position factors (shown in Table 1) provide a meaningful basis for describing and comparing management jobs in terms of their similarities and differences in content. For any specific managerial job, some of these factors are very important and some are of little importance relative to other managerial jobs. Thus, each job can have a unique pattern of important and unimportant factors.

A second type of analysis showed that it was possible to group positions meaningfully on the basis of their profiles on the 13 position factors. It was found that most positions in the sample could be grouped into ten clusters or "job families." Each cluster consists of jobs relatively homogeneous in content.

TABLE 1 Position Description Factors

1. Strategy Planning

A high score on this factor in a management position indicates long-range thinking and planning. The concerns of the incumbent are broad and are oriented toward the future of the company. They may include such areas as long-range business potential, objectives of the organization, solvency of the company, what business activities the company should engage in, and the evaluation of new ideas.

2. Organizational Coordination

A high score on this factor of a management position indicates that the incumbent coordinates the efforts of others over whom he/she exercises no direct control, handles conflicts or disagreements when necessary, and works in an environment where he/she *must* cut across existing organizational boundaries.

3. Internal Business Coordination

A high score on this factor in a management position indicates that the incumbent exercises business controls; that is, reviews and controls the allocation of manpower and other resources. Activities and concerns are in the areas of assignments of supervisory responsibility, expense control, cost reduction, setting performance goals, preparation and review of budgets, protection of the company's monies and properties, and employee relations practices.

4. Products and Services Responsibility

A high score on this factor of a management position indicates activities and concerns of the incumbent in technical areas related to products, services, and their marketability. Specifically included are the planning, scheduling, and monitoring of products and services delivery along with keeping track of their quality and costs. The incumbent is concerned with promises of delivery that are difficult to meet, anticipates new or changed demands for the products and services, and closely maintains the progress of specific projects.

5. Public Relations

A high score on this factor in a management position indicates a general responsibility for the reputation of the company's products and services, questions, or policies. The incumbent is concerned with promoting the company's products and services, the goodwill of the company in the community, and general public relations. The position involves first-hand contact with the customer, frequent contact and negotiation with representatives from other organizations, and understanding the needs of customers.

TABLE 1 Position Description Factors (Continued)

6. Internal Consulting

A high score on this factor in a management position indicates that the incumbent is asked to apply technical expertise to special problems, issues, questions, or policies. The incumbent should have an understanding of advanced principles, theories, and concepts in more than one required field. He/she is often asked to apply highly advanced techniques and methods to address issues and questions which very few other people in the company can do.

7. Autonomy

A high score on this factor in a management position indicates that the incumbent has a considerable amount of discretion in the handling of the job, engages in activities which are not closely supervised or controlled, and makes decisions which are often not subject to review. The incumbent may have to handle unique problems, know how to ask key questions even on subject matters with which he/she is not intimately familiar, engage in free-wheeling, or unstructured thinking to deal with problems which are themselves abstract or unstructured.

8. Financial Commitment Approval

A high score on this factor in a management position indicates that the incumbent has the authority to approve large financial commitments and obligate the company. The incumbent may make final and for the most part irreversible decisions, negotiate with representatives from other organizations, and make many important decisions on almost a daily basis.

9. Staff Service

A high score on this factor in a management position indicates that the incumbent renders various staff services to supervisors. Such activities can include fact-gathering, data acquisition and compilation, and record keeping.

10. Supervision

A high score on this factor of a management position indicates that the incumbent plans, organizes, and controls the work of others. The activities are such that they require face-to-face contact with subordinates on almost a daily basis. The concerns covered by this factor revolve around getting work done efficiently through the effective utilization of people.

11. Complexity

A high score on this factor of a management position indicates that the incumbent has to operate under pressure. This may include activities of handling information under time pressure to meet deadlines, frequently taking risks, and interfering with his/her personal and/or family life.

12. Financial Management

A high score on this factor of a management position indicates activities and responsibilities concerned with the preservation of assets, making investment decisions and other large-scale financial decisions which affect the company's performance.

13. Human Resource Management

A high score on this factor of a management position indicates that the incumbent has responsibility for the management of human resources and the policies affecting it.

Source: Tornow, W. and P. Pinto, "The Development of a Managerial Job Taxonomy: A System for Describing, Classifying, and Evaluating Executive Positions," *Journal of Applied Psychology*, 61, No. 4 (1976), 414.

That is, jobs within a cluster are more alike in content with other jobs in the cluster than with jobs in other clusters. By analyzing these clusters in terms of title, level, function, span of control, and budget, it was found that five of the clusters represent line management and five represent functional areas in the organization (see Figure 2).

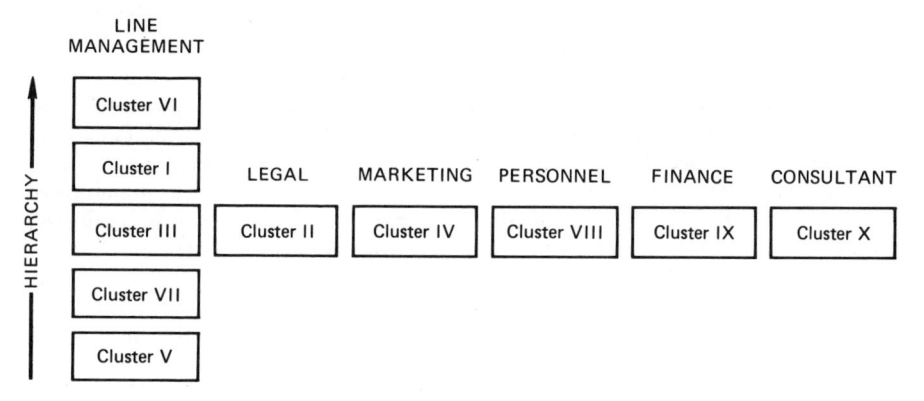

```
         LINE
      MANAGEMENT

    ┌─────────────┐
    │  Cluster VI │
    │             │
    ├─────────────┤
    │  Cluster I  │    LEGAL    MARKETING   PERSONNEL    FINANCE    CONSULTANT
    │             │
    ├─────────────┤   ┌─────────┐ ┌─────────┐ ┌──────────┐ ┌─────────┐ ┌─────────┐
    │ Cluster III │   │Cluster II│ │Cluster IV│ │Cluster VIII│ │Cluster IX│ │Cluster X│
    ├─────────────┤   └─────────┘ └─────────┘ └──────────┘ └─────────┘ └─────────┘
    │ Cluster VII │
    ├─────────────┤
    │  Cluster V  │
    └─────────────┘
```

FIGURE 2, *Clusters of Executive/Management Positions*

Although the clusters are not as distinct as the chart would suggest, the point is that a cluster of jobs can be described in terms of the 13 factors just as a single managerial job can be so described. That is, each cluster has a profile that best represents the jobs which compose it, and each managerial position has a profile that best represents the tasks that comprise it.

Current R&D efforts in this area are focusing on

increasing the objectivity and comprehensiveness of the PDQ

enhancing the usefulness of the PDQ for job evaluation

strengthening the linkage between the 13 position factors and dimensions of managerial performance

In sum, job description research is providing a behaviorally meaningful taxonomy for describing, comparing, and classifying managerial jobs in terms of their content.

Performance Measurement

Like job description, performance measurement has central importance for such applications as staffing, management development, and compensation. Performance measurement therefore should also provide a valid, comprehensive description of the manager's performance that is useful for these various purposes. Performance measurement must include and link (1) *results-oriented* measures (focusing on whether objectives are achieved via, for example, an MBO program) and (2) *process-oriented* measures (focusing on how the objectives are achieved). Process-oriented measures are especially important if we want to identify those performance dimensions which either facilitate or hinder the achievement of objectives.

In addition, the performance measurement system should

- yield similar results from different observers who have the same observation base
- discriminate between managers with clearly different skill and effectiveness levels
- be applicable across companies, positions, and functions
- be acceptable to and usable by managers and facilitate their role as managers of human resources

As a consequence, a major R&D effort has been devoted to developing such a performance measurement tool. The Human Resource Development and Corporate Personnel Research departments (with the assistance of Personnel Decisions, Inc., a local consulting firm) identified the 17 performance dimensions shown in Table 2. These 17 dimensions represent "skill" areas which have been shown to be related to successful managerial performance. Data collected as part of pilot management development programs[1] have indicated that

- the 17 dimensions are seen as relevant to a variety of managerial positions
- raters are able to differentiate managerial personnel along the 17 dimensions
- experienced raters show fewer rating errors than the less experienced
- minor modifications to the form would simplify the process of completing the form and increase the information yield

As a result, a revised tool, the Management Performance Appraisal Form (MPAF), has been developed to describe and evaluate managerial performance along the 17 dimensions. Feedback will be gathered on an ongoing basis on its use and usefulness as quality assurance on its psychometric and operational characteristics.

TABLE 2 Managerial Performance Dimensions

1. Know-How

Demonstrating a thorough knowledge of the technical specialty; keeping informed of the latest developments in the technical specialty; seeking ways to improve managerial and/or consultant proficiency; keeping in touch with events happening outside the organization which impact the functional area.

2. Plan & Allocate

Taking into account all available information to make timely decisions; formulating goals, policies, and plans; monitoring the progress toward objectives and adjusting plans and actions as necessary to meet them; anticipating obstacles and contingencies; allocating and scheduling resources to assure their availability when needed.

3. Document

Processing paper work promptly, properly, accurately, and with attention to details; maintaining accurate and current records about projects, personnel, costs, schedule, and equipment; documenting important aspects of decisions and actions.

4. Effort/Persistence

Working extra hours when necessary to complete assignments; performing "beyond the call of duty," seeking and willingly accepting challenging assignments and added responsibilities; persisting and overcoming difficult obstacles; sacrificing personal convenience in the pursuit of company objectives.

TABLE 2   Managerial Performance Dimensions (Continued)

5. *Innovate*

Developing and applying innovative procedures to accomplish assignments; developing new ideas and unique solutions to planning and problem solving; anticipating and coping effectively with change in circumstances which impact the functional area.

6. *Crisis Action*

Recognizing critical problems and acting promptly and decisively to alleviate them; taking charge quickly in crisis situations; behaving deliberately and rationally under stress; deciding promptly on an alternative course of action when necessitated by unforeseen emergencies.

7. *Responsibility/Accomplishment*

Meeting objectives (that is, budget, profit, headcounts); accepting accountability for the unit's performance; performing duties conscientiously without requiring close supervision; meeting deadlines; being punctual for meetings.

8. *Integrity*

Behaving according to high standards of business, professional, and social ethics; unimpeachably correct ethical conduct.

9. *Organizational Commitment*

Accepting company goals and complying with orders and directives from above; endorsing the policies and actions of superiors; offering constructive criticism about policies and decisions formulated by higher management.

10. *Communicate*

Providing complete, concise, accurate, and prompt information to superiors; disseminating full information to subordinates about company policies and objectives; sharing information with other units as necessary; reporting truthfully job activities and progress toward objectives.

11. *Coordinate*

Coordinating and cooperating with other organizational units to achieve company goals with maximum efficiency; volunteering his/her experience and expertise to assist other units reach their objectives; negotiating with other units for organizational resources; showing broad knowledge about the operations of other units and the company as a whole.

12. *Represent*

Promoting a positive company image to the public; participating actively in community affairs as a company representative; showing genuine concern for the community and society at large; exercising tact and sensitivity while conducting economically advantageous transactions with consumers and suppliers.

13. *Consideration*

Maintaining smooth working relationships among and with subordinates; showing consideration for subordinates' feelings; showing interest in their personal problems; expressing genuine concern for subordinates' morale and general welfare.

TABLE 2 Managerial Performance Dimensions (Continued)

14. Train
Determining subordinates' training needs; instituting standardized training programs to meet those needs; monitoring the training and development of subordinates on technical matters.

15. Delegate
Delegating, giving orders, and assigning tasks; ensuring that assignments are clearly understood; scheduling and allocating work among subordinates equitably and for maximum efficiency; monitoring and evaluating subordinates' performance.

16. Motivate
Setting high performance standards for subordinates; establishing challenging goals for subordinates; giving them increased responsibility and stimulating assignments; setting an example of dedication and conscientiousness for subordinates by working diligently, and putting in long hours when necessary.

17. Coach
Conducting regular performance appraisals; correcting subordinates whose job performance is not acceptable; using appropriate disciplinary techniques when necessary; rewarding subordinates suitably for superior job performance.

Generalizability and Linkage of Job and Person Descriptive Tools

Research efforts also have been directed at determining the generalizability of the 13 position factors and 17 performance dimensions for the broad spectrum of management positions. Rush[2] found that 31 Industrial Relations graduate students and 13 T&D experts rated the factors and dimensions as highly generalizable. Although the generalizability of any one factor or dimension may vary across organizations or jobs, the majority were judged applicable to a variety of settings and individuals.

A matrix linking the 13 position factors with the 17 performance dimensions (shown in Figure 3) was created to identify the specific behavioral requirements for particular factors of management positions. Developed on the basis of pooled expert judgments, the matrix links the descriptions of the job and person by identifying the key management performance dimensions which are judged critical to perform satisfactorily on each of the position factors. As part of Rush's generalizability study, it was found that graduate students and practitioners agreed that a dimension was necessary for performing a given factor in 93 percent of the cases, using a criterion of two-thirds agreement. Both samples agreed with an earlier matrix developed by experts in 61 percent of the cases. As part of the ongoing validation of these tools, managers are being asked to rate the significance of the 17 performance dimensions when completing the PDQ. As sample size permits, data will be analyzed to assess the effects of management level and job cluster on the matrix linkages.

In sum, significant progress has been made in developing standardized, diagnostic questionnaires which permit objective descriptions of managerial job

	POSITION FACTORS														
XIII. Human Resource Management	XII. Financial Management	XI. Complexity	X. Supervision	IX. Staff Service	VIII. Financial Commitment Approval	VII. Internal Consulting	VI. Public Relations	V. Products and Services Responsibility	IV. Internal Business Coordination	III. Organizational Coordination	II.	I. Strategy Planning			
				▓		▓							1. Know-how		
▓								▓	▓			▓	2. Plan and Allocate		
	▓			▓	▓				▓				3. Document		
													4. Effort/ Persistence		
						▓						▓	5. Innovate		
▓		▓						▓	▓				6. Crisis Action		
					▓								7. Accomplishment/ Responsibility		
						▓							8. Integrity		
						▓							9. Commitment		
▓			▓				▓						10. Communicate		
										▓			11. Coordinate		
	▓	▓						▓					12. Represent		
				▓			▓						13. Consideration		
				▓			▓						14. Train		
			▓										15. Delegate		
▓										▓		▓	16. Motivate		
			▓										17. Coach		

PERFORMANCE DIMENSIONS

FIGURE 3 *Job-Person Matrix Showing Which Performance Dimensions Are Thought Most Important in Successfully Accomplishing Particular Position Factors*

content and managerial performance. Research and development efforts are continuing to validate these tools and their linkages. As discussed in the next section, these descriptive tools can provide basic input to such human resource programs as management development, staffing, and compensation.

HUMAN RESOURCE PROGRAM APPLICATIONS

Management Development

A recent paper (Gartland, Rush, Tornow, and Pinto, 1977) describes management development as a risky business. The manager's job is so complex and so conditioned by situational and organizational factors that we can never be sure we have captured enough of the job's content to prepare job-related training programs. All too often new fads and training techniques tend to seduce us away from the basic model of identifying needs, designing programs to meet those needs, and evaluating the impact of these programs.

To improve current performance as well as plan for individual growth and organizational maintenance, management development should follow four key steps. The first step focuses on obtaining comprehensive descriptions of the management job (PDQ) and the individual's performance strengths and weaknesses (MPAF). The second step identifies the relevant behavioral requirements for the particular management development objective via the job-person linkage matrix. If a requirement shows up as a performance weakness, a plan must be created to improve the individual's effectiveness in that area. During this third step, efforts are made to individualize the development program through the prioritization of development areas and the selection of development activities. Finally, an evaluation step is designed to answer such questions as, (a) Does the course/activity achieve its stated objectives? (b) Does achievement of the stated objective result in improved performance, potential, or both? and (c) Does satisfaction with any aspect of the development program moderate its achievement or transfer to job performance?

Development Strategies. The use of the descriptive tools and matrix for identifying development needs is dependent on the kind of development strategy desired. If the objective is to improve the performance of managers on their present job, then *development planning* is the appropriate strategy. The incumbent manager completes the PDQ, and the results are profiled along the 13 position factors. By working through the job-person matrix, those performance dimensions necessary to successfully execute the responsibilities of the three or four most significant factors are identified. The relative importance of any performance dimension is a function of how many of the significant position factors require it. The MPAF then is used to diagnose the manager's strengths and weaknesses on all relevant performance dimensions. Those dimensions identified as weaknesses become the target for development planning.

If the objective is to ready the manager for the requirements of a future job or cluster of jobs similar in content (for example, marketing management), then *career planning* is the appropriate strategy. The three or four most significant factors defining the target job or cluster of jobs can be identified from the continuously updated PDQ data base. Thus, several jobs or clusters can be examined simultaneously in career planning sessions by different individuals without additional data collection. The position profile, job-person matrix, and diagnostic evaluation of current strengths and weaknesses are used in the same fashion as described for development planning. The major considerations in targeting for a specific position versus a cluster of similar positions are the capability to forecast job openings and the individual's preferences (discussed in the next step). Career planning, therefore, differs from development planning in terms of its future orientation and use of previously collected PDQ profiles to identify job or cluster requirements.

If the objective is to identify and develop managers to replace higher level incumbents when those positions are vacated, then *replacement planning* is the appropriate strategy. This activity is distinct from development planning in its focus on a future job and is distinct from career planning in that it is based on organizational needs as opposed to individual interests and preferences. The target position is analyzed and profiled along the 13 factors. Using the job-person matrix, key performance dimensions are then identified. Completed performance appraisals vis-a-vis position requirements are used to rank order candidates for replacement readiness. In the process, weaknesses are identified and replacement-oriented development plans can be established for the candidates.

Management development programs have been constructed which focus on each of these strategies. A modified program is currently proposed (Figure 4) which incorporates an integrated approach to management development, using all three strategies.

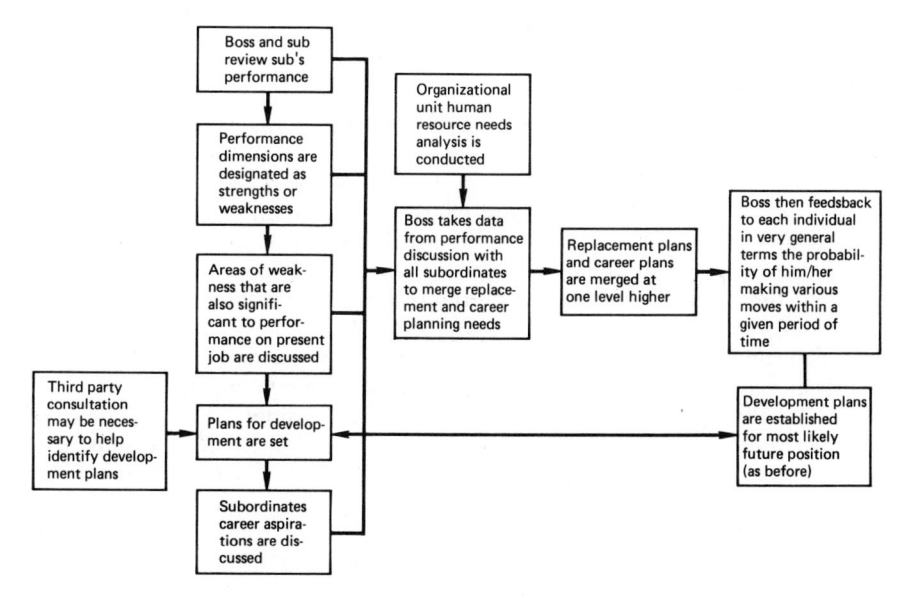

FIGURE 4 *Management and Executive Development: An Integrated Approach Process*

To identify and develop high-level executives and managers, the proposed program uses both a "top-down" and a "bottom-up" approach—top-down to assure that direction and impetus are given to the development effort; bottom-up so that managers discuss their subordinates' performance, developmental plans, and career aspirations with their superiors. This facilitates the merging of organizational and individual development needs.

The core of this approach is performance appraisal. The manager and subordinate review the subordinate's performance against the 17 MPAF dimensions. Dimensions are then diagnosed as strengths or weaknesses. Those areas diagnosed as weak *and* as important for the present job are discussed further to isolate the problem and to arrive at a remedial development plan. Once the needs of the present job have been addressed, the discussion turns to the subordinate's career aspirations.

Parallel with this effort, an organizational human resource needs analysis is recommended. This process will identify key organizational roles that may require replacement and the skill characteristics that incumbents should possess. The manager uses this information, along with the performance review data of all his/her subordinates, to merge individual career aspirations with organizational replacement requirements. These plans are merged one level higher to allow interdepartmental transfer.

The manager then can feed back, in very general terms, the probability of each individual's making certain types of moves within a given time frame, that is, the results of merging career aspirations with replacement needs. Development plans then can be laid for each individual's next most likely position. These development plans must be prioritized with the development plans laid out for improving performance on the present job.

Creation of Development Plan. Once development needs have been identified, a plan must be established to improve performance along these dimensions. Given the limited time available for developmental work, it is often necessary to prioritize the identified needs. An important issue becomes what criteria to use in the prioritization process. From both the individual and organizational perspectives, it makes good sense to focus on those areas where the expected benefits of development efforts are maximum. One such criterion is the relative trainability of various managerial performance dimensions. This knowledge can assist individuals to plan their development more realistically and help the organization determine the relative "development potential" of individuals, thus prioritizing its development efforts.

To determine the relative trainability of the 17 performance dimensions, 24 experts in management development and industrial psychology were surveyed.[3] In making their judgments, raters were asked to consider: (1) the amount of time that would be necessary to change the skill significantly, (2) the amount of money and resources to effect such a change, and (3) the probability that a change would indeed occur. Results indicated a high level of agreement regarding those dimensions adjudged easiest and those most difficult to train. These results are shown in Figure 5. The trainability data have been used in several pilot development programs. Additional research is underway to verify the relative trainability of the 17 performance dimensions by using more objective training and performance criteria.

Another prioritizing criterion is the individual's interests and preferences for various types of activities. Although such information could be used in all three strategies, its major role is in career planning. A Managerial Position Preference Scale (MPPS) has been developed to measure a person's preferences for doing the types of work activities which define each of the 13 PDQ factors. The MPPS yields preference scores along each of the 13 position factors and can be used to help the individual identify jobs or clusters whose content matches his/her preferences. Comparisons of preference and job content profiles also provide input to clarify expectations about future positions. Research is continuing here also to investigate the stability and predictive validity of preference scores.

The second major step in creating a development plan is the selection of activities. Two tools are available to integrate the various development activities and to individualize the developmental plan. The first is a course-person matrix (Figure 6) designed by training managers for internal management education courses to show which performance dimensions come within the scope of each management education course. It can be used to select the appropriate course for each development need. Although these linkages have been determined largely by common sense, research studies are planned to verify the relationships. The results of the linkage research will establish the job relevance (that is, content validity) of the internal management education courses.

The second tool used to integrate and select development experiences is called the *Encyclopedia of Developmental Activities*. This manual lists relevant activities for each performance dimension by such categories as on-the-job development suggestions, readings, audiovisual activities, external seminars/courses, and professional societies. Managers have access to the *Encyclopedia* and are urged to use it in preparing their development plan.

Evaluation. In addition to the ongoing validation of the basic tools used in management development, several types of evaluation studies have been designed to assess the effectiveness of development efforts. The internal validity

MOST TRAINABLE	Document Plan and Allocate Know-How Communicate Train
MODERATELY TRAINABLE	Accomplishment Responsibility Coordinate Represent Consideration Delegate Motivate Coach
LEAST TRAINABLE	Integrity Innovate Crisis Action Effort/Persistance Organizational Commitment

FIGURE 5 *Index of Trainability*

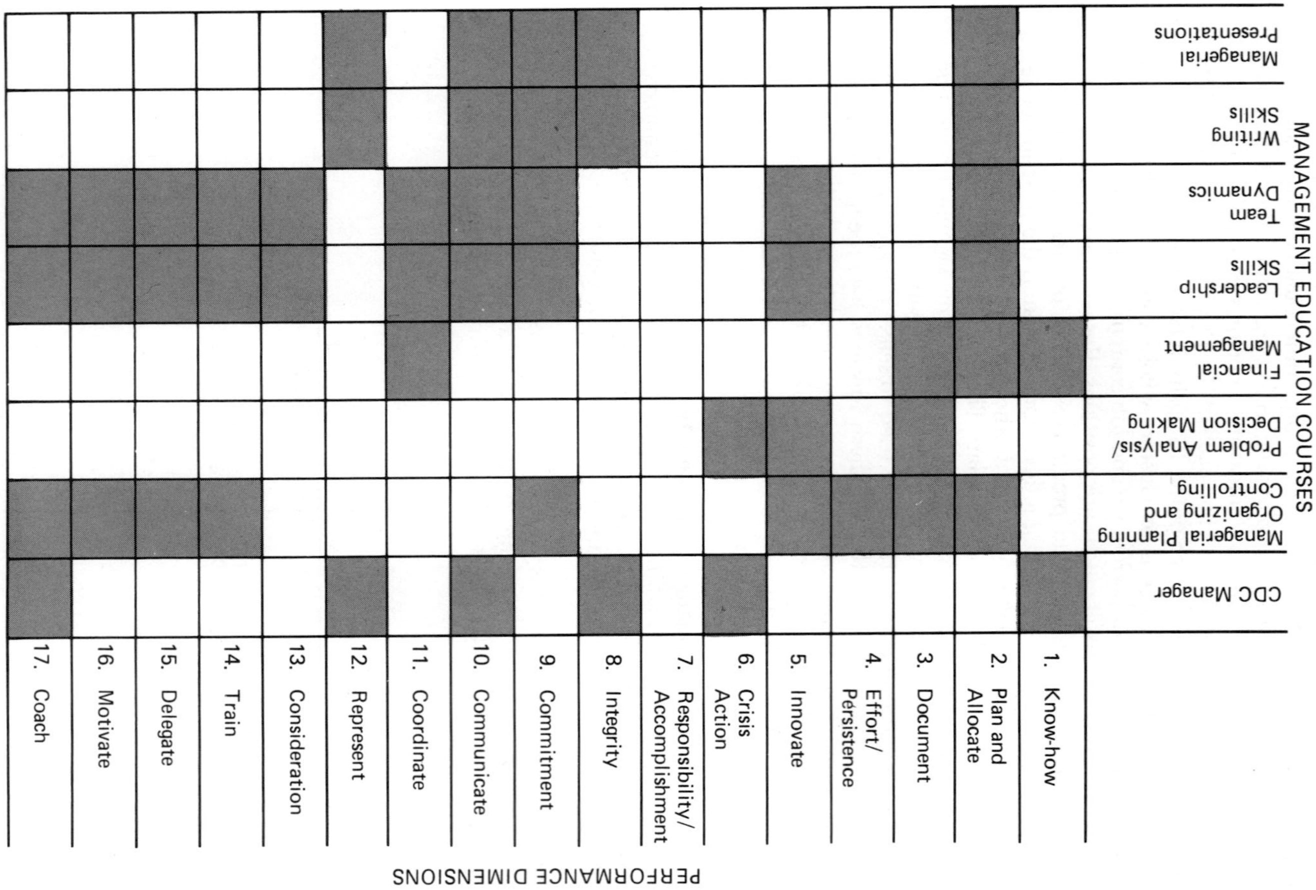

FIGURE 6 Course-Person Matrix Showing Which Performance Dimensions Are Impactable by Which Management Education Courses

Managerial Presentations	Writing Skills	Team Dynamics	Leadership Skills	Financial Management	Problem Analysis/Decision Making	Managerial Planning Organizing and Controlling	CDC Manager		Performance Dimension
				■		■	■	1.	Know-how
■	■	■	■	■		■		2.	Plan and Allocate
				■	■	■		3.	Document
						■		4.	Effort/Persistence
		■	■		■			5.	Innovate
					■		■	6.	Crisis Action
								7.	Responsibility/Accomplishment
■	■						■	8.	Integrity
■	■	■	■			■		9.	Commitment
■	■	■	■				■	10.	Communicate
		■	■					11.	Coordinate
■	■						■	12.	Represent
		■	■					13.	Consideration
		■	■			■		14.	Train
		■	■			■		15.	Delegate
		■	■			■		16.	Motivate
		■	■			■	■	17.	Coach

160

of corporate management education courses is assessed by means of pre- and post-course achievement tests. Paper-and-pencil tests have been used during the pilot phase of course development. This process will be automated as the individualized courses are transformed to a computer-managed instruction mode. External validity means simply the measurement of the impact that development activities have on job performance. By comparing changes in performance of groups completing the management education courses with those of a "no treatment" control group, we will be able to estimate transfer of training. These results will provide empirical feedback for revising the course-person matrix and the trainability index. Finally, a standardized satisfaction measure is administered to all participants completing internal management education courses. This measure, the Learning Experience Evaluation Questionnaire, provides satisfaction scores on such dimensions as content, delivery, context, and outcome. In addition to providing feedback to the management education staff, satisfaction will be investigated as a moderator variable on the internal and external validity of education courses.

Staffing

The staffing process is inextricably linked to job description, performance measurement, and development programs. Effective matches between persons and jobs require knowledge of job characteristics, for example, demands and rewards, and individual characteristics such as skills, needs, and expectations. Selection and training are similarly intertwined. If all persons were perfectly modifiable through training and development, there would be no need for selecting on the basis of individual differences. By contrast, if people could not be changed through development experiences, the organization would have to rely solely on selecting and rewarding those individuals already possessing the desired characteristics.

Figure 7 shows how the descriptive tools and development program can be integrated with the staffing process. Knowledge of the behavioral requirements of a job can be identified by completing the PDQ, profiling the job along the 13 position factors, and working through the job-person matrix to determine the most significant performance dimensions. This information can be used for two purposes. First, it can provide input for writing accurate job descriptions within a standardized framework. Second, it can identify important behavioral skills to use in developing valid selection criteria. What is necessary is to identify the possible predictors of effectiveness along these behavioral dimensions and develop tools which validly measure a person's standing on these dimensions.

Several types of tools may prove to be valid predictors of future effectiveness.

A standardized interview form and procedure should yield quantitative and qualitative information about the person on the important behavioral dimensions.

Improved performance ratings (MPAF) will permit us to investigate the linkages among performance effectiveness in various management positions. Eventually, we might be able to predict future potential on the basis of MPAF profiles.

Preference data (MPPS) may provide input to guide individuals toward those positions whose content most closely matches their preferences. Comparisons of preference and job content profiles may also help to clarify expectations.

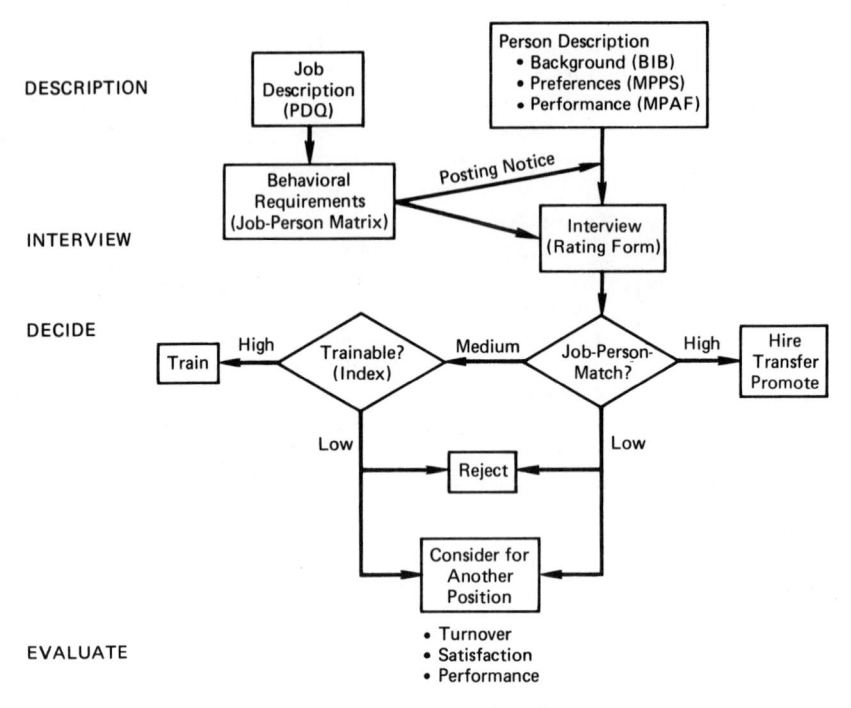

FIGURE 7 *Integrated Staffing Process*

Standardized Biographical Information Blanks (BIB), keyed to previous experiences along the 13 position factors and 17 performance dimensions, should be useful in predicting future success of those with little management experience. Research on BIBs has shown they are capable of such predictions (Owens, 1976).

These and other measures such as situational exercises, tests, and business games have been used by multiple observers in Management Assessment Centers (MAC) to evaluate the management potential of participants. Research on MACs (Howard, 1974; Huck, 1973) have shown great promise.

The purpose of these tools is to provide useful information for determining the degree of job-person match. When there is a high degree of match, the individual should be hired, promoted, or transferred to the target position. When the match is medium, it is appropriate to balance the costs and benefits of training the individual against considering another person. This costs-benefits analysis is too complex to discuss here; it is sufficient to state that the trainability index can be used to determine the "development potential" of the individual. A low job-person match suggests that the individual should be rejected or considered for another position.

As with management development, it is important that staffing decisions be empirically evaluated to determine their impact on the organization and the individual. Ideally, this integrated approach to staffing should improve both the decision making process and actual decisions to reduce undesirable turnover and to optimize individual satisfaction and performance effectiveness.

Compensation

Optimizing job-person matches throughout the organization should have a positive impact on the rewards an individual obtains from his/her job and work environment. Compensation, via equitable systems of job evaluation and pay for performance, also plays a role in enhancing managerial effectivess. The basic tools for objectively describing jobs (PDQ) and performance (MPAF) can facilitate the motivational impact of compensation.

Traditional job evaluation systems describe, compare, and evaluate management positions along such dimensions as knowledge and skill requirements (typically defined by level of education and years of pratical experience), number of people supervised, size of budget, dollar value of products/services responsibilities, autonomy, and contacts. Such information is usually obtained by (1) a job analyst interviewing superiors, peers, and/or subordinates of the target position and then rating the job along each dimension, or (2) a job analyst scoring written descriptions of the target job prepared by the superior. One drawback to this approach is the difficulty of obtaining and processing large amounts of information. That is, the system can only generate and analyze a limited amount of information because of its dependence on trained job analysts. Moreover, as seen in Figure 8, the traditional approach tends to focus on the inputs and, to a lesser extent, outputs side of a systems view of an organization rather than on the throughputs—managerial behavior.

The end result of this approach is to classify jobs into the same grade level on the basis of having similar shares of the input/output pie. That is, the value of a position is determined by how much of the organization's total budget, headcount, and products/services it is responsible for as compared to other positions. However, there is a high risk that such a system can be influenced by factors other than the responsibilities and duties associated with the job—for example, by the personal impact of an incumbent or a superior or by environmental variables—while it ignores job behavior requirements more directly responsible for organizationally valued outputs.

The results of the job description research program showed it was feasible to describe, compare, and classify managerial jobs on the basis of scores along 13 behavior-based position factors. This study also showed that grade levels, established via the existing job evaluation system, could be duplicated 81 percent of the time on the basis of the standardized position profiles. The use of such a standardized position description tool has several advantages:

> Input data can be obtained from a variety of sources without a job analyst. Thus, much more input data can be obtained.
>
> All inputs can be analyzed using a common frame of reference. Thus, inputs from different sources about the same position can be compared and discrepancies can be identified and resolved. Likewise, descriptions of different positions can be readily compared.
>
> All data can be computer scored, thus permitting a number of different jobs to be compared simultaneously.
>
> The descriptive tool (PDQ) can be integrated with other human resource systems, thus utilizing a single, comprehensive job description to provide input to such

applications as staffing, management development, and performance measurement. Consequently, R&D costs and benefits can be shared by the entire system.

It suggests that a position's value to the organization be determined by those *behaviors* required to achieve specific outputs having organizational value.

Research efforts are underway to improve the job description system for such a compensation application. Basing job evaluation procedures more on the behavioral content of positions should result in more content relevance and internal equity in the grading of positions. Thus, positions demanding similar behaviors should be of equal value to the organization and placed in the same salary range. The pay for performance concept then can be realized by basing differential pay within a grade level of measured differences in performance effectiveness (MPAF). By describing and diagnosing managerial effectiveness along multiple performance dimensions, the MPAF provides the organization with an additional leverage point for enhancing its management talent. For example, merit increases can be made contingent on improving performance along one or several of the 17 dimensions.

In sum, the tools for describing positions (PDQ) and job performance (MPAF) can enhance managerial effectiveness by increasing the objectivity of information used for compensation decisions.

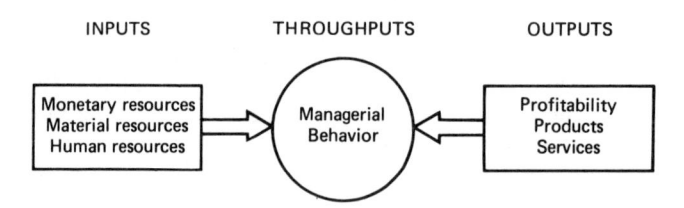

FIGURE 8 *Systems View of an Organization*

IMPLICATIONS

Previous sections have shown how validated tools and procedures that complement each other by drawing on the same or related data bases can permit the different human resource programs/applications in staffing, management development, and compensation to work more synergistically. The benefits of such an integrated approach are based on the following observations.

First, because they originate from different specialties within personnel management, such human resource programs as compensation, training and development, and staffing can suffer from fragmentation and lack of coordination among themselves. This often stems from differences in "jargon," tools, and procedures. However, by having a common R&D effort front-end these programs, bridges in language, tools, and procedures can be built in to assure greater synergy in later program implementation.

Second, R&D efforts and programs/applications must work to complement each other. The problems and needs encountered when implementing and administering programs should spur R&D personnel to devise new tools and procedures for program implementation. As R&D results become available, they should be applied to existing situations, evaluted through actual use, and refined if necessary. In this way, research, development, and application become interrelated steps feeding on each other in an iterative and evolutionary manner.

Third, tools, procedures, and programs/applications cannot be considered in isolation. Just as training and development programs impact staffing practices (and vice versa), a systems view must emphasize the close interrelationship among the tools and procedures for these different human resource functions and must at the same time reflect an integrated R&D approach.

In conclusion, a program that integrates the research, development, and application activities involved in managerial resource utilization can bring personnel management a step closer to standardized hiring, appraisal, development, promotion, and compensation techniques for managerial talent.

Notes

[1] P. J. Pettman, *Psychometric Properties of the Management Development Appraisal Form*, Personnel Research Report No. 94-76 (Minneapolis, Minn.: Control Data Corporation, 1976).

[2] J. C. Rush, *The Feasibility of an External Version of the Individualized Review and Development Planning System*, Personnel Research Report No. 85-76 (Minneapolis, Minn.: Control Data Corporation, 1976).

[3] T. C. Gartland, *Trainability of Managerial Performance Factors*, Personnel Research Report No. 64-75 (Minneapolis, Minn.: Control Data Corporation, 1975).

References

Campbell, J. P., M. D. Dunnette, E. E. Lawler, and K. E. Weick. *Managerial Behavior, Performance and Effectiveness*. New York: McGraw Hill, 1970.

Gartland, T. C., J. C. Rush, W. W. Tornow, and P. R. Pinto. *DICE: Improving the Odds in the Management Development Game*. Paper presented at the Academy of Management, Orlando, Florida, August 1977.

Howard, A. "An Assessment of Assessment Centers," *Academy of Management Journal* 17 (1974), 115-134.

Huck, J. R. "Assessment Centers: A Review of the External and Internal Validities," *Personnel Psychology*, 26 (1973), 191-212.

Owens, W. A. "Background Data," in *Handbook of Industrial and Organizational Psychology*, ed. M. D. Dunnette. Chicago: Rand McNally, 1976.

Tornow, W. W., and P. R. Pinto. "The Development of a Managerial Job Taxonomy: A System for Describing, Classifying, and Evaluating Executive Positions," *Journal of Applied Psychology*, 61 (1976), 410-418.

The Careers of Individuals and Organizations

John J. Leach

Regardless of one's opinion about the quality or value of the great educational push in our country starting in the late 1940s, one inescapable conclusion is that *education elevates expectations.* The more we learn (or believe we have learned), the more we want. As a result we are witnessing today significant shifts in values in what people expect from their work and careers. This paper examines the notion and nature of careers, beginning with the career of the individual, moving next to the career of the organization, and concluding with a section pertaining to career management systems. The central question, for both researcher and human resource professional, is, In terms of a career, precisely what is it about a person's movement through an organization that produces satisfaction, challenge, growth, and commitment for the individual and superior performance and contribution for the organization? In short, how can individual and organizational growth be optimized?

THE CAREER OF THE INDIVIDUAL

It is not an exaggeration to say that for many people, career progress represents a "psychological report card" of how well they are doing in life. Too few people appear satisfied with their "marks." More significantly, as one's career unfolds so, too, does a person's life. Sad to say, unfulfilled dreams and untapped talents seem to represent the norm, not the exception. Peter Drucker's observation that many people "retire on-the-job" years before the official act is verifiable and costly—to both individuals and the organizations employing them (Drucker, 1968).

A career is one of the most fundamental transactions between the individual and the organization. Unlike other work contracts which are explicit, career contracts are typically unclear or suspect and certainly changing over time. It is ironic that what is most precious to many individuals insofar as work is concerned—that is, their career—is given the least attention by the organization, and often surprisingly little conscious study by the individual.

John Leach, "The Careers of Individuals and Organizations," adapted from John Leach, "The Notion and Nature of Careers," *The Personnel Administrator, 22,* 7 (September 1977), 49-55; "The Career of the Organization," *The Personnel Administrator, 22,* 8 (October 1977), 34-39; "Career Management: Focusing on Human Resources," *The Personnel Administrator, 22,* 9 (November 1977), 59-66.

Sources of Career Behavior

Alfred Adler was the first to note that "all life is movement" (Adler, 1958). This somewhat cryptic statement refers to human motivation. Adler assumed that human movement was toward accomplishing three life tasks: being productive in one's occupation, having satisfying love/family relationships, and being able to contribute to the larger community of mankind via a social interest in others. I would add two additional tasks when the notion of careers is discussed, namely, to establish our worthwhileness to ourselves and others, and, to find the unique meaning we intend to give to our lives.

In Adler's view, all human behavior has purpose or, in other words, is goal directed. Furthermore, all comparisons are social comparisons, and successes or failures are defined in terms of our relationships to others in our life space. The goals that we set in life and for our career may be realistic or unrealistic; however, their intent is to propel us through life (and the career) in search for personal significance among others—to satisfy certain fundamental needs for belonging and acceptance. In other words, an individual's goals are blueprints allowing that person to move from a perceived "felt-minus" (in regard to social relationships) to a "felt-plus." If this drive toward independence and superiority becomes overdetermined, that is, competitive urges take over and permanently replace cooperative behavior, the person becomes neurotic. In Adler's view, all neuroses stemmed from interpersonal malfunctioning and, in the final analysis, from excessive vanity. Cooperation, not competition, is the hallmark characteristic of the healthy, mature person. But how does a person determine whether his/her career goals are realistic and psychologically healthy? Figure 1 provides some hints.

A careful examination of Figure 1 reveals the complex, dynamic, and highly interactive processes involved in analyzing career behavior (Leach, 1977). Three major sets of variables affect our life and career movement: heredity, shaping factors, and ages/stages factors. In the process of growing up, we gain some insight into our limitations and potentials toward certain physical, mental, and interpersonal competencies. The shaping factors noted in the figure can be beneficial or detrimental, depending upon how well these socializing impacts prepare us for life and work. The ages/stages factors account for the variability and changing nature of people over time. In adolescence and early adulthood, our interests, attitudes, and values are frequently borrowed or added by the interventions of others and/or their reactions to us. In later life, some or much of this "excess baggage" is shed and a clearer perception of who we are and where we want to go in life results.

It is difficult indeed to focus sharply on who we are until we are approximately 30 years old simply because it requires time to experience and evaluate the impact of heredity, shaping, and ages/stages factors. Significantly, just at this time when one's career is gathering steam and momentum, a person may begin to question and reexamine career direction and progress.

Throughout one's working life, self-esteem and career self-concept grow together. For the person who commits him or herself totally to the occupation life task (at the expense of the love/family and society life tasks), self-esteem and career self-concept become indistinguishable. (In many instances, such persons run the risk of becoming "workaholics.") There is a dynamic interrelationship between self-esteem and career self-concept, and this manifests itself in the career directions that we set for ourselves and the level of aspiration toward which we mobilize our energy and effort. Quite early in life, these are internal career notions only. We have not had sufficient time to reality-test these self-perceptions. When we launch our career, however, we can begin to experiment with actual career roles in the real world of work.

These internal career notions are then altered and modified by the feedback we receive from the real world, a series of perceptions we in turn filter through our needs of the moment and current life stage. These needs form a hierarchy (Maslow, 1954), with psysiological and safety demands forming the base, social, and ego needs constituting the second tier, and the need for self-actualization—becoming what we were intended to become—comprising the apex. Depending upon the person and career examined, and the needs and life stages being encountered, either a blurred or a clear perception of the career universe emerges. The person-in-the-career world (where the person fits and does not fit) also emerges typically in general fashion early in the career and more specifically later in the career.

When the individual is planning a career, consciously or otherwise, the early shapings continue to play a role in the career plan (goal(s) and subgoals) and in the career timetable. These are referred to in the figure as career expectations. The person is constantly grappling with what he/she wants to do versus the "shoulds" and "oughts." The resolution decided upon by the person represents the career conclusions or the foundation for the career plan structure. The productive career plan takes into consideration one's primary career anchor, that is, best fit between the selected career path and the person's overall mix of unique abilities, interests, and values (Schein, 1975).

Bosses managing the careers of others typically see only the behavior exhibited in the spout of the funnel in Figure 1. Management is frequently at a loss to explain what on the surface appears to be confused or even purposeless behavior. Clearly, it is oblivious to the fact that a great deal of psychological material processed much earlier continues to affect career behavior. This behavior—related to career goal-setting, decision making, strategy/tactics, and the methods and styles of executing the career plan—makes *psychological* sense to the individual even if management cannot fathom the *common sense* behind the plan.

The figure is completed by feedback processes, the first directed at outcomes. All elements of the career plan must meet the test of either success or failure.

The significance of the outcome with respect to the person's internal career notions (self-esteem and career self-concept) depends upon how much the person has learned from either outcome. This new learning—if learning indeed has occurred—alters or modifies the person's behavior in subsequent career roles and career situations. The cycle continues as described previously, with new career plans being filtered through existing needs and perceptions of the career universe and the person's place in it, leading to new (or possibly, old) career expectations and conclusions, leaving the funnel in the form of revised or new career goals. One early conclusion that can be drawn for the organization is that the more an organization can "program" career successes for its people, the more positive self-esteem it can count upon in its ranks.

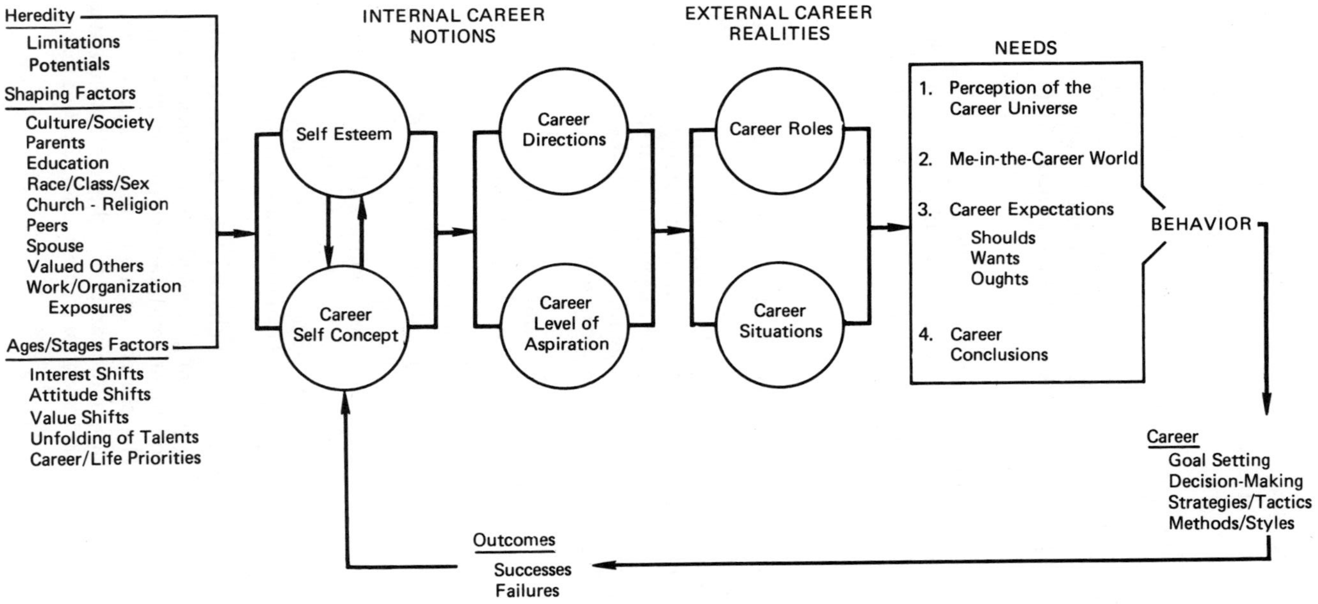

FIGURE 1 *Sources of Our Career Behavior*

The Career Line

Career behavior varies depending upon what phase of the career the person is contemplating. It is useful to look at the career as an unfolding movement line or behavioral pattern. The typical career line can be described as follows.

Career exploration. These random or calculated behaviors are designed to answer the question, What am I going to do with my life? This phase is triggered at numerous stages in life, not solely during preadult or early adult ages, although this is the time of its first appearance. Career choice is the issue here, and frequently people make choices on incomplete, faulty, or even erroneous information.

Career preparation. This refers to one or more educational experiences of varying duration and composition. Career planning traps can include undereducation, over-education, or mis-education in terms of the actual unfolding of a career path. For all practical purposes, this phase constitutes a more specific step in career exploration.

Career entry. Gaining access to the desired career role and career situation is the next phase. Once entry has been made into an organization, it is assumed that the organization will provide career roles and situations that are satisfying, that is, do not depart too widely from the person's internal career notions. One common career planning trap at this stage is prematurely to give up on a chosen career direction because of a hostile or uncaring organization. The individual unwisely decides to leave the career field when, in fact, the career is suitable but the organization is an inappropriate starting point.

Getting established. Apprenticeship and "dues-paying" behavior is activated in this phase. The individual does the best he/she can to incorporate the organization's norms and values into career behavior in order to be accepted. He or she expends energy trying to decode the organization's "career secrets"— for example, which assignments represent career launch pads—in order to move swiftly out of this phase. A common trap in this phase is for the individual uncritically to accept *all* the organization's norms and values, at the expense of submerging one's real feelings and creative reactions to problems and opportunities in the work place. As with the first two phases, career entry and getting established tend to overlap and can be considered together as one phase.

Getting ahead. Pure advancement behavior takes hold in this phase. Career "side-bets," or contingency planning, sometimes emerges. Career-vigilance behavior (in terms of advancement) and career risk/returns are calculated, consciously or otherwise. The search for a mentor or sponsor may also be involved. A person in this phase of the career is highly motivated but also highly anxious; the race is on and there may be only one winner. For this reason, one may encounter executive "burn-outs" during this phase.

Career Stabilization. The plateau of "hold pattern" is characteristic of this phase (Ference, Stoner, and Warren, 1977). Internal career notions and external career realities very probably clash unless the plateau is perceived as a satisfying career option. The first glimmer of the second career may intrude. If concern begins to mount with this plateau, career ambivalence sets in. Life goals are now more seriously examined. The mid-career crisis case is sometimes identified in this phase.

Plateau Resolution. Depending upon the plateau solution selected, the career cycle is either concluded or repeated. The conflict resolution phase, concluding the cycle, has at least four solutions:

Retire-on-the-job behavior, or the fixation pattern

Involuntary career-line exit; that is, the person either becomes obsolete and is terminated, the organization disappears, or the career field itself disappears

Voluntary career-line exit; that is, the person leaves the career blockage or plateau situation and pursues an identical career path in a different organization

Radical career-line exit; that is, the person makes a bold departure in career line and seeks out a distinctively different career, an authentic second career, either within the employing organization or elsewhere

The notion of a career line helps to maintain perspective when studying careers. *Career problems are simply not generalizable.* Therefore, the strategies and programs used to resolve career problems necessarily must vary to fit the case. The organization should be absolutely certain that the programs selected strike at the appropriate phases of career-line problems, otherwise there will be very little return on the investments made. One quick example relates to the use of "fast track" and "promising" lists by organizations. Career development programs frequently focus on the getting ahead phase when a strong cost-benefit case can be made to defend greater spending of programming dollars on career stabilization issues and the employees who fall into this category.

CAREER EPISODES AND NOVELS

It is easy enough to become bewildered by the complexity of career problems. Everything seems to interact with everything else. Indeed, the core problem is that individuals come in every career shape and form imaginable. The organization, on the other hand, is more fixed in its structures, job designs, and other operating mechanisms and finds itself at a loss to accommodate this enormous variety in employee career appetites. There *are* some constants, however, in the career per se and, when combined, these form what will be referred to as career episodes and novels.

One constant is *movement*, which has three components: direction, velocity, and distance. As one navigates through a career, there is definitely a directional factor that can be discerned and analyzed. All career movement has direction (if "going nowhere" is accepted as one plausible movement pattern). The direction of one's career is initiated by the individual's self-determined career goals. Many of the career problems people have relate to unhealthy goal setting; these goals may be impulsive or compulsive, irrational or insatiable, vindictive or egocentric. Often such individuals have little or no conscious insight into the maladaptive directions they set for themselves and wonder why their career progress is stunted or unsatisfying.

The second facet of movement is *velocity*. Some career movements are faster than others. For example, a person can move rather rapidly through the getting established phase but falter or decelerate during the getting ahead phase. The career "burn-out," for example, is a victim of too much velocity. In this context, the words *promotion* and *demotion* take on added psychological significance. In velocity terms, the person may be experiencing "pro-motion" when shunted laterally or even demoted momentarily (if this fits the person's unique career movement needs). On the other hand, the promotion to an assignment falling outside of the person's unique career movement needs may actually represent "de-motion" in career velocity terms. There is at least a little wisdom to Leach's Law, "Getting ahead is not always moving forward," when applied to career planning problems.

The third and final component of movement is *distance*. What is important to remember here is that there are both objective and psychological aspects of career distance. One example of the objective case is when a technologist moves so deeply into a speciality that his/her contribution to the organization becomes increasingly narrow. The seasoned engineer who falls into this trap is only one example of how lack of perspective can lead to insufficient career planning. The psychological aspects of distance relate to the subjective feelings a person has about his/her career. Sometimes an individual will express regret or disappointment when, in fact, significant others (peers, mentors, family, and community members) see the same career as preeminently successful. Distorted career goals generally account for the sense of failure some individuals experience when reviewing career distance—that is, overall progress.

In addition to movement considerations, two remaining major dimensions appear common to all careers. The *career outcome*, which may be either successful or unsuccessful for each of the career-line phases, is perhaps self-explanatory. However, just as with career distance, outcome also has objective and subjective components. Because success is self-defined, a career outcome pronounced as successful by others may be perceived as failure by the person experiencing the career.

The more difficult career constant to describe is the intervening step between the career movement components and career outcomes. I refer to this as a *transition state*. In broadest terms, this represents the objective and subjective costs and demands of career movement. We might think of the transition state as representing the investments and sacrifices (financial and personal) that the person is prepared to make in the pursuit of career advancement. The vital questions here relate to such issues as career goal attractiveness and perceived ability to make both the sacrifices required and also to develop the necessary behaviors to assume the new responsibility. Finally, the person must weigh the probability that the career outcome will indeed be positive and satisfying.

One example of a transition state dilemma relates to the technically trained person who senses that if the career is to advance, he/she will have to consider management, which in this instance also involves returning to college in the pursuit of an MBA degree. Is the career step of "manager" really in his/her best interests? Is there time, money, and energy available to pursue the MBA? Will he or she be able to complete the program successfully and, if so, actually be able to think and act as managers are expected to behave? Finally, will the individual actually get the promotion and find the new role satisfying? The career transition state notion just stated certainly bears resemblance to Victor Vroom's goal-path or expectancy theory of motivation (Vroom, 1964).

These hypothesized career constants (movement, transition states, and outcomes) are crucial career planning data for the individual and significant career development data for the organization. The data, when properly integrated, form a Career Thematic Matrix that relates to career episodes and novels, as outlined in Figure 2.

Examining a given row in Figure 2, say, the Getting Ahead phase, across the various career constants will yield a career episode related to the person's advancement behaviors. Examining a given column, say, the direction career constant, across the various phases of the career line, will yield the person's characteristic approach to goal setting. These data would be generated from interviews, observations, questionnaires, or records, and when the matrix was completely analyzed, a career novel or story would emerge, to include both objective and subjective views of a person's career from start to finish.

A. Career Line Phases
I. Career Exploration/Preparation
II. Career Entry/Getting Established
III. Career Advancement
IV. Career Stabilization
V. Plateau Resolutions/Exits
(Fixation, Involuntary, Voluntary, Radical)

B. Career Constants
I. Direction (Dr)
II. Velocity (V)
III. Distance (Ds)
IV. Transition States (T)
V. Outcomes (O)

C. Career Thematic Matrix

	(Dr)	(V)	(Ds)	(T)	(O)
I					
II					
III			XXX°		
IV					
V					

FIGURE 2 *Career Episodes and the Career Novel*

°xxx = Narratives of career episodes. The box indicated might contain an episode related to a getting ahead strategy, perhaps a consideration of how far a person should go in a personal career path, for example, engineering versus a shift to management.

It has been said that God created mankind because He loves stories. Given that the career is life-unfolding, it is legitimate and useful to examine careers as if they were novels. The content of the story would relate to the sum total of the person's work-life choices, insofar as these are relatively unconstrained. In some cases, the career story might even resemble a picaresque novel, and, in an optimistic vein, may overcome a drab beginning to lead to an exciting mid-career plot.

Also, viewing the career as a story compels researcher and practitioner alike to focus upon the most significant stage in which these stories are located, namely, the organization. Organizations have the option to introduce richness and variety into the work environment, or they can elect to sharply limit when and how employees will execute careers. Conceptually, this schema suggests that there are as many different career stories as there are people—and organizations. Central career themes could vary limitlessly, such as going places, going nowhere, the misfit, the victim, fear of failure, fear of success, underachievement, dilettante, avenger, and so forth.

SUMMARY

It is clear that not to study careers is to miss a significant opportunity to learn what facilitates and obstructs individual and organizational growth in periods of both change and stability. Not to study careers is to miss the opportunity to investigate the limits (and limitations) of growth, technology, and efficiency. Careers impact upon people's destinies. This implies that the organization must give employees the opportunity and wherewithal to intelligently question and evaluate career growth alternatives for "goodness of fit."

Good careers drive out bad careers: good careers make better organizations. As an organization learns to accommodate employee career strivings, it simultaneously learns how to become more effective in human resource planning and utilization. The human resources professional is properly positioned in the organization to deal effectively with these issues: career planning *is* human resources planning; career development *is* organization development. The human resources executive can begin these efforts by taking a fresh look at what is virtually always overlooked, the *career of the organization*.

THE CAREER OF THE ORGANIZATION

Just as people have careers and career lines, so also do organizations. Organizations change over time. These changes are sometimes barely perceptible but, nonetheless, significant. Forgetting for the moment the potential negative impact these shifts have on individual careers, let us consider the organization's dilemma: The organization is noticeably caught by surprise. It finds that it has made and is making numerous costly human resource planning errors. A linear extrapolation of the past no longer suffices as a root strategy. What escaped everyone's notice were subtle changes in organizational mission and dynamics, including the organization's inability to sharply focus upon the demands and problems of new or changing external environments. In brief, the organization failed to anticipate, then failed to accommodate to, emerging shifts in its career line.

CAREER STRUCTURES AND CULTURES

The organization chart is a first approximation of the *career structures* made available to employees to satisfy career objectives and goals. The chart, however, is certainly not the total story. We must look to the informal organization and its dynamic interactions before we can truly appreciate the actual career structures.

In analyzing informal organizations, several *career cultures* invariably emerge. Each culture is described by its own preferred values, knowledge, styles, and beliefs that set it apart from other cultures existing within the organization. As an example, accountants compared to salesmen—or for that matter, scientists compared to managers—frequently represent different career cultures within the same organization. The person embedded within a given culture will attempt to emulate key figures in order to gain acceptance and credibility, and later on the person will look to or depend upon the resources of that culture to act as a launch pad for career advancement.

Because these career cultures must work under the same roof, each culture, to a greater or lesser degree, subscribes to a common core of organizational practice and behavior. In other words, there is always a prevailing philosophy in any organization, and this dominant mode has the strongest impact upon who will or will not advance in the career.

CAREER POWER SYSTEMS

Not all career cultures compete with each other or with the dominant culture. Some coexist and others cooperate. The basis upon which a given career culture decides whether to compete, coexist, or cooperate depends upon the perceived outcomes with respect to *career power*: the power to propel people into more remunerative and higher status roles.

If we now substitute the words *department, managerial function,* and *managerial levels* for the word *culture,* we can begin to understand one ever-present fundamental factor in organizational conflict, namely, *career power battles and skirmishes.* Because career power systems never lie dormant, there is constant jockeying by all cultures for career positioning and leverage for advancement. This is an ongoing preoccupation that consumes considerable psychic and organizational energy.

Major policy decisions rarely receive unanimous acceptance by an organization's career cultures, especially when a high-level decision upsets the current balance of power. Career floors and career ceilings suddenly shift and, in some instances, what were bountiful career opportunities now actually might be buried. Suddenly agitated, all career cultures may assume a ready-alert posture. These facts-of-life are what make the study of the career of the organization so imperative.

It has been said that to be ignorant of history is to run the risk of repeating the mistakes of the past. In attempting to understand an organization's present level of functioning and its human resource problems, one must first have access to the organization's past, a history of the evolution of its career structures, cultures, and power systems. There is an organizational memory which at times resembles the state of the *collective unconscious*, difficult to penetrate or to analyze but nonetheless exerting a felt presence. How does one unlock the door to this career of the organization? The following exercise, developed by the writer, and presented in Exhibit 1 has been useful in revealing stages and demarcation points in the organization's career line. It also has been effective in identifying career next-step departures from that line (Leach, 1977).

Obviously, this technique involves a good deal of projective input. As you might expect, people in different departments, serving different functions at various levels frequently view the career of the organization differently. Consensual as well as divergent points of view represent important data for subsequent analysis and study. In some settings, there is a consensus of opinion regarding certain periods of the organization's career but a lack of consensus on other stages.

Exhibit 1 The Career of the Organization Exercise

Reflect upon the career line and history of your organization (as you have observed it over the years, heard about it from old-timers, and/or as you simply have sensed it to be). Then follow the directions and answer the questions below.

I. Sort the history of the organization (Career Line) into *stages*. Assign descriptive labels or category headings to each stage. The categories selected can include any terms you deem appropriate: A life cycle, evolving product/market trends, changing managerial philosophies, shifting functional dominance (for example engineering to marketing), and so forth.

You are encouraged to use imagination when you sort the organization's Career Line into these categories. For example, one organization was likened to the four movements of a symphony. Select only those labels that best describe the *unique* history of your organization.

II. Next, write a paragraph or two that summarizes to your satisfaction each organizational career stage (including the present stage).

III. Now note how these changes in the Career Line have affected you and others in the firm—for example, with respect to recruitment/selection, morale, job satisfaction, the careers of incumbent employees, training/development practices, climate, business policy, day-to-day practices, managerial controls, delegation, employee attitudes/relations, or power issues between departments.

IV. Anticipate or predict what you think will be the next step in the Career Line of your organization. What impact will this new career stage have upon you and others in the firm? On human resource policies and practices?

V. Retrospectively, what human resource planning mistakes has the organization made? Why did the organization fall into the traps that it did?

VI. What human resource options are open to your organization that will best accommodate the next step in your organization's Career Line? Discuss the pros and cons of each option.

In other organizations, there may be general agreement on all basic themes and stages of the career line, but variations on each theme may be well worth exploring. But the real power of the exercise rests upon its ability to focus sharply on the organization's present status and its career line in the immediate future and, in so doing, to reveal what this implies for career utilization planning and human resources strategy.

CAREER UTILIZATION PLANNING

Figure 3 represents a human resources strategy map. This presentation in terms of a flow diagram is useful in counteracting the professional myopia of planners that sometimes minimizes innovation in career utilization strategy and planning. One can readily see from the figure that there is literally a stream of events bearing upon the careers of individuals and organizations; accordingly, there are numerous points where a human resource planning treatment or intervention can be made.

The figure is relatively self-explanatory. An attraction process takes place whereby the individual and the organization decide who is both interesting and interested in a career opportunity. Many human resource planning problems can be traced to a company's initially poor reputation in the labor market. Once serious negotiations are concluded and the candidate passes through the screening net (the vertical dotted line in the figure), the candidate and the organization mutually decide there is a goodness of fit and the candidate obtains membership. At this point, the organization has created a new career resource.

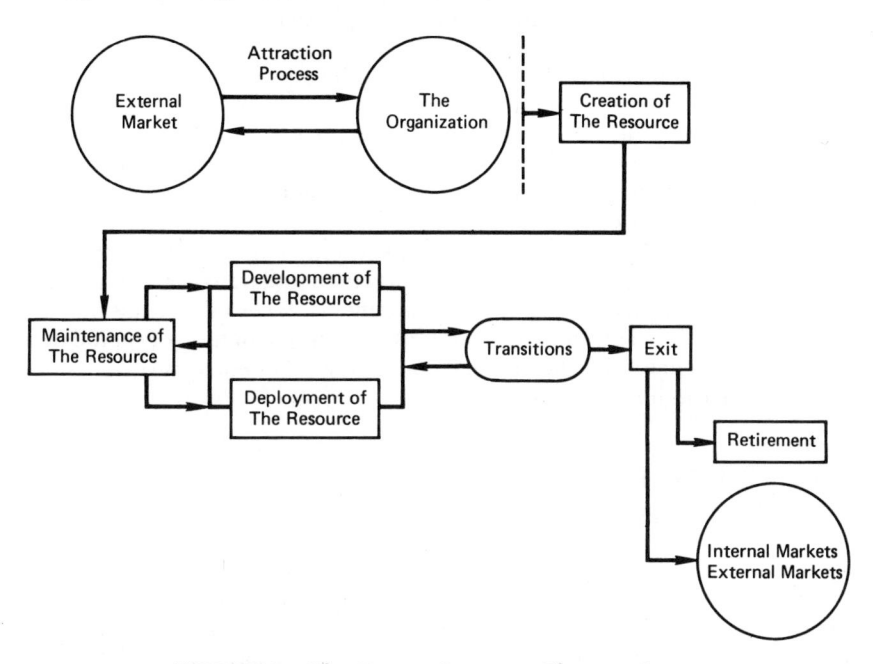

FIGURE 3 *The Human Resources Planning Stream*

Once aboard, each new human resource makes financial and psychological demands on the firm. When the demands are satisfied, the chances increase that the new employees will elect to maintain membership, hence the organization retains these human resources. The issues here all boil down to degree of career satisfaction. Maintenance issues relate to compensation, of course, but also to quality of work life, existing climate and leadership styles, communications, and challenge value of tasks and projects.

In time, most human resources will be found wanting, and development and/or deployment treatments are triggered in order to prepare people for added responsibility. Knowledge or skill training, growth-oriented performance appraisal, and assessment centers are examples of the development treatment. Career intention surveys, career planning programs, job rotation, and formalized mentoring programs are examples of the deployment treatment. The mere activation of development or deployment strategies is assumed to satisfy a greater measure of the employee's career needs, hence the feedback arrow to maintenance.

Development and/or deployment treatments are expected to improve an employee's skill or knowledge level or ability to relate interpersonally. When this expectation is met, the employee is in the midst of a significant transition, say, from technician to supervisor. When such improvements do not materialize, the transition phase becomes a focal point for analysis to determine why there has been no return for these career-utilization investments. One explanation might be that despite organizational investment, the employee is being underutilized or perhaps even incorrectly utilized. Over the span of an employee's career, he or she will need repeated training and career movement treatments, hence the feedback arrow from the transition phase to development or deployment.

So far, the flowchart has painted a rather optimistic picture of the capabilities of the individual and the organization to satisfy their respective needs and demands, both economic and psychological. This obviously is not always the case. There has to be an exit phase to accommodate retirement, of course, but also to account for mismatches over time. In these instances, the employee exits either to the internal labor market (continues the career elsewhere within the organization) or to the external labor market, either through voluntary or involuntary turnover. In other instances, as when an individual cannot or will not respond to development or deployment treatments, he or she may be allowed to "retire on the job." This may be viewed as an example of human capital depletion or obsolescence, with the organization failing to optimize the career utilization value of the human resource.

CAREER UTILIZATION STRATEGY PLANNING

There are many more strategy planning points available to the human resource planner than are typically recognized. When the career line of an organization shifts, tried and true planning approaches of the past may yield little or no returns. Pure strategies, in such cases, have been labeled *one-phase focusing*—for example, investing the major part of the human resource budget in improving the mechanism of the strategy plan, or pouring virtually all investments into the maintenance phase. Mixed strategies, on the other hand, take into account a *combination* of phases in the human resource stream, then set priorities and invest money, manpower, time, and energy accordingly. Some brief illustrations follow.

Creation/Maintenance Strategies. Let us assume that high-priced, well-educated new resources turn over in less than 18 months, well before the organization has realized a return on its investment. To be sure, recruitment sources and specifications need to be audited. In addition, however, the maintenance strategy needs review, for example, in the areas of compensation, quality of work life, communications, and job enrichment.

Creation/Development Strategies. This comparison focuses upon make-or-buy decisions. Let us assume that in the near future the firm will need more technical human resources. It must, therefore, determine whether to bring in this talent already fully trained and seasoned or opt to "grow its own," via increased investment in training incumbents. It might also decide to use an optimal mix approach.

Development/Deployment Strategies. Assume the organization is taking a jaundiced view of what it perceives as heavy training investments with a seemingly poor return. Is the organization unwittingly training people for career paths soon to become obsolete? Would more learning take place if imaginative career pathing were introduced rather than totally relying on classroom training? Are people properly utilized after the development treatments are applied?

SUMMARY

This section has attempted to build the case that shifts in an organization's career line may have serious negative impacts for the careers of incumbent employees. What previously represented desired work-related skills, styles, and values suddenly lacks organizational validity. Career utilization planning should be accorded special attention in times of nonlinear career-line shifts of the organization. But it is evident that this attention should be ongoing because most human resource pools are ineptly utilized. The three major sins of poor human resource planning—shortages, surpluses, and blockages—closely monitor the career of the organization.

CAREER MANAGEMENT SYSTEMS

Many organizations routinely grind out recruitment and succession plans, manpower audits and forecasts, training needs, profiles, and other analyses but do so in a vacuum. This vacuum develops from numerous communications gaps. The most noticeable gap is the one that typically exists between the human resource planners and the business planners of the firm. The most severe failure on the part of management is ignorance of employee career intentions. All too often human resources planning is focused in one direction only—downwards.

The net result of such downward planning is that the data base for the human resource plan is either incomplete or distorted. Human resource plans in these organizations bear little resemblance to the actual career plans of employees and/or to the changing career line of the organization. An effective career management system can close these communications gaps, and in the process a more realistic and complete human resource plan will emerge.

CAREER MANAGEMENT SYSTEMS DEFINED

A career management system relates to the planning, organization, direction, control, and ongoing evaluation of programs and strategies designed to improve the career utilization of employees (Leach, 1977). The system's programs and services are designed to increase upward and downward communications within the firm. The objective is to better inform both parties to the career contract (individual and organization) regarding each other's intentions and capabilities, mutual contributions, and responsibilities in order to optimize growth. Figure 4 outlines several of the more significant requirements, ingredients, and interactions found in the effective career management system.

To properly interpret Figure 4, the reader should visualize the system as a *seesaw*. The employee and the organization represent the participants occupying each side of the plank. The fulcrum, to be discussed shortly, acts as the balancing point. Take away this fulcrum and the career management system disappears.

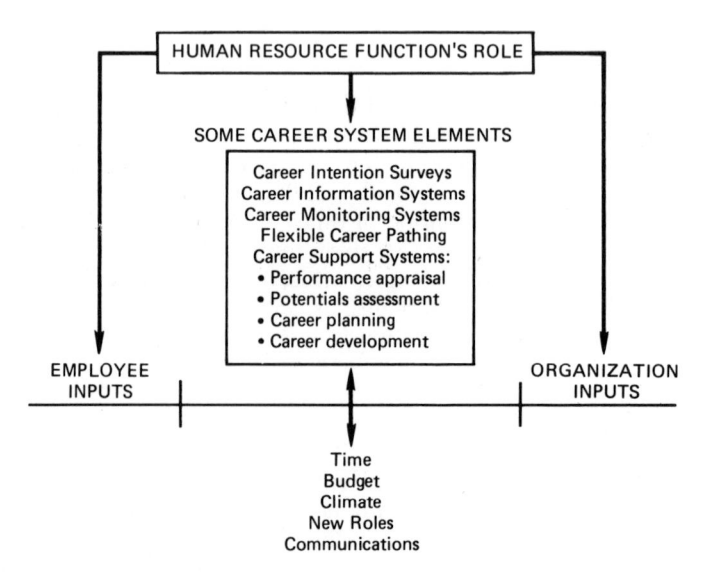

```
                    HUMAN RESOURCE FUNCTION'S ROLE

                    SOME CAREER SYSTEM ELEMENTS

                    Career Intention Surveys
                    Career Information Systems
                    Career Monitoring Systems
                    Flexible Career Pathing
                    Career Support Systems:
                    • Performance appraisal
                    • Potentials assessment
                    • Career planning
                    • Career development

   EMPLOYEE                                    ORGANIZATION
   INPUTS                                      INPUTS

                            Time
                            Budget
                            Climate
                            New Roles
                            Communications
```

FIGURE 4   *Ingredients of a Career Management System*

In our illustration, the seesaw is in equilibrium; that is, the system is in operation and is working satisfactorily. For this to occur, numerous exchanges must have already occurred between the employee and the organization. For example, planning inputs, information that the organization needs from its employees, are developed when the seesaw is activated downward by the organization. The desired data are thereby communicated from employees to the organization. When the seesaw is activated downward on the employee side, career planning inputs important to employees are communicated from the organization to employees.

As this seesaw activity continues, more and more career and human resources data are accumulated. These data then need to be sorted and batched, and transformed into usable information. Once done, this information becomes the major channels through which the career management system operates. These channels ultimately are translated into career management programs and services (see the figure).

Figure 4 gives us a new perspective on the human resources function. According to this model, the human resources group functions as an *internal consultant* to two clients—the individual and the organization. It is further assumed that human resources personnel will take the initiative in providing a base for communications, in determining the communications channels, and in periodically activating the seesaw to generate data. In brief, the human resources function is assumed to represent the *prime mover* of the system; its task is to set into motion, monitor, evaluate, and improve the system to clients' satisfaction.

SYSTEM PREREQUISITES

A review of the five fulcrum requirements of an effective system (Figure 4) reveals that these building blocks represent the most difficult work for the human resources people designing the system. The evolving career programs/services, while requiring some ingenuity, typically fall into place once the proper foundation for the system is laid.

1. Time. The organization must be prepared to free people's time from day-to-day operating matters so that they may analyze and study career utilization problems. While size and diversification represent the major factors in estimating the time needed to install the system, frequently the task can encompass a full calendar year.

2. Budget. Budgets focus effort and energy to ensure that certain things in the organization get done. What is not budgeted for usually never receives any organizational attention. A budget for the study builds commitment and urgency to develop a strong career management system.

3. Climate. This requirement refers to a shared commitment of both individual and organization to the worthwhileness of career utilization efforts. If the climate is one of mutual distrust or disdain, even large amounts of time and money will not produce an effective career management system.

4. *New Roles.* The new role of the human resources function has already been explicated. But there are new roles for the "users" of the system to learn as well. Employees, for example, must learn how to plan their career, how to assess their market worth and career progress, and how to communicate career intentions to the organization. In this system, one basic assumption is that the individual becomes the *manager of his or her career.* The system is expected to provide resources but it is up to the individual to learn how to *negotiate* the career. This can have alarming consequences for that individual who has heretofore delegated personal career management to the organization. Under this new rubric, the individual who is disappointed with career progress or direction is expected to confront the organization with this preception *and* with a plan for change.

On the organization side, management must learn how to relinquish the role of "boss" and feel its way into the role of mentor. Also, at times, managers must accept that they know less regarding subordinates' potential (compared to their present level of performance) and allow other elements of the system to evaluate potential and career direction.

The list goes on and on. Will the hoarding of talent be penalized? Is the organization truly prepared to communicate in detail how people become candidates for promotion, why the winner won, why the losers in the competition lost? Will managers really be rewarded for developing promotables?

5. *Communications.* Users of the system must clearly understand the various elements. Questions such as, Who is responsible for what? How is the system accessed? or What can be expected from each career program and service? must have clear answers for users, set out in a policy statement. Also, since the system generates a great deal of data over a period of time, "privacy" requirements dictate that the rules of accessibility to information be laid out well in advance.

SYSTEM PROGRAMS/SERVICES

When the foundation has been secured, the organization's next step in its career line targeted, and the high-priority career concerns and needs of both individuals and the organization researched, the programs and services of the system can then be set into place. The list of career system elements in Figure 4 is not intended to be exhaustive although the items noted are representative.

Career Intention Surveys. Periodic surveys of employees' career interests and plans are imperative to the system. Information is generated via questionnaires or interviews. The content relates to employees' opinions toward existing recruitment, selection, and upgrading practices, toward opportunities for career progression and the present rate of perceived utilization, as well as impressions of job design, adequacy of training, and so on. Most importantly, employees are asked to disclose career plans, particularly short-range goals.

These surveys frequently yield surprising results. Some employees are found to have no career plans; others are quite happy to stabilize in their present positions; some are more interested in lateral movements, and some are more interested in ladders and paths different from the ones they are presently pursuing.

Career Information Systems. This element is intended to provide employees with the necessary data to make career plans and decisions. One aspect is the provision of career manuals that describe the realities of jobs (as opposed to the sometimes sterile job descriptions new hires inherit). Information related to career ladder options and how one can switch ladders represents another package. Full or modified job posting programs fall into this category.

The test of the adequacy of this element of the system is whether or not employees fully understand the upgrading process and the existing array of career options and are given guidance in how to use and act upon this information when planning their careers.

Career Monitoring Systems. This refers to any program or service that can alert the organization to career plateau or obsolescence situations. One example is routine monitoring of those employees with five or more years in the same assignment to ascertain their feelings about this potential plateau situation. Turnover analyses and exit interview data also fall into this category, especially when effort is made to identify exactly why these career contracts have broken down. Obsolescence audits conducted by outside experts represent another program in this category.

Flexible Career Pathing. Periodic review of the content of jobs should be undertaken to ascertain whether any subtle shifts in demands and/or scope have occurred. These analyses also should determine if new paths and ladders better describe the firm's actual activity. Even if these are deemed adequate, the search should continue for new paths and ladders that aid in career development.

Few organizations give sufficient attention to these factors. Upon analysis, numerous opportunities are found to customize career paths. Moreover, when the established paths and ladders are objectively studied, it is frequently found that the education, experience, and service prerequisites are pitched at unrealistic levels (Walker, 1976). Analyses of many jobs in terms of skill, knowledge, and seasoning requirements reveal a disparity between actual demands and existing screening criteria.

Also, the notion of job families (potential career paths *between* career ladders) needs to be explored. Upon analysis, traditional ladders are frequently seen in a new light. Important bypasses within ladders and potential new connections between ladders inadvertently have been overlooked. Job enlargement/enrichment programs also fall into this category. Finally, the issue of job rotation invariably needs to be reexamined. Job rotation, as a career development tool, can only be effective if there is a comprehensive understanding of the task matrix of the firm and the numerous interrelationships that exist within this matrix.

Performance Appraisal. This element is already well established in most firms today; however, it remains the most poorly understood and executed function in management. The appraisal is an ideal time and place for the boss to enter into the career coach role. To be effective in this role, however, the boss needs to be *both* a sound evaluator and a diagnostician with respect to improvement (Dalaba, 1972).

Potentials Assessment. The individual, particularly early in his or her career, is unable to make an accurate and complete evaluation of career potential. To complicate matters, lower level supervisors are frequently equally inept in making valid assessments of potential. This suggests that somewhere along the career paths, the person must have an opportunity to test potential for a number of positions, not merely accept promotion to the next rung on the present career ladder. In this regard, the assessment center comes quickly to mind as an important program tool. Ideally, the center would examine candidates' potential for a wide range of career options and provide feedback and counseling regarding each option.

Career Planning. Frequently, when a career management system is initiated, the first survey of employee career intentions generates disappointing data. That is, employees have very little awareness of what direction their careers should take. Career planning tools are, therefore, a necessity. Planning a career is foreign to most employees. They need instruction and planning tools before they can gain insights into their abilities, interests, values, and motivations.

Career Development. This input to the system essentially refers to training interventions or deployment treatments via informed job rotation. As the person accesses the career management system at its various points, both the individual and the organization gain a better understanding of career and improvement needs. This phase of the system is intended to provide the education, training, and on-the-job work experiences that better prepare people for the next step in their career progression.

SUMMARY

One patently false conclusion is that people today are lazy or lack ambition. Nothing could be farther from the truth. Their motivation continues at a high level. However, for this motivation to be unleashed, the work must have purpose, it must allow full use of abilities and education and provide at least some measure of autonomy and decision making. People expect to be treated maturely by the organization. They expect to be listened to, and to participate in the decisions that affect them, especially decisions that affect careers. These new—or at least more explicit—expectations set the stage for the requirements of a modern career management system. These expectations bear significantly upon the climates, leadership styles, job designs, and career opportunities that employees seek. When met, these expectations have substantial positive impact for the motivation, productivity, and innovation of any organization's work force.

References

Adler, Alfred. *What Life Should Mean to You.* New York: G.P. Putnam, Capricorn Books, 1958.

Dalaba, O.. "The Dual Responsibilities of Managing Human Resources," *Business Horizons,* 15, 6 (December 1972), 37–48.

Drucker, Peter. *The Age of Discontinuity: Guidelines to our Changing Society.* New York: Harper & Row, Publishers, 1968.

Ference, Thomas P., James A.F. Stoner, and E. Kirby Warren. "Managing the Career Plateau," *The Academy of Management Review,* 2, 4 (October 1977), 602–612.

Leach, John. "The Notion and Nature of Careers," *The Personnel Administrator,* 22, 7 (September 1977), 49–55.

Leach, John. "The Career of the Organization," *The Personnel Administrator,* 22, 8 (October 1977), 34–39.

Leach, John. "Career Management: Focusing on Human Resources," *The Personnel Administrator,* 22, 9 (November 1977), 59-66.

Maslow, Abraham. *Motivation and Productivity.* New York: Harper & Row, 1954.

Schein, Edgar. "How Career Anchors Hold Executives to Their Career Paths," *Personnel,* 52, 3 (May–June 1975), 11–24.

Vroom, Victor. *Work and Motivation.* New York: John Wiley & Sons, 1964.

Walker, James. "Let's Get Realistic About Career Paths," *Human Resource Management,* 15, 3 (Fall 1976), 2–7.

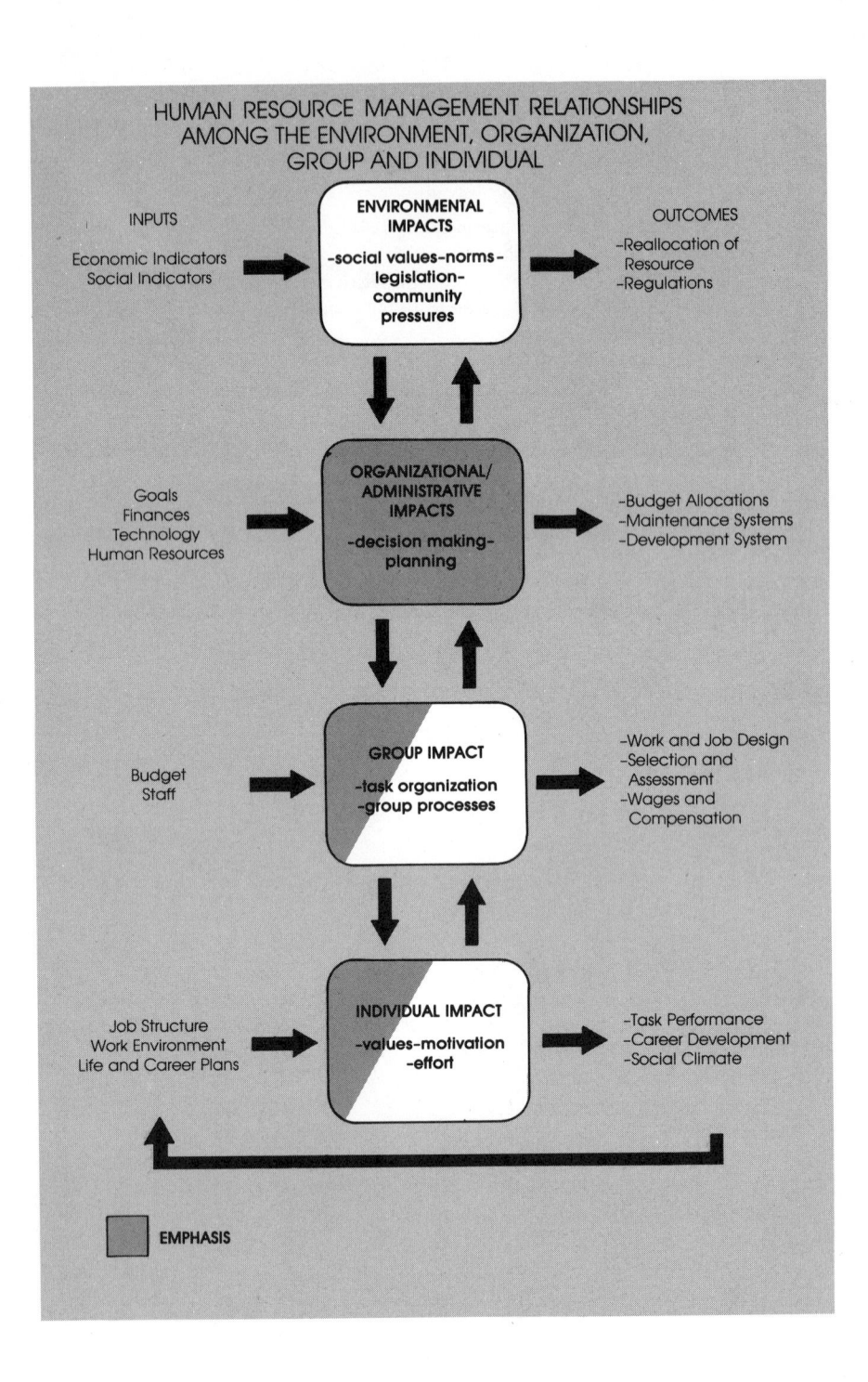

HUMAN RESOURCE MANAGEMENT RELATIONSHIPS AMONG THE ENVIRONMENT, ORGANIZATION, GROUP AND INDIVIDUAL

INPUTS

Economic Indicators
Social Indicators

ENVIRONMENTAL IMPACTS
-social values-norms-legislation-community pressures

OUTCOMES
-Reallocation of Resource
-Regulations

Goals
Finances
Technology
Human Resources

ORGANIZATIONAL/ADMINISTRATIVE IMPACTS
-decision making-planning

-Budget Allocations
-Maintenance Systems
-Development System

Budget
Staff

GROUP IMPACT
-task organization
-group processes

-Work and Job Design
-Selection and Assessment
-Wages and Compensation

Job Structure
Work Environment
Life and Career Plans

INDIVIDUAL IMPACT
-values-motivation
-effort

-Task Performance
-Career Development
-Social Climate

■ EMPHASIS

4

MAINTAINING THE HUMAN RESOURCE MANAGEMENT SYSTEM

Matching the human abilities of the work force and the demands of organizational performance over time requires a flexible blend of human resource management. Also required is a workable yet creative approach to the design of work and work systems. This challenge is made more demanding by complex environmental changes and by the multiple purposes to be served by work activities and the use of information. Growing emphasis on the importance of human rights, the quality of work life, emerging task partnerships between computerized technology and labor, and changes in the social composition of the labor force have encouraged a rethinking of the objectives, design, and implementation of human resource systems. At the same time, the needs for and use of information to support those activities have mushroomed. As a consequence, multilayered changes are taking place to improve human resource processes.

The articles in Part IV give an overview of the contributions professionals have made to update personnel practices, methods, and systems. In response to new needs, professionals have sought not only to devise new methods but to modify systems accordingly. These newer approaches correspond to the modern needs of managers for substantially altered procedures to organize, select, and monitor their work force.

In Part IV we have organized the articles into two sections. The first section treats the basic personnel management activities of recruiting and selecting, training and developing, evaluating, and compensating, while the second deals with various supporting human resource processes.

BASIC PERSONNEL MANAGEMENT ACTIVITIES

Today recruitment and selection activities are being examined from a different perspective. Traditional approaches in which the organization uses tests, interviews, and background information to select and place individuals are being supplemented by a broader concern with the fit between the work experience and an individual's motivation, training, placement, and compensation for a particular job.

In part, this newer conceptualization of a traditional personnel function is a direct response to a policy of equal opportunity for all employees. The first article in this section, "Equal Employment Opportunity Issues: A Perspective," by George T. Milkovich and Frank Krzystofiak is particularly important because it identifies and discusses issues human resource managers confront while implementing EEO policy. Although changes in the composition of the labor force and new legislation have directed the establishment of guidelines for employment practices, the threat or actual launching of lawsuits have brought about changes in the interpretation of these practices. Milkovich's and Krzystofiak's paper keys into these problems of defining discrimination and establishing the standards and models which target potential inequities. Then it addresses some of the major philosophical conflicts involved in defining an equality of opportunity versus an equality of results. The remaining articles in this first section highlight newer models and methodologies which translate that concern for the individual and the organization into effective selection and training programs.

Human resource planning requires active involvement by HRM in training and development activities because personnel planners provide the nexus between the organization's human resource needs and the individual's career needs and desires. In "Training and Development Programs: What Learning Theory and Research Have to Offer," Craig E. Schneier provides the reader with learning principles and findings that can prove useful in all phases of design and implementation of training and development programs. Schneier believes that the dimensions he sets forth form the conceptual base for organizational training and development programs and that they can be applied in a variety of organizational situations.

The experiences at Corning Glass Works provided the basis for the description of a contemporary "performance management system" (PMS) which in the view of company personnel constitutes a significant advance beyond management by objectives (MBO). In "Employee Growth Through Performance Management," Michael Beer and Robert A. Ruh describe an approach that goes beyond traditional performance appraisal and MBO by emphasizing individual development and appraisal, unique instrumentation, and a workable integration of the means of achieving results with the results themselves. The article illustrates the HRM theme through its description of more effective bases for dealing with individuals, developing human potential, and then integrating individual development approaches with the purpose of both organization and individual.

The rewards that managers provide to attract, retain, and stimulate talented employees remain an integral activity in organizational planning. Richard I. Henderson provides a basis for approaching the design of compensation systems based on the relationships between basic work values and the component parts of compensation systems. He identifies those procedures which synchronize different compensation components with the complex needs of individuals. Since compensation systems (alone) cannot meet all of the needs of individuals, Henderson expands the concept of compensation to include the total reward system of the organization, defined as "every inducement a business can offer to an employee that enhances an individual's estimate of personal worth—the fulfillment and satisfaction an employee receives from being a member of the business as well as from being a productive human being." In short, compensation includes both monetary and nonmonetary rewards.

The framework for viewing company compensation approaches described by Henderson is expanded upon by Michael Beer and Gloria J. Gery. In "Individual and Organizational Correlates of Pay System Preferences," the authors describe one company's efforts to take a more systematic approach in revising their pay system in order to more positively influence employee behavior. The company research program focused on nonexempt, salaried employees; and it sought to determine (1) the group's preference for various types of salary systems, and (2) correlates of these preferences. The study helped to bring out the complex relationships between organizational factors and individual behavioral variables; more specifically, it shed light on the "moderating effects of organizational and individual variables on the relationships between the pay system (the administrative entity) and resultant motivation or effort." The four variables identified in this study were organization culture, leadership climate, pay system factors, and individual motivational factors.

Taken together, these studies on compensation provide a significant picture of a key mechanism underlying the HRM model. Part of the cement that joins together individual, group, and organization results from a shared understanding as to contributions and obligations that is formalized through the compensation system. Human resource processes, productivity, bottom-line performance, and individual "benefits" are all bound up in a complex relationship that compensation activities and mechanisms can both strengthen and advance.

Equal Employment Opportunity Issues: A Perspective

George T. Milkovich
and
Frank Krzystofiak

Equal employment opportunity is currently the most significant policy in the management of human resources. This policy influences every personnel decision from recruiting, hiring, upgrading, layoffs, and retirement to compensation, training, performance evaluation, and labor relations. There is no area in human resource management to which it does not apply.

Equal employment opportunity has been confirmed as a basic socioeconomic policy of the nation by over two decades of legislation, executive order, and judicial decision. Yet, while equality of opportunity has been universally accepted as a social policy, signs of potential inequality continue to abound:

> In 1970 over 95 percent of airline stewards were female, over 99 percent of railroad conductors were male (Sommers, 1974).
>
> In 1970 representation of nonwhites in managerial occupations was less than one third of what would be expected from their representation in the civilian labor force (Peake, 1975).
>
> In 1972 the median earnings of women who engaged in full-time year-round work were about 58 percent of the median earnings of men employed on a similar basis (Ferber and Lowry, 1976).
>
> The average earnings paid to women who worked full time in major cities in 1975 were at least $5,000 lower than men's earnings (U.S. Department of Labor, 1978).
>
> In 1974 the unemployment rate for females aged 16 and over was 140 percent of the employment rate for males aged 16 and over (*Employment and Training Report of the President*, 1977).
>
> In 1974 the unemployment rate for nonwhites aged 16 and over was 198 percent of the unemployment rate for whites aged 16 and over (*Employment and Training Report of the President*, 1977).

Equal opportunity in employment is nobly conceived, but it must be translated into practice if desired results are to be achieved. It is with the translation of equal opportunity policy into specific regulations, programs, and actions of managers and agency professionals that the critical questions and issues remain.

This article treats in depth some of the issues that must be faced if equal opportunity policy is to be translated into day-to-day human resource man-

---

Prepared especially for this book and printed with permission of the authors.

agement action. After a brief review of the place of research in the equal opportunity area, we will consider four major issues:

1. the importance of defining equality, discrimination, affirmative action
2. the approaches to establishing standards for the determination of the equality of opportunity
3. the place of human resource modeling techniques in affirmative action planning
4. the philosophical conflict involved in equality of opportunity and equality of results approaches to nondiscriminatory employment

RESEARCH AND EQUAL OPPORTUNITY

According to Dunlop (1977), the contribution of academic research to the formulation of a national economic policy has been minimal. A similar conclusion may be drawn about the impact of academic research on equal employment opportunity policy. Economic researchers have sought primarily to define the role of discrimination in explaining such traditional economic variables as earnings or employment differences among race, ethnic, or sex groups (Blinder, 1973; Cohen, 1976; Gaumer, 1975; Gwartney, 1970). In addition, economists have begun to evaluate the impact of civil rights legislation and employer and compliance agency programs on economic variables (Bergmann, 1972; Flanagan, 1976; Goldstein and Smith, 1976; Heckman and Wolpin, 1976). Behavioral research has tended to either identify discriminatory influences in individual decision making or to investigate the effects of discrimination on employees' and managers' attitudes and behaviors. As we review the major types of research, however, it will become clear that little has been done to assist employers and agencies in their efforts to develop and implement effective EEO policies, programs, and methodologies.

ECONOMIC RESEARCH

Decomposition of economic differences among race/ethnic/sex (R/E/S) groups generally focuses on wages or unemployment (for example, occupations, industries, unemployment). In the area of employment, an attempt is made to divide the total difference in employment across R/E/S groups into discriminatory and nondiscriminatory components. The nondiscriminatory component is associated with (caused by) differences in the endowments or characteristics of the various R/E/S groups, such as age, education, experience, ability, training, motivation. The remaining component reflects differences in the return to (compensation for) the endowments of the groups. This unexplained differential reflects employment discrimination by identifying situations in which minorities or females equal to majorities (typically white males) in objective measures of ability, training, experience, and other relevant endowments, receive poorer treatment with regard to such things as recruitment, hiring, training, promotion, and layoff (Reynolds 1978).

Decomposition of wage differences among race/ethnic/sex groups follows a process virtually identical to that described above. A model is developed relating the endowments of the majority group to their earnings. The empirical weights that show the magnitude of the relationship between white male endowments and earnings are assumed to be the best estimates of how equitable earnings should be distributed. In other words, the model derived from the treatment of majorities (males) serves as the standard against which the earning for minority (female) groups are evaluated. The discrepancy between minority predicted earnings based on the majority model and their actual earnings is assumed to represent wage discrimination. It reflects situations in which minorities (or females), equal to the majority group in objective measures of ability, training, occupation, and other relevant endowments, receive poorer treatment with regard to wages.

An illustration may aid in explanation of this process. Assume that there are two groups (A and B) and that the mean wages and the mean endowment (education is assumed to be the only relevant variable) are presented below:

	Mean Wage	Mean Endowment
Group A	$ 10,000	12 years
Group B	$ 5,800	9 years

In addition, assume that the following empirical model has been established for Group A:

$$\text{Wage} = \$1,000 + (\$750 \times \text{Education})$$

It is clear that not all of the 42 percent wage differential is due to discrimination. Part of this difference is due to the lower endowment or education of Group B, and the remainder is assumed to be discrimination. If Group B were paid according to the same formula as Group A, they would receive $1,000 plus $750 for each of their nine years of education for a total of $7,750. The difference between Group A's actual earnings ($10,000) and Group B's expected earnings ($7,750) reflects a nondiscriminatory productivity difference [$2,250 = (12 years − 9 years) × $750 per year]. The difference between Group B's expected earnings ($7,570) and Group B's actual earnings ($5,800) reflects that difference which is not explained by differences in endowments and therefore is assumed to be discrimination against Group B ($1,950 = $7,750 − $5,800).

The findings of various studies of earning differences show some rather astonishing discrepancies:

> Of a 45 percent difference between male and female wages, Cohen (1976) estimated that 59 percent was due to differences in endowments and 41 percent to discrimination.
>
> Of a 40 percent difference between male and female wages, Gaumer (1975) estimated that 20 percent was due to differences in endowments and 80 percent to discrimination.

Of a 42 percent difference between black and white wages, Gwartney (1970) estimated that 67 percent was due to endowment differences and 33 percent to discrimination.

Of a 51 percent difference between black and white wages, Bliner (1973) estimated that 30 percent was due to endowment differences and 70 percent to discrimination.

Thus, at best, these studies suggest that for females somewhere between 40 percent and 80 percent of wage differences are due to discrimination, and for minorities somewhere between 30 percent and 70 percent of wage differences are due to discrimination. In part, the broad range of findings is due to the use of different variables to control for endowment differences.

The problem of selecting control variables is easily seen. If all control variables are omitted and the total difference in wages is called "discrimination," we have clearly underestimated real productivity differences and overestimated the effect of discrimination. However, if we control for such things as education, we obtain a more accurate estimate of labor market wage discrimination, but we run the risk of ignoring discrimination in other systems such as in the educational system itself. In sum, this approach has well-recognized limitations, not the least of which may be that the unexplained differences may be caused by other factors such as omitted variables, errors in measurement, the use of proxies, or the fact that the world may not be as linear as most research models are.

BEHAVIORAL RESEARCH

Behavioral research tends to investigate attitudinal perceptual differences among white males, minorities, and females (Laws, 1976; Dunnette, 1975) and to study how these differences may affect personnel decisions (Rosen and Jerdee, 1973, 1977; Shinar, 1975; Krefting, Berger and Wallace, in press). For example, a great deal of attention has been devoted to the role that stereotypes and role models may play in personnel decisions. Rosen and Jerdee state, "These negative stereotypes may cause subtle, unintentional discrimination in a variety of decisions" (1977, p. 15). In a series of studies, Rosen and Jerdee (1973; 1974b, c) found that male managers favored men over women in hiring decisions, promotion to managerial positions, acceptance into management development programs, assignments to challenging work, and assessment of tenure. On the other hand, two more recent studies (Hunady and Wahrman, 1977; Briscoe and Mainstone, 1978) do not support this earlier research. The 1978 study found that the subjects, personnel managers, did not favor male over female employees in any of the personnel decisions. Furthermore, female subjects did not indicate either a bias against women as in Goldberg's 1968 study or a pro-woman bias. Briscoe and Mainstone conclude that "this lends a considerable credence to the view that sex stereotyping is not today the problem it is 'made up' to be" (1978, p. 14).

In an interesting series of studies, Newman and Krzystofiak have cast doubts on many of the conclusions drawn from behavioral research. In the initial study, Newman (1978) sent unsolicited resumes to a sample of companies with affirmative action plans. Since only 42 percent of the companies treated black and white applicants equally (despite resumes with equivalent credentials), this study suggests that the companies had a marked tendency to discriminate (against blacks or whites), with the preference for blacks being somewhat more pronounced. In a second study, Newman and Krzystofiak (1978) sent questionnaires to a second sample of firms asking practitioners what they would do if they had received the unsolicited resumes used in the first study. The vast majority of respondents (86 percent) indicated that they would treat the black and white applicants equally. The two studies taken together suggest that any research based on self-reports (the basis of most behavioral research) must be viewed with a good deal of caution.

While much of the academic research, either economic or behavioral, is enlightening, real world events move beyond the researchers. Employers, compliance professionals, and the courts have developed and implemented strategies designed to eliminate discrimination and to achieve equal opportunity.[1] Major court decisions and consent decrees have reshaped the human resource systems of employers. Every major employer has an affirmative action program (AAP) that influences its personnel decisions. All this activity is designed to further the implementation of equal opportunity; yet little of our research has been devoted to gaining knowledge to help design these programs or to evaluating the results of those already implemented. Consider, for example, that in 1974, nine steel companies, representing 73 percent of the industry's employment, the United Steel Workers, and the EEOC agreed to a consent decree which contained provisions to restructure the seniority and transfer rights of employees (Matera, 1976; Moore, 1977). The seniority system was restructured to eliminate the continuing effects of past discriminatory practices and to grant relief to the employees who had been discriminated against. Similarly, in 1973 AT&T agreed to "affirmative action overrides"—minorities and females with less seniority were given promotional opportunities before more senior white males. The effects of these settlements or "treatments" could provide valuable knowledge for future EEO programs.

For example, if seniority is viewed as a major investment by workers, any changes in the rules will influence the value of that investment. If these changes were brought about by an external force such as the courts, rather than the union, several research issues present themselves. What are the consequences of restructured seniority on employee job satisfaction, on absenteeism, on turnover, on unit performance, or on grievances? What do motivation models predict? Do those employees who "benefit" from the restructured seniority system behave or feel differently from those who do not benefit? Are those who benefited the same employees who previously felt discriminated against?[2] Is the new seniority system perceived as fairer or more equitable by the work force? At present, we don't even know if those employees who benefited from the restructured seniority system perceive it to be fairer or provide more equal opportunity.

Another case serves to further illustrate the point. In its settlement, the Bank of America not only set out affirmative action goals but also established trust funds of $3.75 million for women's education, providing an incentive to women to accept and complete training or to develop general creative capacities through travel, education, or public service. This settlement was hailed as forward looking and innovative. What has been the impact of this settlement on women's attitudes, job satisfaction, role perceptions, performance, and feelings about opportunities in the bank? What have been its effects on male employees' attitudes, satisfaction, and performance? On unit performance? Perhaps this "innovative" type of settlement has no identifiable impact on employee attitudes, behaviors, and perceptions of opportunity and equality. The point is simply that each of the major settlements, consent decrees, and affirmative action programs provide research opportunities. The results of this research could help shape future settlements and strategies for compliance agencies, courts, and employers alike.

DEFINITIONS OF DISCRIMINATION

On the face of it, concepts such as equal employment opportunity and employment discrimination seem so simple and intuitive that their recognition would be obvious to all. "Discrimination is discrimination" and "when you've experienced it, you know it" have been definitions exclaimed in the emotion of advocacy (Krzystofiak and Newman, 1978). Yet, considering the enormous volume of regulatory memoranda, the continuing litigation, and the ever-expanding academic literature, these concepts are anything but simple when applied to the real world.

A single definition of employment equality and discrimination agreed upon by concerned parties does not exist! Rather, a variety of definitions exists. Guidelines and regulations issued by the numerous regulatory agencies are designed to translate and clarify equal opportunity into operational terms, yet many of these regulations differ and some even conflict (Morris, 1977; Government Accounting Office, 1976). Similarly, there are the ever-increasing numbers of decisions from the courts. While some serve to clarify, others are in direct conflict (Rosenblum, 1977).

The absence of a definition of discrimination seems to follow from the history of race relations in the United States. It was easy to point to cases of discrimination in the 40s, 50s, and 60s, for discrimination took the form of total exclusion of race/ethnic/sex groups from voting, living in certain neighborhoods, attending certain schools, and occupying positions in certain firms, industries, or occupations. Quite obviously all will agree that total or near total exclusion of minority groups is discrimination in its purest and simplest form.

In the late 60s and 70s, we have begun to move away from total exclusion. Our problem now appears to be deciding which of an almost infinite number of strategies to adopt in working toward a more equitable society. While all thinking individuals agree that total exclusion is unfair or discriminatory, there appears to be nearly complete disagreement as to what constitutes fair or nondiscriminatory representation.

The majority of the systematic efforts to define discrimination have focused on the human resource management areas of testing and selection. Federal selection guidelines of the Equal Employment Opportunity Commission (EEOC) and Office of Federal Contract Compliance Programs (OFCCP) seem to be consistent with Guion's notion that unfair discrimination exists when "persons with equal probabilities of success have unequal probabilities of being

196 Equal Employment Opportunity Issues: A Perspective

hired" (1965). The following quotations from EEOC and OFCCP guidelines shed some light on their concepts of discrimination.

> The use of any selection procedure which has an adverse impact on the members of any racial, ethnic, or sex group with respect to any employment decision will be considered to be discriminatory and inconsistent with these guidelines, unless the procedure is validated in accordance with the principles contained in these guidelines. (OFCCP, part 60-3.3(a))
>
> ... a test should be validated for each minority group with which it is used; that is, any differential rejection rates that may exist, based on a test, must be relevant to performance on the jobs in question. (EEOC, 1067.4(a))
>
> ... where a test is valid for two groups but one group characteristically obtains higher test scores than the other without a corresponding difference in job performance, cutoff scores must be set so as to predict the same probability of job success in both groups. (EEOC, 1607)

A few definitions should serve to demonstrate the complexities involved:

> A test is biased for members of a subgroup of the population if, in the prediction of a criterion ... consistent nonzero errors of prediction are made for members of the subgroup. In other words, the test is biased if the criterion score predicted from the common regression line is consistently too high or too low for members of the subgroup. (Cleary, 1968, p. 115)
>
> Unfair discrimination against a minority group occurs when, over the long run, a firm's personnel decisions yield higher proportions of reject-errors (those erroneous personnel decisions wherein persons rejected from a job could, if placed on the job, have been successful) for members of the minority group than for members of the nonminority group. (Dunnette, 1970, pp. 4-5).
>
> Unfair discrimination exists when persons with equal probabilities of success on the job have unequal probabilities of being hired for the job (Guion, 1965, p. 26)
>
> A test is biased for members of a subgroup if there is a relationship between the test and culture (that is, race/ethnic/sex status) which is independent of the criterion. In other words, if R/E/S status is to enter into selection decisions it must do so only because of the shared relationship of the test and job performance. (Krzystofiak and Newman, 1978, p. 7)
>
> A test is fair if and only if the percentage of minorities selected with the test is equal to the percentage of minorities who would be successful if selection were conducted ... on the criterion measure itself. (Hunter, Schmidt, and Rauschenberger, 1975, p. 1)

It is clear from the above that the following factors may be related to identification of discrimination: errors of prediction, reject errors, the probability of success on a job, the probability of being hired, the relationship between test scores and race/ethnic/sex status, the relationship between test scores and job performance, and the percentage of minorities selected. The questions are: (1) What are the interrelationships between these factors? and (2) What is the relationship between each of these factors and discrimination?

In a discussion of issues faced in the development of standards for the use of tests and other selection devices, Hunter and Schmidt state that they "... have shown that any purely statistical approach to the problem of test bias is doomed to rather immediate failure" (1976, p. 1069). However, the issue of the definition of discrimination in employment selection and testing is still very active (Hunter and Schmidt, 1978; Ledvinka, 1978; Krzystofiak and Newman, 1978). We would disagree slightly with Hunter's position, for we feel that little progress can be made in the integration of our work force without a sound statistical definition of discrimination. The point is, we cannot eliminate "it" if we do not know what "it" is!

STANDARDS FOR DETERMINATION OF EMPLOYMENT EQUALITY

From a practical or operational point of view, the absence of an agreed upon definition of discrimination creates problems when attempting to evaluate the equality of opportunity. For the employer, according to current interpretation, the message from the history of civil rights legislation is that personnel programs and decisions are judged by their *results for protected employee groups* rather than their intent (Blumrosen, 1972).[3] To evaluate these results, standards for the evaluation of employers' personnel behaviors must be agreed upon.

Consider the critical importance of such standards. They are the yardsticks for evaluating the results of human resource decisions. Compliance agents, EEO directors, judges, lawyers, union officials, employees—all involved parties—are continually making evaluations about the results of human resource decisions. Yet the attention and effort devoted to the development of the standards against which the evaluations are made has been minimal at best. By comparison, consider the time and resources devoted to the development of the Uniform Guidelines on Employee Selection Procedures (EEOC, 1970, 1977) and the Employee Testing and Other Selection Procedures (U.S. Department of Labor, 1971, 1977). Representatives from civil rights organizations, agencies, employers, unions, and academia met, testified, and deliberated during the development of these Guidelines, which continue to be refined as experience and knowledge accumulate. No similar effort has been devoted to the development of equal opportunity/affirmative action results.

The determination of such standards is more difficult than it first appears. The illustration given earlier in the article implied that equality of employment opportunity would be achieved if the unemployment rates for minority males and white males were equal. Such a definition overlooks complexities found in society, however. For example, differences in qualifications, interests, education, willingness to relocate, willingness to invest in education, as well as employment discrimination may contribute to differences in unemployment rates. The basic task becomes one of attributing a weight to each of these factors (assuming they are work related)—not an easy task. When one considers that these factors are in turn influenced by practices in the educational systems, cultural differences in child/family situations, role models, and other aspects of society, the true enormity of the task emerges. Many of these factors are not even remotely under the control of the employment systems, so that it may be more correct to say that *differences in unemployment rates among race/sex/ ethnic groups may be determined by many factors, employment discrimination included.* The implication is that equity or parity of unemployment rates, employment rates, and median incomes, for example, among *each* race/sex/ ethnic group is a dubious standard for judging equality of employment opportunity.

Another, perhaps more important, standard currently used to evaluate the results of human resource decisions is the "goal." The concept is that "any politically well defined group (race/sex/ethnic) has the right to ask and receive its fair share of any product or position that is under state control" (Hunter and Schmidt, 1976). In other words, equality of employment is achieved when the composition of the employers' work force mirrors the composition of the relevant labor supply. Thus, if the proportion of black males in an employer's relevant labor supply is 12.3 percent, then an equal percent of blacks should be present in the employer's work force. Further, not only must the employer's total work force be representative of the race/sex/ethnic composition of the relevant supply, but the distribution of these protected employee groups across organization levels, salary grades, and occupations must also correspond to the composition of the supply.

Typically, an employer's goals may not be less than the supply of protected groups. If the representation and distribution of protected groups in the employer's work force is not similar to the relevant labor supply of that group, an employer must justify these differences as work-related (that is, differences in work-related qualifications, education, or interests of each race/sex/ethnic group).

The practical issue can now be stated as, Precisely what is an employer's relevant supply of labor?[4] The definition and measurement of a labor supply becomes extremely significant to all concerned parties when it becomes the standard against which human resource decisions are judged. Unfortunately, civil rights legislation, regulatory agencies, and the courts have been vague and at times seriously inconsistent in their definitions of relevant labor supply.

Rosenblum (1977) cites a lack of consistency in the courts' definitions of relevant supply of labor. For example, in *Griggs* v. *Duke Power* [401 U.S. 424 (1971)], the Supreme Court affimed a lower court ruling that used data saying blacks throughout *North Carolina* could apply to the firm. The Fifth Circuit used data for the *entire South*, as well as *Atlanta*, in *United States* v. *Georgia Power Company* [474 F. 2d 906 (C.A. 5, 1973)]. The Sixth Circuit in *Afro-American Patrolman League* v. *Duck* [503 F. 2d 294 (C.A. 6, 1974)] used the *population of the city of Toledo*, while the Eighth Circuit in *Parkam* v. *Southwestern Bell* [433 F. 2d 421 (C.A. 8, 1970)] considered *state* (Arkansas) data. Recently a District Court used the counties in which a New York union had jurisdiction in *Rio* v. *Enterprise Steamfitters Local 638* [9 CCH EPD, pp. 10, 143, (D.C.—S.D.N. &., 1975)]. Rosenblum (1978) further points out that in *Teamsters* v. *United States* the Supreme Court broadened its decision to apply to an *area-wide population* because the job involved the ability to drive a truck, an ability that many persons possess or can readily acquire. In *Hazelwood School District* v. *United States*, the Court stated that a board of education's appropriate standard for selecting applicants for its teacher work force was the qualified public school teacher population *relevant labor market*. So there are no clear precedents for what is a relevant labor supply.

Agencies also lack consistency in their approaches for determining labor supply. The EEOC uses an aggregate approach that takes into account the protected group representation rates in the entire civilian labor force in the appropriate Standard Metropolitan Statistical Area. Under such an approach, the agency will not consider such factors as education or occupation except when the employer can statistically demonstrate these factors to be work related.

A second agency, the Department of Health, Education and Welfare (1970), recommends the use of a disaggregate approach which permits the use of occupational segmentation of the labor force when estimating labor supply. A third agency, the OFCCP, in Revised Order No. 4 lists eight factors for determining an estimate of labor availability without including any guidance on the sources of data, methods to combine factors, or the relative importance of these factors.[5] The General Services Administration (1978) recently published a scheme for combining the Revised Order No. 4 factors but failed to give rationale for the formula.

McGuiness, in a review of the existing regulations and guidelines and the history of their development, states that:

> There are no known agency memoranda suggesting how this information is to be measured, where the data are found if they exist, the relative significance of the factors, or how they should be combined. Both compliance agencies and contractors have complained about the absence of valid statistical data ... on both a local and national level. (1976, pp. 37-38)

Snider (1977), commenting on the determination of labor supplies for equal employment goal setting, states:

> Bits and pieces of the data are collected by dozens of Federal, State and local agencies and private organizations and published in numerous reports. However, some of the necessary information isn't collected and when it is the data are often conflicting and less than comparable. (1977, p. 2)

The lack of a model that would clarify a firm's "labor supply" underlies this confusion and disarray. Clear definition of such concepts as "labor markets," "labor supplies," "qualified labor force," "applicants," and "qualified applicants" is required. Critical factors that influence the labor supply, such as wage rates and whether an employer is a "wage leader or simply meets competition," have been overlooked by the courts and by regulatory agencies. Further, implicit assumptions and misconceptions remain unexamined; for example, factor 1 of the Revised Order No. 4 states that the entire population of an area must be considered, ignoring the facts that most people 14 years and younger are not permitted employment under law, and that the civilian labor force is a subset of the entire population. In sum, *equality of employment opportunity and discrimination need to be expressed in operational terms.* Meaningful approaches to measuring employers' human resource behaviors and the nation's social progress need to be developed. The absence of a uniform procedure to evaluate these behaviors is enormously costly—to the compliance agencies, to employers, and to the courts—to say nothing of its deleterious effects upon the achievement of equal opportunity. As a consequence of this absence, involved parties seem to have no reliable way to discern their degree of compliance with equal opportunity legislation.

EQUAL EMPLOYMENT/ AFFIRMATIVE ACTION AND HUMAN RESOURCE PLANNING MODELS

A significant and promising trend in human resource management is the development and application of quantitative models to human resource issues. A variety of statistical techniques, stochastic models, and computer simulations have been developed and applied to a wide range of human resource issues (Burack and Walker, 1972; Milkovich and Mahoney, 1976). While many of these techniques remain in the developmental or experimental stage, others have been applied and can be used to assist regulatory agencies and employers in their equal opportunity affirmative action endeavors.

Planning in human resource management is the process of determining how an organization should move from its current human resource status to some more desired human resource position. In this context, affirmative action planning is simply a special application of human resource planning that focuses upon the identification and elimination of disparate treatment in the employment of race/ethnic/sex groups. Equal opportunity policy establishes certain rules for the administration of the various personnel programs including recruiting, upgrading, compensation, and performance appraisal. The affirmative action programs, then, are another in a series of strategies that an organization implements to move from its current human resource position toward its goals.

A common approach to conceptualizing or modeling the human resource system uses the idea of stocks of human resources and flows of these resources from one stock or status to another.[6] Examples of the application of the stocks-flows approach in human resource planning are common (Mahoney and Milkovich, 1971; Bartholomew, 1976; Grinold and Marshall, 1977). Application of the concepts to affirmative action issues has also been advocated (Churchill and Shank, 1976; Ledvinka, 1976; Flast, 1977; Milkovich and Krzystofiak, 1978; Charnes, Cooper, and Niehaus, 1974).

Analysis of stocks of human resources (analogous to balance sheets or inventories) focuses on the distribution or availability of human resources across different status conditions (affirmative action job categories, units, performance levels, or salary grades). Such analysis tends to be static and descriptive because it focuses on a point in time and tends to deemphasize the personnel decisions which determine that particular distribution of human resource stocks.

Churchill and Shank (1976) observe that most agency compliance guidelines for work force analysis—and consequently for implementing employer compliance—tend to emphasize the stock approach. For example, the OFCCP

Affirmative Action Guidelines require an employer to perform the following work force analysis:

> Analysis of all major job groups at the facility, with explanation if minorities or women are currently being underutilized in any one or more job groups ("job groups" herein meaning one or a group of jobs having similar content, wage rates, and opportunities). "Underutilization" is defined as having fewer minorities or women in a particular job group than would reasonably be expected by their availability. (see Part 60-2.11 (b))

Analysis of flows of human resources, on the other hand, focuses on the employment decisions that serve to allocate human resources among various job states. Consequently, flows depict the movement of dynamics of the work force: the proportion of groups receiving promotions, transfers, being laid off, entering training programs, completing training, being terminated, or responding to posted jobs are all illustrations of flows. In affirmative action analysis, flow measures can be used in the evaluation of specific employment practices. The heart of flows analysis is the comparison of a protected group's flow with its availability. For example, if white females comprise 28 percent of the relevant labor pool, then at least 28 percent of promotion and/or training opportunities ought to be allocated to them (Milkovich and Krzystofiak, 1978). Reference to the concept of flows is found in a variety of compliance agency memoranda; however, guidelines for their construction and interpretation are limited (OFFCCP Affirmative Action Guidelines, section 60-2.23). In addition to focusing upon the diagnosis of the work force, personnel flows models diagnose the potential consequences of various EEO programs, agency regulations, and court settlements. Essentially, such an analysis assumes that the proposed programs are the rules which govern or regulate the movement of employees throughout the employing organization. Then, by means of computer simulations, it is possible to analyze the potential consequences, both intended and unintended, of these rules. Such analysis typically focuses on the probability of achieving given goals, the determination of feasible timetables for achievement, and the identification of unforeseen consequences.

Few applications of flow model simulation to actual EEO situations have been reported; however, several employers reportedly use the technique. In one study (Milkovich and Krzystofiak, 1978), EEO goals required an employer to achieve a work force that employed all underutilized, protected employee groups in the same proportion as found in the employer's relevant supply. To achieve this goal, the employer was considering an affirmative action plan that provided for rates of hiring and promoting among underutilized groups that exceeded their representation in the relevant labor supply. Specifically, the plan called for underutilized group hiring rates at 1.5 times their availability in the labor supply and promotion rates twice that of their representation in the internal labor supply. This plan is very similar to the terms of AT&T's 1974 Consent Settlement and to many employers' affirmative action programs, all of which were intended to regulate hiring and upgrading flows under a variety of economic conditions. In this particular instance, however, compliance to the proposed EEO rules would have caused the employer to lay off black females and to promote minority males regardless of their qualifications to achieve the goals. Obviously, the model failed to simulate reality in this case, and modifications of the hiring and upgrading rules were in order. In other studies, Churchill and Shank (1976) and Chew and Justice (1977) used flow model simulations to point out that the rate of change in the distribution of minorities and females in upper levels of the organization and in nontraditional jobs is dependent on the rate of creation of employment opportunities. In other words, for upward mobility to occur, job vacancies or employment opportunities must occur. Employment opportunities, in turn, are determined by two factors: expanding business conditions and employee turnover. Thus, if turnover is reduced (possibly by new legislation that permits later retirements) and if economic expansion is slowed (by downturns in the economy) then the rate at which job opportunities occur sets time limits on the achievement of equal opportunity goals. Currently, most employers and compliance agencies design and implement EEO programs without any idea of whether or not they are even feasible.

The use of human resource modeling techniques, specifically stock and flow models, can greatly assist all concerned parties. Compliance agency professionals, trained in such methods, would then be able to more effectively determine if a given employer is in compliance, and more importantly, to diagnose potential results of proposed actions. Human resource managers could use such methods to more effectively design and evaluate equal opportunity strategies.

PHILOSOPHICAL CONFLICT

The final topic considered in this article is one of the most pressing issues facing contemporary society: How are we to achieve equality? In the late 1960s *equal employment opportunity* seemed to direct human resource managers to seek out and prepare minority groups and women to take full advantage of opportunities and to remove barriers which prevented them from doing so. This approach was *passive* in its attempt to develop *color-blind* systems that focused on *individual merit*. *Equality of opportunity* was a *preventative* approach which would in effect *delay* the ultimate equalization of race/ethnic/sex groups. This system would use *good faith efforts* and *goals* to achieve *equal treatment* or *nondiscrimination*.

In the 1970s *affirmative action* seemed to require human resource managers to seek out and utilize minority groups and women. This new approach was *active* in its attempt to develop *color-conscious* systems which focused on *categorical equality*. *Equality of results* was a *corrective* approach that demanded the *immediate* equalization of race/ethnic/sex groups. This system would use *preferential treatment, quotas,* and *reverse discrimination* to achieve desired *outcomes* (see Table 1).

As students interested in the study of human resources, particularly with respect to employment relationships, we have a responsibility to raise the question, What is equality and how would we achieve it? Indeed, we feel that no amount of data collection or statistical or quantitative model building will provide an answer. Rather, the answer depends in part on values which are perhaps irreconcilable. Nonetheless, we must strive to clarify the terms and investigate the

TABLE 1

Affirmative Action	vs.	Equal Employment Opportunity
Active		Passive
Categorical Equality		Individual Merit
Color Consciousness		Color Blindness
Corrective		Preventative
Equality of Results		Equality of Opportunity
Immediate		Delayed
Outcomes		Good Faith Efforts
Preferential Treatment		Equal Treatment
Quotas		Goals
Reverse Discrimination		Nondiscrimination

behavioral implications of various approaches to equality based on these definitions.

There are two issues involved in the conflict over the equal opportunity-affirmative action approaches to equality. First, when there are identifiable individuals who have experienced discrimination, can affirmative action be legally sanctioned to correct the problem? Second, when there are not identifiable individual victims of discrimination, as in the case of systemic discrimination, is it socially (legally) viable to use affirmative action to correct the problem?

Those who argue against affirmative action as a solution to the problems of identifiable individuals who have experienced discrimination point to Title VII of the Civil Rights Act of 1964:

> Sec. 703 (a) It should be an unlawful employment practice for an employer ... to limit, segregate, or classify his employees in any way which would deprive or tend to deprive any individual of employment opportunities or otherwise adversely affect his status as an employee because of such individual's race, color, religion, sex, or national origin. (j) Nothing contained in this title shall be interpreted to require any employer ... to grant preferential treatment to any individual or to any group because of race, color, religion, sex, or national origin of such individual or group on account of an imbalance which may exist with respect to the total number or percentage of persons of any race, color, religion, sex, or national origin employed by any employer.

In addition, major court cases seem to buttress this position:

> Congress did not intend by Title VII, however, to guarantee a job to every person regardless of qualifications. In short, the Act does not command that any person be hired simply because he was formerly the subject of discrimination, or because he is a member of a minority group. Discriminatory preference for any group, minority or majority, is precisely and only what Congress has proscribed. (**Griggs** v. **Duke Power Company,** 3 FEP 175, 1971)

However, the courts have taken the position that they have the legal right to order necessary remedial action where identifiable victims of discrimination are found·

> The Constitution is both color-blind and color-conscious. To avoid conflict with the equal protection clause, a classification that denies a benefit, causes harm, or imposes a burden must not be based on race. In that sense the Constitution is color-blind. But the Constitution is color-conscious to prevent discrimination being perpetuated and to undo the effects of past discrimination. (**U.S. v. Jefferson County Board of Education,** 372 F. 2d 836, 975; 5th Cir. 1966)

The social issue involving the use of affirmative action as a general remedy to systemic discrimination is somewhat more complex. The proponents of affirmative action seem to argue that reverse discrimination is the only cure for the problem. "When a society has committed past injustices or when a historically disadvantaged group exists side by side with more advantaged groups, it simply is not possible to achieve equality and fairness by applying a neutral 'principle'" (Glickstein, 1977). "Like the infections in the human body which are cured by injections of the same poison, the antitoxin of reverse discrimination is a recognized judicial remedy for the toxin of discrimination" (*Erie Human Relations Commission v. Tullio,* 6 FEP 735). In other words:

> ... Our society cannot be completely color-blind in the short term if we are to have a color-blind society in the long term. After centuries of viewing through colored lenses, eyes do not quickly adjust when the lenses are removed. Discrimination has a way of perpetuating itself, albeit unintentionally, because the resulting inequalities make new opportunities less accessible. Preferential treatment is one partial prescription to remedy our society's most intransigent and deeply rooted inequalities. (Associated General Contractors of Massachusetts, Inc. v. Altshuler, 7 FEP 1160)

The opponents of affirmative actions adopt a "Two wrongs don't make a right" philosophy and argue that reverse discrimination is not a cure because one discrimination cannot compensate for another:

> Discrimination causes individuals to suffer. If they can be individually compensated, well and good. But compensating their grandchildren at the cost of discriminating against someone else does not compensate them in the slightest. It does replace private discrimination (or at least supplement it) with public, government discrimination, sanctioned by the laws. It also sets up another imaginary debt for the social engineer whose successors will one day have to compensate the grandchild of the one victimized today, at the expense of the grandchild of the one benefited today—that is, if moral consistency can be expected.
>
> Put it this way. We object to discrimination against a class of people because it unjustly hurts individual members of that class. If now we argue that it is all right to discriminate against members of other classes in order to compensate the first group, we shall have destroyed the basis of our ob-

jection to the very discrimination we sought thereby to eliminate. (Todorovich, 1977)

At the heart of the controversy is whether the entire concept of providing "equal" opportunity to minority groups and women—through "goals" is constitutional.[7] The issue as posed by the Court in *Bakke* v. *Board of Regents 15*, 18 Cal. 3d 52, 132 Cal. Rpt. 693 (1976) is

> whether a racial classification which is intended to assist minorities, but which also has the effect of depriving those who are so classified of benefits they would enjoy but for their race violates the constitutional rights of the majority.

There has been an outpouring of literature surrounding the Bakke case. In the Bakke decision, the Supreme Court overturned the University of California's admission system which had *reserved* 16 *positions* for minority applicants and the court required that Bakke be admitted to the school. In explaining the action, Justice Powell indicated that, "Preferring members of any one group for no reason than race or ethnic origin is discrimination for its own sake. This the Constitution forbids." (17 FEP 1000) However, the court did allow the University of California to consider race in the admissions process, since "the state has a substantial interest that legitimately may be served by a properly devised admissions program involving the competitive consideration of race and ethnic origin." (17 FEP 1000) While this decision is presumably relevant only to educational institutions, the spillover turmoil in the business community is evident. Further clarification of the role of racial classification in the affirmative admissions/employment setting will be necessary before this turmoil subsides. Similar cases involving employment are winding their way through the courts, for example, *Kaiser Steel* v. *Weber* and *Detroit Police Officers* v. *Young* (16 FEP 1005)

The implications for human resource managers are considerable. At this time, it appears that concepts of preferential treatment, affirmative action overrides, and numerical goals have been upheld, but future tests are in the courts. For the immediate future, equality of results and current affirmative action planning will continue.

If programs to achieve statistical parity, no matter how meritorious or noble their goals, are at sometime in the future declared unconstitutional, then human resource managers and agency professionals must reassess their programs. Not only will many current affirmative action programs need to be changed but employers and perhaps regulatory agencies may be sued because they allegedly discriminated against majority employees.

Perhaps the courts' decisions may require employers and regulatory agencies to focus on affirmative action, upward mobility, and preferential treatment that is race/sex/ethnic blind. Such an approach would take as its target group the "economically disadvantaged." However, this term is as ill-defined as "equality." Ideally, equal opportunity could be based upon individual merit, another term that seems to defy absolute definition. Perhaps our efforts are better devoted to the identifying of merit and disadvantaged groups than racial/sex/ethnic groups and treatments.

CONCLUSIONS

A variety of issues related to human resource management and equal opportunity were discussed in the article. In sum, it was professed that

> Equal opportunity is currently the most significant policy in the management of human resources.
>
> Little progress will be made in the integration of our work force without an agreed upon definition of discrimination.
>
> Meaningful approaches for measuring employers' human resource behaviors and the nation's progress toward equal employment opportunity need to be developed. The absence of a uniform procedure to evaluate these behaviors has costly effects on the achievement of equal opportunity. It should be apparent that judgment and interpretation are inherent in the determination and evaluation of equal employment opportunity. However, a more systematic approach should yield relevant data and insights in making these judgments, reduce the degree of differences that require judgment, and provide a framework within which these judgments can be made. Perhaps in addition to more systematic methodology, there will always remain the need for negotiations and adversary proceedings.
>
> Human resource planning models and techniques, such as personnel flow models and simulations, have tremendous untapped utility for evaluating and diagnosing EEO/AAP. Employers, agencies, and academies should be encouraged to make use of these techniques in both their research and their equal employment endeavors.
>
> Finally, it was observed that as students of human resource management we have a responsibility to examine a basic philosophic issue underlying the general concept of equality.
>
> In employment relationships does equality mean equality of opportunity or equality of results? For managers of human resources, the critical question is, What are the implications of each of these views?

References

Ashenfelter, Orley. "Changes in Labor Market Discrimination Over Time," *Journal of Human Resources*, 5, 4, (1970), 403–430.

Ashenfelter, Orley. "Comment," *Industrial and Labor Relations Review*, 29, 4, (1976), 577–580.

Associated General Contractors of Massachusetts, Inc. vs. Altshuler, 7 FEP 1160.

Axel, Helen, ed. *A Guide to Consumer Markets 1977/78*, New York: The Conference Board, Inc., 1977, p. 107.

Bartholomew, D.J. *Manpower Planning*, New York: Penguin Books, 1976.

Bass, B.J., Krussell, J., and Alexander, R.A. "Male Managers' Attitudes Toward Working Women," *American Behavioral Scientist*, Beverly Hills, Calif.: Sage Publication, Inc., 1971, p. 15.

Bergmann, B.R. and Krause, W.R. "Evaluating and Forecasting Progress in Racial Integration of Employment," *Industrial and Labor Relations Review*, 1972, pp. 399–409.

Bergmann, B.R. "Studying Black-White Differences in the Context of a Microsimulation of Labor Markets," in *Patterns of Discrimination*, edited by G.M. Von Furstenberg, et. al. Vol. 2. (1974).

Biles, George Emery and Mass, Michael A. "Bakke: Death Knell of Equal Opportunity?," *Employee Relations Law Journal*, 13, 2, (1977), 178–189.

Blinder, Alan S. "Wage Discrimination: Reduced Form and Structural Estimates," *Journal of Human Resources*, 8, 4, (1973), 436–455.

Blumrosen, A.W. "Strangers in Paradise: Griggs vs. Duke Power Co. and the Concept of Employment Discrimination," *Michigan Law Review*, 71, (1972), 59–110.

Briscoe, Dennis R. and Mainstone, Larry E. "The Influence of Sex-Role Stereotypes on Personnel Decisions: One More Time," paper presented at 1978 Annual Academy of Management Meetings, San Francisco.

Burack, Elmer H. and Waller, James W. *Manpower Planning and Programming*. Boston: Allyn & Bacon, Inc., 1972.

Burton, Gene W. and Pathak, Dev. S. "101 Ways to Discriminate Against Equal Employment Opportunity," *S.A.M. Advanced Management Journal*, (Autumn 1976), 22–30.

Cain, Glen. Theory of Discrimination. 1976.

Charnes, A., Cooper, W.W., Lewis, K.A., and Niehaus, R.J. *A Multi-Objective Model for Planning Equal Employment Opportunities*, Springfield, VA: National Technical Information Service, Department of Commerce, 1975.

Chew, William B. and Justice, Richard L. *AAP Modeling for Large Complex Organizations*, Conference on Affirmative Action Planning Concepts, Ithaca: Cornell University, 1977.

Churchill, N. and Shank, J. "Affirmative Action and Guilt-edged Goals," *Harvard Business Review*, 54, 2, (1976), 111–116.

Cleary, T. Anne, "Test Bias: Prediction of Grades of Negro and White Students in Integrated Colleges," *Journal of Educational Measurement*, 5, 2, (1968), 115–124.

Cohen, Malcolm S. "Sex Differences in Compensation," *Journal of Human Resources* 6, (1976), 434.

Cohen, S.L. and Bunker, K.A. "Subtle Effects of Sex Role Stereotypes on Recruiters' Hiring Decisions," *Journal of Applied Psychology*, 60, (1975), 566–572.

Department of Labor, Office of Federal Contract Compliance Programs, "Equal Employment Opportunity: Final Rule Making," *Federal Register, Part V*, 42, 12, (January 18, 1977).

Dunlop, John. "Policy Decisions and Research in Economics and Industrial Relations," *Industrial and Labor Relations Review*, 30, 3, 1977, 275–284.

Dunnette, Marvin D. "Personnel Selection and Job Placement of the Disadvantaged: Problems, Issues, and Suggestions," *Technical Report #4001*, Minneapolis: University of Minnesota, 1970.

Dunnette, M.D. "Evidence Related to Differential Participation Rates for Different Occupations by Males and Females," Personnel Decisions Research Institute, 1975.

Erie Human Relation Commission vs. Tollio, 6 FEP 733.

Employment and Training Report of the President, 1977.

"Federal Executive Agency Guidelines on Employee Selection Procedures," *BNA AFEP Manual 401:772, Labor Relations Reporter—Fair Employment Practices Manual*.

Ferber, Marianne A. and Lowry, Helen M. "The Sex Differential in Earnings: A Reappraisal," *Industrial and Labor Relations Review*, 29, 3, (1976), 337–387.

Flanagan, Robert J. "Actual Versus Potential Impact of Government Antidiscrimination Programs," *Industrial and Labor Relations Review*, 29, 4, (1976), 486–507.

Flast, R.H. "Taking the Guesswork Out of Affirmative Action Planning," *Personnel Journal*, 56 (February 1977), 68–71.

Freeman, Richard B. "Availability, Goals and Achievements in Affirmative Action: An Economic Perspective," Washington, D.C.: Equal Employment Advisory Council, in print.

Gastwirth, J.L. and Haber, S.E. "Defining the Labor Market for Equal Employment Standards," *Monthly Labor Review*, 99 (March 1976), 32–36.

Gaumer, Gary L. "Sex Discrimination and Job Tenure," *Industrial Relations*, 14, 1, (1975), 121–129.

General Services Administration, *Handbook on Contract Compliance, Regulations on Availability*, CSL, pp. 2800-2, CH 3-7, 1978.

Glazer, Nathan, *Affirmative Discrimination: Ethnic Inequality and Public Policy*, New York: Basic Books, Inc., Publishers, 1975.

Glickstein, Howard A. "Discrimination in Higher Education: A Debate on Faculty Employment," in *Reverse Discrimination*, B.R. Gross, ed., Buffalo: Prometheus Books, 1977.

Goldberg, P. "Are Women Prejudiced Against Women?", *Trans-Action*, 5 (April 1968), 28–30.

Goldstein, Morris and Smith, Robert S. "The Estimated Impact of Antidiscrimination Programs Aimed At Federal Contractors," *Industrial and Labor Relations Review*, 29, 4, (1976), 523–543.

Griggs vs. Duke Power Company, 3 FEP 195, 1971.

Grinold, Richard C. and Kneale, Marshall T. *Manpower Planning Models*, New York: North-Holland Publishing Company, 1977, p. 257.

Gross, B.R. *Reverse Discrimination*. Buffalo: Prometheus Books, 1977.

Guion, Robert M. "Employment Tests and Discriminatory Hiring," *Industrial Relations*, (1965), 20–37.

Gwartney, James, "Discrimination and Income Differentials," *American Economic Review*, 60, 3, (1970), 396–408.

Heckman, James J. and Wolpin, Kenneth I. "Does the Contract Compliance Program Work?: An Analysis of Chicago Data," *Industrial and Labor Relations Review*, 29, 4, (1976), 544–571.

Heneman, H.G. III and Sandver, M.G. "Markov Analysis in Human Resource Administration: Applications and Limitations," *Academy of Management Review*, 2, 4, 1977, 535–542.

Hudis, Paula M. "Commitment to Work and Wages: Earnings Differences of Black and White Women," *Sociology of Work and Occupations*, 4, 2, (1977), 123–145.

Humanistic Designs. *How to Eliminate Discrimination Practices: A Guide to EEO Compliance*, New York: AMACOM: A division of American Managment Associations, 1975.

Hunady, RoJo and Wahrman, J. "Influence of Sex-Role Stereotypes on Personnel Decisions," Thirty-seventh Annual Academy of Management Meetings, Orlando, 1977.

Hunter, John E. and Schmidt, Frank C. "Differential and Single—Group Validity of Employment Tests by Race: A Critical Analysis of Three Recent Studies," *Journal of Applied Psychology*, 63, 1, (1978) 1–11.

Hunter, John E., Schmidt, Frank L., and Rauschenberger, John M. "Fairness of Psychological Tests: Implications of Four Definitions For Selection Utility and Minority Hiring," Washington, D.C.: United States Civil Service Commission, 1975.

Hunter, John E. and Schmidt, Frank L., "Critical Analysis of the Statistical and Ethnical Implications of Various Definitions of Test Bias," *Psychological Bulletin*, 83, 6, (1976), 1053–1071.

Krefting, L.A., Berger, P.K., and Wallace, M.J., Jr. "The Contribution of Sex Distribution, Job Content and Occupational Classification to Job Sex." *Typing Two Studies, Journal of Vocational Behavior*, in press.

Krzystofiak, Frank and Newman, Jerry. "What is Discrimination? An Evaluation Based on the Word of God (i.e. OFCCP, EEOC)," *Proceedings Academy of Management 1978 Annual Meeting*, in print.

Laws, J.L. "Pschological Dimensions of Labor Force Participation of Women," in *EEO and the AT&T Case*, ed. by P. Wallace, Cambridge: MIT Press, 1976.

Ledvinka, J.L. "Technical Implications of Equal Employment Law for Manpower Planning," *Personnel Psychology*, 28, (1975), 229–323.

Ledvinka, J., LaForge, R.L. and Corbett, T.G. "Testing of an Affirmative Action Goal Setting Model," *Public Personnel Management*, 4 (November 1975).

Mahoney, Thomas and Milkovich, George. *Techniques for Application of Market Analysis to Manpower Analysis*, Minneapolis: Industrial Relations Center, University of Minnesota, 1971.

Metera, V.L. "Steel Industry Equal Employment Consent Decrees," Industrial Relations Research Association 27th Annual Proceedings, Minneapolis, Minn.

McGuiness, K.C. *Government Memoranda on Affirmative Action Programs*. Washington, D.C.: Equal Employment Advisory Council, 1976.

Milkovich, G.T. and Mahoney, T. "Human Resource Planning and Policy," *Handbook of Personnel and Industrial Relations Vol. 4*, ed. by D. Yoder and H. Heneman, Jr., Washington, D.C.: Bureau of National Affairs, 1976.

Milkovich, George T. and Krzystofiak, Frank. "Human Resource Models Applied to Affirmative Action Planning," Invited paper presented at the OFCCP Conference on Affirmative Action Planning Methodologies, Ithaca: Cornell University, 1977.

Milkovich, George T. *An Analysis of Issues Related to Availability, Symposium on Equal Employment Issues*. Washington, D.C.: Equal Employment Advisory Council, forthcoming (1978).

Moore, George A. Jr. "Steel Industry Consent Decrees—A Model for the Future," *Employee Relations Law Journal*, 3, 2, (Autumn 1977), 214–239.

Morris, Frank C. Jr. *Current Trends in the Use (and Misuse) of Statistics in Employment Discrimination Litigation*. Washington, D.C.: Equal Employment Advisory Council, 1977.

Newman, Jerry M. "An Empirical Analysis of Discrimination in Recruitment," *Industrial and Labor Relations Review*, in press, 1978.

Newman, Jerry M. and Krzystofiak, Frank J. "Self Reports vs. Unobtrusive Measures: Balancing Method Variance and Ethnical Concerns," Unpublished Manuscript, 1978.

Oaxaca, R.L. "Male-Female Wage Differentials in the Telephone Industry," In *EEO and the AT&T Case*, ed. by P. Wallace, Cambridge: MIT Press, 1976.

Office of Federal Contract Compliance Programs. "Revised Order No. 14 on Equal Opportunity Compliance Reviews of Non-construction Contractors," in *Daily Labor Report*, No. 98, pp. H-1 - H-8, Washington: The Bureau of National Affairs, Inc., 1973.

Peake, Charles F. "Negro Occupation Employment Participation in American Industry," *American Journal of Economy and Sociology*, 34, 1, (1975), 67–86.

Rabinowitz, D. "The Bias in the Governments' Anti-Bias Agency," *Fortune*, 94 (December 1976), 138–148.

Reynolds, Lloyd G. *Labor Economics and Labor Relations*, 7th ed., Englewood Cliffs, N.J.: Prentice-Hall, 1978.

Rosen, B. and Jerdee, T.H. "Influence of Sex Role Stereotypes on Evaluations of Male and Female Supervisory Behavior," *Journal of Applied Psychology*, 57, (1973), 44-48.

Rosen, B. and Jerdee, T.H. "Effects of Applicant's Sex and Difficulty of Job on Evaluations of Candidates for Managerial Positions," *Journal of Applied Psychology*, 59, (1974), (a) 511-512.

Rosen, B. and Jerdee, T.H. "Influence of Sex Role Stereotypes on Personnel Decisions," *Journal of Applied Psychology*, 59, (1974), (b) 9-14.

Rosen, B. and Jerdee, T.H. "Sex Role Stereotyping in the Executive Suite," *Harvard Business Review*, 52, 2, (1974), (c) 45-58.

Rosen, B. and Jerdee, T.H. "On-the-Job Sex Bias: Increasing Managerial Awareness," *Personnel Administrator*, (January 1977), 15-18.

Rosenblum, Marc. "The External Measures of Labor Supply: Recent Trends and Issues," Conference on Affirmative Action Planning, Ithaca: Cornell University, 1977.

Rosenblum, Marc. "The Use of Labor Statistics and Analysis in Title VII Cases," *Industrial Relations Law Journal*, Vol. 1, No. 4 (Winter 1977), 685-710.

Schmidt, F.L. and Hunter, J.E. "Racial and Ethnic Bias in Psychological Tests: Divergent Implications of Two Definitions of Test Bias," *American Psychologist*, 29, (1974), 1-8.

Shinar, E.H. "Sexual Stereotypes of Occupations," *Journal of Vocational Behavior*, 7, (1975), 99-111.

Snider, Patricia J. "External Data for Affirmative Action Planning," *Conference on Affirmative Action Planning Concepts*, Ithaca: Cornell University, 1977.

Sommers, Dixie. "Occupational Ranking for Men and Women by Earnings," *Monthly Labor Review*, 97, (August 1974), 34-51.

Thurow, Lester G. *Poverty and Discrimination*. Washington, D.C.: The Brookings Institute, 1969.

Thurow, Lester G. *Generating Inequality: Mechanisms of Distribution in the U.S. Economy*. New York: Basic Books, Inc., Publishers, 1975, p. 258.

Todorovich, Miro M. "Discrimination in Higher Education: A Debate on Faculty Employment," in *Reverse Discrimination*, ed. by B.R. Gross, Buffalo: Prometheus Books, 1977.

U.S. vs. Jefferson County Board of Education, 372 F. 2d 836, 876 (5th Cir. 1966) (AFF'D and Corrected en BANC) 380 F. 2d 385 (5th Cir. 1967).

U.S. Commission on Civil Rights. *The Federal Civil Rights Enforcement Effort—1974, Vol. 5: To Eliminate Employment Discrimination*. Washington, D.C.: U.S. Commission on Civil Rights, 1975.

U.S. Department of Health, Education, and Welfare, *Manual for Determining the Labor Market Availability of Women and Minorities*. Washington, D.C.: Office of the Secretary, Office for Civil Rights, 1976.

U.S. Department of Labor. "Affirmative Action Programs," (Revised Order No. 4) *Federal Register*, 36, 23152-23157, U.S. Congress, 1971.

U.S. Department of Labor. Bureau of Labor Statistics. *Employment and Earnings*. 25, 1, (January 1978), 138.

U.S. Department of Labor. "Employee Testing and Other Selection Procedures," *Federal Register*, 36, 19307-19310, U.S. Congress, 1921.

U.S. EEOC. *Affirmative Action and Equal Employment, A Guide Book for Employers*, 1 and 2, Washington. D.C.: U.S. EEOC, 1974.

U.S. Equal Employment Opportunity Commission. "Guidelines on Employee Selection Procedures," *Federal Register*, 35, 12333–12335, U.S. Congress, 1970.

Wachter, Michael L. "Primary and Secondary Labor Markets," *Brookings Papers on Economic Activity*, 3, 637–680, Washington, D.C.: The Brookings Institute, 1974.

Notes

[1] One may ask how is this possible, considering the divergence of opinion about an operational definition of equality and discrimination. A reasonable question; perhaps these definitions keep evolving.

[2] A plausible hypothesis is that they are not the same employees. A reason for this is the frustrating time delay that exists between an employee filing a complaint and an agency investigating and taking any action. However, the current head of the EEOC, Eleaner Holmes Norton, has introduced significant procedural changes designed to lessen the time delay.

[3] There is some evidence that recent Supreme Court decisions can be interpreted as tilting away from "results" toward "intent" (Mounts, 1978).

[4] For an extended discussion of this issue see: *Perspectives on Availabilities*: (Washington, D.C.: Equal Employment Advisory Council, 1978).

[5] OFCCP factors found in Revised Order No. 4: (41: CFR 60-Z)

(1) The minority and/or female population of the labor area surrounding the facility;
(2) The size of the minority and/or female unemployment force in the labor area surrounding the facility;
(3) The percentage of minority and/or female work force as compared with the total work force in the immediate labor area;
(4) The general availability of minorities and/or females having requisite skills in the immediate labor area;
(5) The availability of minorities and/or females having requisite skills in an area in which the contractor can reasonably recruit;
(6) The availability of promotable and transferable minorities and/or females within the contractor's organization;
(7) The existence of training institutions capable of training minorities and/or females in the requisite skills; and
(8) The degree of training which the contractor is reasonably able to undertake as a means of making all job classes available to minorities and/or females.

[6] Stocks are the numbers or proportions of each race/sex/ethnic group employed in a job or salary grade, or some organizational unit. For example, 100 workers may be employed as chemical analysts: 38 percent may be white female, 50 percent white male, 2 percent black females and 10 percent black males.

Flows are the numbers and proportions of employees moving from one stock to another. For example, 10 percent of all the chemical analysts may have been promoted to chemist last year. Four may be white females, two black females, one black male and the rest white males.

[7] An excellent collection of articles and letters representing the several points of view can be found in B.R. Gross (1977) *Reverse Discrimination*.

Training and Development Programs: What Learning Theory and Research Have to Offer

Craig Eric Schneier
University of Maryland

There is little debate among those interested in training and development in organizations that the principles of learning are basic to their programs' design and implementation. This view is evidenced by the fact that training has been equated with learning (for example, Blumenfeld and Holland, 1971), and that many proponents of Organizational Development, notably those favoring laboratory training techniques, have stressed "learning to learn" as a primary objective (for example, Golembiewski, 1972).

Recently, various authors have used learning theory and research effectively in their discussions of training and development programs. Such concepts as anxiety, punishment, and reinforcement are used to help evaluate training experiences. Schrank (1971) has used some learning theory research to help emphasize the degree of similarity between the teacher-pupil role and the supervisor-subordinate role. He has also shed some light on the importance of the teacher's role in determining the pupil's learning success. At least one learning theory, operant theory, has recently been explored as to its application to a wide variety of training and development problems (Murphy, 1972; Beatty and Schneier, 1972).

Despite this sampling of useful ideas generated from learning theory and a widespread recognition that training and development programs are primarily learning processes, there is still much validity in the following remarks by Goldstein and Sorcher:

> Management training—in its several underlying philosophies, its specific conceptualizations and its concrete techniques—is a human learning process. Yet almost without exception, there has been remarkably little reliance in the development and implementation of management training on this vast and relevant body of research literature. (1972, p. 37)

We agree with the statement that there are principles of various learning theories and findings from empirical research that are still relatively unknown and/or not utilized by specialists in training and development. While there is considerable disagreement among the experts as to which one of the several learning theories best explains the human learning process, many principles which logically follow from the various theories are supported by a considerable body of research. Obviously, not all of this research was performed with managers, or even

---

"Training and Development Programs: What Learning Theory and Research Have to Offer," by Craig Eric Schneier. Reprinted with permission of *Personnel Journal*, copyright April 1974

with adults in work situations, but so much of it has been substantiated time and again that the findings are generally agreed upon in the literature.

This article will state some of these principles and findings which are thought to be useful in all phases of training and development programs. The statements will be grouped under the learning environment, the role of the teacher/trainer, characteristics of the learner, basic processes in the human learning activity, reinforcement and punishment, retention and transfer of learning, and practice. (For a more detailed explanation of these principles and findings, the reader is referred to any of the works on learning cited in the references.)

It will be stressed that these seven categories form the interdependent considerations in the design, implementation, and evaluation of effective training and development programs, that they represent the sources of possible contingencies to be dealt with in each unique learning situation, and that they form the conceptual base for many important organizational training and development programs, such as MBO, skill training, and performance appraisals.

PRINCIPLES AND FINDINGS FROM LEARNING THEORY AND RESEARCH

I. The Learning Environment

1. Objectives and success criteria for the learning program should be specified and communicated to all learners before the program begins (see V-7).

2. Tests of the learner's progress should be scheduled. If a learner is not ready for a test, he/she should continue practicing. The learner should have an idea of the types of questions or activities that will be on the test. The "ordeal" aspect of testing should be eliminated.

3. Tasks should be broken into component behaviors that can be learned directly. The behaviors should be sequenced in order of increasing difficulty toward a final target behavior (see V-5).

4. The value of teaching machines and programmed learning devices lies in their ability to help sequence learning, to allow the learner to progress at his or her own pace, and to help control attention by focusing the learner on the stimuli; their value does not lie in their gadgetry or hardware.

5. To measure learning, note observational changes in the frequencies of desired behavioral responses, not necessarily in the strength of responses, in intentions, or in attitudes. Baseline frequencies of behavior must, therefore, be established prior to the learning situation in order to note the differential effects of learning.

6. "Whole" presentation is usually better than "part" presentation. Therefore, give the learner a "feel" for the total task initially.

7. Learning can and does take place in every context, not only in specified locations and in formal programs. Undesirable and desirable behaviors learned in these "informal" settings should be noted.

II. The Role of the Teacher/Trainer

1. Teachers learn a great deal about their learners when they are actually teaching and given responsibility. Having students act as teachers in some situations increases their ability to learn, as well as their empathy for other teachers.

2. The teacher conditions emotional reactions in the learning program, as well as behavioral responses and should, therefore, attempt to condition favorable reactions to himself and to the subject matter.

3. The teacher establishes objectives, methods, sequences, and time limits in learning programs with varying degrees of participation by the learner. The teacher's knowledge of the learner, the situation, and the content of the learning program is vital for specifying both the proper methods and the appropriate degree of learner participation in each learning program.

III. The Characteristics of the Learner

1. People not only learn at different rates, but each person brings a different emotional state or temperament to the learning situation (see II-2). Assessment of temperament facilitates a more effective choice of teaching strategies.

2. The motivational level of the learner is relevant to the type and amount of stimuli to which he/she will respond. Whether the student finds the learning intrinsically or extrinsically rewarding (that is, instrumental for internally mediated or externally mediated rewards) should be considered. The needs the learner has unsatisfied as he/she enters the learning program are also relevant.

3. Each learner's prior conditioning or learning background will influence the amount, frequency, and type of reinforcement and punishment which will be most effective, as well as the method of stimuli presentation (for example, visual, auditory).

4. Individual learners should be encouraged to learn the skills or behaviors of which they are capable and in which they are interested. They should be able to specialize and demonstrate expertise in at least one area in order to take pride in their accomplishments.

IV. Basic Processes in the Human Learning Activity

1. Interest and attention come from successful experiences. These, in turn, facilitate learning as they are seen as rewarding experiences.

2. Attention and curiosity in learning are best facilitated by the use of moderate (not too high nor too low) levels of arousal, curiosity, or anxiety.

3. Learning can occur when the learner merely observes. Active participation is not always necessary, unless motor skills are being taught.

4. Learners should not leave the learning setting after giving incorrect responses. Final responses should always be correct.

5. There are several ways to learn: trial and error, perception-organization-insight, and modeling another's behavior are all effective under certain conditions.

6. Learning usually progresses to a point and then levels off. This leveling (a "plateau" in a "learning curve") may be due to the fact that incorrect responses are being reduced or that small simple steps in learning were learned rapidly and now as the small steps are combined into complex tasks, learning slows. Incentives added in the "plateau" stage are helpful.

7. If motor responses are to be learned, verbal guidance, practice, and a favorable, supportive environment are helpful. If ideas or concepts are to be learned, active participation and the formation of meaningful associations between the new material and more familiar material are helpful.

8. Learning can be inhibited and therefore proper responses decreased if too much repetition or fatigue is evidenced (see VII-3).

9. Avoidance learning occurs when fear is felt and a response is made to eliminate the fear. This fear-avoiding response is often reinforced, and it therefore has little chance of being eliminated, as it is needed to avoid aversive stimuli (see V-2). To eliminate avoidance behaviors, the aversive stimuli must be removed.

10. Incidental learning is learning that remains dormant until the occasion for its demonstration arises (for example, curiosity is stimulated or reinforcement is powerful enough to elicit the response) (see VI-1).

11. Imitation requires that the learner is directly reinforced for matching a model's behavior. "Matched dependence" occurs when the learner models a model. "Same behavior" occurs when two learners respond to the same stimulus, not to each other. Vicarious learning is matching the behavior of another without receiving direct or immediate reinforcement from the model.

12. Complex human learning includes a proper degree of discrimination and generalization. Discrimination requires distinguishing between quite similar stimuli which require *different* responses. Generalization requires noting that similar, but not exactly the same stimuli often require the *same* response.

13. Attitudes can be learned and reinforced in much the same way as behavior is reinforced.

V. Reinforcement and Punishment

1. The "Law of Effect" states that behavior that is reinforced will increase in probability of future occurrence. A reinforcer is, therefore, any object or event that *strengthens* the probability of future occurrence of behavior.

2. Punishment occurs when the probability of a response is *weakened* by an object or event. Punishment leads to escape and avoidance behaviors, as well as frustration.

3. Secondary reinforcers (for example, money) are those objects or events which are linked to or instrumental for receiving other primary reinforcers, such as food, and so also take on reinforcing properties themselves. The many effective secondary reinforcers should be identified and used.

4. Undesired behaviors can be extinguished if they are simply not reinforced and not punished, but ignored.

5. "Shaping" behavior occurs when desired responses are observed which are approximates of a target behavior, and are reinforced. The responses are

continually reinforced as they become closer and closer to the target, until the target is imitated.

6. For punishment and reinforcement to be effective, they must be dispensed immediately and be appropriate in intensity for the particular response they follow.

7. Knowledge of results of performance is basic to learning and is often a reinforcer. It provides necessary feedback for corrective action, and should be related to goal levels, which are predetermined standards of performance communicated to and understood by the learner.

8. A harder, more intense response will not be elicited unless a more intense, more powerful reinforcer is given.

9. If reinforcement is dispensed on a variable ratio schedule (after a random and changing number of responses unknown to the learner), behavior will be most difficult to extinguish. The variable ratio is thus more effective in sustaining desired responses than either a continuous reinforcement schedule (each desired response rewarded) or fixed interval reinforcement schedule (reinforcement given after the passage of an interval of time, for example, weekly).

10. Social reinforcement (in the form of approval or status given by others) can be effective in controlling behavior, depending upon the environment and personal attractions.

11. The personality and position of the reinforcing/punishing agent influences the effectiveness of the reinforcement or punishment he/she dispenses. Therefore, it is not only that the person dispenses rewards, but that his or her manner, sincerity, and tone in these instances is noticed by the learner.

VI. Retention and Transfer of Learning

1. In transferring learning, the teacher/trainer should be aware of latent learning and offer reinforcement to prompt the demonstration of such learning.

2. Time does not cause forgetting per se; it merely allows for interfering learning processes to occur between what was learned and the time recall is desired.

3. Retroactive inhibition refers to the interference of new material on the ability to recall older material. Proactive inhibition occurs when old material interferes with the learning of new material. At times, therefore, it is wise to almost over-learn or repeat some material many times.

4. Some learned material is not recalled, as it is repressed in the subconscious of the learner because its overt demonstration is deemed to be harmful to the learner.

5. Identical stimuli presented in the learning and application settings should result in positive transfer. The learning of principles that apply across situations also aids in transfer of learning.

6. Transfer is aided if responses are given in situations which are similar to those which will be encountered in the post-learning environment.

7. Transfer is aided if the learner is able to demonstrate generalization (see IV-12).

8. Retention is strengthened if a variable-ratio reinforcement schedule is followed (see V-10).

VII. Practice

1. The learner must be encouraged (that is, reinforced) to take practice seriously.
2. Practice should include responses to stimuli different from those encountered in learning, but which may be encountered in actual application (see IV-12).
3. Distributed, rather than massed, practice with frequent short rests is usually optimal.

USES OF THE PRINCIPLES AND FINDINGS

It is obvious that while not all of these findings and principles from learning theory and research are applicable to each type of training and development program, some are of obvious use. Depending on the type of program, exigencies of time and cost, and the characteristics of the trainees and trainers, some will be more relevant than others. Furthermore, the seven categories are not meant to be entirely separate. Many items necessarily overlap. The most important aspect of the categories is their *interdependent* nature. Program developers can benefit from some consideration of each category.

As with so many aspects of organizations, the effective design and implementation of training and development programs depend largely on the recognition of the contingencies the data from the seven categories present to the specialist. In each particular instance, the categories come together in a unique way to form a complex learning situation or set of contingencies to be managed. The use of a particular type of training program can depend upon the characteristics of the trainees, which can depend upon the learning environment and learning content, which may depend upon the role of the trainer, and so on. It can thus be seen that each of the seven categories may influence, or be contingent upon, any or all of the others in any given learning situation. The training and development specialist's success in facilitating learning will, therefore, depend in large part on his or her ability to properly *diagnose* a situation and then develop the most effective learning strategies for that situation. In the diagnostic phase of the facilitation of learning in organizations, the seven categories represent the possible sources of data which can be gathered regarding a training situation (for example, data regarding the environment, the trainer, the trainees and so on) (see Figure 1).

After the diagnosis is completed, the actual *design* of a particular program or learning strategy can begin. The statements in each category can be scanned for their relevance to a specific type of strategy, such as programmed instruction, lectures, or modeling. For example, if a "skill" training program is required, statements concerning practice, knowledge of results, and reinforcement schedules would be helpful. Following design, the *implementation* of the strategy can be aided by the statements, as they suggest points to be noted which can deter or facilitate implementation in a particular situation. For example, as category three notes, certain characteristics of the learner are vital considerations which would make some strategies more effective than others.

```
CATEGORIES OF DATA IN THE
LEARNING SITUATION
  I. The learning environment.
 II. The role of the teacher trainer.
III. The characteristics of the learner.
IV. Basic processes in the human learn-
     ing activity.
 V. Reinforcement and punishment.
VI. Retention and transfer of learning.
VII. Practice.
```

Diagnosis of the learning situation.

Design of the appropriate learning strategy.

Implementation of the learning strategy.

Evaluation and possible *redesign* of the learning strategy.

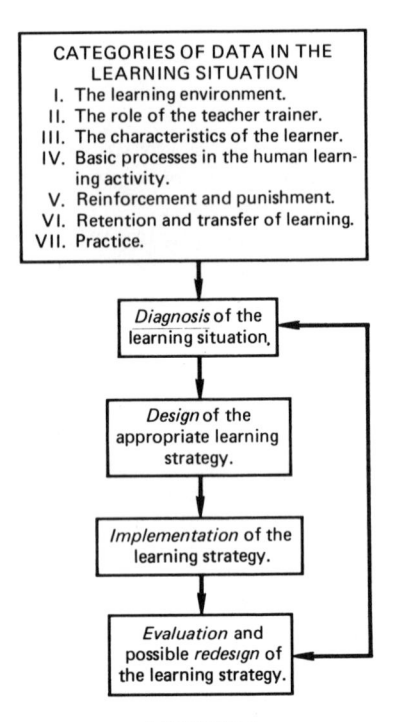

FIGURE 1

The last stage in training and development work is *evaluation* of the strategy and possible *redesign*. This stage can be aided as the seven categories again present the sources of probable success or failure.

The principles and findings from learning theory and research have been presented as an initial list compiled to help those engaged in training and development programs become aware of the scope of the learning literature which is applicable to their programs. The list is also designed for use in the following stages of training and development work: diagnosis of the learning situation, design of the learning strategy, implementation of the strategy, and evaluation and possible redesign. The seven categories are offered as possible sources of data which combine to form each particular training and development situation. Data gathered from the seven categories can facilitate a more rigorous diagnostic effort on the part of the training and development specialist. This diagnosis aids in tying the unique learning situation faced by the specialist to the learning strategy most amenable to that situation. Particular statements within the categories can also be scanned as to their obvious use as guides in implementing specific programs such as MBO, skill training, performance appraisals, and the many other training and development programs which are designed to facilitate learning in organization settings.

References

Bass, B., and J. Vaughan. *Training in Industry: The Management of Learning*. Belmont. Calif.: Wadsworth, 1968.

Beatty, R. W., and Craig Eric Schneier. "Training the Hard-Core Unemployed through Positive Reinforcement," *Human Resource Management, 11,* 4, (Winter 1972), 11–17.

Berrelson, B., and G. Steiner. *Human Behavior.* New York: Harcourt Brace, 1967.

Blumenfeld, W. A., and M. C. Holland. "A Model for the Empirical Evaluation of Training Effectiveness," *Personnel Journal, 50,* 8, (August 1971), 634–640.

Bugelski, B. R. *The Psychology of Teaching,* 2nd ed. Indianapolis: Bobbs-Merrill, 1971.

Goldstein, A. P. and M. Sorcher. "Changing Managerial Behavior by Applied Learning Techniques," *Training and Development Journal, 27,* 2, (March 1973), 36–39.

Golembiewski, R. T. *Renewing Organizations; The Laboratory Approach to Planned Change.* Itasca, Ill.: Peacock, 1972.

Hilgard, E. R., and G. H. Bower. *Theories of Learning,* 3rd ed. New York: Appleton-Century-Crofts, 1966.

Logan, F. A. *Fundamentals of Learning and Motivation.* Dubuque, Iowa: Wm. Brown, 1970.

Murphy, J. "Is It Skinner or Nothing?" *Training and Development Journal, 26,* 2 (February 1972), 2–9.

Schrank, W. R. "Three Experiments in Education," *Personnel Journal, 50,* 9 (September 1971), 702–704.

Skinner, B. F. *The Technology of Teaching.* New York: Appleton-Century-Crofts, 1968.

Staats, A. W., and C. K. Staats. *Complex Human Behavior: A Systematic Extension of Learning Principles.* New York: Holt, Rinehart & Winston, 1963.

Employee Growth Through Performance Management

Michael Beer
Robert A. Ruh

In recent years, management by objectives (MBO) has enjoyed a good deal of popularity. Both personnel specialists and line managers have responded enthusiastically to the emphasis that MBO places on subordinates' results and accountability rather than on their personal qualities. MBO's popularity is easy to understand.

First, many if not most managers feel quite uncomfortable judging the means by which their subordinates accomplish their goals. There are, of course, many

Michael Beer and Robert A. Ruh, "Employee Growth Through Performance Management," Harvard Business Review, July–August 1975, Copyright © 1975 by the President and Fellows of Harvard College; all rights reserved.

reasons for this discomfort. Some managers find evaluating people incompatible with the egalitarian ideals of our society. Others shy away from the role of providing feedback because they fear emotionally laden interpersonal situations. Still others are simply so results-oriented that they have no time for such "personnel stuff."

Second, MBO has proved to be a useful vehicle for increasing the quantity and quality of communication between line managers and subordinates concerning responsibilities, objectives, plans, and results. In addition, research has shown that the setting of specific objectives generally increases the individual's motivation to do certain tasks well.

Despite its usefulness, many managers have found that MBO also has its limitations. In fact, its major strength is its major weakness: MBO focuses the attention of the boss and the subordinate exclusively on task results. For example, a manufacturing manager reviewed the objectives of his plant manager and found that objectives for cost reduction as well as for gross margins had been exceeded. He was pleased. He was not so pleased when he learned sometime later that the MBO process had failed to uncover crucial information: the plant manager had not developed a cohesive plant staff and was not getting along well with managers in other functional areas. MBO does not, therefore, help the manager to observe and evaluate the behavior of his or her subordinates; yet such observation and evaluation are vital to making intelligent promotion decisions and helping employees improve their performance.

Take, for example, the case of a hypothetical sales manager whose job is to improve the performance of his sales force. Suppose that this manager has two salesmen performing substantially below standard; both are achieving only 80 percent of their revenue budgets. How is the manager to help these people improve? Clearly, his first step must be to analyze why each salesman is doing so poorly. It's possible that one salesman lacks the forcefulness and aggressiveness needed to overcome objections and "close" sales, while the other salesman may be alienating customers with his aggressiveness and overconfidence. Obviously, different approaches are called for to help these two people improve, even though their results are about the same.

The dilemma the vice-president of sales would have in the same hypothetical organization illustrates the deficiency of MBO as far as making promotion decisions goes. Let's suppose that the VP has one sales management position to fill and that the two most logical candidates both consistently achieve 150 percent of their quotas. In order to pick the better of the two, the VP must analyze their behavior patterns.

Imagine that one salesman achieves his outstanding results through sheer strength of drive. Fiercely competitive, he is effective because he is a hard worker and persistent. Unfortunately, this salesman is not very organized. Indeed, he is rather sloppy with paper work, and most of his colleagues find him quite difficult to work with. In contrast, imagine that the other salesman performs so well primarily because he does a good job at analyzing his territory and customers and because he plans and organizes effective selling strategies. In addition, he is particularly adept at gaining the help and cooperation he needs from others on the sales force and the marketing staff. Clearly, which of these two people would make the best sales manager cannot be determined by results alone.

For a number of years, managers at Corning Glass Works have used MBO. But because of its shortcomings, staff psychologists and personnel specialists began to look for a system that would incorporate its strengths with a better way to help managers observe, evaluate, and aid in improving the performance of subordinates. After several years of research and development, we produced what we call the performance management system. The PMS is the formal vehicle now used by Corning to manage, measure, and improve the performance and potential for advancement of approximately 3,800 managerial and professional employees.

Our purpose in this article is to describe and analyze this system. It is working at Corning, and we think it can work in other companies. But because a system is only as good as the commitment and skill of people who must use it, we shall also discuss the strategy and tactics used to introduce it as a corporate program and then its strengths and deficiencies. First, however, we would like to share the thinking behind the system with you and why we thought it would be effective.

MANAGING, JUDGING, AND HELPING

One of the most critical problems facing corporations is management development. A central thesis underlying Corning's PMS is that, while classroom learning has its place, effective managerial performance is best developed through practical challenges and experiences on the job with guidance and feedback from superiors. Analysis of current organizational life indicates that the element most frequently missing or deficient in this equation is accurate and objective performance feedback.

PMS was developed to help managers give such feedback in a helpful and constructive manner and to aid the supervisor and subordinate in creating a developmental plan. It is distinguished from other performance appraisal systems by the following characteristics: (1) its formal recognition of the manager's triple role in dealing with subordinates, (2) its emphasis on both development and evaluation, (3) its use of a profile displaying the individual's strengths and developmental needs relative to himself rather than to others, and (4) its integration of the results achieved (MBO) with the means by which they have been achieved.

The development of Corning's PMS was triggered by several problems normally encountered by managers because of their triple role as *managers* responsible for the achievement of organization goals, *judges* who must evaluate performance and make decisions about salary and promotability, and *helpers* who must develop subordinates into more effective and promotable employees. Experience has shown that these functions are not always carried out successfully because they are confused by the manager and they interfere with one another when the manager attempts to communicate with a subordinate.

For example, if you ask a manager who uses only MBO if he reviews his subordinates' performance and helps them develop and improve, he will probably answer yes. Yet, while managing by objectives can play a critical part in ensuring individual and group results, it fails to help subordinates understand what behavior they must modify or adopt to improve those results.

222 Employee Growth Through Performance Management

Another typical problem arises from the conflict between the manager's role as judge and his role as helper. To fulfill his responsibilities to the organization, the manager must submit evaluations to the personnel department, make recommendations about subordinates' promotions, and make salary judgments. Research has shown that his role as judge interferes with his ability to develop a helping relationship with subordinates.[1] A subordinate often begins to feel so defensive that he or she does not hear what the boss is saying, especially when the boss is trying to be a judge and a helper at the same time. Management at Corning developed PMS to help managers differentiate between these roles and to perform each of them effectively.

Management by objectives

- Agree on objectives
- Set criteria
- Make plans
- Execute plans
- Measure results
- Review results
- Begin new cycle

Performance development and review

- Observe behavior
- Describe incidents typical of the person
- Analyze data
- Discuss problems and goals
- Make plans
- Review progress
- Begin new cycle

Performance results evaluation

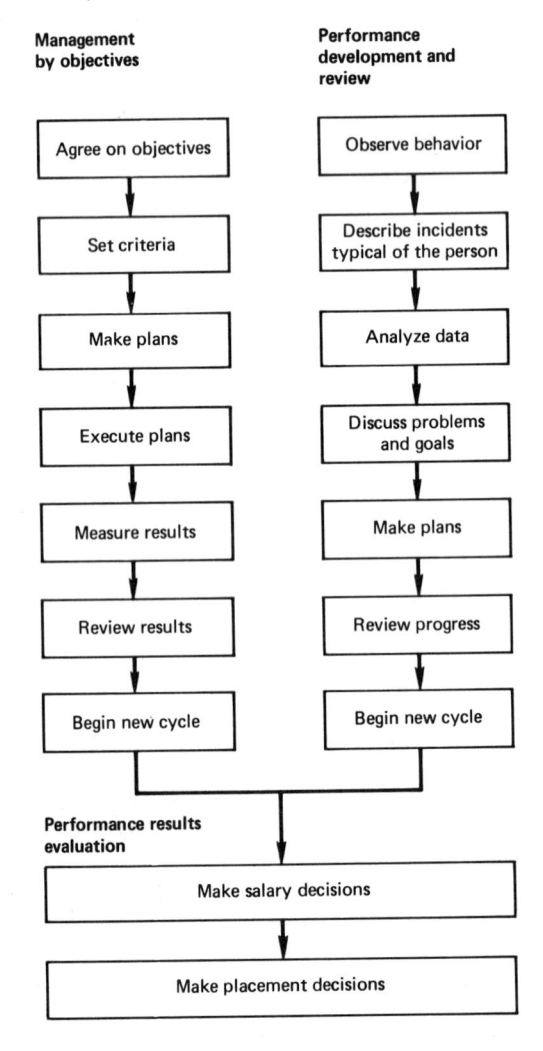

- Make salary decisions
- Make placement decisions

FIGURE 1 *Managing Performance*

DESIGNING THE SYSTEM

Essentially, PMS has three parts—MBO, performance development and review, and evaluation and salary review. Figure 1 indicates how the first two parts, independent and parallel to each other, feed into the third.

What makes the system unusual is a combination of two factors—a careful separation of each part from the other two (that is, each part is carried out separately from the other parts in meetings held at different times between manager and subordinate) and a step-by-step process for company managers to use in performance development and review.

How a Subordinate Performs

While MBO seemed to be a process better designed by each manager to fit his own situation than by the corporation, and the evaluation and salary review process in itself presented few problems, performance development and review was another matter entirely. There were elements of performance common to the various functions and units of the organization, and as we said before, many managers were encountering difficulty in helping subordinates improve their performance. Consequently, to fill this gap, we developed a step-by-step approach.

Using a *performance description questionnaire*, the manager first observes and describes his subordinates' behavior. Then, using a *performance profile*, he analyzes their strengths and weaknesses. Finally, through one or more *developmental interviews*, he attempts to help his subordinates see what changes in behavior are needed and plan for them. In these interviews, boss and subordinate jointly identify areas for improvement and establish plans to develop the abilities needed.

Critical Questions. The performance description questionnaire contains 76 items on which the performance of an exempt salaried person is evaluated by his immediate supervisor. Each item describes a specific type of behavior that has been identified as an important component of effective performance. Table 1 lists eight items from the questionnaire. The supervisor is asked to indicate on a six-point rating scale the extent to which he agrees that his subordinate behaves in ways similar to those described in the questionnaire. Space below each item provides the superior a chance to add comments or examples that substantiate the descriptive rating—"critical incidents" he has actually observed.

Taken together, the behavioral statements represent a comprehensive picture of effective performance within Corning Glass Works. They were identified through extensive research throughout the company and thus reflect the nature of the business environment as well as the company's culture and values and the nature of the tasks to be performed. What this means, of course, is that, while some of the performance items are common to many organizations, others are of significance only to Corning. It also implies that periodic research to update the list is needed as Corning's business, strategy, culture, and tasks change.

Table 1   Items from the performance description questionnaire

Individual performance
1. Objects to ideas before they are explained.
2. Takes the initiative in group meetings.
3. Is unable to distinguish between important and unimportant problems.
4. Has difficulty in meeting project deadlines.
5. Gives sufficient attention to detail when seeking solutions to problems.
6. Gives poor presentations.
7. Sees his problems in light of the problems of others (that is, does not limit his thinking to his own position or organizational unit).
8. Offers constructive ideas both within and outside his own job.

At Corning, the first step in the research was to pool what supervisors considered the critical incidents in the job performance of their exempt employees. We asked 50 supervisors representing a cross section of levels, functions, and divisions within the company to describe subordinates' specific actions that had led to either significant improvements or significant decrements in their departments' performance. The supervisors identified approximately 300 critical incidents, which we then translated into 150 general behavioral descriptions.

After further research to test validity of these general descriptions on 300 employees (selected at random), we arrived at 76 items having a statistically significant correlation with performance and management potential throughout the company.

Individualized Profiles. While a supervisor can easily evaluate each of his subordinates on all 76 items, it would be extremely time-consuming to review all 76 with each of his subordinates. So we had to invent some "shorthand" he could use to transmit to his subordinates the complex information obtained in the questionnaire.

First, we summarized the 76 items along 19 performance dimensions, 8 relating to supervision and 11 to individual performance which are listed on the left-hand side of Figure 2. We will not describe here the statistical methods used to arrive at these dimensions; suffice it to say that problems were encountered.

The most troublesome problem was that the supervisors tended to rate items quite similarly for a particular subordinate depending on whether they saw him as a good performer or a poor one in the first place. This tendency of the rater to allow his initial impressions to influence all subsequent decisions is known as the "halo error." The good performer would not receive feedback that would help him better himself for promotion, and the poor performer would feel "dumped on" and be unable to marshal his energies to work on anything.

We felt that everyone has developmental needs, even the best performers in the corporation. Thus everyone could gain from working on the few performance dimensions for which he had received the lowest ratings.

To break the halo effect, we next developed the performance profile, a tool to help managers discriminate among a subordinate's strengths and developmental

	Subordinate A		Subordinate B		Subordinate C	
	Weakness	Strength	Weakness	Strength	Weakness	Strength
Individual performance						
Openness to influence	●●		●●●●●			○○
Constructive initiative		○○		○○○		○○○○○○
Priority setting		○○		○○○	●●●●●●	
Work accomplishment	●●	●●●●●●●●●●			●●	
Thoroughness and accuracy		○○		○○		○○
Formal communications	●●			○○	●●●●●●	
Organizational perspective		○○	●●			○○○○○○
Credibility	●●			○○○○	●●	
Cooperation		○○	●●		●●	
Decisiveness	●●			○○○	●●	
Flexibility		○○		○○		○○○
Supervisory performance						
Delegation/participation		○○		○○○	●●●●●●	
Support for company		○○ ●●●●●●●●●●			●●	
Communication and positive motivation	●●			○○		○○
Follow-up and control		○○		○○	●●●●●●	
Unit improvement	●●		●●			○○○○○○
Selection, placement, and instruction		○○		○○○○	●●	
Unit productivity	●●		●●		●●	
Conflict resolution		○○		○○○	●●	

FIGURE 2 *Performance Profile*

needs. For each subordinate, the supervisor receives a performance profile like the three samples shown in Figure 2. The center line indicates the person's own average. The dimensions extending to the left are the subordinate's weaknesses; the dimensions extending to the right are the subordinate's strengths. The number of dots indicate specific degrees of weakness or strength. Note that these three profiles should not be compared with each other, since each is structured to reflect only the individual's performance.

We have found that managers are surprised when they receive the profile because they are not used to thinking about their subordinates as having negative qualities, or perhaps at least not the particular ones listed. To us, their surprise indicates that the profile is breaking the halo effect. In fact, the profile has four distinct advantages:

1. It helps both the supervisor and the subordinate to be analytical and discriminating in their evaluation of performance.
2. It, therefore, helps ensure individuals fair recognition for their strengths and constructive criticism for their shortcomings.
3. It reduces the supervisor's defensiveness and his need to "prove" the validity of his judgments.
4. It reduces the subordinate's defensiveness and his need to enhance his superior's judgment of him in relation to his "competitors."

The Interview. A subordinate's performance profile is developed by computer after his supervisor has filled out and sent in his performance description questionnaire. After receiving the profile, the manager is urged to use it to analyze his subordinate's performance in preparation for the developmental interview. Often the supervisor will want to identify the specific behavioral ratings that have caused a dimension to come out as a developmental need. In the interview, the specific behavior that needs attention can be discussed.

Some supervisors have found that asking subordinates to fill out questionnaires on themselves encourages open and nondefensive discussion of their performance. Each dimension can be reviewed and discrepancies between superiors' and subordinates' impressions discussed.

It is not our intent here to describe the ground rules for effective developmental interviews; much has been written about this elsewhere.[2] We do wish to point out that in PMS the developmental interview is a meeting distinct and separate from an MBO session or an evaluation session. The questionnaire and the profile are tools that help the manager differentiate development from MBO and evaluation and that reduce the anxiety associated with the developmental interview.

Finally, it is our belief that developmental plans and objectives are needed if change is actually to occur. The manager needs tools to help him form a developmental plan with his subordinates. These come in the form of (a) an interview guide, for translating explicit developmental needs into specific areas for which training programs have been identified, and (b) a matrix framework as shown in Figure 3, for translating broad needs into general strategies for development.

Strategies for improvement

General areas where improvement is needed	Training: Job-related skills or knowledge	In the laboratory or on the job	Counseling: Professional consulting or counseling	Supervision: Coaching	Observing boss's managerial style	Job enrichment: Job redesign	Job rotation
Understanding of role				●●●		●●●	
Effort, motivation, attitude		●●●		●●●	●●●	●●●	●●●
Knowledge of job or ability	●●●			●●●		●●●	●●●
Interpersonal skills		●●●	●●●	●●●			
Personality traits		●●●	●●●	●●●			

FIGURE 3 *Development Matrix (Intended as an Initial Guide to Getting Some Direction in Consideration Alternative Approaches to Personal Development)*

How a Subordinate is Evaluated

As we mentioned earlier, evaluation interviews of a subordinate's current performance, potential, promotability, and salary increase are distinct from MBO and appraisal sessions. It is best to make these evaluations when the subordinate is due for a salary increase. The manager rates each subordinate's overall performance and potential. The ratings, which are shared with subordinates and endorsed by the supervisor at the next level, reflect both the whats and the hows of performance.

SEEKING COMMITMENT

Since the effectiveness of any personnel system, no matter how well designed, is largely determined by the understanding, commitment, and skills of the line managers who must actually implement the program, we introduced PMS with these managers in mind.

The best way for a staff function to engender resentment or apathy toward a program is to "cram it down the throats" of the people who must implement it, so we did not attempt to introduce the system throughout the corporation all at once. Instead, we gained the approval and support of top corporate management first and then introduced the system to one division at a time on a quasi-voluntary basis. In essence, we sold each division vice-president on the program with no pressure from top corporate management. In accordance with what is known about effective change, we started with the divisions that seemed the most receptive and the most likely to succeed in using the program.

After selling the program to corporate and divisional managers on an individual basis, our primary vehicle for introducing the program within each division was a workshop training session. These sessions, which lasted either two full days or one very long day, covered the following points:

The need for and importance of effective performance appraisal

The rationale for a program that integrates behavior with results-centered approaches to appraisal

The research that led to performance development and review

The MBO approach to performance appraisal and how it is implemented

The use of the questionnaire and the profile

The way to conduct a developmental interview in a constructive, problem-solving manner

In addition to the traditional lecture-and-discussion format, we used a variety of instructional techniques including informal discussion groups, films, and role playing.

GAINING ACCEPTANCE AND MAKING REFINEMENTS

To investigate the extent to which PMS was being used and its effectiveness, we conducted a study in the four divisions having the most experience with the program, ranging from approximately two years to less than one year.[3] We found that 230 of the 351 supervisory personnel in seven plants and four division staff groups had participated in a performance development and review interview, either as bosses or subordinates or as both. Mobility was the primary reason that not all of the managers had participated; an employee or his supervisor very often changed jobs before they had worked together six months. Another reason appeared to be cases of little or no perceived encouragement to use the system.

Through a questionnaire we sent out, however, more than 90 percent of those who had participated in an interview provided us with detailed feedback on their impressions of the program. In addition, we checked our interpretations with the division management staffs during subsequent meetings we held with them. They confirmed and often elaborated on our interpretations.

Of course, there are bound to be some complaints with any new, complex system involving a large number of people. Our data, however, indicated a generally high acceptance of PMS among those who had used it. First of all, supervisors accepted some form of performance feedback as part of their jobs. Second, PMS in general and the questionnaire and profile in particular were seen as greatly helpful in the performance appraisal and development process.

Reduction of Anxiety

It is interesting that the person who found PMS the most helpful was the interviewer. Apparently, the active role of the supervisor placed more responsibility and pressure on him than on the subordinate.

For some, simply having the more formal, scientific-looking results of the questionnaire and profile rather than depending solely on their less systematized observations and conclusions helped set an easygoing tone. For most people, the profile appeared to function as an agenda that furthermore helped stimulate discussion of all aspects of a subordinate's performance. Despite these advances, the supervisors we sampled still seemed to feel that they greatly needed to improve their skills in conducting developmental interviews, and a related study on the effectiveness of the PMS workshop confirmed this finding.

Important Line Relationships

One would think a highly accepted system like PMS would spread itself by word of mouth at least within a single plant. Our results do not confirm this optimistic notion. In fact, it seems that few people communicate their positive views to others in the company. The availability of a good system is not enough to spread its use; a vigorously active program is necessary.

For instance, we found a couple of chains of supervisor-subordinate relationships that had not used PMS. These people reported that although they hadn't been told *not* to use it, they did not feel that they should until the man at the top of the chain told them to or at least had used it with his own subordinates. Other people seemed to want PMS and indicated that they were "waiting for follow-up," that is, pressure from someone in authority.

Organizational Asset

If we accept the premise that the manager's most important task is managing the performance of his subordinates and that constructive performance feedback is a key element in developing managers, then PMS is definitely an organizational asset.

In order to use PMS most effectively, significant resources are needed to follow the introductory workshop with on-the-spot consultation in planning and conducting developmental interviews. Too often, training is thought of as the final step in the introductory process. We recommend, instead, that personnel specialists help managers go through the PMS process at least once. In order to ensure that a performance management system will be used in the first place, key managers at all levels must state their commitment to it and model its use.

At Corning, many managers have found that just identifying the performance dimensions that are important to organizational effectiveness helps develop a common language for discussing performance and making decisions about people, something that is absent in most organizations. Thus, a performance management system can increase the objectivity and enhance the validity of personnel decisions.

Notes

[1] Herbert H. Meyer, Emanuel Kay, and John R. P. French, Jr., "Split Roles in Performance Appraisal," *Harvard Business Review*, January–February 1965, p. 123.

[2] Norman R. F. Maier, *The Appraisal Interview: Gestures, Methods, and Skills* (New York: John Wiley, 1958).

[3] Jack E. Dawson and B. B. (Steve) McCaa, "Performance Management and Review. An Evaluation of its Utilization." Paper presented in *Performance Management System: Research, Design, Introduction and Education*, a symposium of the American Psychological Association Convention, New Orleans, 1974.

Influencing Employee Behavior Through Compensation

Richard I. Henderson, Ph.D.

INFLUENCING EMPLOYEE BEHAVIOR THROUGH COMPENSATION

How often have you walked into a place of business and seen or heard the slogan, "People are our most important resource"? Undoubtedly, this slogan is true. When capable people are actively involved in any business, the productivity, profitability, and growth of the business and the quality of its product are more likely to meet the expectations of its management and the consumers of its output. But how does a business assure itself that those people it employs are most effective in meeting the expectations of its management? One very important way is through its compensation system.

Unfortunately, the actions and responses of a business in its relationship with potential and actual employees frequently do not substantiate its alleged belief that people are truly its most important resource. One indicator of this lack of appreciation is the poor design and implementation of its compensation system. A major reason for compensation system design and implementation failure is inadequate understanding by management and employees of the compensation system and of its influence of all participants in the business. To develop an adequate understanding of just how a compensation system functions, it may be wise to review why people work.

PEOPLE AND THEIR JOBS

Albert Camus once wrote, "Without work, all life goes rotten. But when work is soulless, life stifles and dies." People not only *need* to work, they *want* to. From work, they provide for their physical and mental survival, but the work must be meaningful. One of the primary ways in which people measure the value of their

Introductory Note: An increasing body of literature and research has been addressed to the nonmonetary aspects of organizational membership and approaches for making this a more rewarding experience. Often neglected is the pragmatic side of compensation systems and approaches which focus on the monetary aspects of the employer-employee relationship. Behavioral considerations in this approach become part of a total compensation approach in which the employer attempts to balance the realities of the ability to pay and need to generate profit with the need to attract and retain employees and to motivate performance. The author of the paper that follows attempts to establish this viewpoint and perspective.

The Editors.

Prepared especially for this book and printed with permission of the author.

work is through the compensation and noncompensation rewards they receive in exchange for their efforts.

A major difficulty in understanding the role of work is a failure to appreciate the change the Industrial Revolution has made on the mental as well as the physical well-being of all people. First came machinery that did not require people or animal power as the basic energy source. Then automation relieved employees of much of the effort required to observe, direct, and control the machinery. Now, in the last quarter of the twentieth century, computer-based operating systems have further minimized the requirements for human involvement in the production process. Modern high-technology production systems no longer require massive physical effort in order for human society to survive and grow.

As long as the perception of the role in life of the average worker was one of hard physical work and minimal self-control over work activities, or, for that matter, living conditions in general, aspirations for a life providing more self-determined options were locked deeply inside most human beings. Although work effort in our high-technology society has in most instances been simplified through continuous standardization and specialization of job activities, the responsibility for performing the job correctly has increased dramatically. Increased specialization has brought about greater complexity. The complex processes that produce goods and services for society require the care and concern of each involved worker. The failure of any one worker in the production process can minimize, if not destroy, the value of the final product. Among all of the opportunities available to a business to inform its members that each person is a vital and valuable contributor, none are more important than those made available through the compensation system.

In developing a compensation system, a business must determine what types of employee behavior it seeks to influence. It then must design a compensation system that includes the components most suitable for influencing that behavior.

Worker Expectations

To develop an appreciation of employee job behavior, it is helpful to analyze two basic values that are widespread among people everywhere. These universal values are equality and equity. Equality and equity form the foundation for any reward system that promotes fairness and social justice. It is only within a system that promotes equality and equity and operates within constraints set by fairness and justice that most people feel they will receive honest and impartial treatment. A system that promotes equality and forgets equity is unstable, while one that promotes equity and doesn't recognize equality is unmanageable.

The designers and managers of an equitable compensation system must permit the holders of more responsible positions and the exceptional contributors to lay claim to additional compensation components. Satisfying equity demands requires that there be differences in size or quantity among compensation components offered to employees in various jobs. It also requires that the compensation of employees be differentiated by performance. At the same time, to ensure equality, designers and managers must not only allow but actually encourage employees to compare their compensation components with those of others performing similar types of work and making similar contributions.

Employees measure the relative magnitude of compensation components among themselves and with employees in other work units, in other major organizational groupings, in other firms, or in similar occupations or professions. Compensation system designers and managers must recognize and take into consideration that every individual searches for information. Of all the information sought, none is more important than that used in measuring fairness and justice. In the world of work, measuring fairness and justice invariably includes measuring the relative magnitude of compensation components.

Self-Determination: A Reason to Work

Of the many reasons that people work, one stands out as a universal, underlying motive of the young and the old, the ambitious and the indolent, the expert and the unskilled. This universal reason for working in modern industrial, technical, and service businesses is to enlarge opportunity of choice, enhance self-determination.

The apparently unending spiral of human expectations and aspirations elevates the demands of people everywhere. The job and its accompanying paycheck provide the major opportunity for most people to satisfy a wide variety of demands. Although the paycheck is just one portion of the total compensation received by employees, it is the part that has the greatest impact on their life styles and, therefore, has the greatest opportunity for modifying their behavior.

The compensation offered by the business provides its members with the opportunity to achieve the desirable qualities of modern life. The amount of the paycheck determines, to a significant degree, the choice of housing employees and their families enjoy, their eating habits, and the transportation they use. Employer-provided benefit offerings of health care and a wide variety of protection, educational, and leisure-time services and activities, as well as retirement security, limit the self-determination of employees. Seldom, if ever, do employees have an opportunity for choice among these benefit options. (The major exception to this case is during collective bargaining when unions representing employees negotiate actively and firmly for benefit improvements and changes.)

The great majority of the benefit programs provided by employers, and certainly those that are the most costly, are the result, however, of employee demands. Providing payments for health care or maintaining income during periods of disability or at the lapse or termination of employment are examples of benefits that are extremely costly to the employer. If, however, these benefits were not provided by the employer, their replacement would consume a sizable portion of the employee's disposable income or significantly lessen the actual value of the paycheck.

Compensation provided for superior performance (by the individual, a group, or the business itself) can provide the additional payments that enable employees and their families to afford that extra spice in life—the long-dreamed of vacation, the nonbudgeted but desired "big ticket" purchase, the opportunity to temporarily change life style, or the opportunity to save or invest income for future use.[1]

The desirability for providing these qualities of modern life profoundly affects the relationship of the employee to the business. Having significant influence and control over these qualities of life, the business, through its compensation system, provides its members with the opportunity for self-determination and inner independence, the work itself notwithstanding. By providing opportunity of choice over the largest possible number of options affecting quality of life, the modern business maximizes for its employees freedom from control by others while, in turn, minimizing the feeling of need for assistance or obligation. Herein lies the cornerstone of individual freedom and dignity.

THE COMPENSATION SYSTEM

The compensation system is the allocation, conversion, and transfer of the income of a business to its employees for:

Monetary Claims on Goods and Services. The wage payment received by an employee comes in the form of money. Money as a medium of exchange enables the employee to purchase certain types and amounts of the wide variety of goods and services available at the marketplace. The actual kinds and quantity of purchases made by the employee depend upon the individual mechanisms that motivate choice behavior.

In-Kind Claims on Goods and Services. Many payments an employee receives come in the form of in-kind payments. These payments provide protection through a wide variety of insurances that include, for example, life, health and accident, legal and other claims for such services. In-kind payments also include income protection plans such as unemployment insurance, long-term disability income payments, severance payments, and various types of savings plans and pension plans that provide for security in an uncertain future. In addition to these in-kind payments, many businesses also provide employees with goods and services for individual use. Among these are subsidized cafeteria services, company-provided parking facilities, and discounts on a wide variety of goods and services normally offered by a business to its customers that are desirable to employees. These are only a few examples of in-kind claims on goods and services provided by employers.

In offering employment, the employer agrees to provide compensation in exchange for employee-provided availability, capability, and performance. This contractual agreement establishes an employee-employer income loop. The kind and quantity of compensation in the form of monetary wages and in-kind claims on goods and services vary, however, according to the worth to the employer of the availability, capability, and performance of the employee.

Employers provide for the monetary and in-kind wage claims of their employees through the various components of the compensation system. These include (1) base wages, (2) employee benefits, and (3) incentive components.

Base Wages

The amount of money, before deductions, paid to an employee to perform a specific job is the base wage of that job. The employee usually receives this wage payment in a regular cycle, such as weekly, bimonthly, or monthly. The amount of base wage varies according to how the business values the job. It may also vary according to some plan that recognizes prior employee service or performance contributions.

The variation of base wages from the lowest to the highest paid employee will form a ratio that normally covers a range from 1:15 to 1:30, but in certain businesses, it may form a ratio greater than 1:100. Federally legislated and enforced minimum wage rate standards have a direct effect on the base wages rates of most employees. Even when businesses establish policies to be "pace setters," or market leaders, in setting wage rates or when they negotiate with strong unions in establishing a relatively high acceptable level of base wage rates, the final resulting wage rate structures of the businesses are influenced by federal minimum wage rate standards.

In establishing base wages, three different areas normally require consideration and resolution. These areas are (1) establishment of internal equity, (2) provision for external equity, and, when appropriate, (3) provision for premium and differential payments.

Internal Equity. Each business, whether small or large, goods-producing or service-providing, profit or nonprofit, develops some form of an evaluation procedure for establishing the worth or determining internally equitable relationships among the jobs that comprise its organizational structure. In their most basic form, evaluation procedures provide a hierarchical ranking that states that "this" is the most valuable job, "this" is next most valuable, and so on to the least valuable job. The most sophisticated evaluation procedure will provide a relative ranking of worth from the most valuable to the least valuable job. In this method, job number two may be evaluated as being worth (what is equivalent to) 87 percent of job number one, job number three, 81 percent of job number one, and so on to the point where the least valuable job may be rated as worth 7 percent of job number one. An evaluation procedure that provides this degree of precision requires the use of some quantitative technique that, in turn, provides a specific quantitative value for the worth of each job.

External Equity. Very few businesses have the opportunity to establish base wages without considering the impact of forces external to the business. The locus of external impact on base wages is the job marketplace. Immunity to going market wages, government regulations affecting wage rates, and union influence felt through negotiated collective bargaining agreements is, for all practical purposes, nonexistent. Once a business establishes an internal ordering of jobs, it must then examine its own wage policies and the impact external forces are having on market wage rates. A business may attempt to set wages that replicate what appears to be the market value of the job; it may wish to be a market leader or a market follower, but whatever the case, it does require market wage rate information and must recognize the influences of the marketplace.

Premiums and Differentials. Most businesses provide extra wage payments for work effort that is normally considered burdensome, distasteful, inconvenient, or hazardous. Premiums and differentials range from time-and-a-half premiums paid for hours worked in excess of forty in any one week to differentials paid for shift work. Weekend and holiday work also receive some type of premium.

Working in conditions that are hazardous to health also receive a recognition through wage payment premiums or differentials. Hazardous work applies to such environmental conditions as loud noises, excessive fumes, heat, cold, dampness, and work situations in unsafe areas such as extreme heights and with or around moving machinery.

Employee Benefits

Compensation system designers and managers must feel that attempting to satiate the appetites of the compensation dollar gobblers in the benefits program is an impossible assignment. A decade ago, a respectable and acceptable benefit plan consumed from 20 to 25 percent of the total compensation dollar. Today, many benefit plans are in the 35 percent range and are fast advancing toward 50 percent.

Differences among type (degree) and even quantity of most benefits vary minimally among employees at the various levels of a business. There are many ways of classifying benefits. A simple and commonly accepted taxonomy includes benefit payments for (1) employee security (income protection) and health, (2) time not worked, and (3) employee services. The increase in compensation costs in the benefits area covers the entire gamut of benefits. Taxes paid for government-required benefits continue to increase. Pension costs have doubled and tripled. Social security costs have increased and will advance dramatically in the coming years. There appears to be no end to insurance options to whet the appetites of employees.

Spiraling health-care costs have necessitated larger allocations to the various insurance programs designed to provide health-care services as required. Vacation periods have lengthened and the number of holidays has increased. A review of the trends of the past five years gives one the feeling that, in the near future, many businesses will spend over 50 percent of the income allocated to compensation in providing employee benefits.

Incentives

Designers of incentive compensation plans are forever on the quest of their "Holy Grail." In this case, it is a plan that efficiently and effectively ties employee performance beyond accepted standards to compensation above established base wage payments.

Incentive wages are those wages in which senior management normally has practical means for unilaterally changing the incentive provided to the employees. Management must recognize, however, that unfair manipulation (in the eyes of the employees) of incentive wage plans will lead to employee mistrust and destroy the value of any such plan. An incentive wage component is that part of total compensation that relates to some standard of performance requiring effort above and beyond that normally expected. When employee performance actually exceeds employer expectations, employees gain specific incentive wage returns.

To be effective, incentive compensation must provide opportunity to earn the described incentive in an orderly and consistent manner. Information on performance standards and their related wage incentives must be disseminated to all involved employees. This information must be understood and must meet the rational expectations of those whose behavior it expects to influence.

Incentives have a motivational impact only when employees are able to recognize an incentive component, identify the necessary workplace behaviors they must exhibit to earn the incentive, and accurately forecast the incentives to be earned through specific additional effort.

Those who introduced the concepts of "scientific management" into the world of industrial work at the turn of the twentieth century thought they had found the "one right way" when they developed procedures for measuring the time required to produce a certain output and provided monetary compensation for those who exceeded these standards. Incentive plans today range from these early piecerate incentives for industrial and clerical workers to commissions on sales to executive bonuses based on the overall performance of a division or the entire organization.

Next to motherhood, apple pie, and hot dogs, the most sacred ideal of an American employer is "pay for performance." Most "pay for performance" concepts and plans, however, are more theory espoused than theory applied. Figure 1 outlines the elements of employer-provided compensation and how the employee receives that compensation.

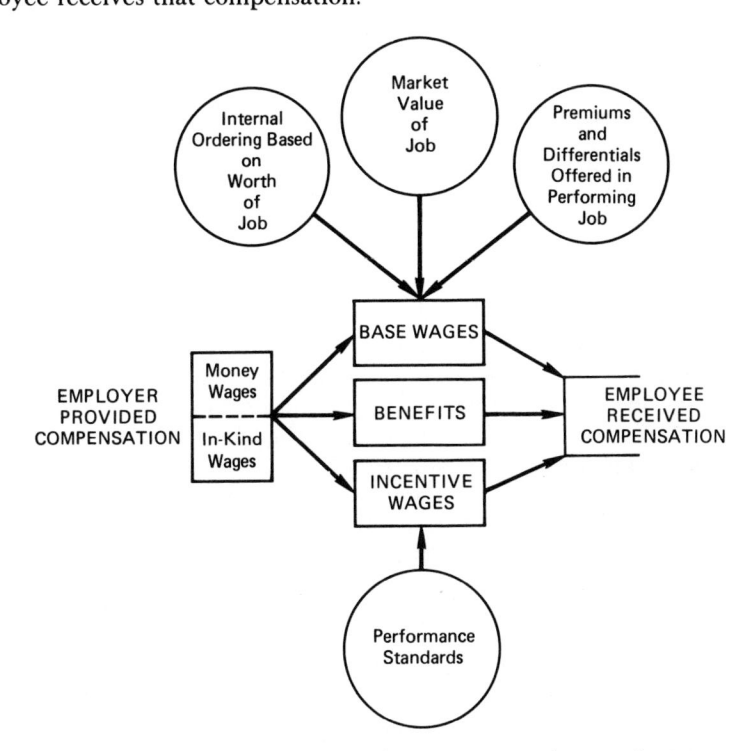

FIGURE 1 *Establishing Employee Money and In-Kind Wage Opportunities*

DESIGNING AND DEVELOPING A MOTIVATING ENVIRONMENT

In providing a motivating environment, a compensation system will only be as strong as its weakest link. The basic reason for the compensation system is to *attract, retain, and stimulate* talented personnel. The phrase *attract, retain, and stimulate* may appear to be trite and commonplace, but it precisely describes what compensation is all about.

Designers and managers of compensation systems face a major difficulty in attempting to identify which components or elements of the system attract desirable talent, which components enable the firm to hold on to those making worthwhile contributions, and, possibly most important, which parts of the compensation system stimulate employees to go that extra mile.

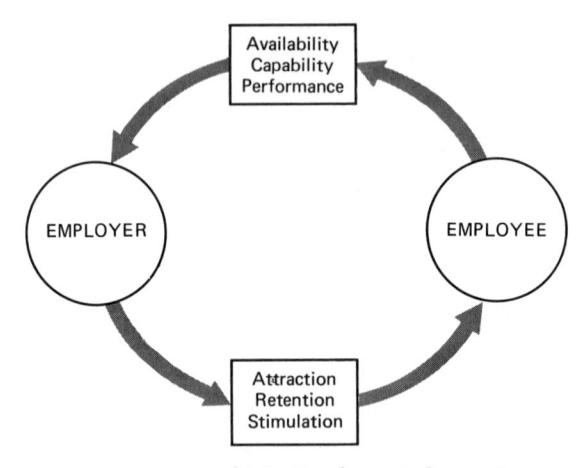

FIGURE 2 *Employer-Employee Behavior Loop*

A possible approach for relating the compensation system of a business to the attraction, retention, and stimulation of talented personnel is to associate wages and benefits to the attraction and retention stages and incentive wages to the stimulation of its members. A reason for categorizing wage payments by (1) base wages, (2) benefits, and (3) incentives is that, in most cases, certain compensation components have a very positive motivational impact on most individuals making an employment decision. Some compensation components assist the business in maintaining a grasp on its employees, but the components that entice and hold personnel are seldom the ones that stimulate excellence (see Figure 3).

Although each compensation component theoretically has an incentive value, some components are far more likely to call forth that extra effort, that superior contribution, from a wide range and majority of employees. Incentive components are those parts of the total compensation system that employees, from the lowest unskilled worker to the chief executive, can expect to receive if benefits or advantages of employee performance actually exceed employer expectations. Of course, each component of the compensation system influences the behavior of each employee somewhat differently, but skilled compensation architecture in combining the various components into a well-designed, synergistic system enhances the potential for attracting, retaining, and stimulating personnel.

There are many employers and managers who feel the money and in-kind wages provided in the base wage and benefits offered in the employment contract are sufficient in themselves to stimulate quality performance. From both contractual and theoretical considerations, there is no reason to doubt the validity of such a rationale. The fatal flaw in this reasoning, however, is the failure to recognize that, to most employees, job retention is not a strong day-to-day concern. After a short time on the job, employees realize that termination is not an action usually practiced by most managers or businesses. Just cause for termination is as much a "reality" in the nonunion business as it is in the unionized business. Workers today realize that most managers find it very difficult to terminate an employee, especially one who has been employed beyond the probationary period. The employee expects continued employment so long as his/her on-the-job behavior is acceptable. Thus, job retention is not a force that normally stimulates high-quality, innovative performance.

The same analytical procedure applies to base wages. Once on the job, base wages will not decrease. Wage expectations reach a high degree of certainty, which clearly runs counter to the employer's desire to stimulate extra or innovative effort.

So, too, with the rather stable and static employment contract, which informs employees that for a certain amount of availability, a certain degree of capability, and a certain quality of performance, a specific amount of base pay in wages and a specific amount of in-kind payments or benefits are available. Operationalizing this information results in the achievement of basic work-related employee expectations that normally discourage performance above and beyond normal or accepted standards. The fairly rigid employment contract with its associated rigid compensation components minimizes opportunity for stimulating vigorous and innovative employee work behavior focused on excellence.

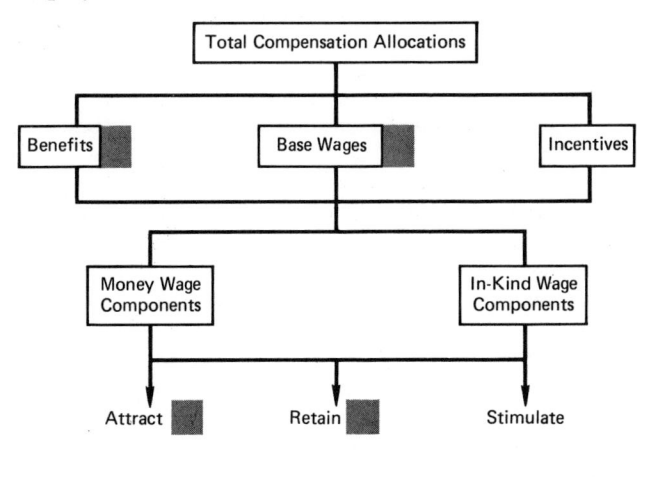

FIGURE 3 *Motivating Desired Behavior Through Compensation*

Thus, job retention, base wage payments, employee benefits, and acceptable standards of performance are not risk oriented or part of a climate of uncertainty. Instead, they center on security, certainty, and dependable mediocrity.

Incentives, on the other hand, require a climate infused with uncertainty or risk. By increasing the size of wage payments being transferred from employer to employee, they provide additional opportunity of choice for the purchase of real goods and services by the employee. The opportunity to earn incentive wage supplements provides the stimulus for risk-taking effort. Developing and managing a compensation system that only attracts and retains employees is fairly simple compared to developing and managing a system that attracts, retains, and *stimulates* the members of the business.

Employee Preference Inputs

Architects responsible for designing understandable, acceptable, and practical compensation systems must take into consideration these major determinants: (1) components of a compensation system overlap and interact in a highly individualistic manner in satisfying employee demand and in eliciting desired employee behavior; (2) either shortly before or after accepting a job, employees develop expectations of what acceptable compensation should be; (3) employees base the value of their efforts and contributions and the compensation they receive primarily on equity relationships based on their own perceptions; (4) compensation components can interact in a mutually reinforcing manner, thus having a synergistic effect when reinforcing one another and a negating/neutralizing effect when one component counteracts another.

In reviewing employee preferences among the various components of existing compensation systems, one point is mentioned time and time again, namely, that neither employer nor employee is adequately informed regarding the bases for establishing the various components of the compensation system, their cost to the business, their worth to the individual as perceived by the business, and their worth as perceived by the employees. The modern, well-educated worker is more interested in and more able to understand economics, economic costs, and compensation values than many managers are willing to recognize. In those cases in which employees' knowledge of economic behavior is not great enough to allow them to use their compensation in personally satisfying ways, businesses should consider implementing educational programs to aid employees in utilizing both base wages and benefits more fully. There is now a shocking lack of communication and understanding of the compensation system, its composition, its costs, and its intended purposes. Until such time as employers are able to communicate a basic understanding of the compensation systems operating in their businesses, the ability to develop valid and reliable compensation preference criteria will remain extremely weak.

When packaging compensation components into a compensation system that is appropriate to a specific employee or group of employees, the compensation system architects must not only be able to identify those elements of compensation that result in specific employee behavior, but also develop a scale that identifies the probability of an employee's gaining a specified compensation component and, above all, the value of the component to that individual. Accomplishing each of these activities is a major challenge facing all involved in designing and managing compensation systems. Success in this area is essential if a compensation system is to provide the motivational qualities necessary to stimulate essential employee contributions.

Although the determinants of motivation to perform a specific act are extremely complex and almost impossible to identify and define, the value of compensation as a motivator lies precisely in its ability to assume a myriad of motivational roles. In its direct or many indirect forms, compensation seems almost magically able to satisfy basic physiological needs while simultaneously satisfying psychological cravings. A well-designed compensation system will provide each member of the organization with a maximum of discretionary options. In some manner, to some degree, compensation is capable of satisfying just about every human need.

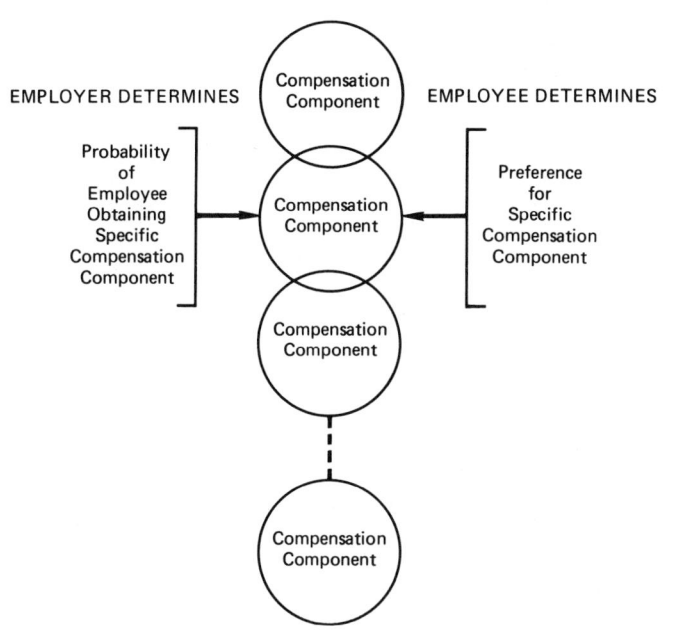

FIGURE 4 *Compensation System Development*

Employee Needs, Demands, Choice, and Compensation

Over the past quarter of a century, much has been written about motivated behavior—individual needs, the drives to satisfy these needs, and the goals that instigate the drives[2] in conjunction with the opportunities available for improving organizational performances through the satisfaction of these needs. The prodigious amount of research focusing on motivation within a behavioral context indicates the interest in needs satisfaction.

The research in this area is diverse, ambiguous, even at times perverse. Researching the area of human motivation requires human participants. Whether the study is a laboratory simulation or one using an actual social setting producing a specific output, the human participants manipulate their responses according to their own unique assessment of the potential benefits and costs of the study. This in itself biases the results of any such study. In addition, individual responses to a specific request involve a series of conscious and subconscious processes that interact in such a way that, although possible, it is still difficult to use the results of these studies for future predictive purposes.

Nevertheless, motivational research provides those involved in managing reward systems in general and compensation systems in particular with a framework that identifies fairly universal human needs and the associated drives that incite action to satisfy these needs. Behavioral scientists have identified two groups of universal needs, one that relates to physiological survival and growth (for example, hunger, reproduction, safety, and shelter) and another, including needs for power, achievement, affiliation, and recognition that relates to psychological survival and growth.

However, the identification and definition of such needs again only provide compensation managers with limited assistance in building compensation systems. An ability to understand needs is vital in developing a sensitivity to the unique qualities of human behavior; but the gap between sensitivity to the demands placed on satisfying human needs and the design of a compensation system that positively affects human behavior from a performance point of view is indeed wide. The reason there is such a gap is that the development of a compensation system that promotes performance and focuses on needs satisfaction requires an understanding of what is happening in the "black box."

The term *black box* as used here signifies one element in a complicated exchange that involves a great number of wide-ranging variables. Our black box, human motivation, is a system whose components are not only difficult to recognize and relate to one another, but whose internal functioning permits very little accurate prediction of future actions. Thus, it is very difficult for the employer to determine at any particular point in time what a given employee is attempting to satisfy and, consequently, to select "strokes" that most adequately fulfill identified needs.

Identifying employee choice considerations and the options available to the business to assist employees in realizing specific goals is not nearly as bleak as it may appear, even if it is well-nigh impossible to use a needs-motivation model to predict human behavior. An option available to management is through the recognition of general relationships between pay and performance. Although much of the research focusing on this relationship is of minimal value to the designers and implementers of compensation systems, it opens the door to considering the roles of compensation and performance activities as stimuli and responses in the behavior of the employer and employee. Put simply, we may not understand fully the "why" of an employee's response to given incentives, but our awareness of the general relationship and continued striving to gain further understanding are what is of importance to the employer. As additional empirical research takes place, our understanding of these complex relationships is bound to grow accordingly.

Employee demands, as opposed to employee needs, are those behaviors that are observable and recognizable. All individuals make demands that relate to their notion of "subsistence" (for example, for food, housing, transportation, clothing) in terms of current and future needs; a second set of demands relates to material requirements beyond subsistence, to leisure-time opportunities and activities, to opportunities for influence, and to saving and investing for future security.

In attempting to identify the effect a given compensation package has on its employees, another analytical tool is to determine, from the employee's viewpoint, which portion of the package provides for "subsistence" and which portion is discretionary.

CHOICE OPPORTUNITIES THROUGH COMPENSATION

Economists have identified income needs according to family size that are necessary to provide basic food, housing, clothing, transportation, health care, and other personal requirements. This is called a "subsistence" income. Although geographic, cultural, and social variations strongly influence the range of "subsistence" income for a particular individual or family, government agencies do identify nationwide subsistence level statistics. The technical definition of this term is very important in public welfare policies and as a reference figure in employer analyses.

The major determinant of the standard of living of most people is their earned income. For the majority of workers, earned income equates to take-home pay, which is primarily base pay minus various payroll deductions.

When applying for a job, whether at the base levels of operation or at the policy levels of senior management, a worker forms a mental picture of what compensation should be. The employee then translates these compensation expectations into standard-of-living spending patterns that establish amount and quality of food, housing, clothing, transportation, health care, and other requirements of life. Although the life style of an employee gained through earned income greater than the subsistence income standard provides more than a basic subsistence style of life, to the employee that life style becomes expected or required. Relative to individual expectations, current standard of living becomes "subsistence" level of life for that individual.

Income Security

One of the most important (if not *the* most important) benefits gained from working is freedom from economic uncertainty and the accompanying fear of being unable to live today or in the future in the manner or style to which one has become accustomed or, at the least, considers acceptable. Freedom from this uncertainty and fear translates into *security*.

The basis of employee security relates directly to subsistence requirements of food, housing, clothing, transportation, and health care. These "subsistence" requirements have both current and future reference points (what the employee demands today and what the employee expects tomorrow).

A view of how employees use their wages in particular and their total compensation in general sheds additional insight on the importance of compensation and its relationships to employee behavior. The first and foremost demand most employees make upon their employers and their jobs is security. Job security in a rather pure sense means the elimination, or at least minimization, of uncertain forces on employees' (source of) income. Some workers would also include the minimization of the impact of adverse natural occurrences and the welcome and unpredictable whims of human forces, both within and outside of the work situation.

The benefits components of the compensation process have a strong influence on the security of each employee, but even with the wide variety of benefits provided to employees, there are limits to their influence on workplace behavior. Most benefit packages by firms are largely cut-and-dried propositions. In many ways, these packages are the last vestige of the employer-employee barter system. Less than a hundred years ago, a large portion of some employees' compensation took the form of shelter in company housing, food and clothing obtained in company stores, and leisure-time activities on company-owned recreational sites. These barter components of the compensation system were deemed unsatisfactory many years ago. They minimized freedom of choice and limited self-expression. No doubt, many benefits are obtainable at a reduced cost and are more available when the business acts as an agent for all of its members, but such efficiency tends to limit *the influence of compensation on employee effectiveness.* With the rapid increase in the share of total compensation cost allocated to providing benefits and the minimal incentive value of business-selected benefits, management is now actively investigating more and better ways of providing choice and self-determination within this area.

Disposable Income

One of the most important elements in an analysis of the effects a compensation package has on a firm's employees is disposable income. The identification of disposable income is quite difficult because of the many variables that determine the amount available to a particular individual and the decisions the individual makes in spending it.

Most workers' sole source of disposable income is the compensation they receive from their employers. A small minority, however, supplement this earned income through return on investments, inheritances, and other wind-fall incomes.

Disposable income often permits employees to make purchase choices that extend their standard of living and quality of life beyond a "subsistence" level. In addition to luxury choices that make living more enjoyable are choices concerning leisure-time activities and opportunities to enhance one's influence.

Beyond "Subsistence"

Although expectations silently and quickly return most styles of living to that of "subsistence," the life style of most workers includes many forms of discretionary purchases. Some forms of housing, food, clothing, and transportation enjoyed by most workers go beyond any reasonable (even subjective) understanding of "subsistence."

Leisure Time. Over the past two decades, much has been written about the boring, routine job and the need for enriching it. The missionaries of job enrichment and job improvement have, at times, forgotten that many, many people are indifferent to whether or not they have more planning and control responsibilities in the overall operation of the businesses. This in no way infers that practically all workers would not enjoy improved supervision or more planning and control responsibilities over how and when they perform their assignments. But the point is that many people work for (1) the compensation received in exchange for their services and (2) the social relations they enjoy on the job. The compensation, in turn, provides additional choices (as well as security and influence) that make life more interesting and palatable. Improving the ability to manage leisure-time activities is in fact one of today's major areas of social interest.

Influence

Over three hundred years ago, John Milton said, "Money brings honor, friends, conquests, and realms." This statement is just as true today as it was then. Most individuals place a good deal of importance on how they are perceived by others and how others respond to them. The compensation package provides an excellent opportunity for employees to achieve influence through increased visibility or greater recognition. The amount of money available and the manner in which the employee uses these funds can enhance acceptance and approval by others. The old adage, "Nothing succeeds like success," underscores the relationship between the use of compensation gained from past efforts and the ability to influence the future. Gaining the confidence of others often arises from the trappings of success made possible through the use of job-earned compensation.

Savings and Investments

For most employees, their base wages (including premiums and differentials) and cash bonuses provide the wherewithal to pay for current consumption. For many employees, these payments require their entire earnings. Changes in the spending pattern of most employees vary directly with increases in wages. The amount of income remaining after making payments for consumables determines the savings and investments made by each employee.

Employee savings and investments provide security beyond that offered by the business. The opportunity to have some choice in future life style or spending patterns is a primary motivation for savings and investments. Job earnings and other currently acquired income determine current living and spending patterns. Savings and investments are that part of discretionary income available for future life style and influence opportunities. The slogan, "Tomorrow is available for those who plan for it today," precisely describes this situation. Those employees who normally have the largest amount of discretionary income available for savings and investments are those who receive the largest share of the compensation provided by businesses.

THE TOTAL REWARD SYSTEM

A total reward system includes every inducement a business can offer to an employee that enhances an individual's estimate of personal worth—the fulfillment and satisfaction an employee receives from being a member of the business as well as from being a productive human being. In the development of the total reward system, those responsible for its architecture must recognize these powerful motivators of human effort and do everything possible to incorporate them as a vital part of the dynamic management system. For this reason, the reader should at least be aware of some important noncompensation variables affecting the success of the reward system.

Every matter that has any expected influence on the productivity, profitability, and growth of the business may also be expected to influence the satisfaction that the individual employee gains from job environment and performance or from compensation.

Each individual brings to the workplace some particular predisposition to work. The specific genetic code that strongly influences the cooperative and competitive behaviors of each individual not only affects the desire to work under set conditions, but also the willingness to provide that extra effort so vital to the success of any operation. In addition, each person develops a unique set of aptitudes and skills from past education, training, and experience. These unique employee qualities have an impact on performance that basically falls outside the domain of compensation.

Many noncompensation, employer-provided variables fall within the realm of basic management skills. Within this category is the quality of managerial expertise at every level in the organization as identified by (1) the ability to integrate and achieve organization, group, and individual objectives and goals which facilitate both worker security and individual growth; (2) the technical skills required of and actually possessed by the manager; and (3) the leadership qualities displayed in developing and furthering constructive social and work-related interaction among members at all levels.

Noncompensation situation (or contingency) variables that are impossible to predict with any degree of accuracy possibly have the most immediate and direct influence on workplace performance. The ability and willingness of each employee to function effectively within the impact of these situation or contingency variables will be the end result of all the many variables having an influence on employee behavior.

Although we have mentioned only a few of the noncompensation variables affecting employee performance, it is important to recognize that compensation influences are so diverse and pervasive that they indirectly affect these variables as well as such important nonmonetary, psychic motivators of human effort as influence, achievement, affiliation, and recognition and these, in turn, powerfully affect employee performance.

Notes

[1] A major American industrial firm paying large annual bonuses noticed a rather significant increase in turnover for employees who had been with the company for ten years. Investigation revealed that these employees had invested the accumulation of these bonuses into businesses of their own.

[2] "Motivation theory is not synonymous with behavior theory. The motivations are only one class of the determinants of behavior. While behavior is almost always motivated, it is almost always biologically, culturally, and situationally determined as well." A. H. Maslow, "A Theory of Human Motivation," *Psychological Review*, 50 (1943), 371.

Individual and Organizational Correlates of Pay System Preferences

Michael Beer
Gloria J. Gery

An organization's pay system is one of the key forces available for influencing the behavior of its members. Little systematic data are available about the effects of different types of pay systems on behavior or attitudes. Pay systems evolve over time, and often administrative considerations and tradition override the more important considerations of behavioral outcomes in determining the shape of the system and its administration.

The research reported in this paper was an attempt to gain a fuller understanding of employee attitudes toward and potential behavioral outcomes of the introduction of a new pay system. Such changes often are planned and executed on the basis of untested assumptions and incomplete understanding. Aside from the contributions to the fields of industrial psychology and personnel administration, we hope that the following discussion of the research study will serve as an illustration of how successful research can be designed and carried out in an organizational setting to help in understanding how individual variables and managerial climate variables interact with pay systems. This should help in predicting the effects of a change in pay systems.

A study of nonexempt[1] salaried employees was conducted at a medium-sized manufacturing organization (23,000 employees, $444 million sales) in 1967 to determine: (1) this group's preference for various types of salary systems, and (2) correlates of these preferences. The study was conducted at a time when the company was considering a change in the salary system, and a major purpose of the study was to attempt to predict potential acceptance of such a change. The proposed shift was from a salary system composed of a guaranteed increase and a single-step merit increase for satisfactory performance to a two-step merit system which would provide increases for satisfactory and outstanding performance and eliminate the provision for a guaranteed annual increase.

Nealey and Goodale (1967) have conducted research on the preferences of blue-collar workers for six proposals for additional paid time off the job and a comparable fringe and wage increase. Using a paired comparison technique, they were able to quantify the relative preference of employees for each of these alternatives. The value of these data for bargaining strategies is obvious, but they do not provide information about preferences for various pay systems. Meyer and Walker (1961) conducted research on the relationship of "need achievement"

Michael Beer and Gloria J. Gery, "Individual and Organizational Correlates of Pay System Preferences," from the book *Managerial Motivation and Compensation: A Selection of Readings*. pp. 325-49. Reprinted by permission of the publisher, Division of Research, Graduate School of Business Administration. Michigan State University.

levels to preference for a salary plan based on a "pay for performance" philosophy and found that managers high in "need achievement" preferred a merit system more than those who were low in need achievement. This relationship did not hold for nonmanagers. There has been no research on the relative preference of white-collar employees for pay systems that differ in provisions for recognizing merit. Such data were obtained in this study on four different pay systems ranging from a guaranteed increase system to a full merit system as a means of predicting acceptance of change.

A second major purpose of the study was to identify various individual and environmental correlates (administrative conditions and managerial practices) of pay system preference. This was done to predict which subgroups of employees (plants, salary levels, age groups, need levels, types, and so forth) would be most receptive to the new pay system and which would be least receptive. Furthermore, correlations between various managerial and/or salary administration practices and pay system preference would provide useful information about the optimum condition for acceptance of change. Since such practices are within the control of management, it was felt that they could be "tuned up" in anticipation of the change, increasing the probability of acceptance of and satisfaction with the new system.

In addition, correlates of pay system preferences were of interest as a means of predicting the potential motivational value of a merit system. While the effects of a pay system change on effort or motivation can be measured directly only after the change has been implemented, correlation of psychological needs with pay system preference provides some insight into the effects of a merit system on motivation.

The relative strength of a series of needs was measured, and the correlation of need strength and pay system preference was examined to draw some conclusions about the instrumentality of four pay systems to need satisfaction and their potential motivational effects. After the study was conducted, a recommendation was made to change the corporate salary system to a merit salary system. Although this change was not made immediately, for a number of significant reasons which are unrelated to our purposes here, as of this writing it is being planned for the near future. Hence, the effects of a change cannot be reported here. However, preferences for pay systems and their correlates have many practical and theoretical implications, which will be discussed.

RESEARCH DESIGN AND ANALYSIS[*]

The first phase of the research consisted of 18 in-depth interviews with a randomly selected representative group of male and female, nonexempt, salaried, clerical, and technical personnel at the company's corporate headquarters. Each interview took approximately one and a quarter hours and followed a general

[*] The data section of this report has been omitted. The relevant tables have been included in the summary section.

protocol relating to the employee's feelings about and experience with the present salary system, his or her preferences for various types of salary systems, attitudes toward employee benefits, and feelings about and experience with performance reviews. The interviews were open-ended and served to provide a framework or structure for the second research phase, the questionnaire survey.

A 95-item questionnaire was developed to measure the basic questions and concerns explored in the interview phase of the study. The questionnaire consisted of Likert-type and paired-comparison items and was pretested on another representative group of 30 nonexempt clerical and technical employees. In addition to pay system preference, a number of a priori factors measured by one or more items were included based on their hypothesized relationship to pay system preference. They are as follows:

1. The relative importance of eight psychological needs
2. Knowledge of the present corporate pay system
3. Background factors, such as age, type of work, and the like
4. Performance feedback experience
5. Quality of superior/subordinate relationship
6. Individual's perception of his/her performance
7. Satisfaction with pay
8. Payroll identification
9. Past experience with pay
10. The perceived relationship between pay and performance

The questionnaire was administered to a stratified random sample consisting of 580 clerical employees and technicians at 28 manufacturing plants, corporate office headquarters, and corporate research and development headquarters. It was composed of approximately 50 percent male and 50 percent female respondents and was representative of all lengths of company service (over six months), salary grades, types of work, and educational backgrounds.

The questionnaire was administered at group meetings by personnel supervisors in various branch plants, corporate offices, and corporate research and development facilities throughout the United States and was anonymously completed and returned to the research group at corporate headquarters.

Descriptive statistical analysis yielded frequencies, mean scores, and standard deviations for each Likert-type item. Paired comparisons of pay system preferences and the importance of work-related needs were reduced to preference indexes for each pay system and for each need. Finally, t tests or Chi Square (x^2) tests were used to test for the significance of relationship between preference for each system and items representing the various a priori factors listed above. No items were combined to arrive at total scores for the factors since these were a priori factors. A Chi Square analysis seemed appropriate in most instances as a measure of relationship because many of the variables consisted of discrete categories or did not meet the assumptions for a parametric test.

SUMMARY AND CONCLUSIONS

We will now summarize our major findings and discuss our conclusions concerning the problems associated with changing a pay system and the overall issue of pay and motivation. The most important data supporting these conclusions are presented in Table 1. The first part of this section will attempt to communicate to the manager the implications of this research for practical application. The second part will deal with theoretical implications.

The study has shown that white-collar, nonexempt employees prefer a two-step differential merit system (5 percent and 10 percent increases) to a general increase system; partial merit system; or a high-risk, one-step merit system (Table 1). This finding confirms that nonexempt, salaried, clerical, and technical employees should not be thought of as significantly different from the managerial and professional work force, and that there is ample possibility for integrating these two groups with respect to pay practices. Management of this group has not always been based on correct assumptions. It is hoped that studies of this type will bring into focus correct assumptions and relevant managerial practices. However, the reader must be cautious about these findings in one important respect. The data on pay system preferences were gathered in the summer of 1967, a period of relatively little inflation. Since that time inflation has significantly increased. It is possible that the broad economic environment affects pay system preferences. In a time of inflation employees may be less willing to work under a merit system that does not provide for annual guaranteed economic adjustment and gives the supervisor complete control over the amount and timing of increases. That is, security and monetary needs may become more important during these periods and, as our study showed, pay systems that provide for some annual increase may be preferred under these conditions. No data are available at the moment to shed light on this matter.

While the overall findings concerning pay system preferences for the white-collar, nonexempt employee are encouraging with respect to the potential integration of pay practices for this group and the exempt, professional and managerial work force, the correlates of pay system preferences indicate that preference is a function of many variables. A strong correlation was found between eight out of ten a priori factors. The ten factors and their relationship to pay system preference have been condensed into five major categories and will be discussed and summarized within this broader framework.

TABLE 1   Rank Order of Pay System Preference and Risk

System	Mean Preference (Maximum Points = 3.00)	Rank of Risk Involved
System B (differential merit system)	2.20	2
System C (combined merit and general system)	1.95	3
System D (above average merit raise only)	1.03	1
System A (all general increase system)	.82	4

Individual Needs

Individual needs for advancement, responsibility, interesting and challenging work, security, vacations, and money were all found to be related to pay system preference (Tables 2 and 3). Individuals high in the first three needs, referred to by Herzberg (1959) as "motivator" needs, were found to favor a merit system more than those low in these needs. Individuals high in the last three needs, referred to by Herzberg as "hygiene" needs, were found to favor a general increase system (no provision for merit increases) more than individuals low in these needs. A person high in the first three needs would appear to be high in the need for achievement and have a life style that places work in a relatively central position. A person high in the last three needs is probably more security-oriented and places less value on achievement and work. Thus, not surprisingly, the basic orientation of the individual toward work, achievement, and risk has much to do with the pay system he or she prefers. The most interesting implications of these findings are that the form of payout, rather than money in and of itself, is the key to the potential motivational value of a pay system and that pay in the form of a merit system could satisfy achievement-oriented needs. Therefore, a merit system can probably be utilized effectively by management in motivating employees. This concept has been in disfavor recently, but our findings indicate that more might be done with money in motivating people, particularly those who are work and achievement-oriented in the first place.

While a merit system would seem to be less need satisfying to the security-oriented individual and, therefore, potentially less motivating, there is probably a net gain in installing a merit system. Those who are high in achievement-oriented needs will be stimulated by such a system to greater heights of performance, while those who are high in security-oriented needs will become more dissatisfied and, it is hoped, will leave. In other words, the human resources available will be better utilized by means of a merit system, and the mix of the work force may change in a favorable direction with turnover of those who do not find such a merit system satisfying. At the same time, it is hoped that greater attraction of new recruits who share concern for achievement and work will occur. The direct effect on individual needs of a merit system is unknown, but it is possible that under a merit system the security-oriented individual may learn to have higher work- and achievement-oriented needs.

Clearly no individual is purely work- and achievement-oriented or purely security-oriented. Since both sets of needs and orientations reside within individuals in different mixes, it would appear that an ideal pay system may include both a general increase and merit provisions. The general increase provision would provide satisfaction of security and equity needs, while the merit part would provide the motivation or incentive to perform. Our study shows that the merit part of the system would have to include several merit steps. Many pay systems in American industry attempt to satisfy both sets of needs with one system, usually a merit system. The management administering such a system must utilize it for the dual purpose of rewarding performance and providing equitable pay and security. The result is that employees do not see a clear relationship between pay and performance which in turn reduces the motivational qualities of the system.

TABLE 2 Relationship Between Motivator Need Strength and Salary System Preference

Need	System A Low need	System A High need	System B Low need	System B High need	System C Low need	System C High need	System D Low need	System D High need
Advancement opportunity	.97	.66°	2.05	2.34°°	1.98	1.95	1.00	1.05
Responsibility	.97	.66°°	2.08	2.32°°	2.01	1.93	.95	1.09
Interesting and challenging work	.91	.72°	2.17	2.24	1.94	1.99	.98	1.05
Recognition	.82	.79	2.20	2.21	2.00	1.94	.98	1.06

° t Test significant at p = .10
°° t Test significant at p = .01
System A—7% general economic increase
System B—5% and 10% merit system
System C—3% general economic increase and 5% merit increase for satisfactory performance
System D—10% merit increase for above average performance only

TABLE 3 Relationship Between Strength of Hygiene Needs and Salary System Preference

Need	System A Low need	System A High need	System B Low need	System B High need	System C Low need	System C High need	System D Low need	System D High need
Job security	.76	.86°	2.30	2.09°°	1.94	2.00	1.00	1.05
Vacations	.69	.94°°	2.28	2.12°	1.96	1.98	1.07	.96
Supervisory practices	.74	.88	2.23	2.17	2.01	1.92	1.02	1.03
Money	.67	.92°°	2.21	2.20	2.02	1.93	1.10	.96°°

° t Test significant at p = .10
°° t Test significant at p = .01

System A—7% general economic increase
System B—5% and 10% merit system
System C—3% general economic increase and 5% merit increase for satisfactory performance
System D—10% merit increase for above average performance only

Several background factors were also found to be significantly related to pay system preference, but these were largely interpreted as being indicative of groups which share similar values and needs. The finding that older and longer-service employees have a higher preference for the highest-risk merit system may indicate that economic security, which is probably more assured for this group, is important if a merit system is to be accepted and is to motivate. This would reinforce the idea that a system combining a general economic adjustment and several merit steps would be optimum. Thus a feeling of security may be helpful in making a merit system an effective motivator and acceptable.

The effects of background factors and needs on pay system preference indicate a strong individual component in the question of what pay system is preferred and which pay system might motivate and satisfy. Perhaps the idea of a cafeteria of pay systems and fringe benefits may hold some promise.

Individual Expectations

An estimate of the individual's expectations under a merit system is available from three of the factors measured:

1. The individual's perception of his or her own performance
2. Individual perception of the relationship between pay and performance
3. Past experience with pay

Past experience with pay and self-perception of performance were clearly related to pay system preference. The more competent an individual perceives himself to be, the more he prefers a merit system and the less he prefers a security system (Table 4). The better the individual's past experience with pay (she has not had to ask for increases and has always been told why she has received an increase) the more she prefers a merit system and the less she prefers a general increase system (Tables 5 and 6).

Clearly individuals' past experiences and perceptions lead them to develop expectations of what it would be like under a given pay system, and this helps determine preference. While differences in expectations may be difficult for management to deal with in planning a pay system change, they can have influence on the practices that lead to these expectations. It would appear that practices which assure individuals that they will not be forgotten by the system enhance preference for a merit system. This finding was strongly supported by the interviews. Perhaps a change to a merit system should be preceded by a period of strenuous effort to administer pay in such a way that it will lead to favorable expectations on the part of the individual employee. Thus effective utilization of the present system may be a prerequisite for the effective change and implementation of new systems.

Leadership Climate

Quality of superior/subordinate relationship and amount and quality of performance feedback were found to be related to pay system preference. The more individuals feel their supervisor understands them and the more freedom they feel to discuss their personal goals with their supervisor, the greater the

TABLE 4 Relationship Between Self-Rating of Performance and Salary System Preference

Self-Rating of Performance	Salary System				
	A°	B	C	D	N
Top 10%	.78	2.23	1.90	1.10	319
Top 10–20%	.89	2.24	1.95	.91	123
Top 20–30%	.78	2.11	2.11	1.00	37
Top 30–40%	.90	1.97	2.29	.84	31
Upper 40–50%	1.11	2.04	1.96	.89	28
Lower 25–50%	.75	2.25	2.00	1.00	4
Lower 25%	1.25	2.00	2.00	.75	4

° x^2 significant at $p = .10$

TABLE 5 Relationship Between Number of Times Asked Supervisor for a Salary Increase and Salary System Preference

Number of Times Asked Supervisor for Salary Increase	Salary System				
	A	B°	C	D	N
None	.80	2.20	1.95	1.04	372
1– 3	.97	2.19	1.90	.94	108
4– 5	.81	2.10	2.12	.98	42
6– 8	.62	2.08	1.69	1.62	13
9–12	.57	2.86	1.71	.86	7
13–30	.50	2.00	2.25	1.25	4

° x^2 significant at $p = .10$

TABLE 6 Relationship Between Perception of Frequency of Asking for a Salary Increase and Salary System Preference

Perception of Frequency	Salary System				
	A	B	C	D	N
Always	.84	2.14	1.96	1.05	56
Frequently	.93	2.00	2.11	.96	45
Sometimes	.70	2.35	1.86	1.09	107
Rarely	.87	2.35	1.88	.90	60
Never	.84	2.15	1.96	1.05	279

preference for a merit system and the lower the preference for a general increase system (Tables 7 and 8). The more frequent the formal and informal reviews of performance and the more individuals are told about reasons for an increase (that is, the more frequent and better the feedback), the greater their preference for a merit increase and the lower their preference for a security system (Tables 9 and 10).

These findings lead us to the strong conclusion that the supervisor is a key link in the preference for pay systems and probably in the satisfaction and motivation of the individual under a given pay system. If preferences are affected by the type of supervision, surely the type of supervision moderates the impact of the pay system on the individual's satisfaction and motivation. This hypothesis has been harbored by many for a long time, and now there appears to be some evidence for it.

Since the perception and intended effects of a pay system probably vary widely, depending on the supervisor, the most carefully designed pay system may be for naught in the hands of a close supervisor who provides little performance feedback. The implications for the acceptance of change to a merit-based system from some more security-based system are clear. Effective supervisory training in performance feedback and effective human relations at the minimum will be essential for the acceptance and potential satisfaction of the employees under such a merit plan. Thus, supervisory training and development should be as much the concern of salary administration departments as any other group in the corporation.

TABLE 7   Relationship Between How Well People Feel Their Supervisor Understands Them and Salary System Preference

Supervisor's Understanding	A°	B°°	C	D	N
Complete understanding	.72	2.01	1.88	1.39	67
Considerable understanding	.71	2.33	1.91	1.04	233
Some understanding	.97	2.13	2.01	.90	167
Little understanding	.86	2.21	1.95	.97	66
No understanding	1.15	1.73	2.15	.96	26

° χ^2 significant at $p = .02$
°° χ^2 significant at $p = .05$

TABLE 8   Relationship Between Perceived Freedom to Discuss Personal Goals with Supervisor and Salary System Preference

Perceived Freedom	A	B	C°	D°	N
Always feel free	.75	2.19	1.89	1.16	226
Usually feel free	.80	2.27	1.95	.99	137
Sometimes feel free	.88	2.22	1.95	.95	95
Rarely feel free	.98	2.00	2.24	.77	66
Never feel free	1.06	2.15	1.76	1.03	34

° χ^2 significant at $p = .05$

TABLE 9 Relationship Between Frequency of Informal Performance Feedback and Salary System Preference

	Salary System				
Frequency	A°	B°	C	D°	N
Almost never or never	1.04	2.02	2.02	.92	179
Yearly	.86	2.12	2.12	.90	97
Every few months or monthly	.73	2.33	1.85	1.09	181
Weekly or several times monthly	.56	2.32	1.84	1.27	99

° x^2 significant at $p = .05$

These frequency categories are combinations of more discrete alternatives in the original questionnaire. Significance was obtained for the original question breakdown.

TABLE 10 Relationship Between Quality of Performance Feedback at Last Merit Increase and Salary System Preference

	Salary System				
Amount of Feedback	A	B°	C	D	N
Reasons behind increase were discussed in full	.74	2.28	1.89	1.09	315
Simply informed of increase; reasons not discussed	.95	2.11	1.99	.95	149
Received increase without being informed by supervisor	.77	1.85	2.19	1.19	26
No increases	.97	2.17	2.02	.84	58

° x^2 significant at $p = .01$

Organizational Culture

Organizational culture is a broad term which has been widely used and variously interpreted. It seemed to us that several of the items in our questionnaire could be viewed as measures of organizational culture. Two items ascertained the payrolls (management and professional salaried, technical and clerical salaried, or blue-collar) with which the individual has had the most contact. One item asked if the individual had been on another payroll before his present job, and which one. A second item asked with which payroll the individual associated most on the job. It seems to us that data from these items are some indication of the values and norms that prevail in the individual's group relative to pay, and the basis for pay.

Several items measured the degree to which individuals had knowledge about the pay system (pay range, their position in it, and so forth). This would seem to measure the openness of the culture, or at least the degree to which a normally taboo topic, such as pay, is openly discussed.

While the items just described are not all-inclusive measures of organizational culture, they do fall into this category. Therefore, the data generated by these items would seem to be some indication of the potential effects of culture on pay system preferences and perhaps satisfaction and motivation under various pay systems.

Our findings are that organizational culture as described above does relate to pay system preference. The more knowledge about pay the individual has, the greater the preference for a merit system and the lower the preference for a security system (Table 11). The more the individual reports previous or present association with a professional or managerial group, the higher the preference for a merit system and the lower the preference for a security-based pay system (Tables 12 and 13).

That culture should have an influence on pay system preference is of interest; that it might have effects on satisfaction and motivation under a given pay system is crucially important. The implications are that planned changes in organizational culture to more openness about pay, greater work involvement, and greater emphasis on reward for performance only (professional and managerial values) may be necessary preconditions for acceptance of new pay systems. The implication is that more motivation and satisfaction may be elicited under merit systems if they are accompanied by complementing cultures. In short, changes in pay systems need to be preceded by or accompanied by cultural changes. The optimization of an existing pay system may also depend on the establishment of an appropriate matching culture. The implication for salary administrators is that they must be concerned about the culture of their organization and its influence on groups of individuals before designing pay systems. It may also mean that in large multi-divisional or multi-plant corporations, differences in cultures that exist between organizational components will mean that differences in pay systems may have to exist for optimum satisfaction and motivation. Since this usually presents difficulties for a corporation that transfers people across these units, it may be desirable for an organization to develop a uniform culture.

Satisfaction with Pay

Satisfaction with pay was measured by several items that ascertained the individual's general attitude toward pay. These items showed that there is a relationship (although not always statistically significant) between degree of satisfaction with the present system and preference for various types of pay systems (Tables 14, 15 and 16). The most consistent finding is that preference for a multiple-step merit system (System B) increases as satisfaction with pay decreases. The relationships between satisfaction with pay and preferences for the security system (System A), partial system (System C), and the high risk, one-step merit system (System D) were generally complex and difficult to interpret. In our opinion, these complexties can be explained in two ways. First, preference for pay systems was measured by a paired comparison system, resulting in lack of independence between preference indexes. Second, the overall measure of satisfaction with pay reflects a multitude of reasons for satisfaction or dissatisfaction. Thus two individuals with the same degree of satisfaction might have different preferences for pay systems because of their reasons for satisfaction or dissatisfaction.

TABLE 11 Knowledge of Present Salary and Salary System Preference

Area of Knowledge	Salary System								
	A		B		C		D	
	Knowledge	No Knowledge	Knowledge	No Knowledge	Knowledge	No Knowledge	Knowledge	No Knowledge
1. His salary grade classification	.72	.92°	2.34	2.07°°	1.91	1.98	1.03	1.03
2. His salary range minimum	.78	.91°	2.25	2.11°	1.92	2.00	1.06	.99
3. His salary range maximum	.77	.94°	2.24	2.10°	1.93	1.99	1.06	.97
4. Type of increases presently available	.82	.93	2.23	2.02	1.93	2.09	1.01	.95
5. Size of merit increases presently available	.69	.88°	2.37	2.12°°	1.82	2.00°	1.11	1.00
6. Frequency of eligibility for merit increases	.79	.89	2.28	2.05°°	1.89	2.05°	1.04	1.01

° t Test significant at p = .10
°° t Test significant at p = .01

TABLE 12   Relationship Between Payroll History and
Salary System Preference

| | Salary System | | | | |
Payroll History	A	B	C	D	N
Exempt salaried	.50	2.42	1.83	1.25	12
No other payroll	.81	2.23	1.96	1.00	347
Both hourly (production) and exempt	.82	2.18	2.00	1.00	17
Hourly (blue-collar production)	.90	2.10	1.93	1.07	182

TABLE 13   Relationship Between Payroll Association and
Salary System Preference

| | Salary System | | | | |
Payroll Association	A	B°	C	D	N
Hourly	1.17	1.72	1.94	1.17	18
Hourly-weekly	.84	2.08	1.72	1.36	25
Hourly-monthly	.90	2.10	1.95	1.05	20
Hourly-weekly-monthly	.88	2.18	1.92	1.02	170
Weekly	.91	1.96	2.09	1.04	55
Weekly-monthly	.79	2.27	1.99	.96	210
Monthly	.64	2.38	1.89	1.10	61

° x^2 significant at $p = .10$

TABLE 14   Relationship Between Satisfaction with Present Pay and
Salary System Preference

| | Salary System | | | | |
Satisfaction	A°	B	C	D	N
Completely satisfied	.88	2.00	1.88	1.23	26
Quite well satisfied	.82	2.12	2.00	1.05	120
Fairly satisfied	.80	2.19	1.95	1.05	239
Somewhat dissatisfied	.81	2.28	1.94	.96	138
Very dissatisfied	1.03	2.23	1.89	.86	35

° x^2 significant at $p = .01$

TABLE 15 Relationship Between Perception of Salary Treatment and Salary System Preference

| | Salary System | | | | |
Treatment	A	B	C	D°	N
Very unfairly	.71	2.00	2.08	1.21	24
Somewhat unfairly	.98	2.28	1.94	.80	99
Fairly	.79	2.24	1.95	1.02	196
Somewhat fairly	.77	2.14	1.95	1.15	124
Very fairly	.86	2.12	1.96	1.06	113

° x^2 significant at $p = .10$

TABLE 16 Relationship Between Frequency of Thoughts of Leaving the Company Due to Salary Dissatisfaction and Salary System Preference

| | Salary System | | | | |
Considered Leaving	A°	B	C	D	N
Many times	.76	2.33	1.81	1.10	42
Several times	.92	2.32	1.83	.92	65
Once or twice	.63	2.38	1.90	1.09	100
Yes, but never seriously	.84	2.20	1.96	.99	134
Never	.90	2.04	2.00	1.06	211

° x^2 significant at $p = .05$

Perhaps the clearest example of this came from the item that asked individuals to check the nature of their complaints about the present system. When those who complained about the lack of incentive in the system were compared with those who had complaints unrelated to lack of incentive, we found a significant difference in pay system preference (Table 17). Those who complained about the lack of incentive in the system had a higher preference for the multiple-step merit system (System B), and the single-step, high-risk merit system (System D), and a lower preference for the partial security system (System C).

The finding that satisfaction with pay is inversely related to preference for a merit system was counter to our hypothesis. We assumed that dissatisfaction with pay would result in distrust, a lack of desire for change in the pay system, and, therefore, greater preference for the existing partial security system than for the multiple-step merit system. In retrospect, however, our findings make sense. Those who are dissatisfied with pay are expressing as much dissatisfaction with the mode of payment as with the amount. Since a large percentage of the sample complained about the lack of incentive in the existing partial security system, satisfaction was found to be inversely related to preference for a merit system. Too often dissatisfaction with pay is assumed to mean dissatisfaction with amount. Our findings suggest that a change to a merit system with no increase in amount payed out by the company will increase satisfaction.

Situational variables can also be expected to influence an individual's pay system preference, although we did not analyze our data in a way that would allow us to test this hypothesis directly. For example, individual's expectations about how they would fare under each alternative system based on their past experience with pay, their relationship with their bosses, and organizational culture could moderate the relationship between satisfaction with pay and pay system preference.

TABLE 17 Relationship Between Whether Complaints About the Present Salary System Refer to the Lack of Merit or Incentive and Salary System Preference

	Mean Salary System Preference		
Salary system	Complaints about lack of merit or incentive[a]	Complaints not related to merit qualities of present pay system[b]	Significance of difference[*]
A	.72	1.21	NS
B	2.47	1.93	.05
C	1.58	2.14	.02
D	1.23	.71	.10

[*]Significance was determined by means of a t Test.
[a]Present System Complaints
  1. Provides little incentive for better performance
  2. Amounts available are too small
  3. Above average performance is not rewarded more than average performance
[b]Present System Complaints
  1. Eligibility periods are too frequent
  2. Not enough information is given to people
  3. Other (open comments)

A Model for Understanding Pay System Preference

The discussion above has been an attempt to summarize the findings of this study in terms of a few broad categories which are conceptually distinct and theoretically meaningful. How do they relate to each other and interact in their effects on pay system preference and potential acceptance of a given pay system?

The model represented in Figure 1 is our estimate of how pay system preferences develop. The existing pay system has only an indirect effect on individual attitudes toward and preferences for various pay systems. More than likely individuals' pay system preferences are heavily moderated by the culture in which the pay system is embedded (the openness of the culture about pay, for example), the particular manner in which their pay is administered, and the way they are supervised by their bosses. Individuals' experience with and subsequent feelings about the present system as filtered through these environmental factors affects expectations about what would happen under various types of systems in the future and to some degree may affect basic needs as well. Then needs and expectations interact in a multiplicative manner (Vroom, 1964) and result in some pattern of pay system preferences. Satisfaction is shown as a final outcome. It is likely to be determined in part by the degree of discrepancy between the existing system and the preferred system. As the data on satisfaction showed, dissatisfaction was associated with stronger preference for systems other than the existing system. Of course, satisfaction is also determined through a comparison by the individual of the amounts actually payed with the amount expected, but this seems to be only part of it. Finally, the model shows a feedback effort on individual needs and expectations resulting from a degree of need satisfaction.

The validity of this model cannot be totally determined from the data presented in this paper, since the data analysis was only of the relationship of each factor with pay system preference. The model represents our estimate of the interaction of the various factors based on past research and theory and our knowledge gained from interviews and observation. For example, it is unlikely that pay system preferences are directly affected by the existing pay system itself. We found in our interviews that supervisory style and cultural factors modify the perception the individual has of the existing pay system. Two people may have radically different feelings about the system because of their experience with it. The experience is largely a function of their organizational setting or culture and their boss. With respect to satisfaction, current theories view it as an outcome variable rather than an independent variable (Porter and Lawler, 1968), and this would seem to make sense here. Furthermore, both our interviews and the data presented above suggest that dissatisfaction is strongly associated with, and probably caused by, preference for a system that would provide more incentive and satisfy achievement needs. Finally, the multiplicative interaction of needs and expectations is hypothesized based on Vroom's work (1964).

If this model is accurate, and we feel more research is necessary to determine this, it has implications for a salary administrator contemplating a pay system change. It is clear that preference for a system and, therefore, potential acceptance of it can be strongly influenced by a number of factors within the control of management. The model and our data strongly suggest that the development of an open culture with respect to pay and the training and development of supervisors in performance feedback and salary administration can materially affect the individual's expectations about what will happen under a merit system and may even affect his needs. Even in the event that needs remain unaffected, the multiplicative interaction of expectations with needs can have a strong effect on final pay system preference and potential acceptance. The conclusion is clear. Plans for a change from a security pay system to a merit system require prior supervisory

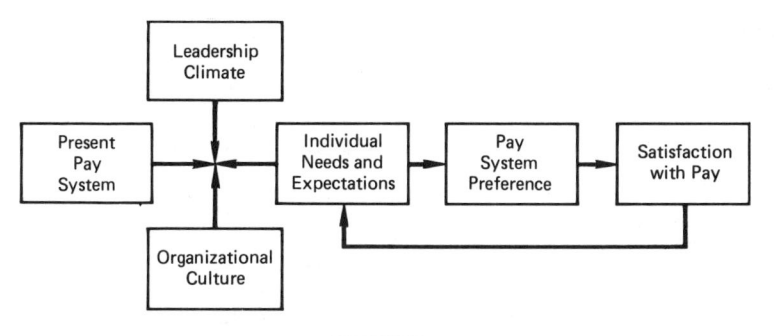

FIGURE 1

and organizational development. At the very least, it requires such steps concurrently with pay system introduction to assure acceptance of the pay system. A merit system will not be accepted and may not have the intended motivational effects if supervisors do not actively administer a performance appraisal system, practice good human relations, explain the reasons for increases, and ensure that employees are not forgotten when eligibility dates come and go. The organization must provide an open climate with respect to pay and a culture where work and effort are valued.

Salary administrators rarely concern themselves with the assessment of these managerial and organizational factors or with their development in advance of a pay system change. This study shows that these factors are as critical as the design of the system itself.

Theoretical Implications

While the research reported in this chapter deals primarily with the question of pay system preference and the problems of change, the data also bear on a number of theoretical issues which are summarized below.

The data show that merit systems are perceived as instrumental to the satisfaction of what Herzberg (1959) has called "motivator" needs (responsibility, challenging and interesting work, and advancement), and security systems are instrumental to the satisfaction of what he calls "hygiene" needs (security, money, vacations). The role of money in motivation has been deemphasized in recent years. Perhaps research findings and current conclusions concerning pay are a function of the fact that most pay systems do not, in fact, reward for performance. Thus Herzberg's findings concerning pay may be a function, not of people's potential response to money, but merely to the form in which it is currently distributed. Our finding that preference for a merit system increases as satisfaction decreases also supports the notion that mode of payment is an important variable in satisfaction. The finding that those who complain about the lack of incentive in the existing pay system prefer a merit system further substantiates that pay systems can be instrumental to the satisfaction of motivator needs and will probably motivate under those circumstances.

The fact that security systems (complete or partial guaranteed annual increases) are perceived as instrumental to the satisfaction of security needs implies that no one system can serve all needs. Since individuals have a whole range of needs, an optimum system may be a combination of a security system and a true merit system. In this system equity would be provided by a general adjustment tied to market changes, and variable increases would be tied to performance only

The relationships of self-perception of performance and past pay experience with pay system preference confirm that expectations play a key role in pay system preference and probably in motivation. The concept of expectations has a long history in psychology, but most recently has been discussed in connection with motivation at work by Vroom (1964) and Porter and Lawler (1968). Our data tend to support the continued importance of this concept in any theory of motivation.

In their recent book, Porter and Lawler (1968) indicate that satisfaction with pay is an outcome in a model of motivation and individual performance with subsequent feedback effects on individual needs and expectations. While the evidence in this study is barely sufficient, our data would support this notion. Higher levels of dissatisfaction were associated with preferences for a different system than now exists, indicating that perhaps needs, but certainly goals, are restructured and rearranged as a result of dissatisfaction. The relationship found between type of dissatisfaction (complaints about the lack of incentive in the system) and preference for a merit system would further support this conclusion.

The finding that the more information the individual had about the pay system, the more he or she preferred a merit system is reminiscent of Lawler's (1967) findings and conclusions about the effects of secrecy on satisfaction and motivation. While preference for a merit system cannot be equated with potential motivation under it, the gap is not so great as to prevent our findings from reinforcing Lawler's. The openness measured by our items implies that merely communication about the nature of the system, as opposed to full disclosure of salaries, may have a positive effect.

The data concerning the effects of supervisory behavior and practices on pay system preference provide the first data known to us concerning the moderating effect of this organizational variable on perception of the pay system and probably its motivational and behavioral outcomes. The evidence is not direct since motivation and behavior were not measured, but the relationship between leadership climate and pay system preference is at least a strong indication that this important variable moderates the effect of the pay system on effort and performance.

We have strongly suggested throughout this discussion that this research has implications for a model of pay and motivation even though the outcome measured by this research is preference for different pay systems. The assumption is that individuals' preference indicates something about their perception of the instrumentality of a pay system to the satisfaction of their needs (our data show this) and, as such, the potential effort they will exert to obtain incentives offered by the system. If this assumption is correct, the data presented in this paper provide some insights into the moderating effects of organizational and individual variables on the relationship between the pay system (the administrative entity) and resultant motivation or effort. We have summarized our view of the interaction between the pay system and the moderating variables in Figure 2. This model suggests that individuals' perception of the pay system and its effects on them (the probability of reward for effort) is probably heavily moderated by how their bosses use the system, supervise them (openness of relationship), and review their performance. It is also moderated by the culture, its openness with respect to pay, and the value placed on achievement and effort. The supervisor and culture are also likely to affect the relative strengths of the individual's needs and expectations, although needs may be a little more fixed due to early development and learning. Satisfaction will relate to effort but only indirectly through its feedback on needs and expectations. Again, satisfaction is viewed as a dependent variable. Our view of the effects of pay on motivation does not differ from that of Porter and Lawler (1968), but we have added our view of the organizational variables that will strongly influence perception of the system and consequently its effects on effort.

Finally, the findings of this research show that we cannot think of changing organizational systems, in this case, a pay system, without considering steps for managerial and cultural changes. Organizational systems and organizational culture are intertwined and must be changed simultaneously or in some planned

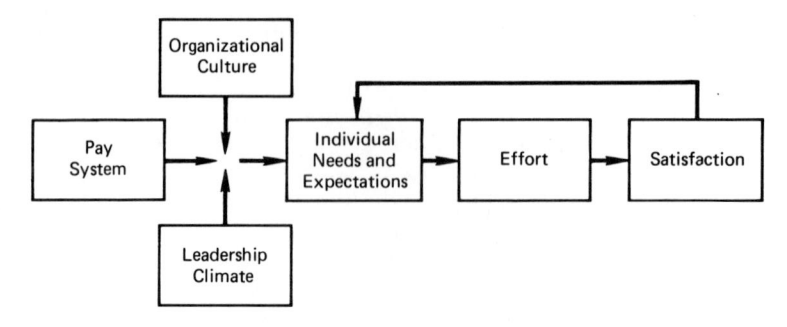

FIGURE 2

sequence for dramatic and permanent changes in organizational effectiveness to occur. This dual consideration, as we are finding in other research (Beer, 1969), is important whether the starting point is culture or system. One without the other does not carry the full intended effects of change.

In general, the findings of this study are encouraging from the point of view of organizational change. The indication is clear that individual attitudes and potential acceptance of new systems (whether pay or other systems) are as much a function of organizational process within the control of management as they are a function of fundamental individual difference.

Note

[1] This study includes employees who are not exempt from the Federal Wage and Hours Laws requiring payment of overtime rates for over forty hours' work per week. In this company these employees are primarily clerical and technical in nature

SUPPORTING HUMAN RESOURCE PROCESSES

The first article in this section illustrates new methods of analyzing the basic skills and characteristics needed for a job (job analysis) and thus relates to the article by Walter W. Tornow and Timothy C. Gartland presented earlier. The next two articles follow through with alternate approaches to job design using these newer concepts. Our final article in this section develops a framework for the modern human resource information system and illustrates the rapidly growing and critical need for information to update the work force, monitor its achievements, and store factual information on the organization.

Against the background of her extensive experience in all manner of service and work organizations, Melany E. Baehr, the author of our first selection, reviews the current objectives, approaches, and applications of job analysis against the background of legislative change and work force themes described in Parts I and III. "Job Analysis: Objectives, Approaches, and Applications" thus emphasizes the human resource need for diagnostic tools which can be used to develop, counsel, and train workers and to validate selection and assessment criteria.

The author goes on to pose some critical questions, the answers to which should be categorizable if significant advances are to be made in job assignment and work performance—for example, What job activities and behaviors are the basis of that set of tasks called a job? What are the characteristics needed by a jobholder to perform a job effectively? After a review of current techniques, various job analysis applications are illustrated by means of projects completed at the work research center of the University of Chicago. These application examples involve such problems as increasing the accuracy of job descriptions, diagnosing training needs, clarifying job requirements, and determining job similarities for the purpose of validating selection tests. Throughout these case examples, the author concentrates on the basic needs of an ongoing personnel (maintenance) program; that is, she uses generalized instruments which can be easily adapted to such systems tasks as human assessment, work design, and career development needs. These basic adaptations of the tools of job analysis provide a foundation for work design and for the division of the work force into productive task groups.

Designing productive and satisfying work systems during a period in which technology, the labor force, and social values are in flux is a complex task. Today that task is made even more challenging by an openness to change among personnel professionals that leads to the generation of new theories and criteria for organizational design. Newer technologies in human resource management and a greater awareness of the organization-environment interface have encouraged a reconceptualization of design strategies. In "Organizational Best Fit: Survival, Change, and Adaptation," Kenyon B. DeGreene provides that reconceptualization as well as some much-needed guidelines for (re)designing organizations to accommodate to internal and external change processes. With the belief that organizational design must help organizations survive in times of turbulent change on all fronts, DeGreene relates concepts from systems theory, systems models, and organization theory to modern design problems. The author begins with a macro view of social systems and organizational environments, then goes on to relate key understandings from these areas to the concept of organizational fit and subsystems. Of particular importance is the author's conceptualization of the social, technological, psychological, and political subsystems within the organization. The article concludes by comparing present design approaches with designs more suitable to a highly turbulent organizational environment.

The approach to job and role design suggested by DeGreene finds application in the article by Richard O. Peterson, "Human Resources Development Through Work Design." Based on some ten years of experience at American Telephone and Telegraph (AT&T) Company, the author examines work and organizational design in terms of various technical options in work systems, organizational structure, and adjustments in the personnel support system. Peterson's article is an excellent illustration of the HRM model as it relates to design options for the individual, the group, the organization, and the work force in a human resource context.

In "The Design and Implementation of Human Resource Information Systems," Robert D. Smith focuses on the use of computers in human resource information systems. Smith's overall model provides an insightful approach to design thinking that integrates in a single information system both human resource data and the information needed for ongoing organizational development. Areas covered include forecasting, development, and planning needs, as well as the storage of key business trends or organizational facts. The article details (1) the planning phases of the information system, (2) its advantages for the selection, training, development, and assessment of human resources, and (3) the storage of information for future organizational development programs. Smith closes with case examples illustrating HRIS for corporate organizational planning and career development.

SUMMARY

Viewed collectively, these articles help to classify the various observations that contribute to an understanding of the worker in a work setting and lead to the design of a human resource management system. Information assumes multiple roles—that derived from human resource activities is in turn processed, analyzed and recycled to human resource and line people in order to improve work study, design, operations, control, and administration. These functions span the full range of HRM functions and touch on the individual, the group, the organization, and the external environment.

Job Analysis: Objectives, Approaches, and Applications

Melany E. Baehr, Ph.D.

OBJECTIVES OF JOB ANALYSIS

Many psychologists have devoted the greater part of their professional lives and research efforts to the measurement of human attributes. Almost as many have been concerned with procedures for describing organizational structures, functions, and climates. By contrast, few have concentrated on the development and refinement of techniques to define and describe any specific job, either in terms of the relative importance of the functions involved in its performance or of the human skills and attributes needed to perform these.

Job Analysis for Human and Organizational Development

Reflection suggests that this is a somewhat anomalous situation. Logically, a comprehensive and accurate knowledge of the functions and human demands of a job is a basic requirement in devising procedures both for the scientific

Reading prepared especially for this book and printed with permission of the author.

management of the organization's human resources and for programs of organizational development.

Job analysis and description are thus prerequisites for such basic procedures as recruiting, selection and placement, performance appraisal, wage and salary administration, and training and promotion. Obviously other basic procedures such as job classification and clarification, job design, and development of organizational structure will also profit. Indeed, job description may be viewed as the natural link between the parallel processes of human resource utilization and organizational development. Examples of practical applications given later in this paper will show that the particular objectives to be achieved will largely determine both the content of the job description and the technique used to obtain it.

JOB ANALYSIS IN SELECTION VALIDATION RESEARCH

Accurate information about the job has always been needed for selection and placement. However, the importance of job analysis for these procedures has accelerated since the passage of the Civil Rights Act of 1964 with its Title VII, which focuses on the elimination of discrimination in employment, and also with the development of successive governmental guidelines on employee selection procedures. Both the 1970 EEOC *Guidelines* (13)[*] and the OFCC 1971 "Order" and its 1974 "Amendment" (24, 23) favor a selection validation procedure which is performance-related and calls for job analysis as a first step. This total procedure requires an empirical demonstration that all criteria used in selection or promotion decisions are related to independently obtained measures of job performance. That the courts take these requirements seriously is evident in such cases as that of *Moody et al.* v. *Albermarle Paper Company* (20). The court minced no words in declaring that "Measured against the Guidelines, Albermarle's validation study is materially defective in several respects...." However, job analysis really comes into its own in the FEA *Guidelines* (14) and the proposed *Uniform Guidelines* (33).

The first major reason for the increasing prominence of job analysis is the acceptance (in addition to performance-related or performance-*criterion* validation) of procedures known as *content* and *construct* validation. The critical need for accurate job analysis is plain from the stated requirements for these procedures. According to the FEA *Guidelines*, a report on *content* validity should contain a full description of the basis on which a performance domain was defined and a comprehensive definition of that domain. In a *construct* validation, the job analysis must provide evidence of the linkage between the construct or skill and the ability to perform important duties on the job and of how this linkage was determined.

A second reason for the increasing importance of job analysis is the new encouragement of consortium or multi-unit selection validation studies. While these use a performance-criterion validation, their results can, if all other conditions have been satisfied, be implemented by units which did not participate in

[*] Numbers in parentheses indicate works cited in the reference section at the end of the article.

the actual study. The primary requirement is to demonstrate, by appropriate job analysis, that the job in the nonparticipating job unit has substantially the same major job duties as one studied. The same conditions hold for the use of a study conducted in one department by another, similar department.

Results obtained through the application of different approaches to job analysis in procedures directed toward human resource and organization development and in procedures used in selection validation research will be described later. These approaches will naturally include methods of observation and interviews with incumbents. However, they will concentrate on some of the newer, quantitative approaches to describing jobs in terms of the relative importance of the specific activities to be performed, the underlying behaviors called for, or the human attributes required for successful performance.

Job Analysis Approaches

The most widely used source for job information in the United States, and the one with the longest history, is probably the *Dictionary of Occupational Titles* (DOT) (34), developed by the U.S. Department of Labor. Indeed, consultation of this source is now specifically mentioned in connection with job analysis requirements in the FEA *Guidelines*. However, definitions obtained from the DOT may be necessary but are certainly not sufficient to fulfill the requirements of a thorough job analysis. Their chief defects are that they are often outdated because of changes in the country's economy and in its job market, as well as the emergence of new occupational fields. In addition, even when a definition is available for the specific occupation being dealt with, it tends to be given in very general terms. *A Supplement to the Dictionary of Occupational Titles* (36) provides somewhat more specific information on selected characteristics of jobs, covering physical demand, and training time.

Interviewing as a Job Analysis Approach

In general, we have found individual interviews to be more successful for defining higher level positions, as illustrated in our occupational analysis of school principalship (7). To provide structure and consistency for our interviews with principals, we developed an Interviewer's Guide consisting of five parts. The first was a summary of the purpose of the study and of the interview. This was followed by a section for data on the school and the principal which would help to interpret the particular content and problems of each principalship. These data included the principal's education and teaching experience and the school's physical size and ethnic composition. The third section contained open-ended questions designed to elicit the principal's perceptions of his or her school and job. The fourth part—Principal's Guide for Describing Specific Activities of the Job—gave an intuitive framework of functions and subfunctions developed on the basis of library research. The interviewer used this framework to probe for items describing each principal's activities in each functional dimension. Finally, there was an open-ended wind-up section in which the interviewer asked for the principal's reactions to the discussion and the project.

Another technique that is often very productive when efficiently handled is "brainstorming" group interviews. We have obtained good results when the group to be interviewed represented a cross section of the organization. In a national validation of a selection test battery for transit operators (3), the group members included the director of personnel, the employment manager, the supervisor of the training school, assistant superintendents, district supervisors, and incumbent operators.

Questions were designed to obtain two types of information—lists of specific activities performed on the job and lists of the skills and attributes needed to perform them. The first list was later systematized to produce a "position description." The listed skills and attributes were utilized by asking the group to classify them into the three categories of "physical," "mental," and "behavioral" characteristics. The psychologists implementing the study then developed, for review, a list of tests thought to measure the listed skills and attributes. Surprisingly, this rather loose-sounding procedure produced some of the most useful job information in the study.

Observation and Analysis of Actual Performance on the Job

It is rather difficult to observe actual on-the-job performance in the case of most higher level positions, such as that of a school principal or executive vice-president. It is, however, a "natural" for such positions as those of transit operators and police patrolmen, where our observations took the form of "ride-alongs" and, in the latter study, also some inadvertent participation in high-speed chases and criminal arrests! The object in this phase of the patrolman selection validation study (9) was to develop a list of behavioral requirements for *successful performance* rather than a list of activities performed. Twenty such global patterns of behavioral requirements were generated for further use. Some examples of these are:

> demonstrate mature judgment, as in deciding whether an arrest is warranted by the circumstances or a warning is sufficient, or in facing a situation where the use of force may be needed
>
> be skillful in questioning suspected offenders, victims, and witnesses of crimes

Standardized and Quantified Measurement of Job Requirements

The rigorous demands made on job-analysis results in selection validation research prompted us to investigate standardized and quantified procedures for job description. An intensive review of the literature revealed four major types of quantified procedures which are briefly described below.

Specific Job Activities. The first logical approach to systematic and quantified procedures for job analysis is to try to obtain precise descriptions of each task performed with estimates of its importance. This approach is perhaps best typified by Morsh (21, 22) in his study of positions in the U.S. Air Force. His work centered around the construction of job inventories which could be economically administered to large numbers of incumbents with the resulting data subjected to a computerized hierarchical grouping procedure to identify and describe job types. Such information served Morsh's purpose of facilitating training and promotion in the various U.S.A.F. career ladders on the basis of knowledge and skill. However, it provided no information on the human attributes required to perform the task or the job.

Underlying Work Behaviors. When jobs are described in terms of specific activities or tasks, quantitative procedures based on job inventories can be applied to only one position or, at best, to only one career ladder. Thus, a special inventory would have to be prepared for each job, a time-consuming and costly process. On the other hand, when jobs are described in terms of underlying behavior, the inventory or other descriptive system can be applied to similar positions across organizations or industries. An example of such an approach is a position-description procedure for executive positions developed by Hemphill (15) that can be used to set forth the similarities and differences among executive jobs regardless of the organization in question. Another instance of an instrument designed to measure underlying work behavior for a particular type of occupation was the Supervisor Position Description Questionnaire developed by Prien (25).

A quantitative job description instrument that could be applied not only across industries but also across a number of different occupations would represent even greater parsimony in the collection of job-description data. According to a review of job-analysis research findings undertaken by Prien and Ronan (26), the most comprehensive study spanning different occupational groups was done by Baehr (1). The instrument developed in this study differentiated between higher level positions in management, marketing, and research and development, where there are a number of overlapping work behaviors. Differences among positions are reported in terms of quantified measures of the perceived relative importance of 12 factorially identified job functions or underlying work behaviors.

A more recent factorial study has identfied 16 job dimensions which have been incorporated in a revised version of the instrument. This instrument, called the Work Elements Inventory (10), makes it possible to analyze (and thus compare) a number of jobs at the same time. This is very useful in job design and in studies of organization structure. However, if the purpose of the job analysis is to put together a trial selection test battery for validation, then the personal attributes required to perform the work behaviors must still be determined, and tests devised to measure these attributes.

Personal Attributes Required to Perform Job Activities and Work Behaviors. Perhaps the widest variety of jobs spanned in a quantitative procedure for job evaluation is found in the extensive work done by Ernest J. McCormick and his associates. Their first and basic step was the development of a standard framework—called the Position Analysis Questionnaire (PAQ)—for describing the activities performed on the job. Ratings made by psychologists were used to establish fixed relationships between the activities performed on the job and the behavior attributes required to perform them. These ratings consisted of estimates of the relevance of each of 67 personal attributes to each of the PAQ job elements. The final estimates of relevance used were those where high inter-rater reliabilities existed (18).

Another PAQ study (19) investigated the concept of "synthetic validity." Mean scores for the nine dimensions of the General Aptitude Test Battery (GATB) were obtained for incumbents in 179 job positions, as well as the traditional validity coefficients of these GATB scores calculated against performance-based criteria for the positions. Attempts were then made to predict both the mean GATB scores and the performance validity coefficients first by the job elements (activities) and second by the personal attributes dimensions. Mean test scores were better predicted than validity coefficients. However, from the point of view of job analysis, the more interesting finding was that, in both instances, the personal attributes predicted almost as well as the job activities. These results raised the interesting possibility of describing jobs directly in terms of the attributes required to perform them.

Psychological Tests for Measurement of Personal Attributes. In an attempt to meet urgent needs to staff proliferating jobs in the early 1950s, Ernest S. Primoff of the U.S. Civil Service Commission developed a systematized, quantified method of matching tests to jobs. This method was based on the J-(Job-) Coefficient (28, 30, 37). Calculation of the J-Coefficient requires

- a list of behavior elements, covering the skills, abilities, and attributes needed for successful performance on the job being analyzed
- ratings made by persons familiar with the demands of the job as to the degree to which each behavior element is important for job success
- a predetermined relationship between the behavior elements and selected tests, expressed through a matrix of standardized and stabilized beta-weights for the elements on each test.

Since its initial use in the 1950s, a vast amount of research has been done on the J-Coefficient. This research has led to use of additive checklists with different types of element measures, such as potential and motivation (31) and knowledge and skill (29), and use of multiple scales in rating the importance of elements (27). Primoff's 1972 review of J-Coefficient procedures (28) described how the calculation of the beta-weights was streamlined through use of employee self-ratings.

The results reported in this review of quantitative procedures for job analysis encouraged us to develop a number of such instruments to be used for a variety of purposes. In constructing such instruments, the objectives to be achieved demand clear choices as to the many possible combinations of the representative variables listed below. Logically, the headings of "Content" and "Response Mode" and those of "Respondent" and "Response Technique" have certain underlying relationships. However, the listed variables and their possible combinations are meant to be suggestive only.

The types of instruments used and their construction are described in the following section, which gives the results of some applications of job analysis.

Content
Specific activities performed on the job
Basic functions of the job (work behaviors)
Skills and attributes needed to perform the activities and functions

Response Mode
Relevance of activity or attribute
Importance of activity or attribute
Time spent on actvity
Ability to perform the activity
Degree to which attribute is possessed

Respondent
Incumbent (comparisons by race, sex, and rank)
Peer
Supervisor
Trained job analyst

Response Technique
Rating scale
Dichotomous choice
Forced choice
Forced distribution

SOME APPLICATIONS OF JOB ANALYSIS

Given the large number of possible applications of job analysis, it seems logical to start with the most direct—actual job description.

Job Descriptions for Different Levels and Types of Industrial Managers

A number of aspects of our work required us to distinguish fairly rapidly between higher level jobs in terms both of the functions to be performed and of the skills required to perform them. To deal with the functional part of our analysis, we developed a quantified job description instrument with factorially determined job dimensions called the Work Elements Inventory (WEI) (10). The items were all related to underlying work behaviors, and they were written in a style suitable for use by job incumbents. The response technique was a forced distribution. In early versions, respondents were first asked to sort all items (each conveniently printed on a separate card) into two piles—one for items regarded as relevant to the job and the other for items that did not apply. Next, they were asked to count the *number* of cards which had been placed in the "relevant" pile. A printed table included with the response materials indicated how many cards out of any number chosen as relevant should be sorted into each of five categories to produce a normal distribution of job-element importance. Thus, each respondent was next asked to distribute the "relevant" cards into five sets reflecting the task's degree of importance and then to place each set into an appropriately labeled envelope.

The basic theory in the construction of the WEI was that there was considerable overlap among the functions performed in even dissimilar higher level positions. Thus sales representatives with dealerships are required to manage as well as to sell. Both line managers and research and development (R&D) staff professionals are at times required to "sell" their ideas. The relatively diverse jobs covered by the WEI are differentiated by the emphasis given, or the relative degree of importance assigned, to the factored job dimensions. In our experience, differences on many performance and skill dimensions that exist across occupations such as R&D professionals, industrial salespeople, and line managers at the vice-presidential level and above are significant at about 1 in 10,000 probability level. Differences between hierarchical positions on a single career ladder, as illustrated by first-line supervisors, middle managers, and vice presidents and up, are generally significant at about the 1 in 1,000 probability level.

Figure 1 shows WEI profiles representing even more stringent comparisons between levels and types of managers. The two profiles on the left represent managers of professionals. Level II are professionals who manage technicians or skilled laborers. Level I are professionals who manage other professionals. The profiles on the right represent line managers. Level II (middle managers) spans the range from second-level manager up to but not including vice-presidents. Level I (executives) are managers at or above ths vice-presidential level.

These profiles make it plain that managers of technicians or skilled laborers (professionals classified as Level II) do not exhibit the same behaviors as traditional managers. The traditional managerial functions begin to emerge only for those who manage other professionals (Level I), where the profile is quite similar to that of middle-line managers (Level II) except that the line managers give considerably less emphasis to the development of employee potential. The executive profile (Line Managers, Level I) gives greater attention to the development of employee potential but concentrates on the three functions of objective setting, decision making, and establishing community-organization relations.

That these visual differences reflect significant differences in function for many job dimensions by both level and type of manager is clear from the results reported in Figure 1. On the left of this table, types of manager are compared, separately, at two levels. On the right, levels of manager are compared, separately, for each type. The greater number of significant differences between levels occurs for line managers. The greatest number of significant differences between types of managers appears at Level II. By the time managers are operating at the vice-presidential level (Level I), differences between types are diminished, with both line and professional managers emphasizing traditional managerial functions.

Diagnosis of Training Needs

In the example given above, we have dealt only with job description. However, respondents can also use the Work Elements Inventory with instruc-

TABLE 1 Significant Differences Between the Mean Importance Ratings for the WEI Job Dimensions for Two Levels and Types of Manager

Job dimensions	Type of manager compared at two levels			Level of manager compared for both types		
	Level I Mgr. of Prof. versus Executives	Level II Mgr. of Tech. versus Middle Mgrs.	Total Group Mgr. of Prof. versus Line Mgrs.	Professional Level I versus Level II	Line Level I versus Level II	Total Group Level I versus Level II
1. Setting Objectives		°°	°°	°		°
2. Improving Procedures		°	°			
3. Promoting Safety			°			
4. Developing Technical Ideas	°		°			
5. Decision Making		°°°	°°	°°		
6. Developing Teamwork		°	°			
7. Coping with Emergencies						
8. Developing Employee Potential		°	°°		°°	
9. Supervisory Practices					°	°
10. Self-development		°°	°		°°	°
11. Community-organization Relations	°	°				
12. Handling Outside Contacts		°				°

° Significant at or beyond the .05 level of confidence
°° Significant at or beyond the .01 level of confidence
°°° Significant at or beyond the .001 level of confidence

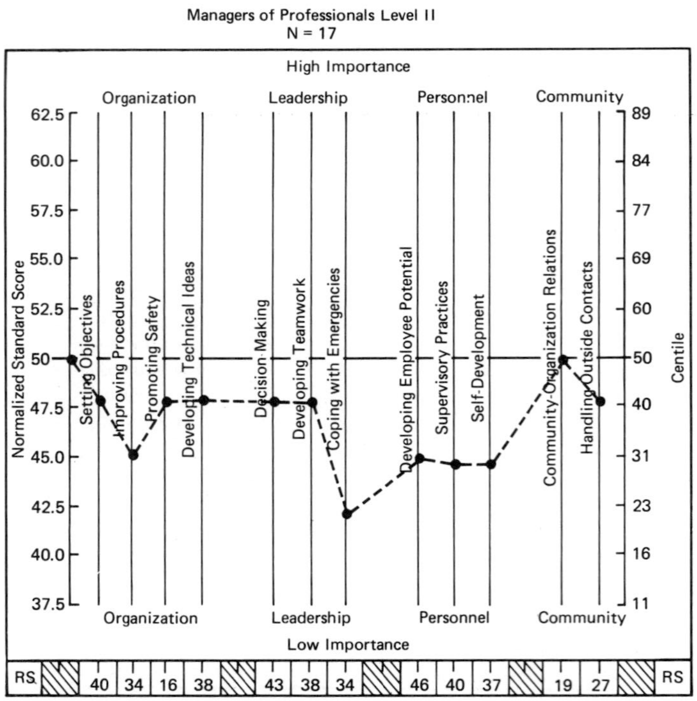

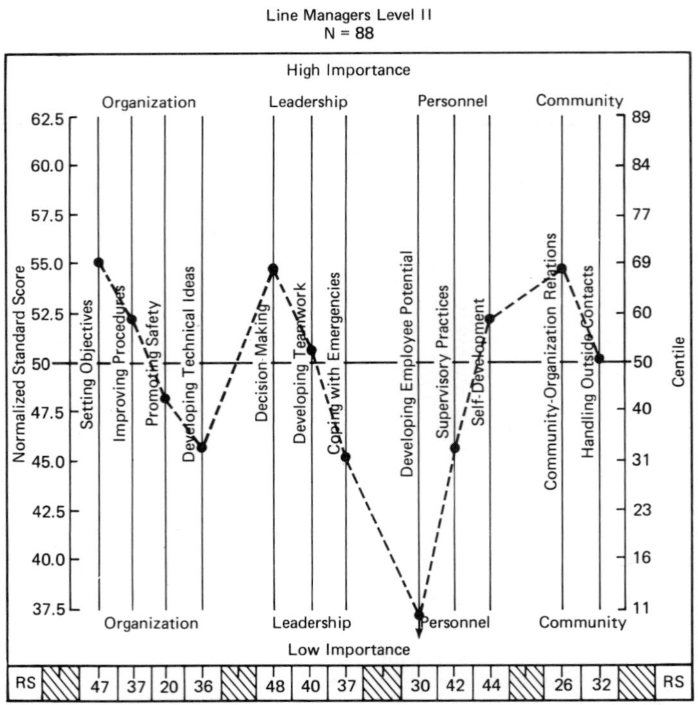

FIGURE 1 Quantitative Job Description: For Different Types and Levels of Industrial Managers

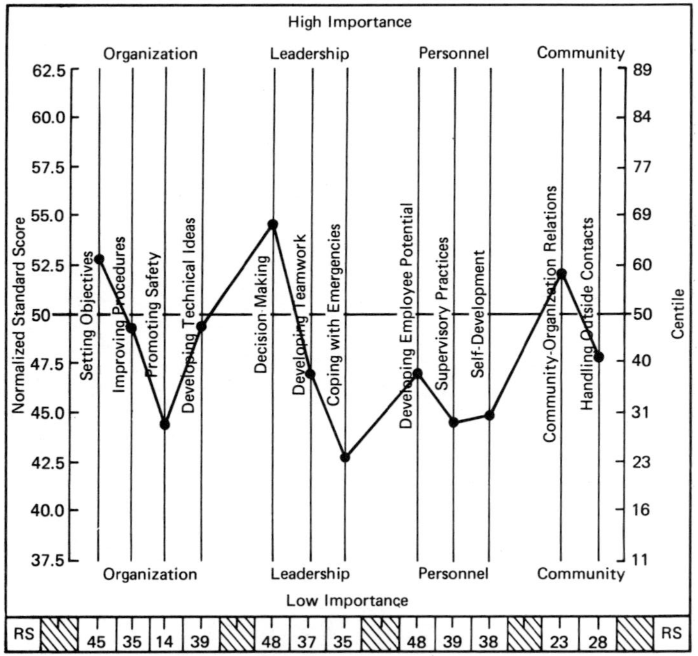

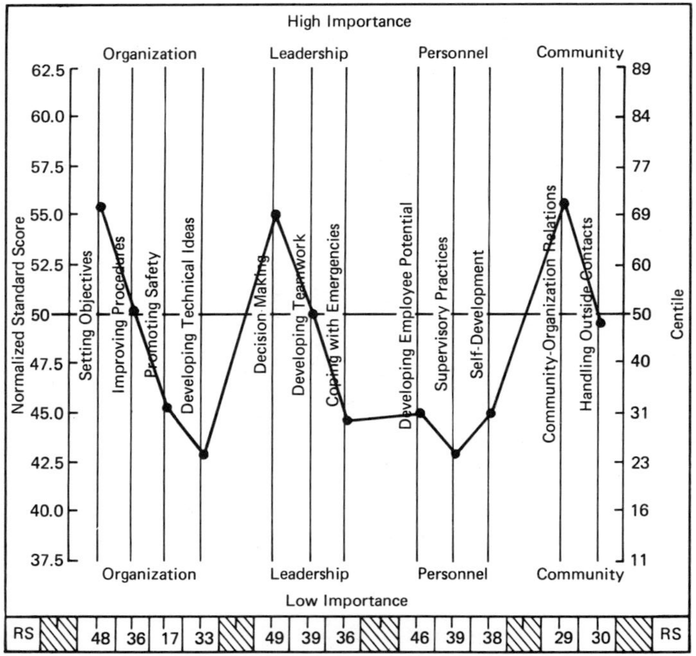

Figure 1 (continued) *Quantitative Job Description: For Different Types and Levels of Industrial Managers*

280 *Job Analysis: Objectives, Approaches, and Applications*

tions to sort the items in terms of how they feel concerning their relative ability to perform the activities. The results can then be used to diagnose training needs. Figure 2 compares "importance" and "ability" profiles for two higher level positions in the Highway Division of a State Department of Transportation (4). The first grid is for district engineers. The second is for office managers who are professionals managing other R & D professionals.

While these profiles are based on the results obtained from a rigorously constructed instrument, we do not regard this approach to the diagnosis of training needs as a psychometric one. Rather, we hope that a study of obvious differences between perceived importance of a job function and perceived ability to perform it, together with an examination of the specific work activities involved in the items which contribute to the job function, will provide a rational basis for group discussion and for custom-designed training programs.

The first grid in Figure 2 shows that the profile for the district engineers closely resembles that of the executives (Line Managers, Level I) shown in Figure 1 except for the extreme importance assigned to the development of employee potential, a function which, ironically, these engineers feel singularly incompetent to perform. They would also probably benefit from development programs in the traditional areas of objective setting and decision making. The second grid in the diagram is for professionals who manage other R&D professionals. As is often the case with managers who are qualified in the physical or computational sciences, they feel that their communication skills do not measure up to the level required by the job. On the other hand, they see themselves as competent to perform the important managerial function of representing the organization in the community, a role in which they appear to be underutilized.

Job Clarification (an Example from the Educational Field)

So far, the individual profiles we have presented have been based on the response of job incumbents at one level in the organization. For *job clarification*, profiles must be developed from responses of an incumbent or group of incumbents and of the supervisor involved, using the same job-description instrument. While this particular approach may not always be the one used, the concepts of job clarification and management by objectives are fairly commonplace in industrial organizations. However, to date they have been much less common in educational institutions. One of our more interesting applications of job clarification was between school principals and their superintendents in two school districts which varied considerably in socioeconomic status and in the ethnic composition of the student body (17).

The clarification was based on the results obtained from implementing a specially constructed job-description instrument called the Job Functions Inventory for School Principals (8). Since the instrument was developed for a single occupation, the items deal with specific job activities performed by the school principal. The response technique is a forced, four-interval, rectangular distribution. In other words, the respondent is asked to sort the items or activities so that there are approximately equal numbers in each of four ranges on

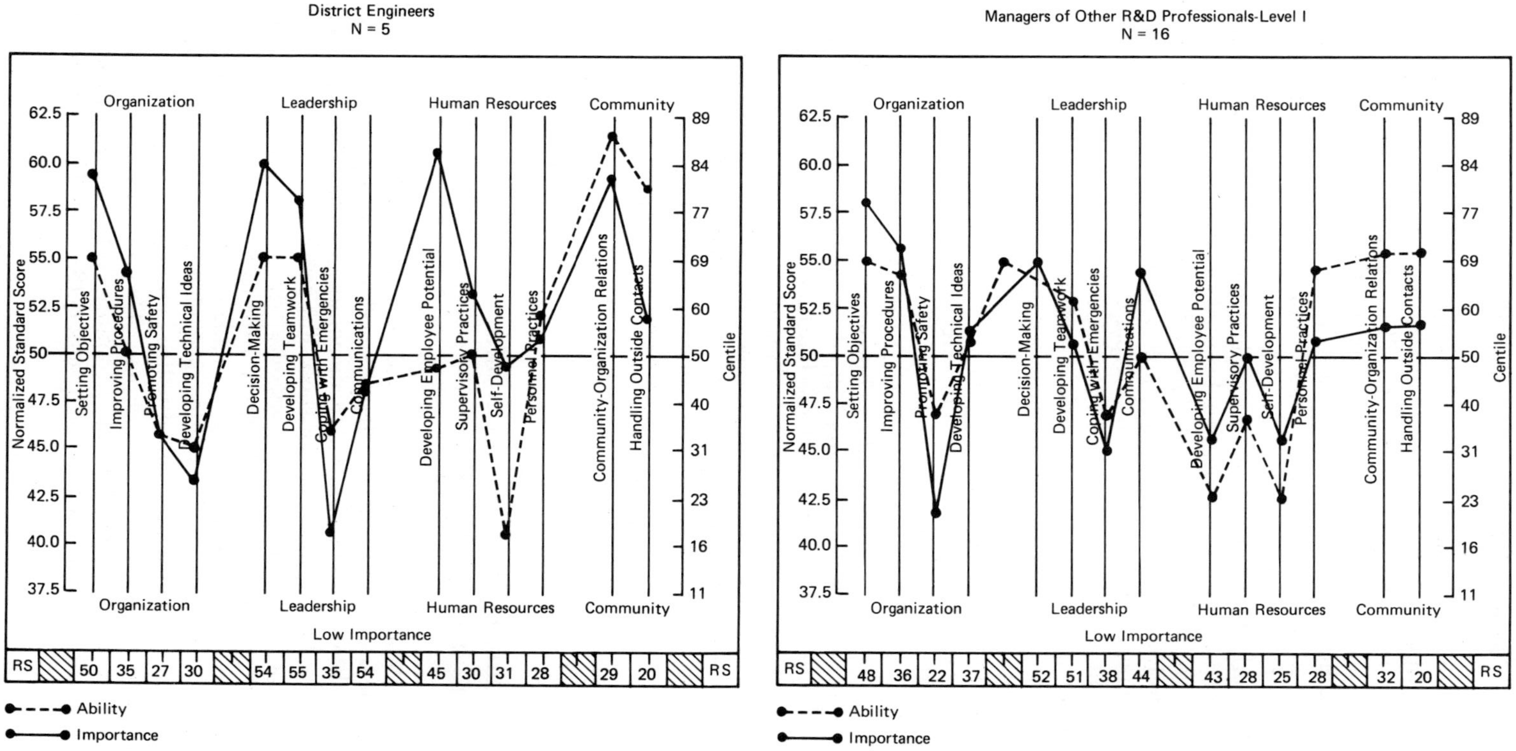

FIGURE 2 *Diagnosis of Training Needs: For Higher Level Line Managers and Managers of Professionals in a State Department of Transportation*

an importance scale. In the final version of the Inventory, this was achieved with a pencil-and-paper instrument adaptable to machine scoring. The respondent was first instructed to read through all the activities and to classify them into approximately equal halves to indicate whether they were of above- or below-average importance for the job. Next, the respondent redistributed those classified as of below-average importance into two approximately equal categories, those of "little or no" importance and those of "less than average" importance. Similarly, the items originally classified as of above-average importance were reclassified into two approximately equal halves as being of "above average" or of "outstanding" importance for the job. A factor analysis of the responses made to 180 items by a national sample of 619 principals produced 17 factors (2) spanning the general areas of interpersonal relations, curriculum, personnel, and administration.

The composite principal and superintendent profiles for the two districts are shown in Figure 3. The job clarification process was first implemented horizontally among the principals in each district. Differences in the two sets of composite principal profiles reflect the different conditions of operation and demands of the job in the two districts. When the composite principal profile for a district is compared with that generated by the relevant superintendent, it is apparent that there are two very different situations. In District A, there are some enormous differences between the two profiles as opposed to District B, where there is reasonable agreement between the superintendent and the principals in their perception of the relative importance of the functions to be performed.

Vertical job clarification between individual principals and their superintendent was quite easily achieved in District B, which, on the basis of observations made over the course of a year, appeared to be rather stable and smoothly functioning. By contrast, District A had experienced considerable turbulence, characterized by both principal and superintendent turnover. The vertical clarification sought, as far as possible, to provide a rational and nonemotional approach to resolving differences in perceptions of the job and to developing a common ground for future operations.

Determining Similarity of Comparable Jobs in Different Organizations

The following three applications of job analysis were used in the course of research programs concerned with selection test validations. The first application was undertaken as one approach to demonstrating that the functions performed, and the human demands for successful performance, were similar for comparable positions in different organizations. This application was designed to comply with requirements in the 1970 EEOC *Guidelines* for implementing a selection procedure already validated for a position in one organization for selection to a similar position in another organization. The position involved in this instance was that of police patrolman.

Two instruments were used for this purpose. They produced very similar conclusions. One was the Work Elements Inventory (WEI) described earlier, and the other was the Skills and Attributes Inventory (SAI) (6). This instrument consists of 95 items describing human skills and attributes, all of which contribute to 13 factorially determined dimensions covering the general areas of mental and special abilities, social skills, and personal attributes. The items are written at a level suitable for job incumbents, and the response technique is a forced-normal, five-interval distribution of relevant items according to the importance of the item for performance of the job. This technique is similar to that described for the WEI on page 275.

The SAI profiles for patrol officers, sergeants, and lieutenants were obtained for both police departments. Those for Department I are shown on the left in Figure 4. Essentially the same profiles were obtained for Department 2. An analysis of variance of SAI dimension scores across ranks indicated that for the first police department, nine and, for the second, ten out of the 13 possible probability values were significant beyond the .05 level of confidence, with the majority of these significant beyond the .01 level. The dimensions on which the significant differences occurred and the direction of the differences "made sense" in the light of other information obtained about these ranks in the course of the job analysis. For example, sergeants and lieutenants scored dramatically higher than patrol officers on the dimension "leadership ability" but considerably lower than patrol officers on "visual acuity" and "physical coordination" skills.

Although there were these marked differences across ranks in both departments, the profile for any given rank was remarkably stable. An analysis of variance of SAI dimension scores between each of the two comparable ranks in the two departments yields a possible total of 39 probability values. Of these, only three were significant beyond the .05 level of confidence. On the basis of these results, the test battery validated for Department 1, was used as an interim selection procedure in Department 2.

The job analysis for the second department produced some additional interesting job-description information. On the basis of SAI profiles compiled for the various groups, we were able to show that white, black, and Hispanic officers, on the one hand, and male and female officers, on the other, evidenced a high degree of consensus on the way in which they viewed the patrol officer's job.

Our second application of job analysis involved two different uses of SAI job profiles in a national or multi-unit selection test validation study for bus operators (3). In the first instance, composite SAI profiles for the bus operator's job, obtained from ratings made by supervisory personnel, were developed for each of the five geographically separate transit authorities participating in the study. Although there was some variation in these profiles, the results of an analysis of variance indicated that only one of the 13 SAI dimensions showed differences significant beyond the .05 level of confidence. On the basis of this finding and of other information obtained in the course of the job analysis, the five authorities were combined for purposes of the validation study. The composite profile for the five participating authorities became the "standard" against which other authorities not participating in the study would assess the bus operator's job.

The "standard" profile and the profile for the first transit authority requesting use of the validated battery are shown in the right-hand grid of Figure 4. The profiles are similar in shape, although the profile for the nonparticipating transit

District A

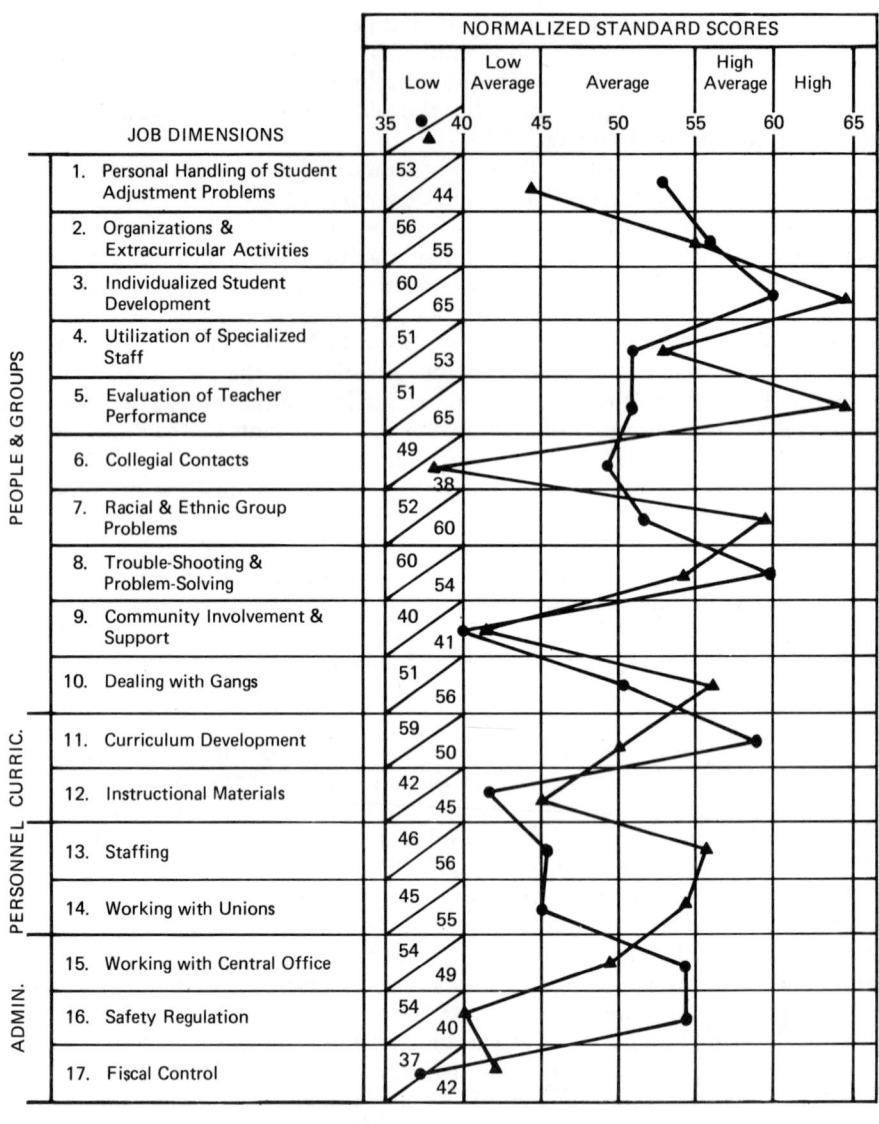

	JOB DIMENSIONS	Low 35	Low Average 40	Average 45 50	High Average 55 60	High 65
PEOPLE & GROUPS	1. Personal Handling of Student Adjustment Problems	53 / 44				
	2. Organizations & Extracurricular Activities	56 / 55				
	3. Individualized Student Development	60 / 65				
	4. Utilization of Specialized Staff	51 / 53				
	5. Evaluation of Teacher Performance	51 / 65				
	6. Collegial Contacts	49 / 38				
	7. Racial & Ethnic Group Problems	52 / 60				
	8. Trouble-Shooting & Problem-Solving	60 / 54				
	9. Community Involvement & Support	40 / 41				
	10. Dealing with Gangs	51 / 56				
PERSONNEL CURRIC.	11. Curriculum Development	59 / 50				
	12. Instructional Materials	42 / 45				
	13. Staffing	46 / 56				
	14. Working with Unions	45 / 55				
ADMIN.	15. Working with Central Office	54 / 49				
	16. Safety Regulation	54 / 40				
	17. Fiscal Control	37 / 42				

●———● Group A – Principals (N=5)
▲———▲ Group A – Superintendents (N=1)

JOB FUNCTIONS INVENTORY FOR SCHOOL PRINCIPALS
...... A standardized and quantitative instrument for defining the basic dimensions of the school principal's job in terms of the specific activities performed and their relative importance for overall successful performance.

FIGURE 3 *JFI Profiles for School Principals and Superintendents in Districts A & B*

District B

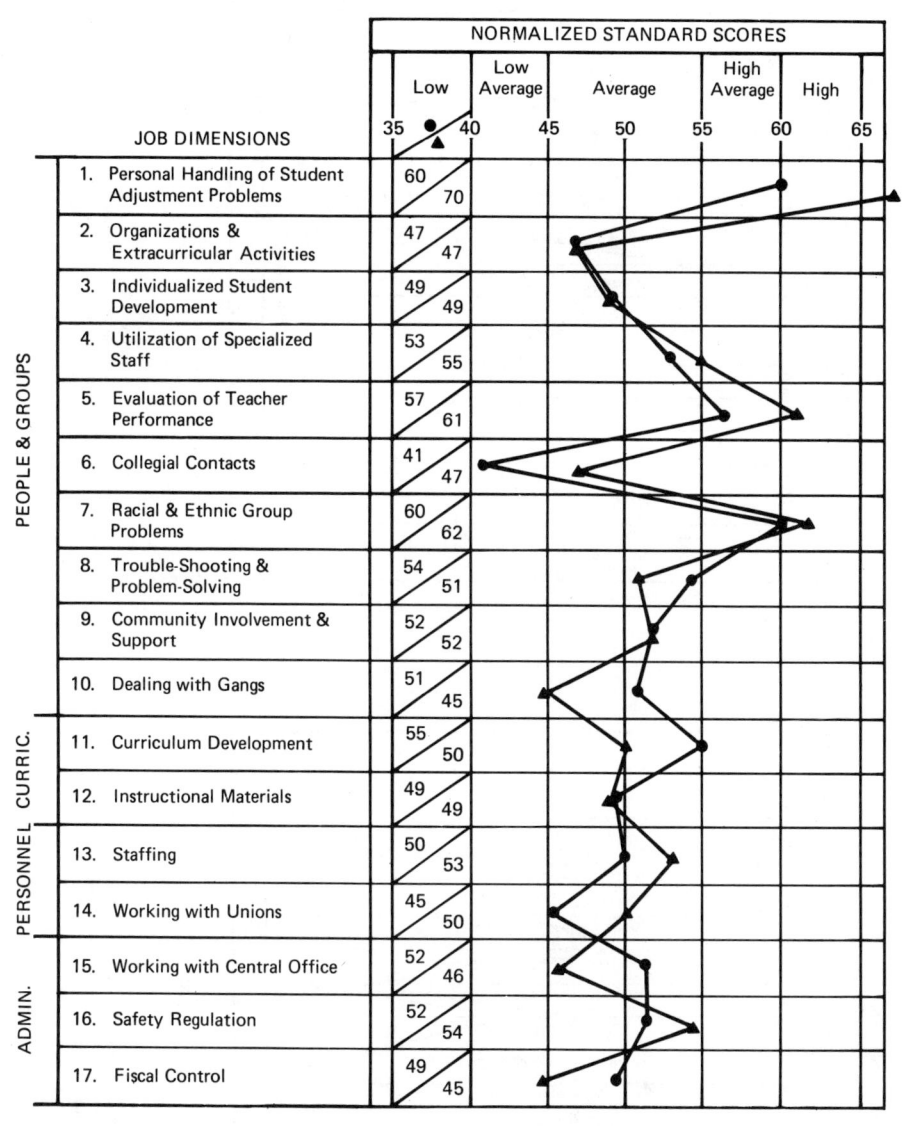

	JOB DIMENSIONS	NORMALIZED STANDARD SCORES
		Low (35) / Low Average (40) / Average (45-50) / High Average (55-60) / High (65)
PEOPLE & GROUPS	1. Personal Handling of Student Adjustment Problems	60 / 70
	2. Organizations & Extracurricular Activities	47 / 47
	3. Individualized Student Development	49 / 49
	4. Utilization of Specialized Staff	53 / 55
	5. Evaluation of Teacher Performance	57 / 61
	6. Collegial Contacts	41 / 47
	7. Racial & Ethnic Group Problems	60 / 62
	8. Trouble-Shooting & Problem-Solving	54 / 51
	9. Community Involvement & Support	52 / 52
	10. Dealing with Gangs	51 / 45
PERSONNEL CURRIC.	11. Curriculum Development	55 / 50
	12. Instructional Materials	49 / 49
	13. Staffing	50 / 53
	14. Working with Unions	45 / 50
ADMIN.	15. Working with Central Office	52 / 46
	16. Safety Regulation	52 / 54
	17. Fiscal Control	49 / 45

●———● Group B – Principals (N=9)

▲———▲ Group B – Superintendents (N=3)

JOB FUNCTIONS INVENTORY FOR SCHOOL PRINCIPALS
...... A standardized and quantitative instrument for defining the basic dimensions of the school principal's job in terms of the specific activities performed and their relative importance for overall successful performance.

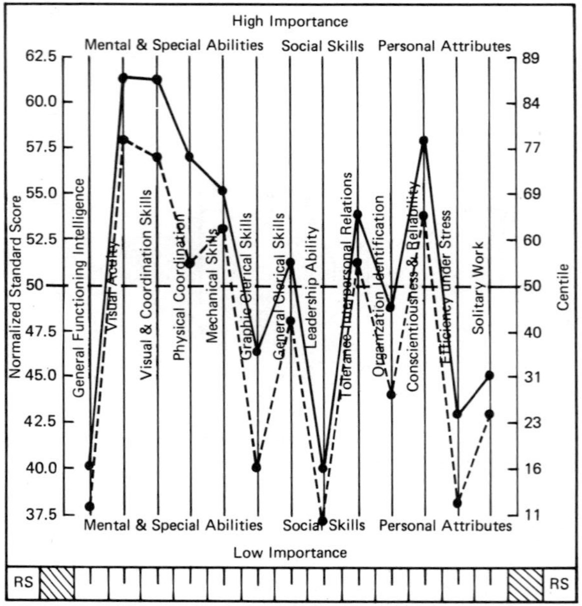

FIGURE 4 *Determining the Degree of Similarity Between Comparable Jobs in Different Organizations*

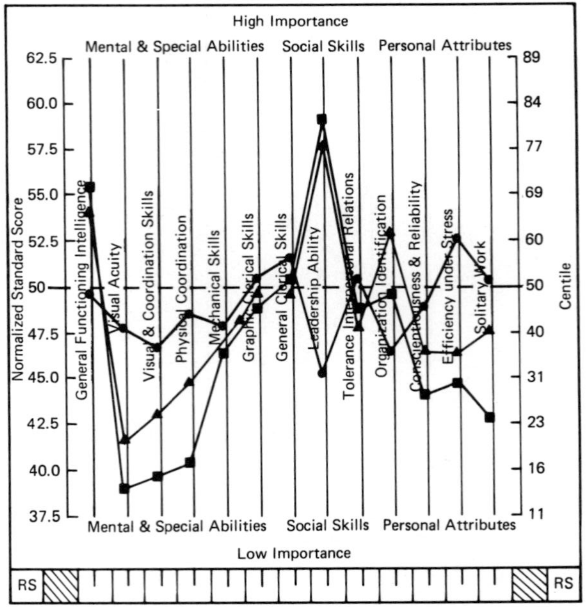

authority is at a slightly lower level than the "standard" profile. However, the results of an analysis of variance indicated that the differences were not significant at a .05 probability level on any of the dimensions. Since the completion of this study, some 35 transit authorities have developed SAI profiles for comparison with the "standard," and a special computer program has been developed to test profile similarity.

The third application of job analysis to be described here occurred in the course of a nationally based, multi-unit study of two police positions, those of municipal patrol officer and state trooper (11). The descriptions of both positions were obtained through use of the SAI and of the behavior attributes included in the Position Analysis Questionnaire (PAQ) by Mecham and McCormick (18). For both instruments, a comparison of the two positions showed no significant differences in the human skills and abilities required to perform them. However, the picture is strikingly different when we use the profile job descriptions produced by the *Job Functions Inventory for Police Officers* (16). The items in this instrument consist of specific activities performed on the job distributed among eight factorially determined dimensions.

The response format was the forced, four-interval, rectangular distribution as was used in the Job Functions Inventory for School Principals. The results showed that the patrol officer's job involved different activities in the five participating cities, that the state trooper's job was different in the five participating states, and that there were also extensive differences between the two job designations. We thus have an apparently anomalous situation in which jobs differ in activities performed but not in the skills and attributes required to perform them. It should be noted, however, that similar results have been found in other occupations, such as between two types of mechanics in the transit industry. In view of results from both studies, we are reasonably convinced that these are not irreconcilable differences. On the one hand, the specific activities to be performed may be observably different and largely determined by on-the-job training. On the other, the underlying work behaviors—and thus the skills and attributes required to perform them—may be similar. The various ways in which these different kinds of information can be utilized are discussed in the following section.

IMPLICATIONS FOR RESEARCH AND PRACTICE

A relatively underemphasized area of personnel research—rigorous job description—has assumed an ever-increasing importance over the past decade, largely because of the legal requirements for the validation of selection and promotion procedures following the Civil Rights Act of 1964 and its Title VII, dealing with discrimination in employment. Results of job-description research can now be applied not only to selection and to the narrower requirements of selection test validation, but also across the entire range of practices for human and organizational development. Indeed, the results open up dazzling vistas of innovative research, leading to the development and refinement of many new techniques.

Some of the procedures for job description and job clarification we have described are excellent preparation, if not prerequisites, for performance appraisal. Some of the measurement instruments used in these procedures, especially those dealing with specific job activities or underlying work behaviors, can be adapted for the development of a variety of performance appraisal techniques. For example, a supervisor can use the total WEI procedure to rate an employee's ability to perform certain functions designated as essential to the job. The employee's performance index could then be simply the sum of the importance scale values of those items which measure the specific functions. This procedure has the advantage of being specially tailored for a position and of reducing personal bias, since only "important" items are used to obtain the index even though the entire series of items is used in the evaluation. However, the procedure clearly has the disadvantage of being time-consuming for the supervisor of any considerable number of employees. A variant of the procedure would be to enlarge the nucleus of "important" items for the job. This could be done through personal interviews or group brainstorming sessions to produce specially tailored behavior-anchored rating scales. In this way, a single instrument, similar to the WEI, can be used very efficiently to develop custom-made appraisal procedures for a variety of positions.

A different approach to performance appraisal is to determine the degree of congruence or association between the profile representing the relative importance of the functions to be performed on the job and the one representing the employee's ability to perform these functions. Such an approach supplies an estimate of the "fit" between the demands of the job and the employee's abilities. It seems a reasonable hypothesis that the closer this "fit" the better the individual's performance is likely to be. This hypothesis has been confirmed in at least one study (32) and will be tested again in the course of research projected for the coming year.

Applying job description to determine the "transportability" of validated selection test batteries has already been described. However, these applications have been limited to determining whether or not the demands of the job in an organization which did not participate in a validation were sufficiently similar to those of job in participating companies to justify use of the test battery. A further step, if necessary, would be to change or adapt the test battery for the new organization in order to account for any differences in the demands of the job in that organization.

Such adaptation could be accomplished by first determining which tests predict the ability to perform each of the functions covered in the job description instrument. It would then be possible to develop or "synthesize" a selection test battery when the important functions to be performed had been identified. This approach has sometimes been called "synthetic validity" and can clearly be used to "synthesize" selection test batteries for high-level or unique positions in organizations where small numbers of incumbents prohibit traditional validation procedures.

A less common adaptation of a job-description instrument for selection was made in our national study of the transit industry (3). The SAI, which describes the job in terms of the skills and abilities required for successful performance, was used as predictor in the trial test battery, along with traditional psychological tests of many of the same skills and attributes. In this context, the SAI becomes a self-report of the degree to which a respondent feels he or she possesses a variety of abilities. Results indicated that, in contrast to results from traditional tests, the self-report of abilities showed no legally adverse impact for any racial group. Furthermore, the SAI was one of three tests out of 11 to survive validation and was found to be more useful in predicting performance than traditional tests of the same constructs (5). Although one study cannot produce definitive results, it can point the direction for future research.

A further step in parsimony in selection procedures would be to avoid the use of tests altogether and base selection on the "fit" between the applicant's self-report of abilities and the established importance profile of abilities required for successful performance on the job. This procedure could be implemented either by using a skills-and-attributes job description, such as that obtained from the SAI, or by utilizing descriptions based on underlying job behaviors. When the latter instruments are used, the process is similar to that which is sometimes referred to as "job/man matching" (12).

The goal of all the various developed and developing personnel procedures is career development and the mapping of career paths in the organization. In achieving this goal, the various forms of job description can make significant inputs. Depending on the content of the items used in the instrument—either activities and work behavior or skills and attributes—cluster hierarchies of job demands may be used to map career paths.

Researchers may be deterred from embarking on some of these more innovative approaches to personnel decisions for fear that these procedures may come up against legal challenges and be judged in default of *Guidelines* requirements. In this connection, it should be pointed out that whenever sample sizes and other conditions make criterion-performance validation feasible, the new simplified procedures discussed here can be implemented concomitantly with little additional time or cost. The results of the simplified procedures may then be "validated" against those obtained in the more detailed procedure. In the opinion of this writer, such an approach should provide sufficient "anchoring" to justify its later independent use in situations where additional validation is not feasible.

The strong impetus given to job-description research, together with the greater choice of personnel procedures afforded by later versions of the *Guidelines*, should be fully explored. When adapted by practitioners, professionally based job description will lead to the greater utilization of individuals by a more scientifically oriented HRM team.

References

1. Baehr, Melany E. "A Factorial Framework for Job Description." Paper presented to the Industrial Section, Illinois Psychological Association Convention, Springfield, Ill., March 18, 1967.
2. Baehr, Melany E. *A National Occupational Analysis of the School Principalship.* Chicago, Ill.: Industrial Relations Center, The University of Chicago, 1975.
3. Baehr, Melany E. *National Validation of a Selection Test Battery for Male Transit Bus Operators: Final Report.* Springfield, Virginia: National Technical Information Service, 1976.

4. Baehr, Melany E. *An Organizational Program for Job Structuring and the Identification of Training Needs.* Unpublished Research Report. Chicago, Ill.: Industrial Relations Center, The University of Chicago, 1976.
5. Baehr, Melany E. "A Practitioner's View of EEOC Requirements with Special Reference to Job Analysis," Occasional Paper 37. Chicago, Ill.: Industrial Relations Center, The University of Chicago, 1976.
6. Baehr, Melany E. *Skills and Attributes Inventory.* Chicago, Ill.: Industrial Relations Center, The University of Chicago, 1971.
7. Baehr, Melany E., and Frances M. Burns. *An Occupational Analysis of the Principalship. Final Report.* A cooperative research project of the Midwest Administration Center and the Industrial Relations Center, both of The University of Chicago. Chicago, Ill.: October 1974.
8. Baehr, Melany E., Frances M. Burns, R. Bruce McPherson, and Columbus Salley. *Job Functions Inventory for School Principals.* Chicago, Ill.: Industrial Relations Center and Consortium for Educational Leadership, The University of Chicago, 1976.
9. Baehr, Melany E., John E. Furcon, and Ernest C. Froemel. *Psychological Assessment of Patrolman Qualifications in Relation to Field Performance.* Washington, D.C.: U.S. Government Printing Office, 1969.
10. Baehr, Melany E., Wallace G. Lonergan, and Charles R. Potkay. *Work Elements Inventory,* research ed. Chicago, Ill.: Industrial Relations Center, The University of Chicago, 1967.
11. Baehr, Melany E., and Arnold B. Oppenheim. "Job Analysis in Police Selection Research." In Charles D. Spielberger ed. *Police Selection,* New York: John Wiley and Sons, in press.
12. Cleff, S. H., and R. M. Hecht. "Job/Man Matching in the 70's," *Datamation,* February 1, 1971.
13. Equal Employment Opportunity Commission. *Guidelines on Employee Selection Procedures.* Washington, D.C.: EEOC, July 31, 1970.
14. *Federal Executive Agency Guidelines on Employee Selection Procedures. Federal Register,* 41, No. 227 (November 23, 1976), 51752-59.
15. Hemphill, John K. "Job Description for Executives," *Harvard Business Review,* 37, 5, (1959), 55-67.
16. *Job Functions Inventory for Police Officers.* Chicago, Ill.: Industrial Relations Center, The University of Chicago, n.d.
17. McPherson, R. Bruce, Columbus Salley, and Melany E. Baehr. *What Principals Do: Preliminary Implications of "A National Occupational Analysis of the School Principalship."* Chicago, Ill.: Consortium for Educational Leadership, 1975.
18. Mecham, Robert C., and Ernest J. McCormick. *The Rated Attribute Requirements of Job Elements in the "Position Analysis Questionnaire."* Lafayette, Ind.: Occupational Research Center, Purdue University, January, 1969.
19. Mecham, Robert C., and Ernest J. McCormick. *The Use of Data Based on the "Position Analysis Questionnaire" in Developing Synthetically-derived Attribute Requirements of Jobs.* Lafayette, Ind.: Occupational Research Center, Purdue University, June, 1969.
20. *Moody et al. v. Albermarle Paper Company et al.* EEOC, Amicus Curiae #72-1267, 5 Fair Employment Practice Cases 613. Washington, D.C.: Bureau of National Affairs, 1973.
21. Morsh, Joseph E. *Evolution of a Job Inventory and Tryout of Task Rating Factors.* Lackland Air Force Base, Texas: Personnel Research Laboratory, Aerospace Medical Division, Air Force Systems Command, December, 1965.

22. Morsh, Joseph E. 'Job Analysis in the United States Air Force." *Personnel Psychology,* 17, 1 (1964), 7–17.
23. Office of Federal Contract Compliance, Department of Labor. "Amendment to OFCC Order on Employee Testing Procedures," *Daily Labor Report,* D-2 (No. 13), 1/18/74. Washngton, D.C.: The Bureau of National Affairs, Inc.
24. Office of Federal Contract Compliance, Department of Labor, "Part 60-3—Employee Testing and Other Selection Procedures" (an amendment to Executive Order 11246), *Federal Rgister, 36,* No. 77 (Wednesday, April 21, 1971), 7532-35.
25. Prien, Erich P. "Development of a Supervisor Position Description Questionnaire," *Journal of Applied Psychology,* 47, 1 (1963), 10–14.
26. Prien, Erich P., and William W. Ronan. "Job Analysis: A Review of Research Findings," *Personnel Psychology, 24,* 3 (1971), 371–396.
27. Primoff, Ernest S. *How to Prepare and Conduct Job-element Examinations.* Washington, D.C.: Personnel Research and Development Center, Bureau of Policies and Standards, U.S. Civil Service Commission, January 1973.
28. Primoff, Ernest S. *The J-Coefficient Procedure* (preliminary draft). Washington, D.C.: Personnel Measurement Research and Development Center, Standards Division, Bureau of Policies and Standards, U.S. Civil Service Commission, March 1972.
29. Primoff, Ernest S. *Research on Efficient Methods in Job-element Examining. Report No. 1—Research on the Additive Checklist.* Washington, D.C.: Personnel Measurement Research and Development Center, Standards Division, Bureau of Policies and Standards, U.S. Civil Service Commission, June 1970.
30. Primoff, Ernest S. *Test Selection by Job Analysis: The J-Coefficient, What it is, How it Works* (Assembled Test Technical Series No. 20). Washington, D.C.: Test Development Section, Standards Division, U.S. Civil Service Commission, May 1955.
31. Primoff, Ernest S. *Use of Measures of Potential and Motivation in a Promotion Examination from Labor-type Positions to Gardner Trainee Park Service.* Washington, D.C.: Personnel Measurement Research and Development Center, Standards Division, Bureau of Policies and Standards, U.S. Civil Service Commission, September 1969.
32. *Technical Appendix to Validation of a Sales Test Battery against Paired-Comparison Ratings of Performance on the Job.* Chicago Ill.: Industrial Relations Center, The University of Chicago, 1967.
33. *Uniform Guidelines on Employee Selection Procedures* Notice of Proposed Rulemaking. Washington, D.C.: Civil Service Commission, Equal Employment Opportunity Commission, Department of Labor. *Federal Register, 42,* No. 251 (December 30, 1977) 6570-06.
34. U.S. Department of Labor, Bureau of Employment Security. *Dictionary of Occupational Titles,* Vol. 1, *Definitions of Titles,* 3rd ed. Washington, D.C.: U.S. Government Printing Office, 1965.
35. U.S. Department of Labor, Bureau of Employment Security, United States Employment Service. *Estimates of Worker Trait Requirements for 4,000 Jobs as Defined in the "Dictionary of Occupational Titles."* Washington, D.C.: U.S. Government Printing Office, 1957.
36. U.S. Department of Labor, Bureau of Employment Security. *A Supplement to the "Dictionary of Occupational Titles, Selected Characteristics of Occupations,"* 3rd ed. Washington, D.C.: U.S. Government Printing Office, 1966.
37. Wherry, Robert J. *A Review of the J-Coefficient* (Assembled Test Technical Series No. 26). Washington, D.C.: Test Development Section, Standards Division, U.S. Civil Service Commission, July 1955.

Organizational Best Fit: Survival, Change, and Adaptation

Kenyon B. De Greene

INTRODUCTION

This paper is about evolution, the evolution of organizations and the increasingly turbulent environments to which they must adapt in order to survive. Perhaps even more importantly, it concerns the evolution of organization theory and design, especially with an anticipated increasing disparity between the demands of environmental complexity and change, on the one hand, and organizational design criteria, on the other.

This paper also represents an implicit synthesis of theories and developments in other fields, which until recently would have been considered at most tangentially related to organization theory and practice. These include the concepts of organismic fit to a given environment and adaptation to demands imposed by environmental change; homeostatic regulation; cybernetic control utilizing comparison of goal and performance information; isomorphy and open and closed systems from general systems theory; information systems; ecosystems; economic and social indicators; futures research; and Forresterian systems dynamics. Collectively the framework is that of sociotechnical macrosystems as explicated elsewhere (De Greene, 1973).

It is only within the last decade or so that the true dynamic complexity of today's organizations and environments has been formally understood. Who ten years ago would have predicted the near bankruptcy of the nation's largest city and one of its most populous states and the failure of some of American's largest corporations? In short, there is considerable evidence that neither theory nor design practice has kept up with, let alone anticipated, the world changes that characterize the last third of the twentieth century.

We examine in turn the life cycle of social systems, the changing environment, organizational di'ferentiation and integration as environmental fit, determinism, psychological and political subsystems, present design approaches, and a design approach consistent with the overall Management of the Interstage. It is my belief that there is no optimum, perfect, final, or universal design applicable to organizations—and for that matter no final solution to any of world society's problems. We can only design for the Interstage, the period between today's sudden and belated awareness of the magnitude of the world's intersecting crises and the day after tomorrow's steady-state post-industrial world.

Kenyon B. DeGreene, "Organizational Best Fit: Survival, Change, and Adaptation," *Organizational Design*, Negandhi and Burack, Eds., The Comparative Administration Research Center, Kent State University Press, 1972, pp. 117-33.

THE LIFE CYCLE OF SOCIAL SYSTEMS

The fossil record is rich in examples of organisms which arose, grew, proliferated, dominated the world of their times, but finally declined and even became extinct. The trilobites, ammonites, and dinosaurs are well known. The historical record is equally rich in examples of civilizations and societies which flourished and grew, only to perish. The Roman and Mayan empires are classic examples. There is thus strong inferential evidence that social systems, including business and service organizations as well as whole societies, go through periods of foundations, youth, maturity, senescence, and extinction.

Scientific studies of organizations longitudinally are unfortunately rare in the literature. Most studies are cross-sectional in nature or deal with a single time slice or at most a segment in the life history of the organization. However, empirical evidence from organizations of many types—railroads, automobiles, airlines, aerospace, land development, postal services, health services, education, social services, the military—suggests organizations do indeed follow an evolutionary sequence.

A major task for the organization scientist is to identify features of misfit to the environment early enough so that ameliorative efforts can be taken. It should be recognized that organizational change is slow, that an organization may be losing fit with its environment without this being immediately evident, and that reliance on a single obvious criterion of success or failure such as size, earnings, or profits may give a totally false picture. Analogously, a person may show good cardiovascular function, but already be dying from an insidious cancer.

Consider General Motors, long one of the largest, most powerful, and wealthiest of American corporations. GM's federal decentralization was long held to be a model for the design of a large, multidivisional manufacturing company. Yet GM appears in at least six ways, involving labor force, perception of market, diversification, and nature of throughput, to be better geared to yesterday's environment than to today's (Drucker, 1974).

One of the few comprehensive studies of the evolution of large, multidimensional organizations was that of Chandler (1962), who analyzed changes in organizational structure at Sears Roebuck, General Motors, DuPont, and Standard Oil of New Jersey. Chandler concluded that the rate of environmental change in technology, markets, and sources of supply provided opportunities for strategic decisions that in turn led the changes in organizational structure.

Greiner (1972) believes organizations move through five major phases of development: creativity, direction, delegation, coordination, and collaboration. Each phase is characterized by a period of evolutionary growth followed by a revolutionary management crisis. The first four phases above are respectively ended by the crises of leadership, autonomy, control, and red tape. Many companies fail along the way if they are unable to abandon past practices; the very practices found applicable to a given period of evolutionary growth lead to decay and a new revolutionary crisis. Thus, a major solution at one phase becomes a major problem later on, and managers must be prepared to dismantle any given structure before crises become uncontrollable.

Hunt (1970), emphasizing the deterministic role of technology, sees two fundamentally different types of organizations, namely, performance and problem-solving. Most organizations for various reasons evolve toward a performance emphasis, that is, to increased routinization. Similarly, Thompson (1969) presents arguments that production orientation and associated bureaucratic structure vary inversely with innovation—the more of one, the less of the other. And Forrester (1969), using complex modeling and computer simulation methodology, has shown a drift over time in social systems to low performance. This is due to counterintuitive behavior (behavior typically the opposite of what we might intuitively predict) and rigid, repeated efforts to solve new problems with old methods.

Modern institutions, however, need not pass inexorably through the stages just discussed to ultimate extinction. Systems science, for example, provides means for designing a self-renewal capability into organizations. A cybernated design is proposed here.

THE CHANGING NATURE OF THE ENVIRONMENT

In the simplest sense the environment of a system consists of those elements, and *interactions* among elements, outside the system boundary that affect the system and are affected by the system. The definition of a system, and especially the concept of system boundary, implies the definition of environment. Nevertheless, in practice, organization theories have tended to ignore or minimize the role of environment. Most models of organizations until recently were closed systems models; that is, the structure and behavior of the organization were determined entirely by forces operating within its boundary. Even the otherwise highly sophisticated systems dynamics simulation methodology represents, by Jay W. Forrester's (1969) own definition, a closed systems approach. In system dynamics materials and people *do* cross the system boundary, but the system does not affect the environment nor the environment the system, and no feedback loops cross the system boundary. The system is, therefore, both closed and open loop. Only in the last few years has open systems theory caught on in organization theory, but even so the appreciation of just what features of the organization interact with which aspects of the environment remains limited.

Obviously, then, the organization designer and organizational management must not only be aware that the environment exists per se, but also must perceive the relevant structural complexity and dynamic change within the environment. There are thus three types of processes of concern: those operating entirely within the organization, those operating mutually between the organization and its environment and those operating within the environment itself. The three types of processes were stated in order of attention paid by both theorists and designers. My emphasis here is on the last two types of processes, namely, organization-environment interactions and new properties emerging in the environmental *field* itself.

Classification of Environments

The concept of *causal texture* of the environment (Emery and Trist, 1965) provides a valuable start at classifying and understanding organizational environments. Emery and Trist differentiate among four types of environments on the basis of the distribution or aggregation, the nature, and the rates of change of the good and bad features of the environments. In a *placid, randomized environment* the goods and bads are relatively unchanging in themselves and are randomly distributed. In a *placid, clustered environment* the goods and bads hang together, and survival becomes critically linked to what the organization knows of its environment. Competent organizations concentrate their resources and subordinate to a main plan; hence, they grow in size and become hierarchical with centralized control and coordination. Both these types of environments are *static*. In a *disturbed-reactive environment* there emerge a number of similar organizations, and competition, action, and counteraction become dominant operations. The required flexibility within a dynamic environment encourages decentralization and decision making at peripheral locations. In a *turbulent-field environment* dynamic processes emerge from the field itself, not merely from the interactions of the elements. The environment itself assumes greater organization and structure.

The organization, the environment, and the organization in relation to the environment are all characterized by dynamic, nonlinear, unpredictable behaviors associated with contact of elements and forces and with positive and negative feedback loop structure. Herein lies the major challenge to modern organization theory. Organizational policies and management practices are likely to be counterintuitive, to produce no effects, or to trigger predetermined, latent destructive forces. Within this frame of reference it can be seen that emphasis on any one determinant of organization structure or behavior is likely to produce misleading results.

To summarize: Not only is the environment becoming more complex in the absolute sense, but our appreciation of this complexity should be increasing. Today there is ever more evidence that the environment is indeed a turbulent field, wherein complexity derives from changes in variety, rates of change, and the emergence of new properties associated with hierarchical jumps or restructurings to hitherto unanticipated configurations of elements. Theoretical formulations have been punctuated by the dramatic events of the last decade. Unfortunately, however, when any attention is paid to the environment at all, it is likely to center deterministically on one or two features such as the market environment or the role of technology. The nature environment, the increasingly better educated labor force, changing values, and the policy-shaping capabilities of new, often informal groups have been ignored. As recent experience with the energy crisis has shown, the behavior of most organizations is reactive rather than anticipatory. In maintaining environmental fit, this can be a fatal flaw.

Finally, we should comment on the *perception* of the environment as opposed to its reality. There may be little relationship between the two. For example, a situation of uncertainty can be reduced by top management to a situation of risk (Michael, 1972). Or the model of the world top managers perceive may, by viture of layers of filters, amplifiers, and attenuators, be only a surrogate of the real world (Beer, 1973).

ORGANIZATIONAL DIFFERENTIATION AND INTEGRATION IN MAINTENANCE OF ENVIRONMENTAL FIT

Just as concern with the interrelations between organization and environment represents probably the main thrust of contemporary organization theory, so concern with internal organizational differentiation and integration provides the meat of classical organization theory. Certain seminal studies performed in the 1960s have provided a bridge between classical and contemporary theory.

The earliest studies of the structure and behavior of twentieth-century organizations scarcely recognized the existence of environment. These included the studies of functional structure of Henri Fayol, studies of work efficiency by Frederick W. Taylor and the Gilbreths, work on the decentralization of authority and centralization of control by Alfred P. Sloan, Jr., at General Motors, and studies of bureaucracy by Max Weber. Collectively such efforts led to a good understanding and effective operation of organizations characterized by specialization of functions, jobs, and personnel; by personal accountability associated with the learning of specific skills, rules, and procedures; and by hierarchical structure and control. Such organizational structure was well fitted to an environment characterized by clear patterns of dominance and subordination among nations, races, and social classes; seemingly unlimited natural and personal resources; relatively low average educational and skill levels; relatively low rate of social and technological change; and relatively great separation of peoples in time and space. More recent studies have provided insights into organizational differentiation and integration that went beyond either-or emphasis on such functions as engineering, production, or sales and on centralized control or decentralized control. Collectively, these studies contribute to a *contingency approach* to organization theory: If certain important environmental parameters can be specified, the best form of a given organization can be determined; however, there is no single universal best form, and any one form is not equally good for all organizations.

Organic Versus Mechanistic Structures

Burns and Stalker (1966) analyzed 20 British firms revealing two basic types of organizational structure, an *organic* structure most effective in rapidly changing markets and technologies and a *mechanistic* structure effective under stable environmental conditions. Firms adapting successfully to the changing (electronics) industry possessed a more holistic concept of their main task and more varied processes for the communication of information necessary for innovation. Flexibility was maintained through introducing new technological and market information to reprogram routine operations. In other words, in these organic firms there was no rigid definition of methods, duties and powers; they were continually reevaluated in the course of interactions with the environment. In contrast, in mechanistic organizations work was successively shredded into smaller and smaller portions and strictly governed by decisions and instructions of superiors. The managerial chain of command was vertical, and information flowed upward to perhaps the one man who "understood" the whole organization. Using an organismic analogy, this management structure is like having the brain decide on spinal reflexes.

Woodward (1965), studying 100 British firms, found a relationship between certain technological variables and management structure. Firms were placed on a continuum expressing predictability and routineness of, and therefore degree of control over, operating processes. At one extreme were unit processors, that is, makers of tailor-made, one-of-a-kind, or prototype articles; in the middle range were large batch and mass-production firms; and at the other extreme were process-control industries. Success in large batch and mass-production firms depended on mechanistic management procedures in which duties were clearly indicated on paper. Standardization had eliminated from production tasks the need for perceptual and cognitive skills, but motor and dexterity skills were still required. In many mechanistic firms, objectives changed in erratic ways, apparently following fragmentation of decision making and control among the specialist departments relative to standards, quantities, schedules, and costs. Even planned changes were in response to internal tension. Eventually, the primary goal became survival of the firm rather than provision of goods and services.

In Woodward's unit-production and process-control firms, on the other hand, management was organic. In the former, difficulties in prediction and control were associated with greater decision making at every level; but an integrated control system was maintained nevertheless. In the latter, routine tasks were highly automated, and the remaining labor force was characterized by large percentages of personnel specializing in exception detection, that is, more highly educated maintenance persons and supervisors. In these organic firms there were repeated periods when reappraisal of objectives and methods took place.

Lawrence and Lorsch (1967) studied ten organizations in the plastics, food, and container industries in terms of internal differentiation and integration as a function of three environments differing in amount of technological and market change. Organizations were also compared both within and among industries on the basis of performance. The high-performing plastics organization, which operated in the most dynamic and diverse environment, was most highly differentiated. Commensurate integration was maintained through the use of both an integrating unit and cross-functional teams which ensured the resolution of conflict among the differentiated units. Participation in decision making by managers of all levels and specialties was high. At the other extreme, the high-performing container organization functioned in a relatively stable and homogenous environment. The functional units were not highly differentiated and the only formal integrating device was the management hierarchy. Nevertheless, this structure met requirements for effective decision making and conflict resolution. In short, two different types of organizational structures were identified, each effective in dealing with its own external environment.

On the basis of review of the work of Burns and Stalker, Woodward, and other authors not cited for sake of brevity here, as well as of their own findings, Lawrence and Lorsch suggested the contingency theory mentioned above. That is, there are complex interrelationships among environmental certainty and diversity, internal differentiation and integration, and conflict resolution. If (1) the organization's differentiation is consistent with the diversity of the environment, (2) integration is consistent with environmental demands for interdependence, and (3) conflict can be resolved at the level wherein lies the required knowledge about the environment, then the organization will be effective in dealing with its environment.

That innovation is dependent on congruency between organization and environment is illustrated by a study of ten innovations of great social impact (Battelle Columbus Laboratories, 1973). The presence in an organization of a technical entrepreneur, who identified scientific and technical information to researchers, was the single most important factor. Next came early identification of a need or "market pull." Supportive and encouraging internal management and the unplanned and planned confluence of technology were also significant factors.

A FURTHER WORD ON DETERMINISM

There is an overreliance on determinism and a deficiency of understanding of mutual causality in explanations of organizational structure and behavior. Thus, technology does not *determine* structure in any real sense. Technologies have different effects depending on their applications. In the process control industries studied by Woodward (1965) and the automated merchant ships studied by Herbst (1974), automation of routine tasks changed the skill levels of the work forces and contributed to a work structure emphasizing problem solving. In contrast, data processing requires exact adherence to rules and procedures. Because of the language and communications barrier between man and machine, the computer is still a hard taskmaster. In a similar vein, a complex environment does not determine organizational structure; for example, an organization can influence or even dominate its market through advertising or acquisition of competitors or sources of resource inputs.

PSYCHOLOGICAL AND POLITICAL SUBSYSTEMS

For epistemological reasons—and not as an invitation to hair-splitting—there is a need to formalize the psychological and political subsystems of organizations. There have, of course, long been steps in this direction, for example, in studies of workers' needs and job satisfaction, in the use of psychological tests, and in the study of power structure and influence. However this work does not explain the evolution of these subsystems, especially the behavior of top management. Bureaucratic organizations and innovative organizations are what they are not just because of technology, hierarchical structure, or rules and procedures, but because of self-selection of personnel from unskilled worker to top executive. Changes in the psychological and political subsystems take place in the evolution of organizations, with personalities reinforcing structure, which encourages more persons with similar and receptive personalities, and so on.

I hold, therefore, that the single greatest test of organizational best fit involves the questions: Are all subsystems within the organization *congruent*, and Is the organization *congruent* with its environment?

There has been some recognition of the importance of managerial, psychological, and political factors to organizational structure and success or failure. For example, Lawrenee and Lorsch (1967, p. 155) suggest that managers in the successful plastics organization may have different personality needs (greater independence and tolerance for ambiguity) from those in the successful container organization (greater dependence on authority and anxiety in the face of ambiguity).

Chandler (1962) highlighted strategic choices among opportunities and needs presented by changing environments. Child (1972), continuing Chandler's line of thought, emphasized strategic choices by the powerful (the "dominant coalition") in organizations as the chief source of variation among organizations. Organizational structure can reflect the distribution of order, security, power, and status that those in power refuse to upset. Existing power structure and associated values provide a perceptual filter through which environmental changes in opportunity or threat must pass. Modification of organizational goals is, therefore, a major source of changes in size, technology, or location. By emphasizing political processes within the organization, Child provides another argument against environmental determinism.

Organizational evolution is thus very much a function of processes within the psychological and political subsystems. These include not only the selective perceptions, the strategic choices as to what to accept and what to avoid and where to go and where not to go, and the personal needs for security, status, economic reward, and power, but also the massive inertia built up over the years as a result of mutual operational reinforcements. It is the inertia and momentum of organizations as much as anything that leads to loss of environmental fit. Relevant personality and other behavioral factors in bureaucracies which contribute to inertia are discussed by Downs (1967) and Fromm (1970).

In this context it is well to reflect on top management's contribution to the recent financial difficulties of Douglas Aircraft, Penn Central, Lockheed Aircraft, Rolls Royce, Boise Cascade, United Airlines, Pan American World Airways, Trans World Airlines, W.T. Grant, and other corporate giants.

PRESENT APPROACHES TO ORGANIZATIONAL DESIGN FOR CHANGING ENVIRONMENTS

The requirements for any specific organizational change differ by sector, industry, and immediately preceding and projected environmental changes. For example, the forestry products and utility companies until recently appeared to be stable, with assured inputs and markets. That was before the energy crisis and the onslaught of the conservationists. Commercial airlines and the aerospace companies will have to change considerably, or many will lose money and markets and disappear, probably through merger. Educational and health services and many government organizations could well heed the handwriting on the wall. Computers, banking, insurance, petroleum, foods, and large-scale retailing appear at present to possess the power to control change without being too much controlled by change.

How then can organizations be designed to minimize buffeting by the environment, to be anticipatory rather than reactive? I have already reviewed features of different organizations that were positively correlated with success or failure in given environments. But these features or design principles were observed *ex post facto* in case studies. Can there be a predictive science of organizational design? Some actual and proposed design criteria justifiable in terms of empirical evidence and theory follow.

Hierarchy and Rigidity

Probably the two paramount questions about organizational structure, both theoretically and pragmatically, are those relating to hierarchy and rigidity. All design alternatives express direct or indirect concern with these two questions.

Paradoxically, in nature, hierarchy enhances not only stability but flexibility and adaptability; in organizations, however, it leads to sluggishness, rigidity, and resistance to change. A fundamental difference is that in nature any given hierarchical level is associated with emergence of new properties; in organizations this is always less true, and in some organizations there is almost no qualitative change setting apart different hierarchical levels. In organisms hierarchy is associated with local option, signal enhancement, synthesis, coordination, and control. In bureaucratic organizations hierarchy can represent compartmentalization, suppression or distortion of signals, and overcontrol.

Rigidity can be thought of in terms of the degree of coupling among the elements of a system. For example, Ashby (1960) determined that the time for a system to adapt to a given disturbance is dependent on the nature of interconnections among the elements. The time required for a system to restore steady state or make an adaptive change was considerably less for a loosely joined system than for systems with coupling only between each element and its environment or with all elements connected to all other elements.

Problems of organizational design, therefore, boil down to utilizing the integrating, coordinative, and emergent properties of natural hierarchies, while enhancing adaptability by means of loose coupling among system elements.

Design Methods

The rigid, restrictive aspects of a tightly coupled hierarchical structure can be reduced by introducing slack into the system, by modifying individuals, and by varying man-hours, money, or scheduled time for a given job. Through use of organizational slack, the tolerable ranges in performance are increased and the detection of exceptions made less necessary. Individuals are modified through selection and training and the use of less formal and liaison-type interpersonal relations. Groups are restructured into autonomous work groups, project teams, program offices, and matrix organizations. Many of such groups are short-lived, because they were set up as task forces to deal with specific problems with short-term solutions.

Project teams and matrix organizations are based on the concept of lateral decision processes. Instead of bucking problems up the hierarchy, managers attempt to solve them at their own levels where information (for example, on the changing environment) originates. At a given level a matrix is formed when a manager or professional becomes a member of both a technical resource department and a product or program office; he has two bosses.

Galbraith (1973) reports particular success in utilizing matrix forms. Businesses with matrix forms are more successful in developing and introducing new products than are businesses without. However, Galbraith (1973; p. 149) acknowledges that matrix designs are really patchwork on the basically bureaucratic structure of organizations with their hierarchically distributed power. They are not new designs, because managers resist really new designs.

From our perspective derived from experience with aerospace organizations, matrix forms, project teams, and program offices are no panacea for problems of organizational design and adaptability. The "Skunkworks" at Lockheed, which produced a number of intelligence-gathering systems such as the high-altitude U-2 and RS-71 aircraft, is widely touted as a successful application of the team approach to project management. The same can be said for the development of the Navy's Polaris missile. However, in these two cases success may have been more a factor of high-priorities, sizable resource inputs, and forceful entrepreneureal leaders than of design. Similarly, the manned space effort involved a successful team approach among organizations on a mammoth scale. At the workaday level in military and aerospace organizations, there are manpower limitations and the matrix group may be saddled with over a hundred projects. Likewise, conflict is common between the project manager and the line manager (who fills out one's rating form!). Further, the Air Force 375-series systems management program seemed to lead to instant bureaucraticization, with contractors complaining that program office demands for paper work interfered with their actual design efforts.

Nevertheless, in spite of misapplications matrix designs are a valuable approach to reintegrating planning, deciding, and doing—behaviors long separated in hierarchical structures (Herbst. 1974). In pure form, matrix organizations have no built-in status differences; it is assumed each member shares values with other members and has a specialized role and a range of competence partly overlapping the competence of other members. Depending on the nature of the task, any member can assume a leadership role. Matrix organizations provide flexible redeployment of people, making it easier for the organization to adjust to technological change. They thus provide an attack on the basic problem of today's organizations: creating conditions for a self-sustaining and continual learning process both at the individual and organizational level.

DESIGN FOR TOMORROW

Designing for tomorrow will not involve radically new ideas so much as the radical implementation of ideas present at least in embryonic form. The design concepts presented here concern sensing, perceiving, and interpreting the present and future states of the organization, comparing both with one another and with their respective environments, and the decision making and action consequent to these comparisons. These design concepts are in no way meant to negate relevant present organizational development methods. Organizational success or failure, as we have already stressed, is a function of many interacting factors. Poor interpersonal relationships and low morale, for example, may seriously degrade organizational effectiveness right now, above and beyond difficulties of keeping an eye on the future. In this case, management would choose to invest, say, in group methods of job enrichment in an attack on the immediate pathology. Further emphasis herein is on management and technical specialists; downstream it may be necessary, for example, to develop new skills and implement different work methods based on management's new and heightened awareness.

Designing for tomorrow involves changes in the structure and function of all four of the organizational subsystems indicated below. Detailed design occurs at the sub-subsystem level. In outline form the overall structure of an organization can be expressed as follows; the areas of emphasis as to design change are *italicized* while the nonitalicized areas represent context and are not discussed further in this brief article.

1. The organization is a sociotechnical system which, as discussed elsewhere (De Greene, 1973), can at once be viewed in terms of human and technological subsystems, hierarchical structure, and information processing expressed in input, throughput, and output terms.

   A. Social subsystem emerging from person-person interactions
      1. *Adaptivity sub-subsystem*
   B. Technological subsystem consisting of hardware, software, facilities, and methods and procedures.
      1. *Sensing sub-subsystem*
         a. *Organizational-state sensing module*
         b. *Present-environment sensing module*
         c. *Future-environment sensing module*
      2. *Central information-processing subsystem*
         a. *Comparator module*
         b. *Modeling and simulation module*
   C. Psychological subsystem consisting of management, staff, and worker motivations, capabilities and limitations, perceptions, feelings, personalities, values, attitudes and beliefs, and actions.
      1. *Management sub-subsystem*
         a. *Personality module*
         b. *Values module*
   D. Political subsystem emerging from the development and use of power and influence.

It must be stressed that these units are *concepts* not necessarily connoting fixed locations, equipment, or personnel. For example, people and information may flow into and out of a unit changing its composition but not its basic raison d'etre over time.

Adaptivity Sub-subsystem

The requirement for this sub-subsystem stems from the realization that the bureaucratic practice of preprogramming and controlling everything results, in a fast changing environment, in an increasing area that is nobody's responsibility. It is also an outgrowth of the recognized need to loosen up or decouple organizational structure. Design reflects the changes in the other subsystems discussed below. And the unit is a descendant of boundary-sensitive or boundary-spanning groups or departments of today variously called market research, advance planning, long-range planning, technological forecasting, futures research, and the like. I propose that organizational adaptability and survival are critically dependent on the strengthening and extending of functions like these.

Experience shows, however, that top management's typical response is to ignore or only pay lip service to such present efforts as human factors, operations research, systems analysis, program planning and budgeting, and futures research. Therefore, the adaptivity sub-subsystem must be a dynamically integral part of line management, not just an advisory or staff group. All top and eventually most middle managers would pass through the adaptivity unit as part of their career development and maintenance of currency. Either internal to the unit or in conjunction with main line management at a given time, the adaptivity sub-subsystem could be viewed as a matrix organization(s). Problem solving and decision making within any matrix would be aided by dynamically updated, organized qualitative and quantitative inputs from the technological subsystem.

Sensing Sub-subsystem

The sensing sub-subsystem consists of three modules. The *organizational-state sensing module* possesses certain counterparts in today's organizations, but they are poorly systematized. *Separate* job satisfaction surveys and work methods studies provide examples. The variables sensed might be conveniently placed into three categories: psychosocial, technological, and output. Psychosocial variables are exemplified by such expressions of job satisfaction and morale as turnover, training costs, absenteeism, pilferage, and vandalism and sabotage. Technological variables include adequacy and currency of equipment, facilities, information flow, work methods, and procedures. Output variables include the major criteria of organizational success or failure and performance factors contributing thereto. Representative measures are earnings, profits, losses, patients treated successfully, graduates placed in jobs, and so on.

The *present-environment sensing module* also has certain counterparts in present designs; but inputs, throughputs, and outputs are commonly poorly interrelated, which is one of the major reasons for organizational ineffectiveness. Discrepancies between sales and inventories provide a classic example. Measures might be classified as source of inputs, effects of outputs, and constraints. Representative sources of inputs include raw material resources, pool of personnel at various educational and skill levels, and available new technologies. Representative effects of outputs include sales, customer complaints, pollution, infractions of government regulations, lawsuits, and accidents. Constraints are exemplified by government regulations, societal acceptance, and competition.

The *future-environment sensing module* is scarcely represented in present designs, but it is absolutely indispensable to organizational adaptation and survival. The more the present environment merges into the future environment, the more important is the reduction of uncertainty dependent on the sensing of multiple variables and, even more importantly, *patterns* of interacting variables. Three types of contemporary developments are of significance here: economic indicators (see Moore, 1975), social indicators (for example, Gross and Straussman, 1974; Sheldon and Parke, 1975), and tehnological forecasting and futures research (see Linstone, 1974). For example, a manager might be interested in new unemployment insurance claims, hiring and layoff rates, and average workweek and overtime as predictors of changes in the business cycle. Single indicators and forecasts of single variables (usually straightforward extrapolations of past and present trends) may be of limited use or downright wrong. Starts toward the determination of patterns of variables are provided by cross-impact analysis and computer simulations.

Central Information-processing Sub-subsystem

The central information-processing sub-subsystem possesses antecedents in today's designs in the form of routine data processing, data banks, management information systems, and command and control systems. There are two main modules.

The *comparator module* is an indispensable feature of the cybernated organization. It (the "machine" or relevant man-machine ensemble) compares goals and objectives with the present state of the system, goals and objectives with forecasted alternative environmental patterns, and the present state of the system with the present state of the environment. "Error signals," that is, disparities between desired and actual conditions, are either output, and displayed to human decision makers, or lead to corrective automatic actions as in-process control, machine control, inventory control, and automatic banking and credit. The error signal reflects present ranges of tolerance.

The *modeling and simulation module* provides the capability for determining alternative future environments and alternative organizational configurations, and for evaluating different strategies. The validity and reliability of a model of complex systems are dependent on (better) understanding of real world variables, forces, interactions, and coalescences. A model's use, and perhaps usefulness, is not necessarily related to validity or reliability but to the forcefulness and persuasiveness of the seller. An invalid model widely used can change policies and hence the future, resulting in a paradoxical self-fulfilling validity.

Management Sub-subsystem

The management sub-subsystem contains two vital modules, a lack of understanding and modification of which will assuredly retard organizational adaptation and perhaps guarantee failure. The *personality module* reflects the needs for power, status, wealth, security, achievement, and self-fulfillment provided by managerial positions; the common managerial resistance to disruption of the status quo; and differences in managers' personalities in different organizations.

The module is based on the assumption that rational behavior exists only in economic, game theoretic, and decision theoretic abstractions; and that managers, like all human beings, distort reality perceptually and accept evidence and "facts" as functions of basic needs and present emotional state. One aspect of human behavior is worthy of special mention here. This is *discounting*, the tendency to place a far lower value on things, people, and events which are far removed in space and time than if they were present here and now (Linstone, 1974). Most managers discount heavily, that is, emphasize immediate problems over remote problems.

The design of the personality module acknowledges the use of individual and group methods of personality modification. In spite of these aids, however, it is likely that many managers will find themselves, or will be found, incongruent with the changing organization and will elect to go to less demanding positions. Those managers personally able and willing to live with certainty and to grapple with the future will receive periodic (or permanent) assignments with the adaptivity sub-subsystem, which continues to be the main boundary-sensitive group of the organization. Here the manager receives a refreshing exposure to the organizational options of tomorrow.

The *values module* design assumes that values, along with needs and personality, are the most basic and important determinants of human behavior in all societies and all organizations. Values represent the intersection of personal needs and societal views of good and bad, right and wrong. They underlie beliefs and attitudes. Understanding values is important to top management for two reasons:

1. Value change is a salient aspect of environmental change and determines, as much as anything, the acceptance of a product *and* of a commitment to a war *and* of business practices *and* of business as a profession.
2. If members of a problem-solving group, matrix or otherwise, do not share values—or at least mutually acceptable values—success is greatly lessened (cf., Herbst 1974, p. 210).

If managers' values are not congruent with one another and with those of society, the chances of maintaining best fit are much reduced. Value change methods are available, but a discussion of them is beyond the scope of this paper.

Political Subsystem

A major purpose of design for tomorrow is adaptation of the political subsystem as discussed earlier through enhancing perception of changing configurations and provisions of dynamically updated learning opportunities. The primary task(s) of the organization will, therefore, be sustained and the familiar degenerative pathology associated with advanced cases of inappropriate bureaucraticization greatly reduced. This does not in any way negate the importance of sensing and interpreting political structure, change, and nuances in the external environment.

Finally, this design for the future, with its emphasis on different managerial personalities and orders-of-magnitude improvements in organizational information-processing and problem-solving capabilities, if it is to be accepted and successful, must have the full understanding and support of top management. The realization that top management itself is frequently a major factor in organizational failure, that career planning in management may require an eventual move out of management, that the hierarchical climb to the room at the top may reflect an obsolescent dream, and that the world will never be certain and secure with problems neatly solved and filed away may be tough pills for many managers to swallow. Yet if these factors are not accepted, organizational adaptation and survival could be seriously threatened. Environmental changes and pressures for organizational change could lead to panic and desperate attempts to maintain the status quo through use of advanced technology. Misuse of sophisticated computer-communications systems, for example, could lead to a frozen, brittle organization. In this context it is well to reflect on Bennis's (1970) surprise at the resistance of large bureaucracies to value change and the acceptance of more organic forms.

CONCLUSIONS

The specific nature, variety, rate, extensiveness, pervasiveness, and uncertainty of environmental change—and especially the nonlinear dynamics and emergence of new environmental structures and properties associated with the meeting and coalescence of forces—greatly reduce the likelihood of survival of contemporary organizations. Macrosystems interactions among psychosocial, demographic, technoglocial, ecological, and economic forces will increasingly stress organizations. Resource-poor and unadaptively managed organizations will fall by the wayside. Even presently large and powerful organizations that have not anticipated changes and planned accordingly will find survival difficult. Organizations which perceive their problems, *or* have their problems perceived by outside consultants, as solvable through behavioral science or operations research *or* information sciences *or* traditional organizational design practice will suboptimize. Suboptimization may produce temporary adjustments, but, analogous to overspecialization in organisms and overdevelopment of anatomical or physiological features, suboptimization may impede long-term survival. Likewise, design approaches that view organizational structure as passively determined by environmental factors and that view management as an essentially unchanging institution detached from survival problems except as to require support, and occasional "development," are likely to fail. Organizational best fit can be maintained, and survivability enhanced, only by facing the reality of designing for an active integration of those dynamic interactions which occur both within the organization and between the organization and the environment. All subsystems will be involved, and a far greater understanding of the environment required.

References

Ashby, W. Ross, *Design for a Brain*, 2nd ed. New York: John Wiley. & Sons, 1960.
Battelle Columbus Laboratories. *Science, Technology, and Innovation*. Washington, D.C.: National Science Foundation, 1973.

Beer, Stafford. "The Surrogate World We Manage," *Behavioral Science, 18* (1973), 198–209.

Bennis, Warren G. "A Funny Thing Happened on the Way to the Future," *American Psychologist, 25* (1970), 595-608.

Burns, Tom, and G.M. Stalker. *The Management of Innovation*, 2nd ed. London: Tavistock, 1966.

Chandler, Arthur D., Jr. *Strategy and Structure: Chapters in the History of Industrial Enterprises*. Cambridge, Mass.: M.I.T. Press, 1962.

Child, John. "Organization Structure, Environment and Performance: The Role of Strategic Choice," *Sociology, 6* (1972), 1–22.

De Greene, Kenyon B. *Sociotechnical Systems: Factors in Analysis, Design, and Management*. Englewood Cliffs, NJ: Prentice-Hall, Inc. 1973.

Downs, Anthony. *Inside Bureaucracy*. New York: Little, Brown, 1967.

Drucker, Peter F. "New Templates for Today's Organizations," *Harvard Business Review, 52* (1974), 45–53.

Emery, Fred E., and Eric L. Trist. "The Causal Texture of Organizational Environments," *Human Relations, 18* (1965), 21–32.

Forrester, Jay W. *Urban Dynamics*. Cambridge, Mass.: M.I.T. Press, 1969

Fromm, Eric. "Thoughts on Bureaucracy," *Management Science, 16* (1970), B699–B705.

Galbraith, Jay. *Designing Complex Organizations*. Reading, Mass: Addison-Wesley, 1973.

Greiner, Larry E. "Evolution and Revolution as Organizations Grow," *Harvard Business Review, 50* (1972), 37–46.

Gross, Bertram M., and Jeffrey D. Straussman. "The Social Indicators Movement," *Social Policy. 5* (1974), 43–54.

Herbst, P. G. "Socio-technical Design: Strategies in Multidisciplinary Research." London; Tavistock, 1974.

Hunt, Raymond G. "Technology and Organization." *Academy of Management,* Journal 13 (1970), pp. 235–252.

Lawrence, Paul R., and Jay W. Lorsch. *Organization and Environment: Managing Differentiation and Integration*. Boston, Mass: Harvard University Graduate School of Business Administration, 1967.

Linstone, Harold A. "Planning: Toy or Tool." *IEEE Spectrum, 11* (1974), 42–49.

Michael, Donald M. "On the Social Psychology of Organizational Resistances to Long-Range Social Planning," *IEEE Transactions on Systems, Man, and Cybernetics, SMC-2* (1972), 578–584.

Moore, Geoffrey, H. "The Analysis of Economic Indicators," *Scientific American, 232* (1975), 17–23.

Sheldon, Eleanor B., and Robert Parke. "Social Indicator," *Science, 188* (1975), 693–699.

Thompson, Victor A. *Bureaucracy and Innovation*. Alabama: University of Alabama Press, 1969.

Woodward, Joan. *Industrial Organization: Theory and Practice*. London: Oxford University Press, 1965.

Human Resources Development Through "Work Design"

Richard O. Peterson

The term *human resources development* is a relatively new one compared to terms like *training, management development,* and *personnel administration.* Yet, the term has already become a kind of catch phrase, used as an "umbrella" for an assortment of traditional personnel functions as well as a symbol of the need to extend concerns and activities beyond the usual functions. The term is already being used uncritically and sometimes inappropriately, with little regard for its direct relevance to *organizational performance.*

The performance of any organization can be assessed in terms of at least four criteria:

> the quality and utility of the products and services it provides
> the efficiency with which it provides those products and services
> the organization's impact on society and the quality of life
> the organization's impact on its employees and their lives

To some organizational managers, human resources development concerns itself primarily with the fourth of these criteria—impact on employees. However, for human resources development to realize its potential in achieving organizational success, it must address itself to the full range of organizational criteria and must optimize the human resources contribution to each of them.

"WORK DESIGN" AND ORGANIZATIONAL PERFORMANCE

One of the most powerful approaches in human resources development for enhancing organizational effectiveness is the emerging technology of work and organizational design. *Work design,* as it will be referred to in this article, is a set of principles and techniques for designing or redesigning the tasks and functions by which the work of the organization gets accomplished, for assigning them effectively among various jobs and job levels, and for supporting them with the necessary personnel-type systems of selection, training, supervision, evaluation, compensation, and so forth.

> Richard O. Peterson, "Human Resources Development Through 'Work Design'." Reproduced by special permission from the August, 1976 TRAINING AND DEVELOPMENT JOURNAL. Copyright 1976 by the American Society for Training and Development, Inc.

No matter what kind of organization is being discussed, the core of the organization must be considered the *work* to be carried out to achieve the organization's objectives. If that work is not effectively designed, arranged and allocated, no amount of elegant organization structure, sophisticated training, or generous compensation system will bring about organization success. Stating this the other way, organizational effectiveness can often be increased by systematic analysis and, where appropriate, by improvement or redesign of its work and jobs. Figure 1 represents the successive layers through which human performance effectiveness must be built. These layers are:

Work: The core of organizational performance; the sum total of activities and processes that must be carried out to achieve specific goals and objectives.

Work Structuring Systems (Methods, Standards, Equipment, and Environment): The direct facilitators or constrainers of performance; ideally, to be designed along with the basic work functions as part of fundamental work design.

Organization Structure: The horizontal and vertical divisions of organizational functions to achieve various degrees of specialization, control, and responsibility; ideally, to be developed as an outgrowth of designing the inner elements of work and its structural factors.

Personnel Support Systems (Selection, Placement, Training, etc): The typical and traditional personnel functions and tasks needed to develop and sustain human performance in the organization; ideally, to be designed on the basis of the more fundamental elements of work and its organization.

Attempts to improve organizational performance are often directed to one or more of the elements of the outer ring—the personnel support systems. Other popular approaches challenge the organizational structure, a somewhat more central issue. However, many problems of organizational effectiveness cannot be solved without going deeper into the design and structure of the work itself—seldom considered as a source of problems. To say it in another way, human resource utilization may not be at its optimum without improving basic work design.

HUMAN RESOURCE UTILIZATION

A number of writers and practitioners point out that the distribution of jobs requiring individual talent, judgment, and creativity does not appear to match the distribution of these capabilities among the employable population. The mismatch is in the direction of having more capability available than is required by existing jobs. Furthermore, the mismatch appears to be getting greater as the population becomes more highly educated. Figure 2, adapted from Whitsett,[1] is one theoretical representation of this mismatch.

One researcher, Lawrence,[2] acknowledges that such a mismatch probably exists, but suggests that not everyone in the "underutilized" segment of the distribution wants work that utilizes his or her capabilities to the fullest. Even if we accept this caution, we must still recognize that there is a vast resource of underutilized talent among people wanting to use their capabilities more fully.

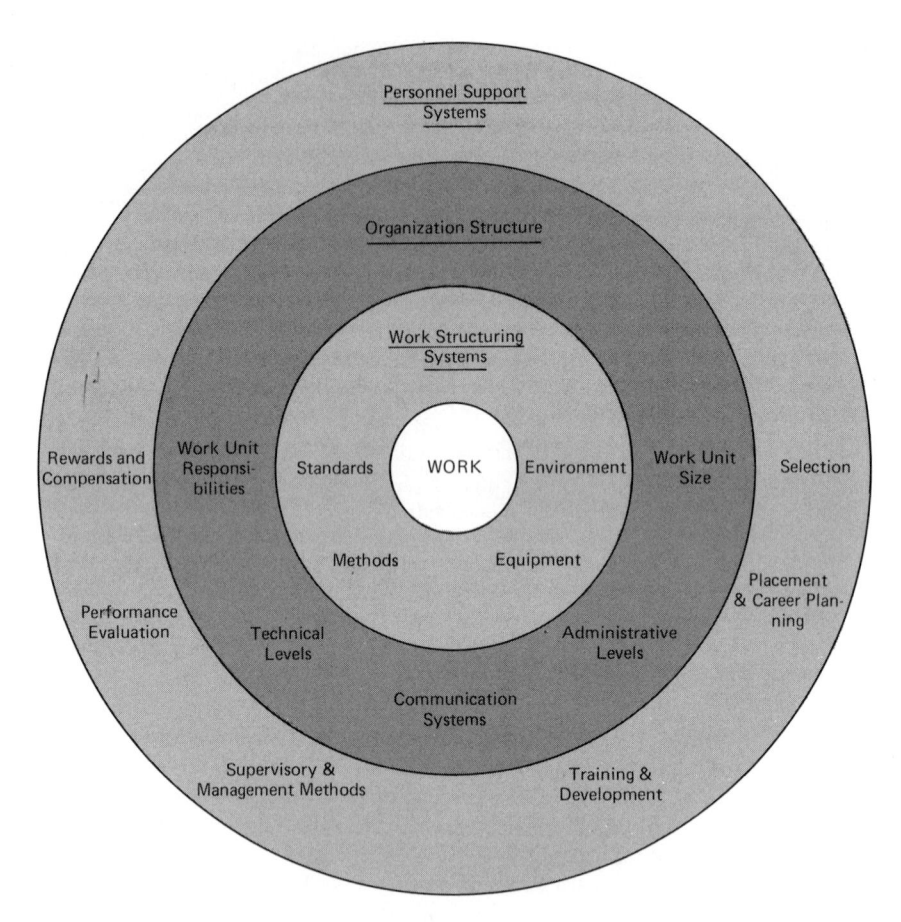

FIGURE 1 *Human Resources Elements in Organizational Performance*

Some cases of underutilization can be reduced or eliminated through improved selection, placement, and career planning or development. But eventually, the long-range solution must lie further into the core of the organization—the design of the work itself and the jobs among which the work is divided.

Thus from both a broad organizational point of view, the achievement of the full range of organization objectives, and from a narrower human resource utilization point of view, work design holds promise as a critical technology of the future.

WORK DESIGN STRATEGY

It is not enough to have techniques available to redesign work. The use of such techniques must be preceded by a diagnosis which determines whether or

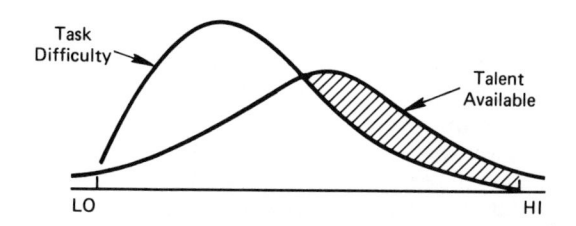

FIGURE 2 *Mismatch Between Task Difficulty of Existing Jobs and the Talent Available Among Employable*

not work design *is* a problem, whether improving work design will contribute to organizational performance, and whether employees are likely to respond favorably to changes in the work design. Hackman[3] has cautioned against undisciplined use of work design techniques and, with his colleagues,[4] has provided a foundation for a systematic strategy which includes an initial diagnosis. The strategy being discussed in the present article has evolved independently over the last ten years of research at American Telephone & Telegraph (AT&T), but it is highly compatible with the Hackman concepts and approach. The AT&T strategy is currently being strengthened to take advantage of the research and experience represented by the strategy of Hackman and his co-workers.

The strategy has three fundamental phases:

  I. Diagnosis of work and organization design
  II. Redesign of work, organization and support systems
  III. Tryout, evaluation, implementation and tracking

PHASE I: DIAGNOSING WORK AND ORGANIZATION DESIGN

Essential to any effort which might result in work design is an initial specification of the problems it is hoped will be reduced or solved, and the criteria of organizational performance by which the overall effort will be evaluated. It is easy to be caught up in the enthusiasm for getting started and to be sure that results will be obvious when everything is carried out, but that is a complacency to be avoided.

When we agree with one of our "clients," an organization somewhere in the Bell System, that we will help them look at work design, we prepare a written project plan intended ultimately as a "contract" for the application of the work-design strategy. The heart of that plan is a statement of the specific objectives of the project and how each will be measured. Some preliminary information and data have to be obtained from the client organization before such a document can be prepared. This information may include organization and job descriptions, current performance objectives and means of measurement and reporting, interviews with top management of the organization as well as with other employees, and interviews with people in organizations which interface with the target organization. The plan also includes a proposed diagnostic process to which the client must agree before actual data are collected.

We find it desirable to collect information and data of several types:

A. *Baseline data* which will be gathered before anything else is done, and again after any changes are made in work design: This baseline should include measures of the project objectives, the dimensions of work, employee attitudes about work and other job satisfaction facets, and any other measures which are likely to reflect on the ultimate success of the project.

B. *Work and organizational process data* which will provide the details of how work gets accomplished, the details on which actual work and organization design decisions can be based: This may include existing task analyses, work-flow diagrams, operating instructions, job descriptions, organization charts and descriptions, and so on. It is usually necessary to supplement whatever is available with either individual or group interviews of job incumbents. Structured time logs have also been used as a source of information on such dimensions as activity, frequency, and length, etc.

C. *Individual and demographic data* which help to define the employee population according to characteristics which may affect the design of the work: This may include data on past experience, training, need for job growth and challenge.

Some measures exist for portions of the baseline data and individual data, such as the *Job Diagnostic Survey* developed by Hackman and Oldham.[5] Standard organizational measures of productivity, efficiency, quality, absence, and so on provide another source of available tools. The remainder of the data is collected with instruments and techniques either especially developed or adapted for the project.

Whenever possible, the data are analyzed by electronic data processing, with some statistical analyzes if appropriate. Most of the process data cannot be so analyzed, but are systematically searched for potential work and organization design problems along the core-work dimensions described below. The baseline data on work dimensions and the process data are compared and combined to produce a summary of the design problems.

The basic dimensions being used to evaluate the existing work design are:

Functional completeness: A complete piece of work with an identifiable beginning and end.

User/turf continuity: An ongoing relationship with one or more specific clients, users, customers, geographical areas, or types of equipment.

Variety of task and skill: The degree to which there are varied tasks and varied skills used in the job.

Power to act: The ability to make decisions concerning your own work functions.

Natural feedback: Individual, specific job-performance information that comes through the work itself or from users.

Opportunity for work-related growth: The degree to which there are job functions which allow for expanded growth and development.

Although measures of some of these dimensions (under different names) are included in the *Job Diagnostic Survey* of Hackman and the *Job Dimensions Checklist* of Suzansky,[6] we felt it was necessary to develop and validate a more behavior-based instrument for measuring work dimensions. Therefore, we are developing and testing a Work Dimensions Inventory under contract to Applied Science Associates. It is currently undergoing validation to determine how each of the work dimensions relates to actual organizational performance.

PHASE II: REDESIGNING WORK, ORGANIZATION, AND SUPPORT SYSTEMS

The results of the diagnosis may show that there is no need for work redesign. If that is the outcome, no work-design activities are undertaken. Problems in other performance support systems (for example, training, instruction manuals, compensation, or selection) would be referred to the appropriate specialist group for their action, if necessary.

If work design is indicated by the kinds of problems identified, design task forces may be formed to begin work redesign. These task forces will probably include employees in the jobs under study. They are not only sources of important job and work information, but their potential contribution to the design of new work configurations is substantial, and their acceptance is critical. Work is redesigned along the six work dimensions defined earlier. Usually beginning with functional completeness, each dimension is examined with an eye to how that dimension can be improved without jeopardy to—and hopefully with improvement in—organization performance.

Alternative configurations and redesign ideas are reviewed with the client. Recommendations are also made regarding changes in other aspects of the personnel support systems needed to effect or sustain the proposed work-design changes. Additional details on the work-design process and its background are presented in the *ASTD Training and Development Handbook*.[7]

PHASE III: TRYING OUT, EVALUATING, IMPLEMENTING, TRACKING

Depending on the scope of the recommended changes, decisions must be made regarding how the redesigned jobs will be "tested." This can range from small-scale tryout in one protected part of the organization all the way to complete conversion of present jobs to new ones. The judicious approach is usually between these two—in as typical a setting as possible, where usual job pressures and situations will be encountered and where organizational performance can be observed and measured.

The newly designed jobs can be further adjusted on the basis of the tryout and its subsequent evaluation. Only then can plans be developed for implementation on a wider basis, to be accompanied by ongoing evaluation wherein the established objectives and measures are tracked through periods of typical operation and variation.

CONCLUSIONS

Human resources development must be oriented toward achievement of all objectives of organizational performance: quality, efficiency, societal impact, employee impact. Human resources activities are often focused on personnel support systems such as training, selection, compensation, and performance appraisal. While it is imperative that these systems be effective to optimize human resource utilization, the more basic core of human performance—the work itself—may be at fault. Techniques and strategies are becoming available for examining and redesigning work and its structuring systems. Current research and experience with this technology of work indicates high payoff when it is judiciously and expertly applied.

Notes

[1] David A. Whitsett, "Job Enrichment, Human Resources and Profitability," in J.R. Maher, ed., *New Perspectives in Job Enrichment*, (New York: Van Nostrand Reinhold, 1971).

[2] Paul Lawrence, "Individual Differences in the World of Work," in E.L. Cass and F.G. Zimmer, eds., *Man and Work in Society*, (New York: Van Nostrand Reinhold, 1975), chap. 2.

[3] J. Richard Hackman, "Is Job Enrichment Just a Fad?" *Harvard Business Review*, September-October 1975, pp. 129–138.

[4] J. Richard Hackman, Greg Oldham, Robert Janson, and Kenneth Purdy, "A New Strategy for Job Enrichment," *California Management Review*, Summer 1975, pp. 57–71.

[5] J. Richard Hackman and Greg Oldham, "The Job Diagnostic Survey: An Instrument for the Diagnosis of Jobs and the Evaluation of Job Redesign Projects." Technical Report No. 4, Department of Administrative Sciences, Yale University, May 1974.

[6] James W. Suzansky, "The Effects of Individual Characteristics as Moderating Variables of the Relation Between Job Design Quality and Job Satisfaction," Stevens Institute of Technology, 1974.

[7] Richard O. Peterson and Bruce H. Duffany, "Job Design and Redesign," in Robert L. Craig, ed., *The Training and Development Handbook*, rev. ed. (New York: McGraw-Hill (in press).

The Design and Implementation Of Human Resource Information Systems

Robert D. Smith

PERSONNEL MEETS COMPUTER: A SCENARIO

John Wheaton is assistant personnel manager for an electronics firm in the Midwest. He has been with the company for about a year following his graduation from college with a major in personnel management. Early in his college career, John became increasingly aware of the computer industry's growth and saw many areas for potential application in the personnel field. Thus he was somewhat disappointed when he began his employment and found that no one within the personnel area had begun to investigate potential computer applications to the field.

One day in late November, John received an unexpected message from the personnel manager who was in Chicago attending an ASPA convention. John had learned about the advanced thinking going on within the American Society of Personnel Administration, especially with regard to organized information management systems, and had asked his boss to attend the yearly meeting. There was a tone of excitement in the manager's voice as he explained to John how a college professor had just spoken about the use of computers in personnel in smaller organizations. He asked John to begin that afternoon to familiarize himself with available computer hardware and software within their company.

John visited the company's data center and spoke with the manager about the on-line terminals, direct access memory devices, storage capacity within the central processing unit, availability of systems programmers, the master plan for systems development within the company, software packages that he might have become acquainted with that were applicable to personnel, and other information matters.

While John did not detect sparks of enthusiasm from the data-processing manager, he did feel that his questions were answered in a courteous although somewhat hurried manner. As soon as his boss returned, he asked for authorization to proceed with the development of a personnel data base which would provide on-line storage, retrieval, and update capability for the personnel records of all employees within the company. The authorization was approved by the company's executive committee and John is now walking to the data center to begin familiarization with the computer terminal system.

Based on an initial development in Elmer H. Burack and Robert D. Smith, *Personnel Management: A Human Resource Systems Approach* (St. Paul, Minn: West Publishing Co., 1977).

316 *Human Resource Information Systems*

Despite his enthusiasm and fervor, John quickly becomes aware of snickers from the data-processing staff as he seats himself at the terminal. There is an intentional remark from the operator about his being "out of place." Undaunted, he begins typing the identification number and password assigned to him the previous day by the data center manager. After several minutes of work with a computer-assisted instruction program dealing with fundamental programming principles, he is asked to leave and return at a time more convenient to the operations staff since an inventory update is about to be run through the machine. John steps aside and watches.

It does not take an experienced eye to note that the operator is lagging and purposely wasting time. After half an hour, John feels he ought to return to his department though he has nothing in the way of new knowledge to report. He tells his superior of the incident and asks that he be allowed to return early the following day as the terminal is usually idle at that time.

Morning comes and John is the first visitor to the operations room. After accessing the computer he begins entering a hypothetical employee record using the management data system provided by the manufacturer of the hardware. He soon finds that the terminal is disconnecting for no apparent reason. After three attempts to log back on the system, he hears muffled laughter and turns to see the entire operations crew smiling and back-slapping behind the plate glass window and now realizes the prank. Without a word, he retreats to his office. He is frustrated, again without progress, and is wondering what to do next.

This case is hypothetical but not far from the real world of personnel information systems. While computers have been important tools in production, marketing, and accounting for over 20 years, their impact on the personnel function has been minimal except in a small number of progressive organizations. There is no doubt that, technologically and economically, the computer is ready for personnel systems but the question arises whether personnel and computer specialists are ready for the computer to enter the field of human resource management.

OVERVIEW OF OBJECTIVES

Systems design, and its commonly applied supportive technology—the computer—can make significant inroads in the areas of tactical and strategic planning and control of human resources in organizations of all sizes. The human resource/personnel function is in special need of decision-oriented information systems because of the growing cost of labor and the increasing need for specialized skills to be brought to bear on organizational problems as quickly as symptoms appear on the horizon.

This paper has the following objectives:

1. to provide a working definition of a human resource (personnel) information system
2. to carry on intelligent dialogue with a systems analyst working in the area of HRIS (PMIS) design
3. to identify guidelines for effective HRIS design
4. to analyze several cases in the HRIS area pointing out strengths and weaknesses

COMPUTERS IN PERSONNEL: THE TRADITIONAL VIEW

Most contemporary human resource systems have failed to keep pace with existing computer technology. Even when the machine is employed in the personnel area it is applied only to fragmented data-processing tasks such as payroll preparation, insurance payments, department phone lists, periodic reports of new hires or terminations, or equal employment reporting.

With these applications, little or no attempt is made to integrate employee records and files in order to provide for fast retrieval, cross-referencing, forecasting, and other types of planning and control models. Data-base technology and distributed processing capabilities (that is, smaller computers allocated to line and staff managers for specialized applications) are generally not brought to bear on personnel problems. Consequently, most personnel computer systems are not oriented toward decision making but rather toward record keeping. Most often they are highly redundant in that the same information is stored in multiple locations. They do not have the flexibility to adapt to changing internal and external situations (Anthony, 1977). Consequently, these systems cannot assist in fulfilling the central personnel mission: planning, selecting, developing, evaluating, and rewarding human resources to meet organizational objectives.

A more encompassing problem exists with regard to computers in personnel. Without an overall systems design, most existing human resource applications have evolved in isolation from the other functional areas in the organization. Sales managers, production heads, and other line managers do not have the opportunity to review performance progress, training history and needs, or compensation problems of their subordinates without a laborious search of disjointed files located in geographically separated offices.

It is not unusual to find that organizations have separate benefits, training, performance, recruiting, manpower planning, affirmative action, compensation, accident, and attendance files. Some data are reported time and again, causing costly duplication and nightmarish search and updating problems. Most importantly, inefficient and fragmented systems place such clerical burdens on personnel staff that human contact and career planning and counseling activities are shortchanged or neglected entirely.

IMPROVING THE DESIGN OF HUMAN RESOURCE SYSTEMS

To improve the traditional situation described in preceding paragraphs, progressive organizations are performing what is known as systems analysis and design projects within the human resource area. Daltas and Schwartz (1976) summarize the immediate and important results which can be expected from such systems analysis efforts:

1. Clear definition of HRIS objectives
2. Consolidation and reduction in amount of stored human resource data

3. Greater status for the human resource function through the linking of its capabilities and activities to the tactical and strategic planning functions within the total organization
4. Provision of information about human assets in a concise, timely, accurate, and objective manner for decision making purposes
5. Development of performance standards for the human resource department
6. Creation of new incentives for using human resource data
7. Enhancement of individual development by relating performance to rewards and job training
8. More meaningful career planning and counseling at all levels
9. Increased capability to quickly and effectively staff nontraditional departments and project teams for ad hoc problem solving
10. Provision of training programs based on organizational needs
11. Improved communications between line and staff
12. Readiness to respond to ever-increasing and always changing government reporting requirements

A MODEL FOR HRIS DESIGN

To achieve even a few of the improvements suggested in the preceding paragraph, careful planning, technical expertise, user participation, extreme patience, and top management endorsement are all important. Initial planning must include an overall model to describe the inputs, transformation, and expected outputs of the system. As an example of such a conceptual model let us refer to Figure 1.

This model uses the components of a general systems model: inputs, transformation, outputs, control, and feedback. It is more comprehensive than the typical personnel model since its inputs include data on leadership styles and organization structure (for example, size of departments, branches, and sections), as well as educational, skills, and demographic data on individual employees. These input data are then transformed into information for decision making in the areas of recruiting, compensation, training, and evaluation. Updated organization charts can be printed. Simulation models can provide for "what if"-type questioning whereby the impact of changes in personnel policies can be evaluated prior to implementation, or, in an advanced system, research can be performed with structural and leadership variables to attempt improvement in individual, team, and organizational performance.

Feedback on systems effectiveness consists of performance measures, both individual and organizational. For example, the effectiveness of a new recruiting and selection strategy can be measured by comparing the performance of personnel selected under the new system versus the performance of a control group selected under traditional guidelines.

Various controls are placed on the system. Governmental regulations, for example, limit the type of data that can be stored on individuals and the manner in which these stored data are shared with the individual. Union policies, organizational objectives, and external labor market conditions also place controls over the collection and use of human resource data.

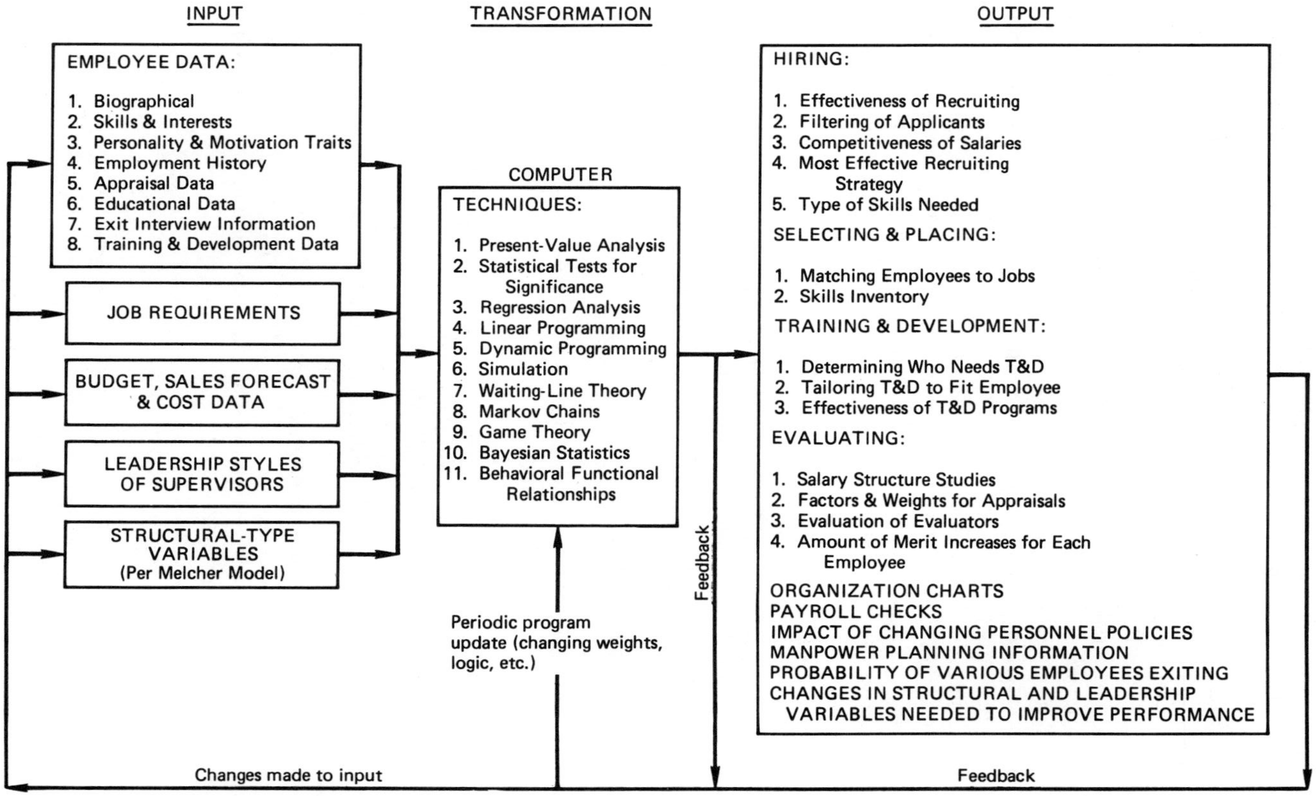

FIGURE 1   Integrated Human Resource Information System

Perhaps a simple example will help illustrate the potential usefulness of the HRIS model. Organization charts have long been considered a necessary tool for management but are useful infrequently because of the difficulties involved in keeping them current. This need not be the case in organizations which maintain a viable HRIS, since sufficient data exist in the system to produce needed charts on demand.

Fried (1977) has designed such a computer-based organization chart system for the State University of New York at Oneonta. Charts are produced for the entire organization or for any subsystem within the university. Users are given a variety of options when requesting a computer-generated chart. They may specify such variables as depth (number of reporting levels), supervisory counts (number of personnel reporting directly to each supervisor), exception classes (such as temporaries, imminent retirees, and so on), vacancies, and others.

This organization chart generator was written as a general computer program easily tailored to output specific charts as detailed by users on a request form designed to lead the requester through selection of desired options. Requests are usually satisfied within a day, since variations in existing charts can be produced without programmer intervention. Designers of the SUNY system suggest the feasibility of simulating organizational redesign alternatives using current data and computer technology. This approach also includes the capability of simulating organizational changes resulting from planned promotions based on career path indicators in the HRIS file.

DESIGNING THE HRIS

Now that an overall appreciation has been developed for the personnel system and its need for improvement, a detailed approach to system design will be presented. The approach consists of five major phases: (1) preliminary systems analysis, (2) systems design, (3) systems engineering, (4) systems testing and implementation, and (5) systems monitoring and evaluation. In an article of this type, detailed explanations of each phase cannot be provided, but Table 1 attempts to summarize the steps involved in each phase. For in-depth discussions of each step and phase, the reader may wish to refer to *Systems Analysis and Design for Management* by Paul Gross and Robert Smith (1976). While it is not possible to provide detailed design explanations, the following sections will help in the understanding of what a good HRIS should do, what objectives should be considered for the system, and the most frequently encountered problems in the design process.

Characteristics of a Successful HRIS

A human resource information system can be considered moderately successful if it meets the following expectations. Its cost should be in line with the size and financial condition of the organization. It should be designed and implemented within a reasonable time. Some systems have been in the design stage for eight to ten years. This length of time is unreasonable since personnel become disillusioned and discouraged over such an extended period. Two to three years, however, should not be considered excessive from the day of problem definition to the day of system implementation.

TABLE 1 Five-Phase Approach to HRIS Design and Implementation

Phase 1   Preliminary Systems Analysis
Perception and definition of problem or situation Definition of environmental constraints affecting system or situation Specification of objectives Specification of operation requirements (detail of problem) Perform feasibility study and submit report
Phase 2   Preliminary Systems Design
Write detailed scenario State alternative systems to meet objectives and constraints Assess alternative systems Select best alternative Make recommendations Define broad engineering requirements Estimate engineering and human factors effects of proposed system
Phase 3   Systems Engineering
Provide detailed specification of engineering components, including hardware, operating systems, facilities design, and so on Make preliminary engineering design alternatives Analyze cost-effectiveness of engineering design alternatives Select best design alternative Recommend to responsible decision maker After approval, provide specifications to programming staff
Phase 4   Systems Testing and Implementation
Test subsystems Test total HRIS system Run parallel system tests Implement system
Phase 5   Systems Monitoring and Evaluation
Measure system performance Evaluate system performance Modify system where necessary Implement total system as modified Perform continual monitoring and evaluation

The HRIS should be capable of modification and expansion without total redesign. Emphasis on the planning activities should be evident. Feedback should be continuous so as to provide for follow-up on new problems. Data files should be integrated for easy cross-referencing among various departments. Critical data should be available upon request such as provided for in on-line, real-time computer-based systems. Such critical information would include: location data for key employees, essential skills data, promotion and performance information, and salary data.

In order to assure that the above characteristics are forthcoming from HRIS design activities, it is very important to establish clear-cut objectives and measures of systems effectiveness. The following section provides guidance in this critical area.

Establishing Objectives for the HRIS

Successful design and implementation of any system requires heavy user involvement, and HRIS is no exception to this principle. If the users of the system are actively involved from the beginning, the chances of successful application are increased a thousandfold.

It is recommended that quantifiable (and thereby measurable) objectives be established for the HRIS, an approach not often discussed in the literature. Some examples of quantified HRIS objectives might be

> To determine the number and types of human resources required for each department for one year, three years, and five years in the future; one-year forecasts should be plus or minus 10 percent of the actual required
>
> To generate a minimum of ten applicants for each open scientific and managerial position
>
> To maintain the recruiting cost per new hire between $300 and $400 for each clerical and semi-skilled position
>
> To place all existing employees (professional level) within one of their top two expressed job preferences within the next two years
>
> To provide a minimum of 40 hours of development seminars within a one-year period for all personnel who have demonstrated potential for promotion to the next higher level
>
> To maintain wage levels within 7 percent of industry averages for all departments

Once such objectives are established and agreed to by both staff and line managers, the effectivess of the HRIS in helping to meet the objectives can be measured. Of course, there are other indicators of systems effectiveness that go beyond the HRIS itself but which the HRIS can be most useful in measuring. These variables include employee turnover, absenteeism, number and quality of suggestions, number and type of grievances, severity and frequency of accidents, participation in tuition refund programs, requests for transfers, and trends in personnel costs.

Further quantifiable measures of systems effectiveness include attitudinal data correlated with demographic, performance, and cost data. This statistical analysis can highlight growing departmental or divisional human problems and perhaps pinpoint some probable causes.

Conditions for Effective HRIS Design and Implementation

In order to develop an HRIS which provides accurate, timely, concise, relevant, useful, and objective information, it is vital that certain organizational, technical, and economic conditions be satisfied. The following set of conditions has been developed through the author's experience in the field coupled with extensive literature documenting the problems, both technical and human, encountered in systems design. Successful HRIS systems meet the following conditions:

Organizational Factors

System effort attracts solid support of top management

Participation of line management, especially production, marketing, engineering, and finance is assured

Human resource information needs of line management accurately defined

Potential system users have positive attitude toward system

Organizational objectives clearly defined

Resistance to change on the part of management and employees carefully planned in educational effort

Technical/Economic Factors

Objectives HRIS specifically defined and communicated

HRIS design team well-qualified technically, functionally, and behaviorally (that is, in communication and leadership skills)

System cost accurately defined and justified

Sufficient time allocated to HRIS design effort

HRIS design team possesses helping attitude toward potential users

Adequate software programs provided by hardware manufacturer or capabilities for program preparation exist within team

Methods provided for maintaining security and privacy of data

Input to system accurately controlled at remote terminal sites

Integrated files provided so that wide application and limited redundancy are possible

Post-implementation audits of system's effectiveness are planned

This listing of factors or conditions is supported through recent field research within 28 organizations in the Pittsburgh area (Schonberger and Buterbaugh, 1976). The research indicates that firms with more comprehensive information systems use the so-called "top down" approach beginning with organizational objectives, top management support, and users rather than computer specialists defining information needs. Most of the firms had recognized the need for an integrated data base and were oriented toward this objective. Sixteen of the firms reported a computerized data base system combined with computer programs directed toward scheduling, forecasting, cost analysis, simulation, estimating, and reporting in support of the functional areas. In other words, over half of the firms reporting a working MIS claimed to be using management science models to refine data stored in an integrated data base. This concept was illustrated by Figure 1.

A major concern for most systems designers is whether to build the system (whether it be a total MIS covering most functional areas of the firm or whether it be an HRIS covering mainly the personnel function) from the top down or from the bottom up. The latter is a piecemeal approach but tends to show quick results in specific and most often unrelated areas. The top-down, holistic approach is directed toward the effectiveness of the whole system rather than toward subsystems. C. West Churchman is one the foremost advocates of the top-down or systems approach (1968). With regard to the bottom-up approach to design, Zani (1970) states: "No tool has ever aroused so much hope at its creation as MIS and no tool has proved so disappointing in use. I trace this disappointment to the fact that most MIS's have been developed in the "bottom up" fashion . . . ." This writer agrees with the holistic or top-down approach, at least to the extent that an overall master plan for systems development is prepared prior to the design of specific and routine data-processing subsystems.

HRIS Output Reports: A Practical Example

As mentioned earlier, an effective HRIS will provide standard as well as special (unplanned) reports on a timely basis. The reports should identify actual and potential problem areas. Grauer (1976) illustrates how the HRIS can be an invaluable tool in dealing with planned and unplanned equal employment opportunity reporting requirements. Using extensive illustrations, he demonstrates how the HRIS can provide for corrective action so that affirmative action goals can be achieved rather than merely monitored.

Using a computer-based HRIS, Grauer has designed a number of report programs which specify applicants interviewed, referrals made, offers granted, and actual hires for all minorities and for any desired time span. For example, the user of the system may request a summary analysis of all applicants interviewed during the year. The report is provided within a day and indicates the following: total referrals, male and female referrals in percentages, and percentage of offers and acceptances for both males and females. By sorting the data on a different key, it may be determined that 10 percent of the males and 25 percent of the females applied for nonexempt (technical/clerical) positions. There are literally thousands of ways the data can be sliced to provide meaningful management information as well as compliance reporting statistics.

Recent computer systems provide software (programming) capabilities that allow the manager-user to obtain special reports without using complicated computer languages or computer professionals. Contemporary report generator programs consist of a series of English commands easily learned by the manager. Some of the most common commands are SORT to arrange data in sequence; SELECT to choose desired characteristics; SUM to obtain totals; AVERAGE to obtain means; and PRINT to get information displayed.

Behavioral Considerations in HRIS Design

In order to obtain reasonable benefits from new technology, greater emphasis must be placed on behavioral impacts of the information system, otherwise engineering efforts will be wasted, unprofitable, or even dysfunctional. Disregard for human needs and values can give rise to conditions similar to those experienced by industry when automation of physical work was first introduced at the turn of the century. At the time of the Industrial Revolution, depersonalization, noise, overtime, rigidity, and shift work increased human tensions and led to high employee turnover, absenteeism, and unionization. Now that we are well into the "second industrial revolution"—automation of routine mental activities—management must be alert to workers' needs for security, self-expression, self-esteem, social acceptance, and self-actualization. Computers and data base systems can easily frustrate these needs and cause much unwanted behavior at all organizational levels.

Computer-based information systems synthesize previously separated tasks into single operations, which not only gives the impression that the employee has lost personal worth but may also diminish the opportunity to communicate with other employees. Computers demand great accuracy from those who supply the input data; then, too, some flexibility is lost in the rate and direction of work flow—certain tasks must be completed at certain times, in prescribed ways, as determined by the equipment used. All these factors contribute to the depersonalizing process and should be carefully analyzed by the personnel department in advance of HRIS implementation.

Furthermore, the older a person becomes, the more likely he or she is to identify with a particular value system. This process of personalizing values can portend that an individual's sense of security and emotional health will be threatened by changes mandated by HRIS. Personality factors become increasingly dominant with advancing age and may play an important role in determining whether people will adjust to changing technology. Warm, outgoing, and friendly persons (typical of many who are attracted by the duties of personnel functions) may have much more difficulty in adapting to technical changes than those who are aloof, cold, unenthusiastic, or fairly thick-skinned.

Designers of the HRIS may be highly rational and logical in their approach to problem definition and solution. Unfortunately (or fortunately) the real-world manager operates under a different set of rules in most cases. Practicing managers are not entirely logical and are influenced by multiple objectives. They are likely to become defensive and perhaps hostile when they lose their ability to sell ideas through their personality. They are not always capable of understanding the value of the computer and may even resist the information it provides if this information differs with their preconceived impressions or previous decisions.

It should be made clear to line and staff personnel that human judgment and creative thinking will be needed for centuries to come regardless of the computer's advances. Managers may be asked to make fewer decisions regarding predefined processes but will constantly be responsible for measuring systems effectiveness, discovering opportunities for improving systems. and making those decisions not already built into the system. Managers must also be shown that their art and skills will now be needed at a more advanced and consequently more valuable stage of the decision-making process. Scheduling, expediting, forecasting, accounting, payroll, and other control functions will probably diminish in importance as computers take over routine tasks. On the other hand, research, planning, systems development, selection and analysis of alternatives, model building, and leadership skills will grow in importance as computer-based systems are integrated in organizations.

Greenlaw (1972) points out a significant relationship between managers with high achievement motivation and HRIS. His study suggests that organizations with integrated personnel information systems provide a number of diverse opportunities to motivate the high achiever type. Immediate feedback on employee turnover, inventory levels, financial ratios, and recruiting results could act as incentives for better decisions and better use of managerial talents.

The great majority of managers are probably not high achievement oriented but those who are tend to be successful and valued members of organizations. If the HRIS is oriented toward those people alone, it may have a significant payoff as well as some side effects which are positive for the other types of managers.

The Matter of Privacy

A final note on HRIS design deals with the very important issue of privacy. Safeguards must be established to assure that unauthorized personnel do not gain access to HRIS files. Employees themselves must be given an opportunity to examine and update their personal files. Graithwaite (1977) suggests that all managers be given a thorough explanation of the Privacy Act of 1974. The HRIS should be reviewed at intervals to ensure that all applications comply with the law. Safeguards, including procedures for disclosing information, should be explained. Policies for handling disputes should be prepared and employee manuals describing the HRIS and its consequences should be discussed by management prior to distribution to all employees. Further changes are expected in the legal aspects of information use and privacy, thus this area requires conscientious monitoring.

CASE ILLUSTRATIONS OF ACTUAL HUMAN RESOURCE INFORMATION SYSTEMS

In this section we provide three short case examples of real-world applications of the theories and principles of HRIS. As the cases are studied, it is recommended that the reader attempt to answer the following questions with regard to each:

1. What are the advantages and potential drawbacks of the HRIS?
2. Could the applications have been made without the aid of computers?
3. Would you like to work for an organization that employs a similar technology? Why or why not?

Cummins Engine Company

The recent addition of a human resource system at Cummins Engine Company is helping to assure that the right person is assigned to the correct position (Infosystems, 1977). The director of the human resource information center states that "it's a whole new world," claiming that a few years ago several thousand prospective employees would apply within any given week and the last applicant in line had his or her application automatically placed on the bottom of the stack. Under the new system, each applicant's skills are input into the data base and all personnel are matched by the computer to company needs regardless of the order of their application.

The entire personnel records of about 2,400 salaried employees are on file, and the computerized system is used to keep records current, produce EEO reports, distribute career profiles, and drive the total payroll system. Clerks are able to retrieve EEO reports for ten operating units within a day, whereas previously it took each unit a full week to prepare a report.

The computer-based system also supports the salaried job announcement program at Cummins. Job postings for salaried positions are announced each week. For the people who apply, a job applicant review profile is generated by the computer and is included with copies of the performance evaluation that the potential supervisor receives. The profile is also used as a turnaround (control) document when a person actually is selected for the position. Other applications of the system include such areas as security, medical, financial, benefits, compensation, and employee development.

Skills Inventories: Some Precautionary Notes. In the preceding case, the concept of a "skills inventory" is introduced from a positive perspective. It should be noted that the skills inventory at Cummins appears to be only part of a total systems plan and in this sense is probably cost justified and reasonably accurate for its purpose. However, as Fahnline (1974) points out, there are many obvious and some not so obvious drawbacks and barriers to effective implementation of the skills inventory concept. First, it should be noted that a computer-stored inventory of the human skills existing within an organization in no way approximates a physical goods inventory in a manufacturing division. Spare parts, for example, are recognized and stored according to certain characteristics, thus an aluminum bracket with four drilled holes is exactly what the name implies. With a human skills inventory, people are identified in terms of a *few* of their total characteristics in the hope that these few characteristics will give an indication of ability to perform a particular function. Such is not always the case, however, since we have not yet learned to measure what people *are* much less what they are capable of *becoming*.

With a physical goods inventory, a single file is required to store and retrieve a particular part number. With people, however, it may be necessary to update two or more files each time a person learns a new skill or changes some demographic characteristic such as address, education, or telephone number. Files and their efficient design become very complex, requiring the services of highly skilled programmers and systems analysts.

Many skills inventories are nothing more than a mechanization of older systems which were not very well thought out in the first place. By automating poorly designed systems, the HRIS merely compounds mistakes made earlier, thus multiplying their negative impact on organizational effectiveness.

In a physical goods inventory, all items of the same kind are, for all practical purposes, identical. If there are 50 aluminum brackets with four drilled holes, it does not make a difference whether one or another is selected for use. With people, the whole purpose of selection is to be able to choose one person over all others. Thus the inventory analogy breaks down further.

If a skills inventory is not really an inventory in the usual sense of the word, at least one can be comfortable in concluding that it is somehow a storehouse for human resource "skills." Not so! In reality, most skills inventories actually contain data about education and experience. But merely knowing that a person worked as a machinist for 12 years at a salary of $14,000 and attended the local vocational school is no indication of the amount of skill the person actually has. Education and experience at best are indicators of skills but not actual measurements of skills. What these indicators say about a person may be quite unreliable.

Much of the early promotion of skills inventories came from computer vendors seeking more applications for excess computer capacity. Because of the high cost of developing and maintaining the inventory, however, caution is recommended before starting on the road to constructing a skills inventory for the sake of the inventory itself. If it is part of a large human resource data base which is cost justified and used for automating most personnel records, statistical analysis, communication, planning, and labor management relations, then perhaps the incremental cost of adding the skills inventory can be justified.

Union Oil Company of California

Bright (1976) describes the Union Oil system as enabling management to know as much about their human resources as they know about other types of resources and that the system is used as an integral part of the overall corporate planning effort.

The human resource system at Union Oil contains five basic programs. The first is the Industrial Relations Information System (IRIS), which is aided by a data base containing some 600,000 bits of information about the company's personnel. The second program, an organizational change model, was designed to keep the information up to date and point out problem areas which may have developed over a five-year period. The third program matches qualifications of current personnel to the future needs of the company via the other two functions. The succession planning program, or AIM (analysis, identification, methodology), is based on five-year forecasts. On the basis of predicted job vacancies, management conducts a developmental program each quarter for prospective aspirants who have been identified by the system. The purpose of the fifth program is to integrate the other four with the overall needs of the organization.

An interesting application of the Union Oil system is described by Bright. Analysis of the age distribution of professional employees indicated significant gaps, some in critical disciplines. Further analysis showed that corporate recruiting had not taken account of replacement needs, either in total or by discipline. A search was then made to attempt to discover a statistical relationship between recruiting and other corporate variables. The best correlation was between a combined series of annual earning and capital expenditures.

The analysts concluded that Union Oil was following a crowd of competitive recruiters to college placement offices when profits were high and cutting back when profits were low. This naturally led to the second conclusion, namely, that most recruiting was being done in expensive years when high-quality people were most difficult to find and employ. Furthermore, since profit crunches hit various divisions at different times, age distribution of vital skills was seriously out of balance across the total company.

Based on these discoveries and after searching the data base and applying statistical methods, the company has been able to develop longer range manpower plans. Cyclical recruiting strategies have been smoothed and emphasis has been placed on replacement needs for critical disciplines. When the Union Oil organization change model reported a sudden rise in attrition rates among key technical people, top management was able to take immediate action to expedite recruiting and replacement in these key areas.

Xerox Human Resource Planning System

The Xerox Corporation is making use of an information system it calls Human Resource Planning (HRP) to identify prospective future managers and facilitate their growth and development toward filling expected management vacancies within the corporation (Reid, 1977). This process is accomplished in concert with an employee career planning program, also part of the HRP system.

The career planning program begins with the completion of a standardized form by the prospective employee. The form includes such information as work experience, education, career objectives, and other personal data. After the form is completed, the employee and his manager discuss and formulate a viable plan to enhance the goal attainment of both the employee and the corporation. Once validated by upper management the plan is activated.

Xerox has identified two major problems with HRP. The first, and most prominent, is the tendency for employees to assume that they will be promoted merely by their inclusion in the program. The second is the tendency for management to become overly enthusiastic about employees' programs and arrange promotions (and/or transfers) before the employees are fully prepared.

One advantage of HRP to management is that once estimates of the expected dates and number of job vacancies are obtained, management can compare these data via the HRP data base to the qualifications of existing employees. If the estimates predict more vacancies than qualified personnel, management can begin preparatory measures by employing the HRP program to correct this inequality. For example, if management's estimates predict a vacancy for a sales manager in the upcoming year, a prospective employee and his manager can organize a schedule of experiences on a timely basis that will prepare the employee to qualify for the particular job. A second advantage to management is that HRP affords them the opportunity to develop their key employees for eventual top-management positions. For the employee, such a system offers the opportunity to share in the planning of his career within the corporation.

Although continually refining the program, Xerox is satisfied with the results thus far, boasting that "practically every senior vacancy in the information systems group during the past five years has been filled from within our own ranks."

SUMMARY AND CONCLUSION

The application of computers to personnel generally lags behind applications in marketing, production, finance, and engineering. This conclusion is based on the results of a survey conducted in 100 leading business organizations (Tomeski, Yoon and Stephenson, 1976).

The most extensive applications of computers in personnel are generally considered routine and operational by computer specialists. These include payroll, benefits, budgeting, employee scheduling, skills inventories, and some statistical analysis. Those areas requiring higher order tactical and strategic decisions are not usually computerized except in more progressive firms such as those cited in this article.

Some of the reasons for the slow and often contested movement of computers and data-based management systems into the personnel arena are as follows. Personnel is often given low priority by upper management and computer specialists, and communication between personnel and systems analysts is weak at best. Consequently, personnel departments frequently play a negligible role in the planning, designing, and implementation of computer systems.

Then, too, personnel departments are not usually designed to function as an integrated system of inputs, processing, and outputs. Payroll, recruiting, training, and compensation are often completely separate entities. A highly trained systems analyst will often avoid the computerization of ill-defined and poorly integrated manual systems for fear of accelerating the rate of ineffective decisions.

Fear of fraud also inhibits computer involvement in personnel. Horror stories of computer crime abound. For example, an employee in the computer section in the welfare department of a large city entered erroneous data into the payroll system and embezzled $2.75 million within a year's time. The employee created a fake work force and paid fictitious workers by checks interrupted by the criminal and cashed as his own.

A third objection is based on the fact that large-scale computer data bases store and retrieve masses of information at the touch of a terminal key. This technology raises the fear and the real possibility of the invasion of personal privacy. Several states have enacted privacy laws and it is likely that future laws will be passed to regulate the use of personnel information. Some companies would rather wait for the laws to be enacted than move forward with the costly computerization of personnel data.

Regardless of the obstacles, however, HRIS can be one of the most valuable human systems in the organization. Its assistance in career planning for managers, professionals, and hourly personnel will more than pay for itself. As Walter (1976) points out, "two of the major tragedies of modern organizations are the failures of large numbers of people to manage their careers in productive and personally rewarding ways and the failure of many leaders to know and understand the career aspirations, interests, skills, and potentials of their subordinates."

A comprehensive HRIS will permit studies of career paths and discovery of pivotal positions for training and development which most key professionals have held during their careers. This knowledge can then be useful in planning future career paths especially in compliance with EEOC requirements.

References

Anthony, W. P. "Get to Know Your Employees—The Human Resource Information System," *Personnel Journal*, April 1977, pp. 179–183.

Braithwaite, T. B. "Privacy Education for Management," *Data Management*, January 1977, pp. 38–41.

Bright, W. E., "How One Company Manages its Human Resources," *Harvard Business Review*, January–February 1976, pp. 37–44.

Burack, E., and R. D. Smith. *Personnel Management: A Human Resource Systems Approach*, Minneapolis: West Publishing Company. 1977.

Churchman, C. W. *The Systems Approach*. New York: Dell Publishing Co., 1968.

Daltas, A. J., and H. M. Schwartz. "Towards Human Resource Management," *Personnel Journal*, December 1976, pp. 628–630.

Fahnline, R. H. "The Skills Inventory Put On," *Journal of Systems Management*, May 1974, pp. 14–21.

Fried, R. "Organizational Charts from Computerized Personnel Data Systems," *Personnel Journal*, June 1977, pp. 284–288.

Grauer, R. T. "An Automated Approach to Affirmative Action," *Personnel Journal*, September–October 1976, pp. 37–44.

Greenlaw, P. S. "The Achievement Motive and Personnel Information Decision Systems," *Personnel Journal*, September 1972, pp. 658–662.

Gross, Paul, and R. D. Smith. *Systems Analysis and Design for Management*. New York: Dun-Donnelley/Harper and Row Publishing Company, 1976.

Hyde, A. C., and J. M. Shafritz. "Introduction to Tomorrow's System for Managing Human Resources," *Public Personnel Management*, June 2, 1977, pp. 70–77.

Mahoney, T. A. "Computerized Simulation: A Training Tool for Manpower Managers," *Personnel Journal*, December 1975, pp. 609–611.

"Managing Human Resources by Computer," *Infosystems*, June 1977, pp. 96–98.

Reid, D. M. "Human Resource Planning: A Tool for Development," *Personnel 54*, 2 (1977), 15–25.

Schonberger, R. J., and T. L. Buterbaugh. "Management Information Systems in Pittsburgh Business Firms," *Pittsburgh Business Review*, Winter 1976, pp. 1–4.

Smith, R. D. "Information Systems for More Effective Use of Executive Resources," *Personnel Journal*, June 1969, pp. 452–458.

Smith, R. D., and K. Klafane. "Computerized Manpower Inventories for Research and Development Planning," *Research /Development*, April 1971, pp. 12–15.

Sylvia, R. A. "TOSS: An Aerospace System That's Go for Manpower Planning," *Manpower Planning*, January–February 1977, pp. 56–64.

Tomeski, E. A., B. M. Yoon, and G. Stephenson. "Computer-related Challenges for Personnel Administration," *Personnel Journal*, June 1976, pp. 300–302.

Walter, V. "Self-motivated Personal Career Planning: A Breakthrough in Human Resource Management," *Personnel Journal*, March 1976, pp. 112–115.

Zani, W. M. "Blueprint for MIS," *Harvard Business Review*, November–December 1970, pp. 95–100.

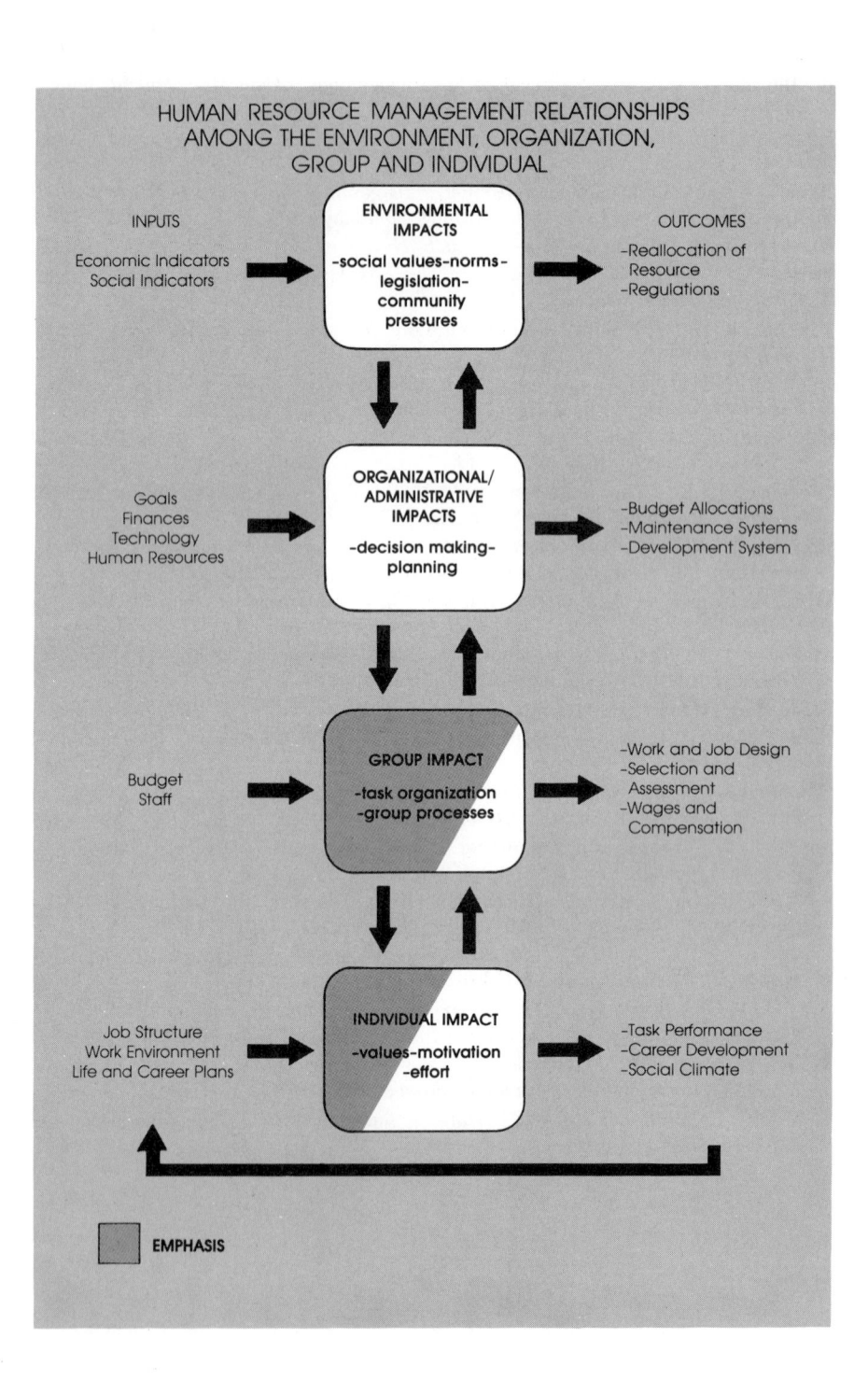

HUMAN RESOURCE MANAGEMENT RELATIONSHIPS AMONG THE ENVIRONMENT, ORGANIZATION, GROUP AND INDIVIDUAL

INPUTS

Economic Indicators
Social Indicators

→ **ENVIRONMENTAL IMPACTS**
-social values-norms-legislation-community pressures

OUTCOMES
-Reallocation of Resource
-Regulations

Goals
Finances
Technology
Human Resources

→ **ORGANIZATIONAL/ ADMINISTRATIVE IMPACTS**
-decision making-planning

-Budget Allocations
-Maintenance Systems
-Development System

Budget
Staff

→ **GROUP IMPACT**
-task organization
-group processes

-Work and Job Design
-Selection and Assessment
-Wages and Compensation

Job Structure
Work Environment
Life and Career Plans

→ **INDIVIDUAL IMPACT**
-values-motivation
-effort

-Task Performance
-Career Development
-Social Climate

■ EMPHASIS

332

5

ASSESSING INDIVIDUAL QUALIFICATIONS

One of the cornerstones of human resource management is the selection and development of the organization's work force. Essentially, human resource management must address itself to the relationship between organizational planning and the fulfillment of those goals through selection and development of employees. Because organizational productivity and individual life styles are linked to this task, the selection and assessment of employees of diverse social backgrounds has become a topic of increasing concern to organizations and to agencies which enforce fair employment practices. For this reason, techniques for predicting an individual's future job performance as well as means for adapting and developing an employee's talents have become increasingly complex and controversial.

The interrelationships between organizational and human resource planning, as well as HRM's responsibility for selecting and developing an organization's work force, should be strikingly apparent. For example, HRM is charged with integrating human resource planning with overall organizational planning, and HRM's selection and development responsibilities are essential to that planning relationship. Predicting future job performance, assessing individual employee potential for advancement, and identifying employee training and development needs provide essential data to the human resource planning process. Furthermore, HRM must be particularly sensitive to social and legislative forces as they impact on the organization's selection and development techniques.

The goal of a selection process is that of making a valid decision about an individual's ability to perform tasks required by the job assignment. The decision problem facing the personnel manager or decision maker is that of trying to predict an individual's future job performance on the basis of work history, education or experience, interviews, biographical data, test scores, or perhaps general impressions. The decision to accept or reject an individual for a job assignment represents the "bottom line" of a complex set of analyses. Currently, human resource managers are reexamining the relationship between this "bottom line," the planning function of management, and the reality of current selection results.

Organizational pressures, social and legislative constraints, changes in the labor force, and technological demands are forcing organizations to reexamine their assumptions about people and the techniques they are using in reaching decisions about accepting or rejecting an individual for employment, transfer, or promotion. Civil rights laws and affirmative action plans have dealt serious blows to many firms' traditional employment practices. These pressures have forced firms to search for and adopt selection techniques that can be demonstrated valid, effective, and practical for staffing decisions.

Once individuals have accepted employment, decisions will be made that will have an impact on their careers, life style, and patterns of work activity and the organization's overall effectiveness. The newly assigned employee will be expected to learn about the work environment, job demands, organizational expectations, and group norms. As the organization attempts to transform the individual into a valuable resource, so also the individual attempts to use the organization to meet his or her specific needs. Adaptation and development activities are embedded within the human resource system, and they must be evaluated in terms of their relationship to organization effectiveness.

Part V consists of two sections; the first contains two articles that present different aspects of the selection process, and the second deals with career development. Each emphasizes a response to the human resource manager's need for information and new approaches to selection and assessment problems. Although each of the human resource functions shape these responses, a central theme is the current importance of selection as a vehicle through which organizational demands and individual needs and qualifications are carefully assessed and matched.

The first article, "Legal and Effectiveness Issues in the Personnel Selection Process," by Helen LaVan and Peter F. Sorenson, Jr., provides the reader with an overall appraisal of current techniques of selection. Because civil rights legislation, court decisions, and governmental enforcement agencies' rulings have had a tremendous impact on selection techniques, the authors have summarized these effects and gone on to suggest procedures with potentially less adverse impact than traditional strategies. Resources useful for maintaining a "state of the art" approach are listed as selected bibliographies within each section of the article.

Because content validity offers a practical, relatively inexpensive, and legally acceptable basis for selection validation, human resource managers are reexamining the assessment center as an evaluation and career guidance tool. One of the advantages of this procedure is that it allows organizations the opportunity to create working environments and test the placement of an individual within the context of that total working environment. "Improving Human Resource Effectiveness Through Assessment Center Technology: Emergence, Design, Application and Evaluation" by Cabot L. Jaffee and Stephen L. Cohen provides a comprehensive picture of the assessment center as a technique and also includes a summary of evaluative research on its validity. First, the authors trace the development of assessment centers and provide a detailed set of guidelines for developing and operating an assessment center that should enable managers to protect individuals' rights while simultaneously meeting organizational needs. The authors conclude that the assessment model can be implemented in ways that provide "fair discrimination" for the qualified candidates and are also beneficial for the career guidance of individuals. Next, the authors summarize empirical research findings on assessment center techniques. The authors conclude that they contribute significantly to newer managerial needs for demonstrably fair employment decisions. The validity of assessment prediction is examined by reports on subsequent job performance and related to both content validity and affirmative action programs. This literature is used to generate procedures for determining the worth of an assessment center program. Because the effectiveness and value of the center have been demonstrated empirically, it is important that an organization carefully examine its goals, jobs, tasks, and assessment exercises **before** implementing as assessment program. Specialized procedures can be used to monitor the content validity of assessment techniques, with careful attention being given to the planning and design of the assessment center program, the affirmative action program, career development, and selection strategies of organizations.

The concluding article of Part V focuses on selection as a post-employment activity which is linked to a carefully planned career development program. The potential impact of advanced training programs on a firm make its design, implementation, and selection procedures particularly challenging. In this article, "Executive Development in the Department of Agriculture," Thomas W. Gill describes a large managerial and executive development program and its "built-in" flexibilities. Gill accomplishes this by outlining the various steps in the program, before presenting examples of development activities which have been tailored to meet agency needs. The author concludes that managerial and executive development must be a comprehensive approach, and that means integrating the department's needs with the individual's qualifications and aspirations. This article clearly shows how human resource activities discussed in earlier sections can be combined in a management and executive development program and prepare the individual for productive work behavior.

THE SELECTION OF HUMAN RESOURCES

Legal and Effectiveness Issues in the Personnel Selection Process

Helen LaVan, A.P.S.
Peter F. Sørensen, Jr., A.P.D.

Perhaps no functional area in personnel administration is at such a complex juncture as personnel selection. At the same time that researchers have started to evaluate the effectiveness of various selection techniques, new laws and their resultant administrative guidelines are emerging to dramatically alter the application of existing techniques.

The major objective of this article is to describe the current state of the selection process from two perspectives: (1) the results of research evaluating the various steps of the selection process, and (2) the current legal requirements of employee selection. It begins by reviewing general philosophies which govern both the selection process and alternative approaches to the process. Discussion then focuses on the state of the art and the legal considerations of the specific steps of the selection process: the application blank, the interview, testing, the use of references and the preemployment physical.

SELECTION PHILOSOPHY

Several different selection philosophies and strategies have appeared in the personnel literature. For example, Strauss and Sayles (1972) identify three alternative approaches to selection:

Screening out applicants who don't fit: When this approach dominates the emphasis is on eliminating those applicants who do not match the organization's notion of a desirable employee.

Fitting jobs to people: Here greater emphasis is on modifying a job to fit applicant characteristics.

Prepared especially for this book and printed with permission of the author.

Fitting people to jobs: Sayles and Strauss identify this as the dominant or typical approach to the selection process. Here the emphasis is on matching jobs to applicants.

Another approach to defining selection strategy is to differentiate between what has been referred to as the "successive hurdles versus the compensatory approach" (Bray and Moses, 1972; Sikula, 1976; Walker, Luthan, and Hodgetts, 1970). The hurdles approach, traditionally the most common in selection processes, requires the applicant to successfully complete or "pass" in sequence each screening device—the application form, tests, and any interviews or other selection techniques. The compensatory approach, on the other hand, involves assessment of the *composite* results of the several screening devices. This latter approach appears to be more favorably received in the recent literature on selection (Miner and Miner, 1977) and is based on the assumption that a deficiency in one set of results can be compensated for by proficiency in another area and that such a comprehensive approach makes for a more valid selection procedure.

Perhaps no area in personnel administration is as subject to as many legal constraints as the functional areas of recruitment and selection. In addition, not only are most of the legal constraints relatively new, but they are subject to continuous interpretational revision by the courts, numerous governmental regulatory agencies, and the current practices of various companies. In this section of the article we attempt to briefly discuss many of these constraints on employee recruitment and selection. For those readers interested in more current discussions of court decisions, regulatory agencies' decrees, and other company practices, additional references are suggested in the bibliography.

The most important legal constraint in the whole recruitment and selection process is undoubtedly Title VII of the 1964 Civil Rights Act, and its companions, the 1972 Equal Employment Opportunity Act and Executive Order 11246, as amended.

Title VII and its 1972 amendment apply to organizations having 15 or more employees that are engaged in interstate commerce, and also to employment agencies, unions, state and local governments, and educational institutions. Such organizations may not refuse to hire, discharge, or otherwise discriminate against employees on the basis of race, color, religion, sex, or national origin. On the other hand, no employer is required to hire anyone unless he or she is qualified or qualifiable, just because the applicant is of a particular race or sex.

While the antidiscrimination provisions apply to all employers having 15 or more employees, those companies having federal contracts in excess of $50,000 are required to develop an Affirmative Action program. While the law itself does not prohibit questions about race, color, religion, or national origin prior to employment, the Equal Employment Opportunity Commission, charged with the enforcement of the law, has in the past regarded such questions as evidence of discrimination. The kinds of questions that may be construed as discriminatory include questions about the applicant's place of birth, family status, color, national origin, and criminal record; also whether the applicant has relatives working at the company or belongs to organizations that are primarily composed of groups of a specific national or religious origin. Unless such factors are "BFOQ" (bona fide occupational qualifications), taking them into consideration in the hiring decision is prohibited, as is the practice of requesting an applicant to affix a photograph. In addition, some states abide by special restrictions. For example, more than half of the states have their own age and sex discrimination laws, which are important primarily because the EEOC will often defer to law enforcement at the state level and also because they cover some organizations not under the federal umbrella.

Postemployment questioning is also restricted. Personnel decisions such as promotions, transfers, or eligibility for training programs should not be based on biographical data that might be construed as discriminatory.

To facilitate compliance, the following were issued:

Executive Order 11246, *Guidelines on Employee Selection Procedures*, issued by the Office of Federal Contract Compliance

Federal Executive Agency Guidelines (developed collaboratively and adopted by the U.S. Civil Service Commission, the Department of Transportation and the Department of Justice, but not the EEOC)

Uniform Guidelines, adopted by all four agencies in 1978

Current selection guidelines specify that it is necessary to validate all recruitment and selection procedures that have an adverse impact on protected classes. In general, any technique that fails to select applicants from protected classes at a rate of 80 percent of majority group selection should be validated in terms of job requirements. For example, if a given test identifies 50 percent of the white male applicants as suitable for employment, it should identify at least 40 percent of the members of a protected class (80 percent of 50 percent) as suitable for employment. This validation requirement as it applies to specific jobs and their selection techniques is, however, suspended when the employer's *total* selection process results in the hiring of minority individuals at a rate of no less than 80 percent of those who form the major part of the organization's work force. Overriding reasons, such as unusually small numbers or special recruiting procedures, also call for exceptions to the four-fifths guideline.

The guidelines recognize that it is not always feasible to validate selection techniques because these techniques might be unscored, informal, or unstandardized. In such cases, the user is encouraged to adopt procedures that are scored, formal, and standardized and that have been validated by other organizations on similar groups; or to adopt reasonable alternate procedures that eliminate the biased adverse impact.

It should be noted that these selection guidelines do not relieve the users of affirmative action obligations, but merely encourage the development and implementation of such affirmative action plans. Guidelines for the development of AA plans have been issued by the Office of Federal Contract Compliance. These guidelines affect employers with 50 or more employees having government contracts totaling $50,000 or more per year. For these firms an affirmative action plan should be written and should contain the following:

1. *Analysis.* In order to determine utilization, it is necessary to consider not only the minority population in a specific labor market but also the number of minority group members with the required skills for the particular job categories. For some

jobs such as president of a firm, the organization may need to consider the regional or national executive market as a target of the recruiting effort. Individuals within and outside of the company need to be considered. Training available to provide the needed skills also has to be considered.

2. *Goals and timetables.* If the study indicates underutilization of minorities, realistic goals for corrective action and timetables for reaching these goals have to be described in writing in the affirmative action plan.

3. *Additional requirements.* In addition, an affirmative action plan should clearly state how affirmative action policy is disseminated and implemented; it should identify problem areas and indicate how the policy will be audited and what actions are being taken to develop linkages with community groups who are making minority referrals.

Three additional laws have an important impact on employee recruitment and selection. They are the Age Discrimination in Employment Act of 1967, the Rehabilitation Act of 1973, and the Viet Nam Era Veterans Assistance Act of 1974. The first act prohibits an employer of 20 or more persons who is engaged in interstate commerce from discriminating on the basis of age. Protected are individuals aged 40 to 65 in private industry and to 70 in government. It is illegal under this law to fail to hire, to discharge, or to otherwise discriminate against individuals in this age group. Even alleged higher costs of doing business because of an older work force does not justify age discrimination. Guidelines that have been issued by the Wage and Hour Division of the Department of Labor indicate that employment ads should not indicate preference for a certain age group. Illustrative of what is specifically prohibited are the following terms: age 25-35, fresh college grad, junior accountant, office boy, and retired person.

The Rehabilitation Act of 1973 requires federal contractors and subcontractors with contracts of $2,500 or more to take affirmative action to provide job opportunites for mentally or physically handicapped individuals who are otherwise employable. While there are many responses required of employers, two kinds are worthy of note—one dealing with reducing barriers in the recruitment and selection process and the other with providing easier access to the work place by means of ramps, special doors, or nearby parking places. The handicapped also benefit when an employer makes simple modifications in tools, equipment, or work benches.

Under the Viet Nam Era Veterans Assistance and Reemployment Act of 1974, federal contractors and subcontractors are required to take affirmative action to hire qualified Viet Nam Era veterans as well as other qualified, but disabled veterans.

Some affirmative action steps that can be taken in the recruitment and selection of the handicapped might be making special arrangements to meet with applicants who cannot get to the interview site; having the interviewer fill in a blind applicant's application blank; and considering the applicant for other positions for which he or she might be more suited. It should be noted that employers cannot use information obtained in a physical examination to determine whether a candidate is a member of a protected category. Applicants or employees who are eligible for affirmative action must reveal themselves to the employer.

References

American Psychological Association, Division of Industrial-Organizational Psychology. *Principles for the Validation and Use of Personnel Selection Procedures.* Dayton, Ohio: *APA Industrial-Organizational Psychologist,* 4 (1975), 19.

Bertram, Francis D. "The Prediction of Police Academy Performance and On-the-Job Performance from Police Recruit Screening Measures." *Dissertation Abstracts International,* 36, 10-A, (April 1976), 6543.

Bray, Douglas W., and Joseph L. Moses. "Personnel Selection," *Annual Review of Psychology,* 23 (1972), 545-576.

Cecil, Earl A., Robert J. Paul, and Robert A. Olins. "Perceived Importance of Selected Variables Used to Evaluate Male and Female Job Applicants," *Personnel Psychology,* 26, 3, (Fall 1973), 397-404.

Combs, Mary J. "Personal Characteristics Influencing the Hiring, Promotion, and Discharge of Women in Selected Groups of Occupations in Clarke County, Georgia." *Dissertation Abstracts International,* 35, 10-A (April 1975), 6582.

Drauden, Gail M. "Entry Level Professionals' Job Analysis and Selection Strategy: A Progress Report." *Catalog of Selected Documents in Psychology,* 7, (February 1977), 26.

EEOC, 1966. *Guidelines on Employee Selection Procedures. Federal Register,* 35, 149 (August 1, 1970); 12333-12336.

Fine, Sidney A. "What's Wrong with the Hiring System?" *Organizational Dynamics,* 4, 2, (Fall 1975), 55-67.

Gorham, William A. "Political, Ethical and Emotional Aspects of Federal Guidelines on Employee Selection Procedures," in *Contemporary Problems in Personnel,* ed. W. Clay Hamner and Frank L. Schmidt. Chicago, Ill.: St. Clair Press, 1977.

Gunderson, E.K. *Psychological Studies in Antarctica,* No. 71-14. San Diego, Calif.: Naval Health Research Center, 1970.

Luke, R. A. "Matching the Individual and the Organization," *Harvard Business Review,* 53, 3 (May-June 1975), 17-34.

Malinowski, Frank A. "Employee Drug Abuse in Municipal Government." *Public Personnel Management,* 4, 1, (January-February 1975), 59-62.

Miner, John B., and Mary G. Miner. *Personnel and Industrial Relations.* New York: Macmillan Publishing Co., 1977.

Norman, Kent L. "Weight and Value in an Information Integration Model: Subjective Rating of Job Applicants," *Organizational Behavior and Human Performance,* 16, 1 (June 1976), 193-204.

Office of Federal Contract Compliance. *Federal Executive Agency Guidelines on Employee Selection Procedures.* Federal Register, 41, 227 (November 23, 1976).

Peterson, Nancy S. "An Expected Utility Model for Optimal Selection." *Dissertation Abstracts International,* 34, 7-A (January 1975), 4258.

Roose, Jack E., and Michael E. Doherty. "Judgment Theory Applied to the Selection of Life Insurance Salesmen," *Organizational Behavior and Human Performance,* 16, 2 (August 1976), 231-249.

Sikula, Andrew F. *Personnel Administration and Human Resources Management.* New York: John Wiley & Sons, 1976.

Schneider, Benjamin. *Staffing Organizations.* Palisades, Calif.: Goodyear Publishing Co., 1976.

Smith, R. D. "Models for Personnel Selection Decisions," *Personnel Journal*, 52, 8 (August 1973), 688–696.

Stone, C.H., and F. L. Ruch. "Selection, Interviewing, and Testing," in *Staffing Policies and Strategies*, ed. D. Yoder and H.G. Heneman. Washington, D.C.: Bureau of National Affairs, Inc., 1974.

Ulrich, J.R., and J.R. Painter. "A Conjoint-Measurement Analysis of Human Judgment," *Organizational Behavior and Human Performance*, August 1974, 50–61.

THE APPLICATION FORM

The application form is probably the most widely used selection technique. There is a minimum of information that should be provided by the application blank, including

1. Basic information—such as full name, address, telephone number, type of work desired, and date available.
2. Work experience—including for example, titles of positions held, rates of pay, and names of employers and immediate supervisors.
3. Education—both academic and other job-related training.
4. References—other than past employers or relatives.

At the beginning of the 70s considerable interest was expressed in systematically identifying and developing *bio-data*, biographical information relevant to the selection process. This interest was reflected in the comments and discussion of bio-data by Bray and Moses (1972) in their review of the field of personnel selection in the early 70s and in a paper by Asher (1972) that reported that "in comparison with other predictors such as intelligence, aptitude, interest, and personality, biographical items had vastly superior validity."

However, this early interest seems to have declined sharply. For instance, in the recent review of selection techniques by Ash and Krocker (1975) the authors report that:

> When Glennon, Albright and Owens published the Catalog of Life History Items (1966), bio-data, standardized and validated, seemed to give great promise for selection. The last three years, however, saw little published on the use of bio-data in employment selection. One possible index of dwindling interest was the experience of the authors of the Catalog who invited reports of validation studies of the items: not one study has been received.

A study reported by Roach (1971) illustrates some of the problems of maintaining the validity of bio-data in a changing environment. Roach showed how the predictive power of a weighted application blank for clerical employment declined over time owing to changes in labor market conditions, manpower needs, and personnel policies. Questions have also been raised concerning the implications of federal and state guidelines for the development and use of bio-data, including its potentially adverse impact on minority applicants and the difficulty in establishing job relatedness (Ash and Krocker, 1975).

Despite the difficulties involved in the development and use of bio-data, there continues to be some degree of activity in this area, particularly concerning the BIB (biographical information blank). For example, one recent study (Hinrichs, Haanpera, and Sonkin, 1976) explores the application of the BIB across national boundaries, including Finland, Sweden, Norway, France, Portugal and the U.S. Results indicate that "it is possible to cross-validate a biographical inventory key for the selection of salesmen across national boundaries." However, the study also indicates that as one moves further from the cultural and occupational groupings in which the key was developed, cross-validity decreases.

An important restriction on the application blank is the Age Discrimination in Employment Act, which prohibits discrimination based on age for individuals aged 40 to 65. It is imperative that any data gathered on the application blank not be used in a discriminatory manner.

References

Ash, Philip, and Leonard P. Krocker. "Personnel Selection, Classification, and Placement," *Annual Review of Psychology, 26* (1975), 481–507.

Asher, J. J. "The Biographical Item: Can it be Improved?" *Personnel Psychology, 25* (1972), 251–269.

Bray, Douglas W., and Joseph L. Moses. "Personnel Selection." *Annual Review of Psychology, 23,* (1972), 545–576.

Dipboye, Robert L., Howard L. Fromkin, and Kent Wiback. "Relative Importance of Applicant Sex, Attractiveness, and Scholastic Standing in Evaluation of Job Applicant Resumes," *Journal of Applied Psychology, 60,* 1, (February 1975) 39–43.

Glennon, J. R., L. E. Albright and W.A. Owens. "A Catalog of Life History Items." Washington, D.C.: American Psychological Assoication, Division 14, 1966.

Guinn, Nancy, L. Johnson and Jeffery E. Kan. *Screening for Adaptability to Military Service.* U.S. AFHRL Technical Report, (May), 29.

Guinn, Nancy, Bart M. Vitola, and Sandra A. Leisey. *Background and Interest Measures as Predictors of Success in Undergraduate Pilot Training.* U.S. AFHRL Technical Report No. 76-9, May 1976.

Hinrichs, J.R., Haanpera, and Sonkin. "Validation of a Biographical Information Blank Across National Boundaries," *Personnel Psychology, 29* (Autumn 1976), 417–421.

Kessler, C. C., and G. J. Gibbs. "Getting the Most from Application Blanks," *Personnel,* January–February 1975, 53–61.

Rosen, Benson, and Thomas H. Jerdee. "Effects of Applicant's Sex and Difficulty of Job on Evaluation of Candidates for Managerial Positions," *Journal of Applied Psychology, 59,* 4 (August 1974), 511–512.

Rosenbaum, Richard W. "Predictability of Employee Theft Using Weighted Application Blanks," *Journal of Applied Psychology, 61,* 1 (February 1976), 94–98.

Schwab, D. P., and R. L. Oliver. "Predicting Tenure With Biographical Data: Exhuming Buried Evidence," *Personnel Psychology, 27* (1975), 125–128.

Sharma, J. M., and H. Vardan. "Graphology: What Handwriting Can Tell You About an Applicant," *Personnel,* March-April 1975, 65-67.

Silberberg, N. E., and M. C. Silberberg. "The Job Application Blank as a Barrier to Jobs," *Rehabilitation Literature*, 35, 12 (December 1975), 364-368.

THE INTERVIEW

In contrast to the rather mixed reception employers have given to bio-data, the interview continues to be a preferred technique. Progress in improving the interview as a selection tool does not seem overly encouraging, however. The following comments appear to be typical of the literature summarizing reported research on the individual interview process:

> Despite a long history as an unrewarding research area, there has been considerable resurgence of interest in the interview. (Bray and Moses, 1972)

> Interest in the interview has continued unabated, but it would be optimistic to conclude that significant advances have been made. (Ash and Krocker, 1975)

> The inevitable conclusion derived from a number of investigations is that interview judgments, as they are usually made in the employment situation, are not closely related to measures of success on the job. In an overall sense, the evidence regarding the validity of the selection interview yields a distinctly disappointing picture. (Miner, 1977)

There is a fair amount of evidence highlighting the problems of interviewer inconsistency, inaccurate information supplied by interviewees, and accuracy of interviewer judgments.

Nevertheless, there is also evidence that these problems can be modified through the training of interviewers and the use of highly structured, patterned interviews (Ash and Krocker, 1975). Problems of objective assessment decrease as the interviewer's knowledge of the job in question increases and as the interviewer receives feedback on the adequacy of his or her decisions.

Although screening applicants before an interview used to be a fairly common practice, the EEOC is now insisting that hiring decisions be based on several factors, not just tests. Hence, most companies are now providing at least one interview.

There is also a trend toward the use of patterned interviews in which a list of questions are provided to the interviewers, so that all applicants receive equal treatment and more systematic comparisons are possible. The standardization of the interview also enables subsequent validation. By avoiding the use of open-ended, nondirected questions that may be influenced by the applicant's manner of speaking, personality, or other subjective qualities, the interview can be made susceptible to subsequent validation.

The OFCC guidelines are far less specific regarding the interview than almost any other aspect of employee selection, although the interview is subject to the same adverse impact restrictions as all other techniques. A general guideline that can be followed is that no question should be asked of applicants in protected classes that is not asked of nonprotected classes.

References

Anstey, Edgar. "Comments on Gardner and Williams' Twenty-five Year Follow-up of Naval Officer Selection Procedures," *Occupational Psychology*, 47, 3-4 (1973), 163-166.

Ash, Philip, and Leonard P. Krocker. "Personnel Selection, Classification, and Placement," *Annual Review of Psychology*, 26 (1975), 481-507.

Austin, David L. "Transactional Interviewing or Who Does What to Whom?" *Personnel Journal*, June 1974, pp. 450-453.

Bernstein, Vicki, Milton D. Hakel, and Anne Harlan. "The College Student as Interviewer: A Threat to Generalizability?" *Journal of Applied Psychology*, 60, 2 (April 1975), 266-268.

Blevins, David E. "Claimed vs. Calculated Cue-Weighting Systems for Screening Employee Applicants," *Journal of Vocational Behavior*, 7, 3 (December 1975), 327-336.

Bray, Douglas W., and Joseph L. Moses. "Personnel Selection," *Annual Review of Psychology*, 23 (1975), 545-576.

Cahn, Dudley D. "The Employment Interview: A Self-Validation Model," *Journal of Employment Counseling*, 13, 4 (December 1976), 150-155.

Gardner, K. E. and A. P. Williams. "A Twenty-five Year Follow-up of an Extended Interview Selection Procedure in the Royal Navy: II. Multivariate Analyses and Conclusions," *Occupational Psychology*, 47, 3-4 (1973), 149-161.

Heneman, Hert G., Donald P. Schwab, Dennis L. Huett, and John J. Ford. "Interviewer Validity as a Function of Interview Structure, Biographical Data, and Interviewee Order," *Journal of Applied Psychology*, 60, 6 (December 1975), 748-753.

Hopper, Robert, and Frederick Williams. "Speech Characteristics and Employability," *Speech Monographs*, (November 1973), pp. 296-302.

Johns, Gary. "Effects of Information Order and Frequency of Applicant Evaluation Upon Linear Information-Processing Competence of Interviewers," *Journal of Applied Psychology*, 60, 4 (August 1975), 427-433.

Kohn, Mervin, "Hiring College Graduates Through Off-Campus Selection Interviewing," *Public Personnel Management*, 4, 1 (January-February 1975), 23-31.

Kopelman, M. D. "The Contrast Effect in the Selection Interview," *British Journal of Educational Psychology*, 34, 3 (November 1975), 333-336.

Landy, Frank J. "The Validity of the Interview in Police Officer Selection," *Journal of Applied Psychology*, 61, 2 (April 1973), 193-198.

Leonard, Russell L. "Cognitive Complexity and the Similarity-Attraction Paradigm," *Journal of Research in Personality*, 10, 1 (March 1976), 83-88.

Leonard, Russell L. "The Delineation of Boundary Conditions in the Similarity-Attraction Paradigm: Cognitive Complexity," *Personality and Social Psychology Bulletin*, 1, 1 (1974), 86-87.

Leonard, Russell L. "Relevance and Reliability in the Interview," *Psychological Reports*, June (1974), 1331-1334.

Loesch, John M. "Development of an Interview Process for the Selection of Life Insurance Sales Managers," *Dissertation Abstracts International*, 35, 9-A (March 1975), 5927-5928.

The process of establishing a statistical relationship between test score and job performance that constitutes *test validation* is an exceedingly difficult one. More is required by the EEOC than merely that the test was developed by an expert.

Additionally, distinctions have to be made between different kinds of tests:

1. *General intelligence* tests, which have recently been held in court to be culturally biased and not predictive of job performance.
2. *Tests of mechanical aptitude, dexterity,* and *clerical aptitude,* which in general are valid.
3. *Personality* tests, which are occasionally used to select individuals for positions that require certain personality characteristics, but which are difficult to validate.
4. *Vocational interest* tests, which are typically used for career counseling and guidance, not for selection.

Care has to be exercised so that only those skills relevant to the job are incorporated into a test. Potential for higher level jobs should *not* be tested unless it can be expected that applicants will in fact attain these higher level jobs within a reasonable period of time.

There are numerous other issues related to testing that are beyond the scope of this paper, including sample size, different prediction scores for different kinds of applicants, and the subject groups for the validation process itself. One precautionary note on sample size: The minimum number of individuals in a group needed to establish statistical validity has been approximated at 30 per job category. Because not many companies have 30 employees (much less 30 applicants) in one job category, the EEOC has in a limited number of cases permitted the pooling of subjects.

There is also the possibility that the same cut-off scores for both minority and majority groups will not necessarily ensure the same level of job performance, precisely because there is never a perfect relationship between test score and job performance. Then there is the more subtle issue of selecting subjects for a validation study: Should current employees, who have had the benefit of work experience and performance appraisals, be chosen or a control group of applicants? A related issue is, What format should the appraisal take? Is the format of the appraisal that is required for validation the one that will accomplish all of the objectives of the appraisal system? Perhaps so, but perhaps not.

REFERENCES

Clarke, Walter V. "Who Gains When you Cheat on a Personality Test?" *Personnel Journal,* (April 1974), pp. 302–303.

Constantin, S.W. "An Investigation of Information Favorability in the Employment Interview," *Journal of Applied Psychology,* 61, 6 (December 1976), 743–749.

Dorin, Philip A. "The Use of the California Psychological Inventory in the Selection of Residence Hall Staff," *Dissertation Abstracts International,* 35, 4–2 (October 1974), 1906.

Ebel, R. L. "Comments on Some Problems of Employment Testing," *Personnel Psychology,* 30 (Spring 1977), 55–63.

London, M., and M. D. Hakel. "Effects of Applicant Stereotypes, Order, aı Information on Interview Impressions," *Journal of Applied Psychology*, 59 (197ᵴ 157–162.

London, Manuel, and John R. Poplawski. "Effects of Information on Stereotyp Development in Performance Appraisal and Interview Contexts," *Journal of Appliec Psychology*, 61, 2 (April 1976), 199–205.

Lopez, F. M. *Personnel Interviewing*. New York: McGraw-Hill Book Company, 1975.

Miner, John B., and Mary G. Miner. *Personnel and Industrial Relations*. New York: Macmillan Publishing Co., 1977.

Pate, Robert H., and Richard K. Harwood. "Employment Interviews: How Critical?" *Journal of Employment Counseling*, (December 1974), pp. 176–182.

Rand, Thomas M. "The Effects of Racial Prejudice, Biographical Similarity, Applicant's Race, and Affiiliation Need on Interpersonal Attraction and Hiring Decision in a Simulated Selection Interview," *Dissertation Abstracts International*, 35, 6–B (December 1974), 3081.

Rand, Thomas M., and Kenneth N. Wexley. "Demonstration of the Effect, 'Similar to Me,' in Simulated Employment Interviews," *Psychological Reports*, 36, 2 (April 1975), 535–544.

Schmidt, Frank L., and Bernhard Hoffman. "Empirical Comparison of Three Methods of Assessing Utility of a Selection Device," *Journal of Industrial and Organizational Psychology*, No. 1 (Spring 1973), pp. 13–22.

Schmitt, Neal, and Bryan W. Coyle. "Applicant Decisions in the Employment Interview," *Journal of Applied Psychology*, 61, 2 (April 1976), 184–192.

Waldron, L. A. "The Validity of an Employment Interview Independent of Psychometric Variables," *Australian Psychologist*, (March 1975), pp. 68–77.

Wiener, Y., and M. L. Schneiderman. "Use of Job Information as a Criterion in Employment Decisions of Interviewers," *Journal of Applied Psychology*, (December 1975), pp. 699–704.

TESTING

Although testing is probably the most "sensitive" area of the selection process in terms of the law, a recent review (Ash and Krocker, 1975) assesses its status in the following terms:

> Despite the pressure, concern, interest, and effort invested, however, progress in both theory and practice in the development of selection procedures to meet these legal and the related technical challenges has been disappointingly limited.

As a result of the careful scrutiny being given employment testing by numerous government agencies, its use in the selection process has been curtailed. Admittedly, some organizations have validated their testing procedures, but some, in the mistaken belief that tests are illegal, have abandoned testing. Whether a test is legal depends on whether adverse impact can be demonstrated. If a test (or any selection mechanism) has an adverse impact on the selection of any of the protected minorities, then the organization has to be able to demonstrate that the test is valid for hiring for that position.

Equal Employment Opportunity Commission, *Guidelines on Employment Testing Procedures*. Washington, D.C.: EEOC, 1976.

"Federal Government Intervention in Psychological Testing: Is It Here?" *Personnel Psychology*, 29 (Winter, 1976), 519–557.

Gael, Sidney, Donald L. Grant, and Richard J. Ritchie. "Employment Test Validation for Minority and Non-Minority Telephone Operators," *Journal of Applied Psychology*, 60, 4 (August 1975), 411–419.

Gatewood, R. D., and L. F. Schoenfeldt. "Content Validation and E.E.O.C.: A Useful Alternative for Selection," *Personnel Journal*, 56 (August 1977), 402–404.

Goeters, Klaus-Martin. "Psychodiagnositics in the Service of Developing Countries: The Selection of Applicants from the Yemen Arab Republic for Pilot Training," *Zeitschrift fur Experimentelle and Angewandte Psychologie*, 22, 2 (1975), 195–217.

Guion, Robert M. "Recruiting, Selection, and Job Placement," in *Handbook of Industrial and Organizational Psychology*, ed. Marvin D. Dunnette. Chicago, Ill.: Rand-McNally, 1976.

Hubbard, Henry F., Thelma Hunt, and Robert D. Kruse. "Job-Related Strength and Agility Tests: A Methodology," *Personnel Management*, 4, (September–October 1975), 305–310.

Matteson, M. T. "Employment Testing: Where Do We Stand?" *The Personnel Administrator*, 20, 3 (January 1975), 17–34.

Office of Federal Contract Compliance. *Validation of Tests by Contractors and Subcontractors Subject to the Provisions of Executive Order 11246*, Federal Register, 33, No. 186 (September 24, 1968), 14392–14394.

Office of Federal Contract Compliance. *Employee Testing and Other Selection Procedures*, Federal Register, 36, No. 192, (October 2, 1971), 19307-19310.

Peterson, D. J. "The Impact of Duke Power on Testing," *Personnel* (March–April, 1974), pp. 30–37.

Robertson, D. E. "Update on Testing and Equal Opportunity," *Personnel Journal*, 56 (March 1977), pp. 144–147.

Sanders, B., and F. Urban. "Employment Testing and the Law," *Labor Law Journal*, 27 (January 1976), 38–58.

Schmidt, F. L., et al. "Job Sample vs. Paper-and-Pencil Trades and Technical Tests" *Personnel Psychology*, 30 (Summer 1977), 187–197.

Schoenfeldt, Lyle F., Barbara B. Schoenfeldt, Stanley R. Acker, and Michael R. Perlson. "Content Validity Revisited: The Development of a Content Oriented Test of Industrial Reading." *Journal of Applied Psychology*, 61, 5 (October 1976), 581–588.

Sharf, J. C. "How Validated Testing Eases the Pressure of Minority Recruitment," *Personnel*, (May–June 1975), pp. 53–59.

Wollack, S. "Content Validity: Its Legal and Psychometric Basis," *Public Personnel Management*, 5 (November 1976), 397–408.

REFERENCE CHECKS

Research on the use of reference checks in the selection process indicates that references serve as poor predictors of later ratings as to job performance and that the degree of validity varies according to the source of the reference and the relationship between the reference and the applicant. However, there is some indication that the use of a forced-choice format may improve the predictive power of references, at least in terms of clerical personnel.

The kinds of references that are typically checked include former employers, schools attended, and personal acquaintances. Former employers can provide information about the applicant's work performance, including specific strengths and weaknesses, and about the person's earnings and reasons for leaving. The commonly accepted practice is to check only five or ten years back, unless the applicant received an unfavorable reference. It is also a commonly accepted practice to ask the applicant's permission to check with the present employer, and some firms also ask for permission to check with prior employers.

The Federal Privacy Protection Study Committee has come up with a series of 162 recommendations affecting the record-keeping relationships that individuals have with many organizations, including employers. One recommendation is that the Federal Fair Credit Reporting Act be amended to require that individuals be informed about what kinds of personal information are being provided to prospective employers and for what reasons. In addition, it was recommended that employees sign authorizations before an employer be allowed to release information to outside parties. Although these are only recommendations at the present time, it can be anticipated that employers will find it difficult to obtain information in the reference check process in the near future.

Similar recommendations were made regarding arrest (but not conviction) records. These should only be considered if they are less than one year old. The recommendation was also made that conviction records be considered only if they are specifically job-related and that both of these be kept separately from other employment and reference data. There is also federal legislation pending that prohibits the use of the polygraph in the employment process, although many states currently have such legislation.

The checking of school references is also becoming more difficult. Unless the former student signs a consent form, many schools will not provide transcripts or other information.

THE PHYSICAL EXAMINATION

Although the preemployment physical is a widely used selection technique, it appears to face the same difficulties of validation as many of the other tests. For instance, existing research, much of it based on the selection of pilots, indicates a good deal of interrater inconsistency (that is, low reliability) as well as difficulty in demonstrating job relevance. Measures obtained on the physical examination do not correlate well with on-the-job performance or with lowered absenteeism and accident rates. However, some degree of success has been reported with the use of health questionnaires such as the Cornell Medical Index Health Questionnaire (Miner and Miner, 1977).

REFERENCES

Miner, John B., and Mary G. Miner. *Personnel and Industrial Relations.* New York: Macmillan Publishing Co. 1977.

A SYSTEMS APPROACH TO SELECTION

In view of the pitfalls to which the selection process has been subject, including the difficult progress in establishing valid selection techniques and the complexities introduced by the expanding influence of governmental legislation, one of the more encouraging trends has been the increased attention to a systems approach to selection (Ash and Krocker, 1975). For example, the CAPER (Sands, 1973) provides information necessary to minimize the estimated total cost of recruiting, selection, inducting, and training personnel. The work of Burack and Smith (1977) represents an additional recent example of a systems approach.

One of the advantages of a systems approach is that it recognizes the importance of the relationships between various aspects of the selection process. The study by Arvey and his co-workers (1976), which focuses on the implications of "time lags" between stages in the selection process, is a particularly relevant example.

REFERENCES

Burack, Elmer H., and Robert D. Smith. *Personnel Management*. St. Paul, Minn.: West Publishing Co. 1977.

Gibbons, Thomas T., and Leonard Rivlin. "A Model for Manpower Utilization," *Industrial Engineering*, 8, 8 (August 1976), 27–29.

Hall, Francine, and Maryann H. Albrecht. *The Management of Affirmative Action*, Palisades, Calif.: Goodyear Publishing Company, 1979.

Menne, J. W., et al. "Systems Approach to the Content Validation of Employee Selection Procedures," *Public Personnel Management*, 5 (November 1976), 387–396.

COMMENTS ON THE STATE OF THE ART

Although the consensus regarding the present state of the selection process is not overly optimistic, it does seem that we can distinguish some areas of progress.[1] So far as the application blank or bio-data are concerned, legislation may well portend a further decline in interest in these techniques. However, the applicability of bio-data for multinationals may stimulate further studies done across national boundaries.

Testing, as with the application blank, may well continue to be a less critical component of the selection process because of the complications created by legislation. These trends will probably place a greater emphasis and burden on the interview as a basis for selection. Although there continue to be difficulties with the interview, it also seems that we are developing a better understanding of the problems with the interview and have developed at least a partial technology for improving the interviewing process. The problem in the near future may well be not that of lack of knowledge, but the implementation of that knowledge for improving the interview as a selection technique. There also seems to be understanding of how to improve the validity of the reference check, some optimism for the application of the health questionnaire, as well as increasing emphasis on a systems approach to selection.

However, it seems clear that there remains a considerable amount of work to be done on each of the steps of the selection process. In any case, it is probably preferable to pool the contributions of each of these techniques in attempting to assess an applicant rather than to view each technique in isolation.

Notes

[1] Because of constraints on article length, we do not pretend to cover all or even most of the complexities of the recruitment and selection process. However, we have attempted to provide an overview of the state of the art. In so doing, we have found the works of Bray and Moses, Ash and Krocker, and Miner of particular value. Each of these works has been cited at least once in the reference sections. The best and most current sources of information on the legal aspects of personnel, written in laymen's terminology, are the following three reporting services. The authors are especially indebted to the Prentice-Hall service from which much of the material on the legal aspects of selection is taken:

Personnel Management: Policies and Practices. Englewood Cliffs, N.J.: Prentice-Hall, Inc., 1977.
Labor Relations Reporter. Washington, D.C.: Bureau of National Affairs, 1977.
Labor Law Reporter. Chicago, Ill.: Commerce Clearing House, 1977.

Improving Human Resource Effectiveness Through Assessment Center Technology: Emergence, Design, Application and Evaluation

Cabot L. Jaffee and Stephen L. Cohen

DEVELOPMENT AND OPERATION OF ASSESSMENT CENTERS

Background

The term assessment, as normally understood in psychology, involves testing and drawing conclusions about the characteristics, traits, or skills of individuals. Assessment centers are not, as the name implies, places where test batteries are

Cabot L. Jaffee and Stephen L. Cohen, "Improving Human Resource Effectiveness Through Assessment Center Technology: Emergence, Design, Application and Evaluation." Copyright © 1978 by Assessment Designs, Inc.

administered, but rather a composite of *techniques* used in applicant selection. The first assessment center in the United States was set up by the Office of Strategic Services (OSS) to evaluate candidates for overseas assignments as agents (Assessment of Men, 1948). In this particular center, a variety of assessment techniques was used, including personality tests, tests of intellectual functioning, and—what has now become the heart of the modern assessment center process—situational tests. Even more important perhaps for the history of the assessment process was the methodology applied by the OSS to arrive at judgments of an individual's capabilities. OSS strategy included the techniques of job analysis, identification of critical determinants of success and failure, development of a specific rating scale for each critical characteristic, design of measures to assess the characteristics, and use of observers to evaluate the candidate for the particular position. Thus the OSS's definition of a methodology for the evaluation process as well as its use of situational tests constituted the beginning of present-day assessment centers.

The OSS assessment center grew out of the efforts of the German and British war boards during the First and Second World Wars. At the end of World War II, the assessment process came into question because of the inability of practitioners to establish validity data to justify its large expense. Although a majority of the participants felt that the process was indeed worthwhile in evaluating patterns of behavior, criteria were lacking by which to compare assessment information.

In 1956, the American Telephone and Telegraph Company began what was to become a milestone in organizational research as well as the major contribution to the development of the present-day assessment center process. Its "Management Progress Study" was an attempt to follow the careers of some 400 young supervisors in a number of Bell System operating companies. One of the techniques utilized in this study was an assessment center in which all individuals participated in a number of simulation exercises as well as personality, interest, and intelligence tests administered by a group of professionally trained staff members. The goal of the study was to follow the progress of these young people over an eight-year period. Long before the results of the study were evaluated, Michigan Bell began the first operational assessment center in 1958. These early centers differed from the "Management Progress Study" centers in two distinct ways: First, their purpose was to select from hourly rank those individuals who might be successful at first-line supervisory positions, and second, the assessors were not trained professionals, but rather line managers. In the period between 1958 and 1965, some 14 Bell operating companies were running about 50 centers for both men and women assessing 6,000 candidates yearly (Jaffee, 1965).

In addition to the Bell System activities, General Electric developed an assessment center for high-potential management personnel in which an emphasis on feedback, developmental recommendations and career planning became an integral, formal aspect of the assessment process. During this same period, AT&T developed a program for the assessment of sales personnel and middle management personnel within the Bell System. Besides the very positive reactions to assessment centers by the large number of managers who served as assessors, the 1958–65 period saw the compilation of a good deal of statistical data for the validity of the process. The statistical support for assessment centers will be discussed in more detail in a later section.

Growth of Assessment Centers

The growth of assessment center technology during the last 20 years has been astonishing. As recently as 1970, there were perhaps 100 in use. By 1975 there were probably 400 assessment centers being employed and by 1980, it is expected that 1000 or more will be employed.° Another aspect of this remarkable growth is a shift in usage from selection to career development techniques. By 1980, probably half of all the applications will involve development, career planning, performance appraisal, or "non-selection" uses.

To say the least, the assessment center concept has endured and is currently thriving. While a number of personnel methods have surfaced over the years, few have stood the test of time as well as the assessment center. Its success probably stems in part from the fact that extensive evaluation has been conducted on the method and its results have been overwhelmingly favorable. This is not to say that improvements in the process are unnecessary, or that the assessment center provides the panacea for all personnel-related problems. Indeed, there are several areas of concern regarding the process and the research that has been conducted to substantiate it. In general, however, the results are very positive and, when compared with those for other similarly used methods, are even more favorable.

Assessment Centers vs. Performance Appraisal

One of the reasons for the successful emergence of the assessment center process has been the inadequacy of traditional performance appraisals to accurately reflect a person's ability to perform. If traditional appraisals of management potential were valid, there would be little need for assessment center evaluations. It is not our purpose to enumerate the myriad reasons that performance appraisals have demonstrated less than adequate success in organizations. However, it is important to keep in mind the major differences between assessment center and typical management appraisals since their differences in format and process provide a clue as to why assessment centers succeed and, thus, how they can be improved. Table 1 summarizes the basis for the differences in the two processes.

These differences reflect divergent approaches to assessing work performance and generalizing it to future performance.

Description and Logic of Assessment Centers

Assessment centers are more than anything a methodology rather than a place. As a methodology, they are based on the application of scientific principles to selection and training programs. The major impetus behind the use of

°Various figures have been cited concerning the number of organizations currently using the assessment center process. These numbers have been as high as 2000. Numbers this high appear to be considerably inflated as they are typically derived from sales of exercises. These sales, from our research, far outweigh actual assessment center use. Simply using a simulation exercise does not by itself indicate an organization is using an assessment center.

TABLE 1 Comparisons of the Bases for Assessment Center Evaluations and Traditional Management Appraisals

Assessment Center Evaluations	Traditional Management Appraisals
Systematic analyses of the job performance requirements and agreement on the specific skills needed to execute them effectively.	Generalized skills for all jobs which are frequently unrelated to performance for a specific job.
Evaluation of multiple performance situations, each of which simulates a critical aspect of the target and job position.	Evaluation of situations of performance on the current job, not on a targeted or higher level position.
Evaluation of future potential typically.	Evaluation of past and/or current performance typically.
Temporally close evaluations of performance in the simulated situations which are designed to resemble a representative cross section of the job's activities over time.	Reliance on memory or recall of performance in relevant job situations that might have occurred months or even years prior to the time of the appraisal.
Multiple appraisers or evaluators.	Single appraiser or evaluator—the boss.
Evaluator agreement on the standards of performance in the simulated situations.	Varying performance standards based on the individual evaluator's frame of reference.
Relatively objective evaluation of behavioral evidence of performance.	Relatively subjective evaluation of evidence of job performance.
Systematic and consistent observation procedures conducted by the evaluator.	Unsystematic and arbitrary observation procedures conducted by the evaluator.
Consensus agreement by the evaluators on the quality of performance observed.	Individual evaluation of the performance quality observed (no call for consensus).

assessment centers came about as a result of fair employment practices legislation and the consequent enforcement guidelines developed by the Equal Employment Opportunity Commission (EEOC) and the Office of Federal Contract Compliance (OFCC). Many companies decided to forego testing because the government placed the burden of proof on the employer to establish that the selection practices do not discriminate. In many cases, the proof rests on a relationship between some sort of an initial judgment based on evaluation instruments and some later performance measure.

Preliminary Analysis. Let us use as an example procedures which might be used in the selection of first-line supervisors, a common selection problem for many organizations. The first task would be to establish a list of critical skills necessary for success on the job.

The following listing contains a number of skills which have been suggested as important for the "effective" supervisor in a variety of different organizations:

1. Leadership
2. Decision making
3. Communication skills
   a. Oral
   b. Written
4. Perception
5. Organizing and planning
6. Resistance to stress
7. Self-confidence
8. Courage
9. Honesty

Briefly, look at this list and assume it covers adequately the requisite skills. Now try to define briefly skill numbers 5, 7, and 8.

Your definition of self-confidence as a skill probably had to do with a person's perception of his or her worth, or with the confidence that a person would have in his/her own ability. We submit that a defintion for a skill which implies congruency or lack thereof between an internal state and something else is of no value for our purposes. In other words, since the phenomenon is not observable, it can be of little practical use because no one can establish what is going on inside another person except that person him/herself.

The first characteristic of a skill, then, is that it be *observable*. If it cannot be seen or heard, then it cannot be the basis for a selection system, be it manager, husband or wife, or personnel trainer.

The second characteristic of a skill is that its definition be *relevant to the situation* to which you wish to predict. In other words, there is a problem with the definition of courage as "the willingness to go into an arena with lions." Obviously, this is a directly observable event since all one needs is a large field surrounded by a high fence and a timer to count how long it takes an individual to enter the arena. The problem with this situation is that it is not a relevant definition of the skill for a business environment, which is the environment to which you wish to predict.

The third characteristic of any selection system skill definition is that it be *quantifiable*. We must be able to determine *how much* of a particular quality or skill one has in order to be able to differentiate between individuals. There are very few qualities which are all or none in degree. The ones we typically deal with exist as degrees of a quality along a continuum. For example, someone is not likely to be purely honest or dishonest, but rather honest some of the time and under certain conditions and dishonest perhaps under others.

In summary then, if one is working with a selection system, the skills, traits, characteristics, or dimensions should be *observable, relevant to the situation*, and *quantifiable*. Unless those three criteria are met, the selection system cannot work and the proper individuals for the management position or any other will not be selected.

Alternatives in Predicting Success. The purpose of a job analysis is to determine the tasks and skills necessary for success. One must also look at the alternative ways of predicting success. Let's consider an analogy involving the owners of a professional basketball team. If you own a professional basketball team, one of the tasks you have each year is drafting basketball players from high school or college for your team. What would you use to make the judgment as to whether you would draft a player from among the alternatives given in Figure 1?

Those of you who suggested the tryout probably did so because you felt it most closely resembled the situation to which you wanted to predict. On the other hand, those of you who felt the scouting report of previous experience would be the better approach probably felt that the longer you could observe someone in a situation which resembles the one to which you wish to predict, the better your predictions will be. Those are the two critical features of a selection program.

Now as you look at the continuum, you realize that everything to the bottom of the "tryout" is inferior as a success predictor. Previous experience as indicated by college statistics would not likely be as accurate a predictor for future success as a professional basketball player as would the tryout. Focus for a moment now on the prediction of success as a manager as depicted in Figure 2. It seems to us that much of the rationale which existed for the basketball player is true in the case of the manager.

For example, intelligence tests asking questions such as "apples are to oranges as pears are to bananas, cherries, or plums" is not a question which comes up very often in most managerial jobs. As such then, the knowledge of these questions would at best be one step removed from a job-related skill or bit of information. There is probably no question that it is better to be "intelligent" than "not intelligent" no matter what you do. However, the critical question becomes the definition of intelligence in the form of "apples are to oranges" versus the skills of decision making or organizing and planning which also utilize intelligence. Obviously the latter definitions are more relevant to the world to which we are interested in predicting.

Consider personality tests or interest tests. To use the answer to the question, "Would you rather be at home reading a book, or at a party mixing with people?" to predict the number of rebounds a basketball player would get, in spite of the

356   Improving Human Resource Effectiveness

fact that it may be one definition of aggressiveness, would be ludicrous. The same problems appear to be true in the case of a manager. To have candidates look at an ink blot and ask them what they see and reject or accept them for a particular position on the basis of their response is looking for symbolic responses as opposed to tangible signs of a person's behavior based on relevant aspects of what they have done.

There are obvious problems associated with the use of tests of personality or intelligence for selection. When one considers previous behavior, critical issues emerge. For example, in the case of an hourly or nonmanagement person moving to a management position, the previous experience is likely to be nonrelevant. In

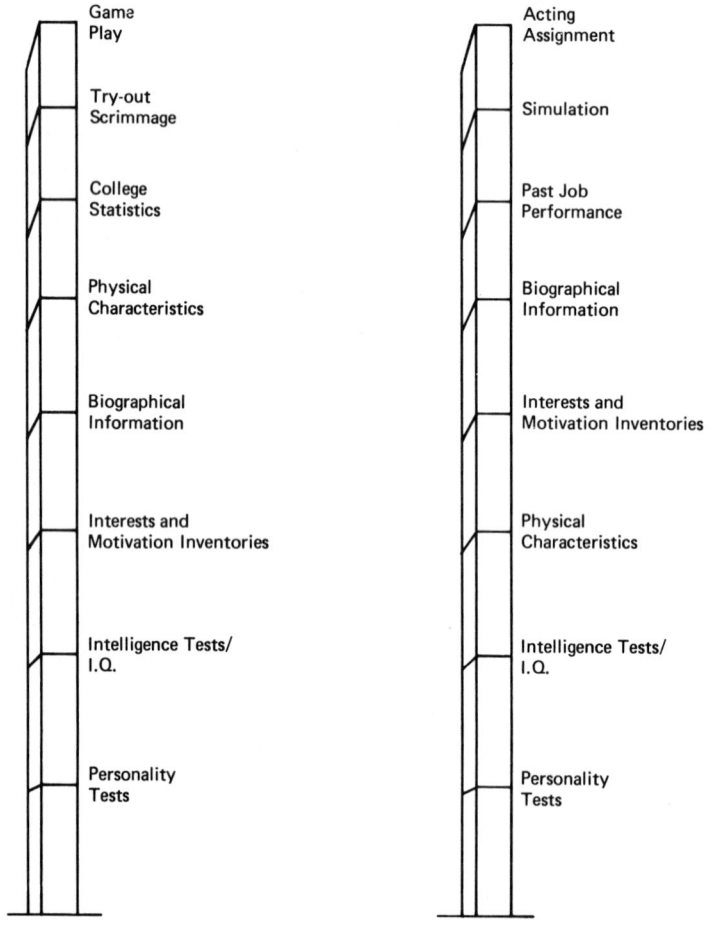

Game Play	Acting Assignment
Try-out Scrimmage	Simulation
College Statistics	Past Job Performance
Physical Characteristics	Biographical Information
Biographical Information	Interests and Motivation Inventories
Interests and Motivation Inventories	Physical Characteristics
Intelligence Tests/ I.Q.	Intelligence Tests/ I.Q.
Personality Tests	Personality Tests

FIGURE 1 *Methods Available to Assess the Skills of a Pro Basketball Player*

FIGURE 2 *Methods Available to Assess the Skills of a Manager*

addition, because performance reviews are generally the definition of past performance and many performance review systems are poor, these often cannot be used as effective predictors. Furthermore, in many performance review systems, everyone is in the top two categories—whatever these are—and it becomes difficult to differentiate between individuals based on this information.

The ultimate predictor, however, using actual acting assignments extensively, may prove impractical. An acting assignment is in many ways roughly analogous to selecting jet pilots and telling him/her to taxi down to the end of the runway, get it up in the air, turn it around, land it, and meet in the hangar. Everyone who arrives at the hangar may know how to fly a jet plane, but the cost of the system may be a bit heavy. In the case of the basketball player given a tryout and cut from the squad, he or she goes home. In addition, in an organization, a good deal of psychological as well as practical problems arise from individuals staying in an acting assignment for a long enough period to have an adequate tryout and yet still providing an opportunity for large numbers of applicants to apply for the position. At times, in specific situations, this system may work, but it certainly does not lend itself to large-scale selection systems which are fair for all concerned employees. A reasonable solution to the problem is simulation, the underlying foundation on which an assessment center is developed.

Assessment Center Testing

Managerial Selection. A good deal of recent literature has attested to the rising use of the assessment center process for management selection and more and more companies every day are beginning to use simulations of the managerial job to predict success as a manager (Rice, 1978; Jaffee and Frank, 1976; Moses and Byham, 1978; McConnell and Parker, 1972; Bray, 1976). One of the interesting findings emerging from some of the studies has been the assessment center's ability to predict success at the second level of management with greater accuracy than success at the first level (Campbell and Bray, 1967; Kraut and Scott, 1972). One reason for this may be quite obviously the greater overlap between the assessment center exercises and what is demanded of an individual at the second level of management. Indeed, two unfortunate and potentially dangerous by-products of all the recent assessment center activity have been the development of off-the-shelf exercises and/or packages that organizations use to judge supervisory potential across various organizations, and the continued reliance on the *original* AT&T design as a model for the development of exercises. Both these directions are fraught with many of the same dangers as the original aptitude testing programs in that a situational exercise designed for one environment will not necessarily predict in another because it is not an adequate simulation of that new environment. It is not sufficient to merely consider *organizing and planning* as a critical skill for a supervisor and use an in-basket exercise to measure it. Organizing and planning demands in one setting may be quite different from the demands in another, in spite of the fact that the best label for both classes of behavior might be organizing and planning. This says something important for the use and design of assessment center programs. More than anything, time and effort must be spent on adequately defining the critical skills and how they are represented behaviorally in a particular organization, as well as designing the best means of observing their presence or absence. All in-baskets are not the same, nor are all business games or leaderless group discussions identical. If this is the case, they cannot all represent the real environment equally well. Much of the remaining variance predicting job success (after the simulation exercises and the pencil-and-paper tests have made their contributions) may well be due to the inadequate sampling of the situational factors rather than to an indictment of simulation in selection.

Minority Selection Issues. Assessment centers have been around for a time and used so that their rationale and experiences have been well documented. One issue for which they have relevance is in the area of minority testing.

Many psychologists have compiled considerable evidence to indicate that job performance is an extremely complex concept and obviously, one that must be dealt with before selection problems can be handled directly. A good deal of the research effort of industrial psychologists has concerned an examination of the questions of test fairness in relation to minority group employment. The fact that attempts to utilize culture-fair tests have not been successful (Bray and Moses, 1972) has made the problem an even more complex one. This seems to suggest that early deprivation in certain critical areas may leave individuals less likely to successfully cope with all our present methods of testing. Another very important issue which cannot be explored at this point because of the problems of criterion measurement is whether or not this early deprivation may decrease the likelihood of certain individuals being successful on the job.

Two alternatives for coping with the prediction problem and minority group testing issues have been suggested. The first of these is the use of moderator variables whereby different groups of people are categorized on a number of possible dimensions, for example, moderators, with race being only one category. Certainly the results of studies in this area have shown some promise. The second direction, however, and the one that appears to have a greater likelihood of providing some reasonable, practical alternatives to many of these prediction problems may be in the use of *samples* of behavior rather than prediction of some set of criteria (Wernimont and Campbell, 1968). In other words, the greater the overlap between the testing situation and the measure of success, the more likely the test will have predictive value. As Cooper and Sobol (1969) aptly put it, "a typist must know how to type and a welder to weld." Tests falling into this category have not presented problems relevant to discrimination in employment because of the obvious parallel between the testing and job situations. Aptitude tests find themselves, in many cases, at the other end of the continuum in that they are asking for responses that overlap very little with subsequent job performance. They (Cooper and Sobol, 1969) go on to say:

> It is sometimes argued that standardized intelligence tests are inherently related to business needs on the grounds that every employer is entitled to prefer more intelligent employees. Similarly, mechanical comprehension tests are sometimes thought of as related to business needs in any industrial situation where machinery is used. This notion misconceives the function of tests.

The responses called for on such tests may not be at all related to an ability to perform on the job in spite of the fact that both behaviors could be definable as intelligence under certain conditions. These types of statements, although not intended as a comment on managerial selection, nevertheless become quite relevant to a number of problems in the use of assessment centers for prediction of supervisory success.

Assessment Centers: Assumptions, Structure, Approach

Assumptions. Let us look for a moment now at the basic makeup of an assessment center.

The following points are of critical importance:

No skill or trait that cannot be defined by observables can be of value in assessing an individual's ability or aptitude.

Nonwork-related behaviors are of no value in assessing an individual's ability for on-job work.

Exercises that do not demand work-oriented behaviors are of no value in determining an individual's ability to perform that work.

It is unfair and invalid to observe and evaluate individuals in situations other than those specific exercises designed to tap the skills required for effective on-job performance.

Reports on the performance of individuals must contain relevant behaviors as their basis rather than conclusions of evaluators relative to inner traits.

All behavior described should consider what the person does at the assessment center only.

Structure. To be considered as an assessment center, the following minimal requirements established by the Task Force on Assessment Center Standards (*Standards*, 1978) must be met:

1. Multiple assessment techniques must be used. At least one of these techniques must be a simulation.

   A simulation is an exercise or technique designed to elicit behaviors related to dimensions or performance on the job by requiring the participant to respond behaviorally to situational stimuli. The stimuli present in a simulation parallel or resemble stimuli in the work situation. Examples of simulations include group exercises, in-basket exercises, and fact finding exercises.

2. Multiple assessors must be used. These assessors must receive training prior to participating in a center.

3. Judgments resulting in an outcome (that is, recommendation for promotion, specific training, or development) must be based on pooling information from assessors and techniques.

4. An overall evaluation of behavior must be made by the assessors at a separate time from observation of behavior.
5. Simulation exercises must be used. These exercises are developed to tap a variety of predetermined behaviors and should be pretested prior to use to insure that the techniques provide reliable, objective, and relevant behavior information for the organization in question.
6. The dimensions, attributes, or qualities evaluated by the assessment center are determined by an analysis of relevant job behaviors.
7. The techniques used in the assessment center are designed to provide information which is used in evaluating the dimensions, attributes, or qualities previously determined.

In summary, an assessment center consists of a standardized evaluation of behavior based on multiple inputs. Multiple trained observers and techniques are used. Judgments about behavior are made, in part, from specially developed assessment simulations.

The judgements are pooled by the assessors at an evaluation meeting during which all relevant assessment data are reported and discussed, and the assessors agree on the evaluation of the dimensions and any overall evaluation that is made.

Approach. The following steps of the assessment center process highlight the major activities involved:

1. Needs analysis
2. Job position(s) analysis
3. Skill identification and definition
4. Simulation development
5. Assessor/observer training
6. Assessee/candidate observation and evaluation
7. Final report writing
8. Feedback to assessee and/or organization
9. Post-assessment center development (for example, skill workshops, job rotation, specialized instructions, management training)

Note that the preliminary steps (1, 2, and 3) serve as the foundation for any assessment center and therefore must be accomplished prior to undertaking the actual activities of the center (steps 4 through 8).

Assessment centers are attempts to gather work samples and other relevant data which might predict managerial success. At these centers, trained managers, psychologists, or staff people observe a group of candidates for either an immediate position or some future situation. The group of candidates goes through a series of especially designed exercises and/or tests and then the assessors make judgments as to the candidates' strengths and weaknesses on a series of predetermined skills or traits. The assessors observe and draw conclusions on each candidate's strengths and weaknesses separately and then attempt to combine data, resolve differences, and generate a comprehensive review of the candidate. This information is usually communicated to the individual as well as to the organization for selection decisions and/or developmental suggestions. Assessment centers have utilized paper-

and-pencil tests, interviews, projective tests, and self-ratings, in addition to simulations (or situational tests).

Paper-and-pencil tests have been used to evaluate general intelligence, reading speed and comprehension, interests, attitudes, and knowledge of current affairs. In some cases, the scores on these instruments have contributed to ratings on skills or variables specifically defined as these test scores, such as academic aptitude or reading ability. In other cases, they have contributed along with other types of instruments to some more general skill or overall composite rating.

Interviews have been used at various stages of the assessment process. The personal interview attempts to evaluate some of the work-related interests and background of an assessment center candidate while the in-basket interview is used to determine the reasons why certain decisions were made in that particular exercise. In the case of personal interviews, the results and judgments made by an evaluator contribute to ratings on a number of different skills.

Projective tests attempt to look at some of the underlying values and motivations of an individual as they might relate to the world of work. Whenever they are used, they are administered by trained professionals and typically, they are not a part of most operational assessment centers. In fact, their only use to date has been in the middle or high level managerial centers.

Peer and self-ratings are gathered at many assessment centers at the conclusion of group exercises in order to evaluate either an individual's perception of his/her environment or his/her self-objectivity.

Simulation instruments are the heart of the assessment center process. In-basket exercises, group discussion problems, and business games or problem analysis exercises are all attempts to take a particular nonmanagerial, supervisory, or managerial job and create an exercise that calls for skills similar to those skills demanded by the particular position. It is the simulation instruments that provide one of the unique features of the assessment center.

Assessors are, for the most part, managers one or two levels above the target position. The basic criteria for the position of assessor have been familiarity with the position in question, a successful career as a manager, and possessing skills much like the ones on which the candidates are to be evaluated. Staff people from within the organization as well as outside psychologists are also involved in many programs. Training time for assessors should range from three days to three weeks and time spent on assessment assignment will vary from one week to one year in duration.

The foregoing section provided an overview of the critical elements in the emergence and development and maintenance of assessment center technology. The next section will describe some of the evaluation of the assessment center process that has taken place and some key research issues that require clarification.

RESEARCH, VALIDITY, AND EVALUATION OF ASSESSMENT CENTER ACTIVITIES

Historically, the assessment center process has been subjected to considerable research and evaluation. The impetus and model for subsequent efforts were provided by the inaugural program at AT&T in 1956. Armed with a sizable and dedicated research team, AT&T has set an example for the type of research that is needed. The call for research, however, was not based merely on the presence of human resources with research skill. It was based on the very pragmatic realization that the purpose of evaluating a person's potential better was ultimately to select and place people in jobs they could most effectively perform. As such, some type of evaluation was necessary to determine the accuracy of the evaluations (or assessments) in predicting the realization of that potential. While assessment center proponents try to avoid the use of the word "test" in describing the assessment situation, the techniques used to validate the assessment center process are typically the same as those used for the more traditional paper-and-pencil tests. Because assessment centers were originally used to identify an individual's management potential, for ultimate selection purposes, it should not be surprising that evaluation research was conducted, as has been the case with most testing programs, to verify the predictions made.

A rough estimate indicates that over 50 definitive research studies, over 50 descriptions and commentaries, nearly ten research review articles/reports, and about seven books have been published specifically about the assessment center process. This does not include the countless number of internal organization reports and unpublished studies. In total, there are probably over 150 different treatments written about the assessment center process—and all approximately in the last 15 years. Close to one half of these treatments have appeared within the last five years.°

While support for the assessment center process has been strong, there are still a number of research issues that warrant discussion. The issues that will be discussed here will help to clarify assessment center results. They include the statistical analysis techniques used in evaluating and interpreting results; the role of content validity in evaluating results; equal opportunity and fairness; reliability versus validity; and the use of return-on-investment computations in determining the worth of a program.

Two types of statistical analyses are usually employed in evaluating assessment center predictions. They both involve the same approach but differ on how the results are presented. The approach involves relating one set of scores with another, typically assessment center performance ratings with those based on job performance. This is the correlational technique that is based on the inference that if the effective or ineffective behavior required of and evaluated by one set of measures (assessment center exercises) is similar to that required of another set of measures (on-job tasks), the two sets of measures are associated or related to each other. In terms of assessment center results, a high positive relationship will be obtained when candidates who do well or poorly in the assessment center also do well or poorly, respectively, on their jobs. If candidates who perform well in the assessment center perform poorly on their jobs and vice versa, the correlation will be strong but in the opposite (or negative) direction from what would be desired. Finally, if little or no discernible pattern between performance in the assessment center and that on the job is found, the correlation would be negligible or near zero. The

° Evidence of the emphasis upon research was further highlighted with the emergence of the *Journal of Assessment Center Technology* in 1978, the only journal devoted entirely to the practice, issues, and research of the assessment center.

results of the correlational approach can be presented in terms of *correlation coefficients* or *expectancy tables*. Assessment center research related to each is presented below.

The Correlation Coefficient

Interpretation. The interpretation of correlation coefficients is not always an easy chore. Two interpretations can be made—one statistical and one practical. The statistical interpretation is based on probability theory: A relationship is statistically significant if it is due to factors other than those associated with chance or luck. A statistically significant correlation obtained between assessment center and job performance ratings would imply that similar types of traits were evaluated in each situation and that indeed the likelihood that a person would perform either effectively or ineffectively on the job was related to the likelihood of that performance in the assessment center.

Statistical significance also takes into account the number of sets of scores that are related such that a certain minimal number of relationships must be obtained in order for significance to occur. The absence of significance might then be due to the fact that enough people weren't evaluated to conclude confidently that the relationship was due to anything other than just a mere coincidence.

The result is that large numbers of candidates are required to obtain statistically significant results. Yet nonsignificant results with small numbers of candidates do not necessarily mean that an assessment program is invalid. On the other hand, statistically significant correlational results do not always mean practical utility of those results. Mathematically the relationship may be significant, but pragmatically it may explain very little. For example, a correlation of .20 (low positive) may be statistically significant because it is based on over 100 sets of scores (candidates). But, it may explain very little about the relationship and therefore, be *insignificant* from a practical standpoint. A correlation coefficient can only tell us the degree to which two or more sets of scores are related. If the correlation is 1.00, we know that the relationship between the two sets of scores is totally (or 100 percent) due to the fact that the same trait(s) is (are) being evaluated by each of the two measures. A correlation of .20, significant or not, indicates that relatively little of the relationship between the two measures is due to the similarity of traits evaluated on each measure. In fact, only 4 percent (calculated by squaring the correlation coefficient) of the relationship is due to the measurement of the same or similar traits. That leaves some 96 percent of the relationship between the two measures unaccounted for. This tells us that there is considerably more to explain about the relationship between the two measures that can be left to the things they measure in common. As such, this correlation has little practical value to us. If the .20 correlation characterized the relationship between assessment center results and subsequent on-job performance, we might question the utility of the former. This doesn't suggest that the assessment center process should be automatically discontinued, but simply that there is quite a lot about on-job performance that could not be explained by assessment center performance. Indeed, it has been shown that when other measures are combined to the assessment center results, the composite accounts for overall better prediction (Wollowick and McNamara, 1969).

Despite these problems with interpreting correlations, the correlation coefficients obtained in the research on assessment centers have generally been very strong. In almost all cases, the correlations are in the positive direction. Out of 23 studies reviewed by one author, only one was found with a negative correlation. Furthermore, 22 of the studies showed the assessment center process to be more effective than other approaches; none showed it less effective. Correlations between assessment center predictions and various on-job performance measures ranged as high as .64 (Byham, 1970). Another review study of 18 research studies on the assessment center approach, showed it to be consistently related to a variety of job criteria. These correlations averaged .40 when a number of promotions beyond the candidate's level was used as the criterion and .63 when manager's ratings of the candidate's promotion potential was used (Cohen, Moses, and Byham, 1974).

Results: The Management Progress Study. The most significant research to date on the assessment center approach has been carried out by AT&T. In the now classic "Management Progress Study," beginning in 1956, over 400 candidates including college and noncollege employees, were assessed (Bray and Grant, 1966). These assessment center ratings were not revealed for eight years at which time the original candidates were tracked for their job progress. The correlations obtained for the relationship of assessment center predictions and level of management research were .44 for the college group and .71 for the non-college group, both statistically significant. Correlations were also obtained between assessment center ratings and salary increments for over 200 of the candidates. These ranged from .39 to .52, all significant, for four different groups.

In another AT&T study, nearly 6000 individuals who were assessed were followed up to determine the relationship between their assessment center ratings and advancement beyond first-level management. The correlation obtained was .44, which was strongly significant (Moses, 1973).

Results: Other Studies. International Business Machines (IBM) and Standard Oil of Ohio (SOHIO) have also researched their ongoing assessment centers over the years. For a total of 12 different groups and various jobs within IBM, correlation results between assessment center ratings and job position level ranged from .29 to .63, 75 percent of which were significant (Wollowick and McNamara, 1969). For the SOHIO assessment center, the results were even stronger using supervisors' ratings of candidate potential as the criteria. Four different studies indicated that these correlations ranged from .63 to .65, which were very significant and highly consistent. (Finley, 1970; Thompson, 1970).

Other organizations have also reported significant relationships between assessment center ratings and a variety of job performance or progress criteria (Bentz, 1971; Meyer, 1972). It appears that in general, the assessment center approach has demonstrated good ability to predict subsequent job progress.

Expectancy Tables and Validity of Results

Even though these results are consistent, positive, and generally significant, the correlation coefficient is still not always easy to interpret. An alternative means of presenting correlational data is the use of expectancy tables. These tables couch results in terms of percentage of individuals in particular classifications. While they are more general in nature, they give a clearer view of results and are more readily interpretable. Categories of predictions make up the vertical side of the table and categories of outcomes the horizontal side. The data making up the cross-cells in the table would be percentages or hit rates. For example, of those predicted to achieve a certain success level, a certain percentage will (hits), and the remainder won't (misses). These percentages can be compared with what might be expected by chance alone with interpretations of the success of the predictions taken from these percentages. A perfect, positive relationship could be explained if predictions were 100 percent accurate. Furthermore, the actual percentages obtained from the predictions could be compared with those that might be expected to occur as a function of normal progress within an organization. This will help to isolate just how much better prediction is with the assessment center method than other methods, or no method at all. While the expectancy table analysis is less precise, it does give a more readily interpretable set of data. The raw percentages can be also analyzed for statistical significance that indicates the extent to which the obtained percentages deviate from what might be expected by chance factors alone. The direction of the deviation from the expected percentages will illustrate whether the predictions favorably or unfavorably compare.

In reviewing assessment center research, a number of studies also have presented their results in terms of expectancy tables. Evidence for the validity of the assessment center process is even more dramatic when these data are presented in this form and they are much more interpretable. For example, Table 2 illustrates the results of the AT&T "Management Progress Study," noted

TABLE 2 Relationship Between AT&T Assessment Center Predictions and Management Level Achieved

	Managment Level Achieved After Eight Years			
Assessement Center Prediction	No. of Assessees	1st Level Mgmt.	2nd Level Mgmt.	Middle Level Mgmt. or Above
College Hires				
Middle Mgmt. Predicted	62	1 (2%)	3 (50%)	30 (48%)
Middle Mgmt. Not Predicted	63	7 (11%)	49 (78%)	7 (11%)
Non-College Supervisors				
Middle Mgmt. Predicted	41	3 (7%)	25 (61%)	13 (32%)
Middle Mgmt. Not Predicted	103	62 (60%)	36 (35%)	5 (5%)

Adapted from Bray and Grant (1966)

earlier (Bray and Grant, 1966). It shows the numbers and corresponding percentages of those candidates' progress eight years after they were assessed.

The advantage of such a table is that several interpretations can be made. One way to look at the results is to determine the relationship between the percent of candidates rated likely to reach or not reach middle management, with the percent that actually did or did not reach that level. For college hires, 48 percent of those predicted to make middle management in fact did, whereas only 11 percent of those *not* predicted to make this level actually did. For the noncollege supervisor sample, these figures are 32 and 5 percent, respectively. Another way to interpret these data is the following: Of the 37 college hire candidates who made middle management or above, 81 percent (30 of 37) were correctly classified. Of the 18 noncollege candidates, 72 percent (13 of 18) were identified correctly. On the other hand, of the 73 candidates in the total group who had not advanced beyond the first level of management, 95 percent (69 of 73) were identified accurately. Regardless of the way the results are interpreted, they provide very impressive support for the assessment center process.

Another illustration of the utility of data presented in this fashion can be seen by reference to Table 3. This table shows the classification data for the previously cited AT&T study with nearly 6000 candidates (Moses, 1973).

It was indicated earlier that a significant correlation of .44 was obtained between assessment center ratings and management progress. Table 3 indicates that candidates evaluated as "more than acceptable" were twice as likely to be promoted two or more times than candidates evaluated as "acceptable." Once again, the data give clear support to the assessment center's ability to provide relatively accurate evaluations of potential managerial progress.

Two Additional Statistical Studies. One of the IBM studies, not reported earlier, also used an expectancy table approach to reviewing its assessment center results (Kraut and Scott, 1972). Table 4 shows the data obtained from that study. The careers of candidates who were assessed and who were subsequently promoted to first-line management were followed. The assessment indicated the degree of management potential for each candidate. The criterion was the incidence of a second promotion. As can be seen from the table, 66 percent of those evaluated as having higher or executive management potential were, in fact, promoted a second time, whereas only 19 percent of those evaluated in the lower two potential categories actually were promoted again.

Results with Sales Personnel. One final table shows that such positive results have also been obtained with nonmanagement candidates, namely sales people. Table 5 reports on their acceptability for sales employment (Bray and Campbell, 1968). Six months later, after sales training had been completed, they were all evaluated by a team of specially trained sales managers to determine whether or not they met standards of sales performance. Incidentally, the team of evaluators had no knowledge of the assessment center ratings. The data show that a substantial difference existed in the percent of assessees meeting review standards as a function of their assessment ratings. Almost three fourths (28 of 41) of those evaluated in the highest two categories met review standards, while only one quarter assessed in the lowest two categories met those same standards.

TABLE 3 Relationship Between Assessment Center Rating and Progress in Management

Assessment Rating	Number of Assessees	No. Receiving Two or More Promotions	Percent Receiving Two or More Promotions
More Than Acceptable	410	166	40.5
Acceptable	1,466	321	21.9
Questionable	1,910	220	11.5
Not Acceptable	2,157	91	4.2
Totals	5,943	798	13.4

Adapted from Moses (1973)

TABLE 4 Relationship Between Assessment Center Potential Ratings and Second Promotions for First-Line Managers

Assessment Potential	Number of Assessees	Number Promoted a Second Time	Percent Promoted a Second Time
Executive management	41	14	34
Higher management	85	27	32
Second-line management	110	30	27
First-line management	88	11	12
Remain nonmanagement	71	5	7
Totals	395	87	22

Adapted from Kraut and Scott (1972)

TABLE 5 Relationship Between Assessment Center Ratings and Subsequent On-Job Sales Performance

Assessment Rating	Number of Assessees	Number Meeting Review Standards	Percent Meeting Review Standards
More Than Acceptable	9	9	100
Acceptable	32	19	60
Questionable	16	7	44
Not Acceptable	21	2	10
Totals	78	37	47

Adapted from Bray and Campbell (1968)

While the results of these studies are impressive, one caution about data presented in the expectancy table form is in order. The percentages themselves can only provide a readily readable overview of the success of the program to predict subsequent performance. Except in certain obvious cases in which the hit and miss rates are clearly different, in order for the data to be utilized appropriately, statistical analyses should be performed. These analyses will provide a firmer foundation for placing confidence in the assessment center's ability to evaluate potential job performance. Incidentally, all the tabular data just presented were found to be statistically significant when subjected to the appropriate analyses. Decisions to expand the assessment center program can be better justified with this information. It should be kept in mind, however, that a decision to use an assessment center does not have to rely solely on its ability to predict significantly subsequent job performance. Such a decision may be made tentatively because the assessment center predictions are far better (significantly) than any other method tried. Justification for its use could be based on the substantial improvement obtained by the assessment center's ability to predict job success over currently used methods (Michigan Bell, 1962; Campbell and Bray, 1967; Jaffee, Bender, and Calvert, 1970; Carleton, 1970; Finley, 1970).

A Note On the Criteria

Prediction models imply two basic things: (1) that the measures used to predict some other performance are indeed relevant to that performance, and the inverse, (2) that the performance measures themselves are equally relevant to the predictors. Both of these must be true in order to validate any predictive measure. The relevance of simulation exercises as predictors has been well documented and will be further discussed under the issue of content validity. However, the relevance of certain criterion measures is frequently suspect and serves as an example of one of the problems alluded to concerning the difficulty in establishing significant correlational relationships. The basis for the issue is somewhat paradoxical. As noted earlier, one of the very reasons for the successful emergence of the assessment center process is the failure of traditional performance appraisals to reflect accurately a person's ability to perform.

Most typically, the criteria against which assessment center results are evaluated are based on the same factors noted above that characterize typical management appraisal systems. With this in mind, it is relatively amazing that assessment center results have been as valid as they have. In brief, assessment center predictions are probably underestimations of their true validity. While obviously implicit in the above comparison, this is not to say that the bases on which assessment center evaluations are made are generally "better" than those on which typical appraisals are based; rather, that the two methods differ markedly. As such, it is questionable that they be used to statistically predict each other. Because the statistical result itself is likely to be contaminated, it reflects an uncharacteristic relationship between the assessment center results and on-job performance as measured by a typical management appraisal.

There are a number of other issues that have recently been raised, concerning among other things the limited range of criteria used from one study to another and the relatively limited number of different organizations that have published results, that need to be addressed (Klimoski and Strickland, 1977). Nevertheless, the consistency of results appears justified enough for other organizations to give serious consideration to using the assessment center approach.

Content Validity

The issues inherent in the types of analyses and criteria problems noted above have largely been responsible for the emergence of the concept of content validity as a more realistic barometer against which to evaluate assessment center results. Content validity refers to the extent to which scores on a test, or other indices, represent performance within the specifically defined content area the tests purport to sample. Related to the assessment center process, this simply refers to the extent to which the simulation exercises represent the performance content of the job which they were designed to sample. This is based on an inference that the factors responsible for performance on one set of measures (i.e., exercises) are similar to those of another set of measures (i.e., job performance). For example, if an exercise is designed to measure the concept of leadership, it is content valid if and only if some evidence exists that it samples the requirements of leadership (however defined) on the job. The definition of leadership can only be defined as the context of the particular job in question. It actually does not matter then what the concept is called but rather how it is behaviorally defined. If you wish, label typical leadership behaviors like delegating, directing, and coordinating under the heading "table." Call it anything you like! Ultimately, the label is unimportant. It is those behaviors, variables, or other factors representing the job that are used to define the label. These serve as the only basis for the content validity of that label. It should be mentioned that the recent joint *Guidelines* classify leadership as a construct and therefore not susceptible to content validation. This becomes an issue of semantics because the concept leadership, while technically construct, can be content validated if it is defined in terms of readily observable behaviors or tasks. Once again, the issue is not the label but rather how the concept, construct, skill, or content is defined.

The difficulty in applying the content validity concept to evaluating the assessment center process, or for that matter, any other predictive tool, is that it does not readily lend itself to statistical analyses. Oddly enough, because of problems in obtaining accurate statistical results, content validity has emerged as a viable alternative to validating such a program. Ironically, as illustrated in an earlier part of the chapter, the concept of content validity always has been the very basis for the design and implementation of the assessment center process—although unfortunately never spelled out as such. This is why "tryout performance" works better as a predictor of basketball playing than other indices less relevant to those behaviors which reflect effective or ineffective basketball playing—and why simulation exercises have had generally greater success in predicting managerial performance than other indices not as closely related to those characteristics which reflect successful managerial job performance.

Content Validity—Its Relevance. Logic notwithstanding, on what objective bases (for example, clout) do inferences of content validity stand as a defense for the validity of an assessment center? First and clearly most important, is the fact that the government, through its *Uniform Guidelines*, endorses the concept as a viable means of determining validity (*Uniform Guidelines on Employee*

Selection Procedures, 1978). Second, the scientific community most interested in such concerns, namely industrial and educational psychologists, have for a long time recognized the concept as relevant to the inference of validity (American Psychological Association, 1970, 1975). More specifically, two recent articles by psychologists from the Civil Service Commission and the EEOC endorsed content validity as a reasonable alternative in evaluating the assessment center process (Gorham, 1978; Taylor, 1978). Coupled with an admission by some of the scientific community that statistically significant validities are difficult to obtain because of certain limitations inherent in the manner in which they are analyzed, support seems to be mounting for more reliance on content validation in evaluating the utility of assessment center techniques.

Third, attention must be brought to the fact that the assessment center process was recently endorsed by a U.S. District Court in a case brought against the city of Omaha, Nebraska (Mendenhall, 1976). In this case, the validity of the city's assessment center for selecting a deputy police chief was challenged. The judge ruled that although the administration of the assessment center used could have been better standardized and controlled, the process itself appeared to be able to measure relevantly the skills required for the position in question. In essence, the judge was saying that the process appeared content valid.

The procedures and guidelines for content validating an assessment center have not yet been well formulated. However, it is agreed that the basis for passing the content validity test will be closely related to the comprehensiveness and accuracy with which initial job analyses are conducted. This is based on the fact that job analyses provide the foundation for the design of relevant simulation exercises, and that the content of the simulation exercises relative to the content of the target job position forms the basis for content validity. It is therefore necessary for any organization using or planning to use the assessment center process to scrutinize carefully the relevance of the simulation exercises prior to the implementation of the program. The case for tailor-designed (specific to the organization's job environment) or modified exercises, as opposed to off-the-shelf versions, appears to be mounting.

In conclusion, it is clear that the future of the assessment center may lie in its ability to demonstrate its content validity. Properly designed and conducted assessment center programs should endure such a test well. However, it is clear from the total absence in the research literature that little thought has been given to determining more standardized and consistent procedures for evaluating the content validity of an assessment center. The need for the procedure is paramount and can only serve to strengthen the position of the assessment center process in personnel administration.

Equal Opportunity and Fairness

Without question, the single issue receiving the most attention over the last decade in personnel administration is that of equal employment opportunity, relating to affirmative action and test fairness. In this context, one of the most attractive characteristics of the assessment center approach is that it provides an alternative to the more traditional and frequently discriminating paper-and-pencil tests. The foundation on which the assessment center process is based, namely observed behavior in relatively controlled settings on simulated job experiences or samples, is more likely to provide fairer employment decisions.

Although simulation type exercises, characteristic of assessment center programs, have been advocated as potentially fairer and more valid for minority employees (Cohen, 1974), there has not been a great amount of research on the fairness of the assessment center per se. The research that has been conducted, however, provides promising results. For example, AT&T has studied the performance of almost 5000 women between 1963 and 1971 (Moses and Boehm, 1975; Moses, 1973). Assessment center performance of these women was positively related to their subsequent promotions into management and advancement within management. More importantly, their overall assessment ratings were similar to the rating distribution for men, and ratings on many of the skills evaluated like decision making and leadership, were relatively the same for both men and women.

Another AT&T study revealed no significant differences between black and white women in the relationship between their assessment rating and actual job performance and potential for further advancement ratings (Huck and Bray, 1976). It also should be noted that in both the black and white women samples, the predictive validity was significant. Finally, in two other studies it has been shown that black males perform similarly to white males in exercises typically used in assessment center programs (Cohen, 1971; Jaffee, Cohen, and Cherry, 1972). These studies, few as they may be, attest to the assessment center's apparent fairness in selecting minority group and/or women managers. Indeed, the assessment of approximately 2000 women at AT&T for affirmative action purposes was endorsed by the federal government as part of the terms of a consent decree. Coupled with the potential for greater reliance on content validity justification for its use, the assessment center approach appears to have considerable promise as a fair and valid means of evaluating the job potential for minority groups and women.

Reliability Results

So far, we have only mentioned the concept of validity in evaluating the assessment center process because of the dependence on this method to evaluate and predict an individual's job performance. But what role does reliability, or the consistency with which these evaluations and predictions can be made, play in influencing how valid the process is going to be?

Reliability typically involves areas of measurement associated with unreliable results such as instability (overtime), inconsistency (between and within measures), and subjectivity (among evaluators). In an assessment center, they relate respectively to those internal process factors such as assess-reassess stability, inter-and intra-exercise consistency, and assessor objectivity. In addition reliability refers to the consistency with which the assessment center process is administered. This consistency actually means fairness in the application of the same measures, standards, and processes to all candidates.

With this in mind, we can examine the effects of reliability on validity. We are not likely to predict validly an individual's subsequent performance if the process is laden with inconsistencies in such things as skill definitions, evaluation standards, exercise design, program administration, and so on. If the process is unsystematically employed with certain standards of operation not adhered to, there is little likelihood that agreement will result. In the absence of any consistency in the process and the manner in which it is used, assessment center validity should suffer appreciably. In the evaluation process culminating in some type of rating used to predict success, inconsistencies between evaluators suggest that there may be disagreement as to what and how certain behavior is to be evaluated. The result of these inconsistencies may be an averaging effect on differences of opinion, thus preventing the likelihood of making fine discriminations between relatively effective and ineffective behaviors. Estimates of validity, then, which are based on successfully predicting different levels of performance will be severely hampered by an unreliable process used to make those estimates.

Fortunately, the reliability reported in assessment center studies is generally very high. One review has summarized a number of these studies on the interrater (assessor) reliabilities reported (Howard, 1974). They range from .60 to .98, with the majority above .75. This result is further confirmed by a more recent study in which 101 potential middle managers were evaluated on 17 skills (Schmitt, 1977). That interrater reliability is high should not be surprising since the assessment center process does its best to insure it. Assessors are similarly trained in how to observe behavior and to use the same standards of performance in evaluating it. Indeed, one study reported quite low interrater reliabilities for untrained assessors while quite high reliabilities for trained assessors (Jaffee, 1971). Interrater reliability should almost always be high if quality and consistent assessor training takes place, but such high reliability does not insure the validity of the process. The issue of reliability or consistency in the assessment center process refers to standardizing the administration of the assessment center. Such standardization will insure that all candidates are treated fairly. Even though the *Standards and Ethical Considerations for Assessment Center Operations* (Standards, 1978) were developed to address these concerns, they have received only minimal direct research attention to date. A summary of these concerns and their related research has been addressed in detail elsewhere (Cohen, 1978).

The standardization issue should be carefully scrutinized. It served as part of the foundation for the previously mentioned court case against the city of Omaha. The assessment center used was claimed by the plaintiffs to be improperly administered and, therefore, unable to provide valid results. The judge's decision included a statement that while this particular assessment center program could have been administratively improved, its results appeared to have been objectively obtained. However, the judge's admittance of the need for administrative improvement in the center suggests that further scrutiny of the assessment center process is inevitable. All assessment center practitioners should carefully review the standardization of their particular programs.

Return on Investment (ROI)

Of all the methods of evaluating the success (or worth) of a program, ROI computations appear the most pragmatic. It is surprising, then, that more effort hasn't been devoted to evaluating the utility of the assessment center method in this manner. To be sure, it is not an easy task. In fact, it would require quantifying many intangible characteristics of success and failure. Nevertheless, most organizations have in their possession some form of the data needed to make these computations. Developing an approach which could make use of the data would be the most challenging task.

Essentially, the task reduces to estimating the costs of relatively ineffective employee performance. One starting point might be to focus on turnover due to lack of ability. If we can enhance the likelihood of job success by better prediction, we will eventually reduce the likelihood of relatively ineffective performance. Some of the costs that could be computed are those associated with (1) start-up time required of a replacement for the incumbent; (2) downtime associated with the incumbent changing jobs either internally or externally (3) training and/or retraining associated with both the replacement and the incumbent; (4) travel and moving expenses if applicable; (5) the difference in productivity (related to dollars) that might have accrued if the incumbent was effective; and (6) the more difficult measure, yet undeniably present, psychological impact on the "failed" incumbent, and also on the morale of those surrounding him.

While we admit to the difficulty of this task, it should be noted that some organizations have taken the time to make such estimates. One estimate of failure costs, based on similar factors to those noted above, was $50,000 for a first-line supervisor's position (Miller, 1972); another was over $250,000 for the cumulative impact of a managerial failure at the upper middle management level (Anonymous, 1978).

Given this information, how then could an organization begin to evaluate the utility of an assessment center program? A simple way to begin would be to estimate the assessment center costs (all things considered) and compare them with the calculated amount it would cost the organization for *just one* person to fail in the target position for which the assessment center was or would be developed. (Our experience indicates that in the vast majority of cases, the latter figure will be considerably higher.) If the assessment center program, then, can prevent just one candidate from being selected who otherwise might have been selected through alternative methods, it proves its worth. This does not even consider the potential for improved productivity (and revenues) with the selection of *just one* person who succeeds.

An ROI analysis is not without its pitfalls. For example, it could conceivably present an interesting dilemma for an organization. It is possible that an assessment center program, for one of numerous reasons, might not demonstrate statistical and/or practical significance according to correlational validation procedures. This same assessment center program might be very useful in isolating potential failures, but of little value in predicting successes. (Such a case would normally not demonstrate very high validity since it only successfully predicts one side of the performance continuum.) Assuming the costs of saving a potential failure outweigh those associated with the program, the use of the program might be continued even with some of its inherent weaknesses. Its continued use for selection, of course, will depend on some initial justification for content validity, and ultimately predictive validity, if possible.

In short, it seems that one area of evaluating assessment center results that has been largely ignored (which appears appropriate) is that concerning its return on investment. While the computations may be tedious and time consuming, it could prove invaluable as an aid in deciding the pragmatic utility of an assessment center program.

FUTURE DIRECTIONS

Uses of Assessment Centers in Overall Human Resources Management

More and more, the assessment center is becoming a tool for training and career development as opposed to merely selection. The reasons for this are many and perhaps include a greater concern for individuals within our society, an emphasis on upward mobility, and an emphasis on each person having the opportunity to develop to full potential. The assessment center provides the basic information necessary for this process to be carried out. As such, the assessment center can fit well into an organization's overall human resource management system. Figure 3 illustrates how the assessment center can fit into a career development and manpower planning system.

The process is initiated by self-nomination. In many organizations, the self-nomination is replaced by management nomination or even a combination of the two methods. In the model presented, the organization retains the right to veto potential candidates for the assessment center. The critical feature of the system is that at all phases the individual is told why particular decisions were made, and developmental opportunities are offered as a result of the information uncovered and the interests of the individual and the organization. So with this particular model, the information generated by the assessment center is used to provide information about further development and career paths.

It should be clear by now that an assessment center cannot be used by itself without a concern for other sources of information and activity within the organization. For career planning purposes, the use of ongoing performance appraisals provides important information concerning managerial skills, technical competency, work attitudes, and perhaps experiences developed by specific assignments. A number of organizations integrate the assessment center information not only with the previous background as covered by performance appraisals, but psychological tests as well. There are a variety of interest inventories and attitude and values tests as well as more traditional psychological testing instruments which provide information that could be used for effective career counseling and the development of individuals within the organization.

Other Future Applications

It has by now become very clear that assessment center methodology will provide the model for legal selection and development within organizations. The assessment center of the future will probably be more sophisticated from the standpoint of accurate simulations of target positions. Reliance on assessment centers for management positions *only* will continue, but its use with nonmanagement positions will escalate. Programs designed for vocational counselors, investigation workers, sales agents, teachers, police officers, research and planning analysts, and others are presently being considered (for example, organization development consultants, employee relations counselors). As the technology becomes more advanced and the pressures increase for content valid instruments, the use of simulation exercises that represent the environment but enable the assessment center to establish situations which would be similar for all participants will become more prevalent. The use of communication equipment, computers, videotape capabilities, more extensive audiovisual equipment, and better means of training assessors and role players will all contribute to simulations of more complex environments which will go beyond the traditional in-basket exercise, business game, and group discussion problems.

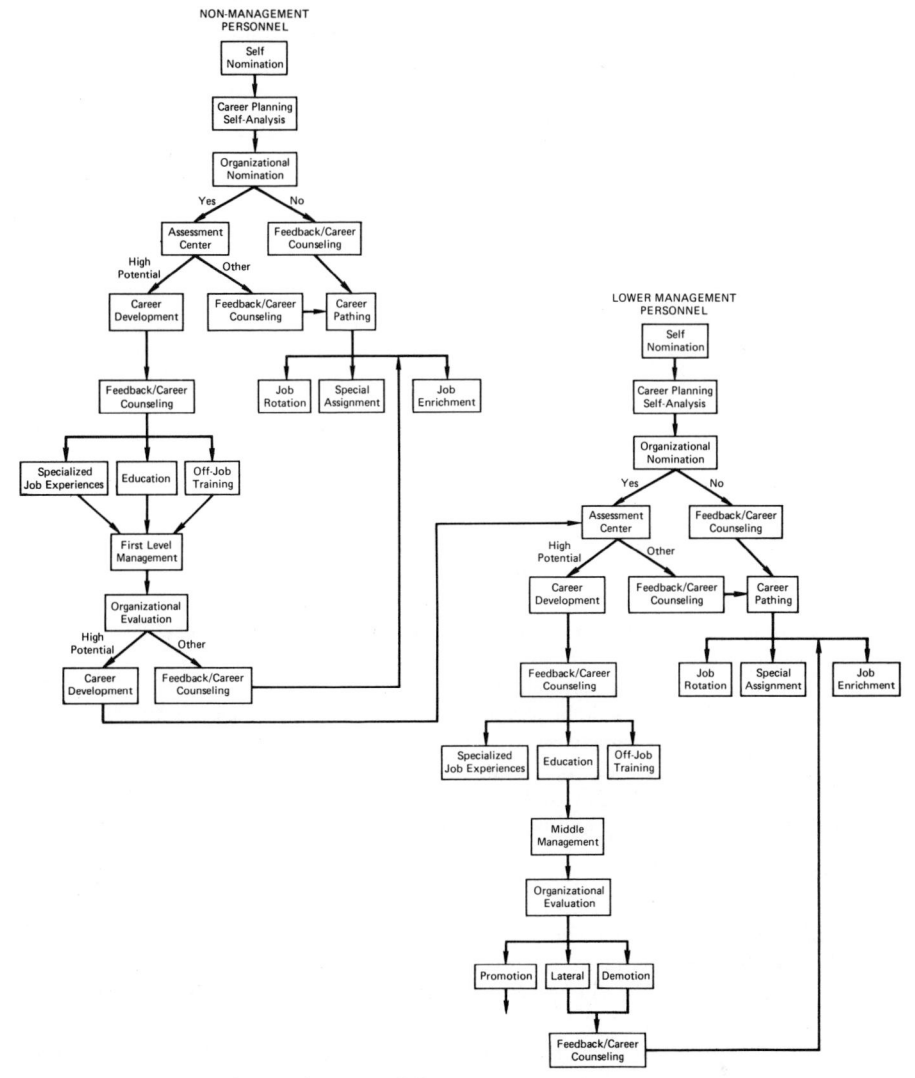

FIGURE 3 *The Application of the Assessment Center to Human Resource Management*

There is another trend which will likely affect the use of assessment centers. As the need to document performance becomes greater, the failure of many existing performance appraisal systems will become more obvious. As retirement laws change, the need to document competency at a present position will become more important. As the economy becomes more worldwide and complex, the need to justify layoffs for particular individuals will become more difficult to effectuate. All in all, whereas the assessment center has been used as a means of defining skills necessary to perform in a target position that is different from an individual's present position a trend for the future might very well be the documentation of competency at that present position. In addition to these trends, a more general exclusion of other alternatives like personality and intelligence measures that have already been virtually eliminated in selection decisions, and interviews and performance reviews which have presented problems for some time, may narrow the range of possible instruments to content valid simulation instruments—the basis of assessment center technology.

SUMMARY

One important question emerges from this review of the assessment center process. Is it a *technology* based on a systematic approach to evaluating human resource ability and potential? We would argue unequivocally that such a technology does indeed exist and furthermore, when applied properly is responsible for the success of the assessment center relative to other personnel-related methods. The basic factors and principles underlying this technology and which are required for its effective use include the following:

> It uses simulations (exercises) that resemble actual job situations. *Principle:* The more similar the assessment "test" is to the actual job, the greater the likelihood of predicting real world job performance.
> It uses trained assessors to observe and evaluate employees/job candidates. *Principle:* The more objective and behaviorally oriented the observation and evaluation stages are, the greater the likelihood of valid and reliable assessments.
> It determines relative skill strengths and weaknesses of candidates. *Principle:* The more that readily observable behaviors predict job success, the greater the likelihood of identifying relative effectiveness across candidates and situations.
> It provides private feedback on candidates' simulation performance. *Principle:* The more behaviorally objective and job-relevant that feedback is, the greater the likelihood of its credibility and impetus for behavioral change.

In summary then, an assessment center demands a job analysis with the skills to be measured being observable, relevant, and measurable. Instruments need to be prepared that reflect the job demands, a staff of assessors needs to be trained, and the process properly integrated into a system that most effectively uses the information for the proper development of the individual and the organization.

While there are a number of research issues that dictate further study of the assessment center process, the general results are extremely favorable. With further attention to these issues, which only can improve an already demonstrated approach, assessment center technology is likely to maintain its position as a very useful technique for improving the management of human resources.

REFERENCES

American Psychological Association, Office of Scientific Affairs. *Standards for Educational and Psychological Tests and Manuals*. 1974, Washington, D.C., p. 76.

American Psychological Association, Division of Industrial-Organizational Psychology. *Principles for the Validation and Use of Personnel Selection Procedures*. 1975, p. 19.

Bentz, V. J. "Validity of Sears Assessment Center Procedures," In *Validity of Assessment Centers*, W. C. Byham (Chairman), Symposium presented at the 70th Annual Convention of the American Psychological Association. (1971), Washington, D.C.

Bray, D. W. "The Assessment Center Method," In *Training and Development Handbook*, ed. R. I. Craig, New York: McGraw-Hill, 1976 1–15.

Bray, D. W., and R. J. Campbell, "Selection of Salesmen By Means of an Assessment Center," *Journal of Applied Psychology, 52*, (1968), 36–41.

Bray, D. W., and D. L. Grant, "The Assessment Center in the Measurement of Potential for Business Management," *Psychological Monographs, 80*, (1966), 1–27.

Bray, D. W. and J. L. Moses, "Personnel Selection," In *Annual Review of Psychology*, ed. by P. H. Mussen and M. R. Rosenzweig, (1972), pp. 545–576.

Byham, W. C. "Assessment Centers for Spotting Future Managers," *Harvard Business Review, 48*, 4, (1970), 150–160.

Campbell, R. J. and D. W. Bray, "Assessment Centers: An Aid In Management Selection," *Personnel Administration, 30*, 2, (1967), 6–13.

Carleton, F. O. "Relationships Between Followup Evaluations and Information Developed in a Management Assessment Center," Paper read at the 78th Annual Convention of the American Psychological Association, 1970, Miami Beach, Florida.

Cohen, B. M., J. L Moses, and W. C. Byham, *The Validity of Assessment Centers: A Literature Review, Monograph II*. Pittsburgh, Pennsylvania: Developmental Dimensions Press, 1974.

Cohen, S. L. "An Investigation of the Utility and Effectiveness of Simulation Techniques in the Evaluation of Disadvantaged Persons for Supervisory Potential," Ph. D. dissertation, Unversity of Tennessee, 1971, p. 170.

Cohen, S. L. "Issues in the Selection of Minority Group Employees," *Human Resource Management, 13*, 1, (1974), 12–18.

Cohen, S. L. "Standardization of Assessment Center Technology: Some Critical Concerns," *Journal of Assessment Center Technology, 1*, 2, (1978), 1–10.

Cooper, G, and R. S. Sobol, "1969 Seniority and Testing Under Fair Employment Laws: A General Approach to Objective Criteria of Hiring and Promotion," *Harvard Law Review, 82* (1969), 1958–1969.

Finely, R. M., Jr. "An Evaluation of Behavior Predictions from Projective Tests Given in a Management Assessment Center," Paper read at the 78th Annual Convention of the American Psychological Association, 1970, Miami Beach, Florida.

Gorham, W. A. "Federal Executive Aging Guidelines and Their Impact on the Assessment Center Process," *Journal of Assessment Center Technology, 1*, 1, (1978), 115–134.

Howard, A. "An Assessment of Assessment Centers," *Academy of Management Journal, 17*, 1, (1974), 115–134.

Huck, J. R., and D. W. Bray,"Management Assessment Center Evaluations and Subsequent Job Performance of White and Black Females," *Personnel Psychology*, 29, 1, (1976) 13–30.

Jaffee, C. L. "Assessment Centers Help Find Management Potential," *Bell Telephone Magazine*, 44, 3, (1965) 18–24.

Jaffee, C. L. *Effective Management Selection*. Reading, Massachusetts: Addison Wesley, 1971.

Jaffee, C. L., J. Bender, and O. L. Calvert. "The Assessment Center Techniques: A Validation Study," *Management of Personnel Quarterly*, 9, 3, (1970), 9–14.

Jaffee, C. L., S. L. Cohen, and R. Cherry. "Supervisory Selection Program for Disadvantaged or Minority Employees," *Training and Development Journal*, 26, 1, (1972), 22–28.

Jaffee, C. L., and F. D. Frank. *Interviews Conducted at Assessment Centers: A Guide for Training Managers*, Dubuque, Iowa: Kendall-Hunt, 1976.

Klimoski, R. J., and W. J. Strickland. "Assessment Centers—Valid or Merely Prescient," *Personnel Psychology*, 30, (1977) 353–361.

Kraut, A. I., and G. J. Scott. "Validation of an Operational Management Assessment Program," *Journal of Applied Psychology*, 56, (1972), 124–129.

McConnell, J. H., and T. Parker. "An Assessment Center Program for Multi-Organizational Use," *Training and Development Journal*, 26, 3, (1972), 6–14.

Mendenhall, M. D. "A Report of an Assessment Center for the Position of Deputy Police Chief," Omaha, Nebraska: Personnel Department, 1976, in C. L. Jaffee and F. D. Frank, ed. *Interviews Conducted at Assessment Centers: A Guide for Training Managers*, Dubuque, Iowa: Kendall-Hunt, 1976.

Meyer, H. H. "Assessment Centers at General Electric," Paper read at the Development Dimensions Conference, 1972, San Francisco, California.

Michigan Bell Telephone. "Personnel Assessment Program: Evaluation Study," P1962, Plant Department. Detroit, Michigan, 1962.

Miller, D. "Assessment Centers at Syntex," Paper read at the meeting of the Personnel Division of the National Pharmaceutical Association, 1972, Hot Springs, Virginia.

Moses, J. L. "The Development of an Assessment Center for the Early Identification of Supervisory Potential," *Personnel Psychology*, 26, (1973), 569–580.

Moses, J. L. "Assessment Center Performance and Management Progress," *Studies in Personnel Psychology*, 26, (1973), 569–580.

Moses, J. L., and V. R. Boehm, "Relationship of Assessment Center Performance to Management Progress of Women," *Journal of Applied Psychology*, 60, 4, (1975), 528.

Moses, J. L., and W. C. Byham, (eds.). *Applying the Assessment Center Method*. New York: Pergamon Press, Inc., 1978.

Office of Strategic Services, OSS Assessment Staff. *Assessment of Men*. New York: Rinehart, 1948.

Rice, B. "Measuring Executive Muscle," *Psychology Today*, (December 1978), Vol. 12, no. 7, 95–110.

Schmitt, N. "Interrater Agreement in Dimensionality and Combination of Assessment Center Judgment," *Journal of Applied Psychology*, 62, (1977), 171–176.

Standards and Ethical Considerations for Assessment Center Operations. Chaired by J. L. Moses, (1978), Task Force on Assessment Center Standards.

Taylor, J. O. "The EEOC Guidelines on Content Validity and Their Application to the Assessment Center Method," *Journal of Assessment Center Technology*, 1, 1, (1978), 9–12.

Thompson, H. A. "Comparison of Predictor and Criterion Judgments of Managerial Performance Using the Multitrait-Multimethod Approach," *Journal of Applied Psychology*, 54, (1970), 496–502.

Wernimont, P. F., and J. P. Campbell. "Signs, Samples, and Criteria," *Journal of Applied Psychology*, 52, (1968), 372–376.

Wollowick, H. B., and W. J. McNamara. "Relationships of the Components of an Assessment Center to Management Success," *Journal of Applied Psychology*, 53, (1969), 348–352.

TRAINING AND LEARNING

Executive Development in the Department of Agriculture

Thomas W. Gill

A noted news commentator wrote recently there was one employee in the Department of Agriculture for every 25 American farmers. The U.S. Department of Agriculture is much more than a department for farmers—it is a department for all 230 million Americans. It is a department of food and a social welfare policy as well as a friend of the farmer. Today, the Department of Agriculture is concerned with the economic production and distribution of essential food and fiber; the wise conservation of natural resources; development of rural areas; some stabilization of agricultural prices and returns; scientific investigation of newer and better methods of agricultural production; regulation of markets and trade in farm products; foreign trade; dissemination of information to farmers and the public on achievement and progress; protection against harmful diseases, insects, and animals; and research for new, improved agricultural products and other products for all citizens.

The Department of Agriculture provides these and other services through over 100,000 employees, 90 percent of whom are in the field. There are 240 executives and 1,100 managers, and because of the complexity of its business, many of the managers and executives occupy regulatory, financial approval, or certification-type positions. Because of the tremendous growth of the Department during the 1940s and 1950s, most of the managers and executives have come up from the program ranks.

It is impossible to look at the formal organization chart of the Department of Agriculture and fully appreciate the interdependence of the various offices and agencies that comprise such an operation. To maintain managerial equilibrium within such a large, complex organization with competing priorities calls for an effective management process. And even more, it calls for effective managers and executives.

Initially, the Department tried to operate a centralized managerial and executive development system from the Career Development Division of the Office of Personnel. In view of the Department's complexity, it was inevitable that such a centralized plan would fail.

Prepared especially for this book and printed with permission of the author.

But certain things were learned.

One cannot ignore manpower needs in planning an executive development program.
One cannot operate an executive development program without money and manpower.
One cannot ignore organizational differences and needs in designing and operating an executive development program.

The Department now has a comprehensive and viable system for identifying and developing managerial and executive talent. It is a system which allows individual agencies and offices considerable latitude to organize their own programs, and it gives the Office of Personnel the manpower to assume a role in executive development.

Currently, the Executive Development Unit in the Career Development Division of the Office of Personnel monitors executive development activities in the various departmental agencies and offices. The present executive development program in the Department has three major thrusts, and they are

1. Need
2. Development
3. Evaluation and feedback

An eleven-step Executive and Managerial Development System has been developed, and it has incorporated the Civil Service Commission's guidelines for the development of managerial and executive personnel. One of the major advantages of the present system is that it provides a logical sequence of steps while allowing the agencies maximum flexibility in meeting the requirements of each step. Table 1 provides a schema of the Department of Agriculture's Executive and Managerial Development System.

TABLE 1 USDA Executive and Managerial Development System

1. Designation of managerial positions
2. Categorization of managerial positions into staff managerial positions, program managerial positions, and managers of scientific and professional personnel
3. Development of knowledges, skills, and abilities for all managerial positions
4. Refinement of knowledge, skills, and abilities (KSA)
5. Assessment
6. Identification of high-potential managers
7. Implementation of individual development plans (IDP's)
8. Development of annual training projections
9. Mid-career counseling
10. Required and KSA training, mobility assignments, optional and self-development training
11. Evaluation

THE EXECUTIVE AND MANAGERIAL DEVELOPMENT SYSTEM IN OPERATION

In this section, we will trace the Department's progress in implementing a managerial development system through each of the 11 phases outlined in Table 1. As a first requirement of the current development system, each of the agencies was expected to designate its management positions. Despite considerable experience with coding positions as "managerial" or "supervisory," and much to the surprise of the Executive Development Unit, there was considerable discrepancy between the various agencies' definitions. Because of these discrepancies, additional guidelines were issued which stressed level of management and budgetary and fiscal accountability. These guidelines have generally led to a consensus of opinion on the designation "management positions."

The *categorization of managerial positions* into staff managerial positions, program managerial positions, and managers of scientific and professional personnel was accomplished without much ado by most agencies. The purpose of this exercise was to make it easier to develop the knowledges, skills, and abilities (KSA) of managers and executives and to get a better grasp of the developmental needs of all managers.

The *development and refinement of the knowledges, skills, and abilities* (KSA) for all managerial positions has not proceeded as smoothly as was hoped. Agencies have used a variety of methods to determine these KSA factors. As a result, the Executive Development Unit developed a *group method* for defining the KSA factors for staff positions.

The group method was essentially a meeting of specialized staff personnel to discuss knowledge, skill, and ability factors required for their job. For example, five agency budget officers would have the task of isolating and defining KSA factors for that position. Their findings would then be cross-checked by a questionnaire, whose rankings might vary somewhat, but whose general import remained the same. Some agencies used the group method, some used questionnaires only, and some relied on individual interviews and a host of other methods. Some used ten or eleven factors for all managerial positions, and a few did intensive individual job analysis.

The *assessment* state of USDA's managerial development program has encountered several problems. One agency which used assessment centers quite extensively discontinued their use when the assessment centers refused to modify their exercises to accommodate the agency. The agency felt the exercise, designed to measure the ability to withstand stress, was weeding out too many of their good managers who were very achievement oriented and perhaps not too sensitive to the needs of individuals. During the course of the exercise, assessors often rejected the more aggressive candidates rather than recognizing this trait as a potential plus for managers.

The *identification of high-potential managers,* which follows automatically from the assessment process, leads to the *implementation of individual development plans.* For a variety of reasons, not all agencies have identified their high-potential managerial personnel. Incumbent managers are assessed by means of performance appraisal systems peculiar to each agency, a policy considered inadequate by many managers and executives. As a consequence, some managers have proposed adopting a new evaluation system every three or four years to avoid the inevitable "leveling" process that results from using the same system over a period of time.

Some agencies have been reluctant to identify high-potential managers not only because of dubious assessment methods but because they are afraid of the "crown prince" image. Second-guessing selections by higher level officials was also a problem in some areas. In addition, since all selection methods must be in conformance with the Federal Merit Promotion System, some agency plans had to be revised. To encourage agencies to identify high-potential managers, the Executive Development Unit offered a program of mobility assignments (Personnel Interchange Process) that will be discussed in greater detail later.

The *creation of Individual Development Plans* (IDP's) for incumbent and high-potential managers has been more successful for the high potentials than for the incumbent managers. Some agencies have developed very detailed and elaborate IDPs and others have adhered to simple guidelines. To encourage greater relevancy of developmental experiences, the Executive Development Unit translated the very general managerial knowledges, skills, and abilities in Civil Services guidelines into more specific Department of Agriculture knowledges, skills, and abilities. For example, the Civil Service Commission lists under Environmental Knowledges: "Federal budgeting system." We translated that into:

Is the manager cost conscious? Are proposals initiated by the manager related to financial or budget constraints?

If the manager needs improvement in this area, then the recommended developmental activity is listed which will enable him or her to improve and develop.

The Executive Development Unit and some committees at the Civil Service Commission are trying to develop a standard individual development plan. Its use, though, would not be mandatory if the agency is happy with existing formats. We also experimented with an Executive IDP which contained functional factors as well as something called "position presence," which can be translated into organizational charisma. It is still under consideration.

The *development of annual training projections* is still a long way down the pike. It includes long-term training and mobility assignments, which are planned and carried out with regularity. The Department sends a substantial number of managers and executives away for training in colleges and universities for periods varying from five weeks to one year.

Mid-career counseling, now called the Agriculture Management Planning Seminar, is unique because it is the first such effort in the federal government, and has met with considerable success throughout the department. This program is designed to help managers in mid-career to gain increased self-awareness, greater self-understanding, improved job satisfaction, and increased work effectiveness. The seminar provides practical, usable, experience-based learning with immediate application to one's work environment and personal life. The manager at mid-career has some clearly identifiable problems, both physiologically and psychologically, and these problems may be more acute in the nonachiever.

This seminar is intended to provide an in-depth exploration of the personal, social, and work-related problems that confront a person in mid-career. It provides immediate experience-based learning for application to the work environment and personal relations, and the small group is the major vehicle for learning. This format creates a learning environment where meaningful growth can occur through collaborative respect for others. The learning process in such a setting encourages the recognition and expression of feelings as an effective way of understanding one's self and one's impact on others. Members of the group have the opportunity to experience a variety of roles and situations including competitiveness, cooperation, stress, success, failure, and conformity and nonconformity.

The *implementation of mobility assignments* is the next step in the management development system. As part of our Personnel Interchange Process, they were originally instituted as an inducement for the agencies to designate high-potential managers. An added side effect is the ongoing creation of a common management philosophy in the Department.

Mobility assignments are designed to provide on-the-job developmental experiences for selected managers and executives through temporary assignments, task force assignments, or special projects on an interagency basis. To date, all but three agencies in the Department are participating in the program. We have made 17 assignments—a small number, but a beginning.

Program evaluation involves continuous feedback from the agencies and offices. We meet informally with agency training officers to discuss problems, and we conduct a formal evaluation on accomplishments of the various steps on an annual basis. To gain greater objectivity, we have considered a formal evaluation by a consultant or task force from outside the Office of Personnel. The results of such an evaluation should be very useful to the future direction of the program.

AN EXAMPLE OF EXECUTIVE DEVELOPMENT PROGRAM— THE FOOD SAFETY AND QUALITY SERVICE

Let us look at one agency's executive development program. Everyone is familiar with the U.S. Department of Agriculture (USDA) stamp of approval on meat and food products. It is the Food Safety and Quality Service which conducts meat and poultry inspections in all states for interstate commerce as well as being responsible for commodity grading programs. With approximately 13,000 full-time employees, this agency is the second largest bureau-level organization in the Department of Agriculture. Most of its managers are in relatively narrow scientific and technical occupations (veterinary medicine, food technology, and chemistry).

The three major programs operated by the Food Safety and Quality Service are Meat and Poultry Inspection, Commodity Grading Programs, and Veterinary Services. These regulatory programs are rigidly controlled by specific statutes and administrative policies which have resulted in a "confederacy-type" of organizational structure. Each of these three major program areas has its own distinct identity, culture, managerial style, and occupational disciplines, so that many agency managers have had little or no formal training in public sector program management.

The agency's executive development program is primarily designed to equip scientific and technical employees with the managerial knowledges, skills, and abilities needed to perform with maximum effectiveness. Although the selection process takes into account the cultures and unique needs of managers in each of the major program areas, the actual screening and selection is agency-wide. Once selected, the participants go through a two-year sequential development program that heavily centers on developmental and managerial behavior assessment. New managers, high potentials, and incumbent managers go through the same training and assessment activities with maximum support for individual self-development efforts.

The Food Safety and Quality Service's program is a compilation of successful features of many executive development systems used in government and private industry. An attempt has been made to avoid the weaknesses and mistakes that surfaced in other programs. The unique aspects of the system are found in an approach to measure executive abilities against a set of behavioral standards.

Screening and Selection

All employees at appropriate grade levels are eligible, and every eligible employee who has not previously participated in the program receives a copy of the announcement. Candidates are selected for the program as a result of scores based upon supervisory potential ratings, interest, and evaluation by an impartial panel. These selection criteria were developed by the Executive Development Committee, and results are submitted annually to the administrator to screen applicants.

Assessments

During the course of the 25-month program, candidates are evaluated and receive feedback on a set of ten behavioral standards:

1. Decision making
2. Decisiveness
3. Flexibility
4. Leadership
5. Oral communications

6. Organization and planning
7. Perception and analytical ability
8. Persuasiveness
9. Sensitivity to people
10. Tolerance to stress

This is strictly a developmental exercise to be used by the trainees only. These standards also serve as the framework for the curriculum and assessment activities.

Curriculum

The curriculum is both sequential and individualized. In view of the trainee's busy work schedule, the same course module is offered across a three-to four-week period, and if the trainee cannot attend the session, he or she can pick it up at a later date. All of the sessions are open seminars, and they are available from time to time throughout the United States.

Counseling Program

This activity is designed to provide executive coaching for participants. There are group meetings of participants and counselors at least once a year, and the participants must maintain contact with assigned counselors for the duration of the program. A select group of retired federal executives (supergrades) are used as counselors.

Time Factor

Phase I of the program includes Orientation, Self-Awareness, Communications, and Dimensions seminars, all four of which are conducted in Washington, D.C.

Phase II consists of a ten-day assignment to another program area within an agency, after which trainees are expected to present an oral report on the experience.

Phase III consists of Assessment activites and the Counseling Program.

Phase IV includes the Models for Management course and a three-day conference.

Another agency in the Department, the Economic Research Service, has a similar executive development program with a unique feature, and that is participation of the participants' spouses. The spouses are invited to attend and participate in the "Communications and Management Dimensions" component. This session is concerned with interpersonal relationships, the art of listening, and some of the dimensions of managing time and resources. It is felt that such an opportunity will give the spouse a better appreciation of what the participant is undertaking, of the relevance of goals and aspirations growing out of the experience, and at the same time provide an interesting exposure to the ideas and concepts presented.

ANOTHER EXAMPLE OF EXECUTIVE DEVELOPMENT— THE AGRICULTURAL RESEARCH SERVICE

The Agricultural Research Service is another agency with an outstanding executive development program. This agency conducts basic, applied, and developmental research in the fields of livestock, crops, pest control, environmental quality, marketing, agricultural health hazards (including food safety), and soil, water, and air resources, all of which contribute to Department of Agriculture missions. The scope and nature of Agricultural Research Service is such that life scientists, physical scientists, and engineers may work as individual contributors, in groups by discipline, and in interdisciplinary teams.

Scientists are thus a large part of the production work force in this agency, and they also occupy most of its managerial and executive positions. Out of a total work force of 8,000 people, 3,000 are scientists, and 101 positions have been identified as executive or managerial.

Executive development efforts in the Agricultural Research Service have focused on facilitating the processes through which a scientist moves beyond the technical field of endeavor and becomes a manager. These processes require careful identification of managerial potential and the acquisition of special skills/knowledges primarily through on-the-job assignments and short attention to individual needs. Thus, executive development is viewed as an integral part of normal management operations rather than as an idiosyncratic body of information; it is a performance-based system in which critical skills and knowledges have been derived from actual job performance requirements. Techniques for assessing and meeting developmental needs feature built-in attention to real-world job performance.

Special features of the program have been the utilization of performance analysis techniques for specifying knowledge and ability requirements of identified positions, pretesting and evaluation of individual developmental planning instruments for new, future, and advancing executives; and incorporation of executive work assignment scheduling into individual development plans. Training and developmental activities are thereby tied to specific, real-world work assignments.

Program improvements and refinements occur through use of feedback from actual operation of the program. Executive work assignments and individual development plans are collected and reviewed in aggregate by the Executive Development Task Force. This provides the agency's top management an opportunity to determine if work assignments are representative of the roles and responsibilities of these management positions. The nature and scope of work assignments provide a check on the *actual* versus the *intended* functioning of the management organization itself.

Manpower studies have indicated that executive turnover in identified managerial positions within the agency is as high as 50 percent in five years, and almost 100 percent in ten years. A nationwide competition was held in order to identify a talent pool of individuals considered to have above-average managerial or executive potential. Twenty-six persons out of 350 applicants were selected, and additional competitions will be announced as vacancies occur.

The selectees participate in an assessment-type workshop based on individual needs. Strong emphasis is placed on developing and improving skills through job-related projects, executive coaching, self-study, and evaluation of current work assignments. It is a unique individualized program.

Each potential executive has been assigned a "mentor," that is, a functioning executive who serves as coach, counselor, helper, and tutor. This mentor/coaching component is regarded as crucial to the success of the program.

Executive work assignments are another important feature of the Agriculture Research Service's Executive Development Program. Trainees carry out real assignments related to future job responsibilities, and learn management skills by "doing" what the agency's executives really do. Most executive work assignments have as their end products *work accomplishments*—tangible, measurable outputs or results. Some examples from an actual Individual Development Plan are presented in Table 2.

Work accomplishments serve a useful purpose for the agency, because they are simultaneously training devices and *products* which focus on real organizational needs. Work assignments are also useful for evaluating an individual trainee's progress.

FUTURE DIRECTIONS

Many of the agencies within the Department have developed executive development programs to meet their specific needs, but the efforts of some have been lagging. In a large organization comprising a confederacy of agencies, a flexible executive development system in which the various agencies can develop their own particular program is the only way to go. The Food Safety and Quality Service has a structured program that is responsive to the organization, and Agriculture Research Service has a very individualized program that is responsive to its needs. The role of the Executive Development Unit is to educate and coordinate, never to coerce.

We have arrived at the following conclusions after monitoring our Departmental Executive Development Program for a reasonable period of time:

> Managerial development is essential if the executive work force is to continue to provide organizational and program leadership.
>
> Managerial and executive development must be a comprehensive approach. It means the *development*, not just the training, of managers and executives for higher level responsibilities. It also means incorporating manpower needs in planning the executive development program, and it means being aware of agency desires in designing and operating such a program. It means money and manpower, too. You cannot operate an executive development program without them.
>
> The organization must think in terms of "payoff" for the individual as well as the organization.
>
> There is no one best way to develop managers.

TABLE 2 Individual Development Plan

Work Assignment	Work Accomplishments
Soil and Water Conservation research problems for MI-MN-WI Area identified and evaluated; low and high priority projects identified.	A. Report prepared for Area Office, NPS, RL's and others. B. Recommend improved management practices, including implementation. C. Charge Area Office with follow-through procedures.
Evaluate, review, and prioritize research activities at Mandan, North Dakota.	Through documentation, inform the Area Director and A. Deputy Administrator of research priorities at Mandan, North Dakota, including a review of the resource and personnel management plans for the location.
Evaluate and prioritize projects and research proposals for WRRC.	Cooperating with the Center Director's staff and professional organizations in the Center, establish impartial procedures to evaluate and prioritize current projects and research proposals in WRRC.
Coordinate planning of the U.S. Meat Animal Research Center Forage Research Program.	1. Establish goals for USMARC forage research relative to the overall USMARC mission and to regional and national forage/livestock programs (written document). 2. Identify research capability necessary to accomplish these goals (written document). 3. Attain consensus support both within and outside ARS for proposed program (formal and informal presentations). 4. Prepare documentation and justification required to gain budgetary approval (written document).

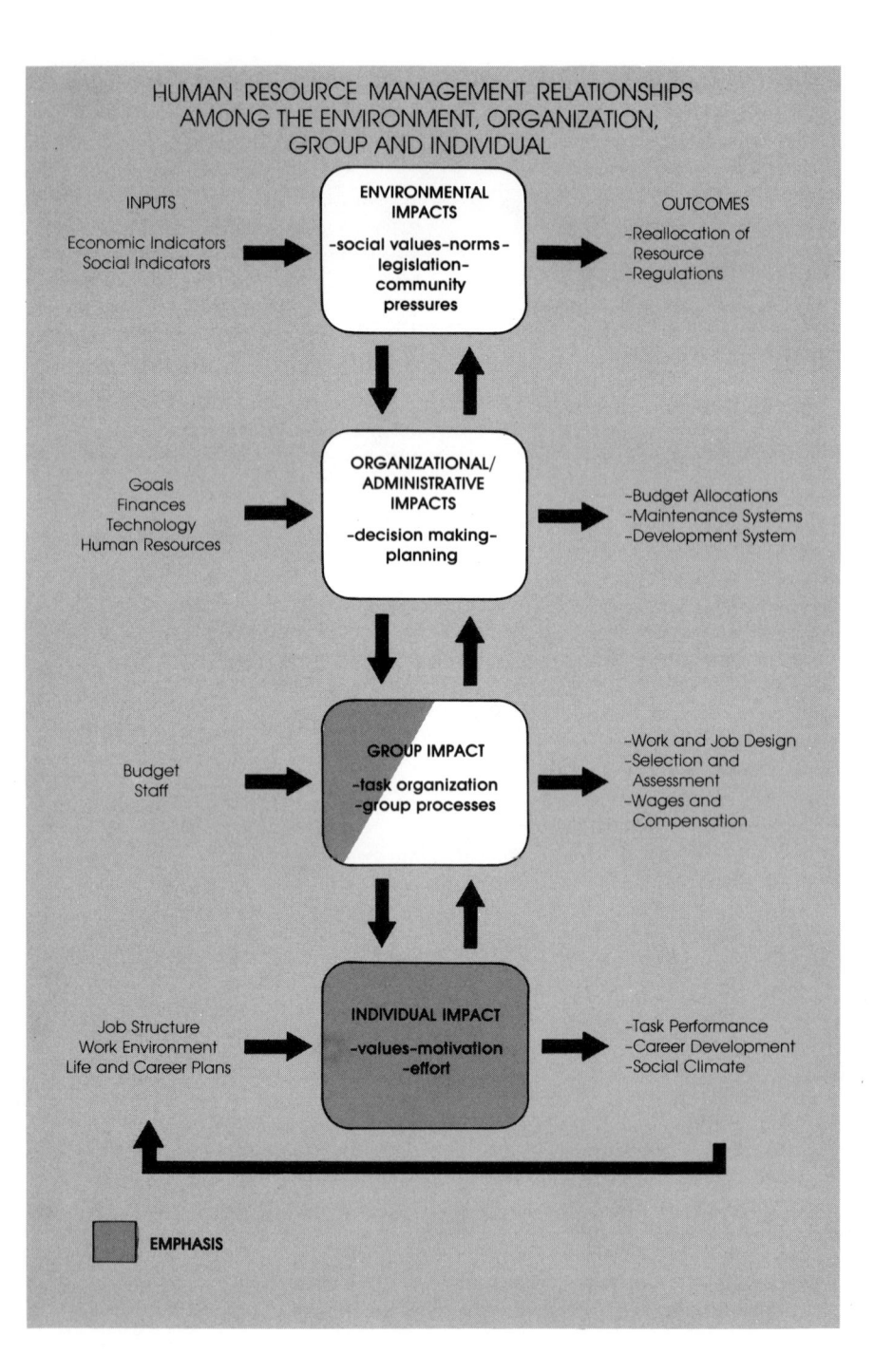

HUMAN RESOURCE MANAGEMENT RELATIONSHIPS AMONG THE ENVIRONMENT, ORGANIZATION, GROUP AND INDIVIDUAL

INPUTS

Economic Indicators
Social Indicators

→ **ENVIRONMENTAL IMPACTS**
- social values–norms–legislation–community pressures

OUTCOMES
- Reallocation of Resource
- Regulations

Goals
Finances
Technology
Human Resources

→ **ORGANIZATIONAL/ADMINISTRATIVE IMPACTS**
- decision making–planning

- Budget Allocations
- Maintenance Systems
- Development System

Budget
Staff

→ **GROUP IMPACT**
- task organization
- group processes

- Work and Job Design
- Selection and Assessment
- Wages and Compensation

Job Structure
Work Environment
Life and Career Plans

→ **INDIVIDUAL IMPACT**
- values–motivation
- effort

- Task Performance
- Career Development
- Social Climate

☐ EMPHASIS

6

EMPLOYEE BEHAVIOR

A job is a **living experience** which has substantial impact on a person's behavior and attitudes in all other contexts. What individuals do at work, the social and physical context of their work, and rewards they receive contribute to their skills, state of health, standard of living, career opportunities, and most importantly, their identity. In turn, those factors affect the future of organizations, workers, and families. For this reason, managers and employees today share the awareness that work is a uniquely important life experience. The implication for the human resource manager is that work activities and resource systems must be considered more in terms of their effect on the motivation, health, and behavior of employees.

Systematic inquiries into the relationship between workers' job activities, personal development, life style in the community, and productivity have expanded our understanding of the causes of employee behavior. Older theories that identified compensation and fringe benefit programs as core stimuli influencing work behavior have been extensively modified. Currently, the influence of the total work environment and the opportunities it provides for interpersonal and career fulfillment often exceed compensation as a major force affecting worker activity. In turn, worker behavior is seen as just one aspect of the total human being, who brings experiences from the external environment to the organization and whose mental, physical, emotional, and social well-being is in turn affected by the activities of the organization and work group.

THE TOTAL PERSON

This deeper appreciation of the interaction between an employee's behavior and the behavior of the organization has added new dimensions to concepts such as motivation, productivity, compensation, health, and even retirement. Thus newly devised systems of compensation, motivation, and health care must be built so as to integrate opportunities for individual self-determination, career development, health, maintenance, human potential, and work behavior in a meaningful way.

Craig C. Pinder directs attention to some of the ethical and practical problems that managers encounter in using compensation and behaviorally based motivation strategies. First he considers the hazards encountered in applying **un**tested theories of motivation. Then he turns to the behavioral implications of using more established theories to direct work behavior, discussing such basic theories as the "VIE" (or path-goal) model of behavior, Herzberg's motivator-hygiene concept and Maslow's needs hierarchy. Problems and limitations in the use of these motivational models lead the author to propose a practitioner's "code of ethics" which can guide the selection and use of strategies based on these models. The concluding section in Pinder's article discusses the implementation of more established approaches to motivation: MBO, participative management, job (re)design, and group incentives. Recognizing that work and health are intimately related, the author cautions that the use of these strategies may place great pressure on individuals to improve their work performance. Since those unsuccessful in increasing productivity are often subject to considerable stress, the careful monitoring of ongoing programs should constitute an area of managerial concern.

INDIVIDUAL BEHAVIOR, PERFORMANCE, AND PROBLEMS OF ADDICTION

Both articles in this section illustrate the imaginative approaches that can be devised by companies to deal with alcoholism. The programs and managerial guidelines of the Illinois Bell Telephone Company were developed during 25 years of experience in the rehabilitation of alcoholic employees. The first article in this section examines the types of programs and interpersonal contacts used to rehabilitate alcoholic employees. Fern E. Asma, Raymond L. Eggert, and Robert R. J. Hilker document the overall success rate of their program (72 percent) and provide an in-depth analysis of the programs used to return these employees to a satisfactory level of job functioning. The authors conclude that their relatively high success rate is a direct result of the company's out-and-out efforts to treat **the health problem of the total person** while providing both organization members and their families with supportive counseling. Since it is often the manager who initially confronts the addicted employee, the company assigns great importance to the managerial role in the rehabilitative system. Their managerial guide "Rehabilitation of the Problem Drinker," is reprinted at the end of this section. The policies, guidelines to symptoms, suggested interview schedules, and procedures contained in the guideline provide a basic operational strategy which can be used by managers to help employees confront any health-related job problem.

RETIREMENT: PROBLEMS AND NEW THINKING

The final articles in Part VI are fitting ones because their dual subject, aging and retirement, (often) represents the termination of full-time work and because the ideas expressed cycle the reader through concepts and programs presented throughout this book. Older workers who have often been treated in a casual, neglectful way in the past, have suddenly moved "front and center" through the attention they have received in legal, ethical, and financial spheres. Management of the older worker now extends to preparation for retirement and the impact of both the work experience and retirement programs on the individual's transition into senior citizenhood. The growing emphasis is on full organizational utilization of the more experienced employee and facilitation of retirement planning.

Within the next 20 years the size of the 35 to 45 year-old age group in the United States will increase by 80 percent and begin to project the "baby boom" generation into older age. This proportionately large group of relatively well-educated and healthy employees requires the attention of human resource managers as they face mid-life and express desires for advancement, retraining, specialized compensation programs, and/or more flexible work arrangements. In "Dealing with the Aging Work Force," Jeffrey Sonnenfeld speaks forcefully to the characteristics of an aging work force, their needs, and the organizational strategies that will help maintain productive and satisfying work relationships for older workers. Because stereotypes of the elderly no longer apply to these employees, Sonnenfeld first discusses the effects of the aging process, the relatively high rates of productivity which can be expected of these workers, and the importance of planning to meet their needs for an active and satisfying work experience. Programs that should help companies establish a forward-looking human resource approach include (1) an analysis of the career paths and performance of workers by age profiles; (2) a careful monitoring of worker performance and appraisal systems; and (3) assessments of employee interests. Such analyses are basic to any human resource system that hopes to select and maintain workers of different age categories through training, counseling, and work designs that support organizational **and** individual goals for a meaningful and active employment experience until retirement.

J. Roga O'Meara's work, "The Problems Retirement Can Bring" addresses the legal, interpersonal, and financial problems of retirees. Because the concerns of the retired center on motivation, compensation, and health problems—areas in which the organization has traditionally played a major role— this piece forcefully illustrates how the organization can continue to influence individual behavior. Workers who leave the organization **and** their families must learn to forge a new self-identity and to create a satisfying daily routine. This process elicits new stresses, copying behaviors, and health problems. The author suggests that these problems can be alleviated through counseling programs which ease the transition between work activities and retirement activities. Programs designed to guide this transition contribute to the preretirement and retirement behavior of the (ex)employee.

MOTIVATION OF THE WORKER

Concerning the Application of Human Motivation Theories in Organizational Settings

Craig C. Pinder

A dilemma shared by any science whose theoretical principles have practical implications concerns the question of when to turn its theory over to the practitioner for application to "real world" problems. On the one hand, an argument can be made that science is useless unless it has some applied value, and that until a theory is lowered from the clouds for testing and application among mortals, the theorist will be unsure of its validity (23). Advocates of application can cite benefits for both the theoretician and the practitioner.

On the other hand, until minimum levels of theoretical specificity and understanding have been attained, the application of many theories may result in little benefit to either the practitioner or the theoretician. In some cases, the theoretician may argue that premature application of theory to real-world problems may be detrimental to both parties of the science making and consumption relationship, because of potential unforeseen consequences. When this is the case, certain ethical issues confront both the practitioner and the scientist.

Defining the Ethical Issues

One can subgroup ethical considerations relating to worker motivation into at least three categories. The first set of issues, most familiar to practitioners and students of organizational behavior (OB), is the problem of when motivation becomes manipulation, and whether managers have the right (explicitly or implicitly) to attempt to shape and/or control the behavior of others. This controversy leads to a discussion of the sanctity of human behavior, individual freedom, and individual dignity. Much has been said and written about this cluster of issues (5, 39, 40, 42, 69), but it is not my intention to treat them here.

A second set of issues revolves around the question of whether "a little knowledge is a dangerous thing." After the manipulation/management prerogative issue has been resolved, what about the dysfunctional consequences

"Concerning the Application of Human Motivation Theories in Organizational Settings," by Craig C. Pinder. Reprinted with Permission from the *Academy of Management Review* (7/72) p. 384-97.

which may accrue to the science, the client, and the members of the organization when *premature* application is attempted?

A third set of ethical issues is concerned with effects on employees of policies based on motivation theories. Assuming that it is legitimate to attempt to control others' behavior, and that present theories are sufficiently refined to justify their application, what are the implications for organizational participants of successful or "nonpremature" implementation of policies grounded in industrial motivational theories and models?

The purpose of this article is to explore the second and third sets of issues. First I will attempt to assess the degree of readiness for application of theories of industrial motivation. Expectancy theory serves as a major example in this analysis, leading to the suggestion that widespread commercial application of most of these theories is still premature. Then, certain consequences which can result from successful application of motivation theories are identified. Since it is a matter of individual values to decide whether the consequences of a particular policy are ethical, throughout the analysis I will simply identify some consequences of application where the question of ethics may appear, leaving the reader to his or her own values in deciding. Finally, implication of these issues for teaching and consulting are discussed.

"How Can I Motivate My Workers?"

This is one of the most common questions asked of behavioral scientists and management consultants by students of business administration and by human resources personnel in ongoing organizations. Usually the question is asked in the belief that relatively simple prescriptions are available, based on reasonably precise theories. Although not an unreasonable question, it is somewhat naive if the asker expects simplistic answers. In many cases simplistic prescriptions are given, to the mutual satisfaction of the practitioner and the profiting consultant. But application of knowledge of human motivation may be somewhat premature, at least in cases where such simplistic applications are attempted. Most premature and oversimplified prescription writing introduces seldom-considered consequences with ethical implications.

AN ASSESSMENT OF THE STATE OF THE SCIENCE

How valid are our most common theories of motivation? Locke's (50) recent review provides only modest grounds for optimism. Most current theories enjoy limited predictive validity. Many suffer from basic problems in their assumptions concerning the nature of people; one or two make predictions which are valid in the short run but which seem to "wash out" in the long run; all are still extremely vulnerable to the influence of individual differences, the nature of which are still being investigated; and several make awkward, contradictory predictions which still have not been adequately reconciled.

As a case in point, consider the currently popular "VIE," or path-goal, models of worker motivation (12, 21, 24, 31, 33, 38, 44, 45, 78, 84). In application, these theories suggest that people will be motivated to perform effectively if supervisors can: (a) determine what sorts of job outcomes are desired by their employees; and then (b) structure the work setting so that effort results in performance; so that (c) performance will result in attainment of these desired outcomes. In other words, the supervisor is expected to conduct a rigorous and accurate survey of employee needs and values, and manipulate the task setting and reward system accordingly in order to maximize employee motivation.

First, recent work by Locke (50), Behling and Starke (6, 77), and Wahba and House (86) at long last has made explicit the important assumptions the theory makes concerning human nature. The gist of these recent theoretical and empirical arguments is that theoretical assumptions concerning human hedonism and rationality are unfounded or at least oversimplified. A conclusion from these studies is that the individual the theory purports to explain is unrealistic. The degree of discrepancy between real person and VIE–assumed person is not yet fully appreciated, but it does seem clear that a gap exists, suggesting that the theory is not yet ready for universal application by practitioners.

Second, the predictive validity typically found by researchers testing VIE theory must be considered. Results such as those found by Pritchard and Sanders (66), Hackman and Porter (29), Reinharth and Wahba (68), or Dachler and Mobley (12) typify the level of validity this theory has to offer in its present forms. Validity coefficients between linear composites of expectancy theory components and hard criteria of effort or performance rarely exceed .40. This means that the theory is seldom able to account for more than 10 to 15 percent of the variance in employee performance. The remainder is "error" variance, attributable to unknown influences of individual and organizational differences. Headway is being made at understanding some of these individual differences. For instance, Lawler's (44, 45) "Hybrid Model" considers the influence of self-esteem and locus of control as partial determinants of expectancies and instrumentalities, respectively. But although VIE theory has been with us in various forms for several years, it is still immature in its ability to predict or explain much of organizational behavior, and thus its widespread application in organizations is premature.

Parenthetically, and in defense of VIE theory, it may be more valid than empirical methods are yet able to demonstrate. Because measures of VIE constructs are of limited reliability (18) and do not possess the ratio measurement scaling properties that the theory's arithmetic expressions require (71), empirical failures may reflect the crudity of research tools as much as invalidity of the theory itself. However, under the norm of science our field embraces, empirical support is necessary for acceptance of a theory, and to date, VIE theory enjoys only mixed empirical support.

Aside from the overall predictive validity of VIE theory, consider the path-goal prescriptions made by the theory. First, to my knowledge, no one has asked VIE–path-goal advocates whether supervisors should have the right to probe employee values, or whether such probing might be considered an invasion of privacy. Most people are sensitive to the privacy of individual values in the context of other social behaviors such as voting, yet no one seems bothered by the possibility that the worker may not want his or her values explored, or that line supervisors may not be competent to perform such an assessment accurately. In other words, we can question the first part of the path-goal prescription by asking: Under what conditions is it ethical to attempt to determine what outcomes are desired by an individual employee? Is it unethical in some circumstances to not attempt such an assessment? Can we assume that these values, once determined, are constant? How accurately can we infer the values of others, and what might be the consequences of being wrong? Answers to these questions are clearly a matter of personal values and specific circumstances. Without implying that such probing is necessarily unethical, I believe that these questions require ethical consideration.

The second prescription of the theory is to structure the work setting so that effort will lead to performance. In terms of other theories, this means manipulation of the difficulty level of the task, or the probability of success. Simply stated, the expectancy theorist suggests maximizing the "expectancy," or the perceived likelihood that effort will lead to performance, in order to maximize employee motivation. One problem with this prescription is that it is contradicted by other theoretical perspectives, such as that of Locke (49), who suggests making tasks difficult (with the proviso that they be accepted by the worker), and that of McClelland and Atkinson (4) who suggest that for some people in pursuit of some outcomes, the probability of success should be set around .5. So the practitioner is left with the question of whether the optimal level of task difficulty for a particular employee is low, medium, or high. Lawler (44) has acknowledged the necessity of building in consideration of the achievement-related outcome in his expectancy model, but we are left, as yet, with no guidelines to assist the practical manager in deciding whether or not achievement motivation is involved in the case of an individual in a job setting.

The third prescription of expectancy theory is for the manager to tie rewards directly to performance. Aside from the fact that empirical tests of this principle are equivocal as to whether the instrumentalities should be maximized or whether rewards should be administered according to a partial schedule (7, 88, 89), there is another potential problem with the contingency principle. Research by Deci (13, 14, 15, 16) and others (26, 47, 64, 65) suggests that a possible consequence of making the administration of organizational rewards, especially money, contingent upon employee performance may be the undermining of the employee's intrinsic motivation to do the work. That is, the individual may come to perceive that his primary reason for doing a job is for the sake of the money it provides.

In the terms of the path-goal theories, this phenomenon is most likely to occur when the person perceives a strong instrumentality, or performance reward probability. A consequence of this perception, according to Deci (16), can be a decrement to the intrinsic motivation of the worker toward the task, and to the intrinsic satisfaction derived from doing the task. This relatively new criticism of VIE theory is still the topic of considerable debate. If further studies confirm the hypothesis, the argument will be made that practitioners may be gaining short-run increases in extrinsic motivation at the expense of long-run losses in intrinsic motivation. Certainly, such a trade-off is undesirable in the context of other management programs aimed at fostering intrinsic motivation (such as job enrichment or participative management).

Another problem with VIE theory is that it differs with other theories on certain significant issues. For instance, VIE theorists and operant theorists still differ on the model of the person, as evident in the recent debate between Scott (73) and Deci (17). Whether the person is more appropriately viewed from the perspective of the behaviorist or the phenomenologist is still not clear, and the debate seems no closer to resolution now than when Hitt (30) reviewed the two arguments years ago. Petrock and Gamboa (63) recently summarized the similarities and differences between the two theories and concluded that they are quite similar in many of their applied prescriptions, so resolution may still be possible. But until some reconciliation is reached over the issues of preferred reward schedules and the nature of the working person, the practitioner is left facing two dilemmas with considerable importance for application.

Lawler (44) has likewise summarized major differences between VIE theory and equity theory in predictions concerning employee performance under different pay situations. This discussion is not meant to be an exhaustive critique of expectancy theory, and I do not mean to suggest that the theory is all wrong and of no value, nor that VIE theory be abandoned simply because it differs from other theoretical perspectives. Although it has been available in several forms for many years, it is still adolescent in its predictive and explanatory ability. It still possesses several limitations—such as unrealistic assumptions concerning the worker, low predictive validity due to individual differences and measurement problems, and critical contradictions with other "established" bodies of theory. Apart from these weaknesses, the theory prescribes probing of employee needs and values—a practice with ethical considerations made all the more profound in view of the validity of the theory itself. As Locke (50) suggested, in order for VIE theory to make substantial progress, it will need to evolve considerably from its present form. In the meantime, its unrestricted application is premature.

Other Popular Theories and Applications

Empirical support of other common motivation theories is generally no better than that for VIE theory. The motivator-hygiene debate now seems to be over: Herzberg's theory is an oversimplification of reality and seems methodologically bound. Equity theory seems to be on the retreat (50) since attempts to extend early laboratory findings into the field have enjoyed only limited success (25). Need hierarchy theory seems to have some utility left, although the debate concerning the number of need levels which exist for most people, and the order in which their gratification proceeds, is not yet finalized (2, 45, 46, 58).

Other managerial and Organizational Development (OD) strategies with roots in motivation theories have found only limited success. Debate has unequivocally demonstrated that job enrichment is not for everyone, although great strides are being made in devising means for identifying individuals for whom enrichment may be suitable (8, 27, 28, 87). Participation programs are not succeeding everywhere and we are just now learning the conditions under which work participation in decision making is appropriate (3, 9, 11, 54, 74, 83, 85). (Critics such as Nord (62) and Jenkins (36) have argued that present approaches to participation and enrichment are doomed to fail because they do not go far enough to change the fundamental legal-socioeconomic structure of Western society.)

The demise of so many Management by Objectives (MBO) programs in recent years (72) has at last led us to reconsider both the systemic and individual/behavioral conditions for goal setting programs to be effective in practice (35, 41, 43, 48, 53, 79, 80, 81). MBO programs are often simply legitimized systems of phony participation, in which the fiction is maintained that the subordinate is making a real input into planning work objectives and procedures. Such situations smack of Machiavellianism and are quickly self-defeating. Compared to most theoretical approaches to motivation in organizations, only goal setting theory based on Locke's (49) original formulation and operant theory (37, 52, 61) seem to enjoy any real success (43). But even in the case of operant theory, there have been instances of misapplication and misinterpretation of the theory's terms, concepts, and principles (56).

In short, the vast majority of familiar theories of motivation, as well as most applied programs which are based upon them, betray the embarrassing state of immaturity of our field. Immaturity is not sufficient justification to indict an academic discipline, but the consequences of hurried and ill-founded attempts to apply its theories may be.

It is a matter of personal values whether theories with limited validity are ready for application in organizations. It is my belief that careful application is a necessary part of the research cycle, needed to determine the validity of theories. However, and this point is crucial, controlled application for the sake of validation should be differentiated from application for the sake of permanently changing organizational systems. Most theories require the former, but cannot yet fully justify the latter.

Some Dysfunctions of Premature Application

In what ways are premature applications of these theories harmful? There are at least three groups whose best interests are at stake every time a premature application is attempted and fails.

First, the OB field itself stands to lose, including academics and practitioners who care about the scientific study of organizations. Every time a new fad or fashion (20) rolls out of our theorizing—or a revised version of an old one (57)—and is sold to industry with unqualified expectations for success, we collectively invest some of the "credit" we have earned with our contacts in the real world. The more we claim our new products to be panaceas, the greater is the investment. Because so many programs require such specific preconditions for their success, the prior probability of their success is usually low. When failure occurs, we lose our credits—not only the consultants or academics who installed the program, but to a certain extent, all who are associated with the discipline. Many practitioners are justified for feeling disappointed and disenchanted with behavioral science and behavioral scientists. It is no wonder that so many of them are skeptical when we approach them with the next latest fashion, either to gain entry for the sake of validation and testing, or for the sake of their adoption of the new programs. In short, the *premature* application of behavioral science principles can move the discipline backward rather than forward, in terms of its credibility and professional stature.

The second group to lose are the client systems which "buy" our premature applications. The time, cost, and energy lost as the result of abortive applications provide sufficient justification for their hostility toward behavioral science and its purveyors.

The third group to lose from these failures are the usual "guinea-pigs"—the lower participants of organizations upon whom most theory-based changes impact. Changes in job content, reporting relationships, status systems, pay systems, working procedures, or other aspects of the work situation can be threatening for the individuals involved.

Most would agree that where it is needed, change is justified. But problems arise where changes are made inappropriately, either because they are too hastily implemented for training to take place; because they involve "blanket treatments" which are not fit for everyone; or simply because the systemic preconditions necessary for success are not in existence. Eager consumers of these theories seldom consider the ethical implications of haphazardly changing people's jobs where the changes are not fully justified and are likely to fail in the long run.

In sum, we should not permit premature application since it harms our prospects for legitimate applications for the purpose of either theory testing or appropriate organizational development. The question seems, then, What do we mean by "premature" applications?

WHAT IS PREMATURE APPLICATION?

It is useful to differentiate between application for the purpose of theory testing and development, and application for the sake of premanent organizational change. The former type of application is scientific in nature; the latter is commercial. I would agree with Garner (23) that eventually all theories require application for the sake of validation. The disappointing field results for equity theory demonstrate the need for such application.

In practice, it is a matter of judgment on the part of the researcher to decide when field application of theories is required for their validation. The researcher should inform the organization's decision makers what the chances for success really are. When practitioners realize that our intentions are scientific, and they are offered no miracles, their expectations cannot easily be violated. The greatest breach of confidence occurs when a fledgling idea is served up as something refined and likely to succeed, and then fails. Thus it may not be the prior degree of validity of the theory so much as the level of expectation engendered by the researcher which determines whether application for the sake of validation is ethical or unethical.

Such humility on the part of researchers may make entree into organizations more difficult than otherwise. Ironically, the difficulties many of us experience at gaining entry are due at least in part to the violated expectations of now-wary practitioners. Regardless, in approaching practitioners for help in our science making, we have a moral obligation to be no more promising of success than our product warrants.

In the case of commercial application, no definite standards exist among academics, consultants, or eager practitioners concerning the minimum degree of validity required of theories before they should be considered ready for organizational consumption (except for consultants belonging to the American Psychological Association or other professional associations for psychologists, which observe a code of ethics). In practice, this decision is usually left up to the parties involved in any application attempt. Because the absolute levels of predictive and explanatory validity of our best motivation theories are extremely low, some form of professional standard is needed to protect practitioners (and the rest of us) from consultants who "sell" theories to organizations for the mutual profit of owners and consultants.

One means of gaining this protection might be a code of ethics for all organizational consultants. It may be that in order for the OB field to attain the status of a profession, a code of ethics is required specifying when and by whom our theories and techniques may be commercially installed. Such a code would consider, apart from the question of when the theories "work" sufficiently well, the question of whether the *correct* application of our theories may entail consequences which are undersirable from the employees' point of view—such as unilateral changes in the psychological contract, threats to intrinsic motivation and satisfaction, or threats to norms of equity and justice. When such dysfunctional consequences can be expected from application of theories, the code of ethics should specify provisions and safeguards to prevent the violation of individual rights.

The code need not preclude the possibility of appropriate commercial application, nor result in compromises in managerial prerogatives. In fact, it might *require* academics to practice the sound principles of validating their theories in the field rather than developing them solely on the basis of laboratory evidence. But when they are taken to the field, the code would require that theories be accompanied by the degree of humility and appreciation for individual differences which is commensurate with their adolescent levels of development. When the consumer has no false illusions, and when the rights of individual lower participants are adequately safeguarded, then the application of adolescent theories would be deemed appropriate. It would be naive to suggest that the mere existence of a code of ethics would prevent all instances of premature application. The considerable room usually left for interpretation from case to case with codes of this kind suggests that a code would provide, at best, only a good first step toward guaranteeing professional and ethical conduct. But a first step is required.

This analysis is not meant to suggest a rigid cloistering of academic ideas in ivory towers. Such a position would be foolish and somewhat iconoclastic. Rather, the arguments should draw to the attention of researchers, teachers, and consultants the ethical implications of premature application of knowledge. What we are lacking in explanatory power we must compensate for with increases in humility and truth when we pass our ideas along to others who wish to apply them.

ETHICAL CONSIDERATIONS SURROUNDING NONPREMATURE APPLICATIONS

Some consequences can arise from successful, nonpremature application of our theory. These pertain to the lower participants upon whom the policies usually impact, and suggest the need for ethical evaluation. Since what is ethical is a matter of individual values, I will only identify the issues and let the reader conduct the moral evaluation.

First, MBO programs should be considered (67). If they are conducted properly, and if pay is tied to performance as Mobley (59) suggests, MBO may lead to the same decrements in intrinsic motivation and satisfaction that Deci (16), Pinder

(65), and others have demonstrated in the context of VIE theory research. If MBO does have this effect, we might judge the consequences at best unfortunate, and at worst, unethical (especially in view of growing sentiment for making work more intrinsically enjoyable).

Another management technique which may also involve a question of ethics is participative management. Since the early Harwood experiments (10), participation in decision making has been heralded as a means of deriving worker acceptance of change, and good performance. The mechanisms of ego-involvement have been posited to explain the success of the technique (84). But as the caveats arising from failure to replicate the original results in other cultures (22)—and the personality considerations found to moderate the effects of the technique—have been reported (83), it is clear that participative management is not the motivational panacea many hoped it would be. Some people like and can benefit from participation while others dislike it and cannot readily accept it. Presumably, for some individuals, the chance (or requirement) to participate involves a radical change in the psychological contract (19, 70) or worse, a significant change in the inducements/contributions balance (55). Although management may genuinely believe that the chance to participate will be seen by employees as an added inducement or reward, some individuals may perceive participation more as an added contribution. To the extent that workers have little *real* choice in whether or not they participate in decisions, and to the extent that they perceive this participation as a change in the psychological contract or the inducements/contributions balance, such programs, for some individuals, may be unfair.

The problem of individual differences as they relate to ethical considerations also emerges in considering job redesign. Whether speaking of job enlargement or job enrichment (following Herzberg's distinction), the perceived desirability of changes in one's job also varies from one individual to another (34). Some people like it and want it, while others do not. In practice, we might permit those who do not want their jobs redesigned to say so—and then respect their decisions. But this alternative is seldom observed by management faced with engineering data and plans which predict savings as the result of job redesign. We could allow disgruntled employees the right to take other jobs in the organization, but the net result is the same—the individual is no longer at the job he or she was occupying before the enrichment or enlargement proposal was made. In cases where the displaced employee is less satisfied with a new job than a former job, his or her rights under the psychological contract may have been violated.

Job redesign or reassignment and displacement of employees may also be examined in ethical terms from another perspective. To the extent that an employee is appropriately assigned to a job, he or she will be satisfied with it, and (following the Theory of Work Adjustment (51)), proficient at it. To the extent that his or her personal profile of work needs is matched by the occupational rewards provided by the job, the worker will be satisfied, provided that he or she is performing adequately. Therefore, any unilateral decision by the organization which redesigns a person's job (and hence changes the nature of the occupation aptitude profile and/or occupational reinforcer profile), or which reassigns the worker to another job for which he or she is less well suited, may result in a reduction of the worker's overall level of work adjustment, as defined by Lofquist and Dawis (51). Again, it is a question of values whether such unilateral changes are ethical or not, but I believe we should at least reconsider job redesign from this perspective.

Group incentive systems provide different, seldom considered ethical considerations. Under most such systems, the norm of "distributive justice" or equity (1) is missing for almost all workers. Above-average performers will be rewarded at rates lower than what their individual contributions would otherwise deserve, while below-average performers, apart from receiving more than their fair share of rewards, may be placed in the awkward situation of social pressure to perform better. When the individual cannot or does not care to increase the level of performance, frustration, dissatisfaction, and conflict may result. To the extent that these undesirable consequences may result from group incentive systems, one might make the argument that such systems are unethical.

Many of the foregoing "dysfunctional consequences" potentially related to application of theories involve disruptions in the psychological contract between worker and organization. Unilateral changes in the contract foisted upon the lower participant by management may be unethical. Theoretically, when the rights of the individual employee under the contract have been violated, three courses of action are open: protesting, to have the violation corrected; seeking alternative employment; or choosing to "put up" with the violation and remain in the organization.

In fact, the number of feasible alternatives open to such an individual is not always great. The relative power of the individual as compared to the organization is usually very small, and unless there is a formal means of rectifying contract violations (such as a union or a company-sponsored grievance system *which really works*), the protest option is not viable. The alternative of seeking other employment is also less viable than suggested by the principles of free enterprise labor markets, especially for workers who are old, somewhat obsolete, or otherwise less than desirable to other organizations. Apart from the questionable feasibility of changing careers later in life, there are often other costs involved for the individual, such as the loss of vested pension benefits, seniority, status, and security. As a result, the only alternative *really* available to many people for whom the contract with the company has been violated ("unilaterally changed") is to stay on board, minimizing the damage and the losses, and possibly taking advantage of opportunities to even the score.

The very act of going to work for an organization in our culture necessarily involves giving up a certain degree of "human freedom and dignity." Obviously, a certain minimum degree of control is necessary, or organizations as we know them could not exist. Most employees understand this, and expect that the organization will attempt to determine and enforce the "rules" of the employment relationship. It is the employee's perception and acceptance of the rules which constitutes his or her side of the agreement. But when the company violates the contract, the individual usually has very little power or recourse; thus, when left unchecked, these violations may be unfair.

IMPLICATIONS FOR TEACHING

Many business students will eventually become the major "consumers" of our theoretical products. After they work themselves into positions of relative power in organizations, they will be responsible for decisions concerning what theories to apply, and when and how to apply them. Consequently, issues of premature application and accompanying ethical implications become especially important for the academic who is planning course curricula.

The constraints of a school term invariably dicatate a decision between "bandwidth" and "fidelity." Bandwidth leads to a smorgasbord-like course where the student is acquainted with as many different variables and theories as time permits. Naturally, the cost in terms of fidelity translates to a superficial and naive understanding of each topic. The extreme alternative is to serve fidelity at the expense of bandwidth, inundating the student with *all* the theory and research pertinent to one or two theoretical models, to the exclusion of alternative perspectives.

On the topic of industrial motivation, as in most areas where the teacher must resolve the issue by compromising between bandwidth and fidelity, students will be only partially equipped to apply what they have learned. When they receive the bandwidth, they are left with the vague impression that myriad variables are relevant, but are not sure how and when. In the case of high fidelity students, a false sense of security grounded in a belief that "VIE (or whatever) is the thing" will result (ten years ago it would have been "Herzberg is where it's at"), and students will be left without the tools to sensibly consume future developments from academe. If Locke (50) is correct in his prediction that VIE theory will need to evolve beyond the point of possible recognition in order to survive, fidelity students will become prematurely obsolete soon after they leave the university.

To this point the familiar bandwidth-fidelity dilemma poses no novelty. But in training practice-oriented business students the trade-off should not be made at all. The potential damage to organizations, and especially to people in them, from application of adolescent theories by graduates with a half-baked knowledge of human motivation, and the false sense of simplicity resulting from undergraduate courses in which the bandwidth versus fidelity compromise was made, is frightening. Without either high levels of professional skill in OB or a moderate level of training supplemented by caution and humility concerning individual differences, business school graduates are likely to perpetuate the kinds of dysfunctional consequences described above.

What Can Be Done?

Assuming that organizations and their members are better off for having practitioners trained in OB, and that only so many hours can be spent during an undergraduate's training in the area of OB, what can be done? To stop teaching OB in business schools and/or reassign the field to psychology departments is one suggestion (60), which this writer rejects. The degree of detail in perception, physiology, and learning theory still found in most psychology departments is superfluous for a student interested in organizations. Traditional psychology departments (or any unidisciplinary departments) cannot provide the degree of interdisciplinary insight required to understand the complexities of organizations.

By leaving OB in business schools, we can continue to interact with, and learn from, professionals devoted to other facets of running organizations, and we can continue to impress on students the importance of the human element in administration. At the same time, we should strive to instill a profound appreciation for the comparative strengths, weaknesses, contradictions, and limitations inherent in the theories we teach.

Students should be as impressed with basic guidelines for *evaluating* theories of motivation as they are familiar with the content of the theories themselves. They should develop the skill to evaluate and consume theories sensibly, both to forestall the likelihood of their growing obsolete once they leave the academic setting, and to avoid the human and organizational costs which can accompany a false sense of simplicity. They should be impressed that what we know about human motivation in organizations is much less than what many single, simplistic theories claim, although we are gradually learning more about systemic conditions and individual differences. Finally, they should be helped to develop the eclectic skills of approaching and understanding motivation or other organizational problems from any of several perspectives, simultaneously drawing on the strengths and weaknesses of various theories. Our combined knowledge, based on the theory and research of several different schools of thought on motivation, is substantial, although the contribution of no one theoretical approach justifies our complete faith. Teaching in this area should demonstrate this and develop the eclecticism this belief suggests.

Discussions with OB instructors from several universities have confirmed my hypothesis that student experience in real organizations can make the educational experience in business schools more valuable. This seems especially true in learning OB. First-hand experience can sometimes supplement the inputs academics provide, making the student appreciate the value of what we offer, and also providing personal case studies or examples which make theories more understandable and applicable. Most of the success and current popularity of the so-called "experiential" approaches to learning OB can probably be attributed to this phenomenon. Perhaps we should expose students to even more experience, either through class assignments requiring them to get involved in organizations during their study, or by requiring minimum degrees of real-world experience before they begin their formal theoretical training. Case studies and novels which illustrate OB principles are used in some schools, to simulate what it is like in real organizations. Arguments in favor of experience as an ingredient of teaching should be separated from arguments in favor of "relevance." I agree with House's (32) recent argument that too much emphasis on application rather than on theory, principles, and analytic skills is a disservice to the student.

In short, if OB teachers relate to their students appropriately, and if consultants do the same with their clients, a little knowledge need not be a dangerous thing in our field.

CONCLUSIONS

The time may be nigh when OB will have to "prove itself" as worthwhile and relevant in order to maintain its respect as a viable academic discipline. We may have to begin demonstrating more frequently the application of and payoffs from our theories, including those concerning human motivation. Although there have already been many attempts to apply our knowledge in organizational settings, too many attempts have been premature, and even when our theories seem to demonstrate enough predictive validity to justify application, certain unforeseen dysfunctional consequences may result—consequences having ethical considerations for everyone concerned, including the OB field itself. The need has been proposed for an explicit code of ethics pertaining to the application of our theories in organizations. Further, it has been argued that in order to achieve and maintain professional status we must begin to conduct ourselves as consultants, researchers, and teachers with the respect for individual differences and for individual and organizational rights befitting a discipline with promising, yet still adolescent theories to offer.

Encouraging signs have appeared recently in professional management journals, wherein other academics concerned with OB application have reminded practitioners of the problem of individual differences and the necessity of remaining aware of the limitations of theories (75, 76, 82). It is hoped that this article will provoke other academics or practitioners to address themselves to the questions of premature application and ethics, if only to formulate counterarguments. To make peace with such issues or to lay them to rest, they must first be articulated.

Note

[1] I wish to thank Vance F. Mitchell and Pravin Moudgill of the University of British Columbia, Walter Nord of Washington University, and Howard Schwartz of Cornell University for their constructive comments on earlier drafts of this article.

References

1. Adams, J.S. "Toward an Understanding of Inequity," *Journal of Abnormal Psychology*, 67 (1963), 422-436.
2. Alderfer, C.P. *Existence, Relatedness, and Growth.* New York: The Free Press, 1972.
3. Alutto, J.A., and F. Acito. "Decisional Participation and Sources of Job Satisfaction: A Study of Manufacturing Personnel," *Academy of Management Journal*, 17 (1974), 160-167.
4. Atkinson, J.W. *An Introduction to Motivation.* New York: Van Nostrand, 1964, see esp. chap. 9.
5. Baritz, L. *The Servants of Power.* New York: John Wiley & Sons, 1960.
6. Behling, O., and F. Starke. "The Postulates of Expectancy Theory," *Academy of Management Journal*, 16 (1973), 373-388.
7. Berger, C., L.L. Cummings, and H.G. Heneman, III. "Expectancy Theory and Operant Conditioning Predictions of Performance under Variable Ratio and Continuous Schedules of Reinforcements." *Organizational Behavior and Human Performance*, 14 (1975), 227-243.
8. Brief, A.P., and R.J. Aldag. "Employee Reactions to Job Characteristics; A Constructive Replication," *Journal of Applied Psychology*, 60 (1975), 182-186.
9. Chaney, F.B., and K.S. Teel. "Participative Management—A Practical Experience." *Personnel*, 49, 6 (1972), 8-19.
10. Coch, L., and J.R.P. French. "Overcoming Resistance to Change," *Human Relations*, 1 (1948), 512-532.
11. Conway, J.A. "Test of Linearity between Teachers' Participation in Decision Making and Perceptions of Their Schools As Organizations." *Administrative Science Quarterly*, 21 (1976), 130-139.
12. Dachler, P., and W. Mobley. "Construct Validation of an Instrumentality-Expectancy-Task-Goal Model of Work Motivation: Some Theoretical Boundary Conditions," *Journal of Applied Psychology*, 58 (1973), 397-418.

13. Deci, E.L. "The Effects of Externally-mediated Rewards on Intrinsic Motivation," *Journal of Personality and Social Psychology, 18* (1971), 105–115.
14. Deci, E.L. "Intrinsic Motivation, Extrinsic Reinforcement, and Inequity," *Journal of Personality and Social Psychology, 22* (1972), 113–120. (a)
15. Deci, E.L. "The Effects of Contingent and Noncontingent Rewards and Controls on Intrinsic Motivation," *Organizational Behavior and Human Performance, 8* (1972), 217–229. (b)
16. Deci, E.L. *Intrinsic Motivation: Theory and Research.* New York: Plenum, 1975.
17. Deci, E.L. "Notes on the Theory and Metatheory of Intrinsic Motivation," *Organizational Behavior and Human Performance, 15* (1976), 130–145.
18. de'Leo, P.J., and R.D. Pritchard. "An Examination of Some Methodological Problems in Testing Expectancy-valence Models with Survey Techniques," *Organizational Behavior and Human Performance, 12* (1974), 143–148.
19. Dunahee, M.H., and L.A. Wangler. "The Psychological Contract: A Conceptual Structure for Management/Employee Relations," *Personnel Journal, 53* (1974), 518–526.
20. Dunnette, M.D. "Fads, Fashions, and Folderol in Psychology," *American Psychologist, 21* (1966), 343–352.
21. Evans, M.G. "Extensions of a Path-goal Theory of Motivation," *Journal of Applied Psychology, 59* (1974), 172–178.
22. French, J.R.P., J. Israel, and D. As. "An Experiment on Participation in a Norwegian Factory," *Human Relations, 13* (1960), 3–19.
23. Garner, W.R. "The Acquisition and Application of Knowledge: A Symbiotic Relationship," *American Psychologist, 27* (1972), 941–946.
24. Georgopoulis, B.S., G.M. Mahoney, and N.W. Jones. "A Path-goal Approach to Productivity," *Journal of Applied Psychology, 41* (1957), 345–353.
25. Goodman, P.S., and A Friedman. "An Examination of Adams' Theory of Inequity," *Administrative Science Quarterly, 16* (1971), 271–288.
26. Greene, D., and M. Lepper. "How to Turn Play into Work," *Psychology Today, 8*, 4 (1974), 49–54.
27. Hackman, J.R., and E.E. Lawler. "Employee Reactions to Job Characteristics," *Journal of Applied Psychology, 55* (1971), 259–286.
28. Hackman, J.R., and G.R. Oldham. "Development of the Job Diagnostic Survey," *Journal of Applied Psychology, 60* (1975), 159–170.
29. Hackman, J.R., and L.W. Porter. "Expectancy Theory Predictions of Work Effectiveness," *Organizational Behavior and Human Performance, 3* (1968), 417–426.
30. Hitt, W. "Two Models of Man," *American Psychologist, 24* (1969), 651–658.
31. House, R.J. "A Path-goal Theory of Leadership," *Administrative Science Quarterly, 16* (1971), 321–338.
32. House, R.J. "The Quest for Relevance in Management Education: Some Second Thoughts and Undesired Consequences," *Academy of Management Journal, 18* (1975), 323–333.
33. House, R.J., and G. Dessler. "The Path-goal Theory of Leadership: Some Post-hoc and A Priori Tests." In *Contingency Approaches to Leadership*, ed. J.G. Hunt, Carbondale, Ill.: Southern Illinois University Press, 1974.
34. Hulin, C., and M. Blood. "Job Enlargement, Individual Differences, and Worker Responses," *Psychological Bulletin, 69* (1968), 41–55.
35. Jamieson, D. "Behavioral Problems with Management by Objectives," *Academy of Management Journal 16,* (1973), 496–505.

36. Jenkins, D. "Beyond Job Enrichment," *Working Papers for a New Society*, 2 (1975), 51-57.
37. Joblansky, S. F., and D. L. DeVries. "Operant Conditioning Principles Extrapolated to the Theory of Management," *Organizational Behavior and Human Performance*, 7 (1972), 340-358.
38. Kafka, V. W. "A Motivation System that Works Both Ways," *Personnel*, 49, 4 (1972), 61-66.
39. Kanfer, F. H. "Issues and Ethics in Behavior Manipulation," *Psychological Reports*, 16 (1965), 187-196.
40. Kelman, H. C. "Manipulation of Human Behavior: An Ethical Dilemma." In *A Time to Speak: On Human Values and Social Research*, ed. H.C. Kelman. San Francisco: Josey-Bass, 1968.
41. Kirchoff, B. A. "A Diagnostic Tool for Management by Objectives," *Personnel Psychology*, 28 (1975), 351-364.
42. Krasner, L. "Behavior Control and Social Responsibility," *American Psychologist*, 17 (1962), 199-204.
43. Lathan, G. P., and G. A. Yukl. "A Review of Research on the Application of Goal Setting in Organizations," *Academy of Management Journal*, 18 (1975), 824-845.
44. Lawler, E.E. *Pay and Organizational Effectiveness*. New York: McGraw-Hill, 1971.
45. Lawler, E.E. *Motivation in Work Organizations*. Belmont, Calif.: Wadsworth, 1973.
46. Lawler, E.E., and J.L. Suttle. "A Casual Correlational Test of the Need Hierarchy Concept," *Organizational Behavior and Human Performance* 7, (1972), 265-287.
47. Lepper, M.R., D.Greene, and R.E. Nisbett. "Undermining Children's Intrinsic Interest with Extrinsic Rewards: A Test of the Over-justification Hypothesis," *Journal of Personality and Social Psychology*, 28 (1973), 129-137.
48. Levinson, H. "Management by Whose Objectives?" *Harvard Business Review*, 48, 4 (1970), 125-134.
49. Locke, E.A. "Toward A Theory of Task Motivation and Incentives," *Organizational Behavior and Human Performance*, 3 (1968), 157-189.
50. Locke, E.A. "Personnel Attitudes and Motivation," *Annual Review of Psychology*, 26 (1975), 457-480.
51. Lofquist, L., and R. Dawis. *Adjustment to Work*. New York: Appleton-Century-Crofts, 1969.
52. Luthans, F., and R. Kreitner. *Organizational Behavior Modification*. Glenview, Ill.: Scott, Foresman, 1975.
53. McConsky, Dale D. "20 Ways to Kill Management by Objectives," *Management Review*, October 1972, pp. 4-13.
54. Malone, E.L. "The Non-Linear Systems Experiment in Participative Management," *Journal of Business*, 48 (1975), 52-64.
55. March, J.G., and H. Simon. *Organizations*. New York: John Wiley & Sons, 1958.
56. Mawhinney, T.C. "Operant Terms and Concepts in the Description of Individual Work Behavior: Some Problems of Interpretation, Application, and Evaluation," *Journal of Applied Psychology*, 60 (1975), 704-712.
57. Miles, R.E. *Theories of Management*. New York: McGraw-Hill, 1975.
58. Mitchell, V.F., and P. Moudgill. "Measurement of Maslow's Need Hierarchy," *Organizational Behavior and Human Performance*, in press.
59. Mobley, W. "The Link Between MBO and Merit Compensation," *Personnel Journal*, 53 (1974), 423-427.

60. Naylor, J.C. "Hickory, Dickory, Dock—Let's Turn Back the Clock," *Professional Psychologist*, 1971, pp. 217–234.
61. Nord, W. "Beyond the Teaching Machine: The Neglected Area of Operant Conditioning in the Theory and Practice of Management," *Organizational Behavior and Human Performance*, 4 (1969), 375–401.
62. Nord, W. "The Failure of Current Applied Behavioral Science: A Marxian Perspective," *The Journal of Applied Behavioral Science*, 10 (1974), 557–578.
63. Petrock, F., and V. Gamboa. "Expectancy Theory and Operant Conditioning: A Conceptual Comparison." In Walter Nord, *Concepts and Controversies in Organizational Behavior*, 2nd ed. Pacific Palisades, Calif.: Goodyear Publishing Co., 1976.
64. Pinder, C.C. *The Moderating Effect of Worker Orientation on the Relationship between Contingent Versus Noncontingent Reward Systems and Intrinsic Motivation and Performance* (Ph.D. dissertation, Cornell University, 1975).
65. Pinder, C.C. "Additivity Versus Nonadditivity of Intrinsic and Extrinsic Incentives," *Journal of Applied Psychology*, in press.
66. Pritchard, R., and M.S. Sanders. "The Influence of Valence, Instrumentality and Expectancy on Effort and Performance," *Journal of Applied Psychology* 57 (1973), 55–60.
67. Raia, A. *Managing by Objectives*. Glenview, Ill.: Scott, Foresman, 1974.
68. Reinharth, L., and M.A. Wahba. "Expectancy Theory as a Predictor of Work Motivation, Effort Expenditure, and Job Performance," *Academy of Management Journal*, 18 (1975), 520–537.
69. Rogers, C.R., and B.F. Skinner. "Some Issues Concerning the Control of Human Behavior: A Symposium," *Science*, 124 (1956), 1057–1066.
70. Schein, E. *Organizational Psychology*, 2nd ed. Englewood Cliffs, N.J.: Prentice-Hall, Inc., 1970.
71. Schmidt, F.L. "Implications of a Measurement Problem for Expectancy Theory Research," *Organizational Behavior and Human Performance*, 10 (1973), 243–251.
72. Schuster, F.E., and A.S. Kindall. "Management by Objectives—Where We Stand Today, A Survey of the Fortune 500," *Human Resources Management*, 13, 1 (1974), 8–11.
73. Scott, W.E., Jr. "The Effects of Extrinsic Rewards on 'Intrinsic Motivation': A Critique," *Organizational Behavior and Human Performance*, 15 (1976), 117–129.
74. Siegel, A.L., and R.A. Ruh. "Job Involvement, Participation in Decision Making, Personal Background, and Job Behavior," *Organizational Behavior and Human Performance*, 9 (1973), 318–327.
75. Sirota, D., and A. Wolfson. "Job Enrichment: What Are the Obstacles?" *Personnel*, 49, 3 (1972), 8–17.
76. Sirota, D., and A. Wolfson. "Job Enrichment: Surmounting the Obstacles," *Personnel* 49, 4 (1972), 8–19.
77. Starke, F., and O. Behling. "A Test of Two Postulates Underlying Expectancy Theory," *Academy of Management Journal*, 18 (1975), 703–714.
78. Stinson, J.E., and T.W. Johnson. "The Path-goal Theory of Leadership: A Partial Test and Suggested Refinement," *Academy of Management Journal*, 18 (1975), 242–252.
79. Steers, R.M. "Task-goal Attributes, *n* Achievement, and Supervisory Performance," *Organizational Behavior and Human Performance*, 13 (1975), 392–403.
80. Steers, R.M. "Factors Affecting Job Attitudes in a Goal-setting Environment," *Academy of Management Journal*, 19 (1976), 6–16.

81. Steers, R.M., and L.W. Porter. "The Role of Task-goal Attributes in Employee Performance," *Psychological Bulletin, 81* (1974), 434–452.
82. Taylor, J.W. "What the Behaviorists Haven't Told Us," *Personnel Journal, 52,* 10 (1973), 874–878.
83. Vroom, V. *Some Personality Determinants of the Effects of Participation.* Englewood Cliffs, N.J.: Prentice-Hall, Inc., 1960.
84. Vroom, V. *Work and Motivation.* New York: John Wiley & Sons, 1964.
85. Vroom, V., and P. Yetton. *Leadership and Decision Making.* Pittsburgh: University of Pittsburgh Press, 1973.
86. Wahba, M.A., and R.J. House. "Expectancy Theory in Work and Motivation: Some Logical and Methodological Issues," *Human Relations, 27* (1974), 121–147.
87. Wanous, J. "Individual Differences and Reactions to Job Characteristics," *Journal of Applied Psychology, 59,* 5 (1974), 616–622.
88. Yukl, G., and G. Latham. "Consequences of Reinforcement Schedules and Incentive Magnitudes for Employee Performance: Problems Encountered in an Industrial Setting," *Journal of Applied Psychology, 60* (1975), 290–294.
89. Yukl, G., K. Wexley, and J. Seymore. "Effects of Pay Incentives under Variable Ratio and Continuous Reinforcement Schedules," *Journal of Applied Psychology, 56* (1972), 19–23.

ALCOHOLISM AND DRUG ADDICTION

Long-Term Experience with Rehabilitation of Alcoholic Employees

Fern E. Asma*
Raymond L. Eggert
Robert R. J. Hilker

The Illinois Bell Telephone Company rehabilitation program for employees with alcoholism was started in 1951 and has been gradually expanded over the intervening years. Other industrial programs had been started as early as 1942.[1] The program was not started because of a certain knowledge that any specific number or percentage of employees suffered from this illness. As a matter of fact, in the early days of the program, it is highly unlikely that alcoholism was recognized as a real illness at all! The program was really started by a farsighted management medical team who knew that the problem was significant. It was significant then in terms of human loss, in loss of business efficiency, in increased sickness disability, and in increased accident disability both off and on the job. We maintain our program today for the very same reasons. However, today we know that it is an effective program in partially solving these problems.

Our knowledge of the number of alcoholic employees in our 42,000-employee group is undoubtedly as rudimentary now as it was when the program was started in 1951. We have really made no effort to survey the problem. You are aware of the various statistics quoted about the incidence of this illness in other companies.[2] Our company is probably no better or no worse than any other similar business. What we do know is that our program has demonstrated that we have enough sick employees to justify continuing and expanding our efforts.

The detection procedure we use to find the employee with alcoholism has undergone a change over the years from the original concept of looking for the alcoholic employee to our present concept of looking for the problem employee. We now look for the problem employee. We now look not only for alcoholism but

---

*Dr. Asma is Assistant Medical Director, Mr. Eggert is Alcoholic Rehabilitation Counselor, and Dr. Hilker is Medical Director of the Illinois Bell Telephone Company, Chicago, Illinois.

for any other medical reason that prevents the employee from doing a good job. We call this a Health Evaluation Program. The immediate supervisor selects an employee for referral to the Medical Department when that employee is not doing a satisfactory job and when the situation cannot be remedied by the usual management procedures. This being the case, the supervisor has a frank discussion of the job problem with the employee. It is indicated to the employee that this type of job performance—whatever it is—will no longer be tolerated and that some effort must be made to change the behavior pattern so that performance will become satisfactory. A visit to the Medical Department is suggested to the employee to determine if a medical problem is the basis for poor job function. This is not a punitive visit in any way. It is explained to the employee that this is one more step our company will take in an effort to aid him in doing his job in a satisfactory way. The employee is free to accept this referral, or to decline it if he wishes. Should he decline referral, he then must make a real effort on his own to change his job performance to that which is satisfactory to the employing department. If he accepts the referral to the Medical Department, we view this as an opportunity to help a patient who has a serious job problem. We do a complete history, physical examination, and laboratory examination on every referred employee. We also arrange and pay for any outside consultations which are necessary. In other words, we do the very best we can to aid in the rehabilitation of the employee. Of course, this has a company-oriented benefit, too, in that it hopefully resolves the job problem as far as the employing department is concerned.

With a detection procedure of this type, it should be quite obvious that the employees who are referred to us usually have emotional illness, alcoholism, are drug users, or have undiagnosed or poorly treated physical illness. The great majority of people we see on this type of evaluation are emotionally ill. The next most frequent cause of job dysfunction is alcoholism.

Here is a brief description of the structure and function of our program. Our Assistant Medical Director is in charge of the Health Evaluations and supervises the Alcoholic Rehabilitation Program. We also have an Alcoholics Rehabilitations Counselor in our department as a full-time employee. After evaluation by the physician, problem drinkers are referred to him. Should it be determined that alcoholism is indeed the problem, regular counseling will be arranged with this counselor. Arrangements will also be made for the employee to participate in meetings of Alcoholics Anonymous. Our physician in charge of this program assists in the rehabilitation when it is determined that professional care above and beyond that which is furnished by the alcoholism counselor is needed. Hospitalization is recommended and arranged for when it is indicated. We also discuss our plans with the employing department. Without their cooperation any successful rehabilitation would be very unlikely. We feel very strongly that the constructive coercion thus initiated is necessary to motivate most employees to participate in the program. The job, after all, is extremely important to the employee and it is only by showing evidence of participation in a serious rehabilitation effort that the job will be secure.

Our program was known only on a "word of mouth basis" until 1969. It, of course, was discussed with management employees in some staff meetings but no general announcement of a company policy on alcoholism was ever made. In 1969, a brochure explaining our policy and program together with a condensation of the book *The Drinking Game and How to Beat It* was mailed to the home of all employees.

We are now reporting on 402 employees on whom we have adequate records. In the early days of our program most records were not adequate for statistical follow-up. In the cases reported, we have records of five or more years before and five or more years after referral to our program.

First, let us consider how these employees were referred to us (Table 1). Ninety percent were referred by the employing department—most of these on a Health Evaluation basis. Four percent were discovered while other examinations were being done in the Medical Department, and 6 percent were self-referrals.

What are the characteristics of these employees (Table 2)? In years of service, the greater number of employees had between 10 and 29 years of service at the time that alcoholism interfered with their doing their job efficiently. Only 77 had less than 10 years of service. These employees were most often between the ages of 35 and 54 years (Table 3). These, of course, are normally the most productive years in the life of the employee and the years in which they could hope to progress in the business. The length of service and age distribution indicates to us that alcoholism had really been present and unrecognized for a considerable time before it finally resulted in a job crisis of sufficient magnitude to demand corrective action.

The great majority of men were married as compared to only about one third of the women (Table 4). The incidence of divorce or separation was much higher in women. This could either indicate a difference of the view of society toward alcoholism in women or indicate that the married dependent woman is willing to endure more to hold on to her marriage. We know that there was severe discord in the marriages of many of our male patients.

We made an effort to estimate the major area of life stress in all 402 employees (Table 5). In 86 percent it was our opinion that the life stress was within the employee himself. Home stress accounted for 25 percent, while job stress accounted for only 9 percent. It should be noted that some patients had more than one area of life stress.

TABLE 1   How Referred to Program

	Women	Men	Total	Percent
Department	86	277	363	90
Medical	5	11	16	4
Self	2	21	23	6
Totals	93	309	402	

TABLE 2   Years of Service When Referred to Program

Years Service	Women	Men	Total	Percent
Under 10	19	58	77	19
10–19 years	23	99	122	31
20–29 years	27	77	104	25
30–39 years	23	56	79	20
40 or over	1	19	20	5

TABLE 3 Age When Referred to Program

Age	Women	Men	Total	Percent
Under 25	2	7	9	2
25–34 years	4	56	60	15
35–44 years	30	95	125	31
45–54 years	50	106	156	40
55 or over	7	45	52	12

TABLE 4 Marital Status of Patients

	Women	Men	Total	Percent
Single	19	39	58	14
Married	33	227	260	64
Widowed	10	5	15	4
Separated	6	9	15	4
Divorced	25	29	54	14

TABLE 5 Estimated Major Area of Life Stress

	Women	Men	Total	Percent
Self	69	277	346	86
Home	42	60	102	25
Job	12	24	36	9
Other	1	13	14	3

Note: Some patients have two or more areas of stress

It is important to make a diagnosis of the type of drinking in order to be most effective in rehabilitation (Table 6). Twenty-one percent were heavy drinkers. These people are not true chronic alcoholics but drink in a serious, damaging recreational way. They are able to control their drinking much easier than other types. Sixty-three percent were typical chronic alcoholics. These are people in whom drinking is compulsive and self-destructive. Six percent of the people were reactive drinkers. They react to life situations by drinking. Ten percent were symptomatic drinkers. These patients were suffering from emotional illness with alcoholism simply a manifestation of the emotional illness. Psychiatric care is necessary for them (Table 7). Psychiatric consultations were obtained in 37 percent of employees referred for evaluation. This figure probably is too high, since in the early days of our program all patients were referred to a psychiatrist. We now have psychiatric consultation only on a selective basis.

What success have we had in obtaining the cooperation of these 402 people and in changing their drinking habits (Table 8)? Of the 402, 230 referrals were rehabilitated—this is 57 percent. By rehabilitated, we mean that these employees had stopped drinking completely for one year or more. Fifteen percent were improved. By this, we mean that these employees were able to function satisfactorily on the job although their drinking had not been completely controlled. This means job rehabilitation was accomplished in 72 percent of employees counseled.

Our rehabilitation rate is very comparable to that of other company programs. Twenty-three percent had accepted our help. This is the group of employees in whom we are unable to predict what will happen. Some will undoubtedly fail and will not be controlled. Others will be improved or even move on to the rehabilitated group. Five percent of all employees were not cooperative and our rehabilitation efforts were a total failure. Of all employees referred to us, 87 percent have accepted counseling by our Rehabilitation Counselor (Table 9). A smaller group participated in regular activities of Alcoholics Anonymous (Table 10). This group, however, was composed almost entirely of chronic alcoholics who benefit most from this fellowship.

TABLE 6 Diagnosis of Type of Drinking

	Women	Men	Total	Percent
Heavy drinker	17	66	83	21
Chronic alcoholic	54	201	255	63
Reactive drinker	7	16	23	6
Symptomatic drinker	15	26	41	10

TABLE 7 Number of Psychiatric Consultations

	Women	Men	Total	Percent
Yes	36	114	150	37
No	57	195	252	63

TABLE 8 Success in Rehabilitation in 402 Referrals

	Women	Men	Total	Percent
Rehabilitated	52	178	230	57
Improved	20	40	60	15
Accepted help	17	75	92	23
Not controlled	4	16	20	5

TABLE 9 Accepted Company Program

	Women	Men	Total	Percent
Yes	77	273	350	87
No	16	36	52	13

TABLE 10 Accepted Alcoholics Anonymous

	Women	Men	Total	Percent
Yes	39	183	222	55
No	54	126	180	45

Now let us consider our success in changing job performance. We had the employing departments estimate job efficiency for the five years prior to coming on the program and for the five years after rehabilitation efforts started. In all, 46 percent of women were rated poor before entering the program whereas only 22 percent were subsequently rated poor (Table 11). Only 10 percent were rated as good employees before coming on the rehabilitation program while 46 percent were rated as good employees after being rehabilitated. Clearly, we were able to change the job efficiency of these employees. In men, approximately the same results were evident (Table 12). The number of employees rated poor was significantly reduced while the number rated good was substantially increased after rehabilitation. The combined effect on job efficiency shows that poor job performance dropped from 28 percent to 12 percent (Table 13). Good job performance was only present in 22 percent prior to rehabilitation and increased to 58 percent after participation in the program. These results indicate that a significant change in job behavior can be accomplished by rehabilitation.

Promotions are another measure of success (Table 14). We are not sure that these statistics are completely accurate. We know that the statistics we are presenting to you are true. However, we have a feeling that some of the promotions may not have been made known to us and that our figures are really not high enough. However, six patients were promoted to management and four patients were promoted to higher pay groups.

It is well-known that the alcoholic employee has many more days of sickness disability absence than does his counterpart who is not alcoholic (Table 15).[3] The statistics presented are for the number of cases—these are cases that lasted for more than seven days of reported illness. We do not have statistics on the first seven days of absence. These 402 employees had 662 cases of sickness disability absence in the five years before participating in our program. In the subsequent five years, the same employees had only 356 cases. This is a significant reduction in sickness disability. However, these employees still are not quite as good in this regard as employees who have never been alcoholic. Nevertheless, cutting our sickness disability rate in these employees by nearly 50 percent is certainly worthwhile.

We are also very interested in our ability to change the accident process. First let us look at off-duty accidents (Table 16). Again, these figures indicate only those cases in which the disability lasted more than seven days. In the five years before rehabilitation, there were 75 cases of off-duty accidents as compared to 28 cases after employees were referred to the program. This is certainly a significant reduction. We are all well aware of the importance of alcohol as a contributing factor in these accidents. We are not all aware that a significant reduction in accidents can be obtained by an effective rehabilitation program.

Alcoholic employees also have many more on-the-job accidents.[4] Our employees were no exception. These figures represent any on-duty accident requiring medical treatment (Table 17). Severity is not indicated in these statistics. In the five years before these employees participated in the program, there were 57 on-duty accidents. This number was reduced to 11 in the five years after rehabilitation. This is a dramatic decrease. There is no doubt that the control of alcoholism will produce a favorable change in the accident process.

The final disposition of our 402 referrals is of interest (Table 18). When this study was completed, 63 percent were still working, 9 percent had been dismissed,

6 percent resigned, 20 percent were pensioned and 2 percent were deceased. In the pension group it should be mentioned that some of these were forced pensions, some were voluntary, and some patients had simply arrived at mandatory retirement age.

In summary, our statistics on 402 employees referred to us for rehabilitation indicate that job efficiency can be increased, sickness disability absences can be reduced, and both off-the-job and on-the-job accidents can be reduced. When these advantages to the business are added to the social advantages to the employee and his family as well as to society in general, it is quite obvious that a rehabilitation program is most desirable.

TABLE 11 Estimate of Job Efficiency

	5 Years Before		5 Years After	
	Women	Percent	Women	Percent
Poor	43	46	20	22
Fair	41	44	30	32
Good	9	10	43	46

TABLE 12 Estimate of Job Efficiency

	5 Years Before		5 Years After	
	Men	Percent	Men	Percent
Poor	69	22	31	10
Fair	158	51	89	29
Good	82	27	189	61

TABLE 13 Estimate of Job Efficiency

	5 Years Before		5 Years After	
	Employees	Percent	Employees	Percent
Poor	112	28	51	12
Fair	199	50	119	30
Good	91	22	232	58

TABLE 14 Promotions in Rehabilitated Employees

	Women	Men	Total
To management	1	5	6
To higher pay group	0	4	4
Totals	1	9	10

TABLE 15 Number of Sickness Disability Cases*

	5 Years Before	5 Years After
Women	229	75
Men	433	281
Totals	662	356

*More than seven days of reported illness.

TABLE 16 Number of Off-Duty Accidents*

	5 Years Before	5 Years After
Women	32	6
Men	43	22
Totals	75	28

*More than seven days absence.

TABLE 17 Number of On-Duty Accidents*

	5 Years Before	5 Years After
Women	4	1
Men	53	10
Totals	57	11

*Any accident requiring medical treatment.

TABLE 18 Final Disposition in 402 Referrals

	Women	Men	Total	Percent
Working	51	204	255	63
Dismissed	9	27	36	9
Resigned	8	17	25	6
Pensioned*	22	56	78	20
Deceased	3	5	8	2

*May be forced, voluntary, or mandatory.

Notes

[1] See S. Pell and C.A. D'Alonzo, "Sickness Absenteeism of Alcoholics," *Journal of Occupational Medicine*, 12 (1970), 198–210; and C.F. Wilcox, "The Alcoholic in Industry," *Ohio Medical Journal* 64 (1968), 77–78.

[2] R.E. Winter. "One for the Plant," *Maryland Medical Journal*, 19 (1970), 97-99; and W.W. Davis. "Practical Experience with an Alcoholism Program in Industry," *Ohio Medical Journal*, 66 (1970), 814–816.

[3] R.W. Stevenson. "Absenteeism in an Industrial Plant due to Alcoholism," *Quarterly Journal of the Study of Alcoholism*, 2 (1942), 661–668.

[4] Maxwell Observer. "A study of Absenteeism, Accidents and Sickness Payments in Problem Drinkers in One Industry," *Quarterly Journal of the Study of Alcoholism*, 20 (1959), 302–312.

Rehabilitation of the Problem Drinker

Illinois Bell Telephone Company, Medical Department

THE PROBLEM DRINKER—HOW GREAT A PROBLEM?

About 80 million adults in this country drink alcoholic beverages. Most of these people are able to indulge *without* harming themselves or anyone else. The government estimates at least 9 to 11 million of them are problem drinkers, who are letting alcohol interfere with, and perhaps ruin, their lives.

Approximately 85 percent of these problem drinkers work in industry. A percentage of Illinois Bell people belong to this group, since it is estimated that 5 to 7 percent of the employees in any company are problem drinkers.

Problem drinkers have a compulsive, uncontrollable urge to drink. Their drinking interferes with normal living by creating problems with their lives. They become physically and mentally unable to handle alcohol. To them, the importance of alcohol eventually outweighs all other considerations, including family, friends, and job.

Because compulsive drinking gets progressively worse, it's very important that we discover an employee who has a drinking problem as soon as possible. By identifying problem drinkers early enough, we may be able to rehabilitate them. *We must remember that alcoholism can be just as relentlessly progressive and destructive as cancer if it is not treated in its early stages.*

WHEN DOES DRINKING BECOME A COMPANY PROBLEM?

Alcoholism can be defined as habitually poor job performance resulting from excessive drinking. This definition can be easily understood by a busy supervisor as well as the alcoholic himself. The problem drinker's repeated poor work in turn has a bad effect on smooth job operations as far as the boss, peers, and union representatives are concerned.

Examples of when an employee's drinking becomes a company problem:

1. Work performance is less efficient and dependable.
2. The employee's drinking affects personal health.
3. The employee's drinking affects interpersonal relationships on the job.
4. The person has alcohol on his/her breath during working hours.
5. There is an attendance problem.
6. There are complaints from customers or other employees.

"Rehabilitation of the Problem Drinker," Reprinted with permission of Illinois Bell Telephone Company, Medical Department.

7. There are frequent on- or off-the-job accidents.
8. There are unexplained disappearances from the work assignment.
9. Off-the-job problems emerge.

WHAT IS IBT'S POLICY ON PROBLEM DRINKING?

Illinois Bell's policy on employees with drinking problems has four basic premises:

1. Alcoholism is an illness and should be treated as such. All employees with drinking problems will receive the same consideration under the company's medical and benefit programs as do employees with other illnesses if they cooperate in treatment and attempts at rehabilitation.
2. Our efforts will be directed toward rehabilitation of the employee whenever possible. Employees will receive the best advice we are able to provide.
3. Cooperation will be maintained between the employing department and the Medical Department. No one-sided action will be taken in any case. Conferences will be held about employees who have repeated problems.
4. The employee will be given every reasonable opportunity and all reasonable help to overcome the problem. If the employee does not cooperate and rehabilitation efforts are unsuccessful, the case will then be handled as an administrative problem and the employee's future with the company decided by the employing department.

HOW ARE EMPLOYEES REFERRED TO THE MEDICAL DEPARTMENT FOR HELP?

1. Any employee who knows he or she has a problem with alcohol may make an appointment and bring this problem directly to the attention of the Medical Department. The employee will receive all of the rehabilitation services of the Medical Department in the same confidential manner as an employee with any other illness.
2. Management may refer an employee to the Medical Department when it is felt that the employee might have a drinking problem and/or job problem. Most cases will be best handled by initiating a Request for Employee Health Evaluation. *Complete written documentation* of the problem and any interviews with the employee will be included to help evaluate the case.

YOUR ROLE AS A MANAGEMENT REPRESENTATIVE

As a management representative, you are in the best position to identify and help an employee with a drinking problem. You know the employee's job performance, attendance record, condition and appearance on the job, the person's habits, and very likely something about his or her family and community relationships.

You're one of the few people—perhaps the only one—who can motivate the problem drinker to seek treatment. A problem drinker who ignores the pleading of friends or the urging of family often will recognize the problem and seek treatment when faced with the possible loss of employment.

HOW TO RECOGNIZE THE SYMPTOMS

A person with a drinking problem will have certain behavior patterns such as:

1. Frequent Monday, Friday, post-holiday and post-payday absence and/or tardiness.
2. A variety of poor excuses for frequent absences for minor illnesses. Such people claim to be suffering from colds, gastritis, flu, stomach conditions, and other ailments more often than do other employees.
3. Frequent on- and off-the-job accidents.
4. Moodiness and unusual sensitivity leading to arguments or disinterest in the job.
5. Decreasing reliability, evidenced by an inclination to put things off; a tendency to neglect details formerly pursued; placing blame on other workers; a desire for different job assignments; seeking loans from the company or associates.
6. A marked change in appearance, such as swelling of the face, flushed face, red or bleary eyes. These changes are often accompanied by increasing carelessness in dress and appearance.
7. Hand tremors.
8. Memory blackouts.
9. Drinking habits which differ from those of companions (faster drinking, sneaking drinks, drinking longer, or heavy spending on alcoholic drinks).
10. Evidence of domestic discord or increasing financial troubles.
11. Marked sensitivity to suggestions that alcohol is a problem.

REMEDIAL STEPS TO BE TAKEN

Don't Cover Up

If you have a person with a suspected drinking problem in your organization, the sooner you face the situation the better. Don't cover up for them. No matter how well meant such an attitude is, it is a disservice to a person heading toward a compulsive drinking problem. One of the underlying facts about this illness is that the victim can recover only with outside assistance, however, often cannot see the necessity for such assistance. The earlier the treatment, the greater the hope of rehabilitation. Alcoholism is like cancer. You can help by catching it early.

The First Interview

Instead of covering up, start as soon as possible with a down-to-earth discussion with the employee. Do this when he or she is sober if possible.

Plan the interview meticulously and be well-armed with facts and observations to back up the firm approach you'll take. Prepare a carefully written documentation of the interview.

1. The employee should be told that he or she is in serious trouble on the job and that this behavior will *no longer be tolerated.*

2. The employee should also be told that the company has an excellent program for rehabilitation and that he/she will be sent to the Medical Department for evaluation and help. This should be suggested in a genuine spirit of help and not as a disciplinary action.

Explain in detail the reasons you are concerned about the person's performance, for example,

1. Those aspects of the person's work which are not meeting your expectations for a person with that amount of training and years of experience
2. The person's record of tardiness and sickness absence, compared with records of all employees in your own group, office or area, or in the company
3. Evidence of interpersonal relationships with other employees suffering
4. A diminishing safety record on and off the job
5. Changes in personal and physical appearances
6. Alcohol on the breath
7. Complaints from customers and other employees

You'll need all the understanding, patience, perseverance, and firmness you can muster if you're to succeed. Be firm about the job deficiencies and the fact that you will no longer tolerate them.

The first and perhaps the biggest challenge is to convince the employee that he/she has a problem and that the job is in jeopardy.

Don't be surprised if the employee strongly disagrees with you, and comes up with excuses like these:

"I haven't been feeling well."
"I've had a lot of trouble lately."
"All my friends drink more than I do."
"I can stop drinking anytime I wish."
"I never drink on the job—so it's none of your business."

Tell the employee that you want to send him/her to the Medical Department for a Health Evaluation to aid in rehabilitative efforts. If the person agrees, refer him/her to the Medical Department.

If the employee refuses to go to the Medical Department, be sure the individual understands that he or she must show improved performance. Watch the employee's performance closely thereafter for signs of continued deterioration. If the performance does not improve, talk with the individual again and *insist* on a referral to the Medical Department.

If the employee refuses a second time, follow your usual administrative procedures dealing with unsatisfactory job performance. Also, call the Medical Department to see if they have anything further to suggest.

WHAT THE MEDICAL DEPARTMENT DOES

The Request for Employee Health Evaluation should include *a complete written report* of all the facts and personal interviews in the case. It is *important* to tell the employee that this information will be made available to the physician.

The physician will do a complete examination, evaluate the seriousness of the health problem, and recommend a plan of action. Consultation with outside specialists will be obtained when necessary.

The Medical Department has a trained counselor who is responsible for coordinating rehabilitation efforts. If the examination indicates that rehabilitation should be attempted, and if the employee agrees to cooperate, he/she will then be referred to the counselor. The counselor and the physician will outline a program of therapy and follow-up for the employee. Basically, this program uses Alcoholics Anonymous and regular counseling in the Medical Department. Other specialized care will be suggested when needed. The Medical Department welcomes, and seeks, the cooperation of the employee's family, personal physician, and clergyman.

APPLICATION OF BENEFIT PLAN

An employee who is absent because of a drinking problem may be entitled to sickness disability under the "Plan for Employees' Pensions, Disability Benefits and Death Benefits." Sickness disability will be granted if the employee is cooperating in following a medically prescribed course of treatment, and if the Medical Department advises that he/she is cooperating but is unable to work. Based on facts in each case, the Benefit Committee will determine whether or not the employee will receive benefits.

YOUR RESPONSIBILITY CONTINUES

Once the decision is made to attempt rehabilitation, your role as a management representative continues to be a vital factor. The Medical Department will continue to need your close cooperation. You must remain an understanding friend of the employee, alert to the changing state of mind and moods, and be prepared to take the initiative when personal problems arise relating to the course of treatment. For example, it may be necessary to assist by getting the help of the employee's family or church. Your assistance may also be needed in persuading the employee to seek aid from a local clinic, Alcoholics Anonymous, or some other selected agency.

You should keep in close contact with the Medical Department and immediately report any new evidence of drinking.

THE EMPLOYEE HAS A RESPONSIBILITY TOO

As you try to help the employee, you should make it clear that

1. It is the individual's responsibility to gain complete control of his/her drinking problem.
2. The company expects the individual to make favorable progress toward complete rehabilitation.
3. The company will not tolerate continued unsatisfactory job performance.

If a relapse occurs, an understanding attitude should be shown if the employee is cooperative and continues to demonstrate a sincere interest in his/her rehabilitation.

ACTION IN DIFFICULT SITUATIONS

When the employee is not cooperating in the individually outlined program, disciplinary action may be necessary, such as warnings, suspensions, or a leave of absence. Final disposition of all cases rests with the employing department *after* consultation with the Medical Department.

It is important that the employing and the Medical Department cooperate in close supervision of the employee at all times.

DOCUMENTATION

Frequently, in the administrative handling of an alcoholic case, the alcoholic will deny that anyone has ever talked to him/her concerning the problem.

It is very important to keep complete records concerning each episode, interview, or conference. Also include facts relating to the supervisor's contacts with the Medical Department Staff or other interested parties. All of a supervisor's records must be detailed, complete, dated, and signed. It should be explained, for example, that the employee spoke incoherently, was unsteady in stance or walking, was untidy or shaky — rather than stating the simple conclusion that the employee was intoxicated. If disciplinary action is taken, there should be a written record of the reasons for the action. This record should describe the warnings given to the employee about his/her future with the company, as well as evidence indicating that the employee understood these warnings.

SOME FINAL THOUGHTS

Rewards to the company, to the individual employee, and to his or her family and friends can be great when rehabilitative efforts succeed. Conversely, the penalties can be severe when rehabilitative efforts fail.

426   *Rehabilitation of the Problem Drinker*

The earlier rehabilitative efforts start, the greater the chances for success.

When the supervisor procrastinates or does nothing, individual cases may "go too far" to accomplish rehabilitation.

Time alone will not "cure" the alcoholic — it requires the marshalling of all the rehabilitative forces outlined in this booklet.

Our program can best be summed up in the following diagram which follows the problem case through circumstances that may develop — either to the successful conclusion of rehabilitative measures or to ultimate disciplinary action.

References

Literature:

Alcoholism and the Employee: One out of 10	Illinois Bell Telephone Company 212 W. Washington St., HQ 14-F Chicago, Illinois 60606
Alcoholism in Industry, Modern Procedures	National Council On Alcoholism 733 Third Avenue New York, New York 10017
Long-term Experience with Rehabilitation of Alcoholic Employees (Reprint)	Illinois Bell Telephone Company 212 W. Washington St., HQ 14-F Chicago, Illinois 60606
Manual on Alcoholism	American Medical Association 535 N. Dearborn Chicago, Illinois 60610
The Supervisor's Role with the Problem Drinker Employee (Reprint)	Illinois Bell Telephone Company 212 W. Washington St., HQ 14-F Chicago, Illinois 60606
What to Do about the Employee with a Drinking Problem (Code-X01804-8)	Kemper Insurance Co. Communications and Public Affairs Dept. D-1 Long Grove, Illinois 60049
"What To Say To An Alcoholic," *Management* Review (Reprint)	American Management Association 135 W. 50th Street New York, New York 10020

Films – CCTV Videocassettes:

°°*Alcoholic*	Produced by Illinois Bell Telephone Co. and ABC-TV, Chicago (1963)
°°*Alcoholism*	CCTV Videocassette
°°*Drink, Drank, Drunk*	CCTV Videocassette of CBS-TV Special (1975)

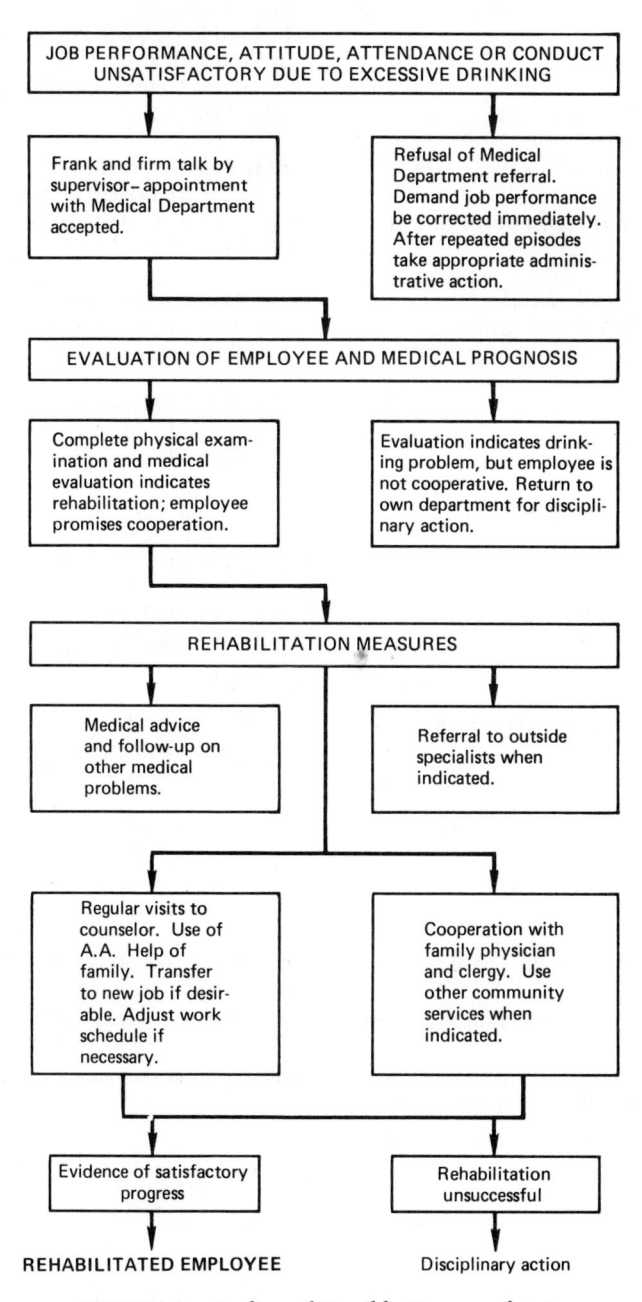

```
┌─────────────────────────────────────────────────────────┐
│  JOB PERFORMANCE, ATTITUDE, ATTENDANCE OR CONDUCT       │
│      UNSATISFACTORY DUE TO EXCESSIVE DRINKING           │
└─────────────────────────────────────────────────────────┘
            │                              │
            ▼                              ▼
┌──────────────────────┐      ┌──────────────────────────┐
│ Frank and firm talk  │      │ Refusal of Medical       │
│ by supervisor –      │      │ Department referral.     │
│ appointment with     │      │ Demand job performance   │
│ Medical Department   │      │ be corrected immediately.│
│ accepted.            │      │ After repeated episodes  │
│                      │      │ take appropriate adminis-│
│                      │      │ trative action.          │
└──────────────────────┘      └──────────────────────────┘
            │
            ▼
┌─────────────────────────────────────────────────────────┐
│       EVALUATION OF EMPLOYEE AND MEDICAL PROGNOSIS      │
└─────────────────────────────────────────────────────────┘
            │                              │
            ▼                              ▼
┌──────────────────────┐      ┌──────────────────────────┐
│ Complete physical    │      │ Evaluation indicates     │
│ examination and      │      │ drinking problem, but    │
│ medical evaluation   │      │ employee is not          │
│ indicates rehabili-  │      │ cooperative. Return to   │
│ tation; employee     │      │ own department for       │
│ promises cooperation.│      │ disciplinary action.     │
└──────────────────────┘      └──────────────────────────┘
            │
            ▼
┌─────────────────────────────────────────────────────────┐
│                  REHABILITATION MEASURES                │
└─────────────────────────────────────────────────────────┘
            │                              │
            ▼                              ▼
┌──────────────────────┐      ┌──────────────────────────┐
│ Medical advice and   │      │ Referral to outside      │
│ follow-up on other   │      │ specialists when         │
│ medical problems.    │      │ indicated.               │
└──────────────────────┘      └──────────────────────────┘
            │                              │
            ▼                              ▼
┌──────────────────────┐      ┌──────────────────────────┐
│ Regular visits to    │      │ Cooperation with family  │
│ counselor. Use of    │      │ physician and clergy.    │
│ A.A. Help of family. │      │ Use other community      │
│ Transfer to new job  │      │ services when indicated. │
│ if desirable. Adjust │      │                          │
│ work schedule if     │      │                          │
│ necessary.           │      │                          │
└──────────────────────┘      └──────────────────────────┘
            │                              │
            ▼                              ▼
┌──────────────────────┐      ┌──────────────────────────┐
│ Evidence of          │      │ Rehabilitation           │
│ satisfactory progress│      │ unsuccessful             │
└──────────────────────┘      └──────────────────────────┘
            │                              │
            ▼                              ▼
   REHABILITATED EMPLOYEE           Disciplinary action
```

FIGURE 1 *Outline of Possible Courses of Action*

428 Rehabilitation of the Problem Drinker

The Dryden File (27½ min.)   Motivision, Ltd.
Richard S. Milbauer Productions
21 West 46th Street
New York, New York 10036
(212) 757-4970

° *Escape from Addiction* (27½ min.)   FMS Productions, Inc.
1040 North Las Palmas Avenue
°° *Father Martin's Guidelines* (45 min.)   Los Angeles, California 90038
(213) 466-8289

° *For Those Who Drink*   L. L. Cromien & Company
°° Complete Version (38 min.)   284 Delaware Avenue
    Abridged Version (29 min.)   Buffalo, New York 14202

° *Frank Lovejoy Story*   Illinois Bell Telephone Company
212 W. Washington St., HQ 14-F
Chicago, Illinois 60606

° *Need For Decision*   Illinois Bell Telephone Company
212 W. Washington St., HQ 14-F
Chicago, Illinois 60606

° *To Your Health*   American Medical Association
535 North Dearborn
Chicago, Illinois 60610

°° *Social Drinking: Fun or Fatal*   National Safety Council
444 North Michigan Avenue
Chicago, Illinois 60611

°° *We Don't Want to Lose You*   The Oz. of Prevention
15900 W. 10 Mile Road
Suite 302
Southfield, Michigan 48075

° Available from the Office of Illinois Bell Alcoholism Rehabilitation Counselor.

°° Available from the Illinois Bell Employee Film/Videocassette Library.

Additional literature on alcoholism is also available from the office of the Illinois Bell Alcoholism Rehabilitation Counselor.

RETIREMENT: PROBLEMS AND PROGRAMS

Dealing with the Aging Work Force

Jeffrey Sonnenfeld

DEMOGRAPHICS, EARLY RETIREMENT, AND INDIVIDUAL LIFE CRISES

The extension of mandatory retirement to age 70, signed into U.S. law last April, has caught most organizations off guard and has surfaced latent fears about the general age drift in the work force. Management experts and journalists over the last year or so have become quite vocal in their prophecies about the changing complexion of the work force.

We used to hear predictions about the "greening of America." Now we hear references to impending problems resulting from the "graying of America," as the country belatedly awakens to the composite effects of demographic trends, improvements in life expectancy, and changes in social legislation. Executives are being warned to anticipate changes in employee performance and attitudes, performance appraisals, retirement incentives, training programs, blocked career paths, union insurance pensions, and affirmative action goals, among other worrisome issues.

Business managers have been the target of superficial and conflicting admonitions appearing in the press. As the chief executive of a leading paper company recently complained to me, "At first we were interested in the warnings. Now, they all say the same things. We hear all the fire alarms being sounded, but no one suggests where we should send the engines."

The needs of a very different work force overshadow many of the other issues of the 1980s for which managers must prepare their organizations. Just as other organizational activities must adapt to a changing environment, human resource planning dictates a major overhaul in recruitment, development, job

Jeffry Sonnenfeld, "Dealing with the Aging Work Force," Harvard Business Review, November–December 1978, Copyright © 1978 by the President and Fellows of Harvard College; all rights reserved.

structure, incentives, and performance appraisal. Thus management attention should now be focused on specific problems in mid- and late-career planning.

It is hard enough to comprehend the individual aging process without at the same time assessing the effects of an entire population growing older. If Congress and President Carter had not extended the work years, leaders of America's organizations would still have had to face troublesome human resource changes.

As a consequence of the 43 million babies born in the years immediately following World War II, a middle-aged bulge is forming and eventually the 35- to 45-year-old age group will increase by 80 percent. By the year 2030, this group will be crossing the infamous bridge to 65, increasing the relative size of that population from 12 percent of all Americans to 17 percent, a jump from 31 million to 52 million people.[1]

Some labor analysts point out that even those Department of Labor statistics are conservative, for likely changes downward in the mortality rate due to advanced medical treatment are not reflected in the predictions. Today, the average life expectancy is about age 73, which is 10 years longer than the years of life expected at birth in the 1950s.

On examining the rate of this change, one sees that the size of the preretirement population, between the ages of 62 and 64, will not be affected dramatically until the year 2000. Until that time this group will expand at an annual rate of 7.6 percent above 1975 figures. Between 2000 and 2010, however, it will grow by 48 percent. For one to assume, however, that there are at least 22 years before major problems arise would be incorrect. This population bulge will be moving through several critical career phases before reaching the preretirement years.

One should pause and reflect on how, in just the next ten years, the population bulge will be lodged in the "mid-life crisis" age. This added strain will magnify the traditional work and nonwork problems associated with the sense of limited opportunity at that age. Even sooner, the decline in youth population, which is currently causing the consolidation of secondary schools, will shift the balance of power and the approach in company recruitment.

As a consequence, a dwindling young work force will make it more difficult to fill entry-level positions. Already there are predictions about shortages in blue-collar occupations by the mid-1980s.[2] It is not at all too soon for managers to start investigating their company demographics.

On top of the foregoing, the recent legislation on extending mandatory retirement further heightens the concern about job performance in the later years. Sooner than even the advocates of this legislation dreamed, business managers find themselves faced with contemplating the implications of long-tenured senior employees.

The immediate impact of this legislation depends, of course, on how older workers respond to the opportunity to remain on the job. Many companies are looking at the well-publicized trend toward earlier retirement and concluding that this trend will counteract the effects of extended tenure possibilities. Labor force participation rates are dropping for workers age 55 and older and for those age 60 and over.

A retirement expert on the National Industrial Conference Board, a business research organization, said, "People want to retire while they are still young and healthy enough to enjoy the activities of their choice."[3] Another Conference Board researcher reported that these younger retirees are interested in education, in traveling, and in spending more and more money on themselves.[4]

Also, Victor M. Zin, director of Employee Benefits at General Motors, commented, "There used to be a stigma to going out. He was over the hill, but now it's a looked-for status. Those retirement parties, they used to be sad affairs. They are darn happy affairs now. The peer pressure is for early retirement."[5]

Research suggests, however, that such a trend reflects worker income, education, job conditions, and retirement security. Dissatisfied workers and those with better pension plans seem to be more likely to opt out earlier. The experience of Sears and Roebuck, Polaroid, and several insurance companies which have already introduced flexible retirement, shows that at least 50 percent of those workers reaching age 65 remain on the job. In contrast, only 7 percent of auto workers take advantage of the opportunity to continue past age 65.

Gerontologists also do not support an early retirement trend. They cite the greater political activity of older Americans, the increasing average age of nursing home occupants, and a 1974 Harris Poll survey of retirees over 65 who claimed they would still work if they had not been forced out.[6] Such a reversed trend might be strengthened as age 65 becomes early retirement and workers see extended career opportunities.

Gerontologist Bernice Neugarten, reporting on her research that indicated a new perspective on "time" appears in the mid-to-late 30s, commented:

> Life is restructured in terms of time-left-to-live rather than time-since-birth. Not only the reversal in directionality, but the awareness that time is finite is a particularly conspicuous feature of middle age. Thus "you hear so much about deaths that seem premature—that's one of the changes that come over you over the years. Young fellows never give it a thought...." The recognition that there is "only so much time left" was a frequent theme ... those things don't quite penetrate when you're in your 20s and you think that life is all ahead of you.[7]

Harvard psychiatrist George E. Vaillant likens this period to the stresses of adolescence and rebellion against authority and structure. His original clinical research tracks people through 40 years of life, and provides a valuable in-depth analysis of adult development. Vaillant feels that, by 40, people "put aside the preconceptions and the narrow establishment aims of their 30s and begin once again to feel gangly and uncertain about themselves. But always, such transitional periods in life provide a means of seizing one more change and finding a new solution to instinctive or interpersonal needs."[8]

From his clinical studies of people progressing through their middle years, Yale psychologist Daniel Levinson argues, "This is not an extended adolescence, but a highly formative, evolving phase of adult life." He found that, while a smooth transition is indeed possible, more often dramatic chaos is likely to characterize mid-life transition. One's former life structure (for example, occupation, marital life) suddenly seems inappropriate and new choices must be made.

According to Levinson, "If these choices are congruent with his dreams, values, talents, and possibilities, they provide the basis for a relatively satisfactory life structure. If the choices are poorly made and the new structure seriously flawed, however, he will pay a heavy price in the next period."[9]

Regardless of the causes of this stressful period, several events in society indicate that the symptoms will soon spread in epidemic proportions:

First, those persons reaching the mid-career period in the next ten years will have achieved far higher educational levels and associated higher aspirations than ever experienced by this group previously. By 1980, one out of four workers will have a college degree.

Second, the pattern of occupational growth suggests increasingly insufficient opportunities for advancement in a narrower occupational hierarchy. Unfavorable predictions of future needs through 1985 by the Bureau of Labor Statistics confirm the cause for distress. Professional positions will remain scarce, and the expanded demands of the 1960s for engineers, scientists, and teachers, which influenced so many young people to undertake higher education, will remain history. Clerical, sales, service, and operative workers are expected to be in demand.

Third, the size of the postwar baby boom means intense competition for whatever opportunities do exist. This competitiveness is due to the bulk of the population being at the same career point rather than being more evenly distributed.

Finally, the new legislation on mandatory retirement threatens to further limit opportunities for advancement.

Organizations should prepare now for the inevitable frustrations of career stagnation in the middle years. Already there are individual and organized complaints from those who say that somehow society has cheated them. After investing valuable years in expensive higher education, following glowing promises held out by society, graduates are entering a stagnant labor market. In many cases, academic degrees have become excess baggage to those recipients who are forced to enter the labor market at inappropriate levels.

Many research studies have warned about the growing expectations for self-fulfillment in work. Poor physical health, mental maladjustment, and social disenchantment are consequences of status conflict.

Some social analysts have suggested that anarchistic tendencies of the terrorists in Italy and other parts of Europe are expressions of rage against betrayal by the social order. The fury that burned college buildings in this country in the last decade may strike again in the coming decade, as that generation reacts in frustration to limited opportunities and a sense of defeat.

Stereotyped Perception

One of the fears of businessmen is that they will no longer be able to ease out older workers. Much of the initial reaction to the recognition of a graying work force has been to try to figure out new ways of "weeding out the deadwood." Pension inducements, less generous and "more realistic" performance appraisals, and other rationalizations for eliminating older, less desirable workers are being developed.

Who should be the target of those designs? Columnist William L. Safire has echoed the fears of many businessmen who link age to performance:

... old people get older and usually less productive, and they ought to retire so that business can be better managed and more economically served. We should treat the elderly with respect which does not require treating them as if they were not old. If politicians start inventing "rights" that cut down productivity, they infringe on the consumer's right to a product at the lowest cost...."[10]

THE LATER YEARS

It is important to explore how much factual evidence there is to support the stereotyping and the prejudices that link age with senility, incompetence, and lack of worth in the labor market. Age 65 was an arbitrarily selected cutoff age used by New Deal planners who looked back historically to Bismarck's social welfare system in nineteenth-century Germany.

Certainly, one does not have to look hard to find the elderly among the greatest contributors to current society. The list is long of older citizens who have made major contributions in all fields including the arts, industry, science, and government, and who continue to be worthy and inspiring members of our society.

Age-Related Change

Physiological changes are most pronounced and most identified with old age, but vary markedly in degree between individuals of the same age. It is not clear what changes are actually a result of aging and what can be attributed to life styles. Researchers indicate, however, that after age 50 life style becomes a less influential factor in physiological change than aging itself.

Among age-related changes are declines in the sensory processes, particularly vision, failures in the immunity system that lead to cardiovascular and kidney problems and to degenerative diseases such as rheumatoid arthritis. While 85 percent of workers over 65 suffer from chronic diseases, these are not sudden afflictions. Hence 75 percent of those 60 to 64 years old suffer from these diseases, many of which can be controlled by modern medical treatment. The major effects of these diseases are loss of strength in fighting off invaders and loss of mobility.

Reaction time seems to be affected by the increase in random brain activity, or "neural noise," which distracts the brain from responding to the proper neural signals. A fall in the signal-to-noise ratio would lead to a slower performance and increased likelihood of error. To correct for this possibility of error, performance is delayed to permit time to gain greater certainty. Research on cognitive abilities shows that older people are more scrupulous in the use of decision criteria before responding or forming associations required for decision making. Older people are less likely to use mnemonic or "bridging" mechanisms to link similar concepts. They require a 75 percent chance of certainty before committing themselves, while younger people will take far greater risks.[11]

When time pressure is not a relevant factor, the performance of older people tends to be as good, if not better, than that of younger people. In self-paced tests and in self-paced learning situations, older people do not have to make speed versus accuracy trade-offs and, consequently, their performance is higher.

Learning is also inhibited by the delayed signal-to-noise ratio since it interferes with memory. Most of the learning difficulties of older people stem from acquisition and recall rather than from retention. This relates to the two-step process of memory involving an initial introduction and a later retention period. That is, older people have a harder time holding information in short-term memory, awaiting long-term storage, due to neural noise. This is the same sort of problem older people have with recall.

However, once the information reaches long-term storage, it can be retained. The process of in-putting the information, and retrieving it, can become blocked for intervals of time. Cognition is perhaps the most important difficulty of older workers and relates to problem solving, decision making, and general learning ability. Training in appropriate mental techniques can overcome many of these short-term memory blockages.

Similarly, intelligence tests often have age biases built in with the inherent speed versus accuracy trade-off. Recent researchers have tried to avoid such a bias and have found problem solving, number facility, and verbal comprehension to be unaffected by age. The ability to find and apply general rules to problem solving are more related to an individual's flexibility and education than to age.

Work Attitude

Research studies on all sectors of the American work force have found that age and job satisfaction seemed to bear positive relationships, but it has become apparent that it is hard to consider job satisfaction without considering what aspects of the work experience are important to the individual.[12] Organizations must carefully consider the type of satisfaction which they are measuring, and try to determine how both the more productive and less productive workers in different age groups vary. Perhaps the types of incentives built into a company's rewards package may encourage the less productive, rather than the more productive, older workers to remain with the company.

Along the same line, increasing monetary benefits but not expanding opportunities for job variety would be a serious mistake if the desired workers are more interested in personal growth and achievement than in financial incentives. Mastery and achievement are closely related to job satisfaction. As such, the need for mastery, or recognized accomplishment, becomes increasingly important.

Thus sudden change in job structure and social networks can be threatening to older workers. Their niche in society is defined largely by their contribution in the work place. The job presents friendship, routine, a sense of worth, and identity. Obsolescence and job change are major fears of older workers.

Job Performance

In reviewing studies of performance by occupation for different age groups, it is important to be aware of biases built into the performance appraisals themselves. On top of this, cross-sectional studies of different age groups are also viewing different individuals. It is quite possible that selection factors in older populations explain much of the difference between older and younger populations. In other words, the older workers staying on the job may be different somehow in their skills or interests in that they have managed to remain on the same job.

Looking first at *managers,* one once again sees the manifestation of the tendency toward caution with age. Victor H. Vroom and Bernd Pahl found a relationship between age and risk taking and also between age and the value placed on risk.[13] They studied 1,484 managers, age 22 to 58, from 200 corporations and used a choice-dilemma questionnaire. It seemed that the older managers were less willing to take risks and had a lower estimate of the value of risk in general.

These findings are supported by another study on determinants of managerial information processing and decision-making performance; 79 male first-line managers ranging in age from 23 to 57 years (a median of 40 years) were measured by the Personnel Decision Simulation Questionnaire.[14] Older decision makers tended to take longer to reach decisions even when the influence of prior decision-making experience was removed.

However, the older managers were better able to accurately appraise the value of the new information. Hesitancy about risk taking was also supported in this study; older decision makers were less confident in their decisions.

Another study focusing on task-oriented groups also found that older group members once again sought to minimize risk by seeking more reliable direction.[15] Younger members were more willing to shift authority within the group and to make better use of the experience of others. In this way, younger members of the group were more flexible and more tolerant.

Studies of professionals generally concentrate on *scientists* and *engineers.* Perhaps this is because their output is so easy to measure (for example, publications, patents). Such studies have found bimodal distributions of innovativeness as a function of age. That is to say, there were two peaks of productivity separated by ten-year intervals in research laboratories compared with development laboratories. The first peak in research laboratories occurred by age 40, and the second peak did not appear until age 50. In the development laboratories, the first peak occurred around age 45 to 50, and the second appeared around age 55 to 60.[17] These studies tracked contribution longitudinally over a person's career.

Wider studies of scholarship and artistic contribution revealed a similar first peak at about age 40 and a second peak in the late 50s. Looking more broadly at productivity, it is clear that creative activity was lowest for the 21- to 50-year old group and generally increased with age.[17] It is also a fact, however, that younger scholars and scientists have a more difficult time achieving recognition in the journal networks than do their senior colleagues.

Older people seem to have achieved superior standing among *sales workers* as well and to have remained higher performers. Reports from insurance companies, auto dealers, and large department stores suggest that age is an asset, if a factor at all, in performance.

In a large study of sales clerks in two major Canadian department stores, performance improved with age and experience, the actual peak performance of the sales clerks being about age 55.[18] In several organizations, particularly high technology companies, however, morale plummeted corresponding to length of service. These latter organizations may have used sales as a traditional entry position for managerial development. Those employees remaining on the job over ten years began to perceive frustration in their personal goals of managerial advancement.

Age has had surprisingly little effect on *manual workers*. In several studies, performance seemed to remain fully steady through age 50, peaking slightly in the 30s. The decline in productivity in the 50s never seemed to drop more than 10 percent from peak performance. Attendance was not significantly affected, and the separation rate (quits, layoffs, discharges) was high for those under age 25 and very low for those over 45.[19]

These findings may not only indicate greater reliability among older workers, but also suggest that those who have remained on the job are, in some way, the most competent. Such a sorting out of abilities may not take place equally well across all industries. While tenure among factory workers within industries is reduced with age, absenteeism rates in heavy industry and construction do increase with age. This may be a more evident consequence of mismatches between job demands and physical abilities.

Finally, the high variation of manual labor performance within age groups, compared with the variation between age groups, suggests that individual differences are much more important than age group differences. The need to evaluate potential on an individual basis, and not by age group, has been convincingly established in these studies.

Considerable variation within age groups is found in studies on *clerical workers* as well. A study of 6,000 government and private industry office workers found no significant difference in output by age. Older workers had a steadier rate of work and were equally accurate. Researchers in many studies found that older clerical workers, both male and female, generally had attendance records equal to that of other workers, as well as lower rates of turnover.[20]

Corporate Experience

Many well-publicized reports identify particular companies in various parts of the country which have never adopted mandatory retirement policies yet have continued to be profitable and efficient with workers well into their 70s and 80s. For example, Thomas Greenwood, president of Globe Dyeworks in Philadelphia, who has retained workers hired by his grandfather, commented, "As long as a man can produce, he can keep his job."[21] The 87-year-old president of Ferle, Inc., a small company owned by General Foods which employs workers whose average age is 71, commented, "Older people are steadier, accustomed to working discipline."[22] Sales workers at Macy's department stores in New York have never had to conform to a mandatory retirement age, and have demonstrated no apparent decline in performance attributable directly to age.

Banker's Life and Casualty Company proudly points to its tradition of open-ended employment, retaining top executives, clerks, and secretaries through their late 60s, 70s, and 80s. Of the 3,500 workers in Banker's home office, 3.5 percent are over 65 years of age. Some have been regular members of the Banker's work force, while others have come after being forced into retirement from other companies. The company reports that older workers show more wisdom, are more helpful and thorough, and perform their duties with fewer personality clashes. Studies on absenteeism at Banker's Life and Casualty show that those over 65 have impressive attendance records.

Large companies that have changed to flexible retirement plans in recent years have had similar satisfactory performance reports. U.S. Steel has permitted more than 153,000 nonoffice employees to continue working as long as they can maintain satisfactory levels of performance and can pass medical examinations.

Polaroid has found that those employees who choose to remain on the job after age 65 tend to be better performers. Company retirement spokesman Joe Perkins explained, "If you like to work, you're usually a good worker." He added that attendance is also exemplary as older workers ". . . often apologize for having missed work one day, three years ago because of a cold. There is a fantastic social aspect as people look forward to coming to work." No one is shifted between jobs at Polaroid unless the worker requests a change. Even among older workers whose jobs entail heavy physical demands high performance is maintained.

Performance Appraisal

Generally the companies just mentioned have not had to deal with older workers who remain on the job despite poor performance. There is no guarantee that workers will always be able or willing to perform well and to relinquish their jobs when they are no longer capable of fulfilling the job requirements. Even if both the company and the individual want to continue their relationship, it is not always possible to effectively match an employee's skills with the company's job opportunities.

This need to identify differences between more and less productive older workers is a difficult distinction to make with current performance measurement techniques. The process must be objective, consistent, and based on criteria that are uniformly applied and which will endure court challenges. Arthur C. Prine, Jr., vice-president of R.R. Donnelley & Sons Company, recently explained, "As soon as you pick and choose, you'll scar a lot of people when they are most sensitive. I just dread the thought of calling someone and saying, 'You've worked for forty-five years and have done a wonderful job, but you've been slipping and you must retire.' "[23]

Instead of carrying less productive older workers near retirement on the payroll, employers may begin to weed them out earlier in an effort to deter age-discrimination charges. Richard R. Shinn, president of Metropolitan Life, forecasts that "employers are going to make decisions earlier in careers if it appears that someone is going to be a problem as time goes on."[24]

Thus predictions of future performance will be important criteria in performance appraisal. Even the use of formal standard evaluations does not eliminate age bias or avoid self-fulfilling prophecies which prejudice the evaluation process.

Such a bias was shown in a recent poll of managers. A 1977 questionnaire of *Harvard Business Review* readers concluded that "age stereotypes clearly influence managerial decisions."[25] *HBR* readers perceived older workers as more rigid and resistant to change and thus commended transferring them out rather than helping them overcome a problem. The respondents preferred to retain but not retrain obsolete older employees and showed a tendency to withhold promotions from older workers compared with identically qualified younger workers.

Part of this discrimination problem is that many companies consider an employee's potential to be an important element in his evaluation. As mentioned in the section on basic abilities, chronological age never has been a valid means of measuring a worker's potential and now is illegal under the Age Discrimination in Employment Act. The strength of various faculties may slightly correlate with age in certain aspects, but there is no categorical proof that age has an effect on capabilities. Individuals vary greatly, and useful measures of potential must recognize such differences.

One of the best-known functional measures was the GULHEMP system designed by Leon F. Koyl, physician from DeHaviland Aircraft.[26] This system had two dimensions, the first being a physical-mental profile and the second a job-demand profile. Workers were examined on seven factors of general physique, upper extemities, lower extremities, hearing, eyesight, mental features, and personality attributes. These individual factors were plotted on a graph and superimposed on similarly graphed job task profiles. Individuals were then viewed in relation to the job profiles available. While successful in its pilot experience, this federally supported project was not seen as a high priority government expenditure. Thus the project in functional age measurement was terminated.

Functional measures, however, are not the answer to the performance appraisal question. While they can provide the quantifiable "expert" criteria companies might need for age-discrimination suits, their strength lies largely in assessing the potentials of physical labor. The sensitive areas in performance appraisal are evaluations of the more nebulous factors.

Ratings of "mental abilities" and "personality attributes," which were the poorest factors on the GULHEMP scale, are the most sensitive areas in the appraisal process, and the only truly relevant dimensions in most white-collar and managerial jobs. Some consulting firms have been assessing the important elements of successful job performance, appraising corporate personnel, and establishing appropriate organizational recruitment and development programs.

WHAT MANAGERS CAN DO

How can companies resolve the kinds of frustration expressed at the beginning of this article by the chief executive of the paper company? Where can they send the fire engines? It is far easier to read about social trends than to perceive ways of preparing for them. It is clear that America's work force is graying. Older workers will tend toward caution, will experience far greater levels of frustration, and will show signs of age individually at very different rates.

However, companies are not fated for stodginess. In this section let us look at six priorities for managers to consider in preparing for the impending dramatic change in their own internal environments:

Age profile. It has been demonstrated that age per se does not necessarily indicate anything significant about worker performance. Instead, executives should look at the age distribution across jobs in the organization, as compared with performance measures, to see what career paths might conceivably open in the organizations in the future and what past performance measures have indicated about those holding these positions.

Job performance requirements. Companies should then more precisely define the types of abilities and skills needed for various posts. A clear understanding of job specifications for all levels of the organization is necessary to plan for proper employee selection, job design, and avoidance of age-discrimination suits. For example, jobs may be designed for self-pacing, may require periodic updating, or may necessitate staffing by people with certain relevant physical strengths.

Several companies have looked at the skills needed in various jobs from the chief executive down to reenlisted older and even retired workers who have the needed experience and judgment. For example, as Robert P. Ewing, president of Banker's Life and Casualty, stated, "Our company sets performance standards for each job and these standards are the criteria for employment. Age doesn't count. Getting the job done does."

Such an approach requires careful assessment of needed job competence where traits, motives, knowledge, and skills are all evaluated. When this information is considered in relation to the magnitude and direction of planned company growth, future manpower needs can be predicted. Obsolete job positions can be forecast and workers retrained in advance. Necessary experience cannot be gained overnight, and development programs should be coordinated with precise company manpower needs.

Performance appraisal. Corresponding with improved job analyses, companies must improve their analyses of individual performance as well. Age biases are reflected in both the evaluation format and the attitudes of managers. Management development programs should be aware of the need to correct these biases. Both Banker's Life and Polaroid have teams that audit the appraisals of older workers to check for unfair evaluations. These units have also been used to redress general age prejudice in the work place.

Companies need a realistic understanding of current work force capabilities for effective human resource planning. A company cannot adjust its development, selection, and job training strategies appropriately without knowing the current strengths and weaknesses of its workers. Additionally, potential courtroom challenges on staffing and reward procedures necessitate evidence of solid decision criteria.

Work force interest surveys. Once management acquires a clearer vision of the company's human resource needs, and what basic abilities its workers have, it must then determine what the current workers want. If management decides that it wants to selectively encourage certain types of workers to continue with the organization while encouraging turnover of other types, it must next determine what effects different incentives will have on each group.

In addition, management must be well aware of workers' desires and values so that it can anticipate and prepare for morale drops. Understanding work force aspirations is essential in reducing the harmful organizational and personal consequences of mid-career plateauing. For example, companies might offer counseling programs to those who frequently but unsuccessfully seek job changes, or might consider making alterations in the prevailing company culture and in the norms which link competence and mobility.

Education and counseling. Management may discover that its workers are also confronted with a variety of concerns regarding the direction of their lives after terminating current employment. Counseling on retirement and second-career development are becoming increasingly common to assist workers in adjusting to the major social disengagement following retirement.

IBM now offers tuition rebates for courses on any topic of interest to workers within three years of retirement, and continuing into retirement. Subject matter need not have any relation to one's job, and many workers include courses in preparation for second careers (learning new skills, professions, and small business management).

Counseling is also important to address problems of the work force which remains on the job. Career planning to avoid mid-career plateauing and training programs to reduce obsolescence must be developed by each company. The educational programs must reflect the special learning needs of older workers. Self-paced learning, for example, is often highly effective. Older workers can learn new tricks, but they need to be taught differently.

Job structure. A better understanding of basic job requirements and employee abilities and interests may indicate a need to restructure jobs. Such restructuring cannot be done, however, until management knows what the core job tasks are in the organization and what types of changes should be instituted. Alternatives to traditional work patterns should be explored jointly with the work force. Some union leaders have expressed reservations about part-time workers whom they fear may threaten the power of organized labor. Management, too, wonders about its ability to manage part-time workers. Some part-time workers have found that they "lack clout and responsibility" in their jobs in small companies.

Management may have more flexibility than anticipated in changing such conditions as work pace, the length or timing of the work day, leaves of absence, and challenges on the job. With a tightened reward structure for older workers, satisfaction with the job may shift increasingly to intrinsic features of one's current job.

America's work force is aging, but America's organizations are not doomed to hardening of the arteries. Older workers still have much to offer but organizations must look at certain policies to ensure that their human resources continue to be most effectively used. Organizations must be alert to changing work force needs and flexible in responding to meet those needs.

Notes

[1] U.S. Bureau of the Census, *Current Population Reports*, Series P-25, No. 61, "Projections of the Population of the United States, 1975 to 2050" (Washington D.C.: U.S. Government Printing Office, 1975).

[2] Neal H. Rosenthal, "The United States Economy in 1985: Projected Changes in Occupations," *Monthly Labor Review*, December 1973, p. 18.

[3]Jerry Flint, "Early Retirement Is Growing in U.S.," *New York Times*, July 10, 1977.
[4]Jerry Flint, "Businessmen Fear Problems from Later Age for Retirement," *New York Times*, October 2, 1977.
[5]*Ibid.*
[6]"The Graying of America," *Newsweek*, February 28, 1977, p. 50.
[7]Bernice Neugarten, *Middle Age and Aging* (Chicago: University of Chicago Press, 1968), p. 97.
[8]George E. Vaillant, *Adaptation to Life* (Boston: Little Brown, 1977), p. 193.
[9]Daniel J. Levinson, "The Mid-Life Transition: A Period in Adult Psychosocial Development," *Psychiatry*, 40 (1977), 104.
[10]William L. Safire, "The Codgerdoggle," *New York Times*, September 3, 1977, p. 29.
[11]For an example of research on cognitive abilities, see A.T. Welford, "Thirty Years of Psychological Research on Age and Work," *Journal of Occupational Psychology*, 49 (1976), 129.
[12]See, for example, John W. Hunt and Peter No. Saul, "The Relationship of Age, Tenure, and Job Satisfaction in Males and Females,,' *Academy of Management Journal*, 20 (1975), 690; also, Bonnie Carroll, "Job Satisfaction," *Industrial Gerontology*, 4 (Winter 1970).
[13]Victor H. Vroom and Bernd Pahl, "Age and Risk Taking Among Managers," *Journal of Applied Psychology*, 12 (1971), 22.
[14]Ronald N. Taylor, "Age and Experience as Determinants of Managerial Information Processing and Decision Making Performance," *Academy of Management Journal*, 18 (1975), 602.
[15]Ross A. Webber, "The Relation of Group Performance to Age of Members in Homogeneous Groups," *Academy of Management Journal*, 17 (1974), 570.
[16]Ronald C. Pelz, "The Creative Years in Research Environments,,' Indsutrial and Electrical Engineering, *Transaction of the Professional Technical Group on Engineering Management*, 1964, EM-II, p. 23, as referenced in L.W. Porter, "Summary of the Literature of Personnel Obsolescence." Conference on Personnel Obsolescence, Dallas, Stanford Research Institute and Texas Instruments, June 21-23, 1966.
[17]Wayne Dennis, "Creative Productivity Between the Ages of 20 and 80 Years," *Journal of Gerontolgoy*, 21 (1966), I.
[18]"Age and Performance in Retail Trades," Ottawa, Canadian Department of Labor, 1959, as referenced in Carol H. Kelleher and Daniel A. Quirk, "Age, Functional Capacity, and Work: An Annotated Bibliography," *Industrial Gerontology*, 19 (1973), 80.
[19]U.S. Department of Labor, *The Older American Worker*, Report to the Secretary of Labor, title 5, sec. 715 of the Civil Right Act of 1964 (Washington, D.C.: U.S. Government Printing Office, June 1965).
[20]See, for example, U.S. Department of Labor, Bureau of Labor Statistics, *Comparative Job Performance by Age: Office Workers*, Bulletin No. 1273 (Washington, D.C.: U.S. Government Printing Office, 1960); and U.S. Department of Labor, Bureau of Labor Statistics, *Comparative Performance by Age: Large Plants in the Men's Footwear and Household Furniture Industries*, Bulletin No. 1223 (Washington, D.C.: U.S. Government Printing Office, 1957).
[21]J.L. Moore, "Unretiring Workers: To these Employees, the Boss is a Kid," *Wall Street Journal*, December 7, 1977.
[22]S. Terry Atlas and Michael Ress, "Old Folks at Work," *Newsweek*, September 26, 1977, p. 64.
[23]Irwin Ross, "Retirement at Seventy a New Trauma for Management," *Fortune*, May 8, 1978, p. 108.
[24]*Ibid.*
[25]Benson Rosen and Thomas H. Jerdee, "Too Old or Not Too Old," *Harvard Business Review*, November-December 1977, p. 105.
[26]Leon F. Koyl and Pamela M. Hanson, *Age, Physical Ability and Work Potential* (New York: National Council on the Aging, 1969).

The Problems Retirement Can Bring

J. Roga O'Meara

An employee reaches a dramatic turning point in his life when he/she retires. His/her career job, whether he/she wanted it so or not, is no longer his/hers; and he/she has to adopt new attitudes and develop new habits for the different kind of life that lies ahead of him/her. Undergoing such a transition can (and often does) lead to a wide range of problems—problems that affect not only the retiring employee, but his or her employer and society as well.

PROBLEMS FOR RETIRING EMPLOYEES

Not all employees, of course, run into problems when they retire. There are many thousands who wind up happier after they retire than they were before. Relieved of the pressures and responsibilities of their career jobs and receiving both Social Security and liberal pension benefits, they are left free to devote as much time as they please to activities in which they had developed strong interests before they retired. Some are finding greater happiness in running small businesses of their own, in doing volunteer work, or in returning to school as teachers or students. Others are content not to commit themselves to any central activity; instead, they settle for a life of relaxation and ease—swimming, trying their hand at painting or writing, or just doing nothing at all, as the fancy moves them.

It would seem, then, that the retirees who stand the best chance of steering clear of problems are those who (1) cultivated outside interests or learned how to enjoy leisure time before they retired, and (2) worked for companies that provide them with adequate pension benefits. A vice-president of personnel, who took early retirement to engage in research work, put it this way:

> The unique and rewarding thing about retirement is that it gives you relative financial independence. Your income is reduced rather substantially. But even if you're not lucky enough to obtain a second career job, you still have enough money to get by on. And that's what makes the difference.
>
> While I was climbing the corporate ladder and had growing family responsibilities, there were times when changes at the top gave rise to personality conflicts and other predicaments I had to stomach because I couldn't afford to lose my regular paycheck.
>
> Now, the change in my financial circumstances puts me in the driver's seat. Our children are through school and out on their own, and my wife and I are assured of continuing and adequate retirement income. Should I find

J. Roga O'Meara, "The Problems Retirement Can Bring," from J. Roga O'Meara, *Retirement: Reward or Rejection,* Report No. 713. New York: The Conference Board, 1977.

myself in a disagreeable job situation, I can quit and seek more congenial employment elsewhere. If I don't land a job that appeals to me, we can still eat regularly, and I can keep myself pleasantly occupied playing golf, reading, or just dozing in a comfortable chair.

A large segment of the working population, however, is not provided with this kind of relative financial independence at retirement time. It has been pointed out that only 29 million (44 percent) of the 65.9 million nongovernment wage and salary workers in the nation's civilian labor force at the end of 1973 were covered by employer-financed retirement benefit plans.[1] What is more, the retirees covered by such plans are not always paid enough retirement benefits to supplement adequately their Social Security benefits. It would appear, therefore, that unless they have other sources of income to fall back on, most retiring employees encounter some financial problems.

Nor are financial problems the only ones that can make retirement a trying time. There may have been one or more problems—failing health, for example, or family troubles—that were bothering some retiring employees during their final years on their career jobs. Such problems not only carry over into retirement, but the concern they cause is aggravated by the addition of financial and other problems directly attributable to the advent of retirement.

Here, then, is a random sample of the broad range of problems that retirement can bring to retired employees.

Financial Problems

As has been said, a great many retirees are confronted with financial problems because all, or nearly all, of their retirement income is derived from Social Security benefits. In New York City, for example, where retirees have been especially hard hit by inflation, there are now over a million persons 65 or more years of age.[2] The City's Office for the Aging reports that about nine tenths of these persons are paid Social Security benefits. Relatively few of them, it adds, receive income from any other source: only about a third (which is higher than the national average) derive income from pensions, less than a third realize income from assets such as dividends or rents, and less than a fifth earn income from wages or salaries.[3]

Thus, the only income that a majority of elderly New Yorkers have to subsist on is Social Security and Supplemental Security Income (SSI). SSI, which is federally financed, guarantees older persons (and the blind or disabled) a certain amount of income as a substitute for local welfare allowances. In New York City, for example, the maximum SSI payment for an elderly person living alone is $219 per month ($158 in federal funds plus a $61 state supplement). When the SSI is being computed, however, the first $20 of a recipient's *unearned* income (Social Security benefits, pensions, dividends, rents, and so on) and the first $65 plus half the balance of his *earned* income (wages or salary) are not counted.

Illustration. The monthly SSI payment for a single elderly person receiving $105 in Social Security benefits, $26 in pension benefits, $15 in dividends, and $75 as wages for part-time work would be $88 [$219 *less* $126 unearned income ($105 + 26 + 15 = $146 − $20) and $5 earned income ($75 − 65 = $10 − ½ of $10)]. By the same token, were his sole income $100 a month in Social Security benefits, then his monthly SSI payment would be $139 [$219 *less* $80 unearned income ($100 − $20)].

A retiree qualifies for SSI if he or she owns a home that is valued at no more than $25,000 and that is furnished reasonably, and if the value of his or her convertible assets (cash, stocks, and so on) does not exceed $1,500. "For a frighteningly large proportion of New Yorkers," a reporter comments, "inflation is making old age the ultimate calamity."[4]

Retirees in other sections of the country, whose income is limited largely to Social Security benefits, are also under constant financial strain. Many residing outside metropolitan areas, for example, need a car. But if the car breaks down, paying cost of repairing or replacing it can necessitate sacrificing on food and other essentials for long periods of time. Some elderly couples cannot even afford to get married, since the woman's Social Security benefits as a wife would be only half what she receives as a single individual.

But even when retirees are provided with employer-financed pensions or other retirement income, they can still be plagued by financial problems.

> Dave Munson, for example, is 60 years old. Not long ago, he was pensioned off in a plant closing and has not been able to find another job. The early age at which he had to retire militates against him in two ways: it reduces his pension benefits substantially, and it also leaves him too young to qualify for Social Security and Medicare benefits.

> Tom Curtis is about to retire at the age of 65 with a pension equal to about one third of his working salary. He will also get Social Security and Medicare benefits. But when he was 45, he married a much younger woman. Both he and his wife are resolved to give all four of their children, ranging in age from 13 to 19, a college education. This will be extremely difficult unless they have additional sources of income.

> Bob Hartman is also retiring at age 65. Although his combined retirement benefits will add up to about half his working income, he and his wife have lived for many years in a Manhattan apartment where their rent is $700 a month and they travel and entertain often. It takes all of Bob's preretirement income to keep pace with this life style. What happens after he retires and his income is cut in half?

Housing Difficulties

Employees generally stick to familiar surroundings when they retire. The 1970 Census figures show that, between 1965 and 1970, a sizable 72 percent of persons 65 or more years of age did not change residence, that another 20 percent transferred to new housing but without leaving the county or state where they had been residing, and that only 4 percent went across state lines to find new homes (including a few who relocated in foreign lands).[5] All of the remaining 4 percent moved, but the location of the residences they left was not reported.

Despite these statistics, the Federal Council for the Aging has said that with better health, higher incomes, and improved housing, some greater mobility among older persons may be expected in the future. And there can, of course, be numerous reasons that would prompt a retired employee to pick up stakes and settle in a distant destination. He may have been relocated by his employer some five to ten years earlier and wish to return to the area where he spent most of his life; he and his wife might want to move to a different part of the country to be near their children and grandchildren; it might be advisable for him or his wife to be in a warm climate for health purposes; or he may have landed a second career job with a company in another state.

Undertaking a long-distance move, however, can lead to serious problems unless all the possible drawbacks of the new locations are investigated in advance.

> Larry Peterson, for example, had been a successful salesman. He and his wife had enjoyed several visits to Florida and decided to retire there. They sold their house in Connecticut, bought a trailer home, and drove down. All their previous visits, though, had been during the in-season winter months. When they settled there on a year-round basis, they found that the Florida climate was too hot for them most of the other months of the year.

> Bill and Beth Hughes were apartment dwellers in New York City who had spent all their vacations with their daughter and her family in Minnesota. When Bill retired, they moved to the town where their daughter lived. But, less than a year later, the daughter's husband was transferred by his company to California. His company paid to relocate him and his family. The Hughes, however, could not afford a second move.

> Frank and Virginia Fenton were New Yorkers who had gone to see friends who had bought a home in a retirement community in Southern California. The visit had been pleasant and the Fentons made up their minds to retire there also. After becoming permanent residents themselves, however, they soon realized they had made a mistake in confining all their contacts to old folks; they missed the stimulation of being able to mix with and talk to people of all ages.

Even local moves can bring problems if the possible disadvantages are not duly considered before the final commitment is made.

> Nell Crowley was a widow who worked in Chicago. Her son and his wife had a large house in the suburbs, and they invited Nell to come live with them when she retired. Having only a small retirement income, she welcomed the invitation. But although she and her daughter-in-law had gotten along well before, they soon became a constant irritation to each other when dwelling under the same roof. Life turned sour not only for Nell, but for her son and daughter-in-law as well.

> Eddie and Irene McAuliffe found the house they owned in the suburbs of New York City big and burdensome when the children had gone off on their own and Eddie had retired. They decided to sell it and move to an apartment in Manhattan, because they loved concerts and the theater. Not long after they settled in the city, however, Irene was mugged one evening while returning from church. Ever since, both she and Eddie are so crime conscious they are afraid to go out after dark.

There are some, though, who find New York City an ideal place for retirement. A retirement counselor tells the story of a native Manhattanite who had moved to the suburbs when her husband's company relocated there, but resolved to move back to Manhattan when he retired. The real estate agent, knowing they could afford the rent, suggested an apartment overlooking the East River. "No," she replied, "who wants to live by the river where you look out the window and maybe you see a boat go by? Give me Third Avenue where, when you look out the window, maybe you see an accident."

Legal Complications

Retiring and retired employees can face a great number of situations that involve a need for legal advice. They stand at a crucial crossroad in their lives and may want to rewrite their wills, buy or sell property, start a business, or find out how to deal with a newly acquired tax status. If their employers make legal assistance available to them in such matters and they take advantage of the offer, their best interests are protected. But if they have to pay for such legal assistance themselves and feel they can avoid incurring the high fees lawyers charge by handling the matters themselves, they could wind up with more problems than they started out with.

George and Viriginia Garland, for example, had planned to spend their retirement in New Mexico and invested their savings in a house there. The purchase was made on the basis of sales-talk promises; the Garlands had not seen the property or consulted a lawyer. On reaching the home site, they found it in an isolated area and without some of the necessities for normal living, such as water, electricity, roads, and medical and shopping facilities.

Vince Hodiak had taken up painting as a retirement hobby. As his skills developed, the number of his paintings multiplied. Soon his neighbors and many of their friends offered to buy paintings from him and he set up a spare room as a display studio. He had gone into business—but without seeking advice on the legal implications of the venture. When the licensing and tax authorities finally caught up with him, he had to pay fines for failing to comply with applicable federal, state, and local laws.

Jeff Thompson's wife left him soon after he retired, and he decided to leave his house to his sister. Without the help of a lawyer, he drew up a will in his own handwriting (a holographic will) that clearly expressed his intention. He failed, however, to meet technical requirements of the laws of the state in which he lived; and when he died, the distribution of his property under the laws of that state gave the house to his estranged wife.

Shortly after he retired at age 65, Bart Wilson sold the house that had been his home more than 20 years for $40,000. He had paid $25,000 for the house; and because he had attained age 65 before the date of sale and had owned and used the house as his principal residence, Section 121 of the Internal Revenue Code entitled him to exclude $10,000 of his capital gain from tax.[6] He lost the advantage of his tax benefit, however, because he had not sought professional advice.

Estate planning, once considered a problem area restricted to the very wealthy is, as a result of spiraling inflation, rising salaries, and long-range benefit plans, becoming a matter of crucial concern to more and more employees.[7]

Loss of Prestige

On the whole, retired executives would seem less prone to financial problems than retired rank-and-file employees, since they are usually provided with higher retirement incomes. But there is at least one retirement problem that is more likely to beset executives. It is the void that follows a loss of prestige.

An executive occupies a position in the company that gives him authority and certain privileges. Having to give these up when he retires can leave a letdown feeling. There was an executive in a small company in New England, for example, who reluctantly agreed to retire. He refused, however, to surrender the key to the executive washroom. Every workday thereafter, at a set time each morning and afternoon, he walked from his home to the company office and made use of the key.

Retirement can mean a letdown even for chief executive officers. After years at the helm of a company, deciding its destinies, they suddenly become forgotten men. What they think no longer matters; someone else has taken over the top spot. If they return for a social function, they have to hail their own cabs when they depart—the company's chauffered limousine is no longer at their disposal. When they retired, their prestige in the company retired with them.

Second Career Problems

Employees who wish to continue working after retiring from their career jobs are often disappointed—unless, of course, they are willing to perform volunteer services for worthy causes. The job market is especially bad now as a result of the recession. But, even in good times, retirees intent on second careers can be hampered by certain disadvantages.

For one thing, the business world is strongly youth oriented. As already indicated, one of the reasons that led companies to establish mandatory retirement and to encourage early retirement was to ease out older employees and open their jobs to younger employees who, in the consensus of management thinking, are considered generally more productive.

Another difficulty encountered in second career job seeking is that if a retiree is offered a job, it is apt to involve far less satisfying job duties than his career job did. Many employers regard training older workers for responsible jobs as an unsound investment. Furthermore, there are some employers who know the amount of the pension that retired applicants receive and deduct a portion of this amount from the pay offer they make them.

Lack of Purpose

It was the industriousness of its settlers that built the United States into a great nation. Throughout its history, work has always been held in high regard. A man's job was his contribution to progress, his means of earning a livelihood. If he lost his job, he was deprived of his basic purpose in life.

Many of the men and women now being forced to retire were brought up in this traditional belief, and it makes it extremely difficult for them to adjust to the prospect of a future without a career job. In their eyes, idleness is what seventeenth-century prelate Jeremy Taylor called it, "the death of a living man." They are convinced they could perform their career jobs productively for many more years.

Adding to their problems is the fact that their career job was largely instrumental in directing their mode of existence. It determined what time they got up in the morning, when they ate their meals, and what time they went to bed at night. Even their periods of leisure (their evenings and weekends and vacations) were part of a fixed routine that centered around the job.

Such employees can be left at a total loss when they retire. Being deprived of their career job strips them of a needed sense of purpose and continuing achievement. But it does more than that. It also takes away the discipline that had regulated their daily habits. They become too disorganized to seek another job successfully. More than one company has had a retired employee who committed suicide and left a note containing these sad words: "I had nothing to live for."

Alcoholism

No broad-scale statistics are available to show how extensively the problem of alcoholism affects retirees as a group. "To my knowledge," the Executive Secretary of the National Institute on Alcohol Abuse and Alcoholism (an arm of the National Institute of Health) informed The Conference Board, "no one has yet surveyed the relative incidence of alcoholism among the various age groups in this country."

But there does seem to be ample evidence that some employees take to drinking excessively after they retire. Many cooperating executives cite numerous instances that have come to their attention, especially among employees who had developed drinking habits (social or otherwise) while still on the job.

> The case of Don Lennon is typical. He and his wife Kate had fallen into the nightly routine of a couple of predinner martinis as soon as he got home from the office. When Don retired, the martini drinking was started before lunch. Less than a year later, both Don and Kate were chronic alcoholics.

Two other types of retirees found to be susceptible to drinking problems are those who had not learned to make constructive use of their leisure time and those who settled in retirement communities. "Every time I go to Florida," a personnel director recounts, "I visit one of the best salesmen we ever had. I always leave with the impression that he and the other residents of the retirement village where he lives can't wait until sundown so they can have or go to a cocktail party that runs well into the night."

Marital Rifts

When a married man retires, a new dimension is added to the marriage for both him and his wife. Suddenly he stops spending five days of each week at work; he is home nearly all the time. Many couples welcome the new arrangement; they see it as an opportunity to plan and carry out trips and projects they had long wanted to share together.

It can prove disturbing for other couples, however—especially for the wife. As someone has remarked, she winds up with twice as much husband but only half as much income. Having him underfoot all day every day can throw an accustomed schedule that she enjoys out of kilter.

> Bea and Arthur Bennington, for example, had no serious rifts in their marriage until he retired. That made the difference. Bea had sent him off to work every morning with a good breakfast. At night, when he returned, there was an excellent dinner awaiting him. Evenings and weekends, the two of them engaged in pursuits of mutual interest. Weekdays, however, while Arthur was at work, Bea had a rotation of concerts, bridge clubs, and other social activities she attended. These activities had become an important part of her life. When Arthur retired and suggested that she give them up so that she could get him his lunch every day, the emotional eruption that followed eventually led the couple to divorce proceedings.

Loneliness

There are employees who, when they have to leave their career jobs, lose contact with the people they hold most dear.

> Hank Green's only close friends, for example, were the men and women he worked with in a brokerage house in downtown Manhattan. After he was retired on reaching age 65, he spent day after endless day sitting by himself in his cheap hotel room in midtown or feeding the pigeons in Central Park. He had no one to joke with or confide in; his friends were still on the job. For him, retirement proved a long and lonely time.

> Mike Casino's job was different. His retirement, however, brought the same results. For 40-odd years, he had been a mailman in a small town in California. During those years, he had not only delivered letters and packages to the people along his route but had become the friend and confidant of most of them. When he brought them good news, he shared in their joy; when the news was bad, he comforted them. His daily contacts with them, which had always been an important part of his life, became the most important part after his wife died ten years before he had to retire. That turned his life into a lonely one when retirement time did come. He was cut off from the daily contacts of his route; although he occasionally met some of the people in town, the relationship had changed. Someone else was sharing their joy when good news came in the mails, comforting them when the news was bad.

Loss of Identity

One of the most touching problems retirement can bring is the fear it engenders in some retirees that they will lose their identity as individuals. They feel—especially if it becomes necessary for them to enter nursing or old-age homes—that they are no longer recognized as human beings with treasured memories and a great need for love.

Not many years ago, for example, an old woman died alone in the geriatric ward of a hospital in Ireland. Found among her scant possessions was a poem that ended with this poignant plea:

> ... But inside this old carcass a young girl
>   still dwells.
> And now and again my battered heart swells.
> I remember the joys; I remember the pain;
> And I'm loving and living life over again.
> I think of the years, all too few—gone too
>   fast.
> And accept the stark fact that nothing can last.
> So open your eyes, nurses, open and see
> Not a crabbit old woman, look closer—
>   See **me!**

Failing Health

A handicap of reaching retirement age is that it increases the likelihood of failing health. On top of that, the sicknesses that strike retired employees tend to be more serious, to last longer, and to cost considerably more to doctor than the sicknesses of younger employees. In mid-1974, the annual per capita medical bill was $183 for persons under 19 years of age, $420 for persons between the ages of 19 and 64, and $1,218 for persons 65 years of age or more.[8]

While it is true that part of the medical expenses of those 65 and over is covered by Medicare, this probably entitles them to less protection than they had under their employer's health care program while still active employees. Furthermore, the wives of married employees who retire at age 65 are usually a few years younger and not yet eligible for Medicare. In such instances, the wife's developing a grave illness can bring ruinous financial problems.

Possibly even more damaging than such financial problems are the unsettling psychological reactions that the greater possibility of failing health can arouse in retirees. For some of them, for example, momentary pains and other medical symptoms that they were inclined to ignore during their younger years now become sure signs of cancer or an impending heart attack.

But even for retirees who maintain a more temperate attitude, the threat of failing health can still pose problems. One of the questions put to TIAA-CREF annuitants in an extensive survey asked what they liked least about retirement.[9] Here are a few of the replies:

> I like least the process of aging, living with ailing and aging flesh. As someone has said, "Old age is not for sissies."—A single female, age 82.

> I am afraid I shall live too long and I do not anticipate inactivity with pleasure.—A single female, age 86.

> Least-liked aspects: declining energy, shortness of breath, some loss of hearing. To think I almost forgot!!—declining sex energy!!!!—A married male, age 66.

Fear of Death

Perhaps the most critical consideration related to retirement is seldom mentioned openly. It is the growing awareness of the inevitability of death and the consequent fears it can evoke. This is a problem that most employees have learned to keep in proper perspective.

For instance, a married 72-year-old woman in the TIAA-CREF survey remarked: ". . . considering the alternative, growing old isn't so bad." Or as Victor Borge, the 67-year-old entertainer put it: "It's marvelous to be growing old. If I weren't getting old, I would be dead."[10] But no matter how rationally retirees may cope with it, fear of death is a problem that not only persists but is apt to become more bothersome with each retirement year that passes.

PROBLEMS FOR COMPANIES

The retirement revolution poses at least three types of problems for companies: legal problems, people problems, and financial problems.

Age-Discrimination Suits

From time to time, adverse business conditions make it necessary for companies to reduce their work forces. Many of them do so by liberalizing the early retirement provisions of their pension plans on a selective basis. This enables them to ease out long-service employees whose usefulness has declined, even though they are not yet 65 years of age.

Ever since 1967, however, when enactment of the Age Discrimination in Employment Act barred employers from depriving individuals between the ages of 40 and 65 of jobs because of their age, companies have had to worry about being sued for violations of this Act every time they "encourage" older employees to retire early. Such suits have proved costly to some employers.

> In 1974, the Standard Oil Company of California, in an out-of-court settlement of an action brought against it by the U.S. Labor Department, consented to pay about $2 million to 160 employees after a federal district court ruled it had let a discriminatorily large number of older employees go over a 25-month period.

> The heirs of an EXXON Research and Engineering Company chemist, found in another federal district court action to have been forced into retirement at age 60, were granted a jury award of $750,000 "for pain and suffering" (later reduced by court order) and $30,000 "for out-of-pocket compensatory damages" (later increased). An appeal is pending in this case.

> In still another federal district court case, the Labor Department is asking payments totaling $20 million for 300 employees forced into retirement by the Baltimore and Ohio Railroad and the Chesapeake and Ohio Railway before they had reached age 65.

It should be noted, however, that the federal district court has upheld the right of a company to retire an employee who is younger than 65 if its right to do so is stipulated in a bona fide retirement income plan [*Brennan versus Taft Broadcasting Company*, Civil No. 72-426 (N.D. Alabama, 6/27/73; CCH 7 EDP #9232), affirmed 500 F. 2d 212 (5th Cir. 1974)]. The company in this case has a profit-sharing retirement plan which made the normal retirement date for each participant "the first day of June coinciding with or next following the date on which he has attained age 60." An employee who was retired under this provision had signified his desire to participate in the plan by signing a form in which he agreed to all of the plan's provisions. The Labor Department, suing on this employee's behalf, claimed that his being retired involuntarily violated the Age Discrimination in Employment Act of 1967. But the court, declaring the company's plan "a bona fide one," ruled that it "was not used as a subterfuge to evade the purposes of the Act."

On October 1, 1976, on the other hand, the U.S. Court of Appeals for the 4th Circuit heard a case that involved a comparable factual situation (*McMann versus United Airlines, Inc.*, 542 F.2d 217) and reached a conflicting conclusion. It held that, inasmuch as the 1967 Act was intended "to prohibit arbitrary age discrimination in employment," there must be a reason other than age for a provision in a retirement plan which requires employees to retire before age 65. Any other interpretation, this court explained, would produce the "absurd result" of an employer's being able to discharge an employee under a retirement plan for no reason other than age and then being precluded by the same Act from refusing to rehire the same employee, since the Act specifies that "no such employee benefit plan shall excuse the failure to hire any individual."

This case was remanded to the lower court, but only to afford the employer (whose sole argument had been that its plan was exempt from the Act because it predated it) an opportunity to show that the early retirement provision was justified by some economic or business purpose other than arbitrary age discrimination. "Our reversal," the appeals court declared, "does not finally decide this case .... United may have other valid defenses. For example, we note that the Act provides another exemption where age is a 'bona fide occupational qualification' ... United may raise this defense on remand."

Further evidence of conflict in judicial thinking was disclosed in a judgment handed down by the 3rd Circuit of the U.S. Court of Appeals, on January 20, 1977, in the case of *Zinger versus Blanchette, Bond and McArthur, Trustees of the Property of Penn Central Transportation Company, Debtors, and Penn Central Transportation Company* (Case No. 76-1249). This court agreed that a retirement plan is not entitled to exemption by the mere fact that it predated the 1967 Act, but it disagreed with what it termed the "implication" of the decision in the United Airlines case that all programs providing for involuntary retirement before age 65 are outlawed. Convinced by an examination of the Act and its legislative intent that "Congress has chosen to exclude retirements pursuant to bona fide retirement plans so long as the plan is not a subterfuge," the court ruled that Penn Central's plan, since both parties concede it to be bona fide and not unreasonable with regard to the amounts of pensions provided for early retirees, is not an illegal subterfuge to avoid the purposes of the Act.

Morale and Productivity Losses

Because compulsory retirement at any age is a rather recent development, there are still large numbers of active employees who feel it is unfair. They resent the prospect of having to retire when they reach a specified age, with no regard for their personal wishes or their capability to continue working effectively. Such resentment can give rise to problems that could cause their employers irreparable harm.

Many reluctant retirees, for instance, are long-service employees who are versed in the intrigues of plant or office "politics." During the last five to ten years they are on the job, they can spread the seeds of discontent among their fellow employees. This not only disrupts the morale of the work force, it also diminishes productivity.

One-way Cooperation

Some companies have found they can reduce the number of active employees who resent the approach of retirement by sponsoring programs designed to show older employees that retirement is not a rejection of them as older employees but a reward for their years of faithful service and that, if they plan for it in advance, the time they will spend in retirement could turn out to be the most satisfying period of their lives. But no matter how much thought, time, and money companies invest in these retirement preparation programs, they can never be sure of complete success. This is because the ultimate decision as to whether he or she will or will not prepare for retirement has to be left to each individual employee.

Were a company, for instance, to launch a seminar program that offered retiring employees valuable group and individual counseling by medical doctors, psychiatrists, financial experts, and other high-priced professionals, it would be wasting its money if it required the employees to attend the counseling sessions. Attendance has to be made optional if the purpose of the program is to be achieved. Yet experience proves that there are always some eligible employees (and they are usually the reluctant retirees) who refuse to take advantage of the retirement preparation opportunities made available to them. The excuse they most generally give, when questioned, is that they do not want their fellow employees to know how old they are. But companies suspect that the more likely reason is that they are unwilling to face up to the inevitability of retirement or that they are afraid the preparation program is a scheme for hurrying them into early retirement. Such employees, of course, remain a potential source of morale and productivity problems for their employers.

Corporate Image Uneasiness

It has been noted that many companies have, of their own volition, granted pension boosts to their retired employees. They did so out of concern for the financial welfare of the retirees, whose fixed incomes were being steadily devalued by inflation.

But they were also motivated by a less altruistic concern. They realized that retirees keep gaining strength, as their ranks increase, and that the impressions they leave when they talk to others about the treatment they are receiving from the company they retired from carries much weight in determining the character of that company's corporate image.

High Cost of Early Retirement

Companies that have to reduce their work force frequently try (as has been indicated) to hold on to younger employees by encouraging their older employees to take early retirement. This approach can bring financial problems, however, because the encouragement is given in the form of specific bonuses and other costly monetary incentives that are seldom provided for in the regular provisions of corporate pension plans.

What is more, if companies make these monetary incentives available to all employees eligible for early retirement, they run the risk of losing highly skilled employees whom they do not want to retire early. Should they then ask such employees to stay on the job until their normal retirement age, they have to offer them extra pension benefits that add a further financial burden.

PROBLEMS FOR SOCIETY

As companies keep hurrying more and more of their older employees into retirement at earlier and earlier ages, opposition to the trend is growing in government and other nonbusiness circles. Retired employees are transformed from contributing members of society to continuing liabilities, because society—now that it is no longer accepted custom for children to take care of their elderly parents—has to assume responsibility for their welfare.

A Drain on the Economy

Inasmuch as a majority of retired employees derive all their income from Social Security benefits, which usually do not provide them with enough money to satisfy even their basic needs, they have to be subsidized through Supplemented Security Income (SSI). This, of course, imposes a heavy finanical burden on society.

It is a burden, too, that will get heavier with the passing years, since the declining birth rate will steadily lower the numbers of employees paying Social Security taxes at a time when there will be a substantial boost in the numbers of employees qualifying for Social Security benefits. Furthermore, as retirees build up more and more voting strength, society will find it increasingly difficult to deny their demands for repeated hikes in Social Security benefits.

Unresolved Conflict

Set on forestalling these emerging social problems, the government is pressing for a reversal in the trend to earlier retirement. It feels the nation's economy could be bolstered and the health and happiness of older citizens enhanced if companies would adopt more flexible policies and give their employees more say in the determination of when they are to retire.

To date, neither side has taken any action to resolve this conflict. Should companies, however, continue to refuse to make concessions to the government's point of view, the eventual outcome could be an outlawing of mandatory retirement at any age.

Notes

[1] Walter W. Kolodrubetz, "Employee-Benefit Plans, 1973," *Social Security Bulletin*, May 1975, Table 1, p. 23.

[2] In the New York-Northeastern New Jersey area, the Bureau of Labor Statistics reports, living costs for a retired couple at an intermediate level of living were more than $1,000 (or 18 percent) above the autumn 1974 national average for urban areas. Furthermore, the area's increases at all the three living levels were significantly above the national urban average rise for the seven-year period from 1967 to 1974. *BLS News Release*, August 31, 1975.

[3] Menachem Daum, "Recent Developments in the Economics of Aging: Their Impact on the Elderly of New York City." New York City Office for the Aging, *Facts for Action*, 7, 2 (June 1975).

[4] Clinton Cox, "Some Days I Just Sit in My Room and Listen to the Radio," *New York Sunday News*, April 6, 1975, p. 26 et seq.

[5] United States Census Detailed Characteristics Booklet, Volume 1, Part 1, U.S. Summary, Section 2, Chart 196.

[6] Section 121 permits exclusion of all of the capital gain if the adjusted sales price (price less selling expenses) is $20,000 or less. But if the adjusted sales price exceeds $20,000, then the ratio that $20,000 bears to the actual adjusted sales price is applied to the actual capital gain (adjusted sales price less cost basis).

Example: $40,000 (sales price) less $10,000
(expenses of sale) =
$30,000 (amount realized on sale)
$30,000 (realized on sale) less $15,000
(cost basis) =
$15,000 (capital gain)
$15,000 (capital gain) $\times \dfrac{\$20,000}{\$30,000} =$

10,000 (excludable amount)

[7] See also Burton Teague, "Estate Planning and the Executive Taxpayer," *The Conference Board Record*, November 1974, pp. 60–64.

[8] Marjorie Smith Mueller and Robert M. Gibson, "Age Differentials in Health Care Spending, Fiscal Year 1974," *Social Security Bulletin*, June 1975, p. 3.

[9] Mark H. Ingraham, with the collaboration of James M. Mulanaphy, "My Purpose Holds: Reactions and Experiences in Retirement of TIAA-CREF Annuitants," Educational Research Division, Teachers Insurance and Annuity Association—College Retirement Equities Fund, 730 Third Avenue, New York, New York 10017.

[10] Charles McHarry, "On the Town," *New York Daily News*, April 10, 1976.